THE KISSINGER TRANSCRIPTS

Also by the National Security Archive:

Bay of Pigs Declassified: The Secret CIA Report on the Invasion of Cuba
Edited by Peter Kornbluh

White House E Mail: The Top Secret Computer Messages the
Reagan-Bush White House Tried to Destroy
Edited by Tom Blenton

The Cuban Missile Crisis, 1962: The Declassified History
Edited by Laurence Chang and Peter Kornbluh

The Iran-Contra Scandal: The Declassified History
Edited by Malcolm Byrne and Peter Kornbluh

South Africa and the United States: The Declassified History
Edited by Kenneth Mokoena

THE
KISSINGER
TRANSCRIPTS

THE TOP SECRET TALKS WITH BEIJING AND MOSCOW

EDITED BY
WILLIAM BURR

THE NEW PRESS   NEW YORK
1998

Requests for permission to reproduce selections from this book should be made through our website: https://thenewpress.com/contact.

Originally published in the United States by The New Press, New York, 1999
This paperback edition published by The New Press, 2000
Distributed by Two Rivers Distribution

ISBN 978-1–56584–480–3 (hc.)
ISBN 978-1–56584–568-8 (pbk.)

The New Press publishes books that promote and enrich public discussion and understanding of the issues vital to our democracy and to a more equitable world. These books are made possible by the enthusiasm of our readers; the support of a committed group of donors, large and small; the collaboration of our many partners in the independent media and the not-for-profit sector; booksellers, who often hand-sell New Press books; librarians; and above all by our authors.

www.thenewpress.com

—Contents

Preface

This book presents for the first time in print declassified transcripts of Henry Kissinger's conversations with the leaders of China and the Soviet Union when he was special assistant to the president for national security affairs, and later secretary of state, during the presidencies of Richard Nixon and Gerald Ford. Although many important transcripts remain classified, these extraordinarily detailed records of conversations allow readers to see at first hand how key figures in modern world history—Chinese Communist Party Chairman Mao Zedong, Premier Zhou Enlai, Deputy Vice Premier Deng Xiapoing, Soviet Communist Party General Secretary Leonid Brezhnev, and Soviet Foreign Minister Andrei Gromyko, among others—interacted with Henry Kissinger, one of the most celebrated and criticized diplomat-policymakers in recent U.S. history.

What makes these transcripts extraordinarily significant is the light they shed on the conduct and diplomatic interactions of major historical figures during a critically important phase in the history of the Cold War, the years when the Nixon administration tried to achieve a détente—a relaxation of tensions—with its powerful adversary, the Soviet Union, and a rapprochement with its former enemy, the People's Republic of China. Nixon, his successor Gerald Ford, and Kissinger carried out these initiatives in part to minimize the risks of future confrontations with either of the nuclear states. China and the Soviet Union were deeply antagonistic toward each other; so, by developing a closer relationship with both nations, the Nixon-Ford policy sought to maximize U.S. leverage over Moscow and Beijing and thereby preserve a central U.S. role in world affairs. "Triangular diplomacy"—the effort to manipulate relations with Beijing and Moscow to Washington's advantage—was at the heart of U.S. foreign policy under Nixon and Ford. These declassified transcripts illuminate Kissinger's efforts to carry out this policy.

Few secretaries of state have reached the celebrity status or notoriety associated with Henry Kissinger. Even when he was Nixon's special assistant for national security affairs, Kissinger appeared on the covers of *Time* and *Newsweek* and was often seen at parties in the company of a succession of actresses. His gift of flattery had taken him far in winning media support and attention; so had his willingness to leak information selectively and to brief the press as an anonymous "senior administration official." Kissinger found his celebrity status quite useful in enhancing his prestige, but, as much as he relished the limelight, he did not want his work as policymaker and presidential adviser exposed to public scrutiny. His personal views about American power, the decision-making and negotiating processes through which he wielded power, and his communications with foreign leaders remained largely hidden—and Kissinger wanted it kept that way.[1]

Secrecy was one of Kissinger's most important methods for maintaining policy control as well as room for diplomatic maneuver. Although executive secrecy had been customary in the Washington bureaucracy since World War II, Kissinger carried it far beyond its usual bounds. He took great pains to exercise personal control over the classified documents whose creation he supervised, whether back-channel messages to the president or memoranda of conversations with presidents and foreign leaders. He believed that tight control over sensitive information was necessary for achieving the element of surprise in diplomatic maneuvers, preventing various interlocutors from seeing through deceptive statements, preserving White House mastery over policy, and winning bureaucratic battles.[2] Leaks to the press by others in the administration infuriated Kissinger, and in order to identify and punish the perpetrators, he would vainly authorize wiretaps of journalists and subordinate officials. Indeed, to minimize the possibility of leaks as well as to strengthen White House policy control (and sometimes even to protect Nixon from himself), Kissinger's staffers routinely prepared sanitized versions of presidential conversations for distribution to other agencies.[3]

Until he became secretary of state, Kissinger refused to allow State Department professionals with Chinese or Russian language skills to attend high-level meetings with the Chinese and the Soviets. Thus, when Nixon and Kissinger met with Mao Zedong or Leonid Brezhnev during the early 1970s, they had to rely on Chinese or Russian interpreters, had no means to check how accurately their statements were rendered, or knew whether various nuances were understood. Apparently, Kissinger found it easier to accept this hardship than the risk of a transcript falling into the hands of bureaucratic rivals.[4]

During his six years at the White House and the State Department, Kissinger was remarkably successful at preserving executive secrecy; the main exceptions were leaks of documents during the South Asian crisis and the sensational revelations of his role in the wiretaps of his NSC aides. After President Ford's defeat, Kissinger was determined to retain a tight hold over his papers, largely to protect his reputation after he left government.[5] Therefore, in January 1977, when he left the State Department, he transferred to the Library of Congress copies of his White House and State Department files as part of a larger collection of his papers. Under his deed of gift to the Library, Kissinger retained access to them for writing his memoirs but exempted them from public access until 2001 or five years after his death, whichever occurred later. Although Kissinger often had contentious relations with Congress during his tenure in office, a loophole in the Freedom of Information Act (FOIA) provided him congressional protection after he left office. With the FOIA limited to documents in the custody of the executive branch, Kissinger's decision to house his papers at the Library of Congress protected documents deemed Kissinger's personal papers—including notes of telephone conversations held while he was acting as Secretary of State and National Security Advisor—from FOIA requests of historians, journalists, and the general public.[6]

Kissinger's personal control over the most comprehensive collection of U. S. government records on the diplomacy of the Nixon–Ford era amounts to a deliberate inconvenience for researchers. Even with this inconvenience, however, government agencies and archives hold significant primary sources on Kissinger's role in Nixon–Ford diplomacy. For example, the National Archives has custody over the Nixon White House National Security Files, including Henry Kissinger's Office Files. Undoubtedly, those files duplicate part of the Kissinger collection at the Library of Congress. The National Archives is slowly opening the Nixon National Security file; eventually, systematic declassification will make available almost all records of Kissinger's daily briefings to Nixon, the memoranda of his and Nixon's conversations with foreign leaders, and their back-channel communications.[8] Moreover, thanks to inexpensive photocopying and the necessities of policy coordination, Kissinger's close assistants had their own copies of the transcripts of his discussions with foreign leaders. The National Archives and the State Department have also begun to open such papers, thus ensuring the early availability of some of the most important documents.

One of Kissinger's assistants was Winston Lord, later ambassador to the People's Republic of China (PRC) during the Bush administration and assistant secretary of state for East Asian and Pacific affairs during the Clinton administration. Lord joined Kissinger's National Security Council staff in 1969 at the age of thirty-two, after working in the foreign policy bureaucracy since the early 1960s. He would become Kissinger's special assistant and right-hand man on China policy. He took notes at meetings with the Chinese, prepared transcripts, wrote back channel messages, and chose appropriate wine and lighting for dinner meetings. Even though Lord learned in May 1973 that Kissinger had approved FBI wiretaps on his phone to determine who had leaked information in early 1969 on the secret bombing of Cambodia, he chose to stay rather than leave the heady world of secret diplomacy.[9] When Kissinger became secretary of state in September 1973, he appointed

Lord as director of the department's Policy Planning Staff (PPS). At the PPS, Lord continued to play a central part in China policy and accumulated a highly sensitive collection of documents that provide an extraordinary close-up view of Kissinger's conduct of relations with Beijing during the 1970s.

Under its statutory mandate to declassify older materials, the State Department has opened up all of Kissinger's memoranda of conversations, among other documents, in Winston Lord's PPS files at the National Archives. These files were a critically important source for this volume. Pursuant to FOIA requests by the editor, the State Department has also declassified additional transcripts of Kissinger's conversations with Soviet leaders that were collected by other associates and left in departmental archives. Kissinger's memoranda of conversations (memcons) with Soviet General Secretary Leonid Brezhnev and Foreign Minister Andrei Gromyko from 1972 to 1973, when the détente process was at its peak, remain closed; but the memcons released by the State Department — documenting the period 1974–76 period, when détente was under pressure and starting to weaken — have been released. These detailed transcripts record Kissinger's discussions with the Soviets on the second phase of the Strategic Arms Limitations Talks (SALT II), the Conference on Security and Cooperation in Europe (CSCE), economic cooperation, and the Angolan situation. Taken together, the transcripts in the Lord papers at the National Archives and those released by the State Department provide extraordinary evidence of Kissinger's efforts to carry out triangular diplomacy.

What is remarkable about the transcripts is the detail they provide. Before Kissinger, the preparation of more or less literal transcripts of high-level meetings in government had been a haphazard occurrence. Memcons had often been very detailed, but even records of presidential meetings were not necessarily verbatim.[10] Apparently dissatisfied with old-style memcons, and no doubt convinced that an exhaustive record with no nuances overlooked (even if U.S. translators were absent) would best serve current policymaking and perhaps eventual memoir-writing, Kissinger had his NSC aides, Winston Lord and Peter Rodman, among others, take notes at meetings and prepare the records. Everything was recorded: not only small talk but also the atmospherics, and the activities, including Brezhnev's pacing the room or Deng Xiaoping's habitual use of a spittoon.

With such great detail, the transcripts shed light on Kissinger as a person — his erudition, vanity, considerable intellectual acumen, use of flattery and deception, self-deprecating humor, and propensity to deride those not present. More importantly, they provide us with an independent basis for evaluating Kissinger as a diplomat and policymaker; so we are not forced to rely solely on his memoirs of the Nixon administration, *White House Years* and *Years of Upheaval.* In many respects, the transcripts confirm Kissinger's memoir accounts of his meetings with Mao Zedong and Zhou Enlai during 1972 and 1973, but they also show how the memoirs tell only part of the story of triangular diplomacy, at times prompting us to wonder what else Kissinger has left out. Most significantly, the transcripts record Kissinger's persistent and in some respects risky effort during 1973 to develop a tacit strategic "alliance" with Beijing, including his failed attempt to persuade the Chinese to approve a hotline agreement. Moreover, the transcripts dramatically expand our knowledge of a period that Kissinger has not yet described in published memoirs—his role during the administration of Gerald Ford.[11] The transcripts of meetings with Deng, Mao, Brezhnev, and Gromyko during the 1974–76 period are essential for assessing crucial developments in these years.

To put these transcripts in context, this volume begins with an Introduction that provides an overview of Kissinger's thinking about world affairs on the eve of the Nixon administration, the development of his working relationship with Richard Nixon, and their joint effort to preserve a central U.S. role in world affairs by forging new relations with old adversaries. Although their interest in reaching a Vietnam War settlement shaped the approaches to Beijing and Moscow, other objectives took on great importance as the war continued. For Nixon and Kissinger, détente and a "linkage strategy" involving arms control and economic agreements could provide a more effective means of containing the Soviet Union while avoiding the dangers of nuclear confrontation. Even a new relationship with China was part of their containment strategy. With both Beijing and Moscow locked in mutual enmity, Nixon and Kissinger believed that ending the adversarial relationship with China would give them "leverage" over the Soviets and enhance American power generally.

Following the Introduction, nine chapters document Henry Kissinger's conversations from 1971 to 1976 with the Chinese and the Russians or with his staff on policy issues concerning China and the Soviet Union. Each chapter includes introductory material to put the documents in historical context, and each document is annotated to clarify references that might otherwise be obscure. In general, I have reproduced documents in their entirety; some of the most important transcripts, for example, Nixon's and Kissinger's talks with Mao, are published in full. Many transcripts are quite lengthy, though.

In the interest of providing the fullest possible coverage of Kissinger's role in East-West relations, presenting the most revealing material, and avoiding some of the intricacies of arms control and other negotiations, a number of documents are reproduced only in part. In such cases, the excluded material is faithfully summarized. In several instances, short excerpts of certain transcripts are presented when they are especially illuminating. For those readers not wholly satisfied with excerpts and summaries, the National Security Archive will publish in full on its World Wide Web site a selection of transcripts that are published in part in this volume or could not be included for reasons of space.[12]

Chapter 1 provides an overview of the U.S.-China rapprochement and the U.S-Soviet détente that accelerated after 1971. Excerpts from important conversations between Richard Nixon and President Georges Pompidou of France suggest the broad strategic and political interests that motivated White House initiatives toward Beijing and Moscow. A transcript of a back-channel Kissinger-Dobrynin meeting suggests Moscow's apprehension of Washington's new China policy, while records of the celebrated Nixon-Mao meeting in February 1972 and of Kissinger's secret meetings with Chinese diplomats show the extent to which "deep suspicion" of the Soviets informed American policy. Even when the U.S.-Soviet détente appeared to be on firm footing after the May 1972 summit, the transcripts show Kissinger warning the Chinese of the possibility of a Soviet attack during the mid-1970s.

Kissinger's interactions with the Chinese were perhaps at their most intense during 1973; he met with Mao and Zhou twice, in February and November, and had numerous secret meetings with Chinese diplomats in between. Chapters 2, 3, and 4 document Kissinger's trips to Beijing and his incessant efforts during 1973 to keep the Chinese apprised of U.S.-Soviet negotiations and other developments, including extremely revealing briefings on U.S. policy during the Middle East October War. Transcripts from 1973 also disclose elements of tension and disagreement; Kissinger found it difficult to convince Mao and Zhou that détente with Moscow was not at Beijing's expense, while his efforts to enlist China in a secret negotiation to end the fighting in Cambodia ended with ill will on both sides.

Difficult moments notwithstanding, the record of Sino-American exchanges during 1973 show the establishment of a more formal "liaison" relationship and Kissinger's concurrent efforts to establish a "tacit" Sino-American alliance to contain the Soviet Union. Although 1973 was the year in which U.S.-Soviet détente was peaking, the transcripts disclose Kissinger's growing, if exaggerated, apprehension of the possibility of a Soviet military action against China and his briefings of PRC officials on Brezhnev's latest anti-Chinese fulminations. By the year's end, despite Moscow's warning against U.S.-China military cooperation, Kissinger had offered Zhou hot line communications links that could be used to provide strategic warning of a Soviet attack. The Chinese never responded to Kissinger's hotline proposal, but intelligence cooperation did deepen in the years ahead.

Kissinger's offer to the Chinese did not mean that he was abandoning détente. Chapter 5 portrays Kissinger's March 1974 discussions with Brezhnev to negotiate a SALT II agreement (in preparation for what was to become Nixon's final Moscow summit), discuss bilateral economic cooperation, and review pending international negotiations, including the CSCE process. Yet, the discussions showed that detente was becoming more problematic and not only because the Nixon presidency was starting to collapse. The divisive issue of multiple independently targetable reentry vehicles (MIRVs) alone was making SALT negotiations very difficult (the Soviets resisted Kissinger's efforts to put limits on multiple warheads), and his successes at excluding Moscow from the Middle East peace process angered Brezhnev. Moreover, Sen. Henry Jackson (D-Wash.) was waging guerrilla war against détente, most prominently by demanding that the Soviets reform their emigration practices before Congress would grant them economic benefits. Both Kissinger and Brezhnev were contemptuous of efforts to interject human rights issues into détente, but they nevertheless remained optimistic about resolving these complications.

The strains in the U.S.-Soviet détente process paralleled a somewhat more strained relationship with China. Chapter 6 documents Kissinger's efforts to deepen the Sino-American rapprochement with Beijing when new circumstances—Nixon's resignation and a new U.S. president and Zhou's decline and the rise of Deng Xiaoping as Kissinger's primary Chinese interlocutor—made that difficult indeed. Even though the acerbic Deng found U.S.-China relations basically "good," the transcripts show how the Taiwan problem and continued Chinese aversion to dénte contributed to a "cooling" process during 1974. Not only had Kissinger and the State Department taken steps on Taiwan that had irritated the Chinese, but his efforts to test the waters on formal diplomatic recognition revealed that Beijing had taken a hardline policy on normalization, which excluded the protection for Taiwan that Washington found politically essential. Moreover, where Kissinger had been warning Beijing of the threat from Moscow, he now found the tables turned, with Deng cautioning him that the Soviet threat to the West was far greater. That Mao declined a meeting with Kissinger during the latter's November 1974 visit suggested how much U.S.-China relations had stagnated.

Chapter 7 documents the mixed picture of U.S.-Soviet détente in late 1974 and in 1975. Kissinger's October 1974 discussions with Brezhnev in Moscow produced the basis for a major SALT agreement, which Ford and Brezhnev approved in Vladivostok a few weeks later. Disputes over the status of the Soviet "Backfire" bomber and U.S. cruise missiles made it very difficult to finalize an agreement, although negotiations continued. Another sore spot was economic détente: the transcripts show Brezhnev raging about Henry Jackson, and Kissinger making assurances that he would be able to subdue Senate critics. Nevertheless, Kissinger failed to stave off congressional action restricting economic cooperation arrangements, in part because of inattentiveness to detail and possibly because of his ambivalence to credits to the Soviets. The final agreement of the CSCE, signed at Helsinki in July 1975, was a high-water mark for détente, but transcripts of Kissinger's talks with Andrei Gromyko earlier in the month disclose Soviet anxieties about U.S. nuclear policy. Moreover, an aside by Kissinger about "competition" in the Third World hinted at troubles to come.

Transcript material in chapter 8 highlights Kissinger's unsuccessful efforts to reverse the growing stagnation in U.S.-China relations during 1975 and 1976. Although Richard Nixon had promised diplomatic normalization in 1976, President Ford's election plans made it impossible for him to meet that promise: neither Ford nor Kissinger wanted the Taiwan problem to generate attacks from the Republican right. (Indeed, Ford's concerns about his election prospects induced him to end Kissinger's tenure as his national security assistant, although keeping him as secretary of state). U.S. decisions to delay normalization, however, would produce exasperation in Beijing and rebuffs to Kissinger's initiative for improved relations short of full diplomatic recognition. Although Kissinger believed that Beijing still needed Washington as a counterbalance to the Soviet Union, Beijing was more interested in keeping Washington and Moscow apart. Deng's biting attacks on détente, a difficult meeting between Kissinger and Chairman Mao, and what Kissinger saw as "insolent" Chinese behavior made problems in the relationship evident. A visit by President Ford would signal a temporary improvement in relations, including a more lenient aproach to Beijing's purchase of U.S. computers with potential military application. Nevertheless, the Taiwan issue remained a sore point with the Chinese, and the political struggles that unfolded after Zhou's death in January 1976 and Mao's demise the following

September would make Kissinger and his advisers wonder about the future of the rapprochement with China.

As U.S.–China relations stagnated, U.S.–Soviet relations declined too during 1976. Transcripts in chapter 9 of Kissinger's talks with Brezhnev and Gromyko during his January 1976 visit to Moscow show that SALT remained a key agenda item; both sides made conscientious efforts to narrow their differences and may even have achieved a "breakthrough." Fearful of political attacks in an election year, however, President Ford decided not to build on this achievement, and the negotiations remained dormant for the rest of the year. However, the specter of an Angolan civil war was beginning to overshadow SALT. Kissinger interpreted the conflict in familiar geopolitical terms, overlooked its indigenous nature, and treated the Soviet role in Angola as a threat to American credibility—a departure from the "restraint" needed to make détente work. His warnings to Brezhnev were to no avail; indeed, Brezhnev refused to discuss Angola. To serve notice on Moscow and to counter attacks from Republican primary hopeful Ronald Reagan, Kissinger's rhetoric hardened, and he began to espouse a tougher line against the Soviet Union. The future of détente was now uncertain.

The detail provided by the transcripts is useful for throwing light on a critical period in the history of U.S. foreign relations. While U.S. records of conversations cannot in themselves explain the deeper motivations or decision-making processes of all of the participants—for that, much more Chinese, Russian, and U.S. documentation is essential—they, at least, provide a basis for preliminary assessment of the Nixon-Ford era foreign policy, especially Henry Kissinger's conduct of U.S. diplomacy.[13] Some readers may feel that the documents vindicate their assessment of Kissinger as a shrewd practitioner of balance-of-power diplomacy. Others, taking the longer view, may see him as a transitional figure in the complex passage to a post-imperial world in which America would be less central than it had been.[14] Some may be less impressed by Kissinger as a diplomat and see him as a vain and power-hungry flatterer or even a counterrevolutionary who tolerated human rights abuses and was guilty of war crimes in Indochina. Still others may see him as an appeaser of totalitarian governments. Nevertheless, critics may be slightly more tolerant, and boosters more critical once they have read the transcripts that follow. Whatever one may think of Kissinger now, the growing availability of significant primary source material will enable us to make more objective evaluations of this important figure and his role in world politics.

A NOTE ON THE TEXTS

In all of the transcripts, all Chinese names were originally rendered in Wade-Giles. Since the documents were prepared, however, pinyin transliteration has become standard. On the advice of experts in Sino–American relations, and for the sake of consistency throughout the book, the editor changed the Wade-Giles transliterations into pinyin. For example, while those who prepared transcripts and other documents wrote "Peking" or "Chou En-lai," the editor has instead rendered them as "Beijing" and "Zhou Enlai." I wish to thank Professors Chen Jian, Department of History, Southern Illinois University, and Lyman Miller, Paul H. Nitze School of Advanced International Studies, for their kind assistance in providing pinyin transliterations for a number of names.

Also, nonsubstantive changes—involving punctuation, diacritical marks, and so on—have been amended throughout for reasons of clarity and consistency. Parentheses indicate comments and intrusions in the original text, whereas brackets indicate comments and clarifications introduced for this volume.

In a very few cases, a speaker's name has been expanded for clarity.

Notes

1. For significant studies of Kissinger's rise to prominence, first at Harvard and then in government, see Walter Isaacson, *Kissinger: A Biography* (New York: Simon and Schuster, 1992), and Robert D. Schulzinger, *Henry Kissinger: Doctor of Diplomacy* (New York: Columbia University Press, 1989). For a comprehensive study of U.S.–Soviet détente, with shrewd analysis of Kissinger as a policymaker, see Raymond Garthoff, *Détente and Confrontation: American–Soviet Relations from Nixon to Reagan* (Washington, D.C.: Brookings Institution, 1994). Franz Schurmanns, *The Foreign Politics of Richard Nixon: The Grand Design* (Berkeley: University of California Institute for International Studies, 1984) offers important insights (despite its idiosyncracies), as does John L. Gaddis, "Rescuing Choice from Circumstances: The Statecraft of Henry Kissinger," in *The Diplomats, 1939–1979*, ed. Gordon A. Craig and Francis L. Loewenheim (Princeton, N.J.: Princeton University Press, 1994), pp. 564–92.

2. "Back-channel" refers to telegrams and other documents relating to private communications with foreign governments that only Nixon, Kissinger, and their immediate staff saw. By design, Nixon and Kissinger used the back channel, or "presidential channel" as Kissinger liked to call it, to keep important information away from the State Department and other agencies; see Isaacson, *Kissinger: A Biography*, pp. 205-9. For Kissinger's fury over leaks and his role in decisions to wiretap, see ibid, pp. 212-27, and Harrison E. Salisbury, *Without Fear or Favor: The New York Times and Its Times* (New York: Times

Books, 1980), pp. 218–30. Kissinger's use of deception is analyzed in Gaddis, "Rescuing Choice from Circumstances," pp. 590–93.

3. For an example of the transmission of a "severely truncated and sanitized" record of a "spicy" presidential conversation to the State Department, see Lord to Kissinger, "Memcons of Meetings Between the President and Heath, Brosio," 17 Nov. 1970, National Archives, Record Group 59, Department of State Records, Records of Policy Planning Staff (Director's Files), 1969–1977, box 334, Winston Lord—Chron—Nov. 1970.

4. See Isaacson, *Kissinger: A Biography*, p. 426; Gerard C. Smith, Memorandum for the File, " Report of Visit to Washington, April 26-May 2, 1972," 3 May 1972, copy at the National Security Archive (hereafter referred to as *NSA*).

5. Even before he became secretary of state, Kissinger had extralegally squirreled away sensitive files at the Pocantico Hills, New York estate of his patron and friend Nelson Rockefeller. See Isaacson, *Kissinger: A Biography*, p. 231.

6. See ibid., pp. 231–32. Kissinger's deputy at the National Security Council, Alexander Haig, also deposited his papers at the Library of Congress, further restricting access to records of the Nixon and Ford administrations.

7. Some important Nixon-era records are not at the National Archives, however; records of meetings of the National Security Council and its subcommittees remain under the Council's control.

8. Significantly, the Gerald Ford papers at the Ford Library also include significant Kissinger material from 1974–77.

9. See John Prados, *Keepers of the Keys: A History of the National Security Council from Truman to Bush* (New York: William Morrow, 1991), p. 311; and Isaacson, *Kissinger: A Biography*, pp. 212–27.

10. Any volume of the State Department's *Foreign Relations of the United States* series will include numerous examples of pre-Kissingerian memoranda of conversations.

11. Reportedly, Kissinger is at work on his memoirs of this period.

12. All transcripts of Kissinger's talks with Soviet leaders obtained through FOIA are available for inspection at the National Security Archive's reading room. Material from the Winston Lord files at the National Archives (described in endnote 3, above) used in this collection is fully cited in footnotes and endnotes throughout the text. The National Security Archive's World Wide Web address is: http://www.seas.gwu.edu/nsarchive. Besides Kissinger material, the Archive's Web site has wide-ranging declassified Cold War-era documentation on nuclear weapons issues and U.S. relations with, and policy toward, East and South Asia, and Latin America.

13. As valuable as the transcripts are for illuminating Henry Kissinger as a diplomat and presidential adviser, they cannot stand alone. Establishing a clearer picture of the Nixon–Kissinger foreign policy strategy will require the opening of Kissinger's own papers, the NSC files in the Nixon papers at the National Archives, and NSC materials at the Gerald Ford Library, not to mention Chinese and Russian source materials.

14. For the concept of "post–imperialism," see David Becker and Richard L. Sklar, *Postimperialism: International Capitalism and Development in the Late Twentieth Century* (Boulder, Colo: L. Rienner, 1987).

Introduction:
Henry Kissinger and American
Power in a Multipolar World

To put the transcripts of Henry Kissinger's meetings with Chinese and Soviet leaders in the fullest possible context, we must consider the assumptions he brought to the discussions, the political relationship with Richard Nixon that enabled Kissinger to act on his assumptions, and the innovative policies toward China and the Soviet Union that were at the heart of the Nixon–Kissinger "grand design" for world politics. Although the total volume of declassified records remains far too slim and permits only tentative conclusions, what has been declassified, taken together with important published accounts, makes it possible to provide an overview of Nixon's and Kissinger's efforts to put the Cold War on a new footing by accommodating the two Communist giants. However new these policies may have been, though, Nixon and Kissinger sought to manipulate international relations so as to achieve very traditional goals—preserving a central role for American power in world politics and thwarting hostile political configurations abroad that could "isolate" and potentially endanger American society.

In early 1969, Kissinger went to work at the White House as assistant to the president for national security affairs. At that time, the Vietnam War had raised troubling questions about the nature and scope of America's role in the world. Kissinger himself worried that the United States was losing clout in world affairs after a long stretch of supremacy and saw new circumstances—for example, a more independent Europe, the growing autonomy of Third World nations, and U.S.-Soviet nuclear parity—as forces that were making American power "irrelevant." Yet within nearly five years—soon after being elevated to secretary of state—he would find international conditions far more satisfactory: he mused that it would be possible to conceive of "different worlds in which we have to live" where power alignments were less acceptable to the United States. He thought that current alignments were then altogether favorable. "It is extremely in our interest, I believe, to keep the present world going as long as possible."[1]

Why did Kissinger believe that the world in November 1973 was the best of all plausible ones compared with the more volatile conditions of early 1969? As one who, in classical realist terms, defined the nations with impressive military power or industrial resources as those that counted in world affairs, Kissinger saw the United States, Western Europe, the Soviet Union, China, and Japan as central to the structure of modern international relations. At the time he was speaking, in 1973, the U.S.-Soviet détente was a going concern with an apparently promising future, not withstanding the recent tensions during the Middle East October War. Indeed, Kissinger saw the Middle East outcome as one that promised a central U.S. role as peacemaker while excluding Moscow from the essentials of the diplomatic process. Moreover, having liquidated—at enormous human cost—the direct U.S. military role in Vietnam, Kissinger had moved forward in cultivating a relationship, after more than twenty years of hostility, with the People's Republic of China, which was becoming the Soviet Union's foremost adversary. Thus, as long as Moscow and Beijing were antagonistic, Kissinger saw limitless possibilities for subtly influencing both and balancing one against the other so that Washington could keep its options open while preserving its influence.

The other two power centers, Western Europe and Japan, he saw as stable: they had close political, economic, and military relationships with the United States that were codified by formal alliances or security treaties and backed up by U.S. nuclear weapons. Even though relations with both had been strained, no crisis threatened to sunder them. While Japan now had diplomatic relations with China and the West Europeans were forging their own détente with the Soviets, both still looked to Washington for security. (The Chinese had even begun to accommodate themselves to the U.S.-Japan security relationship as a counter to any incipient militarist tendencies in Japanese society.) Moreover, the situation in Central Europe was calm—an agreement with the Soviets had stabilized the once-threatening Berlin situation, and the two German states now had diplomatic relations. Kissinger had worried about West German Chancellor Willy Brandt's efforts to forge a détente with Eastern Europe and the Soviet Union—*Östpolitik*— but there was no danger of a German-Soviet entente.

The September 1973 coup in Chile against Salvador Allende's Socialist government must also have pleased Kissinger because a left-wing challenge to the status quo had been quashed. Yet with oil-producing nations now wielding power in world markets, he could not be complacent about the Third World. Nevertheless, U.S.-Soviet and U.S.-China relations were moving forward, so Kissinger could be content that there was no danger of Sino-Japanese or European-Soviet—or for that matter German-Soviet or Sino-Soviet—power centers that would exclude U.S. political and economic influence, such specters had been the stuff of nightmares for Washington policymakers for many years. The world power configuration was congenial precisely because the United States was closer to each of the other major power centers than they were to each other. American power was certainly "relevant" and, for better or worse, Kissinger had played a central role in making that possible.[2]

Kissinger reportedly had said, when discussing his success with Italian journalist Oriana Fallaci, that he "always acted alone," like the "cowboy who leads the wagon train." The truth, of course, was far more complex.[3] Clearly, he was a central participant in decision making and a critically important source of ideas and rationalizations for presidential decisions. Nevertheless, he also acted under presidential authority, and Richard Nixon played a key role in charting the administration's strategy. It was Nixon, far more than the somewhat hesitant Kissinger, who pushed hard for a new approach to China. While the paucity of archival evidence makes it difficult to determine who had more influence in day-to-day decision making, the available records show that Nixon thought hard, in his own manipulative way, about international relations and the role of American power in influencing them.

A skillful servant of power whose ascendancy and authority derived from his relationship with the president, Kissinger nevertheless believed that Nixon's ideas were often defective. After their long meetings in Nixon's hideaway office at the Old Executive Office Building, Kissinger took it upon himself to sift out the sound ideas from Nixon's harebrained schemes. After meeting with Nixon, Kissinger occasionally denigrated Nixon to his National Security Council colleagues by referring to him as the "meatball mind" and "our drunken friend." Kissinger once indiscreetly observed near an open microphone that "he was a very odd man, an unpleasant man."[4]

A combination of personal and policy considerations explains how Kissinger—a talkative, pessimistic, insecure, Harvard-educated, Jewish émigré, and Rockefeller adviser—was able to develop a close, if never comfortable, working relationship with Nixon, a California Republican legendary for being remote, insecure, and contemptuous of intellectuals, Jews, and the Northeastern internationalist establishment that had nurtured Kissinger. Nevertheless, Nixon had found Kissinger useful even before hiring him. Kissinger's role as foreign policy adviser for Nelson Rockefeller had brought him into contact with Nixon's law partner and campaign manager, John Mitchell. Even before Nixon had conceived of a role for Kissinger, the Harvard professor was passing information on the Johnson administration's Vietnam negotiations to Mitchell and Nixon. Kissinger's professional reputation, his penchant for manipulation and secrecy as shown by his campaign services, his access to other foreign policy experts, and Mitchell's endorsement, among other qualifications, must have persuaded Nixon that Kissinger could help him in Washington. Undoubtedly, Kissinger's gift of flattery and readiness to relay "insider" gossip helped; Nixon's anxieties led him constantly to seek the blandishments that his National Security assistant was always ready to provide.[5]

Nixon must also have found Kissinger's unsentimental thinking, with its emphasis on international stability and "order," wholly congenial. In an essay prepared shortly before the election, Kissinger identified "historical trends" that were producing global instability: U.S. nuclear superiority was fading, the "generation gap" limited the use of American power abroad, while old allies and proliferating new nations alike had growing capabilities to act independently. Showing some contempt for Third World revolutionaries and the nationalism of small countries, he wrote that with their "little sense of responsibility to an over-all international equilibrium," Third World leaders could "blackmail" one or both superpowers—or even threaten the peace—by exploiting their rivalries.[6]

The problem of the new era, Kissinger believed, was finding a way for American power to meet the critical need for "an agreed concept of order." Drawing on his studies of nineteenth-century European diplomacy, Kissinger believed that order required an "equilibrium of power," a system wherein the predominant powers had more of a stake in acting with restraint and in restraining the actions of less cooperative nations than in trying to overthrow the equilibrium. For Kissinger, stability was the central objective of equilibrium; he saw it as the duty of all nations to cooperate in maintaining a balance and avoiding divisive actions that could upset the world's "moral balance." Indeed, for Kissinger, a regime's legitimacy depended not so much on its internal characteristics as on whether its policies were compatible with international equilibrium.[7]

With its considerable resources and "sense of mission," Kissinger believed the U.S. could play a central role in promoting political stability and military security but not unilaterally. In part, this was because of the Vietnam War–induced breakdown of the domestic Cold War consensus. As Kissinger put it, "One of the legacies of the war . . . will be a strong American reluctance to risk overseas involvement." Even if Washington had the will to intervene, its power now had less reach. Nuclear capabilities meant little in an increasingly "multipolar" world, where the greater dispersal of economic and military power meant that "other nations have an unprecedented scope for autonomous action." Moreover, in spite of Cold War enmities, the United

States needed to find a way to limit its rivalry with the Soviets: "The nuclear age imposes a degree of cooperation and an absolute limit to conflicts." Furthermore, U.S.-European relations faced a "profound crisis"; given Western Europe's greater "economic strength and political confidence," the old pattern of U.S. tutelage was no longer tenable.

Although Western Europe's power had grown, Kissinger believed that only the United States had the resources and the "view of its destiny" that would enable it to play a "global role," however circumscribed by new conditions. Rather than directly involving itself in policing operations or vainly trying to reform the Third World's political systems, the United States would be "concerned more with the over-all framework of order." The role that he envisioned for American power was to encourage the "initiative of others," for example, by providing military assistance to regional powers so that they would police their "immediate areas," an idea that would find expression in the so-called Nixon Doctrine. Implicit in this doctrine was the hope that nations that acted "irresponsibily" would be subject to pressure or even intervention by the United States or its regional partners.

Besides the obvious international complexity of establishing this new equilibrium, the policy also involved domestic obstacles. Kissinger believed that innovative policymakers with "comprehensive concepts" would have to find ways to circumvent the foreign policy bureaucracy, especially the State Department, lest the decision-makers become little more than "referee[s] among quasi-autonomous bureaucratic bodies." Also dangerous, in Kissinger's view, were the changing values of the most idealistic youth, who saw the "management of power" as practically "immoral" and were "indifferent or even hostile to systems and notions of order." Partly because of the generation gap, the mood of the American public—including leadership groups— was now "oscillating between being ashamed of power or expecting too much of it." If Americans became "content with simply managing their 'physical patrimony,'" Kissinger worried, U.S. power would become "irrelevant" and "prospects of world order will decline."

With his preoccupation for stability, Kissinger saw a U.S.-organized equilibrium as essential to avoid international "chaos" but also believed that a central U.S. role in establishing international balance was necessary to realize other important objectives. Statements that he made later in the Nixon administration, when he was worried that the Soviets might translate their bellicose rhetoric about China into action, help explain why he saw an "equilibrium of power" as so essential.[8] In February 1973, Kissinger told a rather surprised and skeptical Mao Zedong that if the Soviet Union attacked

China, "it would dislocate the security of all other countries and will lead to our own isolation."[9] A few months later, in a May 1973 statement to President Georges Pompidou of France, Kissinger conveyed a similar thought when he argued that it was a vital U.S. interest to prevent the Soviets from destroying China. If Moscow "managed to render China impotent, Europe would become a Finland and the United States would be completely isolated."[10]

Put another way, Kissinger conjectured that China's collapse would make the Soviet Union the hegemonic power in Eurasia, and that such a tremendous shift in the balance of power would lead Western Europe to seek an accommodation with the Soviets and relinquish alliance connections with the United States. With Europe neutralized or "Finlandized," the United States would be left "isolated" in an unfriendly world environment.

Kissinger's notion that an "isolated" America was a prospect to be avoided had its parallel in the efforts of Lord Castlereagh—one of the protagonists in Kissinger's first book, *A World Restored*—to create a balance of power in post-Napoleonic Europe whereby the British isles would not be cut off from important continental developments. It may also have been related to the understanding of national security common among globally oriented U.S. elites since World War II—the belief that the United States could not survive as a constitutional democracy with a liberal capitalist political economy if it was "isolated" in a world dominated by statist command systems (communist or fascist), particularly if they dominated the strategically vital Eurasian continent. In such a scenario, unless the United States could find a way to overcome adverse international trends and to compete with rival power blocs politically, economically, and militarily, it too would have to adopt state-command methods and become a "Fortress America" or a garrison state.[11]

We can speculate further that Kissinger's Harvard patron, William Y. Elliott, a member of the prestigious Business Advisory Council, may have acquainted him with the political-economic arguments against isolation. Elliott took it for granted that that the "American system" required free access to world markets.[12] Many of Kissinger's predecessors in Washington held similar views. Walt W. Rostow, for example, who became Lyndon Johnson's national security assistant, had written in 1962 that an unfavorable shift in the Eurasian balance of power could turn the United States into a "beleaguered island and a garrison state." Later, in early 1968, Robert S. McNamara explained to Congress why it must reject an isolationist "Fortress America" stance: if it did not, the United States would face a "more dangerous and uncertain world" where pressures for nuclear proliferation would increase, and where "we would . . . have to reorient our industry and commerce to achieve a maximum degree of economic self-sufficiency with . . . considerably less economic freedom for all."[13]

Kissinger's assumptions—the importance of a balance of power and the necessity for a central U.S. role in world politics—were entirely compatible with Nixon's. So was Kissinger's interest in negotiating with the Soviets and in finding ways to readjust American power to new international conditions. Nixon had already written in *Foreign Affairs* that the United States' "role . . . as world policeman is likely to be limited in the future." As the 1968 presidential campaign came to a close, he spoke of the danger of nuclear confrontations and the need to move into a "new era—the era of negotiation." Nixon had also speculated publicly about the possibility of an accommodation with China, although, like Kissinger, he tended to regard China more as a near-term threat than a potential associate.[14]

At their early meetings, Nixon and Kissinger made significant decisions about policymaking procedures for the new administration. During the campaign, Nixon had criticized President Johnson's supposedly disorderly foreign policy process and vowed that he would "clean house," but he kept to himself the changes he envisioned. In particular, Nixon was contemptuous of the State Department, suspicious that it was full of Democrats who would sabotage his administration, and determined to shape foreign policy in ways that would support his political objectives. If he did not know it already, Nixon would quickly find out, that Kissinger also regarded the State Department as an obstacle to policymakers with a "sense of direction." Given Kissinger's own inclination for manipulation, it was easy for him to agree with Nixon that the president had to "direct foreign policy from the White House." Certainly, he was ready to help Nixon accomplish that objective.[15]

By early January 1969, Nixon had approved a set of recommendations giving Kissinger, as his national security assistant, unprecedented authority over the national security policymaking apparatus. Kissinger held the power to issue National Security Study Memoranda (NSSMs) to direct the agencies—State, Defense, CIA, and the Arms Control and Disarmament Agency (ACDA)—to prepare special studies so that Nixon and he could determine where policy changes needed to be made. Moreover, by allowing Kissinger to chair a National Security Council Review Group, Nixon gave him the authority to approve departmental proposals before they reached the president.[16]

Kissinger's adept use of secrecy and his penchant for deception—his tight control over the record of Nixon's conversations and his routine employment of "back-channel" methods to communicate with foreign governments while keeping the State Department in the dark—were central in his success in helping Nixon to win control over the levers of policy. Even with his leading position, though, Kissinger attained his preeminent role in policymaking, at others' expense of course, only gradually, in fits and starts. Secretary of Defense Melvin Laird, former chairman of the House Armed Services Committee, who had his own power base and was no slouch at bureaucratic maneuver, managed to preserve considerable autonomy as well as direct access to Nixon. Others were not as shrewd and effective. Nixon had chosen an old associate, William P. Rogers, as his secretary of state, precisely for his lack of knowledge of international affairs, in order to facilitate White House control over foreign policy. While Rogers was reluctant to accept Kissinger's authoritative position, he was neither ruthless nor resourceful enough to mount an effective challenge.[17]

Some months into the administration, the perceptive Soviet ambassador Anatoly Dobrynin, who had been meeting regularly with Kissinger, sized him up and assessed his role in policymaking. Writing to Foreign Minister Andrei Gromyko and the Politburo, he described Kissinger as a "smart and erudite person, . . . extremely vain [and] not averse to boasting about his influence." As evidence of Kissinger's conceit, Dobrynin quoted him: "Only two people can answer precisely at any given moment the position of the USA on this or that question: these are President Nixon and Kissinger." Nevertheless, Dobrynin believed that the boasting had some foundation: Kissinger had a "solid position" at the White House and was the "dominant influence on the president in the area of foreign policy."[18]

If Nixon's and Kissinger's extraordinary manipulations to control policy took place out of the public's eye, their more visible moves showed the significant degree of continuity with prior administrations. For example, in February 1969, Nixon acknowledged a central element in U.S. foreign policy since World War II when he paid his first presidential visit to Western Europe. With U.S.–European relations frayed due to disagreements over the Nonproliferation Treaty and nuclear use consultation, and Europeans wondering over the implications of Nixon's talk of limits to the U.S. role as an international "policeman," Nixon affirmed his commitment to U.S.–European relations and to NATO—a " 'blue chip' investment which must on no account be discarded." In conversations with British prime minister Wilson, Nixon reassured him that even if the "role that US leadership can play has receded," the United States remained a "very powerful country with a major role to play" and it would sustain its transatlantic defense commitments. Further, Nixon assured Wilson that he was not "perturbed" by Moscow's improved strategic capabilities because Washington retained a "'sufficiency' of nuclear deterrence," in other words, even if the Soviets launched a surprise first attack against the United States, it had enough nuclear forces to launch a devastating response.[19]

In trying to reassure NATO allies, Nixon gave them a partial sense of his basic foreign policy strategy: to settle the Vietnam War and to reach a strategic arms limitation agreement [SALT], among other goals, by trying to manipulate the Soviet Union. Even if Nixon was reasonably confident about U.S. nuclear "sufficiency," in a secret talk to NATO Permanent Representatives, he suggested that strategic arms limitation talks were necessary to "reduce the danger to peace." This emphasis on arms control as a balm for superpower tensions was by no means novel; Lydon Johnson had made abortive arms control initiatives during 1967-68 as a step toward detenté. Nevertheless, Nixon was in no hurry to start negotiations; he would not "rush into [SALT] just for the sake of talking; progress should be made on all other matters as well." He did not want to create "Western euphoria" or imply a "détente when there was not détente" because that could lead to dangerous concessions to the Soviets while "great political problems"—the Vietnam War and the Middle East crisis—remained unsolved.[20]

To try to maximize their leverage with the Soviets, Nixon and Kissinger upheld the concept of *linkage*, the idea that diplomatic contacts with a particular nation must be carefully correlated to ensure their consistency with basic policy goals. However, as Nixon told the Europeans, he would not use the term *linkage* in public, presumably because of its manipulative implications. He certainly regarded it as a policy tool that could induce the Soviets to help bring the Vietnam war to an end and help solve the Arab-Israeli conflict. Nixon was only hinting at his and Kissinger's considerable optimism that the Soviets had enough influence over Hanoi to bring about an early settlement. Similarly, Nixon also believed, as he had told Harold Wilson that the Soviets wanted a SALT agreement more than he did, suggested that Washington had some leverage with Moscow.[21]

Nixon's deep-seated anti-communism cast the Soviet Union as a dangerous rival while recognizing that new circumstances could entice Moscow to relax tensions. Nixon believed that the Soviets, although rhetorically "less belligerent," nevertheless favored weakening and fragmenting NATO as a "long-term" policy objective. Even if the Soviets had not changed their "hearts," however, he speculated that certain factors might produce a "changing of the head" in Moscow: Western Europe's strength, the "nuclear cloud above [their] heads," and an "overriding concern about China."

Nixon wanted to explore the possibility that Leonid Brezhnev and other Soviet leaders were taking a new approach but, in the meantime, NATO would have to ensure that it possessed a "credible" military threat to Moscow.[22]

Clearly, Nixon was not entirely candid with his European allies. Although his hint about the "threat to peace" conveyed a sense that arms control talks had a certain urgency, perhaps he did not find it necessary, or even wish, to observe that it was not only the Soviets who had to worry about the "nuclear cloud." In late 1970, Nixon may have been more forthright with Wilson's successor, Edward Heath, when he told him that "[w]hat disturbs me is the change in the strategic balance . . . The period of nuclear standoff has at last arrived." If U.S. nuclear war plans were put into effect, 50 or 60 million Americans would die. With a "nuclear standoff" in effect, it was evident that the United States would have to substitute negotiations for Cold War confrontations.[23]

Nixon's desire for a slow approach suggests that he had no grand vision of détente at the beginning of his administration, even if he did believe that a negotiating track was essential. Nevertheless, the frank discussion of linkage shows that Nixon and Kissinger were formulating a concept that would guide their approach to U.S.–Soviet relations. In part, they came to see linkage as denoting progress on a range of issues—Vietnam, SALT, or Berlin—as prerequisite for relaxing tensions with the Soviets. More specifically, linkage was the means by which Nixon and Kissinger tried to use incentives and penalties (carrots and sticks) to encourage Soviet conduct that was compatible with international stability, and even to give Moscow a stake in preserving it.[24] Thus, as Kissinger explained in the fall of 1973, the object of détente was not to change Moscow's basic philosophy or its brutal political system but, rather, to create a structure of international relations that would provide Moscow with "more incentive to pursue a peaceful course than a military course." If détente could be sustained long enough, he speculated, the Soviets could even develop "Western interests"—political and economic interests structured around cooperation—that "will change not so much their ideology, but their calculation of risks every time they have a tough decision to make." To the extent that the Soviets began to show self-restraint in exercising influence, they would, in Kissinger's terms, become a legitimate member of the international system.[25]

If, as Nixon suggested, Vietnam was a central focus of his early efforts to employ linkage, in his talk with NATO officials, he never fully conveyed how preoccupied he and Kissinger were with ending the war. The Vietnam War had become a central focus of domestic political crisis as well as a strain in

U.S. foreign relations, and it had to be resolved. Moreover, Nixon believed that his prospects for reelection depended on a settlement. As Dobrynin correctly observed of his talks with Kissinger some months later, "For Nixon foreign policy problem No. 1 remain[ed] the question of how to find an exit from the Vietnam war under acceptable conditions."[26]

The definition of "acceptable conditions" was the clincher. Kissinger observed in late 1973 that the war had to be settled "in a certain way if any of the other opportunities were to be seized." Any arrangement involving the "sacrifice of a government that we had been instrumental in creating" was not to be countenanced. The fate of the Saigon regime over time was necessarily an open question, but Nixon and Kissinger refused to sponsor its formal overthrow in a peace agreement. Doing so, they believed, would diminish the credibility of American power, cause dominoes to fall throughout Southeast Asia, put the administration in a politically untenable position, and ultimately make "other opportunities," such as a different relationship with Beijing or Moscow, more difficult to pursue. Nixon's professed commitment to "peace" notwithstanding, he and Kissinger, no less than their immediate predecessors, were determined to validate American credibility in Vietnam, a misguided obsession that would lead to four more years of war, immeasurable casualties, and tragedies and anger at home.[27]

The Nixon–Kissinger decision to follow a strategy of linkage by tacitly interweaving Vietnam and SALT — and, as it turned out, a Berlin settlement — caused relations with the Soviets to develop slowly, as Nixon had predicted. SALT talks began in the fall of 1969, but neither side made any specific proposals until 1970. Nixon wanted to end the Vietnam War "fast"; but the cumulative impact of diplomatic linkage, secret diplomacy, American troop withdrawals, and military pressure (for example, secret and sustained bombings of Cambodia), the means that Nixon hoped would produce a settlement, only caused the war to drag on. Kissinger made repeated appeals to Dobrynin, but Moscow could offer little help because its influence on the fiercely nationalistic North Vietnamese was limited. Following conventional Cold War assumptions that Hanoi was under Moscow's control, Nixon and Kissinger interpreted this as simply Soviet uncooperativeness. In early 1970, they publicly declared that Moscow's failure "to exert a helpful influence" on Hanoi "cannot but cloud the rest of our relationships with the Soviet Union."[28]

Believing that they needed more leverage over the Soviets to induce cooperation, Nixon and Kissinger began to play hardball in 1970. During the fall 1970 "mini-crisis" over a prospective Soviet submarine facility in Cienfuegos, Cuba, Kissinger took a tough approach with Dobrynin. He warned that "the Soviets were at a turning point in our relations," and that it was Moscow's responsibility "to decide whether we should go the route of conciliation or that of confrontation."[29] Although Kissinger would later claim that an uncompromising line had contributed to "changes in Soviet policy," he acknowledged that the parallel secret initiatives toward China had more impact. However much White House officials believed that a Soviet role in settling the Vietnam War was necessary, they did not bank solely on Moscow's assistance. Kissinger knew that China had provided significant economic and military aid to Vietnam, and he later wrote that one reason the White House sought an opening to the PRC was "to generate pressures on Hanoi which would move the North Vietnamese toward a reasonable settlement of the Indochina conflicts."[30]

Nixon had already taken a lead role on initiatives toward China in early 1969, when he asked Charles de Gaulle to transmit a message to the Chinese leadership that the United States was "going to withdraw from Vietnam come what may." Understanding that Beijing had been anxious about the huge U.S. military presence in Southeast Asia, Nixon was signaling the Chinese that troop withdrawals would begin, and that he wanted no hostilities with China over Vietnam. Nixon and Kissinger hoped gradually to draw China into an interest in a Vietnam settlement and in dealing with Washington.[31]

Ultimately, though, Vietnam was only one facet of the administration's interest in restoring relations with Beijing after more than twenty years of animosity. Certainly, with the Chinese economy weakened by Mao's experiments and the Cultural Revolution, U.S. leaders no longer saw China as a dangerously threatening "model" of social development to be isolated from international forums and the Western commercial system. Once the Sino–Soviet split deepened and escalated into border clashes during 1969, Nixon believed that it was time for Washington to seek an opening with Beijing and even to warn the Soviets against threatening China. To some extent, Nixon believed that rapprochement with China was necessary to prevent Asian countries from worrying about a U.S.–Soviet détente. If Washington and Moscow grew too close to each other, he told Kissinger and Ambassador to Poland Walter Stoessel, East Asian countries might begin to fear a Soviet–American "cabal against the Chinese." That would be "bad enough," Nixon observed, but an even worse outcome would unfold if Moscow grew so strong that it could "take over China in the sense of controlling its policies and actions." Tacitly reaching back to Secretary of State John Hay's "open door" policy, Nixon believed it essential to uphold China's territorial integrity so that it remained an independent power free from foreign control. Otherwise, he declared to Stoessel and Kissinger that a recreated Sino-Soviet bloc "would be dangerous to world peace."[32]

Though Sino-Soviet tensions gave rise to alarming scenarios, Nixon and Kissinger also saw the advantages they held for American power. They believed that in spite of Beijing's rhetorical hostility toward American policy, fears of a Soviet threat were leading China to seek a counterbalancing relationship with the United States. Kissinger was not interested in either exacerbating or lessening Sino-Soviet tensions, but he was convinced that exploiting them could enhance American power: the United States would have "much greater leverage with Moscow and induce it to establish a more constructive relationship with us." Given that Washington shared Beijing's "basic mistrust" of the Soviets, creating a new equilibrium would not merely expand the scope of containment but would even make a cruel dictatorship like Mao's China a more legitimate member of the world system. Not only would the Soviets be more nervous about U.S.-PRC relations, but they would feel some pressure to improve their relations with the United States.[33]

Nixon and Kissinger saw an opening to China as compelling for other reasons. Given the extent of U.S. involvement in Southeast Asia and the Cold War, they could not overlook the possibility that "miscalculations" might someday embroil Beijing and Washington in war.[34] A divided Korea was a potential tinderbox; and an economically ascendant Japan was becoming more nervous about a nuclear China, while the Chinese in turn were wary of a revival of Japanese militarism. China was still "strategically weak and vulnerable" and before it had the "the strategic weaponry to directly threaten America's security," Nixon and Kissinger wanted to calm the East Asian situation by developing a more "positive relationship" with Beijing.[35]

In famous remarks in Kansas City, delivered on 6 July 1971, three days before Kissinger arrived in Beijing, Nixon gave some economic underpinnings to the security-oriented analysis of his national security assistant. In a briefing to media executives, Nixon speculated on the future of American power and competitive economic strength in an emerging multipolar world. While he realized that American power was eroding, he nevertheless wanted the United States to keep its "preeminent position" in world markets, particularly in the face of potent industrial competition from Japan and Europe. No doubt trying to flatter Mao and Zhou (who quickly learned of the speech), Nixon also spoke of China as one of the great economic powers. In order to prevent China from becoming "isolated" and out of touch with "world leaders," he said that "doors must be opened" and relations between Beijing and

Washington normalized. Whether China became a great economic power or not, in a world where commercial and industrial rivalries were becoming intense, Nixon could not risk American isolation from a potentially significant area of economic development; he could not, however, risk provoking Beijing's anti-imperialism by saying so openly.[36]

As one analyst has written, there was "nothing foreordained about Sino–American détente."[37] Despite the series of public and private overtures to Beijing that Nixon and Kissinger orchestrated during 1969 and 1970, not all of their signals were harmonious. Events such as Nixon's public statement in mid-1969 that China was the "greatest threat" to world peace may well have slowed, or at least confused, the process of rapprochement. Chinese Communist Party policy assumed a "dual confrontation" with the United States and the Soviet Union, during 1969 and 1970, Mao's lieutenants were holding serious and sustained debates over whether Washington and Moscow were equally threatening. While Mao and Zhou believed that it was possible and necessary to mend fences with its distant adversary, Mao seems not to have announced this until the late summer of 1970. At a conference in Lushan, he apparently startled party leaders when he told them about the secret communications with Washington and his acceptance of a U.S. proposal for a visit by one of its representatives.[38]

However, the U.S. invasion of Cambodia in the spring of 1970 led to a temporary breakdown in communications. By the end of the year they were back on track, and in the spring of 1971 Beijing startled the world with "ping-pong diplomacy," when, during the world championship table tennis games in Japan, the PRC team invited its U.S. counterpart to China. Even more dramatic but secret was the fact that Washington and Beijing had agreed in principle to a clandestine visit by Kissinger and a later trip by Nixon. Although the transcripts of Kissinger's secret talks with Zhou in July 1971 remain classified, their basic conclusion became public when Nixon and the Chinese announced to the world that he would travel to China.[39]

Nixon and Kissinger believed that their startling maneuverings to change the balance of power had paid off. Kissinger later remarked, "Everything moved that was very difficult before." Within weeks of his China trip, the Soviets suddenly showed more flexibility on the timing of a Nixon–Brezhnev summit in Moscow, which hitherto they had stalled, and tried to link to other issues, such as Berlin. Upstaged by Washington and Beijing, they agreed to a Nixon visit to Moscow in June 1972. Nevertheless, Nixon and Kissinger kept pressure on the Soviets during December 1971 through the South Asian war when they weighed in on the side of China's ally, Pakistan, against India, whom they treated as a Soviet proxy. With these threatening signals to Moscow and New Delhi, Nixon and Kissinger sought to demonstrate their reliability to the Chinese as a prelude to Nixon's talks with Zhou and Mao.[40]

Nixon's dramatic visits to Beijing and Moscow in 1972 were media spectacles. In China, Nixon met with Mao and Zhou and signed off on the Shanghai Communiqué, in which both nations announced their opposition to "hegemony," that is, Soviet expansionism, while the United States formally confirmed its intent to reduce and then terminate its military presence in Taiwan. Already running for reelection, Nixon boasted that his China trip was the "week that had changed the world." A few months later he traveled to Moscow, met with Brezhnev, and approved major agreements on strategic weapons, anti-ballistic missiles (ABMs), and principles of U.S.–Soviet conduct. In promoting these arrangements, Nixon would use more grand rhetoric. In an address to Congress on his return, he would declaim that "we witnessed the beginning of the end of an era," in which millions of people lived "under the shadow of a nuclear war which could be touched off by the arms race." By slowing the spiral of nuclear weapons buildup, "we have begun to reduce the level of fear by reducing the causes of fear."[41]

Despite the overselling of U.S.–Soviet détente, which would haunt its architects in later years, the Nixon administration had indeed taken major steps toward establishing a new international balance of forces. The agreements with Moscow began to define concrete ways by which mitigating U.S.–Soviet rivalry could contribute to Kissinger's goal of an "equilibrium of power." With the ABM treaty, the superpowers had closed off the possibility of a spiraling, potentially dangerous competition in anti-ballistic missile systems; and with the SALT I agreement, the Nixon administration had put a ceiling on the buildup of Soviet ballistic missiles while (in what turned out to be a short-sighted move) preserving the U.S. advantage in nuclear warheads deployed on lethal multiple independently targetable reentry vehicles (MIRVs). While Nixon and Kissinger would deprecate the value of the "Basic Principles of Relations Between the United States and the Soviet Union" that Nixon signed, the document nevertheless established a code of conduct for superpower competition, including peaceful coexistence, "sovereignty, equality, non-interference in internal affairs," mutual restraint, and crisis avoidance.[42]

Notwithstanding Kissinger's general indifference to economic policy issues, at least in this stage of his career, economic problems on both sides — Washington's need to expand exports in order to correct balance of payments problems and Moscow's agricultural shortfalls and need to modernize its economy—created powerful incentives for détente. In keeping with the linkage tactics, Nixon and Kissinger held back on delivering economic benefits until détente was fairly advanced; consequently, it became necessary to create incentives for encouraging Soviet foreign policy restraint. Thus, soon after Nixon's visit, the administration followed up on its promises of U.S. agricultural credits and the Soviets purchased hundreds of millions of dollars worth of U.S. grain. In October 1972, Washington and Moscow signed a comprehensive trade agreement and a settlement of World War II lend-lease aid to the Soviets was linked to the provision of most-favored-nation treatment for Soviet exports. Moreover, the United States committed itself to provide substantial Export-Import Bank credits to underwrite U.S. industrial exports. Efforts to implement these arrangements had significant implications for the détente process in the following years.[43]

Parallel to and interrelated with the U.S.-Soviet détente were Western European efforts, in which West Germany played a key role, to establish a process of détente with the Soviets. West German *Ostpolitik* provided important impetus; both Nixon and Kissinger had to move forward on détente with the Soviets because of their exaggerated concerns that West German Chancellor Brandt's diplomacy would increase Soviet influence and turn the Federal Republic into a "Finland" in which U.S. influence would be lost or diminished severely. A key development, very much shaped by Kissinger's back-channel efforts, was the 1971 Quadripartite Agreement on Berlin; this agreement stabilized Western access to Berlin and made that divided city less a flashpoint for superpower confrontation. Important in itself, the Berlin agreement also made the White House receptive to the upcoming Moscow summit and raised interest on both sides in multilateral talks on European security and on force levels in Central Europe.[44]

A European security conference to ratify postwar borders had been a Soviet goal for some years; Washington, on the other hand, supported talks on Mutual and Balanced Force Reductions (MBFR) in part to dampen Congressional pressure to withdraw U.S. troops from Western Europe. For Nixon and Kissinger, and for NATO more generally, the popular "Mansfield Amendment" posed many risks; Brezhnev, too was apprehensive of it, because of the impact U.S. troop withdrawals might have on Germany's military role in Europe, including Bonn's attitude toward nuclear weapons. At the 1972 summit Nixon and Brezhnev agreed to MBFR talks and also approved the Conference on Security and Cooperation in Europe (CSCE). The latter began with a preliminary meeting in Helsinki in November, and the MBFR talks started in Vienna in January 1973. Kissinger would routinely disparage the CSCE as a "loser for the West, because of the weakening of the alliance in a period of illusions," but it was the price to be paid for the MBFR negotiations he saw as essential for safeguarding the U.S. military presence in Europe.[46]

Nixon and Kissinger reached a Vietnam settlement—initially the central objective of their contacts with Moscow and Beijing—in the fall of 1972, months after their meetings with Mao and Brezhnev. Determined to preserve the Thieu regime, at least for a "decent interval," Washington continued to expend blood and treasure in order to coerce Hanoi to desist its efforts to overthrow Washington's Vietnamese client. In fact, after the Beijing and Moscow summits, both the Chinese and the Soviets began to increase pressure on the North Vietnamese to compromise. Eventually, Hanoi acquiesced, if only temporarily, to the Thieu regime; Washington, in turn, had to accept the North Vietnamese troop presence in the South. The precise impact of Chinese and Soviet pressure on North Vietnam's diplomacy remains to be learned, but whatever it was, the U.S. direct military role in Vietnam nevertheless came to an end in January 1973.[47]

Settling the Vietnam War certainly played an important role in Nixon's and Kissinger's early interest in détente with Moscow and rapprochment with Beijing. Nevertheless, a more complex logic, derived from Cold War rivalries with the Soviets and a commitment to reinforcing a central U.S. role in world politics, was fundamental to White House efforts to improve relations with both Communist giants. Putting Cold War containment policy on a new basis, the Nixon administration sought an equilibrium based on Sino-Soviet estrangement, cooperation with Moscow, and a covert tilt toward Beijing, while trying to ensure that neither power became too close to U.S. allies in Asia and Europe. Those endeavors provide the context for and the substance of the transcripts that follow.

Neither Kissinger nor Nixon had any illusions about the difficulty of repairing, much less improving, relations with decades-old political and ideological adversaries. They had their own anti-Communist suspicions, and significant domestic political forces militated against détente with Moscow and looked askance at going too far in placating Beijing. Thus, the following transcripts disclose not only serious efforts to achieve rapprochement with both Beijing and Moscow but also the souring of U.S.–Soviet détente and the stagnation in U.S.-China relations during the mid-1970s. The "present world" that Kissinger found so satisfactory in late 1973 had become within a few years, less appealing or certain. Not only did U.S.–China relations stagnate during the mid-1970s, but the Nixon–Kissinger effort to forge a U.S.–Soviet détente began to unravel. U.S.–China relations stopped developing in part because of Beijing's deep suspicions of U.S.–Soviet negotiations, and in part because of the Ford administration's reluctance to cut off formal political ties with Taiwan—the condition for further progress in relations with the mainland. Hampering U.S.–Soviet relations were the growing domestic U.S. criticisms of détente, which contributed to the impasse in the SALT II talks and the controversy over Soviet assistance to the winner in the Angolan civil war, the Popular Movement for the Liberation of Angola (MPLA).

The transcripts in this book cannot by themselves account for the problems that frustrated U.S.–China and U.S.–Soviet relations. U.S., Russian, and Chinese archival sources that are still classified or otherwise unavailable are essential for clarifying the developments of the mid-1970s. However, even the available materials show how the troubled relations with Beijing and Moscow stemmed in part from flaws in Nixon–Kissinger diplomacy and policymaking procedures, some of which ultimately brought down Nixon himself and reduced Kissinger's status. Such flaws included their preoccupation with secrecy, their exaltation of presidential authority and control, their contempt for bureaucracy and Congress, and their deeply manipulative conception of politics in United States' international relations.[48]

Nixon–Kissinger efforts to aggrandize presidential power and to use it secretly engendered adventurous actions that, once detected, made it impossible for Nixon to govern and raised suspicions of Kissinger that eventually undermined his authority. By late 1973, with Watergate bedeviling and then ruining his presidency, Nixon could no longer focus on the steps needed to sustain détente. Moreover, after Nixon's resignation, his promise to normalize relations with Beijing in 1976 became virtually null and void and discomfited U.S.–China relations in the following years. Kissinger's inclination toward deception also impaired his pursuit of détente. When he tried to negotiate a SALT II agreement in 1975 and 1976, mistrustful Pentagon officials successfully insisted that he be put on a short leash.

Both Nixon and Kissinger expected a certain amount of "trust" and deference from Congress and the public, but the weakened Cold War consensus, growing suspicion of their conduct of diplomacy, and Watergate made acquiescence and trust problematic, not only among antiwar critics but also among influential and ambitious Cold Warriors in Congress.[49] Thus, their "grand design" for détente partially collapsed from lack of congressional support for economic benefits to the Soviet Union—Most Favored Nation access to U.S. markets and Export-Import Bank credits—that Nixon and

Kissinger believed were necessary to induce Soviet cooperation. Particularly determined opposition to economic détente from Sen. Henry Jackson complicated Kissinger's efforts immeasurably. His studies of the adroit maneuvers of nineteenth-century statesmen had not prepared him for real-world dealings with legislative bodies. That Kissinger shared Jackson's suspicions of Soviet leadership may have further reduced his effectiveness in getting credits for Moscow: neither man wanted to make the Soviet Union more robust economically.

The virtual denial of economic benefits was not the only impediment to détente. The Angolan situation—particularly in light of Kissinger's insistence that it represented a Soviet challenge to American credibility—also soured U.S.-Soviet relations. Even without conflict over southern Africa, however, Kissinger's policies were in trouble domestically. Though he had high, if declining, approval ratings in public opinion polls during the mid-1970s, the polls also showed that the public believed that Soviet power was increasing.[50] Apparently, Kissinger's diplomacy had not put the public at ease, much less convince it that détente was the best means to contain Soviet power.

Kissinger's emphasis on elite policy management and public acquiescence led him to overlook one of his own maxims: "The acid test of a policy is its ability to gain domestic support."[51] It was only in 1975 that he began to make public education a priority or develop significant reservoirs of support for détente, especially among conservatives. The concept of détente as regulated competition between adversaries was not an impossible sell, but Americans had little experience in subtle dealings with antagonists, accustomed as they were to regarding the Soviet Union as an archenemy than a rival. In the wake of the Angolan crisis, it became very easy for Kissinger himself to emphasize the idea that the Soviet Union was a competitor to be contained.[52]

Despite problems in execution, though, the U.S.-Soviet détente that Kissinger helped to launch set an extraordinarily important precedent, one that future policymakers could not easily ignore. Even Ronald Reagan, who had attacked Kissinger's détente during the 1970s, found, when U.S.-Soviet tensions reached disturbing levels between 1981 and 1983, that he had alternative to reviving communications with Moscow and developing "constructive cooperation." Reagan, of course, was lucky to face in Mikkail Gorbachev a Soviet leader who was far more able than Brezhnev to deal with the challenges of his time. But even before Gorbachev came to power, Reagan reluctantly concluded that a hostile policy offering the Soviets no incentives to cooperate was incompatible with American security. As Reagan put it, even if "neither of us likes the other system . . . living in this nuclear age makes it imperative that we do talk."[53]

From any standpoint, though, the Nixon–Kissinger effort to establish dialogue with China was a significant and substantially more successful initiative than détente. Gerald Ford's decision not to fulfill his predecessor's promise to normalize U.S.–China diplomatic relations in 1976 displeased Beijing, but the manipulative diplomacy underlying the Nixon–Kissinger approach to China may well have contributed to the impasse that developed during 1974 and 1975. Kissinger, wanting to develop a "tacit" alliance with Beijing and believing that the administration had "leverage" over both China and the Soviet Union, had repeatedly warned the Chinese of the Soviet threat.[54] His fears were overstated, however, and his warnings may have led some among China's elite to conclude that he had tried to manipulate them. The Chinese were not willing to put relations with Washington at risk, nor were they fond of Kissinger's overtures. In the meantime, to Kissinger's dismay, Vice Premier Deng Xiaoping proved himself adept at manipulating the Soviet threat and criticizing U.S. détente policy.

Even if Beijing–Washington relations did not unfold smoothly, Kissinger's precedent remained important for succeeding administrations. In trying to establish a special security relationship with Beijing—by expanding intelligence cooperation, proposing a hotline to provide Beijing with strategic warnings, and supporting relaxed controls over sensitive technology exports—Kissinger sought to strengthen Sino–American cooperation as a bulwark against Moscow. This policy of favoring close security relations almost to the point of incorporating Beijing into the Western security system presented a serious dilemma in 1989 when human rights abuses in China became the subject of world opprobrium after the Tiananmen Square repression. When Kissinger had policymaking authority, he did not see Beijing's internal political practices as relevant to policy because they had little to do with a regime's international legitimacy. Even today, when there is no "Soviet threat" and U.S. policymakers have broader notions of legitimacy, they tend to follow Kissingerian logic by treating human rights concerns as secondary to overall strategic and economic relationships.[55]

Although it is easy to find fault, Kissinger nevertheless deserves credit for playing a central role in moving U.S.–China relations toward normalization and reducing tensions with the Soviet Union. The transcripts that follow illuminate a crucial phase in the history of the Cold War, when U.S. policymakers sought to move beyond the confrontations of the past. They show as well how concerns for credibility and the centrality of American power, a manipulative conception of international relations, and exaggerated fears of the Soviet Union made it very difficult to transcend the conflicts of the past.

Notes

1. See "East Asian Chiefs of Mission Conference- Tokyo, Japan, Thursday, Nov., 15 1973, Afternoon Session"; copy at U.S.-Japan Collection, National Security Archive (hereafter referred to as NSA). Franz Schurmann, *The Foreign Politics of Richard Nixon: The Grand Design* (Berkeley: University of California Institute for International Studies, 1986), pp. 7–13, provides an incisive depiction of the socio-political problems facing Nixon when he came to power.

2. For Kissinger's assumptions about U.S. predominance, see Robert Beisner, "History and Henry Kissinger," *Diplomatic History* 14 (Fall 1990), pp. 511–27. For basic concepts of U.S. national security that had emerged during the 1940s and would show their influence in Kissinger's thinking, see Melvyn P. Leffler, *A Preponderance of Power: National Security, the Truman Administration, and the Cold War* (Stanford, Calif.: Standford University Press, 1992).

3. See Oriana Fallaci, *Interview with History* (New York: Liveright, 1976), pp. 40–41.

4. For a detailed account of the Nixon-Kissinger relationship, see Walter Isaacson, *Kissinger: A Biography* (New York: Simon and Schuster, 1992), pp. 129–51.

5. For the origins of the Nixon–Kissinger association, see ibid. as well as Stephen E. Ambrose, *Nixon*, Vol 2: *The Triumph of a Politician* (New York: Simon and Schuster, 1989), pp. 231–33. For John Mitchell's role as an intermediary, see Harrison E. Salisbury, *Without Fear or Favor: The New York Times and Its Times* (New York: Times Books, 1980), p. 229. For insightful sketches of the relationship, see Walter LaFeber, *The American Age: United States Foreign Policy at Home and Abroad Since 1750* (New York: Norton, 1989), pp. 599–602 and Joan Hoff-Wilson, *Nixon Reconsidered* (New York: Norton, 1994), pp. 149–57.

6. This paragraph and those that follow draw on Henry Kissinger, "The Central Issues of American Foreign Policy," in *Agenda for the Nation*, ed. Kermit Gordon (Washington, D.C.: Brookings Institution, 1968), pp. 585–614. See also the discussion in Mike Bowker and Phil Williams, *Superpower Detente: A Reappraisal* (London: Royal Institute of International Affairs, 1988), pp. 50–51.

7. For insight into Kissinger's thinking about equilibrium and stability, see Robert Litwak, *Detente and the Nixon Doctrine: American Foreign Policy and the Pursuit of Stability, 1969–1976* (New York: Cambridge University Press, 1984), esp. pp. 61–62.

8. For "chaos" and "survival," see Kissinger, *A Necessity for Choice: Prospects of American Foreign Policy* (New York: Anchor, 1962), p. 8.

9. Mao laughed, "How will that happen? How would that be?" Kissinger did not elaborate. See p. 107 of this volume.

10. See memorandum of conversation, [memcon] 29 May 1973, National Archives, Record Group 59, Department of State Records Policy Planning Staff (Director's Files), 1969–1977 (hereafter referred to as *PPS* with archival box number and file information), box 328, China Exchanges 16 May–13 June 1973. On 4 August 1972, Kissinger made a comparable statement in a discussion with China's ambassador to the United Nations,

Huang Hua: "We believe also that it is against our interests to permit the establishment of an hegemony in Eurasia dominated from Moscow." See chapter 1 of this volume.

11. See John A. Thompson, "Another Look at the Downfall of 'Fortress America'," *Journal of American Studies* 26 (Dec. 1992), 405-6, and Leffler, *Preponderance of Power*, pp. 19-23. For some of the origins of internationalist opposition to exclusive power blocs in Eurasia, see Martin J. Sklar, "The Open Door, Imperialism, and Post-imperialism: Origins of U.S. 20th Century Foreign Relations Circa 1900," in *Postimperialism and World Politics*, ed. Richard L. Sklar and David Becker (Westport, Conn.: Praeger, forthcoming).

12. For Kissinger's association with Elliott, see Isaacson, *Kissinger: A Biography*, pp. 62-64. In a 1946 lecture at the School for Advanced International Studies, Elliott had spoken of foreign trade as "very important" for the U.S. economy and had said that if the United States failed to make a loan to the British "state monopoly capitalism" could dominate the "world system" with deleterious consequences for international order and the "American system." "American Economic Foreign Policy Interest in Britain's Future," n.d., William Y. Elliott Papers (Archives, Herbert Hoover Institution), box 64.

13. See Rostow to Rusk, "Alliances and Their Inhibiting Effect . . . ," 15 Nov. 1962, *RG 59*, Policy Planning Staff Records for 1962, box 228, Chron—File Nov.-Dec. 1962; and "Statement of Secretary of Defense Robert S. McNamara Before the House Subcommittee on Department of Defense Appropriations on the Fiscal Year 1969-1973 Defense Program and 1969 Defense Budget," n.d., Nuclear History Collection (copy at *NSA*).

14. See Richard Nixon, "Asia After Vietnam," *Foreign Affairs* 46 (Oct. 1967), pp. 111-25; Raymond L. Garthoff, *Détente and Confrontation: American-Soviet Relations from Nixon to Reagan* (Washington: D.C. Brookings Institution, 1994) p. 15; and Allen S. Whiting, "Sino-American Detente," *China Quarterly* 82 (June 1980), p. 335.

15. See Stephen Ambrose, *Nixon: The Triumph of a Politician, 1962-72* (New York Simon and Schuster: 1989), pp. 231-33; and Isaacson, *Kissinger: A Biography*, pp. 151-56.

16. See Isaacson, *Kissinger: A Biography*, pp 151-56; and Litwak, *Detente and the Nixon Doctrine*, pp. 64-67. For Nixon, Kissinger, and their NSC system, see John Prados, *Keepers of the Keys: A History of the National Security Council from Truman to Bush* (New York: William Morrow, 1991), pp. 261-378, and Hoff, *Nixon Reconsidered*, pp. 159-66.

17. Garthoff, *Détente and Confrontation*, p. 79; and Isaacson, *Kissinger: A Biography*, pp. 195-205.

18. See "Dobrynin and Kissinger, 1969—Opening the Back Channel," *Cold War International History Project Bulletin* 3 (Fall 1993), pp. 62-67. Dobrynin's evaluation of Kissinger in his memoirs was rather more circumspect. See Dobrynin, *In Confidence: Moscow's Ambassador to America's Six Cold War Presidents* (New York: Times Books, 1995), pp. 199-200.

19. See memcon with Harold Wilson, 24 March 1969, National Archives, Record Group 59, Department of State Records, Executive Secretariat Conference Files, 1966-72 (hereafter referred to as *Conference Files*, with archival box number and file information), box 484, President Nixon's Trip to Europe 23 Feb-2 March 1969 Chronology Memcons vol. I of VIII. Nixon credited Kissinger with inventing the term "sufficiency."

20. See State 032316 to U.S. Embassy Paris, 1 March 1969, *Conference Files*, box 484, Presi-

dent Nixon's Trip to Europe 23 Feb.–2 March 1969 Chronology Memcons vol. I of VIII; and Garthoff, *Detente and Confrontation*, pp 84, 279–81. For an important study putting détente in the context of developments during the 1960s, see Keith L. Nelson, *The Making of Détente: Soviet–American Relations in the Shadow of Vietnam* (Baltimore: Johns Hopkins University Press, 1994).

21. See State telegram 032316 to U.S. Embassy Paris, 1 March 1969; and Garthoff, *Detente and Confrontation*, pp. 279–81; William B. Bundy, *A Tangled Web: The Making of Foreign Policy in the Nixon Presidency* (New York: Hill and Wang, 1998), p. 56.

22. Nixon's speculations about a shift in Soviet thinking on international relations were correct. See Nelson, *Making of Détente*, pp. 119–28.

23. See Memcon, 3 Oct. 1970, attached to Lord to Kissinger, "Memcons of Meetings Between the President and Heath, Brosio," 17 Nov. 1970. *PPS* box 334, Winston Lord-Chron-Nov. 1970. For substituting confrontation with negotiations, see Garthoff, *Détente and Confrontation*, p. 217.

24. Garthoff, *Détente and Confrontation*, pp. 32–27; and Bowker and Williams, *Superpower Détente*, pp. 52–55. See also John Lewis Gaddis's interpretation of linkage in his thoughtful essay, "Rescuing Choice from Circumstances: The Statecraft of Henry Kissinger," in *The Diplomats, 1939–1979* ed. Gordon A.Craig and Francis L. Lowenheim (Princeton, N.J.: Princeton University Press, 1994), pp. 577–80.

25. See "East Asian Chiefs of Mission Conference November 14–16, 1973, Afternoon Session" (copy at *NSA*). In the same talk, Kissinger stated that it was not inconceivable that Soviet domestic structure would change under the impact of détente, but that would only be a "welcome bonus," not a key goal.

26. See "Dobrynin and Kissinger, 1969—Opening the Back Channel," *Cold War International History Project Bulletin 3* (Fall 1993), pp. 62–67.

27. See Garthoff, *Détente and Confrontation*, pp. 279–81; and "East Asian Chiefs of Mission Conference November 14–16, 1973, Afternoon Session," (copy at *NSA*). For the administration's Vietnam policy generally, see George Herring, *America's Longest War: The United States and Vietnam, 1950–1975* (New York: McGraw-Hill, 1996), pp. 243–83. For the role "credibility" played in U.S. policy, see Robert J. McMahon, "Credibility and World Power," *Diplomatic History* 15 (Fall 1991), pp. 455–72; and Robert H. Johnson, *Improbable Dangers: U.S. Conception of Threat in the Cold War and After* (New York: St. Martin's, 1994). For a critique of Kissinger's notion of credibility, see Gaddis, "Rescuing Choice from Circumstances," pp. 578–80.

28. See Garthoff, *Détente and Confrontation*, pp. 279–87; and Herring, *America's Longest War*, 243–47. For the often-troubled Soviet–North Vietnam relationship, see Ilya V. Gaiduk, *The Soviet Union and the Vietnam War* (Chicago: I. R. Dee, 1996).

29. See Lord to Kissinger, "Your Recent Meetings with Dobrynin," 14 Oct. 1970, box 334, Winston Lord—Chron Oct. 11–31 1970. For Cienfuegos and U.S.–Soviet relations during 1970, see Garthoff, *Détente and Confrontation*, pp. 87–100; and Isaacson, *Kissinger: A Biography*, pp. 281–315.

30. See "East Asian Chiefs of Mission Conference—Tokyo, Japan, Thursday, November 15, 1973, Afternoon Session," n.d., (copy at *NSA*); and Kissinger to the President, "Your Trip to the People's Republic of China: A Scope Analysis . . . ", 20 Nov. 1975, *PPS*, box 380, China Notes.

31. See Garthoff, *Détente and Confrontation*, p. 286. For China's role in Vietnam during the 1960s, see Chen Jian, "China's Involvement in the Vietnam War, 1964–1969," *The China Quarterly* 142 (June 1995): pp. 357–87; and Qiang Zhai, "Beijing and the Vietnam Conflict, 1964-1965 . . . ," *Cold War International History Project Bulletin* 6–7 (Winter 1995/96), pp. 233–50.

32. See memcon, "Conversation with the President Concerning China and U.S.-Chinese Contacts," 9 Sept. 1969, National Archives, Record Group 59, Department of State Records, State Department Foreign Policy Files, 1967–69, POL Chicom-US. For U.S. China policy during earlier phases of the Cold War, see Rosemary Foot, "The Eisenhower Administration's Fear of Empowering the Chinese," *Political Science Quarterly* 111 (1996), pp. 505–21; and *The Practice of Power: U.S. Relations with China Since 1949* (Oxford: Clarendon, 1995). For the Open Door policy and its origins at the beginning of the century, see LaFeber, *American Age,* pp. 204–11.

33. See Kissinger to the President, "Your Trip to the People's Republic of China: A Scope Analysis . . . ," 20 Nov. 1975. See also NSSM 106, "China Policy," 19 Nov. 1970; copy at *NSA*. For comprehensive treatments of the opening to China, see Garthoff, *Detente and Confrontation*, pp. 227–78; Robert S. Ross, *Negotiating Cooperation: The United States and China, 1969-1989* (Stanford, Calif.: Stanford University Press, 1995), pp. 17–54; Bundy, *A Tangled Web*, pp. 100-110, 231–45, and 305–7. For Nixon-Kissinger strategy, see also Foot, *Practice of Power*, pp. 135–38.

34. For perceptive analysis of the relationship between Nixon-era security policy in East Asia and the administration's diplomatic initiatives, see Earl Ravenal, *Large-scale Foreign Policy Change: the Nixon Doctrine as History and Portent* (Berkeley: University of California Institute for International Studies, 1989).

35. See Kissinger to the President, "Your Trip to the People's Republic of China: A Scope Analysis . . . ," 20 Nov. 1975. See also "People's Republic of China," 14 Aug. 1974, *PPS*, box 376, China—Sensitive 1 July.-16 Aug, 1974. U.S. intelligence agencies anticipated that Beijing could start fielding long-range ICBMs capable of striking Washington by 1976, if not earlier. See U.S. Defense Intelligence Agency, "Soviet and People's Republic of China Nuclear Weapons Employment Policy and Strategy," March 1972 (copy at *NSA*).

36. See *Public Papers of the President of the United States: Richard Nixon, 1971* (Washington, D.C., U.S. Government Printing Office, 1972), pp. 802–7. For an astute commentary on Nixon's speech, see Foot, *Practice of Power*, p. 222; and John Judis, *Grand Illusion: Critics and Champions of the American Century* (New York: Farrar, Straus and Giroux 1992), pp. 210–12.

37. See Garthoff, *Détente and Confrontation*, p. 227.

38. See Ross, *Negotiationg Cooperation*, pp. 26–27; and Garthoff, *Détente and Competition*, pp. 227–54. For Chinese debates, see John W. Garver, *China's Decision for Rapprochement with the United States, 1968-1971* (Boulder, Colo.: Westview Press, 1982). For Zhou's important role in encouraging a rapprochment with Washington, see Shu Guang Zhang, "In the Shadow of Mao: Zhou Enlai and New China's Diplomacy," in *The Diplomats*, ed. Craig and Loewenheim, pp. 364; and Dick Wilson, *Chou: The Story of Zhou Enlai* (London: Hutchinson, 1984), p. 272.

39. For a detailed chronology of U.S.-Chinese secret communications, see Peter Rodman

to Kissinger, "Who Invited Whom?" 13 Oct. 1971, National Archives, Nixon Presidential Materials Project, HAK Office Files, box 13, China.

40. See Garthoff, *Détente and Confrontation*, p. 108; and Dobrynin, *In Confidence*, pp. 326–27.

41. See *Détente and Confrontation*, pp. 216–17, 226–67.

42. For the SALT negotiations and the 1972 summit, see ibid., pp. 146–223, 325–59; and Isaacson, *Kissinger: A Biography*, pp. 316–32, 424–38.

43. See Garthoff, *Détente and Confrontation*, pp. 341–45; and Nelson, *Making of Detente*, pp. 33–35, 98–99.

44. See Garthoff, *Détente and Confrontation*, pp. 125–27, 135–39; and Kissinger memorandum for the President, "NSC Meeting (1) Germany and Berlin; (2) Burden Sharing," 14 Oct. 1970, National Archives, Nixon Presidential Materials Project, President's Office Files, box 82, Beginning 11 Oct. 1970. For Kissinger's overstated concerns about *Ostpolitik*, see Johnson, *Improbable Dangers*, pp. 62–65.

45. Beginning in 1966, Senator Michael Mansfield (D-Mont.) (b. 1903) periodically tabled a "sense of the Senate" resolution calling for significant reductions of U.S. forces in NATO Europe to induce other NATO members to share more of the conventional defense burden. In May 1971, a version of the "Mansfield amendment" that called for a fifty percent decrease in U.S. forces was close to passing when Brezhnev undercut it by delivering a speech calling for negotiated force reductions in Central Europe. Garthoff, *Détente and Confrontation*, pp. 132–33.

46. See Garthoff, *Détente and Confrontation*, pp. 127–35; and NSC staff briefing paper, "European Security," n.d., Nixon Presidential Materials Project, Ronald Ziegler Files, box 37, Issues Briefing Book (Soviet Summit, May 1972). For Kissinger's thinking about the relationship between MFBR talks and undercutting support for Mansfield, see Kissinger, *White House Years* (Boston: Little, Brown, 1979), pp. 399–401 and 947–48.

47. For the Vietnam negotiations and détente, see Garthoff, pp. 288–94; and Herring, *America's Longest War*, p. 243. For significant accounts of the 1972 negotiations, see Issacson's account, in *Kissinger: A Biography*, pp. 439–90; and Seymour Hersh, *The Price of Power: Kissinger in the Nixon White House* (New York: Summit, 1983). For significant primary source material on Kissinger's efforts to work with Beijing in shifting Hanoi's negotiating position, see *PPS*, box 329.

48. For trenchant evaluations raising issues outside the scope of this book, see Beisner, "History and Henry Kissinger," pp. 520–24; Judis, *Grand Illusion*, pp. 191–224; and Hoff-Wilson, *Nixon Reconsidered*. For emphasis on the role of deception in Nixon-Kissinger diplomacy, see William Bundy's significant study, *A Tangled Web: The Making of Foreign Policy in the Nixon Presidency*, which appeared just as this volume was being finished.

49. According to Nixon's 1971 foreign policy statement, "the leadership" could not expect a "moratorium on criticism," but it could "ask the American people for some degree of trust, and for acknowledgment of the complexities of foreign policy." See Ravenal, *Large-scale Foreign Policy Change*, p. 54.

50. See *The Gallup Opinion Index* no. 126 (Jan. 1976), p. 25, and ibid., no. 131 (June 1976), p. 28. In April 1975, 56 percent approved and 25 percent disappoved; in May 1976, 49 percent approved and 36 percent disapproved.

51. See Kissinger, *A World Restored* (Boston, Mass.: Houghton Mifflin, 1957), p. 326, as quoted in Beisner, "History and Henry Kissinger," 517.
52. See La Feber, *The American Age*, pp. 637–38. For the "weakness of the pro-détente forces," see Bowker and Williams, *Superpower Detente*, pp. 164–67. Ravenal has noted that Kissinger's balance-of-power concepts were difficult to reconcile with U.S. political traditions. See *Large-scale Foreign Policy Change*, pp. 83–84.
53. Quotation from Raymond Garthoff, *The Great Transition: American-Soviet Relations and the End of the Cold War* (Washington, D.C.: Brookings Institution, 1994), p. 144. For an overview of Reagan's Soviet policy during the early 1980s, see pp. 757–67.
54. For "leverage," see Kissinger to the President, "My Trip to China," 2 March 1973, *RG 59, PPS*, box 374, China—Sensitive Special WL File Misc & Reports, Nov. 1974.
55. See Garthoff, *Great Transition*, pp. 758–85, 819–25, and 1093–1101, for the developing security relationship with China during the Carter years.

1

"See How Those Pieces Could Be Moved to Our Advantage":

Washington–Moscow–Beijing, 1971–72

Henry Kissinger's ascendancy to chief presidential adviser and formulator for national security policy gave him a central part in Richard Nixon's efforts to develop new relations with old adversaries. Yet the new era of negotiations that Nixon proclaimed in his 1969 inaugural address unfolded slowly and unevenly. While continuing negotiations with North Vietnam, Nixon's and Kissinger's insistence on "peace with honor"—the preservation of American credibility—prolonged the bloodshed until the January 1973 settlement ended the direct U.S. military role there. Although the fighting in Indochina complicated efforts to forge détentes with the Chinese and the Soviets, a negotiating track nevertheless unfolded, even if it hardly put an end to the saber-rattling. Not only did Nixon realize his vision of a new relationship with an old Cold War antagonist, the People's Republic of China, but he presided over significant changes in U.S.–Soviet relations. The material results of the administration's triangular diplomacy—the Nixon's visit to Beijing in February 1972 and the Moscow summit in May—were significant accomplishments and especially felicitous in an election year. Nevertheless, Nixon's rhetoric about a "lasting peace" rested on a foundation of Cold War mistrust: ultimately, it was suspicion of Moscow that had drawn Nixon and Kissinger closer to Beijing. The goal was a détente that would contain the Soviets and sustain American power.

The documentary record of initial White House-level efforts to initiate rapprochement with China and détente with the Soviet Union remains slim. While federal agencies have released important documentation on the Strategic Arms Limitations Talks (SALT), White House files on China and the Soviets remain for the most part closed. As valuable as the Winston Lord/Policy Planning Staff (PPS) files are, even these do not include transcripts of Kissinger's secret talks in Beijing in July 1971 or of the other visits in 1971 and 1972. Nevertheless, Lord's papers contain extremely significant material—the record of the Nixon–Mao meeting in February 1972 and transcripts of Kissinger's back-channel discussions with Chinese diplomats in Paris and New York—which greatly advance knowledge of Sino-American relations during the 1971-1972 period. In addition, Nixon's Office Files at the National Archives include records of important meetings with foreign leaders that shed light on the thinking about relations with Moscow and Beijing, which animated Nixon-Kissinger secret diplomacy.

The story has been told many times of the complex and secret U.S.-China minuet that led to, after nearly two years of contacts, Kissinger's clandestine mission in July 1971. However, a key development that made other moves possible was the series of gestures Washington made during the last of the periodic meetings between U.S. and Chinese representatives in Warsaw. In February 1970, U.S. ambassador Walter Stoessel informed the Chinese that the U.S. military bases in Taiwan were not meant as a threat and that as "peace and stability in Asia grow," that is, as the war in Vietnam ended, "we can reduce those facilities on Taiwan that we now have." This was the United States' intention, he said. Beijing had already made clear that it expected some movement on the U.S. military presence in Taiwan, the most divisive issue in U.S.-China relations, so this was an important concession. Although it undoubtedly received Mao's favorable attention and facilitated further discussion, Kissinger failed to mention this exchange in his memoirs.[1]

With both Washington and Beijing concerned about the Soviets, and Mao wanting a presidential visit to confirm China's status in the world of nations, other deft moves enabled both sides to reach their goals.[2] Beijing's public diplomacy—inviting the U.S. ping-pong team to China in the spring of 1971—and a new round of secret U.S.-Chinese communications, facilitated by Pakistani President Yahya Khan, were crucial. On 21 April, after Nixon had publicly expressed interest in visiting China, Zhou Enlai suggested the possibility of a presidential visit.[3] In a 10 May response, Nixon wrote Zhou that he was "prepared to accept" the suggestion and proposed preliminary secret meetings between Kissinger and Zhou to exchange views and to explore a possible presidential visit. Writing on 29 May, Zhou authorized a Kissinger visit and increased the pressure by adding that Mao "welcomes President Nixon's visit." On 4 June, Nixon sealed the bargain by replying that "he looked forward to the opportunity of a personal meeting" with Chinese leaders. In early July, Kissinger made his sensational secret trip; and, on 15 July, Nixon and Zhou simultaneously announced a summit in Beijing in early 1972.[4]

One subtext of Nixon's announcement was his and Kissinger's pursuit of a complex balance-of-power strategy designed to increase U.S. leverage in world politics while avoiding the rekindling of a Sino-Soviet understanding. With Beijing and Washington engaged in a dialogue, Kissinger reasoned, the Soviets would have to work harder to sustain and improve relations with Washington just to keep China and the United States from becoming too close. Kissinger also sought leverage with the Chinese leadership, whom he saw as "tough ideologues who totally disagree with us where the world is going." Ultimately, though, his primary interest was in exploiting their anti-Soviet animus. Thus, during the 1971 India-Pakistan War, Kissinger viewed India as a Soviet proxy to be countered by leaning toward Beijing's ally, Pakistan and, if necessary, by providing military support for China. Kissinger, no doubt worried that some of Mao's lieutenants may have questioned the opening to Washington, acted as if a tough line was essential to a demonstration of U.S. reliability, lest Mao and Zhou have second thoughts about their decision.[5]

In his memoirs, Kissinger was careful to downplay any tilt toward Beijing. As he put it, he had to manage the triangular relationship carefully so that both Moscow and Beijing would fall prey to "simplifications" about Washington's allegiances. Whatever the Chinese may have thought, though, Kissinger gave them special treatment and his memoirs barely hinted at actions suggesting an evolving special relationship with Beijing, such as his decisions to supply sensitive intelligence information, including satellite photography, on various occasions. In this regard, Kissinger was treating the Chinese, but not the Soviets, as well as he treated the United States' NATO allies.[6]

Nixon's visit to China, an achievement symbolized by his meeting with Mao Zedong on 21 February 1972, was both a public relations and a geopolitical success.[7] However, their talks were far from substantive. When Nixon tried to steer away from the commonplace toward policy issues, Mao asked him to "do a little less briefing." Nevertheless, Nixon's willingness to make concessions on Taiwan and their mutual agreement that both powers had a more menacing adversary in common provided the underpinnings for the "Shanghai Communiqué" of 28 February 1972 that was issued on Nixon's departure. Thus, while China affirmed its support for wars of national liberation and social revolution and the United States affirmed its commitment to peace, both euphemistically conveyed their opposition to "hegemony"—Soviet influence—in Asia and the Pacific. Not only did this confirm the anti-Soviet underpinnings of the Beijing-Washington rapprochement, but it represented a rebuff to Moscow's earlier proposals for a U.S.-Soviet partnership in the event that Beijing turned hostile to both.[8]

The communiqué also disclosed an initial meeting of the minds on the

Taiwan question. The United States made no specific public concessions on when or whether it would break diplomatic relations with the Republic of China, but it did "acknowledge" Beijing's position that there is "but one China" and that "Taiwan is part of China." In addition, Washington reaffirmed the promises it had first made in 1970 that, as "tensions in the area" diminish, Washington would "progressively reduce its forces and military installations in Taiwan."

The United States also stated its interest in a "peaceful settlement" of the Taiwan problem, but the communiqué did not mention the specific concessions on Taiwan that Nixon had proffered the Chinese in order to cement the new relationship. Most significant, especially because of it implications for the Ford administration, was Nixon's assurance that he would "actively work toward" and complete "full normalization of U.S.-PRC relations by 1976, the year that would end his second term in office. Besides promising not to support any Taiwanese military action against the mainland or any Taiwan independence movement—apparently a source of particular concern to Beijing—Nixon also agreed to "discourage Japan or any other third countries from moving into Taiwan as the U.S. presence diminished." The last point reflected Beijing's concern about Japanese power in the region, an apprehension that Kissinger tried to alleviate by taking a gradual approach to the withdrawal of U.S. military forces from Taiwan. To avoid antagonizing Taiwan and its U.S. supporters who opposed any relaxation of commitments to the Republic of China, Nixon made all of these pledges secretly.[9]

The understanding on Taiwan was linked with a less explicit one on Vietnam. U.S. force reductions from Taiwan were dependent on the lessening of tensions in the area. Implicitly, China would also have to help lessen those tensions by encouraging North Vietnam to settle at the conference table. While China's (or for that matter the Soviet Union's) impact on the negotiations remains to be learned, in the months after Nixon's visit, Kissinger was assiduous in briefing PRC diplomats on the Paris peace talks and in asking them to intervene with Hanoi. The Chinese would express criticism of U.S. bombings, but Kissinger found the remarks "moderate." When the peace talks broke down in the wake of Kissinger's famous "peace is at hand" statement, the Chinese criticized him and argued that only the Soviets could benefit from extended conflict. Vice Foreign Minister Qiao Guanhua admonished that "one should not lose the whole world just to gain South Vietnam." Nevertheless, the Chinese kept listening to Kissinger and presumably delivered his December 1972 warnings of possible bombing attacks. While Beijing would strongly condemn the Christmas bombings, it continued to play a role as intermediary until the signing of the Paris peace agreement.[10]

The belief that U.S.–Soviet relations were fundamentally competitive was the the basis of the Nixon–Kissinger Soviet policy; nevertheless, their search for a Vietnam settlement and the recognition that the "nuclear cloud above our heads" made unchecked rivalry quite dangerous encouraged them (as it did the Soviets) to find a way of coexisting with Moscow.[11] The latter concern had shaped the Quadripartite Agreement on Berlin (3 September 1971) that substantially eased Cold War tensions over that divided city and improved the climate for further agreements at the summit level. It was the SALT process, however, that assumed even greater importance in the administration's calculations and served as a valuable political property because of domestic support for arms control. It was also a safety valve for U.S.–Soviet relations by exemplifying the idea that "negotiations could substitute for confrontation." Public interest in reducing the strategic arms competition was growing, and SALT embodied the possibility of superpower dialogue as a way to reduce tensions and the dangers of conflict. As Nixon put it, a SALT agreement would be a "boon to civilization."[12]

At the May 1972 summit, Nixon and Brezhnev approved two agreements reached in the SALT I negotiations: the Antiballistic Missile (ABM) Treaty and an Interim Agreement on Certain Measures with Respect to Strategic Offensive Arms. Eliminating an expensive and possibly dangerous competition in defensive anti-missile systems, the ABM treaty permitted each signatory to build two systems only: one to protect ICBM sites, the other to defend National Command Authorities (NCAs) in Washington and Moscow from missile attack. The interim agreement established ceilings, lasting for five years, for deployment of land-based and submarine launched ballistic missiles (SLBMs). SALT I was not exactly a freeze—it would allow the Soviets to build more SLBMs in exchange for dismantling older ICBM launchers—but it nevertheless was an important step in checking strategic competition. It was in the second phase of SALT that Washington and Moscow would begin to negotiate additional constraints and even cuts in forces.

Kissinger's penchant for back-channel negotiations had been a central element in the SALT talks, one that the agency chiefs behind whose backs he worked found exasperating. Secretary of State Rogers and the Arms Control Disarmament Agency director Gerard C. Smith, among others, believed that Kissinger's secretive diplomacy had produced less-than-optimum results, e.g., on levels of Soviet SLBMs.[13] Kissinger, however, was less interested in the substance of SALT I than in the fact that agreements with Moscow had been reached. It may have been enough for him that the Interim Agreement preserved the U.S. lead in multiple independtly targetable reentry vehicles (MIRV), the latest deadly innovation in the strategic nuclear competition. Even though SALT I force levels gave the Soviets an edge in ICBMs, 1,618 to the United States' 1,054, and multiple warheads deployed on Minutemen ICBMs and Poseidon submarine-launched ballistic missiles [SLBM] gave Washington an advantage. With MIRVs, U.S. missiles carried more than double the number of warheads that the Soviets had on their strategic forces, about 4,764 to 1,982. Kissinger would later observe in private that the U.S. edge was politically significant; the implication was that Washington's greater firepower might make the Soviets more cautious.[14]

Summit agreements on "Basic Principles" of U.S.-Soviet relations, on a European security conference, and on talks on Mutual and Balanced Force Reductions received little fanfare in Washington because Nixon and Kissinger were not very enthusiastic about them. The Soviets, however, treated the Basic Principles solemnly, as a "juridical basis" or code of conduct for superpower relations. For them, reaching agreement on a joint declaration of peaceful coexistence, "reciprocity, mutual accommodation . . . and mutual benefit," and mutual restraint was a significant achievement: It meant recognition of U.S.-Soviet parity, of an equal relationship. For Nixon and Kissinger, however, the Basic Principles were no more than a "road map," a set of "aspirations." As for the European Security Conference, a long-standing Soviet goal, now linked to prospective MBFR talks, both Nixon and Kissinger were decidedly skeptical. As Nixon put it a few months before the summit, "the Soviets may . . . hope to break up NATO" by coupling SALT with the security conference.[15]

Nixon and Brezhnev did not sign major economic agreements at the summit, but the prospect of economic détente encouraged cooperation in other areas, SALT in particular. Not long after Nixon's visit, the administration followed up promises of U.S. agricultural credits, and the Soviets purchased hundreds of millions of dollars worth of U.S. grain. In October 1972, Washington and Moscow signed a comprehensive trade agreement, and a settlement of World War II lend-lease aid to the Soviets was linked to the provision of most-favored-nation treatment for Soviet exports. Furthermore, the Nixon administration committed itself to provide substantial Export-Import Bank credits to underwrite U.S. industrial exports.[16]

The real achievements of the Moscow summit encouraged Nixon and Kissinger and their Soviet counterparts to treat détente as a process worth sustaining. While Nixon's postsummit hype conveyed the public impression that détente was about creating a "durable peace" and transcending the era of power politics, private remarks he made to advisers a few months earlier made clear that he viewed the superpowers as fundamental rivals, even if they were making significant cooperative agreements. Calling the Soviets "aggressive," he observed that "each side is out to do the other in." Indeed, Nixon suggested that the Soviets would not be interested in arms control or cooperation if it were not for internal economic problems and their worries about the "neighbor to the East." Implicitly, the Soviets were a power to be managed although in the age of nuclear parity this might take cooperative, nonconfrontational forms.[17]

The following two documents, although out of order chronologically with the others in this chapter and not Kissinger transcripts, help to put Kissinger's activities in context. Prepared by General Vernon Walters, the U.S. defense attaché in Paris, the documents show Nixon frankly describing to President Georges Pompidou of France some of the elements of his "grand design" for U.S. relations with China, the Soviet Union, and Western Europe. The meeting resulted not from China initiatives but, rather, from the impact of the United States' New Economic Policy decisions—to control inflation, to correct a gaping trade deficit and a weakening dollar by terminating dollar–gold convertibility, and to impose a 10 percent import surcharge and wage–price controls. Nixon and Kissinger, worried that European countries might retaliate against the United States, arranged meetings in December with European heads of state to help forge a consensus on international economic policy.

However much Nixon's Quaker background may have disposed him to talk about "structures of peace," these documents reflect the mixture of hardboiled Cold War thinking and sober recognition of international configurations of power that shaped his thinking. Thus, Kissinger, for all his dislike of Nixon as an individual, later admitted that in "these general surveys, Nixon was at his best" because of his "excellent grasp of overall relations."[18]

Top Secret Memorandum of Conversation
Subject: Meeting at Junta Geral, Angra do Heroismo, Terceira, Azores
Date and Time: 13 December 1971; 0900 AM
Present: The President; President Pompidou; Mr. Andronikof; Major
    General Walters[A]

[A] Source: National Archives, Nixon Presidential Materials Project, President's Office Files, Box 87, Memoranda for the President Beginning December 12, 1971.

[Nixon and President Georges Pompidou of France discuss procedure and agenda for the discussions and then agree to begin with a general review of relations between the United States, Europe, and the Soviet Union. Before briefing Nixon on his recent trip to the Soviet Union, Pompidou describes how the Soviets' "great apprehensions" of Germany have led them to want a strong French role in Europe, lest European leadership fall "by default" to Bonn.]

[Pompidou] had seen Kosygin three times and Brezhnev three times. He had been to the USSR as Prime Minister and had seen both Brezhnev and Kosygin. He had seen Kosygin as Prime Minister. He had returned to the USSR as President and, as President Nixon knew, Brezhnev had recently been in France. They were very different men. Kosygin's temperament is not very gay. He was very studious on economic and technical problems. He was fascinated by industrial progress. He was from Leningrad and in this respect he was perhaps more reserved towards Germany than others. He was afraid of the Germans and if pushed might react violently. Brezhnev was a Ukrainian and a Southerner. He was jovial and cordial and liked to eat and drink. He was folksy, liked good cars. He owned a Rolls Royce, a Mercedes, a Citroen and a Maserati. He did not yet have a Mustang. President Nixon commented that Brezhnev had all kinds of cars but not an American one. President Pompidou said that a Zil looked like an American car. Brezhnev liked good living. He was easy in conversation but in depth he was very tough. He was permanently conscious of the importance of military power but was also aware that he had to raise the living standards of his fellow citizens. We were close to a period of anniversaries. The U.S. would soon celebrate its 200th Anniversary, the French were celebrating the 100th Anniversary of the Republic. Brezhnev wanted to celebrate the 50th Anniversary of the Soviet Constitution and to them commemorate means to distribute more consumer goods to the people. Brezhnev counted on France and Germany and the West in general to furnish the means of rapidly producing more consumer goods. He is determined to import consumer goods if necessary. Despite all of this he never forgets the importance of power and at the bottom of things Soviet policy presents two characteristics:

1. It is like a river—if it finds a hollow, it flows in until stopped by rock.
2. It is obsessed by China constantly.

For now the Soviets are desirous of accentuating détente in Europe and would like to conclude their agreements with the Germans and obtain the ratification of the treaties. They are in a hurry. They watch without pleasure the formation of the Common Market. Above all they are concerned with everything that happens in Asia and try to cut the ground from under Chinese ambitions. They are presently more concerned with Chinese potential than ambitions.

President Pompidou said that he had mentioned that the Soviet leaders were obsessed with China. The dream of Yalta may not be over for Soviets who may still dream of sharing the world with the U.S. This is a deeply rooted idea. China disturbs this idea and they don't like it. President Pompidou said that leaving aside current events (Indo–Pakistan War) he believed the Soviets would seek to reach agreement with the U.S. But one must understand, and this President Nixon knew as well as he did, that to them an arrangement means retreat nowhere and advance whenever possible. This is true of all powerful people.

President Nixon said that this analysis by President Pompidou was very perceptive and very candid. It was extremely helpful and he could assure the French President that his candor would be respected and his confidence would not be betrayed. He would like to ask a question: Which did the Soviets fear most—China or the U.S.? President Pompidou replied that they feared China most, not immediately but they felt they could do nothing against China which was indestructible by its mass and in 20 to 50 years it will be so enormous that they will not be able to cope with it. Next they fear Germany. They feel Germany is capable of fomenting something. With the U.S. they feel complicity.

President Nixon said that there was one difference. They feared China certainly and Germany possibly because they are neighbors and might be a threat from a territorial standpoint. While they fear American power, they do not fear any U.S. territorial ambitions against them. He believed that in the broad landscape President Pompidou had painted we should now look at the pieces and see how those pieces could be moved to our advantage rather than theirs. To begin with, in respect to the relationship between Western Europe and the U.S., it was no secret that the Germans felt that the U.S. could not be depended on. The reasons were they felt that it was inevitable that the U.S. would withdraw from Europe except perhaps for a small force but the U.S. could not be counted upon to risk its survival to defend Europe in a nuclear war. The actions of the U.S. Senate, the Mansfield Amendment reinforces that point of view. It was all well and good for us to make the usual protests that the U.S. would stand by the European countries and that we could be counted on. In the final analysis what determines U.S. and French policy is self-interest. This was the basis for his contention that the U.S. and Western Europe, despite some differences of which they were aware, were inextricably tied together. In the long term it would be disastrous for the U.S. to leave Europe as a hostage to the USSR. That is why it was necessary for the U.S. and Europe to have close economic relations. Militarily it was vital to the U.S. to preserve Europe and to remain and not to reduce its forces unless on a very clear multilateral basis such as a reduction vis-à-vis the Communist bloc would be disastrous.[19] MBFR had begun in 1968 before he was elected.[20] U.S. policy was that it must be pursued on a multilateral basis. We had yet to find any formula by which such a reduction would not downgrade our interests in relation to the Soviet bloc. We could continue the Brosio discussions and consult to the extent that President Pompidou desired.[21] Personally the President was very skeptical. His concern was that MBFR be used simply to obtain a U.S. withdrawal. Only with a visible U.S. presence could we maintain our interest. The Soviets know this and that is why they want us out as soon as possible.

In the matter of our talks with the Soviets either at SALT or in May when the President would meet with Brezhnev and Kosygin he wished to assure President Pompidou that there would be absolutely no U.S.-Soviet talks apart from or at the expense of the European Alliance. President Pompidou had spoken of the Soviet interest in a Yalta type agreement with the U.S. Many in the U.S. felt that Yalta was very detrimental for Europe politically and economically and basically beneficial to the USSR and detrimental to the U.S. Therefore the President looked on the forthcoming talks as very tough and hard. The Soviets want progress on trade. This is possible but will not be nearly as great as many think. Some progress on arms limitation may be possible if there is an equal deal on other subjects. However, there must be a clear understanding that during this period when the Soviets have nuclear parity with the U.S. this does not mean that the Soviets can get away with a policy to humiliate the U.S. or weaken the U.S. in defense of the position of its allies in Europe.

It seemed to the President that in this framework the maintenance of strength and cohesion was more important then ever. The U.S. in the long run cannot have a viable world without Europe. Europe cannot survive without the U.S. contribution to nuclear strength at this time. The Soviets know this and would like to divide the U.S. and Europe. The Soviets also know that at the heart of the European problem are the Germans. President Pompidou could not be more correct when he pointed out that Germany, which is the heart of Europe, is always potentially, despite its cultural and economic ties to the West, drawn towards the East. The East holds millions of Germans as hostages. This is why we must keep Germany economically, politically and militarily tightly within the European Community. Ostpolitik is a nice concept and can win a Nobel Prize. President Pompidou or himself in Brandt's place might do the same. But politically it was dangerous to risk old friends for those who would never be friends. We should be very tough with the Soviets on the matter of European security. The agreements with Brandt should be signed sealed and delivered. Into this picture now come France, Britain and Germany. If President Pompidou and he, in the course of their meetings, could, without being belligerent (which neither he nor President Pompidou wanted), reach a strong understanding on principles, it would be helpful and not just for both countries. It would help his meetings with the Germans and with the U. K. to make progress on Europe. We must realize that many cynics and some honest people felt that when France left NATO [sic] that this meant the end of the European Alliance. The President was aware that France remains in the Alliance but is outside the Integrated Military Structure. He felt we would play in to the hands of our potential opponents if it appeared that France, except for some economic ties, was determined to go her own way in a race to Moscow. The President was not suggesting that France and others should not have independent policies towards the East. This was why he was having meetings with our Western European Allies so as to make crystal clear in our initiatives with the Soviets and the Chinese that our primary allegiance is to the West, not in any sense of belligerence but that is where our interests lie. This will help in making a better deal with the Soviets.

[After Pompidou raises doubts about the Mansfield Amendment— "more significant than Pearl Harbor" because Western Europe not just part of the U.S. fleet could be "lost to the Soviets"—he questions West German interest in reduction of U.S. and Soviet forces in Europe.]

They should be the most hostile to the reductions envisaged in MBFR. After all, they would be the first to be endangered. He must say that Brandt had told him that he was hostile to the neutralization or "Finlandization" of Germany. But the day the U.S. leaves Germany, the U.K. and France will not be far behind and then Germany would not be far from neutralization.

President Nixon said that the problem in the U.S. as in Europe was largely psychological. Many Americans were naive and softhearted. Many intellectuals, the media and professors don't believe there is any threat from the Russians. Some of the young also. President Pompidou interrupted to say, "Bishops too." President Nixon said that some of the Protestant and Catholic clergy feel this way too and the inherent difficulties are increased when political leaders who know the Soviets add fuel to the fire. What used to be called the cold war rhetoric is no longer salable. What was needed was the type of spirit with which President Pompidou had met the Soviets and in which he himself planned to meet them. A totally pragmatic meeting of Eastern and Western leaders. He had no illusions regarding the difficulties of his forthcoming meetings. There would be no "spirit of Moscow or Beijing" arising out of his trips. He remembered Khrushchev. He had a sense of humor. He was tough and impressive. He would not allow the almost passionate desire of so many of our people to believe the best about the Soviet leaders' desire to seek peace to blind them to reality. Not because the Russians were Communists but because they were a powerful country who saw their goals as antagonistic to ours.

The French had lived too long to be so naive. His attitude towards both the Communist Superpowers was that we cannot live with them but then we cannot live without them. Live and let live based on fantasies of our own. Our society and civilization need to recognize that their attitudes, desires and foreign policies are different from our own basically because they are Communists. From time to time they may recede from their policies of expansion but Communist theology requires a dedication to expansion taking advantage of every temporary circumstance. By that he did not mean that non–communist nations did not try and take advantages but not in areas of fundamental policy of conquest. The nations of Europe and the U.S. do not have this as part of their national policies.

The President did not know why the Soviet leaders and the Chinese leaders had arrived at the decision to meet with U.S. leaders. Not primarily because they wanted better relations or liked us. If there was not a strong Europe and if the Soviets did not have a threat in the East they would not be interested in talking to the U.S. By the same token he would like to have Dr. Kissinger tell President Pompidou what the Chinese think. He did not believe that Mao would be talking to the leader of the capitalists and courting the U.S. unless he was concerned by the Soviets and to a lesser extent by the Japanese. If one said this publicly they would deny it. Some in our country said when the President announced his trip to Peking that the Soviets would refuse to talk with us. Actually the Soviets were more willing to talk SALT, Europe and Berlin after Peking announced the visit than they had been before. After the announcement of his visit to Moscow the Chinese had showed a greater interest in talking to us than before.

President Nixon recalled that he had told President Pompidou before that when he had seen General De Gaulle while he (President Nixon) was out of office and ha[d] asked him whether he had any advice for the U.S., President De Gaulle had replied that rather than put all of its eggs in the Soviet basket the U.S. should have a more open policy towards the Chinese like France. His responsibility was like President Pompidou's. They must go into these things with their eyes open and try to defend our point of view.

[Regarding an East – West European security conference, Nixon suggests that it might not be an "unmixed blessing" for the Soviets: One result might be to open up Eastern Europe to the West. Nevertheless, he is concerned that it could "lead to the letting down of our guard and the belief that . . . the cold war is finished."]

Overhanging the whole area of Soviet–U.S. relations is the sober, somber fact that if the Soviet leader decided to risk nuclear war and the U.S. was involved, he knew that he had the power to kill 70 million Americans and we had the power to kill 70 million Russians. The U.S. President knows this too. There are limitations on power and a restraining influence not because of love but because of fear. It was essential that the two nations pursue the ne-gotiating track rather than the confrontation track. We have impressed this on the Soviets with regard to Southern Asia in the last 24 hours. The Presi-dent wished to add in regard to the desire for détente that he totally agreed with President Pompidou. The people of the U.S. and Europe wanted it, at least a majority of them did. In Europe perhaps for different reasons. The Germans want it because the Soviets can give them East Germany, U.K., France and Italy because they are convinced that we live in a dangerous world. The danger presently represented by nuclear war, not the loss of 3,000 men as at Pearl Harbor. The whole place would be turned into a grave-yard. No one wanted that. It was very important to look at the two attitudes on détente. Some sought a European Conference on the naive assumption that the Soviet aims have changed and that their designs in Europe and in the rest of the world are basically peaceful. On the other hand, some who seek détente on our side have no illusions and recognize that a different relation-ship and good relations between Europe and the USSR and the U.S. and the USSR are a practical necessity, that there are dangers in a policy of confron-tation. But we must have no illusions about the basic aims of the Communist States. They are quite different from one another. Even if they wanted it would be impossible for European or U.S. leaders to take an intransigent stand and refuse to talk. Ten years ago this was possible in the U.S. It is no longer. On the other hand, it is important that the leaders recognize that naive public opinion often demands talks that will make the whole world peaceful. We should seek such negotiations but for the right reason. By the facts of

Soviet power, the risks of confrontation in the Middle East or elsewhere are unacceptable. Therefore, we should seek to lessen the risk of war and seek, as President Pompidou had indicated, to make Europe a more viable area and to open Eastern Europe whose peoples' hearts are with the West.

The President wished to add in a different sense. He would like to discuss the motives for his trip to Peking in the afternoon. China today was a major power with the largest population in the world. She was a mini economic power with a production less than half of Japan's although she had 800 million people to Japan's 100 million. China was a mini nuclear power in relation to the USSR but we take the long view as do the Soviets and President Pompidou. Twenty years from now China will be a major nuclear power if they so wish. Do we allow that to come about with China isolated. We should make an effort for a new start. The President had made this choice himself with his eyes open to seek by necessity a peaceful relationship with them.

[The two presidents begin to close their discussion and agree that Kissinger will attend their afternoon meeting, which will include discussions of China and international economic issues. "President Pompidou then expressed the belief that the Chinese were much more complicated than the Soviets. The President said that they were perhaps more sophisticated and more subtle." They conclude by agreeing to tell the press they have discussed the President's forthcoming trips to Beijing and Moscow.]

Memorandum of Conversation, Top Secret
Subject: Meeting at Junta Geral, Angra do Heroismo, Terceira, Azores
Date and Time: 13 December 1971; 4 PM
Present: The President; President Pompidou; Dr. Kissinger; Mr. Andronikof; Maj Gen Walters

President Nixon opened the discussions by saying that he felt that they had had a good talk that morning and that President Pompidou had expressed a most perceptive view of the Soviet leaders. What was important was not so much their views as what they were like. The President then said that if President Pompidou found it useful, Dr. Kissinger could give him on a confidential basis his appraisal of where the China initiative stands. The President and President Pompidou had talked together concerning Sino–Soviet relations. They had skirted the Chinese Soviet confrontation in South Asia that was going on. The President said that if President Pompidou had different views, he would appreciate hearing them.

Dr. Kissinger then said that the President had given the background. His trip had been a chance to explore with the Chinese. It was rather complicated but we had put a series of propositions up to the Chinese. They did not have to accept or refuse. We had used intermediaries trusted by them. After contact was established, the original initiative for the invitation came more from the Chinese side than from ours. Vietnam was almost not discussed.

Our analysis was that they were concerned principally by four main countries of which three were their immediate neighbors. With a common frontier or close by. Before he had gone, the President had given him detailed instructions to explore their views of the world situation to see whether there was a basis for a discussion. He had spent 20 hours with Zhou Enlai the first time and had had 35 hours with him on the second visit.

Dr. Kissinger said that as an illustrative anecdote, on the second visit there had been a sign at the airport which said, "Defeat the American Imperialists." He had mentioned it to the Foreign Minister and that afternoon the sign had been replaced by one greeting the Afro–Asian Tennis Team.

Mostly the Chinese feared the Soviet Union, and to a lesser degree Japan. There were underground shelters in Peking and other cities. They were not against us. They had showed some of these tunnels and they were 35 kilometers long. The Chinese were far more exercised by the million Soviet troops along their borders than they were by our forces in Japan.

With regard to Vietnam it was our basic impression that the Chinese would like this to be settled, but they do not know how to go about it without moving Hanoi closer to Moscow and increasing their feeling of being encircled.

The President said that in our discussions with the Chinese there seemed to be two separate problems. We had a whole series of matters to discuss. They do not and this may complicate the problem. At the beginning of the evolution of the Chinese situation they had to set the direction and their difficulty in doing this was understandable. Chinese policy was affected by three conflicting motives: ideology which was hostile to us, their requirements for survival and their desire to lead the third world would often lead them into opposition to both the USSR and to [the] U.S. and would lead them to zigzags.

The President then asked Dr. Kissinger to explain what was planned in the way of meetings there.

Dr. Kissinger said the President would have extensive talks with Prime Minister Zhou Enlai and would also see Chairman Mao. It is expected that he will see Mao twice. It was impossible that he should not see him. There will be simultaneous meetings at different levels with the experts. Prime Minister Zhou Enlai expects to accompany the President. This has not been announced. Discussions will be far reaching. There is no agenda and each side can submit for discussion anything they want. The talks will be bilateral.

The President then said that he gathered from Dr. Kissinger's talks with the Chinese that they take the long view. They do not view the talks as producing immediate results in Taiwan or elsewhere and tend to regard these talks as the beginning of a long process. In the case of the Russians they will probably insist upon shorter range discussions when he goes to Moscow and will want decisions.

Dr. Kissinger said that there was a different style between the Soviets and the Chinese. The Russians like general statements that can be interpreted in many different ways. The Chinese prefer declarations which can be carried out and like to state differences as well as agreements.

The President then said that the attitude of the Chinese towards their neighbors can be summed up in this way. The Russians they hate and fear now. The Japanese they fear later but do not hate. For the Indians they feel contempt but they are there and backed by the USSR.

[The discussion turned to the India–Pakistan War and then to international economic policy. In order to avoid economic tensions, Nixon and Pompidou approve an agreement on exchange rates, which presages the Smithsonian Agreement to be signed in Washington a week later. That agreement will codify new currency alignments, including a devaluation of the dollar by about ten percent against the Group of Ten European currencies in order to help the United States to correct its balance of payments deficit.][22]

COMMENTARY

In briefing Pompidou, Kissinger did not discuss the back-channel communications he had routinely used for White House approaches to the Chinese and negotiations with the Soviet Union. Kissinger worked hard at preserving the secrecy of these communications; even today only a handful of memoranda of conversations with Soviet Ambassador Dobrynin have been declassified.[23] The one that follows documents a meeting that took place only a few weeks after Kissinger's first trip to China, and only a few days after Nixon's announcement of import quotas. Besides dealing with some of the key issues of détente—the Berlin negotiations and SALT—it suggests some implications of the new U.S. China policy for U.S.-Soviet relations.

Before Nixon announced his visit to China the Soviets had been stalling on a proclamation of the U.S.-Soviet summit, but now they were suddenly cooperative. Dobrynin told Kissinger that Moscow saw "no difficulty" in announcing a May 1972 Nixon visit to Moscow. The conversation made it clear enough that the China initiative had raised some hackles in Moscow, not only did the Soviets see the opening to China as aimed at them, but they also worried about the impact of U.S. moves on Japan. Dobrynin's worried suggestion that the Nixon "shocks"—the ten percent surcharge on imports and the failure to provide Tokyo with due notice of the administration's *volte face* on China policy—could prompt the Japanese to move closer to Beijing was not the last time that the Soviets would express concern to Kissinger about a Sino-Japanese entente.

The exchange on Berlin showed some of the problems created by Kissinger's secretiveness. U.S. diplomats, unaware that Kissinger and Dobrynin had already reached an agreement, had to "go through a procedure of negotiation" at the risk of a deadlock involving "overwhelming difficulties" that could derail the prearranged agreement.

Before this conversation took place, a serious crisis between India and Pakistan began to unfold, a crisis triggered by Karachi's brutal suppression, involving the massacre of hundreds of thousands of people, of the independence movement in East Pakistan (now known as Bangladesh). Despite wide opposition in the U.S. government, the White House was already tilting toward China's ally, Pakistan, and against India, which Kissinger regarded as a Soviet proxy. Well before war broke out between India and Pakistan, Kissinger was secretly encouraging "friends of Pakistan" in the Middle East to provide military aid because the U.S. Congress severely limited direct assistance to that country.[24] Dobrynin understood very well the direction of U.S. policy and was not about to accept Kissinger's assurances that "we were not lined up with anybody" in South Asia.

THE WHITE HOUSE
TOP SECRET/SENSITIVE/EXCLUSIVELY EYES ONLY
MEMORANDUM OF CONVERSATION
DATE & TIME: August 17, 1971-Luncheon
PLACE: The Map Room, The White House[B] [25]

[B] Source: National Archives, Record Group 59, Department of State Records, Policy Planning Staff (Director's Files), 1969-1977 (hereafter referred to as *PPS*, followed by archival box number and file information).

The meeting took place so that I could give Dobrynin the answer to the Soviet invitation to a summit in Moscow.[26]

Dobrynin opened the conversation by speaking about the new economic policies announced by the President on Sunday evening. He said it was the second jolt we had given to Japan.[27] I said "Well, maybe this gives you an opportunity." He said "No, this gives China an opportunity." The real danger to the world was a combination of China and Japan, and he wondered whether we took that sufficiently into account. I said that the total effect of our policies might be healthy. Dobrynin was noncommittal.

Summit

We then turned to the business at hand. I gave him the date of May 22 for the summit and September 16 or 15 for the announcement. Dobrynin said that the announcement sounded good to him and that the date would have to be confirmed in Moscow; however, he saw no difficulty. He asked why we picked that particular date. I replied that the primary reason was that the President would be in San Clemente and would not be back in Washington until September 7 and that therefore it was important for him to have a week of preparing allies and telling the bureaucracy. Dobrynin said if we told the bureaucracy it would leak. I said that nothing that we have handled in the White House has ever leaked and this would not either. Dobrynin said that he would have an answer for us very soon.

Berlin

Dobrynin then pulled out a slip of paper and discussed the Berlin issue. He said he had received instructions to get in touch with me immediately on the basis of a cable he had received that [Valentin] Falin had sent to Moscow. Apparently [Kenneth] Rush had said that he was bound by Presidential instructions to deviate from the agreements already reached.[28] Dobrynin said that this was making a very bad impression, if an agreement reached by the highest authorities was overthrown again later due to bureaucracy. I explained to Dobrynin that our problem was as follows. Neither our bureaucracy nor our allies knew of the agreement that therefore had to go through a procedure of negotiations. Sometimes the formulations might have to be altered. I wanted him to know, however, that if there were a deadlock we would break it in favor of the agreed position, unless overwhelming difficulties arose. I read to him the telegram from Rush speaking of Abrasimov's rough tactics towards the British Ambassador which certainly didn't help matters. Dobrynin said that speaking confidentially the Soviet Ambassadors in Eastern Europe were not used to diplomacy. They were usually drawn from party organizations and when they met opposition they didn't realize that they were not dealing with party subordinates. This was the trouble with Abrasimov. Falin would certainly have acted differently.

China

Dobrynin then asked whether there were any difficulties in our relations with the Chinese. Why, for example, were we delaying so long in announcing the date of our visit? I said that there were no difficulties and that the visit would be announced in due time, but that we wanted everybody to settle down for a bit first. Dobrynin reverted to his usual line that he hoped we were not engaged in an anti–Soviet maneuver. I said that events would demonstrate that this was groundless. He referred to the Alsop column that we had exchanged ideas on military dispositions. I said, "Anatoliy, do you think I would be this amateurish, and do you think that could be of any precise concern to us?" He said he certainly hoped that this were true.[29]

Subcontinent

We then turned the conversation to India. Dobrynin said he wanted us to be sure to understand that the Soviets were doing their best to restrain India. They wanted peace in the subcontinent. It was an ironic development where they were lined up with what looked we had always thought was the pillar of democracy while we were lined up with the Chinese. I said as far as the subcontinent was concerned, we were not lined up with anybody. We above all wanted to prevent the outbreak of a war, and we hoped that they did not inadvertently give the Indians enough backing so that they felt it was safe to engage in war. Dobrynin said that their interest was stability, and in fact they had invited the Pakistani Foreign Secretary to come to Moscow in order to show that they were pursuing a balanced policy. I said that they should not encourage Indian pressures for an immediate political solution since that would only make the problem impossible. I stated it would be best if we worked on the refugee and relief problems first and on political accommodation later. Dobrynin said that he was certain that the Soviet Union basically agreed.[30]

Dobrynin then asked me whether it was correct what the Indians had told them, namely that we would look at a Chinese attack on India as a matter of extreme gravity and might even give them some support. He said that the Indians had been puzzled by my comment but had then put it all together after my trip to Beijing. I said that I never commented about meetings in other countries, but that we certainly were not aligned with any country against India.[31] Dobrynin commented that he admired the general conduct of our foreign policy even when it was objectively directed against the Soviet Union, but he felt that our arms policy towards Pakistan escaped his understanding. We were paying a disproportionate amount for what we were shipping. I said that we never yielded to public pressure and that he knew very well that the arms we were shipping were minimal and inconsequential with respect to the strategic balance.

SALT

We then turned to SALT. Dobrynin said that whether I believed it or not the Soviet military were deeply concerned about a three site system, because they believed it provided the basis for an area defense and could be tied together.[32] Even a two site system was in principle hard for them. He said he thought there might be a possible compromise if we accepted one site for us with a wider radius than the Moscow radius, and if this were done there might be a basis for a compromise. I avoided an answer and told him that we would study this proposition.

Dobrynin said that he was ordered to stay here until the summit issue was settled, but he was very eager to leave because he knew he had to be back on September 20.

COMMENTARY

Parallel to the back-channel with Dobrynin, which Kissinger had institutionalized early in the Nixon administration, were secret communications with Chinese diplomats that Kissinger had initiated within weeks of his secret trip in July 1971. One of the channels was the PRC's ambassador to France, Huang Zhen. Before Huang's later assignment to Washington in 1973 as the PRC liaison to the United States, Kissinger would meet with him regularly to discuss U.S.–Soviet relations and the state of the Paris peace talks with North Vietnamese diplomats, among other issues. In part, these confidential discussions fulfilled Kissinger's assurance to Zhou that he would keep

Beijing informed on the substance of U.S.–Soviet relations. He never discussed with the Soviets the substance of U.S.–China relations, much less the details of his talks with PRC officials.[33] In this and other ways, then, Kissinger was showing the tilt of U.S. policy toward China.

Another important channel to Beijing was Ambassador Huang Hua, who headed the PRC's United Nations Mission when it was established in November 1971, a few weeks after the U.N. General Assembly voted to seat Mainland China.[34] Huang and Kissinger began holding secret meetings at a CIA safehouse in the Lower East Side of Manhattan and quickly developed a comfortable relationship across the ideological divide. Although they were able to keep their meetings secret, within months some neighbors began to wonder "what is going on." Security officials asked that Kissinger "arrive in something other than a large limousine," arrive on time, and bring a less obtrusive Secret Service detail. (Apparently the agents had "been leaping out of the car and stopping traffic.")[35]

On 10 December 1971, Kissinger met with Huang Hua to brief him on the U.S. stance toward the South Asian crisis. A week earlier, the Bangladesh crisis had exploded into war when Pakistan launched a surprise attack on India. With the U.S. public generally supporting India and the cause of Bangladeshi independence, Nixon and Kissinger secretly and deceptively tilted policy toward Pakistan, in part because of President Yahya Khan's important role in facilitating communications with Beijing during 1970 and 1971. Moreover, Nixon and Kissinger saw India as a Soviet proxy and believed incorrectly that Indian prime minister Indira Gandhi aimed to destroy West Pakistan in order to humiliate the government that had helped to forge U.S.–China relations. Kissinger told Huang how the White House was sustaining its tilt toward Karachi with veiled threats to the Soviets, secret requests to Middle Eastern governments to provide military equipment to Karachi, and instructions to send an aircraft carrier fleet through the Straits of Malacca into the Bay of Bengal.[36]

Secretary of State Rogers was furious with White House policy toward Pakistan, although he failed to realize that Nixon was as much its architect as Kissinger. Nixon and Kissinger continued to make key decisions in secret. Only they knew that their naval deployments were to ensure "maximum intimidation" of India and the Soviet Union. Although the Indians were puzzled by U.S. maneuvers, Kissinger later argued that this action had been "the first decision to risk war in the triangular Soviet–Chinese–American relationship."[37] However, he did not admit in his memoirs that he had counseled Ambassador Huang that if Beijing decided to intervene in the war "to protect its security, the U.S. would oppose efforts of others to interfere with the People's Republic." Huang's rhetoric in the conversation was militant; Kissinger concluded incorrectly that the Chinese were about to join the fighting. Beijing had as little interest in intervening as the Indians had in escalating the fighting. A week after this meeting, on 17 December, the Indians accepted Pakistan's offer of an unconditional cease-fire.

TOP SECRET/SENSITIVE/EXCLUSIVELY EYES ONLY
MEMORANDUM OF CONVERSATION
DATE & TIME: Friday, December 10, 1971; 6:05 P.M.–7:55 P.M.
PLACE: New York City, East Side
PARTICIPANTS: Ambassador Huang Hua, PRC Permanent
    Representative to the United Nations and Ambassador to Canada;
    Chen Chu, PRC Deputy Permanent Representative to the United
    Nations and Director, Information Department, Ministry of Foreign
    Affairs; Tang Wensheng, Interpreter; Shi Yanhua, Interpreter;
    Henry A. Kissinger, Assistant to the President for National Security
    Affairs; Ambassador George Bush, US Representative to the United
    Nations; Brig. General Alexander M. Haig, Jr., Deputy Assistant to
    the President for National Security Affairs; Winston Lord, Senior
    NSC Staff Member[C]

Dr. Kissinger: I see you in the newspapers all the time. You're a great publicity expert. And very argumentative.
Ambassador Huang: No, I always argue in self-defense.
Chen Chu: He counterattacks in self-defense.
Dr. Kissinger: Preemptive attack.
    Mr. Ambassador, what we have is not strictly UN business, but our contact in Paris is not there.
Miss Tang: Mr. Walters?[38]
Dr. Kissinger: He is not in Paris right now. He is going to be with the President in the Azores.
    This may turn out to become UN business, but we wanted the Prime Minister urgently to know certain things we are doing. Therefore we have taken

---

[C] Source: *PPS*, box 330, China Exchanges 20 Oct.–31 Dec. 1971.

the liberty of this slightly irregular procedure. (Ambassador Huang nods.) The apartment is slightly improved over last time. Next time we meet we will really have a suitable place. (Looking at a Chinese scroll on the wall.) There seems to be a wandering Chinese painting that we hang up every time we have an apartment. (Chinese laughter.) I hope those sentences are friendly.

Ambassador Huang: I can't see them from such a distance.

Chen Chu: (Looking at the scroll) It is an ancient poem.

Dr. Kissinger: I have some great colored pictures of you (Ch'en). I will send them to you. They were taken at the Great Wall.

Let me explain to you what we have done in various categories. Incidentally, just so everyone knows exactly what we do, we tell you about our conversations with the Soviets; we do not tell the Soviets about our conversations with you. In fact, we don't tell our own colleagues that I see you. George Bush is the only person outside the White House who knows I come here.

You know we have made a number of public declarations about India. I held what is known as a press backgrounder this week in which I pointed out that India is at fault. I will give you the text of it before you leave so that you can read it.[39] And we will continue to pursue this line publicly.

You know what we have done in the United Nations so there is no point in reviewing this with you.

[Kissinger explains to Huang the administration's decisions to cancel current economic and military aid to India, including $87 million in loans, $31 million in military aid, and $72 million in food aid, and its efforts to defer World Bank loans to India. He also describes recent warnings to the Soviets, including a letter from Nixon to Brezhnev on 6 December, that their "support of Indian aggression endangers the relationship between the Soviet Union and the United States."[40] Brezhnev's reply on 9 December is conciliatory; it proposes a cease-fire and political settlement between the Government of Pakistan and East Pakistan leaders. Nixon responds the next day after the Pakistani commander in the East had asked for a cease-fire. Without a cease-fire between India and Pakistan, Nixon argues, "we would have to conclude that there is in progress an act of aggression directed at the whole of Pakistan, a friendly country, toward which we have obligations."[41]

Dr. Kissinger: . . . In order to underline what we have said, we worked with a number of countries to provide aid to Pakistan.

Ambassador Huang: But this is not in the letter that you are quoting.

Dr. Kissinger: No, I am telling you about this. This is terribly complex. We are barred by law from giving equipment to Pakistan in this situation. And we also are barred by law from permitting friendly countries which have American equipment to give their equipment to Pakistan.

So we have worked out the following arrangements with a number of countries. We have told Jordan and Iran and Saudi Arabia, and we will tell Turkey through a channel other than the ones with which Ambassador Bush is familiar. We said that if they decide that their national security requires shipment of American arms to Pakistan, we are obliged to protest, but we will understand. We will not protest with great intensity. And we will make up to them in next year's budget whatever difficulties they have.

On this basis, four planes are leaving Jordan today and 22 over the weekend. Ammunition and other equipment is going from Iran.[42]

Ambassador Huang: You mean over the weekend?

Dr. Kissinger: We don't know the exact time, but immediately we understand. And six planes from Turkey in the near future. This is very confidential obviously, and we are not eager for it to be known. At least not until Congress gets out of town tomorrow.

In addition, we are moving a number of naval ships in the West Pacific toward the Indian Ocean: an aircraft carrier accompanied by four destroyers and a tanker, and a helicopter carrier and two destroyers. I have maps here showing the location of the Soviet fleet in the Indian Ocean if you are interested. These are much smaller ships. They are no match for the US ships. (Showing Ambassador Huang the map) Here is a merchant tanker, . . . submarine . . .[43]

Ambassador Huang: (laughing) I'm no expert.

Dr. Kissinger: I'm not either. There is no difficulty.

There is not much in the Soviet fleet. What is the total number, Al? (to Haig) I've read it somewhere.

Ambassador Huang: There's a cruiser coming in now.

Dr. Kissinger: Their ships are not much.

I now come to a matter of some sensitivity. We have received a report that one of your personnel in a European country, in a conversation with another European, expressed uncertainty about the Soviet dispositions on your borders and a desire for information about them. We do not ourselves concentrate on tactical intelligence. We only have information about the general disposition, and we collect it at irregular intervals by satellite. But we would be prepared at your request, and through whatever sources you wish, to give you whatever information we have about the disposition of Soviet forces. I don't have it with me, but we can arrange it easily wherever you wish and in an absolutely secure way.

Secondly, the President wants you to know that it's, of course, up to the People's Republic to decide its own course of action in this situation, but if the People's Republic were to consider the situation on the Indian subcontinent a threat to its security, and if it took measures to protect its security, the US would oppose efforts of others to interfere with the People's Republic. We are not recommending any particular steps; we are simply informing you about the actions of others.

The movement of our naval force is still East of the Straits of Malacca and will not become obvious until Sunday evening when they cross the Straits.

I would like to give you our assessment of the military situation on the subcontinent. I don't know whether you have any assessments. I would like to give this to you and then tell you one other thing

The Pakistani army in the East has been destroyed. The Pakistani army in the West will run out of what we call POL — gas and oil — in another two to three weeks, two weeks probably, because the oil storage capacity in Karachi has been destroyed.[44] We think that the immediate objective must be to prevent an attack on the West Pakistan army by India. We are afraid that if nothing is done to stop it, East Pakistan will become a Bhutan and West Pakistan will become a Nepal. And India with Soviet help would be free to turn its energies elsewhere.

So it seems to us that through a combination of pressures and political moves it is important to keep India from attacking in the West, to gain time to get more arms into Pakistan and to restore the situation.

We sent yesterday the relevant paragraphs, the non-rhetorical paragraphs, from Brezhnev's letter to President Yahya for his opinion. (To Ambassador Huang and Miss Tang) Why don't you read what we told him? It is an unusual method of proceeding, but we have to understand each other. This is just a quotation, an extract. (To Miss Tang) Don't write it down word for word, Nancy.

You don't need a master spy. We give you everything. (handing over his file) We read that you brought a master spy with you. You don't need him. He couldn't get this by himself. (Chinese laughter) Next time he (Ambassador Huang) will show me one of his dispatches, but it will do me no good at all, since I can't read it. (Chinese laughter)

(To Ambassador Bush) Don't you discuss diplomacy this way.

Ambassador Bush: I'm trying to understand it. I'm waiting for the Chinese translation.

[After the Chinese read the cable to Yahya, Kissinger summarizes Yahya's response, which proposes a cease-fire monitored by U.N. observers, troop withdrawals, and "negotiations looking toward the political satisfaction of Bengali aspirations."]

Dr. Kissinger: . . . Our judgment is if West Pakistan is to be preserved from destruction, two things are needed—maximum intimidation of the Indians and, to some extent, the Soviets. Secondly, maximum pressure for the cease-fire.

At this moment we have—I must tell you one other thing—we have an intelligence report according to which Mrs. [Indira] Gandhi told her cabinet that she wants to destroy the Pakistani army and air force and to annex this part of Kashmir, Azad Kashmir, and then to offer a cease-fire. This is what we believe must be prevented and this is why I have taken the liberty to ask for this meeting with the Ambassador.[45]

One other thing. The Acting Secretary of State—the Secretary of State is in Europe—called in last night the Indian Ambassador and demanded assurance that India has no designs, will not annex any territory. We do this to have a legal basis for other actions.

So this is where we are.

Ambassador Huang: We thank Dr. Kissinger very much for informing us of the situation on the subcontinent of India–Pakistan, and we certainly will convey that to Prime Minister Zhou Enlai.

The position of the Chinese Government on this matter is not a secret. Everything has been made known to the world. And the basic stand we are taking in the UN is the basic stand of our government. Both in the Security Council and the plenary session of the General Assembly we have supported the draft resolutions that have included both the cease-fire and withdrawal, although we are not actually satisfied with that kind of resolution. But we feel that the draft resolution which had support in the Security Council and especially the one which we voted in favor of in the General Assembly, reflect the aspirations of the overwhelming majority of the small and medium countries. And in the plenary session of the General Assembly this draft resolution was put forward by Algeria and Argentina and 38 more and it was adopted by a majority of 104. The opposition consisted in effect of only two—the Soviet Union and India. The others were either their followers or their protectorates. We feel that this reflects the aspirations, it shows where the hearts of the people in the world turn to.

Miss Tang: (To Dr. Kissinger) Do you understand?

Dr. Kissinger: Oh, yes.

Ambassador Huang: It shows what the majority of the people in the world support and what they oppose. Because if India, with the aid of the Soviet Union, would be able to have its own way in the subcontinent then there would be no more security to speak of for a lot of other countries, and no peace to speak of. Because that would mean the dismemberment and the splitting up of a sovereign country and the creation of a new edition of Manchukuo, the Bangladesh.[46] It would also mean aggression by military force and the annexation of sovereign territory.

[Huang, explaining further that Beijing's minimum criteria for a U. N. resolution were cease-fire and withdrawal, suggests that Washington's position is "weak." He advocates linking it with British and Soviet support for negotiations between West and East Pakistan. Kissinger demurs and argues that "we don't want . . . to have West Pakistan go the way of East Pakistan."]

Ambassador Huang: (The Soviet proposal for negotiations) means legalizing of the new refurbishment of another Manchukuo, that is, to give it legal status through the UN, or rather through the modalities of the UN.

This goes against the desires of the people in Pakistan, against the desires of the peoples of the world that was expressed in the voting of the General Assembly on this issue. The Soviet Union and India now are progressing along on an extremely dangerous track in the subcontinent. And as we have already pointed out this is a step to encircle China.

Dr. Kissinger: There is no question about that.

Ambassador Huang: And you also are clear about our activity, that is we are prepared to meet attacks coming from the east, west, north, and south.

Dr. Kissinger: When we have an exchange program between our countries, I hope to send a few State Department people to China. I'll send you a few of our State Department people for training. I may look weak to you, Mr. Ambassador, but my colleagues in Washington think I'm a raving maniac.

Miss Tang: We didn't finish.

Ambassador Huang: We are prepared for attacks on the east, west, north, and south. We are prepared to engage in guerrilla warfare once again with millet and rifle, and we are prepared to begin our construction over again, after that eventuality. And the private attitude adopted by Brezhnev which we see now, in which he talks about so-called political negotiations is in fact direct and obvious intervention in the internal affairs of a sovereign country and something we feel is completely unacceptable, is inadmissible.

Of course we have nothing here about the military situation in the India – Pakistan subcontinent except what we read in the newspapers. But from our experience of a longer period we feel that the struggle waged by the people in Pakistan is a just struggle and therefore it is bound to have the support of the Chinese people and the people of the world. Whoever upholds justice and strives to defend their sovereignty, independence and territorial integrity . . .

We have an old proverb: "If light does not come to the east it will come to the west. If the south darkens, the north must still have light." And therefore if we meet with some defeats in certain places, we will win elsewhere. So we keep persevering. So long as we persevere in principle and a just struggle, then final victory will still be ours. I don't think there's need for any more elaboration on that, because the history of the Chinese people's revolution itself is a good example.

Dr. Kissinger: Mr. Ambassador, we agree with your analysis of the situation. What is happening in the Indian subcontinent is a threat to all people. It's a more immediate threat to China, but it's a threat to all people. We have no agreement with the British to do anything. In fact we are talking with you to come to a common position. We know that Pakistan is being punished because it is a friend of China and because it is a friend of the United States.

But while we agree with your theory, we now have an immediate problem. I don't know the history of the people's revolution in China nearly as well as you do. I seem to remember that one of the great lessons is that under all circumstances the Chinese movement maintained its essence. And as an article on the Chungking negotiations makes clear, it is right to negotiate when negotiations are necessary and to fight when fighting is necessary.

We want to preserve the army in West Pakistan so that it is better able to fight if the situation rises again. We are also prepared to attempt to assemble a maximum amount of pressure in order to deter India. You read the New York *Times* every day, and you will see that the movement of supplies and the movement of our fleet will not have the universal admiration of the media, to put it mildly. And it will have the total opposition of our political opponents.

We want to keep the pressure on India, both militarily and politically. We have no interest in political negotiations between Pakistani leaders and East Pakistani leaders as such. The only interest that we possibly have is to get Soviet agreement to a united Pakistan. We have no interest in an agreement between Bangladesh and Pakistan.

We are prepared also to consider simply a cease-fire. We are prepared also to follow your course in the UN which most of my colleagues would be delighted to do and then Pakistan would be destroyed.

If we followed your course of insisting on cease-fire and withdrawal and do nothing then Pakistan will be destroyed, and many people in America will be delighted. If you and Pakistan want this then we will do it. That is no problem for us. That is the easiest course for us.

So we will . . . we agree with your analysis completely. We are looking for practical steps in this issue which happens to be a common fight for different reasons. We will not cooperate with anyone to impose anything on Pakistan. We have taken a stand against India and we will maintain this stand. But we have this problem. It is our judgment, with great sorrow, that the Pakistan army in two weeks will disintegrate in the West as it has disintegrated in the East. If we are wrong about this, we are wrong about everything.

What do you think of cease-fire without political negotiations? The only reason we want political negotiations at all is to preserve East Pakistan, not to weaken it.

Ambassador Huang: Are you prepared to take the step in the UN of putting forward a proposal simply for cease-fire, along this course?

Dr. Kissinger: No, that's why I'm talking to you. Let's be practical—by tomorrow the Pakistan Army in the East will have surrendered. Therefore should one have a resolution for a ceasefire in the West?

Ambassador Huang: Why should we not condemn India for its aggression against East Pakistan? Why should there not be a demand for the resolution already passed in the General Assembly which calls for withdrawal? And if it is . . . if you find it impossible to condemn India . . .

Dr. Kissinger: We do. We don't mind condemning India.

Ambassador Huang: . . . A step should not be taken backward from the resolution already passed in the General Assembly.

Dr. Kissinger: There are two separate problems. The resolution in the General Assembly is one for the whole problem—that can be maintained. We are not saying we accept the occupation of East Pakistan; we don't have to accept that. But this would be a resolution for a cease-fire only. And the Arabs would not accept the occupation of their territory even though there is a cease-fire. So . . . but we are not here to tell you . . . When I asked for this meeting, I did so to suggest Chinese military help, to be quite honest. That's what I had in mind, not to discuss with you how to defeat Pakistan. I didn't want to find a way out of it, but I did it in an indirect way.

But this is for you to decide. You have many other problems on many other borders. What is going to happen is that the Pakistani commander in East Pakistan, independent of anything we did, has asked the UN to arrange a cease-fire in East Pakistani. We will not take a stand in opposition to you on this issue. We think we are on the same side. So . . .

Ambassador Huang: We feel that the situation on the subcontinent is very tense and is in the process of rapid development and change. And therefore, as I expressed earlier, we will immediately report what you tell me.

Dr. Kissinger: I don't want the Prime Minister to misunderstand. We are not looking for a way to get out of the situation. We are looking for a way to protect what is left of Pakistan. We will not recognize Bangladesh. We will not negotiate with Bangladesh. We will not encourage talks between Pakistan and Bangladesh.

We have the immediate practical problem—is it better to have a cease-fire or is it better to let the military events continue? In either event both of us must continue to bring pressure on India and the Soviet Union.

(There is an exchange in which Dr. Kissinger confirms to Bush that he talked to Bhutto, that he was meeting him the next morning and that Bush's appointment with him was confirmed for later this night.)

I shall tell him (Bhutto) he should take his direction from you on whatever resolution he wants and that we will support him. I shall tell him to disregard any American official except me and General Haig. He doesn't have to take his direction from you, but I will tell him to check with you. Usually you criticize us for sticking too much to our friends, so we will not in this case create the wrong impression.

Ambassador Huang: As for Bangladesh, has Ambassador Bush recently met with anybody from Bangladesh?

Ambassador Bush: The Ambassador is referring to a squib in the New York *Times*.

[Bush explains an inadvertent and embarrassing meeting arranged by a Pakistani judge during which the latter's associates had tried to initiate a conversation on the Bangladesh problem.]

Dr. Kissinger: In any event, no matter what you read, no one is authorized to talk to the Bangladesh. We don't recognize Bangladesh and will not recognize it.

Ambassador Huang: I thank Ambassador Bush very much for his explanation.

Ambassador Bush: One of the men had defected from the Pakistan Embassy in Washington and came here. Ambassador Shahi would kill me.

Dr. Kissinger: My former personal assistant is now working for Senator Muskie.[47] There are many defectors around these days.

Mr. Ambassador, I am going to the Azores on Sunday afternoon with the

President for 48 hours. General Haig has my complete confidence, and we have very rapid communication, so if you have some communication for us . . .

But I want Beijing to be clear that my seeing you was for the purpose of coordinating positive steps, not to prepare you for negative steps.

Ambassador Huang: I don't have anything else.

Dr. Kissinger: Good. I wish happier occasions would bring us together.

We have particular affection for Pakistan because we feel they helped to reestablish contact between the People's Republic and the United States.

So we are prepared to listen to any practical proposals for parallel action. We will do our best to prevent pressure against any country that takes unilateral action. I shall speak to Mr. Bhutto tomorrow in the sense that I have indicated to you.

Ambassador Huang: Of course, we will also contact Mr. Bhutto and, of course, as you later clarified yourself, we of course will give no directions. Yahya Khan is the President, and we only have friendly exchanges.

Dr. Kissinger: Of course the word "direction" was not well chosen.

Ambassador Huang: We think that is all there is today. What we need to do is to relay this to Prime Minister Zhou Enlai.

(There were then a few minutes of closing pleasantries while the Chinese waited for their automobile.)

[Huang tells Kissinger that Shi Yanhua will replace Nancy Tang as principal liaison to the U.S. side. When Kissinger asks whether his secretaries can have "social contact with the girls in the Chinese delegation," Huang assents. They discuss possible housing arrangements for the PRC U.N. mission.]

COMMENTARY

The White House tilt toward Pakistan raised questions about the White House's stance regarding human rights, but Kissinger was more interested in other aspects of the crisis. In January, according to Dobrynin, Kissinger acknowledged that excessive apprehensions about Soviet intentions had led the White House to take "unreasonable" steps. No doubt, he was referring to U.S. naval maneuvers, but he may also have meant his statement, intended as a veiled warning to the Soviets, that they should stay away from Third World crises lest they precipitate another unreasonable U.S. reaction. This use of threats and military signals in the South Asian crisis appears to have strengthened Kissinger's belief that such methods would prevent the Soviets from helping Washington's adversaries in regional or internal conflicts.[48]

While Kissinger's authority at the White House seemed unchallenged, by the end of the month Nixon was thinking about the possibility of firing him. Nixon was envious of Kissinger's growing celebrity status, and he had problems with Kissinger's handling of the South Asian war; his domestic advisers, John Ehrlichman and H. R. Haldeman, were now privately expressing their concerns about Kissinger's "mood swings." During the South Asia crisis, Kissinger was deeply upset with press criticism, and livid over Secretary of State Rogers's opposition to his Indian policy; in the following weeks, he became distraught and then gloomy when he learned that the Joint Chiefs of Staff had spies working inside the National Security Council. Nixon, said by some to have wondered if Kissinger needed "psychiatric care," had stopped taking his calls. While Kissinger thought hard about resigning in January, the situation changed as the trips to Beijing and Moscow approached, and Nixon found it useful to speak with him again.[49]

Nixon's visit to China in February 1972 was tremendously successful and put the tentative rapprochement on much firmer ground with formal understandings on Taiwan and "hegemony."[50] However, no one in the U.S. party knew how close Mao had been to death only days before the visit. A few weeks before Nixon arrived, he had been suffering from heart problems and a lung infection which he had refused to allow his doctors to treat until 1 February. Mao, for whom the President's visit would confirm China's "equal" position in the world of nations, was eager to meet with Nixon. As a result, he conceded to undergoing physical therapy so he could walk and be in a condition to receive visitors.[51] Although he could barely speak and was bloated from edema, Mao nevertheless surprised his close advisers by summoning Nixon soon after his arrival on the morning of 21 February. Although Mao had nearly died, Nixon and Kissinger were only told that he had been suffering from bronchitis.[52]

The discussion was mostly banal, but Nixon and Kissinger may have gotten what they wanted out of it—the opportunity to leave China's "fanatic" but pragmatic leaders with an impression of "our seriousness and reliability." Kissinger advised Nixon that it was Mao's and Zhou's pragmatism that led them to deal with one "barbarian" nation in order to control another, but the relationship would not develop unless the Chinese believed they could depend on Washington. Because the United States would be making important commitments on force withdrawals from Taiwan and normalization of relations, Kissinger emphasized that "our basic task is to get across to them that we can make certain moves they will want in the future because it is in our own self-interest." Nixon, perhaps taking Kissinger's advice, made statements that he hoped would encourage Mao and Zhou to view him as reliable, even though they had no reason to trust him: "You will find I never say something I cannot do. And I will always do more than I can say." Indeed, not long after Nixon had left Beijing, he ordered the withdrawal of nuclear-capable F-4 Phantom bomber units from Taiwan to validate his pledge to withdraw U.S. military forces from the island.[53]

THE WHITE HOUSE
February 21, 1972
TOP SECRET/SENSITIVE/EXCLUSIVE EYES ONLY
MEMORANDUM OF CONVERSATION
PARTICIPANTS: Chairman Mao Zedong; Prime Minister Zhou Enlai;
   Wang Hairong, Deputy Chief of Protocol of the Foreign Ministry;
   Tang Wensheng, Interpreter; President Nixon; Henry A. Kissinger,
   Assistant to the President for National Security Affairs; Winston
   Lord, National Security Council Staff (Notetaker)
DATE AND TIME: Monday, February 21, 1972—2:50-3:55 P.M.
PLACE: Chairman Mao's Residence, Beijing[D]

(There were opening greetings during which the Chairman welcomed President Nixon, and the President expressed his great pleasure at meeting the Chairman.)

President Nixon: You read a great deal. The Prime Minister said that you read more than he does.

Chairman Mao: Yesterday in the airplane you put forward a very difficult problem for us. You said that what it is required to talk about are philosophic problems.

President Nixon: I said that because I have read the Chairman's poems and speeches, and I knew he was a professional philosopher. (Chinese laugh.)

Chairman Mao: (Looking at Dr. Kissinger) He is a doctor of philosophy?

President Nixon: He is a doctor of brains.

Chairman Mao: What about asking him to be the main speaker today?

President Nixon: He is an expert in philosophy.

[D] Source: *PPS*, box 372, "Mao Book December 1975 Mr. Lord."

Dr. Kissinger: I used to assign the Chairman's collective writings to my classes at Harvard.

Chairman Mao: Those writings of mine aren't anything. There is nothing instructive in what I wrote. (Looking toward photographers) Now they are trying to interrupt our meeting, our order here.

President Nixon: The Chairman's writings moved a nation and have changed the world.

Chairman Mao: I haven't been able to change it. I've only been able to change a few places in the vicinity of Beijing.

Our common old friend, Generalissimo Chiang Kai-shek, doesn't approve of this. He calls us communist bandits. He recently issued a speech. Have you seen it?

President Nixon: Chiang Kai-shek calls the Chairman a bandit. What does the Chairman call Chiang Kai-shek?

Prime Minister Zhou: Generally speaking we call them Chiang Kai-shek's clique. In the newspapers sometimes we call him a bandit; we are also called bandits in turn. Anyway, we abuse each other.

Chairman Mao: Actually, the history of our friendship with him is much longer than the history of your friendship with him.

President Nixon: Yes, I know.

Chairman Mao: We two must not monopolize the whole show. It won't do if we don't let Dr. Kissinger have a say. You have been famous about your trips to China.

Dr. Kissinger: It was the President who set the direction and worked out the plan.[54]

President Nixon: He is a very wise assistant to say it that way. (Mao and Zhou laugh.)

Chairman Mao: He is praising you, saying you are clever in doing so.

President Nixon: He doesn't look like a secret agent. He is the only man in captivity who could go to Paris 12 times and Peking once and no one knew it, except possibly a couple of pretty girls. (Zhou laughs.)[55]

Dr. Kissinger: They didn't know it; I used it as a cover.

Chairman Mao: In Paris?

President Nixon: Anyone who uses pretty girls as a cover must be the greatest diplomat of all time.

Chairman Mao: So your girls are very often made use of?[56]

President Nixon: His girls, not mine. It would get me into great trouble if I used girls as a cover.

Prime Minister Zhou: (Laughs.) Especially during elections. (Kissinger laughs.) Dr. Kissinger doesn't run for President because he wasn't born a citizen of the United States.

Dr. Kissinger: Miss Tang is eligible to be President of the United States.[57]

President Nixon: She would be the first woman President. There's our candidate.

Chairman Mao: It would be very dangerous if you have such a candidate. But let us speak the truth. As for the Democratic Party, if they come into office again, we cannot avoid contacting them.

President Nixon: We understand. We will hope that we don't give you that problem.

Chairman Mao: Those questions are not questions to be discussed in my place. They should be discussed with the Premier. I discuss philosophical questions. That is to say, I voted for you during your election. There is an American here called Mr. Frank Coe, and he wrote an article precisely at the time when your country was in havoc, during your last electoral campaign. He said you were going to be elected President. I appreciated that article very much. But now he is against the visit.

President Nixon: When the Chairman says he voted for me he voted for the lesser of two evils.

Chairman Mao: I like rightists. People say you are rightists, that the Republican Party is to the right, that Prime Minister [Edward] Heath is also to the right.[58]

President Nixon: And General de Gaulle.

Chairman Mao: De Gaulle is a different question. They also say the Christian Democratic Party of West Germany is also to the right. I am comparatively happy when these people on the right come into power.

President Nixon: I think the important thing to note is that in America, at least this time, those on the right can do what those on the left talk about.

Dr. Kissinger: There is another point, Mr. President. Those on the left are pro-Soviet and would not encourage a move toward the People's Republic, and in fact criticize you on those grounds.

Chairman Mao: Exactly that. Some are opposing you. In our country also there is a reactionary group which is opposed to our contact with you. The result was that they got on an airplane and fled abroad.[59]

Prime Minister Zhou: Maybe you know this.

Chairman Mao: Throughout the whole world, the U.S. intelligence reports are comparatively accurate. The next was Japan. As for the Soviet Union, they finally went to dig out the corpses, but they didn't say anything

Prime Minister Zhou: In Outer Mongolia.

President Nixon: We had similar problems recently in the crisis on India–Pakistan. The American left criticized me very heavily for failing to side with India. This was for two reasons: they were pro-Indian and they were pro-Soviet.

I thought it was important to look at the bigger issue. We could not let a country, no matter how big, gobble up its neighbor. It cost me—I don't say this with sorrow because it was right—it cost me politically, but I think history will record that it was the right thing to do.

Chairman Mao: As a suggestion, may I suggest that you do a little less briefing? (The President points at Dr. Kissinger and Zhou laughs.) Do you think it is good if you brief others on what we talk about, our philosophic discussions here?

President Nixon: The Chairman can be sure that whatever we discuss, or whatever I and the Prime Minister discuss, nothing goes beyond the room. That is the only way to have conversations at the highest level.

Chairman Mao: That's good.

President Nixon: For example, I hope to talk with the Prime Minister and later with the Chairman about issues like Taiwan, Vietnam and Korea.

I also want to talk about—and this is very sensitive—the future of Japan, the future of the subcontinent, and what India's role will be; and on the broader world scene, the future of US–Soviet relations. Because only if we see the whole picture of the world and the great forces that move the world will we be able to make the right decisions about the immediate and urgent problems that always completely dominate our vision.

Chairman Mao: All those troublesome problems I don't want to get into very much. I think your topic is better—philosophic questions.

President Nixon: For example, Mr. Chairman, it is interesting to note that most nations would approve of this meeting, but the Soviets disapprove, the Japanese have doubts which they express, and the Indians disapprove. So we must examine why, and determine how our policies should develop to deal with the whole world, as well as the immediate problems such as Korea, Vietnam, and of course, Taiwan.

Chairman Mao: Yes, I agree.

President Nixon: We, for example, must ask ourselves—again in the confines of this room—why the Soviets have more forces on the border facing you than on the border facing Western Europe. We must ask ourselves, what is the future of Japan? Is it better—here I know we have disagreements—is it better for Japan to be neutral, totally defenseless, or is it better for a time for Japan to have some relations with the United States? The point being—I am talking now in the realm of philosophy—in international relations there are no good choices. One thing is sure—we can leave no vacuums, because they can be filled. The Prime Minister, for example, has pointed out that the United States reaches out its hands and that the Soviet Union reaches out its hands. The question is which danger the People's Republic faces, whether it is the danger of American aggression or Soviet aggression. These are hard questions, but we have to discuss them.

Chairman Mao: At the present time, the question of aggression from the United States or aggression from China is relatively small; that is, it could be said that this is not a major issue, because the present situation is one in which a state of war does not exist between our two countries. You want to withdraw some of your troops back on your soil; ours do not go abroad. Therefore, the situation between our two countries is strange because during the past 22 years our ideas have never met in talks. Now the time is less than 10 months since we began playing table tennis; if one counts the time since you put forward your suggestion at Warsaw it is less than two years. Our side also is bureaucratic in dealing with matters. For example, you wanted some exchange of persons on a personal level, things like that; also trade. But rather than deciding that we stuck with our stand that without settling major issues there is nothing to do with smaller issues. I myself persisted in that position. Later on I saw you were right, and we played table tennis. The Prime Minister said this was also after President Nixon came to office.

The former President of Pakistan introduced President Nixon to us. At that time, our Ambassador in Pakistan refused to agree on our having a contact with you. He said it should be compared whether President Johnson or President Nixon would be better. But President Yahya said the two men cannot be compared, that these two men are incomparable. He said that one was like a gangster—he meant President Johnson. I don't know how he got that impression. We on our side were not very happy with that President either. We were not very happy with your former Presidents, beginning from Truman through Johnson. We were not very happy with these Presidents, Truman and Johnson.

In between there were eight years of a Republican President. During that period probably you hadn't thought things out either.

Prime Minister Zhou: The main thing was John Foster Dulles' policy

Chairman Mao: He (Zhou) also discussed this with Dr. Kissinger before.

President Nixon: But they (gesturing towards Prime Minister Zhou and Dr. Kissinger) shook hands. (Zhou laughs.)

Chairman Mao: Do you have anything to say, Doctor?

Dr. Kissinger: Mr. Chairman, the world situation has also changed dramatically during that period. We've had to learn a great deal. We thought all socialist/communist states were the same phenomenon. We didn't understand until the President came into office the different nature of revolution in China and the way revolution had developed in other socialist states.

President Nixon: Mr. Chairman, I am aware of the fact that over a period of years my position with regard to the People's Republic was one that the Chairman and Prime Minister totally disagreed with. What brings us together is a recognition of a new situation in the world and a recognition on our part that what is important is not a nation's internal political philosophy. What is important is its policy toward the rest of the world and toward us. That is why—this point I think can be said to be honest—we have differences. The Prime Minister and Dr. Kissinger discussed these differences.

It also should be said—looking at the two great powers, the United States and China—we know China doesn't threaten the territory of the United States; I think you know the United States has no territorial designs on China. We know China doesn't want to dominate the United States. We believe you too realize the United States doesn't want to dominate the world. Also—maybe you don't believe this, but I do—neither China nor the United States, both great nations, want to dominate the world. Because our attitudes are the same on these two issues, we don't threaten each others' territories.

Therefore, we can find common ground, despite our differences, to build a world structure in which both can be safe to develop in our own ways on our own roads. That cannot be said about some other nations in the world.

Chairman Mao: Neither do we threaten Japan or South Korea.

President Nixon: Nor any country. Nor do we.

Chairman Mao: (Checking the time with Zhou) Do you think we have covered enough today?

President Nixon: Yes. I would like to say as we finish, Mr. Chairman, we know you and the Prime Minister have taken great risks in inviting us here. For us also it was a difficult decision. But having read some of the Chairman's statements, I know he is one who sees when an opportunity comes, that you must seize the hour and seize the day.

I would also like to say in a personal sense—and this to you Mr. Prime Minister—you do not know me. Since you do not know me, you shouldn't trust me. You will find I never say something I cannot do. And I always will do more than I can say. On this basis I want to have frank talks with the Chairman and, of course, with the Prime Minister.

Chairman Mao: (Pointing to Dr. Kissinger) "Seize the hour and seize the day." I think that, generally speaking, people like me sound a lot of big cannons. (Zhou laughs.) That is, things like "the whole world should unite and defeat imperialism, revisionism, and all reactionaries, and establish socialism. "

President Nixon: Like me. And bandits.

Chairman Mao: But perhaps you as an individual may not be among those to be overthrown. They say that he (Dr. Kissinger) is also among those not to be overthrown personally. And if all of you are overthrown we wouldn't have any more friends left.

President Nixon: Mr. Chairman, the Chairman's life is well-known to all of us. He came from a very poor family to the top of the most populous nation in the world, a great nation.

My background is not so well known. I also came from a very poor family, and to the top of a very great nation.[60] History has brought us together. The question is whether we, with different philosophies, but both with feet on the ground, and having come from the people, can make a breakthrough that will serve not just China and America, but the whole world in the years ahead. And that is why we are here.

Chairman Mao: Your book, "The Six Crises," is not a bad book.[61]

President Nixon: He (Mao) reads too much.

Chairman Mao: Too little. I don't know much about the United States. I must ask you to send some teachers here, mainly teachers of history and geography.

President Nixon: That's good, the best.

Chairman Mao: That's what I said to Mr. Edgar Snow, the correspondent who passed away a few days ago.[62]

President Nixon: That was very sad.

Chairman Mao: Yes, indeed.

It is all right to talk well and also all right if there are no agreements, because what use is there if we stand in deadlock? Why is it that we must be able to reach results? People will say . . . if we fail the first time, then people will talk why are we not able to succeed the first time? The only reason would be that we have taken the wrong road. What will they say if we succeed the second time?

(There were then some closing pleasantries. The Chairman said he was not well. President Nixon responded that he looked good. The Chairman said that appearances were deceiving. After handshakes and more pictures, Prime Minister Zhou then escorted the President out of the residence.)

[Besides the Nixon–Mao conversation, the only available declassified record of the February 1972 trip is a document that includes excerpts from three talks—each one indicated by its date—that Nixon and Kissinger had with Zhou and Vice Foreign Minister Qiao Kuanhua on Taiwan and the Shanghai Communiqué. In them, consistent with Beijing's wishes, the Americans agree that Taiwan was not an "international dispute" between Americans and Chinese but an "internal matter" for the Chinese to settle. Nevertheless, Nixon and Kissinger, intent on offsetting criticism from the Right about "selling out" an old Cold War ally, delicately try to elicit assurances from the Chinese that Taiwan's reunification with the Mainland— "liberation" from the Chiang Kai-shek regime as Beijing put it—will occur peacefully. While Zhou expresses "confidence" that the PRC will "liberate" Taiwan in a "friendly way," no formal commitment appears in the communiqué. Kissinger will not give up on this issue; but his inability to secure a commitment from Beijing will contribute to President Ford's decision in 1975 to delay normalization until after the election.]

STATEMENTS MADE BY PRC LEADERS TO SECRETARY KISSINGER OR PRESIDENT NIXON REGARDING THE PEACEFUL LIBERATION OF TAIWAN, n.d. [circa Nov. 1974] [excerpts][E]

February 22, 1972 (President Nixon and Premier Zhou)

President Nixon: . . . We will support any peaceful resolution of the Taiwan issue that can be worked out. And the reduction of the remaining third of our military presence on Taiwan will go forward as progress is made on the peaceful resolution of the problem.

Premier Zhou: . . . We have already waited over twenty years (regarding Taiwan)—I am very frank here—and we can wait a few more years. I can go a step further. Even when Taiwan comes back to the motherland, we will not establish any nuclear bases there. . . .

February 24, 1972 (Dr. Kissinger, VM Qiao, and Premier Zhou)

Dr. Kissinger: Let me ask you this. We will be able, on the basis of the preceding paragraph, to say to the press that on international disputes we have renounced the use of force. Then on Taiwan I would say that China does not consider Taiwan an international dispute.

[E] Source: *PPS*, box 373, China–Sensitive Oct. 16–Dec. 31, 1974

Vice Minister Qiao: So there is no need to add this phrase here.

Dr. Kissinger: But is it all right if we explain the meaning of the communiqué in this sense afterwards—can we say after we get back that one of the results of our trip was that we have renounced the use of force in our disputes with one another? Then we will say—we will not embarrass you—that you do not consider Taiwan an international dispute. We will not be tricky on this.

Vice Minister Qiao: Our position on the Taiwan question we have stated on many occasions.

Dr. Kissinger: I understand. We will not apply it to the Taiwan question. We know your position—you have stated it since 1955, and we will not use this communiqué as a way of making you change your position on this.

Vice Minister Qiao: We have always considered that the Taiwan question had two aspects. One is your military presence, which we should try to resolve through negotiations, whereas the question with Chiang Kai-shek is a domestic matter.

Dr. Kissinger: Let us drop this then. . . .

Premier Zhou: . . . You want a peaceful liberation (for Taiwan).

Dr. Kissinger mentioned in his private talks on the last day (of his July trip) and in reply to Dr. Kissinger we said that we will strive for peaceful liberation. This is a matter for both sides. We want this. What will we do if they (the leaders in Taiwan) don't want it? While your armed forces are there (on Taiwan) our armed forces will not engage in military confrontation with your armed forces. . . .

Premier Zhou: And so it is our hope, it would be good if the liberation of Taiwan could be realized in your next term of office. That, of course, is only a hope. Of course that is our internal affair. We cannot express the hope that you should not interfere in this internal affair. You should not impose anything on us nor should we impose anything on Chiang Kai-shek. But also, Mr. President, you should be aware that there are not too many days left to Chiang Kai-shek.

Premier Zhou: I should say very frankly that when Dr. Kissinger said that it would take ten years (to solve the Taiwan question), that would be too long. This was at a briefing conference (held by Dr. Kissinger). You said that maybe it would take ten years, but that would be too long. It is better not to mention any date. I can't wait ten years. You have ten years. . . .

Premier Zhou: So we hope to solve this question (of Taiwan) in a friendly way since already more than twenty years have passed. According to the solution to the question put forward by John Foster Dulles at the Warsaw talks, the time limit has already been passed. Dulles put forward the proposal through the American ambassador that so long as China did not use force for a period of ten, fifteen, or twenty years, he would be satisfied. If we had concluded such an agreement then the fifteen years would have long passed by now. . . . But if we accepted such a principle, it would be equivalent to accepting interference in our internal affairs. So we cannot accept that. . . . We are not asking you to remove Chiang Kai-shek. We will take care of that ourselves.

President Nixon: Peacefully?

Premier Zhou: Yes, we have self-confidence. . . .

February 25, 1972. (Dr. Kissinger and Vice Minister Qiao)

Vice Minister Qiao: You can say that (the final withdrawal of U. S. forces from Taiwan will come about) entirely as your own initiative, not as an agreement betweeen you and us. That is, you consider there is such a prospect. And you consider that this prospect is coming closer. And so you are able to make the progressive reduction. As for what happens finally, you can entirely link that up with the peaceful settlement.

Dr. Kissinger: But if we can do that in language, then we have no problem.

COMMENTARY

Kissinger later wrote that Nixon's trip to Beijing had a favorable impact on relations with the Soviets because Brezhnev and his colleagues moved more quickly to complete agreements before Nixon's arrival. Only Soviet archives can corroborate Kissinger's assessment, although memoir accounts of the summit do confirm that Nixon's trip to Beijing had triggered sensitivities in Moscow.[63] No memcons of the May 1972 U.S.–Soviet summit have been declassified, however, and only declassification of the secret record will shed light on discussion of the more sensitive issues—such as China but especially Vietnam—about which the memoir accounts provide little information.[64]

According to U.S. observers, "good personal relations" characterized most of the summit; the U.S.'s recent bombing campaign over North Vietnam, however, did elicit an angry reaction from the Soviet leadership.[65]

Otherwise, the SALT I agreements, and the Basic Principles all made for an atmosphere of bonhomie. However, one Soviet proposal made the Americans uncomfortable and suspicious. Brezhnev had already approached Kissinger, during his secret trip in April, about an understanding that

Washington and Moscow would not use nuclear weapons against each other (the initiative that resulted in the 1973 Prevention of Nuclear War Agreement). The Soviets saw their proposal as a step toward a nuclear no-first-use agreement—a logical step toward putting the Basic Principles into effect, but Kissinger, on the other hand, readily interpreted it as a gambit for an implicitly anti-Chinese condominium that could provide cover for a Soviet nuclear strike against Beijing. As he later put it, the Soviets were "trying to embarrass us in our relations with Beijing" because they realized that the Chinese would find it "anathema": Not only did the Soviet proposal contravene China's official support for a comprehensive ban against nuclear use, but it would not prevent Moscow from using nuclear weapons against another power such as Beijing.[66]

Nixon offered Brezhnev a counterproposal, but he avoided a discussion by suggesting that the Soviets use the back-channel for further dialogue. Disturbed by the proposal's anti-Chinese implications, Kissinger briefed Zhou on Brezhnev's proposal during his June 1972 visit to Beijing. Kissinger told Zhou, in effect, that Nixon would accept it only if "there was an assurance [that the Soviets] were not free to make nuclear attacks on our allies or other countries in whose independence we have an interest," meaning China, among others.[67]

In late July, Dobrynin delivered a more specific proposal that Kissinger also found objectionable: Moscow and Washington would foreswear first use of nuclear weapons against each other, even if other countries used them, but they could use them to defend allies. During one of his regular meetings with Huang Hua at the CIA safehouse in New York, Kissinger reviewed the state of play, explaining that the proposal was unacceptable because it would interfere with U.S. "freedom of action" to preserve "international peace" by using nuclear weapons to defend a country not covered by the agreement. "We are looking for a formulation that expressed nuclear non-use as an objective rather than an obligation." In other words, Kissinger wanted nothing that would limit the United States' power to use nuclear weapons first.[68]

The next week Hua presented Beijing's deeply critical evaluation of the Soviet proposal. After Kissinger disclosed his suspicions about West German Ostpolitik, his reply to Hua gave him an opportunity to expound on his dim view of Moscow's "aggressive intent in the East" and intention to use détente to establish a Eurasian hegemony. Kissinger may have already made the same point to Zhou Enlai, but now he informed the Chinese that, even without a formal agreement, Washington would come to their aid if the Soviets attacked them. In effect, he was treating the PRC as a de facto *component of the U.S. security system.*

The gloomy analysis of a Soviet drive for Eurasian "hegemony" that informed Kissinger's assurances reflected what was becoming a characteristically exaggerated notion of the Soviet threat to China; whether it was overstatement calculated to exploit Sino-Soviet tensions in order to draw Beijing closer to Washington, remains to be seen, as more documents are declassified. In any event, the Chinese were not persuaded by Kissinger's explanations; the Soviet initiative on nuclear war would continue to be a controversial element in Sino-American relations, even after Kissinger believed he had watered it down to a "bland set of principles."[69]

U.S. Ambassador to the United Nations George Bush had attended earlier Kissinger-Huang meetings, but Kissinger cut him out of the loop in 1972. In March he had told Huang that "Bush doesn't know about our meetings any longer" and would be invited to attend "only if United Nations business is involved."[70]

THE WHITE HOUSE
TOP SECRET/SENSITIVE/EXCLUSIVELY EYES ONLY
MEMORANDUM OF CONVERSATION
PARTICIPANTS: Dr. Henry A Kissinger, Assistant to the President for National Security Affairs; Winston Lord, NSC Staff; Huang Hua, PRC Ambassador to the United Nations; Shi Yanhua, Interpreter
DATE & TIME: Friday, August 4, 1972—5:15-6:45 P.M.
PLACE: New York City[F]

(There were some opening pleasantries, including Dr. Kissinger's favorable remarks on the Ambassador's light-weight, light grey Chinese outfit.)
Dr. Kissinger: I saw Ambassador Bush this morning. You scared him about Korea. You intimidated him. We will have to give him more backbone.
Ambassador Huang: (Immediately pulling out a piece of paper and reading from it.) Following our talk last time, I would like to express the following views regarding the primary point of the message of July 26 given by Dr. Kissinger, that is the idea that the United States and the Soviet Union sign a treaty on a mutual nuclear nonaggression. "First, the Chinese side considers

F Source: *PPS*, box 323, China Exchanges, 25 June-17 Oct. 1972.

the Soviet proposal to be nakedly aimed at the establishment of nuclear world hegemony.

"Secondly, the Soviet proposal only stipulates that the Soviet Union and the United States should not use nuclear weapons against each other or their allies. This is obviously an attempt, following the Partial Nuclear Test Ban Treaty and the Nuclear Non-Proliferation Treaty, to go a step further and monopolize nuclear weapons, maintain nuclear superiority and make nuclear threats against countries with few nuclear weapons, non-nuclear countries, and countries in which the production of nuclear weapons is barred, and force them into spheres of influence of either this or that hegemony so that the two hegemonies may have a free hand in dividing up the world and manipulating the destinies of countries of the world at will.

[Huang further explains that a U.S. - Soviet agreement on nuclear non-use is "impermissible"; it is contrary to the equality of nations and because of its overtones of superpower collusion, the antihegemony clauses of the Shanghai Communiqué. The only agreement on nuclear weapons that Beijing found permissible would be one calling for the destruction of nuclear weapons, with a treaty on non-use — especially non-use against non-nuclear nations as a first step.]

Ambassador Huang: . . . We hope that the U. S. side will give serious consideration to this.

[Huang also read three aide-mémoires, one calling for action to end U. N. commissions and commands on Korea, the second thanking the United States for assistance for Cambodia's Prince Sihanouk's security during an overseas trip, and the third thanking Kissinger for trying to promote PRC - West German contacts. However, Kissinger objected to China's insistence on a U. N. debate on Korea; instead, he suggested the possibility of taking action on some of China's concerns in ways that would not alienate South Korea.]

Kissinger: Now on the German question . . . I have a direct channel to the German Chancellor which does not go through the diplomatic line.
Ambassador Huang: The Chancellor?
Dr. Kissinger: Chancellor Brandt. He (the "direct channel") is the Chancellor's assistant for Foreign Policy, who has roughly the same job I do for the President. He has asked my opinion about the establishment of diplomatic relations between Beijing and Bonn. He has stated as his own personal opinion that he thinks there is no enormous hurry and that the weight of Germany's interests is in Europe.

Now I am considering what reply to give to him. We know from certain information that [Egon] Bahr—that's the name of the man—is very close to the Soviet Union, and he reports almost every conversation to the Soviet contact that he has. So I have to be somewhat careful in my reply. But as I told you I may be in Germany early in September and I can talk to Brandt directly.

As for us, we are in favor of diplomatic relations between the Federal Republic and the People's Republic. The question is whether you want to establish those before the general elections which are in December—December 3, he tells me in his cable; December 3, it hasn't been announced yet—and to what extent you want to deal with this group.

Ambassador Huang: We haven't gotten specific instructions.

Dr. Kissinger: Of course. I will give him a noncommittal reply until I hear from you.

Ambassador Huang: The message indicates (looking at it) that during Mr. Schroeder's visit to China he indicated the desire of various quarters of West Germany for the establishment of diplomatic relations at an early date and the Chinese side responded positively.

Dr. Kissinger: The question now is the definition of "early date." I am prepared, if you want, to indicate to the Germans that you are prepared to do this, but perhaps you will let me know. I will have to do this through a channel other than him.

Mrs. Shi: What?

Dr. Kissinger: Through someone other than Bahr because Bahr will report it immediately to the Soviet Union. But if you have any views, you let me know, and I will wait for a reply.

[Huang notes that establishing relations with the Federal Republic will be relatively easy because there are no preexisting ties with the "Chiang Kai-shek clique," and Kissinger observes that decisions on timing and whether to work through the governing Social Democrats or the Christian Democrats is "primarily a tactical question." He then says, "I will reply only in a general way and simply say that I have always found you very honorable to deal with, without indicating anything on the timing."]

Dr. Kissinger: . . . Now let me talk to you about the nuclear issue. First of all, we agree with the general analysis you have presented, although we, of course, cannot accept the motives you have ascribed to us. (Ambassador Huang corrects Mrs. Xia on the word "ascribe.") Because if those were our motives we wouldn't consult with you.

Let me give you our analysis of the situation and of the strategy we intend to pursue, and then we can talk about this. Our analysis is that there is a deliberate Soviet policy to isolate you, and that the many agreements the Soviet Union has made in the last two years and the patience they have shown in the face of setbacks in the West, can only be explained to us in terms of aggressive intent in the East. (Ambassador Huang questions Mrs. Xia on something.) This is our analysis. We believe the period of greatest danger in this respect is likely to come in the period 1974–76. We believe also that it is against our interests to permit the establishment of an hegemony in Eurasia dominated from Moscow. And therefore, it is in our interest to resist this without any formal agreement (with the PRC) simply out of our own necessity.

Now the problem is how to accomplish this. We cannot artificially maintain tensions in the West when our allies pursue the policies they do, and when we have no direct interest in tensions in the West.

Ambassador Huang: You mean you don't have a direct interest in the West?

Dr. Kissinger: In tension in the West. We have no interest in maintaining tension in the West, but we have an interest in maintaining our *position* in the West. And if we remain in office, we shall not reduce our forces in Europe unilaterally, and as I told the Prime Minister, even by agreement we will not reduce them by much more than 10 percent.

But what we have to try to accomplish before that time period that I mentioned to you is to establish enough of a relationship with you so that it is plausible that an attack on you involves a substantial American interest. And you would make a great mistake if you thought that we had primarily commercial interests, because with this Administration at least, that's of a third order of interest. Our basic strategy is what I mentioned to you. In order to have a plausible basis and in order to avoid giving the Soviet Union the pretense of claiming that they are being encircled, we want to do enough with the Soviet Union to maintain a formal symmetry. (Ambassador Huang checks Mrs. Xia's translation, then smiles and indicates that Dr. Kissinger should continue.)

It is a very complicated policy, but it is a very complicated situation. And we will not participate in any agreements that have the objective tendency of isolating you, or can be directed at you. But what we are looking for is to find some formulation that deprives this proposal of its substantive content but gives it some general abstract qualities, that gives it no operational significance. We have not yet replied, so I am telling you our thinking.

For example—I want to tell you this is an internal paper which we are considering now—we are playing with the idea of a proposal that in the first paragraph, when they say there is an obligation not to use nuclear weapons against each other, we might say we agree to do the utmost to create conditions in international relations in which nuclear weapons are not used by anybody. And then have a second paragraph which says that in order for this condition to be realized, there cannot be either a threat or the use of force by one side against the other, by one side against the allies of the other, or by either side against a third country. And furthermore, that neither side will encourage the threat or use of force by any of its allies or by any other third country.

We have not submitted this, and we are debating it. This makes it very general. It isn't confined to nuclear countries and it isn't an obligation. If you have any views, we would welcome them. And I said, we have not responded and we will certainly not accept the proposal I mentioned to you.

Ambassador Huang: The Chinese sides attitude is very clearly stated in the first message (looking at the message), that is, the Chinese side hopes the U.S. side will give serious consideration to the Chinese side's proposal that an agreement on the complete prohibition and thorough destruction of nuclear weapons will be reached through the consultation of all countries. (Repeating) . . . through the consultation of all countries.

Dr. Kissinger: I understand your point.

Ambassador Huang: (Looking at the message) As a first step, an agreement should be reached on the non-use of nuclear weapons by nuclear countries against each other and by nuclear countries against non-nuclear countries. We would consider that only such an agreement is correct and would really solve the problem.

Dr. Kissinger: I understand this point and it is not inconsistent with our views.

Ambassador Huang: Do you think the Soviet side will accept such a proposal? What is the possibility?

Dr. Kissinger: (Pausing) Will they accept such an agreement?

Mrs. Shi: Yes.

Dr. Kissinger: You made it before.

Ambassador Huang: At the session of the General Assembly last year, we reaffirmed our statement on this question and asked Mr. Malik to reply, and he didn't. In the past, the Soviet side had proposed a similar view, similar proposals.

Dr. Kissinger: I can't judge. I doubt it, but I can't be sure.

You can be certain that you will be informed of every step that is taken in this matter before it is taken.

Ambassador Huang: And does the U. S. side agree to our proposal?

Dr. Kissinger: (Pausing) We are trying to avoid a situation where the Soviet

Union can threaten our allies with conventional forces, and we are then prohibited from using nuclear weapons in defense of Western Europe.

Ambassador Huang: Because the Chinese proposal for the prohibition of the use of nuclear weapons is not an isolated step. It is proposed as a first step.

Dr. Kissinger: This is our principal concern, the Soviet military concentration in Europe which none of our allies are capable of resisting themselves.

Ambassador Huang: Well, I hope when the U. S. side has considered this question, you will let us know.

Dr. Kissinger: You can be certain. We will not make any move which you are not aware of and have not had a chance to make a comment on. You can assure the Prime Minister now that we will not accept the Soviet proposal.

Ambassador Huang: I will report this to the Premier.

[Kissinger discussed his back-channel efforts through British Cabinet Secretary Burke Trend to develop a U. S. - U. K. consensus on triangular strategy.]

Ambassador Huang: (Interrupting) Just a matter for clarification. You said that you have an interest in avoiding this situation. Was this sentence directed against the Soviet's proposal? You said "avoid this situation."

Dr. Kissinger: We are interested in trying to avoid a situation of Soviet aggressive actions in East Asia. We also discussed the Soviet proposal with them, but we have not yet received their reaction. We discussed this in somewhat less detail than with you. But those are the only two countries that I have discussed it with . . .

Ambassador Huang: Would you elaborate on your view that the greatest danger is the period 1974-76?

Dr. Kissinger: It is my impression that it will take until then, or maybe just before then, to complete the pacification of the West, the European Security Conference and maybe some more progress in disarmament, and the shift of military forces.

Ambassador Huang: So when the European Security Conference and disarmament will make some progress . . .

Dr. Kissinger: Yes, and when it has established a basically peaceful intent or reputation has been established, and their military buildup is completed. One reason is that there are new nuclear weapons introduced which will not be completed until 1974.

Mrs. Shi: You mean nuclear weapons introduced . . . ?

Dr. Kissinger: In the strategic forces. They are more directed against us.

Ambassador Huang: Directed against you?

Dr. Kissinger: Some. I don't want you to think you are in a monopoly position in receiving all the attention. The strategic forces to keep us . . . are directed mostly against us, some against you, but they are mostly against us.

Ambassador Huang: I thank you for the clarification.

Dr. Kissinger: I don't want to mislead you. This is our interpretation in the White House. Not everybody agrees with it. If you get a change of Administrations they would take a less cataclysmic view of the probable evolution.

Mrs. Shi: What?

Dr. Kissinger: Our opponent in the campaign takes a different view as you probably know.[71]

* * * * *

[Kissinger briefly discusses the Vietnam peace negotiations, shows Huang some documents, and notes that the North Vietnamese are trying to "play on our domestic politics."]

Ambassador Huang: That finishes our work?

Dr. Kissinger: Yes.

[In the closing pleasantries, Kissinger asks Huang how people who want to make movies in the PRC should contact the government. "For example, Bob Hope, a good friend of the Administration, had just asked for help with his request to shoot background shots of China for a show." Although Kissinger does not want to get involved in such requests, he observes "it would be nice if certain people got a personal response." Huang responds that Hope could write the PRC embassy in Ottawa or write to him directly.]

Notes

1. See Raymond L. Garthoff, *Détente and Confrontation: American Soviet Relations from Nixon to Reagan* (Washington, D.C.: Brookings Institution, 1994), p. 252, quoting Seymour Hersh, *The Price of Power: Kissinger in the Nixon White House* (New York:Summit, 1983), pp. 360–61. For background on the Taiwan question, see Nancy B. Tucker, *Taiwan, Hong Kong, and the United States, 1945–1992: Uncertain Friendships* (New York: Twayne, 1994). For signals from Beijing about concessions on Taiwan, see Marshall Green to the Under Secretary, "Next Steps in Taiwan Policy," 6 Oct. 1969, National Archives, Record Group 59, Department of State Records, State Department Foreign Policy Files, 1967–69, POL Chicom–US.

2. See He Di, "The Most Respected Enemy: Mao Zedong's Perception of the United States," *China Quarterly* 137 (March 1994), pp. 154–55.

3. Nixon would want the China trip even more when he learned that Beijing had been making approaches to his Democratic party rivals about possible visits. See Allen S. Whiting, "Sino–American Détente," *China Quarterly* 82 (1980), p. 338.

4. For a detailed chronology of U.S.-Chinese secret communications, see Peter Rodman to Kissinger, "Who Invited Whom?" 13 Oct. 1971, National Archives, Nixon Presidential Materials Project, HAK Office Files, box 13, China. For Kissinger's account of White House China initiatives, see Henry Kissinger, *White House Years* (New York: Little, Brown, 1979), pp. 163-94 and 684-732. For a recent memoir of the July 1971 secret trip by a participant, see John H. Holdridge, *Crossing the Divide: An Insider's Account of Normalization of U.S.-China Relations* (Lanham, Md: Rowman and Littlefield, 1997), pp. 45-66.

5. For "tough ideologues," see Kissinger to the President, "Your Encounter with the Chinese," 5 February 1972, Nixon Presidential Materials Project HAK Office Files, box 13, China. For an important study of the 1971 India-Pakistan War, see Robert Jackson, *South Asian Crisis: India, Pakistan, and Bangladesh: A Political and Historical Analysis of the 1971 War* (London: Chatto & Windus for the International Institute for Strategic Studies, 1975).

6. *White House Years*, p. 1076.

7. For accounts of Nixon's visit and the meetings, see ibid., pp. 1049-76; Walter Isaacson, *Kissinger: A Biography* (New York: Simon and Schuster, 1992), pp. 399-407; Garthoff, pp. 266-68; and Stephen Ambrose, *Nixon*, vol. 2: *The Triumph of a Politician, 1962-1972* (New York: Simon and Schuster, 1989), pp. 512-19.

8. For the text of the Shanghai Communiqué, see Holdridge, *Crossing the Divide*, pp. 263-67. For Soviet overtures, see Garthoff, *Detente and Confrontation*, p. 272.

9. See Kissinger to the President, "Your Encounter with the Chinese," 5 Feb. 1972.

10. For a full record of U.S.-PRC exchanges on Vietnam during 1972, see *PPS*, box 329. For "moderate" criticisms of bombing in Vietnam, see Kissinger to the President, "My May 16 Meeting with the Chinese," n.d., *PPS*, box 329, China Exchanges 1 March-24 June 1972. For Qiao's statement, see memorandum of conversation, 13 Nov. *PPS*, box 329, China Exchanges 24 Oct.-31 Dec. 1972. For "We have gone beyond the limits," see memcon, 7-8 December 1972.

11. For "nuclear cloud," see State 032316, 1 March 1969, National Archives, Record Group 59, Department of State Records, Conference Files, 1966-72, box 484, "President Nixon's Trip to Europe, 23 Feb.-2 March, 1969, Chronology Memcons, Vol I of VIII."

12. For significant accounts of the SALT process, Garthoff, *Détente and Confrontation*, pp. 146-223; Mike Bowker and Phil Williams, *Superpower Detente: A Reappraisal* (London: Royal Institute of International Affairs, 1988), pp. 67-76, and John Newhouse, *Cold Dawn: The Story of SALT* (Washington, D.C.: Pergamon-Brassey's, 1989). For "substitute for confrontation," see Garthoff, *Détente and Confrontation*, p. 217.

13. For discussion of Kissinger's role in the SALT talks and evaluation of his performance, see Garthoff, *Détente and Confrontation*, pp. 166-70, 179-88, and Isaacson, *Kissinger: A Biography*, pp. 322-27.

14. See Robert S. Norris and Thomas B. Cochran, *US-USSR/Russian Strategic Offensive Nuclear Forces 1945-1996* (Washington, D.C.: National Resources Defense Council, 1997), Tables 1 and 2; and SecState to U.S. Embassy Belgrade, "Secretary Kissinger's July 4 Report to North Atlantic Council on 1974 Summit Meeting," State Department telegram 148542, 10 July 1974 (copy at *NSA*).

15. See Garthoff, *Détente and Confrontation*, pp. 326-34; "Meeting of the President with

the General Advisory Committee on Arms Control and Disarmament," 21 March 1972, National Archives, Nixon Presidential Materials Project, President's Office File, box 88, Beginning March 19.

16. See Garthoff, *Détente and Confrontation*, pp. 341–45; and Bowker and Williams, *Superpower Detente*, pp. 77–79.

17. For detailed discussion of U.S. and Soviet concepts of détente, including the problems raised by the tension between cooperative goals and the search for unilateral advantage, see Garthoff, *Détente and Confrontation*, pp. 27–73, which, at p. 39, characterizes Nixon's policy toward the Soviets as one of "competitive coexistence and containment." See also Bowker and Williams, *Superpower Détente*, pp. 43–57. "Meeting of the President with the General Advisory Committee on Arms Control and Disarmament," 21 March 1972, National Archives, Nixon Presidential Materials Project, President's Office File, box 88, Beginning March 19.

18. See Kissinger, *White House Years*, p. 963.

19. Garbled syntax and perhaps inaccurate notetaking failed to get across Nixon's point that it was a unilateral U.S. reduction that he saw as "disastrous."

20. MBFR refers to "Mutual and Balanced Force Reductions" of conventional forces deployed in Europe. At a meeting in Reykjavik in mid-1968, NATO ministers had called for a "process leading to mutual force reductions." See Garthoff, *Détente and Confrontation*, p. 128.

21. In October 1971, NATO ministers selected NATO Secretary General Manlio Brosio (1897–1980) to represent NATO in discussions with the Soviets on MBFR. The Soviets, however, were more interested in a European security conference and objected to a "bloc-to-bloc" approach on forces reduction. See Garthoff, *Détente and Confrontation*, pp. 132, 134.

22. For a review of the 1971 international monetary crisis, see Robert Solomon, *The International Monetary System, 1945–1981* (New York: Harper and Row, 1982), pp. 188–215.

23. For the creation of the Dobrynin-Kissinger back-channel, see Garthoff, *Détente and Confrontation*, p. 82; Dobrynin, *In Confidence: Moscow's Ambassador to America's Six Cold War Presidents, 1962–1986* (New York: Times Books, 1995), pp. 199–206; and Isaacson, *Kissinger: A Biography*, pp. 205–9.

24. For the White House tilt toward Pakistan, see memcon, 19 Aug. 1971, *PPS*, box 330, China Exchanges July–Oct. 20, 1971.

25. Kissinger used the Map Room, established by Franklin D. Roosevelt during World War II, for secret back-channel discussions with Dobyrnin, among other foreign diplomats. See Isaacson, *Kissinger: A Biography*, p. 207.

26. On 5 August 1971, for the first time, Nixon sent a letter to Brezhnev as Communist Party general secretary; earlier presidential letters had been sent to Prime Minister Kosygin, the nominal head of state. Officially recognizing Brezhnev's first place in the hierarchy, Nixon wanted to establish "closer personal contact" with Brezhnev so the two could have wide-ranging dialogue on foreign policy problems at the summit level. On 10 August, Dobrynin told Kissinger that the leadership would like Nixon to visit sometime in May or June 1972. See Anatoly Dobrynin, *In Confidence*, pp. 229–32.

27. For the impact of the Nixon "shocks" on U.S.-Japan political and economic relations, see Isaacson, *Kissinger: A Biography*, p. 348; William B. Bundy, *A Tangled Web: The*

Making of Foreign Policy in the Nixon Presidency (New York: Hill and Wang, 1998), pp. 238–40 and 265–70; and Robert Angel, *Explaining Economic Policy Failure: Japan in the 1969–1971 Crisis* (New York: Columbia University Press, 1991).

28. Kissinger and Dobrynin, working with U.S. Ambassador to West Germany Kenneth Rush and Willy Brandt's national security assistant Egon Bahr, secretly negotiated the Berlin agreement. Kissinger only brought the State Department in once the "back channel" negotiators had completed the draft agreement. For secret Berlin diplomacy, see Garthoff, *Détente and Confrontation*, pp. 137–38; Isaacson, *Kissinger: A Biography*, 324–37; and Kissinger, *White House Years*, pp. 805–10, 822–33.

29. Even if Kissinger and the Chinese had not exchanged "ideas on military dispositions," the former had already (or was about to) provide intelligence information, including satellite photography, on Soviet force deployments in the Far East. See Garthoff, *Détrente and Confrontation*, pp. 261–62, and Isaacson, *Kissinger: A Biography*, p. 345.

30. Dobrynin later observed that the Indian–Soviet friendship treaty was "not the mutual assistance pact Indira Ghandi was seeking." See Dobrynin, *In Confidence*, p. 238.

31. Dobrynin's sources were accurate. On 7 July 1971, Kissinger told the chairman of the Indian Atomic Energy Commission "that under any conceivable circumstances the U.S. would back India against any Chinese pressures" because the "U.S. knew that foreign domination of India would be a disaster"; see memcon, 7 July 1971, *PPS*, box 340, July 1971. Dobrynin later commented that the Indians estimated that by making these assurances, Kissinger was trying to "neutralize unfavorable reaction in Delhi to some yet unknown American move in Asia—the nature of which they only discovered when his mission to Beijing was disclosed"; see Dobrynin, *In Confidence*, p. 236.

32. This is a reference to ongoing negotiation in SALT over how many antiballistic missile sites each side would be allowed to have. Ironically, while the Soviets had been interested in a complete ban on ABMs, Kissinger rejected any serious exploration of the proposal. See Garthoff, *Détente and Confrontation*, pp. 170–74.

33. See Garthoff, *Détente and Confrontation*, pp 262–63.

34. The U. N. action took place when Kissinger was returning from his second trip to Beijing; he was subsequently criticized for agreeing to a visit when the U. N. would be voting on China's membership, because it undercut the efforts of the U.S. delegation to the U.N. to preserve Taiwan's seat. Kissinger would later tell a dismayed U.S. Ambassador to the United Nations George Bush, who had lobbied hard to save Taiwan's seat, that he was "disappointed" by the U.N. action. See George H. W. Bush with Victor Gold, *Looking Forward* (Garden City, N.Y.: Doubleday, 1987), pp. 115–16; Isaacson, *Kissinger: A Biography*, p. 352, and Garthoff, *Détente and Confrontation*, p. 264.

35. See Jon Howe to General Haig, "Precautions in Special Place," 24 April 1972, *PPS*, China Exchanges 1 March–24 June 1972.

36. For Kissinger's account of the crisis, see his *White House Years*, pp. 842–918. For informed accounts that cast doubt on Kissinger's understanding of the crisis, see Garthoff, *Détente and Confrontation*, pp. 294–322; Christopher Van Hollen, "The Tilt Policy Revisited: Nixon–Kissinger Geopolitics and South Asia," *Asian Survey* 20 (1980): 339–62; Isaacson, *Kissinger: A Biography*, pp. 371–78; Bundy, *A Tangled Web*, pp. 268–92. For "impress," see Kissinger to President, "My December 10 Meeting with the Chinese in New York," *PPS*, box 330, China Exchanges, 20 Oct.–31 Dec. 1971.

37. See Kissinger, *White House Years*, p. 909.

38. During the early 1970s, the U.S.-born Foreign Ministry official Tang Wensheng was, with Wang Hairong, a member of a small liaison group that controlled the Politburo's access to the Chairman. See Dr. Li Zhisui, *The Private Life of Chairman Mao: The Memoirs of Mao's Personal Physician* (New York: Random House, 1994), p. 530.

39. For the text, see Jackson, *South Asia Crisis*, 207–9.

40. For quotations from Nixon's letter, see Kissinger, *White House Years*, pp. 900–901.

41. Kissinger opposed a separate cease-fire as "counter to what we had just proposed to the Soviets," so he worked to persuade the Pakistani government to revoke the commander's offer; see Kissinger, *White House Years*, pp. 905–6. He did not mention to Huang, at least during this meeting, that during the Sino–Indian War in November 1962 the Kennedy administration assured the Government of Pakistan, then angry over U.S. military aid to India and fearful of Indian deployments on its borders, that "it will come to Pakistan's assistance in the event of aggression from India against Pakistan." See U.S. Department of State, *Foreign Relations of the United States, 1961–1963*, vol. 19 (Washington, D.C.: U.S. Government Printing Office, 1996), pp. 369–73. Kissinger, however, did inform the Soviets of the pledge; see *White House Years*, p. 905.

42. On 12 December, Kissinger's deputy, Alexander Haig, informed Huang that the King of Jordan had just sent six of a total of fourteen fighter aircraft to Pakistan, and that the Shah of Iran would compensate Jordan with six of its own aircraft. In addition, Iran and Saudi Arabia were sending small arms and ammunition. Turkey might send "up to twenty-two aircraft" and "we are doing all we can to facilitate this." See memcon, 12 Dec. 1971, *PPS*, box 330, China Exchanges, 20 Oct.–21 Dec. 1971.

43. On 12 December, Haig also reported to the Chinese that the Seventh Fleet "will go through the Straits of Malacca tomorrow and proceed to the Indian Ocean by Wednesday" (ibid.).

44. "POL" refers to petroleum, oil, and lubricants.

45. From all accounts, only Kissinger and Nixon believed that the Indians aimed to destroy the Pakistani army, much less annex Azad Kashmir, a disputed border territory. For background on this report—which, among other points, mentioned destroying Pakistani "armor," *not* the army—see Garthoff, *Détente and Confrontation*, pp. 301–2, and Van Hollen, "The Tilt Policy Revisited," pp. 351–52. For the text of CIA chief Richard Helms's report to the Washington Special Action Group, see Jackson, *South Asia Crisis*, p. 225.

46. This is a reference to the puppet state that the Japanese created in Manchuria during the 1930s.

47. A reference to Anthony Lake, who had resigned in protest from the NSC Staff after the invasion of Cambodia. See Isaacson, *Kissinger: A Biography*, p. 276.

48. See Dobrynin, *In Conference*, p. 238. This may have been a variation of the Nixon "madman theory" on the value of intimidating adversaries such as North Vietnam with the prospect that the United States might take any action, however irrational, in a military confrontation. See Isaacson, *Kissinger: A Biography*, pp. 163–64, 369.

49. See Isaacson, *Kissinger: A Biography*, pp. 380–97; John Ehrlichman, *Witness to Power: The Nixon Years* (New York: Simon and Schuster, 1982), pp. 302–12; and Ambrose, *Nixon*, vol. 2, pp. 488–90.

50. For Nixon's and Kissinger's accounts, see Ambrose, *Nixon*, vol. 2, pp. 560–64; and Kissinger, *White House Years*, pp. 1057–62.

51. For Mao's health during this period and its implications for the Nixon visit, see Li, *The Private Life of Chairman Mao*, pp. 553–65. Kissinger mistakenly believed that Mao had suffered a series of strokes before the meeting. *White House Years*, p. 1061.

52. For the apparent surprise of Mao's subordinates at the Nixon meeting, see Chen Jian, "Sino–American Studies in China," in *Pacific Passage: The Study of American East–Asian Relations on the Eve of the Twenty–first Century*, ed. Warren I. Cohen (New York: Columbia University Press, 1996), p. 25.

53. See Kissinger to the President, "Your Encounter with the Chinese," 5 Feb. 1972, and "Mao, Chou, and the Chinese Litmus Test," 19 Feb. 1972, Nixon Papers, National Security Council Files, HAK Office Files, box 13, China; Briefing Paper, "Taiwan," n.d., *PPS*, box 370, Secretary Kissinger's Visit to Peking Oct. 1973 S/PC Mr. Lord vol. 1.

54. This may have been more than flattery. Apparently, Nixon played the leading role on China policy, while Kissinger was initially more skeptical about the possibility of a rapprochement and, at the outset, was "intellectually insecure on Chinese affairs." See Garthoff, *Détente and Confrontation*, pp. 242–43

55. Possibly a reference to TV producer Mararet Osmer who met Kissinger in Paris just after he had returned from his clandestine trip to Beijing and while he was in the midst of secret negotiations with the North Vietnamese. According to a *Newsweek* correspondent, "Kissinger was the only person who used his personal life to conceal his professional activities." See Isaacson, *Kissinger: A Biography*, p. 39.

56. Given Mao's many concubines, he may have assumed that Nixon and Kissinger made as free and easy "use" of women as he had. See Li, *Private Life of Mao*, for a detailed account of Mao's personal life.

57. Mao is referring to Nancy Tang's birth in the United States.

58. According to Li Zhisui, when Mao first spoke with him about the possibility of an approach to the United States, he said that "America's new president, Richard Nixon, is a longtime rightist, a leader of the anticommunists there. I like to deal with rightists. They say what they really think — not like leftists, who say one thing and mean another." See Li, *The Private Life of Chairman Mao*, p. 514.

59. This is a reference to the mysterious flight and death in an airplane crash of Defense Minister Lin Bao in September 1971. Much about the "Lin Bao affair" remains obscure, but there are more allegations than there is evidence to support Mao's claim of Lin's opposition to overtures to the United States. For the most recent study, see Frederick C. Teiwes and Warren Sun, *The Tragedy of Lin Bao: Riding the Tiger During the Cultural Revolution* (Honolulu: University of Hawaii Press, 1996), esp. pp. 123–26. See also Chen Jian, "Sino–American Relations Studies in China," p. 25.

60. The statement about a "very poor family" was a standard Nixon line. While Richard Nixon's family was close to poverty when he was born in 1910, by the 1920s and 1930s, his father Frank Nixon owned a gas station and a grocery store, making him considerably more prosperous than others in his Yorba Linda, California neighborhood, especially when the Great Depression broke. See Stephen Ambrose, *Nixon*, vol. 1: *The Education of a Politician 1913–1962* (New York: Simon and Schuster, 1987), pp. 32, 35–36.

61. After losing the 1960 presidential race, Nixon wrote a partial memoir entitled *Six Crises*

(Garden City, N.Y.: Doubleday, 1962) which detailed the major "crises" of his career—among them the Alger Hiss case, the campaign finances controversy in 1952 that led to his Checkers Speech, Eisenhower's heart attack, and his encounter with an angry mob during his 1958 visit to Latin America.

62. A close friend of Mao Zedong, the American left-liberal journalist Edgar Snow had reported on China since the 1930s; his books *Red Star Over China* (New York:Random House, 1938)) and *The Other Side of the River: Red China Today* (New York: Random House, 1962), among others, had an important impact on U.S. perceptions of China during the 1950s and 1960s. On 1 October 1970, during the National Day celebration in Beijing, Snow sat in the reviewing stand with Mao; he met with Mao and Zhou Enlai several times that fall. In one meeting Mao expressed his desire to host a visit by Nixon. Mao believed that Snow worked for the CIA and assumed that anything he said would reach official Washington. However, no one in Washington took note of Snow's presence on the reviewing stand, and NSC officials discouraged efforts to debrief Snow on his exchanges with Mao. See Li, *The Private Life of Chairman Mao*, p. 532; Garthoff, *Détente and Confrontation*, pp. 254–55; Hersh, *Price of Power*, pp. 366–67; and Allen Whiting, "Sino–American Détente," *China Quarterly* 82 (1980), p. 338.

63. See Garthoff, *Détente and Confrontation*, p. 290. Even Kissinger had difficulty learning what had transpired at some of the meetings between Nixon and Brezhnev, from which he had been excluded. See Kissinger, *White House Years*, p. 1208; Isaacson, *Kissinger: A Biography*, p. 426.

64. For detailed accounts and analyses of the Moscow summit, see Garthoff, *Détente and Confrontation*, pp. 325–58; Ambrose, *Nixon*, vol. 2, pp. 544–48; and Isaacson, *Kissinger: A Biography*, pp. 425–38. For Kissinger's and Nixon's recollections respectively, see *White House Years*, 1202–57, and Ambrose, *Nixon*, vol. 2, pp. 609–21.

65. Winston Lord and John Negroponte to Larry Higby, "President's May 24 Evening at the Soviet Dacha," 30 June 1972, *PPS*, box 335, Winston Lord—Chron—June–Aug 1972; Garthoff, *Détente and Confrontation*, pp. 113–14, 121.

66. Garthoff, *Détente and Confrontation*, pp. 377–78; Dobrynin, *In Confidence*, pp. 277–78; and Kissinger to the President, "My Trip to China," 2 March 1973, *PPS*, box 374, China—Sensitive—Special WL File Misc and Reports, Nov. 1974.

67. See "Talking Points July 26, 1972," *PPS*, box 327, China Exchanges 25 June–17 Oct. 1972; and Garthoff, *Détente and Confrontation*, pp. 377–78.

68. See Memcon 26 July 1972.

69. Garthoff, *Détente and Confrontation*, p. 377. Years later, Kissinger acknowledged to Dobrynin that "he had been wrong in basing his concepts on the inevitability of a Soviet attack against China." See Dobrynin, *In Confidence*, p. 277.

70. See memcon, 14 March 1972, *PPS*, box 329, China Exchanges 1 March 1972–24 June 1972.

71. This line of asterisks may denote discussion of even more sensitive issues of which the transcripts have not yet been declassified.

"Two Former Enemies":

Kissinger in Beijing, February 1973

In February 1973, Henry Kissinger traveled to Beijing for the fourth time. Not only did he get to meet with Chairman Mao, but, as he later reported to Nixon, the "talks were the freest and most candid, and our reception the most cordial . . . of any of my visits." Kissinger believed that a number of things had made this possible, among them, the end of the U.S. fighting in Vietnam, Washington's "meticulous handling of the Chinese," and the aging Chinese leadership's desire to hasten "normalization and the institutionalization of our bilateral relationship." In order to establish regular communication channels and to cultivate the relationship until the United States had broken diplomatic ties with Taiwan, Kissinger and the Chinese agreed to create special liaison offices in each other's capitals. Making this possible were mutual concerns about the Soviets; as Mao put it, both countries needed to "work together to commonly deal with a bastard." As before, China's needs dovetailed with Nixon's and Kissinger's conviction that the triangular relationship with Beijing and Moscow increased Washington's leverage with both, thereby strengthening American power generally.[1]

As confident as Kissinger was in evaluating the talks with Mao and Zhou, he could not deny that both had doubts about American policy even while they confirmed U.S.-China "friendship." Indeed, both Mao and Zhou "replayed the theme" that Washington "might be helping the Soviet Union" against China, although perhaps not by design. Kissinger believed that a "strong and independent China [was] clearly in our interest and the interest of world peace," he also believed in the need for U.S. policy to relax tensions with Moscow. Consequently, he found himself trying to reassure the Chinese that he would not allow détente to endanger Beijing. The Chinese remained suspicious; and in the months that followed Kissinger renewed his efforts to win Beijing's confidence.

Despite Mao's and Zhou's questions about détente, Kissinger took to heart the evident fact that they were receptive to the international power alignment that Washington had forged during the postwar decades. For example, the Chinese had ceased to denounce the Tokyo-Washington connection; instead they understood the purpose of the U.S.-Japan Security Treaty as a "brake on Japanese expansionism and militarism." Indeed, the Chinese had come to view Japan as an "incipient ally . . . to counter Soviet and Indian designs." With respect to Western Europe, Mao and Zhou, among others, were becoming enthusiastic supporters of NATO and strong European defenses—and strong critics of European "illusions of peace" with Moscow. David K. E. Bruce, chief of the U.S. Liaison Office in Beijing, later observed, the reason for the Chinese *volte* face on NATO was simple enough: A "reduction of allied troop strength would mean the release of a certain number of Soviet divisions that could then be turned eastward—not only be available but probably be stationed somewhere in the East."[2]

During Kissinger's talks with Zhou, the two began a delicate negotiation over one item of unfinished business in Southeast Asia, the continuing war in Cambodia. Committed to the Lon Nol dictatorship since the 1970 coup, the Nixon administration had begun another undeclared war by bombing Cambodia, to disable the Khmer Rouge insurgency and to bolster its South Vietnam client state. For the Chinese, a settlement depended not on bombing but on U.S. talks with Prince Norodom Sihanouk, Cambodia's deposed ruler who was in exile in Beijing. Despite the support for Lon Nol, Kissinger would consider political alternatives, even to the point of bringing Sihanouk back for a major role in Cambodian political life. Kissinger, however, linked negotiations to a cease-fire: The Khmer Rouge would have to lay down their arms if the United States was to stop the bombing.[3]

Kissinger clearly relished discussing sensitive political and military issues with Zhou. In areas where he had less interest or expert knowledge, such as commercial and financial policy problems, he was more willing to share responsibility with the State Department. Thus, consistent with President Nixon's explicit interest in finding ways to "open" China to world trade and investment, during the course of 1973, it fell to State Department officials to try to reach an agreement with the Chinese on the thorny question of blocked Chinese financial assets and the private claims of U.S. nationals against the Chinese government (for example, for property seizures).[4] Settling these issues, Kissinger's advisers noted, was important for reestablishing banking and other private commercial connections with China. But they remained politically charged, and the pervasive influence of Marxist and Leninist ways of thinking in Chinese politics and society complicated the efforts to settle the assets and claims controversy. Mao frankly told Kissinger that the "ideological influence" was likely to persist on both sides; sometimes that Americans will want to say "away with you Communists" while the Chinese will want to say "away with you imperialists." Kissinger could only agree; both sides had to be faithful to their principles.[5]

For Kissinger, a central achievement of his visit was the agreement to establish liaison offices in Washington and Beijing. He was prepared to suggest a U.S. office in Beijing, but he did not expect the Chinese to reciprocate. What made it possible, he reported to Nixon, was Zhou's statement that Beijing had "no intention to liberate Taiwan by armed force." At that point, Kissinger reaffirmed Nixon's pledge to normalize relations. That prompted the agreement to establish liaison offices. By May 1973, the two governments had set up shop in their respective capitals, establishing what Kissinger saw as "embassies in everything but name" with Chinese and U.S. representatives enjoying diplomatic immunity and privileges.[6] Although Kissinger's report to Nixon had all but misrepresented the premier's statement, Zhou had said no plans "at the moment," not "no intention," Kissinger was not going to let an ambiguity hold up a major agreement.[7]

Kissinger realized that the future of Taiwan was a difficult problem for the administration, a "painful" situation that would unfold when Washington eventually broke off political ties with that "decent" ally. But he was also concerned about the possibility that Mao and Zhou might soon pass on made him worry that continuity in U.S.–Chinese relations might lapse. Washington had scant knowledge of Beijing's internal political dynamics, much less of the next generation of leaders and their attitudes. Nevertheless, Kissinger believed that the United States' leverage would sustain close relations with Beijing. "Assuming continued hostility with the USSR," he wrote, the Chinese have "no real alternative to us as a counterweight." If Washington handled this important relationship carefully, Kissinger assured Nixon, "it should continue to pay us dividends—in relaxing tensions in Asia, in furthering relations with Moscow, and generally in building a structure of peace."[8]

Most of the record of Kissinger's visit remains classified. The only accessible memcons at present are of his meeting with Mao Zedong on 17 February and several excerpts from conversations with Zhou Enlai on Cambodia. However, his declassified report to Nixon on the trip partly compensates for the dearth of material because of its detailed summary of his talks with Zhou on strategy toward the Soviets. However, a key document—the record of Kissinger's first private meeting with Mao—is declassified in full.

Kissinger received his summons to Mao's villa late in the evening while he and Zhou Enlai were meeting. At that time, the Chairman's health was substantially better than a year earlier, but he was still recovering; later in the year,

Kissinger would report that Mao "looked much healthier and thinner than in February." [9] Kissinger's memoir account of the discussion is detailed enough and conveys its often droll character as well as some of the more serious moments, such as Mao's warnings about Soviet intentions. Nevertheless, he excluded the most sensitive parts of the discussion, such as Mao's suspicions that the West might be pushing "Russia eastward, mainly against us," or that Washington might even want China to get into a war with Russia as a way to destroy the Soviet Union. Kissinger also withheld the exchanges on the French elections—notably, his claim that "we are doing our utmost" to help Georges Pompidou—and on Japan–Soviet relations, where both he and Mao agreed on the need to prevent Moscow and Tokyo from becoming too close.

TOP SECRET/SENSITIVE/EXCLUSIVELY EYES ONLY
MEMORANDUM OF CONVERSATION
PARTICIPANTS: Mao Zedong, Chairman, Politburo, Chinese
  Communist Party; Zhou Enlai, Premier of the State Council; Wang
  Hairong, Assistant Minister of Foreign Affairs; Tang Wensheng,
  Interpreter; Shen Zuoyun, Interpreter; Dr. Henry A. Kissinger,
  Assistant to the President for National Security Affairs; Winston
  Lord, NSC Staff
DATE AND TIME: Saturday, February 17, 1973, 11:30 P.M.–Sunday,
  February 18, 1973, 1:20 A.M.
PLACE: Zhungnanhai, Chairman Mao's Residence Beijing People's
  Republic of China[A]

(At 11:00 p.m. February 17, 1973 at a meeting in a villa near the Guest House where Dr. Kissinger and his party were staying, Prime Minister Zhou Enlai informed Dr. Kissinger that he and Winston Lord were invited to meet with Chairman Mao Zedong at 11:30 p.m. that evening. He told Dr. Kissinger that he would come to the Guest House shortly to escort him to the Chairman's residence.

Dr. Kissinger and his delegation members at the meeting went back to the Guest House. Prime Minister Zhou Enlai came to the Guest House at 11:20

[A] Source: National Archives, Record Group 59, Department of State Records, Policy Planning Staff (Director's Files), 1969–1977 (hereafter referred to as PPS, with archival box number and file information), Mao Book, Dec. 1975, Mr. Lord.

p.m. and rode with Dr. Kissinger to Zhungnanmhai. Mr. Zhu, Deputy Director of Protocol, accompanied Mr. Lord. Prime Minister Zhou Enlai escorted Dr. Kissinger into the outer room of the Guest House and then through another room to Chairman Mao's sitting room.

The Chairman was helped up from his chair by his young female attendant and came forward to greet Dr. Kissinger. Photographers took pictures. He welcomed Dr. Kissinger and Dr. Kissinger pointed out that it was almost exactly a year ago that he had first met the Chairman. The Chairman then greeted Mr. Lord and commented that he was so young, younger than the interpreters. Mr. Lord replied that he was in any event older than the interpreters. The Chairman then motioned to the large easy chairs and the parties sat down. The photographers continued to take pictures.)

Chairman Mao: (As he headed toward his chair.) I don't look bad, but God has sent me an invitation.

(to Mr. Lord) You are a young man.

Mr. Lord: I am getting older.

Chairman Mao: I am the oldest among those seated here.

Prime Minister Zhou: I am the second oldest.

Chairman Mao: There was someone in the British Army who was opposed to the independence of your country. Field Marshal Montgomery was one of those to oppose your policy.[10]

Dr. Kissinger: Yes.

Chairman Mao: He opposed the [John Foster] Dulles policy. He probably doesn't oppose you anymore. At that time, you also opposed us. We also opposed you. So we are two enemies. (laughter)

Dr. Kissinger: Two former enemies.

Chairman Mao: Now we call the relationship between ourselves a friendship.

Dr. Kissinger: That's our sentiment.

Chairman Mao: That's what I am saying.

Dr. Kissinger I have told the Prime Minister that we speak to no other country as frankly and as openly as we do to you.

Chairman Mao: (to the photographers) That's all for you.

(The photographers leave.)

But let us not speak false words or engage in trickery. We don't steal your documents. You can deliberately leave them somewhere and try us out. Nor do we engage in eavesdropping and bugging. There is no use in those small tricks. And some of the big maneuvering, there is no use to them too. I said that to your correspondent, Mr. Edgar Snow. I said that your CIA is no good for major events.

Dr. Kissinger: That's absolutely true. That's been our experience.

Chairman Mao: Because when you issue an order, for example, when your President issues an order, and you want information on a certain question, then the intelligence reports come as so many snowflakes. We also have our intelligence service and it is the same with them. They do not work well. (Prime Minister Zhou laughs.) For instance, they didn't know about Lin Bao. (Prime Minister Zhou laughs.) Then again they didn't know you wanted to come.

I read two articles in 1969. One of your Directors of your China desk in the State Department wrote an article later published in a Japanese newspaper.

Dr. Kissinger: I don't think I read that.

Prime Minister Zhou: I hadn't mentioned it to you before.

Dr. Kissinger: No.

Chairman Mao: Your business was done well. You've been flying everywhere. Are you a swallow or a pigeon? (laughter) And the Vietnamese issue can be counted as basically settled.

Dr. Kissinger: That is our feeling. We must now have a transitional period toward tranquility.

Chairman Mao: Yes, that's right.

Dr. Kissinger: The basic issues are settled.

Chairman Mao: We also say in the same situation (gesturing with his hand) that's what your President said when he was sitting here, that each aide has its own means and acted out of its own necessity. That resulted in the two countries acting hand-in-hand.

Dr. Kissinger: Yes, we both face the same danger. We may have to use different methods sometimes but for the same objectives.

Chairman Mao: That would be good. So long as the objectives are the same, we would not harm you nor would you harm us. And we can work together to commonly deal with a bastard. (laughter)

Actually it would be that sometime we want to criticize you for a while and you want to criticize us for a while. That, your President said, is the ideological influence. You say, away with you Communists. We say, away with you imperialists. Sometimes we say things like that. It would not do not to do that.

Dr. Kissinger: I think both of us must be true to our principles. And in fact it would confuse the situation if we spoke the same language. I have told the Prime Minister that in Europe you, because of your principles, can speak more firmly than we can, strangely enough.

Chairman Mao: As for you, in Europe and Japan, we hope that you will cooperate with each other. As for some things it is alright to quarrel and bicker about, but fundamental cooperation is needed.

Dr. Kissinger: As between you and us, even if we sometimes criticize each other, we will coordinate our actions with you, and we would never participate in a policy to isolate you. As for Japan and Europe, we agree that we should cooperate on all essential matters with them. Europe has very weak leadership right now.

Chairman Mao: They don't unite with each other.

Dr. Kissinger: They don't unite, and they don't take farsighted views. When they are confronted with a danger they hope it will go away without effort.

Prime Minister Zhou: I told Dr. Kissinger you (the U.S.) should still help Pompidou.[11]

Chairman Mao: Yes indeed.

Dr. Kissinger: We are doing our utmost, and we will do more.

Chairman Mao: (gesturing with his hands) Now Mr. Pompidou is being threatened. It is the Socialist Party and the Communist Party putting their strength against him.

Dr. Kissinger: Yes, and they have united.

Chairman Mao: (pointing at Dr. Kissinger) They are uniting and the Soviet Union wants the Communist Party to get into office. I don't like their Communist Party, just like I don't like your Communist Party. I like you, but not your Communist Party. (laughter)

In the West you always historically had a policy, for example, in both World Wars you always began by pushing Germany to fight against Russia.

Dr. Kissinger: But it is not our policy to push Russia to fight against China, because the danger to us of a war in China is as great as a war in Europe.

Chairman Mao: (Before Dr. Kissinger's remarks are translated, he makes remarks in Chinese and counts on his fingers. Miss Tang then translates Dr. Kissinger's remarks and after that Chairman Mao's remarks.)

What I wanted to say is whether or not you are now pushing West Germany to make peace with Russia and then push Russia eastward. I suspect the whole of the West has such an idea, that is to push Russia eastward, mainly against us and also Japan. Also probably towards you, in the Pacific Ocean and the Indian Ocean.

Dr. Kissinger: We did not favor this policy. We preferred the German opposition party which did not pursue this policy. (Chairman Mao, smoking a cigar, offers cigars to Dr. Kissinger and Mr. Lord who decline.)

Chairman Mao: Yes, that's our feeling. We are also in favor of the opposition party in Germany.

Dr. Kissinger: They conducted themselves very stupidly.

Chairman Mao: Yes, they were defeated. The whole of Europe is thinking only of peace.

Prime Minister Zhou: The illusions of peace created by their leaders.

Dr. Kissinger: Yes, but we will do our best to strengthen European defenses and keep our armies in Europe.

Chairman Mao: That would be very good.

Dr. Kissinger: We have no plan for any large reduction of our forces in Europe for the next four years. (Chairman Mao turns to Prime Minister Zhou)

Prime Minister Zhou: In talking about reducing your troops, you mean only at the most 10 to 15 percent.

Dr. Kissinger: That is exactly correct.

Chairman Mao: What is the number of American troops in Europe? They are probably mostly rocket units.

Prime Minister Zhou: There are between 300–350,000 including the Mediterranean.

Chairman Mao: That probably does not include the Navy.

Dr. Kissinger: It does not include the Navy. There are about 275,000 in Central Europe. That does not include the Sixth Fleet in the Mediteraneann.

Chairman Mao: And your troop deployment to Asia and the Pacific Ocean is too scattered. You have them in Korea. I heard the number is about 300,000.

Dr. Kissinger: About 40,000.[12]

Chairman Mao: And from 8,000 to 9,000 with Chiang Kai-shek.

Prime Minister Zhou : In Taiwan.

Chairman Mao: Then it is said that there are two groups in Japan, 40,000 in Okinawa and 20,000 to 30,000 in Japan proper. I don't know how many there are in the Philippines. Now you have remaining in Vietnam a bit over 10,000.

Dr. Kissinger: But they will all be withdrawn.

Chairman Mao: Yes, and I heard that you have 40,000 in Thailand.

Dr. Kissinger: That is correct. But all the units the Chairman mentioned are mostly air force units and therefore they probably cannot be measured by the number of personnel.

Chairman Mao: You also have ground forces, for instance, in South Korea.

Dr. Kissinger: In South Korea we have ground forces.

Chairman Mao: That was all begun by Truman and Acheson. So this time you held a memorial service for Truman and we didn't go. (laughter)

Dr. Kissinger: When you have a liaison office in Washington it will be more possible in the future.

Prime Minister Zhou : You've held all these memorial services, both for Truman and Johnson. (Chairman Mao and Prime Minister Zhou laugh.)

It seems to me that your voice is hoarse today. You should have a day's rest tomorrow. Why do you want to continue to talk so much?

Dr. Kissinger: Because it is very important that you and we understand what we are going to do and to coordinate our actions, and therefore we always tell the Prime Minister what our plans are in various areas of the world so that you can understand the individual moves when they are made.

Chairman Mao: Yes. When you pass through Japan, you should perhaps talk a bit more with them. You only talked with them for one day and that isn't very good for their face.

Dr. Kissinger: Mr. Chairman, we wanted this trip's emphasis to be on the talks in Beijing, and I will take a separate trip to Tokyo.

Chairman Mao: Good. And also make clear to them. You know the Japanese feelings towards the Soviet Union are not so very good.

Dr. Kissinger: They are very ambivalent.

Chairman Mao: (gesturing with his hand) In a word, during the Second World War, Prime Minister Tanaka told our Premier, what the Soviet Union did was that upon seeing a person about to hang himself, they immediately took the chair from under his feet.[13]

Dr. Kissinger: Yes.

Chairman Mao: It could be said that they didn't fire a single shot and yet they were able to grab so many places.[14] (Prime Minister Zhou chuckles.) They grabbed the People's Republic of Mongolia. They grabbed half of Xinjian. It was called a sphere of influence. And Manchuko, on the northeast, was also called their sphere of influence.[15]

Dr. Kissinger: And they took all the industry out of it.[16]

Chairman Mao: Yes. And they grabbed also the islands of Sakhalin and the Kuriles Island. (Chairman Mao and Prime Minister Zhou discuss among themselves.) Sakhalin is the southern part of the Kuriles Island. I will look it up in the dictionary to see what its Chinese translation is.[17]

Dr. Kissinger: The Japanese are tempted by the economic possibilities in Russia.

Chairman Mao: (nodding yes) They want to grab something there.

Dr. Kissinger: But we will encourage closer ties between Japan and ourselves, and also we welcome their relationship with the People's Republic.

Chairman Mao: We also believe that rather than Japan having closer relations with the Soviet Union, we would rather that they would better their relations with you. That would be better.

Dr. Kissinger: It would be very dangerous if Japan and the Soviet Union formed closer political relations.

Chairman Mao: That doesn't seem likely.

Prime Minister Zhou: The prospects are not too good.

Chairman Mao: We can also do some work there.

Dr. Kissinger: The Soviet Union has made overtures but the Japanese have not responded. They have invited [Japanese Foreign Minister Masayoshi] Ohira to go to Moscow.

Prime Minister Zhou: Yes, this year, the second half.

Dr. Kissinger: This year.

Prime Minister Zhou: And it seems on this question that Ohira has a clearer idea of the Soviet Union than others. But there are some not so clear in their understanding as their Foreign Minister.

Dr. Kissinger: That is correct.

Prime Minister Zhou: That is also the bureaucracy as you term it.

Dr. Kissinger: We are prepared to exchange information with you on these matters.

Prime Minister Zhou: (to Chairman Mao) We have decided besides establishing a liaison office in each capital to maintain the contact between Huang Hua and the White House.

Chairman Mao: (to Prime Minister Zhou) Where is the stress?

Prime Minister Zhou: The liaison office will handle the general public exchanges. For confidential and urgent matters not covered by the liaison office we will use the channel of Ambassador Huang Hua.

Chairman Mao: Huang Hua has met an ill fate. (Prime Minister Zhou laughs.) He was doing very well in your place and immediately upon his return to Shanghai, he twisted his back.

Dr. Kissinger: We will find a doctor for him when he returns.

Chairman Mao: Yes. (Prime Minister Zhou laughs.) He seemed more safe in your place. Immediately upon his return to Shanghai he collapsed. From the atmosphere with which your President received our acrobatic troupe, I thought that the Vietnamese issue was going to be settled.

There were some rumors that said that you were about to collapse. (laughter) And the women folk seated here were all dissatisfied with that. (laughter, especially pronounced among the women) They said if the Doctor is going to collapse, we would be out of work.

Dr. Kissinger: Not only in China.

Chairman Mao: Yes, and the whole line would collapse like dominos.

Dr. Kissinger: Those were just journalists' speculation.

Chairman Mao: Only speculation?

Dr. Kissinger: Only speculation.

Chairman Mao: No ground whatsoever?

Dr. Kissinger: No ground whatsoever. In fact the opposite was true. We have now been able to place our men into all key positions.

Chairman Mao: (nodding yes) Your President is now saying that you are proposing something as if you were moving the Great Wall from China to the United States, that is, trade barriers.[18]

Dr. Kissinger: What we want to do is lower barriers.

Chairman Mao: To lower them? Then you were doing that just to frighten people. You are saying that you are going to raise tariffs and non-tariff barriers and maybe you do that to intimidate Europe and Japan.

Dr. Kissinger: Partly. We are proposing a trade bill which gives both the power to raise and lower barriers, in order to get it passed through Congress. We must create the impression that we might increase barriers. We want executive authority to do it without Congressional approval, but if we ask Congress to reduce barriers they would refuse. (Prime Minister Zhou laughs.) And this is why we are asking for executive authority to move in either direction.

Chairman Mao: What if they don't give it to you?

Dr. Kissinger: We think they will give it to us. It will be a difficult battle, but we are quite certain we will win. We are proposing it also in such general language that we can remove discrimination that still exists towards the People's Republic.

Chairman Mao: The trade between our two countries at present is very pitiful. It is gradually increasing. You know China is a very poor country. We don't have much. What we have in excess is women. (laughter)

Dr. Kissinger: There are no quotas for those or tariffs.

Chairman Mao: So if you want them we can give a few of those to you, some tens of thousands. (laughter)

Prime Minister Zhou : Of course, on a voluntary basis.

Chairman Mao: Let them go to your place. They will create disasters. That way you can lessen our burdens.[19] (laughter)

Dr. Kissinger: Our interest in trade with China is not commercial. It is to establish a relationship that is necessary for the political relations we both have.

Chairman Mao: Yes.

Dr. Kissinger: That is the spirit with which we are conducting our discussions.

Chairman Mao: I once had a discussion with a foreign friend. (The interpreters hold a discussion with Chairman Mao.) I said that we should draw a horizontal line—the U.S.-Japan-Pakistan-Iran (Chairman Mao coughs badly.)-Turkey and Europe.

Dr. Kissinger: We have a very similar conception. You may have read in a newspaper that Mr. Helms has been moved to Iran, and there was a great deal of speculation how this affected my position.[20] In fact we sent Helms to Iran to take care of Turkey, Iran, Pakistan and the Persian Gulf, because of his experience in his previous position and we needed a reliable man in that spot who understands the more complex matters that are needed to be done. (Chairman Mao lights his cigar again.) We will give him authority to deal with all of these countries, although this will not be publicly announced.

Chairman Mao: As for such matters we do not understand very much your affairs in the United States. There are a lot of things we don't know very well. For example, your domestic affairs, we don't understand them. There are also many things about foreign policy that we don't understand either. Perhaps in your future four years we might be able to learn a bit.

Dr. Kissinger: I told the Prime Minister that you have a more direct, maybe a more heroic mode of action than we do. We have to use sometimes more complicated methods because of our domestic situation. (Chairman Mao queries about the translation and Miss Tang repeats "mode of action.") But on our fundamental objectives we will act very decisively and without regard to public opinion. So if a real danger develops or hegemonial intentions become active, we will certainly resist them wherever they appear. And as the President said to the Chairman, in our own interests, not as a kindness to anyone else.

Chairman Mao: (laughing) Those are honest words.

Dr. Kissinger: This is our position.

Chairman Mao: Do you want our Chinese women? We can give you ten million. (laughter, particularly among the women)

Dr. Kissinger: The Chairman is improving his offer.

Chairman Mao: By doing so we can let them flood your country with disaster and therefore impair your interests. In our country we have too many women, and they have a way of doing things. They give birth to children and our children are too many. (laughter)

Dr. Kissinger: It is such a novel proposition, we will have to study it.

Chairman Mao: You can set up a committee to study the issue. That is how your visit to China is settling the population question. (laughter)

Dr. Kissinger: We will study utilization and allocation.

Chairman Mao: If we ask them to go I think they would be willing.

Prime Minister Zhou: Not necessarily.

Chairman Mao: That's because of their feudal ideas, big nation chauvinism.

Dr. Kissinger: We are certainly willing to receive them.

Chairman Mao: The Chinese are very alien-excluding. For instance, in your country you can let in so many nationalities, yet in China how many foreigners do you see?

Prime Minister Zhou: Very few.

Dr. Kissinger: Very few.

Chairman Mao: You have about 600,000 Chinese in the United States. We probably don't even have 60 Americans here. I would like to study the problem. I don't know the reason.

Miss Tang: Mr. Lord's wife is Chinese.

Chairman Mao: Oh?

Mr. Lord: Yes.

Chairman Mao: I studied the problem. I don't know why the Chinese never like foreigners. There are no Indians perhaps. As for the Japanese, they are not very numerous either; compared to others there are quite a few and some are married and settled down.

Dr. Kissinger: Of course, your experience with foreigners has not been all that fortunate.

Chairman Mao: Yes, perhaps that is some reason for that. Yes, in the past hundred years, mainly the eight powers, and later it was Japan during the Boxer Revolution. For thirteen years Japan occupied China, they occupied the major part of China; and in the past the allied forces, the invading foreigners, not only occupied Chinese territory, they also asked China for indemnity.[21]

Dr. Kissinger: Yes, and extraterritorial rights.[22]

Chairman Mao: Now in our relations with Japan, we haven't asked them for indemnity and that would add to the burden of the people. It would be difficult to calculate all the indemnity. No accountant would be able to do it.

And only in this way can we move from hostility to relaxation in relations between peoples. And it will be more difficult to settle relations of hostility between the Japanese and Chinese peoples than between us and you.

Dr. Kissinger: Yes. There is no feeling of hostility of American people at all toward the Chinese people. On the contrary. Between us right now there is only essentially a juridical problem. (Chairman Mao nods agreement.) Which we will solve in the next years. But there is a strong community of interest which is operating immediately.

Chairman Mao: Is that so?

Dr. Kissinger: Between China and the U.S.

Chairman Mao: What do you mean by community of interest? On Taiwan?

Dr. Kissinger: In relation to other countries that may have intentions.

Prime Minister Zhou: You mean the Soviet Union?

Dr. Kissinger: I mean the Soviet Union.

Prime Minister Zhou: Miss Shen understood you.

Chairman Mao: (looking toward Miss Shen) The Chinese have a good command of English. (to Prime Minister Zhou) Who is she?

Prime Minister Zhou: Miss Shen Zouyun.

Chairman Mao: Girls. (Prime Minister Zhou laughs.) Today I have been uttering some nonsense for which I will have to beg the pardon of the women of China.

Dr. Kissinger: It sounded very attractive to the Americans present. (Chairman Mao and the girls laugh.)

Chairman Mao: If we are going to establish a liaison office in your country do you want Miss Shen or Miss Tang?

Dr. Kissinger: We will deal with that through the channel of Huang Hua. (laughter)

Chairman Mao: Our interpreters are truly too few.

Dr. Kissinger: But they have done a remarkable job, the interpreters we have met.

Chairman Mao: The interpreters you have met and our present interpreters who are doing most of the work are now in their twenties and thirties. If they grow too old they don't do interpretation so well.

Prime Minister Zhou: We should send some abroad.

Chairman Mao: We will send children at such a height (indicating with his hands), not too old.

Dr. Kissinger: We will be prepared to establish exchange programs where you can send students to America.

Chairman Mao: And if among a hundred persons there are ten who are successful learning the language well, then that would be a remarkable success. And if among them a few dozens don't want to come back, for example, some girls who want to stay in the United States, no matter. Because you do not exclude foreigners like Chinese. In the past the Chinese went abroad and they didn't want to learn the local language. (looking toward Miss Tang) Her grandparents refused to learn English.[23] They are so obstinate. You know Chinese are very obstinate and conservative. Many of the older generation overseas Chinese don't speak the local language. But they are getting better, the younger generation.

Dr. Kissinger: In America, all, or the vast majority, speak English.

Prime Minister Zhou: That is the younger people. The first generation ones don't learn the local language. There was an old overseas Chinese who came back to China after living abroad. She was old and died in Beijing in the 1950s when she was in her nineties. She was a member of our People's Government. She didn't speak a word of English. She was Cantonese, extremely conservative.[24]

Dr. Kissinger: Chinese culture is so particular that it is difficult to assimilate other cultures.

Chairman Mao: Chinese language is not bad, but the Chinese characters are not good.

Prime Minister Zhou: They are very difficult to learn.

Chairman Mao: And there are many contradictions between the oral and written language because the oral language is monosyllabic while the written language develops from symbols. We do not use the alphabet.

Dr. Kissinger: There are some attempts to use an alphabet I am told.

Prime Minister Zhou: First we must standardize the oral language.

Chairman Mao: (gestures with his hand and points to his books) But if the Soviet Union would throw its bombs and kill all those over 30 who are Chinese, that would solve the problem for us. Because the old people like me can't learn Chinese. We read Chinese. The majority of my books are Chinese. There are very few dictionaries over there. All the other books are in Chinese.

Dr. Kissinger: Is the Chairman learning English now?

Chairman Mao: I have heard that I am studying it. Those are rumors on the outside. I don't heed them. They are false. I know a few English letters. I don't know the grammar.

Miss Tang: The Chairman invented an English word.

Chairman Mao: Yes, I invented the English term "paper tiger."[25]

Dr. Kissinger: "Paper tiger." Yes, that was all about us. (laughter)

Chairman Mao: But you are a German from Germany. But your Germany now has met with an ill fate, because in two wars it has been defeated.

Dr. Kissinger: It attempted too much, beyond its abilities and resources.

Chairman Mao: Yes, and it also scattered its forces in war. For example, in its attack against the Soviet Union. If it is going to attack, it should attack in one place, but they separated their troops into three routes. It began in June but then by the winter they couldn't stand it because it was too cold. What is the reason for the Europeans' fear of the cold?

Dr. Kissinger: The Germans were not prepared for a long war. Actually they did not mobilize their whole forces until 1943. I agree with the Chairman that if they had concentrated on one front they would almost certainly have won. They were only ten kilometers from Moscow even by dispersing their forces. (Chairman Mao relights his cigar.)

Chairman Mao: They shouldn't have attacked Moscow or Kiev. They should have taken Leningrad as a first step. Another error in policy was they didn't cross the sea after Dunkirk.

Dr. Kissinger: After Dunkirk.

Chairman Mao: They were entirely unprepared.

Dr. Kissinger: And Hitler was a romantic. He had a strange liking for England.

Chairman Mao: Oh? Then why didn't they go there? Because the British at that time were completely without troops.

Dr. Kissinger: If they were able to cross the channel into Britain. I think they had only one division in all of England.[26]

Prime Minister Zhou: Is that so?

Dr. Kissinger: Yes.

Prime Minister Zhou: Also Sir Anthony Eden told us in Germany at that time that a Minister in the Army of Churchill's Government said at that time if Hitler had crossed the channel they would have had no forces. They had withdrawn all their forces back. When they were preparing for the German crossing, Churchill had no arms. He could only organize police to defend the coast. If they crossed they would not be able to defend.

Dr. Kissinger: It also shows what a courageous man can do because Churchill created by his personality much more strength than they possessed.

Chairman Mao: Actually by that time they couldn't hold.

Prime Minister Zhou: So Hitler carried some romantic feelings about Britain?

Dr. Kissinger: I think he was a maniac, but he did have some feelings about Britain.[27]

Chairman Mao: I believe Hitler was from the Rhine area?

Dr. Kissinger: Austria.

Prime Minister Zhou: He was a soldier in the First World War.

Dr. Kissinger: He was in the German Army, but he was a native of Austria.

Prime Minister Zhou: From the Danube.

Dr. Kissinger: He conducted strategy artistically rather than strategically. He did it by intuition. He had no overall plan.

Chairman Mao: Then why did the German troops heed him so much?

Dr. Kissinger: Probably because the Germans are somewhat romantic people and because he must have had a very strong personality.

Chairman Mao: Mainly because during the First World War the German nation was humiliated.

Dr. Kissinger: Yes, that was a very important factor.

Chairman Mao: If there are Russians going to attack China, I can tell you today that our way of conducting a war will be guerrilla war and protracted war. We will let them go wherever they want. (Prime Minister Zhou laughs.) They want to come to the Yellow River tributaries. That would be good, very good. (laughter) And if they go further to the Yangtse River tributaries, that would not be bad either.

Dr. Kissinger: But if they use bombs and do not send armies? (laughter)

Chairman Mao: What should we do? Perhaps you can organize a committee to study the problem. We'll let them beat us up and they will lose many resources. They say they are socialists. We are also socialists and that will be socialists attacking socialists.

Dr. Kissinger: If they attack China, we would certainly oppose them for our own reasons.

Chairman Mao: But your people are not awakened, and Europe and you would think that it would be a fine thing if it were that the ill water would flow toward China.

Dr. Kissinger: What Europe thinks I am not able to judge. They cannot do anything anyway. They are basically irrelevant. (In the midst of this Chairman Mao toasts Dr. Kissinger and Mr. Lord with tea.) What we think is that if the Soviet Union overruns China, this would dislocate the security of all other countries and will lead to our own isolation.

Chairman Mao: (laughing) How will that happen? How would that be? Because since in being bogged down in Vietnam you met so many difficulties, do you think they would feel good if they were bogged down in China?

Dr. Kissinger: The Soviet Union?

Miss Tang: The Soviet Union.

Chairman Mao: And then you can let them get bogged down in China, for half a year, or one, or two, or three, or four years. And then you can poke your finger at the Soviet back. And your slogan then will be for peace, that is you must bring down Socialist imperialism for the sake of peace. And perhaps you can begin to help them in doing business, saying whatever you need we will help against China.

Dr. Kissinger: Mr. Chairman, it is really very important that we understand each other's motives. We will never knowingly cooperate in an attack on China.

Chairman Mao: (interrupting) No, that's not so. Your aim in doing that would be to bring the Soviet Union down.

Dr. Kissinger: That's a very dangerous thing. (laughter)

Chairman Mao: (using both hands for gestures) The goal of the Soviet Union is to occupy both Europe and Asia, the two continents.

Dr. Kissinger: We want to discourage a Soviet attack, not defeat it. We want to prevent it. (Prime Minister Zhou looks at his watch.)

Chairman Mao: As for things, matters, in the world, it is hard to say. We would rather think about things this way. We think this way the world would be better.

Dr. Kissinger: Which way?

Chairman Mao: That is that they would attack China and be defeated. We must think of the worst eventuality.

Dr. Kissinger: That is your necessity. (Prime Minister Zhou laughs.)

Chairman Mao: We have so many women in our country that don't know how to fight.

Miss Tang: Not necessarily. There are women's detachments.

Chairman Mao: They are only on stage. In reality if there is a fight you would flee very quickly and run into underground shelters.

Miss Wang: If the minutes of this talk were made public, it would incur the public wrath on behalf of half the population.

Chairman Mao: That is half of the population of China.

Prime Minister Zhou: First of all, it wouldn't pass the Foreign Ministry.

Chairman Mao: We can call this a secret meeting; (Chinese laughter) Should our meeting today be public, or kept secret?

Dr. Kissinger: It's up to you. I am prepared to make it public if you wish.

Chairman Mao: What is your idea? Is it better to have it public or secret?

Dr. Kissinger: I think it is probably better to make it public.

Chairman Mao: Then the words we say about women today shall be made nonexistent. (laughter)

Dr. Kissinger: We will remove them from the record. (laughter) We will start studying this proposal when I get back.

Chairman Mao: You know, the Chinese have a scheme to harm the United States, that is, to send ten million women to the United States and impair its interests by increasing its population.

Dr. Kissinger: The Chairman has fixed the idea so much in my mind that I'll certainly use it at my next press conference. (laughter)

Chairman Mao: That would be all right with me. I'm not afraid of anything. Anyway, God has sent me an invitation.[28]

Dr. Kissinger: I really find the Chairman in better health this year than last year.

Chairman Mao: Yes, I am better than last year. (The photographers enter the room.)

They are attacking us. (The Chairman then gets up without assistance to say goodbye to the Americans.) Please give my warm regards to President Nixon. Also to Mrs. Nixon. I was not able to meet her and Secretary Rogers. I must apologize.

Dr. Kissinger: I will certainly do that.

Prime Minister Zhou: We will send you a press release in one hour. (Chairman Mao escorts Dr. Kissinger into the outer room where he says goodbye to Dr. Kissinger and Mr. Lord. Prime Minister Zhou then escorts Dr. Kissinger to his waiting car.)

COMMENTARY

Among Winston Lord's papers at the National Archives is a special file on Kissinger's highly secret and sensitive negotiations with the Chinese on Cambodia from 1973 to 1975. All of the documents in the file are excerpts from longer conversations with Zhou Enlai, Huang Hua, and Huang Zhen, among other officials. Apparently, Kissinger asked Lord to compile these documents in 1975, the year of the Khmer Rouge military victory in Cambodia, perhaps for his use in testimony before Congress or to facilitate a new round of talks with the Chinese.

With the full text of other Kissinger-Zhou talks during this visit still classified, these excerpts give the reader a good sense of the character of Kissinger's exchanges with Zhou at the zenith of their political relationship.

However much their relationship was driven by instrumental purposes, they, nevertheless greatly enjoyed speaking with one other. Certainly, these documents provide an unparalleled view of the intelligence, wit, and cynicism that informed Zhou's negotiating style; and they suggest as well how he had so easily captivated Kissinger, who became one of the premier's most enthusiastic Western admirers.[29]

When Kissinger and Zhou held their discussions, Prince Sihanouk had been living in political exile in Beijing since the 1970 coup. Although the Chinese had provided assistance to the Khmer Rouge insurgency, the exiled Sihanouk had also received political support from Beijing. Without Chinese primary sources, Beijing's motivations remain unclear; no doubt, however, Zhou perceived a Chinese role in expediting a Cambodian settlement as advantageous for strengthening relations with the United States. Moreover, Zhou may have seen Sihanouk's neutral policies as a way to reduce U.S. influence in a neighboring state while preventing overly close relations with Vietnam, a traditional Chinese antagonist. For their part, Saloth Sar—later known as Pol Pot—and the Khmer Rouge had no use for Sihanouk and were determined to revolutionize Cambodia, but Zhou seemed to believe that war-torn Cambodia was hardly ready for Communist rule; as he put it, "It is impossible for Cambodia to become completely red now." The implication was that the Khmer Rouge would have to accept Sihanouk's leadership for the time being.[30]

Zhou made no secret of his strong opposition to Washington's support of Lon Nol; indeed, Chinese criticism grew as the United States resumed the bombing of Cambodia in early 1973.[31] Nixon had announced a cease-fire in Vietnam only a few weeks earlier, but he continued to provide military aid to the Lon Nol regime. Under article 20 of the Agreement on Ending the War and Restoring Peace in Vietnam, both Americans and North Vietnamese were to remove troops from Cambodia and to refrain from granting any military aid to the parties there. North Vietnam had already taken most of its forces out of Cambodia and was urging the Khmer Rouge to accept a cease-fire and negotiations, but they refused to negotiate. To warn Hanoi to avoid offensive action against the Saigon regime, to force remaining North Vietnamese forces from Cambodia, and to compel the Khmer Rouge to stop fighting, Nixon and Kissinger ordered a new bombing campaign. In so doing, they violated a congressional ban on direct U.S. military support in Cambodia: the U.S. air attaché used embassy facilities to control air strikes and communicate with the spotter planes supporting them.[32]

Kissinger's emphasis on bombing to achieve political ends flowed from dubious assumptions—that the Khmer Rouge were the creatures of the North Vietnamese and that the Cambodian conflict was, as he put it to Zhou, essentially a "foreign war." Forcing the North Vietnamese to withdraw, Kissinger seemed to believe, would turn the Cambodian conflict into a "civil war," and perhaps a more manageable situation. Nevertheless, he must have recognized that bombing could not stabilize Lon Nol's politically weak position. That and his interest in developing a strategic relationship with Bejing may have made him willing to meet Zhou half-way on a political settlement that included Sihanouk.[33]

What does not come across in these transcripts is that, in the last stages of the Vietnam negotiations, the Chinese had hinted to Kissinger that they would be willing to arrange a meeting between him and Prince Sihanouk. Kissinger responded that the Cambodian opposition would have to stop fighting ("a period of quiet") before there could be discussions with the Prince. Thus, rather than meet the nominal head of the Cambodian insurgency, Kissinger preferred to work through Beijing and Hanoi while the fighting and bombing continued. Future declassifications may help historians determine whether Kissinger's decisions to turn down these overtures represented a tragic lost opportunity to settle a bloody conflict.[34]

TOP SECRET/SENSITIVE/EXCLUSIVELY EYES ONLY
MEMORANDUM OF CONVERSATION PARTICIPANTS: Zhou Enlai, Premier, State Council; Ji Pengfei, Minister of Foreign Affairs; Qiao Guanhua, Vice Minister of Foreign Affairs; Wang Hairong, Assistant Foreign Minister; Tang Wensheng, Interpreter; Shen Zouyun, Interpreter; Two Notetakers; Dr. Henry A. Kissinger, Assistant to the President for National Security Affairs; Richard T. Kennedy, NSC Staff; Miss Irene G. Derus, Notetaker
PLACE: Villa #3, Beijing, China
DATE AND TIME: February 16, 1973, 2:15–6:00 P.M.[B]

PM Zhou: Yes, we also don't know very well what happened. We only know that the Soviet Ambassador is carrying on certain activities. And the Soviet Ambassador to Phnom Penh has gone back to Phnom Penh.
Dr. Kissinger: As Ambassador?

[B] Source: *PPS*, box 381, PRC–Cambodia–Secretary Kissinger.

PM Zhou: The Soviet Ambassador.

Dr. Kissinger: They have a Chargé there.

PM Zhou: Recently there was a Chargé there, and according to information they are going to send an Ambassador there.

Dr. Kissinger: I didn't know that.

PM Zhou: That is recent information. As for the Cambodian country, why can't you accept to have negotiations with Norodom Sihanouk as head of state?

Dr. Kissinger: I don't know him as well as the Prime Minister. I understand it is a nerve-wracking experience. (Zhou laughs.)

PM Zhou: Did Senator Mansfield say any words or discuss with you?

Dr. Kissinger: Oh, yes, Senator Mansfield is prepared to conduct negotiations with Sihanouk.[35]

PM Zhou: But unfortunately Prince Sihanouk wasn't in Beijing. He was elsewhere. So your people say that after the President was elected for a second term, then Senator Mansfield would come again to China.

Dr. Kissinger: Yes, but he is not qualified to discuss that for us, and he would only confuse the situation. He is too emotional about this. This is not an emotional problem. I will—is the Prime Minister finished with his observation?

PM Zhou: I have just raised this question and see what you have.

Dr. Kissinger: I have been told that (pointing to a paper being held by the Chinese side). Is this the article? I haven't read the text. I just read a summary. Actually the Prime Minister, Pham Van Dong, was astonished when we said that once we give them money for certain categories they can use it for anything within that category. He apparently wasn't used to treatment like that from other countries.[36] (Zhou laughs.)

But it is important for us to be able to do this. We want the countries of Indochina to be independent. We have no other interest in that area. We don't need any bases in Indochina. But for us to be able to establish this relationship, the DRV [Democratic Republic of Vietnam] must cooperate to some extent. If there is no cease-fire in Laos and no withdrawal of forces, how can we ask our Congress to give money? It is psychologically impossible. Article 20(b) of the Agreement says foreign forces must be withdrawn from Laos and Cambodia without any condition. And we are prepared to withdraw our forces, and we have talked to Thailand, and it will withdraw its forces. So the DRV must live up to this obligation. Now they are very close to a cease-fire in Laos, and I frankly do not understand what is delaying it. Perhaps they will conclude it today.

PM Zhou: We will be able to get information everyday from official sources as to whether or not it has been signed.

Dr. Kissinger: Well, I will find out when I get back. Now about Cambodia. It is obviously a very complex situation, and we have no particular interest in any one party.

PM Zhou: From the very beginning you would not admit that. I refer to the coup d'état. It was not done by the CIA. So after you examine your work, you will find how it was not done by them.[37]

Dr. Kissinger: It was not done by them.

PM Zhou : Like the situation in Laos.[38]

Dr. Kissinger: It is a different situation.

PM Zhou: Then who did it?

Dr. Kissinger: I have told the Prime Minister once before when I first learned of the coup d'état I thought Sihanouk had done it, that he would come back after three or four days. I thought he had done it so he could show Hanoi that (their) troops there made the population very unhappy. That was my honest opinion.[39]

PM Zhou: Yes, you have told me about it.

Dr. Kissinger: That was my sincere conviction.

PM Zhou: But I was quite skeptical about the CIA so I asked you to make a study of it.

Dr. Kissinger: I did make a study of it. Why should I lie to you today? It makes no difference today. The CIA did not do it.

PM Zhou: So it was done by France?

Dr. Kissinger: It could have been done by France. It could have been done by other interests. It could even perhaps have been done independently by Saigon. But it was not done by America nor did we know about it. At that time our policy was to attempt to normalize our relations with Sihanouk, and you will remember that the Prime Minister and I exchanged some letters at that time. We have always been opposed to the presence of North Vietnamese troops in Cambodia. We are opposed to that today. We think the North Vietnamese should withdraw their troops into Vietnam. We did not think they had the right to maintain troops on foreign territory.

Now we believe that there should be a political negotiation in Cambodia, and we think that all the political forces should be represented there. And that does not mean that the existing government must emerge as the dominant force, but how can we, when we recognize one government, engage in a direct negotiation with Sihanouk? This is out of the question. But if there were a cease-fire and if North Vietnamese forces were withdrawn we would encourage a political solution in which Sihanouk would play a very important role. We don't want necessarily Hanoi to dominate Laos and Cambodia, but we will not support in either of these countries, and certainly not in Cambodia, one political force against the others.

But if the war continues—first of all, if the North Vietnamese—they are violating Article 20(b) of the Agreement. Secondly, it will be almost impossible for us to go to our Congress and ask for economic support for a country that has its troops on foreign territory. It is difficult enough as long as they have troops in the South, but that we can treat as a special case.[40] We believe a solution consistent with the dignity of Sihanouk is possible, and we have so far refused overtures from other countries that have different views. But there has to be some interruption in military activity because otherwise our Air Force will continue to be active on one side, and there is no end to it. My difficulty in meeting with Prince Sihanouk is no reflection on Prince Sihanouk. It has to do with the situation there.

PM Zhou: France has maintained relationships with both sides. And the same is true of the Soviet Union, so things have been so complicated.

Dr. Kissinger: France wants to pick up what is left over without any risk and without any investment. (laughter)

PM Zhou: Three years ago during the time of the occurrence of the Cambodian incident, the French had sent Prince Sihanouk to the Soviet Union so Lon Nol at the time took a further step to announce the overthrow of the Cambodian monarchy and to abolish the royal system. So as a result Kosygin sent Sihanouk to Beijing. So in standing on the just side we should give them support. Further, Lon Nol at the time counted on us to maintain the original relationship, and Lon Nol even said that it was permissible to use Sihanouk Harbor to transport weapons to South Vietnam as was done by Sihanouk before. And prior to that Sihanouk also asked Lon Nol to be in charge of this matter—that is to transport weapons to South Vietnam, and he gained money out of that.[41] So Lon Nol was most familiar with this matter. And now after engaging in subversive activities he wanted to directly collect the taxes so that was too unreasonable and unjust so we rejected him. During that month—more than one month, they continued their initiative—our Ambassador proved that. At the beginning he refused to let our Ambassador leave Cambodia.

Dr. Kissinger: Well, I have always believed that if Sihanouk had returned to Phnom Penh rather than Moscow, he would still be King or Prime Minister.

PM Zhou: And he might be arrested.

Dr. Kissinger: Yes, possibly.[42]

PM Zhou : Because Lon Nol would do anything he wished to.

Dr. Kissinger: Well, we will never know this, but in any event . . .

PM Zhou: Do you know Lon Nol very well?

Dr. Kissinger: Once. I didn't think he is an extremely energetic man.

PM Zhou: He is half paralyzed.[43]

Dr. Kissinger: He is actually very anxious still to establish relations with you.

PM Zhou: No, we wouldn't do that with such a person. You should also not deal with such a man who carries on subversive activities against the King. It is just for you not to support India in dismantling Pakistan. On that one we stood together because you supported justice. But we think it is not very—it is not fair for you to admit Lon Nol.

Dr. Kissinger: But I think it might be possible to find an interim solution that is acceptable to both sides and I think, for example, that the Lon Nol people would be willing to negotiate with the Chief Minister of Sihanouk here. (To Mr. Lord: What is his name again?) Penn Nouth. And that might lead to an interim government which could then decide who should be Chef d'état. This possibility has also occurred to us.

PM Zhou: Would that do if you go without Lon Nol?

Dr. Kissinger: The end result could well be without Lon Nol.

PM Zhou: Not only the Prime Minister of Sihanouk wouldn't engage in such a negotiation, but there is the Khmer resistance in the interior area in Cambodia.[44]

Dr. Kissinger: What would not be acceptable?

PM Zhou: To take Lon Nol . . .

Dr. Kissinger: Well, it doesn't have to be Lon Nol himself. It could be somebody from that government.

PM Zhou: Have you had any contact with the Soviet Union and French on this point, or would they go to you for that?

Dr. Kissinger: No we have not talked to France at all. The Soviet Union had very vague conversations, their Ambassador with me. But I thought they were leaning more towards Lon Nol than the other side. They were certainly not leaning towards Sihanouk.

PM Zhou: Because he is not so fond of Sihanouk at all.

Dr. Kissinger: But they made no concrete—because I said to the Vice Minister when he was in New York, "I want to talk to the Prime Minister." I have talked to Le Duc Tho about it, and he said he is in favor of negotiation.[45] He said they wouldn't make the final decision in Hanoi, but, of course, you will be in direct contact with them.

PM Zhou: And he told me that you said that you would go to me and talk.

Dr. Kissinger: That is right. He said to me first, that it would be best if I talked to you, and then I said I would be glad to. Le Duc Tho always has a slight problem with his time sequence.

PM Zhou: So this question is quite similar to the question of the Secretary General. (laughter) Of course, since Sihanouk is in China we cannot but tell him your opinion in our wording, but of course, we have our own position on this question.[46]

Dr. Kissinger: We would appreciate it if he would not repeat it in newspapers and interviews. His self-discipline isn't up to Chinese standards.

PM Zhou: It is impossible. He often told others what I had told him, and also sometimes when I hadn't told him. (laughter) So the word wouldn't be very clear what the Premier had actually told him. So after learning about your ideas and what we learned about it, we wouldn't tell him all about it. Perhaps he would broadcast it and it would be carried in Chinese newspapers, and it wouldn't be all right for us not to carry it in our newspapers. The freedom our *People's Daily* has given to Sihanouk is much greater than any freedom granted to any Heads of State by any country at all. General De Gaulle didn't get freedom like that when he was in Britain.[47] He would be sure to include it in his message if he was told something.

We support his Five Point Declaration of March 23, 1970.[48] That time you were not involved. And we also supported the declaration issued jointly by the Head of State, the Prime Minister and the Deputy Prime Minister of Cambodia which was issued on January 26.[49] And later the three other Ministers in the interior area of Cambodia also supported this declaration. This is still our position. Do you know the Five Point Declaration of March 23, 1970?

Dr. Kissinger: No.

PM Zhou: At that time you were not involved with it.

Dr. Kissinger: This is an extremely unusual event. None of my colleagues have ever heard me admit I didn't know something, but I will know it as soon as I can get a copy. Have you English or French copies?

PM Zhou: Both.

Dr. Kissinger: Either one I can read. I have not studied it, but the major problem, frankly, is not the formal position but what evolution we foresee. And from our side we are prepared to cooperate with you, if we can find a way with him to come up with a solution consistent with his dignity.

PM Zhou: You have told us your ideas and we have learned about it, but at the moment perhaps this is not possible. We will consider it again, and next time I will tell you our ideas.

Dr. Kissinger: All right.

[The next day, Cambodia came up again briefly. Kissinger assured Zhou that, once the Chinese had consulted Sihanouk, the United States was prepared in principle, "to discuss with you who might be acceptable negotiators on both sides and acceptable principles in an interim government." The point was to find a solution that was "consistent with the dignity of all sides," both the Lon Nol government and its opposition.[50] Zhou and Kissinger had more substantive discussions on Cambodia the following afternoon.]

TOP SECRET/SENSITIVE/EXCLUSIVELY EYES ONLY
MEMORANDUM OF CONVERSATION

PARTICIPANTS: Zhou Enlai, Premier, State Council; Ji Pengfei, Minister of Foreign Affairs; Qiao Guanhua, Vice Minister of Foreign Affairs; Zhang Wenchin, Assistant Foreign Minister, Acting Director of American Pacific Affairs Department; Wang Hairong, Assistant Foreign Minister; Tang Wensheng, interpreter; Shen Zuoyun, interpreter

Two Chinese notetakers; Dr. Henry A. Kissinger, Assistant to the President for National Security Affairs; Richard T. Kennedy, NSC Staff; Alfred Le S. Jenkins, Department of State; Winston Lord, NSC Staff; Peter W. Rodman, NSC Staff; Miss Irene G. Derus, Notetaker

PLACE: Great Hall of the People, Beijing, China

DATE AND TIME: February 18, 1973, 2:43 P.M. - 7:15 P.M.[C]

PM Zhou : Now there are two other matters I would like to discuss with you. One is Cambodia. Because it seems this time during this visit it will be difficult to make further progress. We know your ideas. You are more clear about our position. We gave you the documents in English and French. We gave you already the 5-point statement of March 23, 1970, and also the January 26, 1973, but we should further give you the January 23 one of the three Vice Ministers of the Royal Government of National Union in the interior part of Cambodia.[51] And we are in agreement with Vietnam in respecting the position of the Front of National Union of Cambodia and also the Royal Govern-

---

[C] Source: *PPS*, box 381, PRC – Cambodia – Secretary Kissinger.

ment of National Union of Cambodia. Our tendency would be that you should cease your involvement in that area. Of course you would say in reply that other parties should also stop their involvement.

Dr. Kissinger: That is right.

PM Zhou: If it was purely a civil war the matter would be relatively more simple. Of course it wouldn't be easy to immediately confine it to a civil war. The situation would be like China in the past. Of course it is not possible to hope for Cambodia entirely copying the previous China situation.[52] But one thing can be done, that is, we can talk in various ways to make your intention known to the various responsible sides in the National United Front of Cambodia. Because the National United Front of Cambodia is not composed of only one party; it also is composed of the left, the middle and the right.

Of course, Samdech Norodom Sihanouk wishes to be in a central position, as is the King of Laos and Prime Minister Phouma.[53] They actually now have two leading persons; one is the head of state, the other is the Prime Minister, Penn Nouth. Of course in the interior the strength of the left is larger. And we also believe that differences will also occur in the Lon Nol clique.

France is also active, and so is the Soviet Union. The Soviet Union is also attempting to fabricate their own Red Khmer but they can't find many people.[54] But it might in the future appear. So, in the future, if there is some information you would like to give us in this respect, we can also give you some too. But it would only be information. It would not be—we have not yet reached the stage where we could provide any views or suggestions.

Dr. Kissinger: I understand.

PM Zhou: And we would like to take very prudent steps, because we wish to see the final goal of Cambodia realized; that is, its peace, independence, unity, sovereignty and territorial integrity.

Dr. Kissinger: We completely agree with these objectives.

PM Zhou: But we will still have to wait and see in which way these objectives can be realized. And you know and Samdech Norodom Sihanouk also knows, that we would never want to turn Samdech Norodom Sihanouk into someone who would heed to our beck and call. If we did that, that would be like hegemony. Many of the views he expresses in our *People's Daily* are not necessarily our views, but we give him complete freedom. Although he has written songs about nostalgia about China—in Beijing he wrote a very good poem about China being his second motherland—and although he is writing such poems we do not cherish illusions. I was going to try to persuade him not to try and publish the second song. I advised him to use "homeland" because, "motherland" was too excessive. He insisted on "motherland." We must be prepared for the day when he says it doesn't count! Anyway it was all written by him; it has nothing to do with us. Of course he is now saying I am one of his best friends, friends, "as Mr. Mansfield is." It doesn't matter. That is only personal relations. He is still the Head of State of the Buddhist State of Cambodia. So we still have to wait and see the developments of that issue.

So if we wish to see Southeast Asia develop along the lines of peace and neutrality and not enter a Soviet Asian security system, then Cambodia would be an exemplar country.

Dr. Kissinger: We are in complete agreement with that objective. And we have the same difficulty determining in exactly which direction to put our influence.

PM Zhou: We still have to study that problem.

Dr. Kissinger: We are prepared to exchange information. It would be kept in strictest confidence. And we also believe . . .

PM Zhou: Anyway I believe you to a certain degree answered me, when I said about the fact that Lon Nol will not do. I do not mean that the forces that he represents do not count.

Dr. Kissinger: I understand that. But before one can act on that, one has to have some idea of the alternative. I also agree that if it can become a Cambodian civil war rather than a foreign war, that would be the first step toward realizing these objectives.

PM Zhou: We understand the directions. We understand our respective orientations. Because it is impossible for Cambodia to become completely red now. If that were attempted, it would result in even greater problems. It should be settled by the United Front, on the basis of the policy I just now mentioned; that is, independence, peace, neutrality, unity and territorial integrity.

Dr. Kissinger: Those principles we agree with, and we now have to find some framework for achieving them in a way that takes account of all the real forces.

PM Zhou: So, one [once?] we agree.

[The discussions on Cambodia became more difficult during the following months, but Kissinger remained hopeful in the short term, in light of his positive assessment of the talks with Mao and Zhou. As Kissinger's report to Nixon indicated, however, the focus of his talks with Zhou, however, was not Southeast Asia but the Soviet Union and U.S.–Soviet relations.]

SECRET/SENSITIVE/EXCLUSIVELY EYES ONLY
March 2, 1973
MEMORANDUM FOR: THE PRESIDENT
FROM: HENRY A. KISSINGER
SUBJECT: My Trip to China[D]

The Soviet Union dominated our conversations. In 1971 there were somewhat guarded references by the Chinese to Soviet designs, but they ritualis-
tically linked the US and the USSR as the two superpowers seeking
hegemony. By the time of your visit the Chinese leaders were quite candid
about the Soviet menace but stayed away from extended discussion. By last
June the Soviet Union had become one of the two major topics in my conversations, the other one being Indochina. On this trip it was the centerpiece
and completely permeated our talks. The Chinese views generally surfaced
in the regional discussion and are detailed later in this report. Following are
the more general observations.

Zhou raised the USSR in our first meeting and kept coming back to it. He
called a special meeting the night of February 17 to discuss this subject and at
the end of his presentation he announced my meeting with Mao, where again
it was a major topic. We discussed it at length the next day as well. In literally
every region of the world the Chinese see the Soviet hand at play. As you will
see in the area discussions below, Mao and Zhou urged us to counter the
Russians everywhere — to work closely with our allies in Europe and Japan,
and to take more positive action to prevent the Soviets filling vacuums or
spreading their influence in areas like the Middle East, Persian Gulf, Near
East, South Asia and Indian Ocean.

In our first meeting, after my opening statement, Zhou asked me in effect
whether we thought the world was moving toward peace or war. I said that
there were some positive developments, but we were not naive about potential dangers, such as the intensive Soviet military buildup. I made clear that
we had major business to do with Moscow, but we were under no illusions
about its possible motivations. We would continue our policy of keeping the
Chinese fully informed and not concluding any agreements that could be
directed against Beijing.

Zhou pointed to developments in Europe and said perhaps we sought to
"push the ill waters of the Soviet Union eastward." He also cited our diver-

---

[D] Source: *PPS*, box 374, China – Sensitive Special WL File Misc and Reports, Nov. 1974.

sion of fighters from Taiwan to South Vietnam last fall in ENHANCE PLUS as an example of our taking advantage of Beijing; somewhat out of context, he said that this showed we might be standing on Chinese shoulders to reach out toward the Soviet Union.[55]

The next day I purposely detailed our proposed force reductions on Taiwan and then made a more sweeping analysis of our policy toward the Soviet Union. I said that the nature of our relationship meant that we had to pursue a more complicated policy than the PRC which could oppose the Soviet Union outright on issues. We were making several agreements with Moscow, but we would not let these constrain us in the event that our interests were jeopardized. I pointed out that the USSR could follow one of two courses. If they truly wanted peace, we would welcome that course, and the agreements we were making, might contribute to that end. If, however, as seemed more likely, they were bent on a more threatening road, we had shown in the past that we would react strongly if our interests were jeopardized. In any event, I emphasized, we would maintain strong defenses and improve our strategic forces so long as the Soviet buildup continued. And on issues of direct concern to Beijing we would take Chinese interests into account, such as on the Soviet initiative on a nuclear understanding, where we have been fighting a delaying action ever since last spring.[56]

Zhou and then Mao, however, both replayed the theme that we might be helping the Soviet Union, whether or not purposely. Whereas we saw two possibilities, i.e. that the Soviet Union would either pursue a peaceful or menacing course, the Chinese saw only the latter. They were spreading their influence everywhere with the help of their satellites, like India, and were out to isolate the Chinese. The "new czars" were neurotic and omnipresent. It was the Chinese duty to try and expose their designs wherever possible, however lonely their efforts in a world enamored with false détente.

Mao even went so far as to suggest that we might like to see the Russians bogged down in an attack on China; after wearing themselves out for a couple of years, we would then "poke a finger" in Moscow's back. I rejoined that we believe that a war between the two Communist giants was likely to be uncontrollable and have unfortunate consequences for everyone. We therefore wished to prevent such a conflict, not take advantage of it.

Given Mao's and Zhou's skeptical comments on this issue, I treated it at considerable length the day after my meeting with the Chairman. I said there were three hypothetical US motives in a policy that contributed to pressures on the PRC from the USSR. First, we might want the Soviet Union to defeat China. I stressed emphatically that whether Moscow defeated China or Europe first, the consequences for us would be the same; we would be isolated and the ultimate target. Thus this could never be our policy.

The second possible motive was the one Mao mentioned — our wish for a stalemated Moscow attack on Beijing, so as to exhaust the Soviet Union. I pointed out that even partial Soviet dominance of China could have many of the consequences of the first option. In any event, such a major conflict would have unpredictable consequences. The Soviet Union might take rash actions if they were stymied as the Chairman claimed we had been in Vietnam. And we would be forced either to demonstrate our impotence and irrelevance, or make a series of extremely complex decisions.

The third possibility was that we might contribute to a war between China and the Soviet Union through misjudgment rather than policy. This I recognized as a danger despite our intentions. I then analyzed at length our policy around the world, with emphasis on Europe, to demonstrate that we plan to maintain our defense, continue a responsible international role and work closely with our allies. In short, while seeking relaxation with Moscow, we would also ensure that if it did not choose a peaceful course we and our friends would be in a position to resist and defend our national interests. And I made it evident that we would consider aggression against China as involving our own national security.

It is not at all clear that we have fully allayed Chinese suspicions. While they have nowhere else to go in the short term, they will certainly watch our Soviet moves with wariness, and take out insurance with Japan and Europe.

COMMENTARY

In his report to Nixon, Kissinger also reviewed his talks with Zhou and Mao on another sensitive issue, the problem of Taiwan. He restated secret pledges that Nixon had made a year earlier — for example, normalization, withdrawal of forces from Taiwan, and "dissociation from any Taiwan independence movement" — and briefed Zhou on U.S. plans to withdraw F-4 squadrons and half of the U.S.'s 9,000 military personnel from the island. In his talks with Zhou, Kissinger also reaffirmed Nixon's pledge to establish diplomatic relations by mid-1976, and he went on to make a new commitment as well: "to move after the 1974 elections toward something like the Japanese solution with regard to diplomatic relations."[57] When Japan normalized relations with China in 1972, it closed down its embassy in Taiwan while maintaining a private, nongovernmental office to maintain trade and cultural connections. Although ambiguous, Kissinger's statement implied that Washington would start to cut back its diplomatic presence in Taiwan after 1974, a step that he realized could be "painful" because of the long history of U.S.-Taiwan relations.

In *Years of Upheaval* Kissinger was silent on the Taiwan discussions perhaps because he believed that it would expose him to attacks from Taipei as well as from U.S. friends of Taiwan, especially among Republican conservatives. When he published the book in the early 1980s, he was trying hard to curry favor with Republican rightists, partly in order to neutralize their opposition to him in the event that he might have an opportunity to return to government. Relations with Taiwan had reached their nadir when the Carter administration broke diplomatic ties in 1979. Kissinger may well have wanted to avoid accusations that he had contributed to the process of weakening Taiwan's position by supporting the withdrawal of U.S. forces and by affirming commitments about Taiwan's status for the sake of better relations with the regime on the mainland.[58]

Kissinger concluded his report to Nixon by observing that even if the outlook for the relationship with Beijing was "positive," important developments might lead to "trouble":

Our dealings with the Soviet Union.

To date the Soviet factor has been the main leverage in our dealings with the PRC. At the same time—and contrary to the predictions of almost all Soviet experts—our opening to Beijing has paid us substantial dividends with Moscow as well. With conscientious attention to both capitals we should be able to continue to have our mao tai and drink our vodka too.[59] Beijing, after all, assuming continued hostility with the USSR, has no real alternative to us as a counterweight (despite its recent reaching out to Japan and Western Europe as insurance). And Moscow needs us in such areas as Europe and economics.

But this is nevertheless a difficult balancing act that will increasingly face us with hard choices. Mao and Zhou both suggested that inadvertently or not, our Soviet policies could increase the pressures on China. It was even intimated that we might favor a Sino-Soviet conflict, so as to bog down the Soviet Union and weaken it for our own attack. A cutting edge is the Soviet initiative on a nuclear understanding. One of Moscow's motives is certainly to embarrass us in our relations with Beijing, since they know their initiative is anathema to Beijing. We have fought a delaying action on this issue for almost a year now, but Brezhnev is apt to push it to a head in conjunction with his visit here. To satisfy him and not dissatisfy Zhou at the same time will be a challenge. Other concrete awkward areas in our triangular relationship include European security policies and the granting of credits to Moscow.

The coming change in Chinese leadership.

Mao is in his 80s and has received an "invitation" from "God." Zhou is 75 and has just publicly noted the need for new leadership soon in his country. They obviously control PRC policy now but it is not at all clear that they can assure continuity in their policy lines. The Lin Bao affair was obviously a major challenge and may have been a close thing. They have not managed to fill many key party and military posts since then. Mao constantly referred to the difficulties posed by women in China, undoubtedly a reference to his wife who represents the challenge from the left. All of this is reflected in Chinese eagerness to institutionalize our relationship, even if it means bending the sacred "one China" policy to do it.

We know little about power relationships in the PRC and even less about the succession problem. We can only assume—both from the above indices and because of the objective choices facing China—that substantial opposition to present policies exist and that this includes foreign policy. There are undoubtedly those who favor accommodation with Moscow over Washington, for example. Thus, before the present dynasty passes from the scene, we must strengthen bilateral ties, get our two peoples used to a closer relationship, and reach out to more layers of Chinese leadership so as to strengthen the advocates of an opening to America.

There are two other potential problems, but these would seem to be more manageable and under our control:

The need for a strong American world role.

We are useless to Beijing as a counterweight to Moscow if we withdraw from the world, lower our defenses, or play a passive international game. Mao and Zhou urged a more aggressive American presence—countering Soviet designs in various areas, keeping close ties with our allies, maintaining our defense posture. If the Chinese became convinced that we were heeding the inward impulses of voluble sectors of Congress, the public and the press, we would undoubtedly witness a sharp turn in Peking's attitude. You and I have, of course, assured the PRC leaders privately, as well as proclaiming publicly, our intentions to maintain a responsible international role. So long as you are President, Peking should certainly be convinced that we will be a crucial factor in the world balance.

The issue of Taiwan.

The Chinese have been farsighted and patient on this question. Their willingness to ease our predicament is now most dramatically shown in their setting up a liaison office in Washington while we maintain diplomatic relations with the GRC [Government of the Republic of China]. On the other hand, we have largely bought their public reasonableness with your own private assurances—to normalize fully our relations by 1976 and to withdraw our forces from Taiwan now that the Vietnam War is over. Taiwan is a problem we should be able to control, both internationally and domestically, as we continue to add to the handwriting on the wall and condition our audiences. However, we should be under no illusions that our final step will be anything but painful—there are few friends as decent as our allies on Taiwan.

Notes

1. For Kissinger's report on the visit, see Kissinger to the President, "My Trip to China," 2 March 1973, National Archives, Record Group 59, Records of the State Department, Policy Planning Staff Records (Director's Files), 1969-77 (hereafter referred to as *PPS* with archival box number and file information), box 374, China—Sensitive Special WL File Misc. and Reports, Nov. 1974. For Mao's reference to a "bastard," see memcon, 17 Feb. 1973 (p. 96.).

2. Statement by Bruce in "East Asian Chiefs of Mission Conference—Tokyo, Japan, Thursday, November 15, 1973 Morning Session," p. 117, copy in U.S.-Japan Collection, National Security Archive (hereafter referred to as *NSA*).

3. For Kissinger's account of the Cambodian initiative in 1973, see Henry Kissinger, *Years of Upheaval* (Boston: Little, Brown, 1982), pp. 335-53. For a useful overview of the U.S. invasion of Cambodia and its impact, see George Herring, *America's Longest War: The United States and Vietnam, 1950-1975* (New York:McGraw-Hill, 1996), pp. 267-64. See also William Bundy's account in *A Tangled Web: The Making of Foreign Policy in the Nixon Presidency* (New York: Hill and Wang, 1998), pp. 373-74, 385-87, 391-94.

4. The proposed deal covered U.S. private claims against China and Chinese claims of financial assets that the United States and its allies had blocked or "frozen" in 1950 during the Korean War. The U.S. private claims validated by the U.S. Foreign Claims Settlement Commission totaled $196.8 million. The Chinese frozen assets totalled $70-80 million. The Nixon administration came to regard settlement of this issue as "essential for further normalization of US/PRC economic and trade relations in a number of areas, including banking and finance, insurance, transportation, and trade exhibits" (Briefing

Paper, "U.S. Private Claims and PRC Frozen Assets," n.d., *PPS*, box 370, Secretary Kissinger's Visit to Peking, Oct. 1973 S/PCS Mr. Lord vol. 1 [folder 2 of 2]).

5. Later in the year, David Bruce would tell U.S. ambassadors that the liaison office staff was "getting accustomed" to routine denunciations by the Chinese, but "always in the second place to the Soviet Union. We are now Number Two for purposes of public propaganda." Yet he emphasized the "unvarying courtesy [of Chinese officials] and the ease of negotiations." See East Asian Chiefs of Mission Conference — Tokyo, Japan, Thursday, November 15, 1973 Morning Session," pp. 65-66 (copy in U.S.-Japan Collection, at *NSA*).

6. See Kissinger to the President, "My Trip to China," 2 March 1973. For a fascinating account of the creation of the U.S. Liaison Office and U.S.-China relations in this early period, see John H. Holdridge, *Crossing the Divide: An Insider's Account of Normalization of U.S.-China Relations* (Lanham, Md.: Rowmand and Littlefield, 1997).

7. See "Private Statements Made by PRC Leaders to Secretary Kissinger or President Nixon Regarding the Peaceful Liberation of Taiwan," n.d., *PPS*, box 372, Nov. 1974.

8. See Kissinger to the President, "My Trip to China," 2 March 1973.

9. See Kissinger to the President, "My Visit to China," 19 Nov. 1973.

10. World War II General Bernard Law Montgomery (1887-1976) had visited China twice in 1960 and 1961 to meet with Mao Zedong and Zhou Enlai. He subsequently condemned the Eisenhower-Dulles policy of opposition to recognizing the PRC. See Alun Chalfont, *Montgomery of Alamein* (New York: Atheneum, 1976), pp. 313-14.

11. This is a reference to forthcoming French legislative elections on 11 March, in which the Gaullists prevailed.

12. As of 30 September 1971, U.S. military personnel stationed in South Korea numbered 40,740. Official Department of Defense file information provided by Washington Headquarters Services, Statistical Information Analysis Division.

13. This seems to be a reference to the August 1945 Soviet declaration of war on Japan and attack on Japanese forces in Manchuria. By that point the U.S. Navy's blockade had crippled the Japanese economy, and the U.S. Army Air Corps bombing raids had pulverized its key urban-industrial centers.

14. It was an exaggeration to say that the Soviets "didn't fire a single shot" during the Manchurian campaign at the close of World War II; they certainly had a greater margin of resources, which allowed them to prevail quickly. The Soviets did not seize the Kurile Islands easily, though, and the fighting there provided them with an "inkling of the island campaigns in the Pacific"; H. P. Wilmot, *The Great Crusade: A New Complete History of the Second World War* (New York: Free Press, 1990), pp.466-70.

15. In postwar negotiations with Stalin, the Chinese Nationalists relinquished claims to Outer Mongolia and granted it independence, thus allowing the Soviets to incorporate it into their defense system. See Xiaoyuan Liu, *A Partnership for Disorder: China, the United States, and Their Policies for the Postwar Disposition of the Japanese Empire, 1941-1945* (New York: Cambridge University Press, 1996), pp. 260-62. Mao, during his negotiations with Stalin in 1949-50, had signed a secret agreement giving the Soviets a preferred position in Manchuria and Xinjiang. See Sergei N. Goncharov, John W. Lewis, and Xue Litai, *Uncertain Partners: Stalin, Mao, and the Korean War* (Stanford, Calif.: Stanford University Press, 1993), pp. 121-22.

16. Beginning in the fall of 1945 the Soviets undertook, as reparations from Japan, an immense campaign to dismantle and remove industrial machinery, raw materials, and inventories of finished goods from Japanese mines and factories in Manchuria. In 1946 a U.S. investigation estimated the damage at $858 million; the cost of replacement to compensate for removals, destruction, and deterioration of remaining plant was said to be about $2 billion. Historian Steven Levine has concluded that "within weeks of the end of the war much of Manchuria's industrial wealth had been destroyed." See Tang Tsou, *America's Failure in China, 1941–1950* (Chicago: University of Chicago Press, 1963), p. 335; and Steven Levine, *Anvil of Victory: The Communist Revolution in Manchuria, 1945–1948* (New York: Columbia University Press, 1987), pp. 68–70.

17. The Yalta agreements authorized Soviet annexation of Sakhalin and the Kurile Islands on the condition that Moscow declare war on Japan within two to three months after the German surrender. See Melvyn P. Leffler, *A Preponderance of Power: National Security, the Truman Administration, and the Cold War* (Stanford, Calif.: Stanford University Press, 1992), p. 81.

18. The Nixon administration was then preparing to present to Congress a trade policy proposal to expedite American participation in the latest General Agreement on Trade and Tariff [GATT] negotiations, later known as the "Tokyo Round" because the meeting that launched them had taken place in Tokyo. In April 1973, Nixon requested authority to adjust tariff and nontariff barriers, provide relief for areas adversely affected by imports, extend trade preferences to developing countries (the generalized system of preferences), and grant most-favored-nation status to the Soviet Union. Among the provisions of the Trade Act of 1974, signed into law by President Ford in January 1975, were procedures requiring Congress to approve or reject in their entirety trade agreements negotiated under the law, later known as "fast track" arrangements. For useful accounts, see Gilbert Winham, *International Trade and the Tokyo Round Negotiation* (Princeton, N.Y.: Princeton University Press, 1986), pp. 129–37, and I. M. Destler, *Making Foreign Economic Policy* (Washington, D.C.: Brookings Institution, 1980), pp. 129–90.

19. As Kissinger noted in his memoirs, this was undoubtedly a reference to Mao's wife, Jiang Qing, an important figure in the Chinese Communist Party's radical wing; see his *Years of Upheaval*, p. 68.

20. Apparently as punishment for Director of Central Intelligence Richard Helms' refusal to cooperate with the administration over Watergate, Nixon fired the DCI, but let him choose a job as ambassador. Helms chose a posting in Iran, where he believed he would have more autonomy than in one of the embassies in Western Europe; he served there from April 1973 to December 1976. For background on his appointment, see Thomas Powers, *The Man Who Kept the Secrets: Richard Helms and the CIA* (New York: Knopf, 1979), pp. 241–45.

21. After the Sino-Japanese War of 1894–95, the Japanese seized Taiwan and the Pescadores and forced China to pay an indemnity of over 300 million yen. After the Boxer uprising of 1900, the foreign powers — Germany, Japan, Britain, Russia, France, and the United States — assessed an indemnity of $330 million. Secretary of State John Hay had unsuccessfully tried to scale the charge down, and the United States later used its share of the proceeds to pay for the education of Chinese students at American universities. For the indemnity to Japan and the Boxer indemnity, as well as much useful background

on Western and Japanese imperialism in China, see, respectively, Stewart Lone, *Japan's First Modern War: Army and Society in the Conflict with China, 1894–1895* (New York: St. Martin's Press, 1994), pp. 174–75, and Michael Hunt, *The Making of a Special Relationship: The United States and China to 1914* (New York: Columbia University Press, 1983), p. 200.

22. Beginning in the 1840s, with Britain in the lead, but rapidly followed by the U.S., foreign powers with commercial operations negotiated treaties with the Chinese that provided foreigners with extraterritorial legal rights. Thus, if an American killed a Chinese national, special U.S. consular courts would dispense "justice." The United States surrendered its extraterritorial privileges only in 1943. See Warren Cohen, *America's Response to China: An Interpretative History of Sino-American Relations* (New York: Wiley, 1971), pp. 9, 156, and Te-Kong Tong, *United States Diplomacy in China, 1844–1860* (Seattle: University of Washington Press, 1964), pp. 3–4, 103-7.

23. A reference to Nancy Tang's U.S. background.

24. The subject is not further identified.

25. In a 1946 interview, Mao said that "the atom bomb is a paper tiger, which United States reactionaries use to scare people. It looks terrible, but in fact it isn't." See David Holloway, *Stalin and the Bomb: The Soviet Union and Atomic Energy, 1939–1956* (New Haven: Yale University Press, 1994), p. 282.

26. Montgomery's Third Division was the only combat-ready organization in England after Dunkirk. See Chalfont, *Montgomery of Alamein*, p. 116.

27. This is a reference to Hitler's hope that the British would separate their interests from Poland and not declare war against Germany in 1939.

28. According to Mao's doctor, it was one of his "games" to tell foreign leaders that he would not live much longer as a way to "test foreign reaction to his possible death." See Li Zhisui, *The Private Life of Chairman Mao: The Memoirs of Mao's Personal Physician* (New York: Random House, 1994), p. 568.

29. For thoughtful, excellent sketches of Zhou as diplomatist and of the Zhou–Kissinger relationship, see respectively Shu Guang Zhang, "In the Shadow of Mao: Zhou Enlai and New China's Diplomacy," in *The Diplomats, 1939–1979*, ed. Gordon A. Craig and Francis L. Loewenheim (Princeton, N.J.: Princeton University Press, 1994), pp. 337–70, and Dick Wilson, *Chou: The Story of Zhou Enlai* (London: Hutchinson, 1984), pp. 275–85.

30. See Thomas Engelbert's and Christopher E. Goscha's important study, *Falling Out of Touch: A Study on Vietnamese Communist Policy Toward An Emerging Cambodian Communist Movement, 1930–1975* (Clayton, Victoria, Australia, Centre of Southeast Asian Studies, 1985), pp. 107–8. For some new details on China's Cambodian policies, see the extraordinary material in Odd Arne Wested *et al.*, eds., *77 Conversations Between Chinese and Foreign Relations on the Wars in Indochina* (Washington, D.C.: Cold War International History Project, 1998), pp. 187–88, 191–92. For Chinese sphere of influence policy, see Ben Kiernan, *How Pol Pot Came to Power: A History of Communism in Kampuchea, 1930–1975* (London: Verso, 1985), p. 298.

31. Thus, on 11 April, Zhou "strongly condemned" Washington for its "wanton bombings" in Cambodia. Briefing paper by Solomon, "Peking Indicates Continued Strong Support for Sihanouk," 13 April 1973, *PPS*, box 329, China Exchange 1 Jan. 1973–14 April 1973.

32. See David Chandler, *The Tragedy of Cambodian History: Politics, War, and Revolution Since 1945* (New Haven: Yale University Press, 1991), p. 227; Kiernan, *How Pol Pot Came to Power*, pp. 357–58, 360–61; Randall Ebnnett Woods, *Fulbright: A Biography* (Cambridge, Eng.: Cambridge University Press, 1995) p. 631.

33. See Kissinger, *Years of Upheaval*, p. 344.

34. See Memcon, 13 Nov. 1973, *PPS*, box 329, China Exchanges Oct. 24–31 Dec. 1972; Tad Szulc, *The Illusion of Peace: Foreign Policy in the Nixon Years* (New York: Vikings, 1978), p. 687.

35. An old friend of Prince Sihanouk's and an early critic of the Vietnam War, Mansfield had proposed defusing the conflict by making South Vietnam a neutral country. His interest in neutral solutions to the Indochina crisis dovetailed with Sihanouk's efforts to steer the same course for Cambodia. For Mansfield and Sihanouk, see Szulc, *The Illusion of Peace*, p. 55.

36. This is a comparison between Soviet foreign aid practices and the secret protocol of the peace agreement between the United States and the Democratic Republic of Vietnam stipulating U.S. $3.25 billion in financial aid for post-war reconstruction. no aid was ever given, of course; and it is very unlikely that Nixon or Kissinger devoted much time to planning ways to obtain the money from Congress. See Woods, *Fulbright*, p. 629.

37. Controversy lingers over the origins of the coup in March 1970 that drove Prince Sihanouk out of power and brought Gen. Lon Nol to the helm. For Kissinger's account, see his *White House Years*, pp. 457–64. For one that suggests greater U.S. complicity and/or foreknowledge, see William Shawcross, *Sideshow: Kissinger, Nixon, and the Destruction of Cambodia* (New York: Simon and Schuster, 1979), pp. 112–23. For an important account suggesting significant collaboration between U.S. and Australian intelligence in Cambodia, see Justin J. Corfeld, *Khmers Stand Up! A History of the Cambodian Government* (Clayton, Victoria, Australia: Centre, of Southeast Asiah Studies, Monarh University, 1994), pp. 52–83.

38. This is a sarcastic reference to the CIA's heavyhanded manipulations of Laotian affairs since the late 1950s. For important studies of U.S. policy in Laos, see Charles A. Stevenson, *The End of Nowhere: American Policy Toward Laos Since 1954* (Boston: Beacon, 1973), and Roger Warner, *Back Fire: The CIA's Secret War in Laos and its links to the War in Vietnam* (New York: Simon and Schuster, 1995).

39. What helped to set the coup in motion were demonstrations on 11 March 1970, no doubt with Sihanouk's permission, outside the National Liberation Front and North Vietnamese missions in Phnom Penh which ended in the sacking and burning down of the buildings; this in turn prompted a wave of looting and attacks on Catholic churches. See Chandler, *The Tragedy of Cambodian History*, p. 194. Kissinger's emphasis on the opposition to Hanoi is consistent with his presentation in *White House Years* (Boston: Little, Brown) p. 463, where he quotes a memo to Nixon suggesting that "it is quite possible that this is an elaborate maneuver to permit Sihanouk to call for Soviet and Chinese cooperation in urging the VC/NVA [Viet Cong/North Vietnamese Army] to leave, on the grounds that he will fall and be replaced by a 'rightist' leader if [they] stay in Cambodia." The original text of this memorandum of conversation refers to "his troops" but "their" is more in keeping with Kissinger's meaning.

40. By treating the DRV troops in the South as a "special case," Kissinger had agreed with

the North Vietnamese that they could remain there. To obscure this concession, he had made a unilateral statement accompanying the peace agreement that the United States did not "recognize the right of foreign troops to remain on South Vietnamese soil." In the agreement, the United States had pledged to recognize the "unity and territorial integrity of Vietnam"; consequently, DRV troops were not "foreign." Walter Isaacson, *Kissinger: A Biography* (New York: Simon and Schuster, 1992), pp. 481–82.

41. By agreement with the PRC, during the 1960s the Cambodian government took 10 percent, over and above the charges for transport and storage, of Chinese aid to the Vietnamese National Liberation Front. Lon Nol and his spouse, among others, financially benefitted from these arrangements; they even embezzled a special fund used to consolidate the revenue. See Corfield, *Khmers Rise Up!*, pp. 35–36, 38, 51. Lon Nol's role in this enterprise was well known in Washington: see, for example, Woods, *Fulbright*, p. 633.

42. It would be more accurate to say "most likely." After the 1970 coup, the Lon Nol government tried Sihanouk in absentia and sentenced him to death. See Milton Osborne, *Sihanouk: Prince of Light, Prince of Darkness* (Honolulu: University of Hawaii Press, 1994), p. 222.

43. Lon Nol had had a stroke in February 1971. A year later, the American ambassador Emory Swank cabled Washington that Lon Nol was a "sick man, mentally and physically." See Chandler, *Tragedy of Cambodian History*, pp. 211, 214. For a devastating portrait of the Lon Nol's regime, with its widespread corruption and brutal repression of noncommunist opposition, see Chandler, *Tragedy of Cambodian History*, pp. 215, 223–26.

44. A reference to Pol Pot's Khmer Rouge.

45. A top member of the DRV politburo, Tho had been Kissinger's counterpart in the secret talks in Paris on Vietnam. See Isaacson, *Kissinger: A Biography*, pp. 251–53.

46. In other words, Zhou agrees to pass on Kissinger's proposal "in our wording" for talks between Sihanouk and Lon Nol's representatives.

47. This is a reference to De Gaulle's work in London on behalf of Free French forces during World War II.

48. After Sihanouk was deposed, he broadcast a message from Beijing calling on Cambodians to take up arms against the Lon Nol regime and to ignore laws issued from Phnom Penh. He further called for the the creation of a "Government of National Union," a "National Liberation Army," and a National United Front" to fight Cambodia's enemies. See Chandler, *Tragedy of Cambodian History*, pp. 200–201.

49. This might correspond to a three-point elaboration issued by Khmer Rouge leaders on 28 January: "total withdrawal of U.S. and allied forces from Cambodia," "dissolution of the Lon Nol regime," and creation of an "independent, peaceful, neutral, democratic, and prosperous Cambodia." See State Department Briefing Paper, "Cambodia," n.d., *PPS*, box 370, Kissinger Visit to Peking, Oct. 1973, Cambodia.

50. See memcon, 17 Feb. *PPS*, box 381, PRC–Cambodia–Secretary Kissinger.

51. See endnote 49 above.

52. This may be a reference to the U.S. efforts, led by General George C. Marshall during 1946–47, to mediate the Chinese Civil War.

53. Since 1959, the King of Laos had been Savang Vatthana. Souvanna Phouma, a leader of

the Laotian independence movement and a neutralist, Souvanna Phouma was Savang's Prime Minister.

54. Pol Pot's Khmer Rouge was ideologically indebted to Mao Zedong and the Chinese revolution. See Kiernan, *Pol Pot Regime*, p. 330.

55. Undertaken during the fall of 1972, during the final phases of U.S. military operations in Vietnam, "Enhance Plus" was an emergency operation to strengthen the South Vietnamese military with some $1 billion in military hardware, some of it provided by a number of U.S. allies. For example, the Republic of China transferred 48 F-5A fighter jets to Vietnam. By the end of the effort, South Vietnam had the fourth largest air force in the world. See Kissinger, *White House Years*, p. 1366; Herring, *America's Longest War*, p. 279; Briefing paper, "Taiwan," n.d., *PPS*, box 370, Secretary Kissinger's Visit to Peking, Oct. 1973 S/PC Mr. Lord, vol. 1.

56. This refers to the Soviet proposal to the United States first advanced in April 1972 that led to the Prevention of Nuclear War Agreement signed in June 1973. See Raymond Garthoff, *Détente and Confrontation: American–Soviet Relations from Nixon to Reagan* (Washington, D.C.: Brookings Institution, 1994), p. 377.

57. Ibid.

58. For reactions to the Carter decision to normalize relations with Beijing and break off formal diplomatic ties with Taipei, see Nancy B. Tucker, *Taiwan, Hong Kong, and the United States, 1945–92: Uncertain Friendships* (New York: Twayne, 1994), pp. 132–37. For Kissinger and the Republican Right, see Isaacson, *Kissinger: A Biography* pp. 721–22.

59. Mao tai is a powerful Chinese liquor derived from wheat and sorghum.

3

From Cambodia to the October War:
Beijing – Washington, March – October 1973

As the American and Chinese governments established their liaison offices in Beijing and Washington, the U.S.-China dialogue began to focus on two issues—Cambodia and U.S.-Soviet relations. The U.S. Air Force continued its secret bombing of Cambodia; Kissinger, who had convinced himself that congressional edicts to force a bombing halt undercut U.S. diplomacy, tried in vain to promote his proposals for negotiations and a cease-fire. His Cambodian initiative may have been futile from the beginning; and the bombing itself may have crippled any chances for an early settlement. Also central to Kissinger's China diplomacy was the perennial but thorny issue of U.S.-Soviet relations. The June 1973 Brezhnev – Nixon summit represented another milestone in the evolution of détente, but the signing of the U.S.-Soviet agreement on the Prevention of Nuclear War (PNW) Agreement greatly troubled Beijing. Kissinger labored to convince the Chinese that PNW would strengthen their security, but they nevertheless interpreted it as a potentially dangerous step toward a superpower condominium. However, these tensions did not outweigh the strategic interests that were fueling the U.S.-China relationship.

Heading the liaison offices in Beijing and Washington were two respected and seasoned diplomats, both of whom were key figures in the political establishments of their respective nation. The U.S. Liaison Office (USLO) in Beijing was led by David K. E. Bruce, a scion of upper-class Maryland and Virginia families and a financial contributor to Democratic Party campaigns, who had served in the Office of Strategic Services during World War II. During the postwar decades, he had served Democratic and Republican administrations in diplomatic and policymaking roles, including ambassadorial positions in France, Germany, and the United Kingdom. The Chinese office in Washington was led by Huang Zhen, a member of the Chinese Communist Party Central Committee who had risen to the rank of major general during the civil war. Huang had held diplomatic posts since the 1950s, serving as ambassador to Hungary, Indonesia, and France (his most recent posting).[1]

In Kissinger's talks with Bruce and his deputies, as they made preparations for Beijing, Kissinger made it plain that the USLO was primarily a creature of the White House, a means to effect the back-channel to Beijing. As he told Bruce in March 1973, his effectiveness depended on the Chinese understanding that "from beginning that [you are] the President's man." He wanted CIA technicians to run the USLO's communications system, lest anyone in the State Department have the ability to measure the volume of back-channel communications. Kissinger insisted that the White House "deal with [Beijing] completely openly" and believed that the Chinese would "welcome" the emphasis on a sturdy back-channel arrangement. He soon told the Chinese about the planned CIA role at the USLO. As he told his advisers, the CIA man "can't do anything they [the Chinese] won't know about anyway."[2]

As established figures were playing new roles in U.S–China relations, Henry Kissinger's own part in the policymaking process changed. Interactions between Nixon and Kissinger were tense during the final stages of the Vietnam War, making their collaboration more difficult than ever; but the developing Watergate crisis made it virtually impossible for Nixon to dismiss Kissinger. Not only did Kissinger's celebrity status strengthen his position, but the demands imposed by the Senate's continuing Watergate investigation made Kissinger essential for policy continuity. Thus, on 22 August 1973, while briefing the press on William Rogers's resignation as secretary of state, Nixon perfunctorily announced Kissinger's appointment. A month later, the Senate approved the nomination, and Kissinger was sworn in as secretary of state, he retained his role as assistant to the president for national security affairs. Kissinger's authority over U.S. foreign policy had become more comprehensive than ever.[3]

While Kissinger believed that the administration's efforts to "enmesh" the Soviets in a framework of political obligations and economic connections would "paralyze" them, Mao and Zhou were less confident. They expressed concern about U.S.–Soviet cooperation at their expense and showed particularly sensitivity about the PNW. While the Soviets pushed hard for a PNW agreement, more to reduce U.S.–Soviet tensions than for anti-Chinese reaons, Kissinger worked to ensure that an agreement could not be used against "third countries" like China. He had kept Beijing informed throughout the negotiations but Kissinger and his associates found it difficult to convince PRC officials that the agreement would let Washington come to their defense against the Soviets or that the agreement represented a form of anti-PRC collusion. Zhou's criticism were relatively subdued, [in] sorrow but not in anger", David Bruce wrote, but the Nixon-Brezhnev summet, along with the flap over Cambodia, cooled U.S.-China relations that summer.[4]

During the months after the June 1973 summit Kissinger briefed Huang and then Zhou on one of the most sensitive events of the summit, Brezhnev's unsuccessful efforts to enlist Washington in a crusade against the Chinese nuclear program. This episode pointed to an interesting role reversal in U.S.-Soviet relations: where ten years earlier the United States approached the Soviets about possible joint action to check the Chinese nuclear program, now the Soviets were worried.[5] Whether the Chinese knew about U.S. thinking in the earlier period is not known, but they assuredly learned about Soviet concerns in 1973. Although Kissinger's assistant, Lawrence Eagleburger, speculated that the Chinese must have found his boss's "revelations . . . unnerving," only the Chinese archives can disclose just how unnerving this news was.[6] Kissinger might have calculated that his briefing would bring China closer to the United States, but he also concluded that lessening Chinese concerns would require the United States to profide special aid to strengthen China's strategic capabilities.

During the months after Kissinger's February visit to Beijing, his secret dialogue with the Chinese (as well as with the North Vietnamese) on Cambodia dragged out in New York, Paris, Washington, and Beijing. By early June 1973, the Chinese were willing to convey to Sihanouk U.S. proposals for evacuating Lon Nol to the United States for supposed medical treatment and for establishing a "coalition structure" that included the Prince. With Sihanouk in a leadership position, Kissinger believed, it would be possible to "keep things balanced" internally. Kissinger soon believed that if the requisite cease-fire was arranged, he could meet with Sihanouk during his anticipated visit to Beijing in early August.[7]

In the meantime the Senate Foreign Relations Committee had learned that the U.S. Air Force was, in Kissinger's words, "bombing the bejesus" out of Cambodia, in violation of prohibitions on U.S. participation in combat operations there. Kissinger later denied that the bombing was in any way indiscriminate, but during the first months of 1973 the U.S. Air Force killed thousands of noncombatants with over 250,000 tons of bombs—more than the United States had dropped on Japan during World War II. By May and June, an angry and impatient Congress was moving to shut down the American military role there. At the end of June 1973, Congress forced Nixon, already weakened by the unfolding Watergate scandal, to halt the bombing on 15 August.[8]

Within a few weeks the Chinese told Kissinger that they could no longer serve as go-betweens with Sihanouk, and the Cambodian initiative collapsed. Kissinger later claimed that Congress had derailed a negotiated settlement by setting a deadline for the bombing halt and thereby depriving the Chinese and Sihanouk of the necessary political leverage—with the Khmer Rouge—to negotiate a bombing halt with the United States. Indeed, Kissinger later blamed anti-war critics for the Khmer Rouge's grisly triumph in 1975, while denying his own responsibility for the bloodshed.[9]

Although Chinese sources will be essential to a clearer understanding of the Cambodian situation, we can only wonder if the bombing halt had the decisive impact that Kissinger claims. Other problems already made a negotiated settlement unlikely. Sihanouk bitterly opposed any concessions to Lon Nol; instead, he wanted the "total humiliation" of the regime and its supporters. Moreover, with Sihanouk's base of support growing in 1973, the Khmer Rouge wanted nothing to do with him or with any negotiations or cease-fire arrangements. Indeed, contrary to Kissinger's assumption about Vietnamese influence, the Khmer Rouge rejected Hanoi's recommendations for a cease-fire. The U.S. bombing kept the Cambodian Communists from seizing power in 1973, but it did not weaken their determination to destroy the U.S.-backed regime; if anything, the bombing may have radicalized the Party and strengthened the hard-liners led by Pol Pot. Kissinger argued that bombing could expedite a settlement; more likely, it only postponed the Khmer Rouge's triumph.[10]

Kissinger had expected to discuss Cambodia and other issues with the Chinese in early August, but Zhou stalled on setting a date, either because he wanted to assess the post-bombing situation in Cambodia or had to overcome internal opposition to his U.S. policy. Nevertheless, close consultations continued, despite the setback over Cambodia and the frictions over U.S.-Soviet relations. Kissinger's schedule was frantically busy during the October 1973 Arab-Israeli War, but he regularly apprised Ambassador Huang of changes in U.S. policy and U.S.-Soviet relations. For example, on 25 October he provided Huang with a full briefing of the reasoning behind his decision to support a worldwide alert of U.S. military forces in order to rebuff Brezhnev's initiatives for a joint force to stop the fighting. He reminded the ambassador that détente was one way to wage the Cold War, and explained that one of his principal objectives was to "keep the Soviet military presence out of the Middle East and to reduce the Soviet political influence as much as possible."[11]

In his memoirs, Kissinger seldom discussed his handling of Chinese diplomats, especially when it involved subjects that unsettled U.S.-PRC relationship. The document that follows, a record of a secret meeting at the White House is a good example of Kissinger's efforts to reassure, in this case, to convince Beijing that the United States' intentions were benign in negotiating the PNW agreement with the Soviets. This conversation took place in mid-May, as Nixon's efforts to cover up the Watergate affair were slowly destroying his presidency. A few weeks earlier, his close advisers H. R. Haldeman and John Ehrlichman had resigned because of their roles in the coverup. Nixon had just brought in General Alexander Haig to replace Haldeman as chief of staff and had also appointed a special prosecutor, Archibald Cox, to conduct an investigation. Hearings on Watergate by the Senate Select Committee on Presidential Campaign Activities were only two days away, as were newspaper headlines that Kissinger himself had approved wiretaps of his close aids, including Winston Lord.[12]

THE WHITE HOUSE
TOP SECRET/SENSITIVE/EXCLUSIVELY EYES ONLY
MEMORANDUM OF CONVERSATION
PARTICIPANTS: Dr. Henry A. Kissinger, Assistant to the President for National Security Affairs; Winston Lord, NSC Staff; Han Xu, Deputy Chief of the PRC Liaison Office; Qian Dayong, Official of the PRC Liaison Office; Ji Chaozhu, Official of the PRC Liaison Office; Mr. Guo, Official of the PRC Mission to the United Nations
DATE AND TIME: Tuesday, May 15, 1973 10:20 A.M. – 11:00 A.M.
PLACE: The Map Room, The White House[A]

(While waiting for Kissinger to arrive, the Chinese discuss with Lord their efforts to find accommodations. "Mr. Guo said that he had heard about Mr. Lord's departure from the staff from the newspapers. Mr. Lord confirmed this, and he noted that he had talked to Mrs. Shi about this and earlier to members of the Liaison Office. Mr. Lord reviewed the reasons for his leaving, namely, rest, reflection, recharge his batteries, and see more of his family.[13] He reiterated that he would stay in the Washington area and hoped to see the Chinese on a personal basis. He said that he might be back in government some day, perhaps working for Dr. Kissinger, but that he needed to take a

---

[A] Source: National Archives, Record Group 59, Department of State Records, Policy Planning Staff (Director's Files), 1969–1977 (hereafter referred to as *PPS, with archival box number and file file information*), box 328, China Exchanges 15 April 1973–15 May 1973.

break at this point. If he did come back, he would then be all the more efficient. The Chinese repeated their regrets that Mr. Lord was leaving and their hope to see him on a private basis and inquired about his replacement. Mr. Lord responded that the staff was being somewhat reorganized and Dr. Kissinger was bringing in some good new people, but that in any event there would be continuity. He cited Messrs. [Jonathan] Howe (temporarily), [Peter] Rodman, and [Richard] Solomon.")[14]

[When Kissinger appears, he asks about the Liaison Office's house-and office-hunting activities.]

Dr. Kissinger: . . . I'm eager for your cook to arrive. (laughter)
Ambassador Han: We are also hoping for an early arrival.
Dr. Kissinger: I am sure of that.

I appreciate your agreeing to see me here, Mr. Ambassador. It is very difficult for me to go to New York since I'm leaving tomorrow for Paris. I wanted the Prime Minister to have an account of our meeting. (Mr. Lord indicated to Dr. Kissinger while this was being translated that the Chinese wished to keep the meeting secret. They had told Mr. Lord this as they were walking from their car to the Map Room.) We can keep this meeting secret very easily. The entrance at this point of the White House is not known to the press. If you are seen, we will say that it concerned preparations for housing and technical things. But there is no possibility that it will be seen.

Ambassador Han: Our hope is that this meeting will be, as previous meetings, kept secret.

Dr. Kissinger: You can be sure that from our side there will be no discussion of it. Just on the one chance in a thousand that someone sees you drive out — this has never happened before — we will just say this is a routine visit connected with technical arrangements for housing. There's no possibility. I'm just protecting against the possible chance. I use this room for meetings when I do not want them to become known.

Let me talk about my visit to Moscow and my general impressions. I spent four days in Zavidovo, which is the hunting lodge of the Politburo. Most of my time was in conversations with General Secretary Brezhnev. First I'll talk to you about matters that concern the United States and the Soviet Union. Then let me talk about what we said concerning China. And then let me tell you what our policy is, because it is important that Beijing and Washington understand each other completely.

First let me talk to you about the various drafts of the nuclear proposals that the Soviet Union has made to us. (He pulls out his folder.) We've given you every previous draft, and I have attached the last draft that the Soviet Union gave us, and where it stands now after discussion there. (Dr. Kissinger writes an addition on one of the attachments that he is about to hand over.)

Let me explain what we are trying to do. If we want to establish a condominium with the Soviet Union, we don't need a treaty. We've had many offers to that effect. If we want to gang up with China against the Soviet Union we don't need to make any arrangements, as I will explain to you later. What we are trying to do first of all is to gain some time. Secondly, to establish a legal obligation as between us and the Soviet Union that requires the Soviet Union to consult with us before taking any military acts, so if they do take any military actions without consulting us, they will have taken unilateral acts which gives us the basis for common action, which we do not now possess with regard to third countries. So what we have done in our discussions, which are not yet finally completed, is first of all to insist that any obligation that applies between us and the Soviet Union applies also between the Soviet Union and third countries. Secondly, (sic) that the objective of not using nuclear weapons can be realized only if there's a renunciation of the use of any force. Thirdly, any consultations that occur between us and the Soviet Union are confined to those cases where the two countries might go to war against each other or they might threaten a war against a third country. Thirdly (sic) where it says in the draft that nothing should impair existing agreements, etc., the Soviet Union wanted only to say when there are treaties and formal agreements, and we insisted that it should include "other appropriate instruments" such as letters and communiqués.

Ambassador Han: That's the fourth point.

Dr. Kissinger: Yes.

Mr. Ji: Nothing should impair . . .?

Dr. Kissinger: (reading from the draft treaty) "Nothing in this agreement shall affect or impair the obligations undertaken by the United States and the Soviet Union toward their allies or other countries in treaties, agreements, and other appropriate instruments."

We have prepared a document on where this now stands with our explanation of what it means, for whatever views you want to express. There are three basic objectives. First, to gain time. Secondly, to force the Soviet Union if it engages in military actions to do so out of a posture of peace rather than an atmosphere of tension. Thirdly, it gives us legal obligations for our position in case of countries where we don't have formal arrangements. (He hands over the annotated current draft and the previous version that the Chinese had seen, attached at Tab A.)

Mr. Ji: The second principle concerned . . . could you kindly repeat this?

Dr. Kissinger: We want to make sure that when the Soviet Union attacks it will be from a posture of relaxation of tension immediately to war, rather than from a prolonged period of tension which confuses the issue.

Of course, no one knows we are giving you this. The single-spaced part is our comment.

While talking on this subject, let me mention a discussion with Mr. Brezhnev that concerned China. Brezhnev took me hunting one day, which is a sport I have never engaged in. (The Chinese smile.) In fact he went hunting, and I just walked along. In the Soviet Union one hunts from the stand in the trees with the animals below, so it is not excessively dangerous. After the shooting was over Brezhnev had a picnic lunch brought in, and it was just he and I and one interpreter. In this conversation he expressed his extremely limited admiration of China. (laughter from the Chinese) And he is a somewhat less disciplined and controlled leader than your Prime Minister. That is not new. That has been done before.[15]

But then he said the Soviet Union and the United States had a joint obligation to prevent China from becoming a big nuclear power. And he said, "do you consider China an ally?" I said, "No, we don't consider it an ally — we consider it a friend." He said, "well you can have any friends you want, but you and we should be partners" — he meant Moscow and Washington. He repeated again that we have a joint responsibility to prevent China from becoming a nuclear power. And I said we recognize no such joint responsibility. That was it, in effect. The rest was simply tirades about China which there is no sense in repeating — things like big power chauvinism, and as soon as you are strong enough you will also turn on us. That sort of thing, immaterial.

Then on the last day, I flew from that lodge to Moscow just to stop at our Embassy for 15 minutes, and I was accompanied by Dobrynin, their Ambassador here. He said that Brezhnev had asked him to make sure that I understood that the conversation at the hunting stand was meant to be serious and not a social conversation. He said he wanted to know whether there existed a formal agreement between the People's Republic and the United States. I said there didn't exist any agreement, but there existed appropriate instruments which we took from this draft, and that in any event we will be guided by our national interest — which we had expressed in the President's Annual Report.

These were all the conversations which concerned China . . . except every time we mentioned third countries here, Gromyko would say that we were acting as the lawyer for China. Our views remain exactly as expressed by me to the Chairman and the Prime Minister, and by the President in his letters to the Chairman and Prime Minister. We continue to believe that it should be the objectives of both our governments to continue to accelerate normalization to the point where it becomes clear that we have a stake in the strength and independence of the People's Republic.

I would be prepared if the Prime Minister wanted, to come to Peking in August after the summit here in order to make a visit. It wouldn't have to be as long as previous visits because we've had basic talks. Maybe two days, or two or three days. If the Prime Minister — we mentioned this in New York once — were considering a visit to the United Nations, we would, of course, give him a very warm reception here in Washington, or if he would come only to Washington. Then we could announce that in the summer. But we could think of other measures to symbolize this.

I have a self-interest in this anyway because if those two things happen, Winston Lord would certainly come back from vacation. So you should also consider it from this wide perspective.

This is the general perspective. I also want to tell you that even though there are many changes in the staff, such as the departure of Winston Lord, there are also some compensations like the return of General Haig to the White House. And you can count on the continuity of our policy that we have been pursuing.

Those are the most important things from Moscow. Now I want to tell you a few minor things.

With respect to SALT, we do not foresee an agreement this year on anything except general principles.[16] (To Lord.) Did we give them our latest proposal?

Mr. Lord: (To Kissinger) We gave them the Soviet proposal.

Dr. Kissinger: By the end of this week we will give you our proposal, so you know what is being discussed in Geneva. We are working on this proposal this week. From my conversations in Moscow it's quite clear that there will be no concrete agreement except on general principles, and those principles are not yet worked out. When they are, we will show them to you. They will not be distinguished by excessive precision.

On MBFR there was practically no discussion except for the timing of negotiations later this year. We will also give you a summary of the position we are discussing with our allies. We have not yet discussed it with the Soviet Union. We will do that next week.

We are also preparing for the Summit a number of bilateral agreements of the same sort as last year—agricultural research, oceanography, cultural exchange, civil aviation.

On the economic side, it was simply another reiteration by the Soviet leaders of their need for long term credits.

Again, we want to repeat that anything we are prepared to do with the Soviet Union we are prepared to do with the People's Republic. And conversely, we may be prepared to do things with the People's Republic what we are not prepared to do with the Soviet Union.

Those are the major things I discussed in the Soviet Union.

As to the visit of Brezhnev, he will be here eight days. He will spend five probably in Washington and two in Los Angeles or San Clemente. We haven't decided yet on some place in between, it may be Key Biscayne, it may be Detroit—he is crazy about automobiles.

You know I'm going to Paris on Thursday to meet with—I can't call him Special Advisor anymore, he's the Deputy Prime Minister now.[17] (Laughter). Again I want to repeat what I've said to Ambassador Huang Hua and the Prime Minister, that it is really in the interest of all countries to bring about an observance of the ceasefire.

Let me say one thing about all the domestic excitement you find in the United States at this point. Once you are here for some time you will see that there are always fits of hysteria descending on Washington in which people talk about nothing else. And six months later it's difficult to remember exactly all the details of the controversy. The conduct of foreign policy is unaffected, and may in fact be even slightly strengthened in some fields, because many of our opponents may even want to show how responsible they are. It will become clear within the next two months that control of foreign policy in the government is being strengthened.[18]

So the lines laid down in the conversations in February in Peking were fixed and will be pursued with vigor, and I would not let the noise here in Washington be too distracting.

On Korea we would like to give you an answer in two weeks. Frankly I have not had time to prepare an adequate answer.

Cotton textiles. You sent us a note. We've asked the agencies not to pursue this subject until your Ambassador comes here. We have certain legal obligations imposed on us by the Congress. I can tell you now that if our relations are ever impaired it will not be because of cotton textiles. (Laughter) This is an issue that will be easily settled.[19]

I don't know whether the Ambassador has anything. (The Chinese discuss among themselves.)

Ambassador Han: I have two things I would like to take up with Dr. Kissinger. The first thing is that the day before yesterday, on the 13th, there was a demonstration here against us in which, according to reports, they burned the national flag.

Dr. Kissinger: We regret this deeply. It is inexcusable. We will do the maximum permitted under law to prevent this. We cannot prevent demonstrations in authorized places. We will do our best to minimize these incidents. And when we can physically stop them, we will, of course, stop them. I know I express the view of the President and the whole U.S. Government when I speak of our regret over this incident.

Ambassador Han: Another thing—this is a minor matter. The American columnist, Mr. Marquis W. Childs, he is in Peking now, and he told our people that Dr. Kissinger suggested that he call on the Premier.[20]

Dr. Kissinger: I'm a great admirer of the Premier and therefore I always think it is of benefit for someone to see him. I think Marquis Childs is basically so well disposed toward China and eager to be helpful that it might be in your interest if the Prime Minister saw him. He will certainly write very favorably, and is socially well-connected so that what he brings back will be very positive. But except for this I have no personal interest. If the Prime Minister is too busy it would not be considered a personal affront to me. (There is discussion among the Chinese.)

Ambassador Han: About keeping this meeting secret from the press. If in the one of a dozen possibilities we were seen as you mentioned . . .

Dr. Kissinger: I won't say anything. I will deny that I saw you.

Ambassador Han: . . . We will say that it was an ordinary call and in addition to an ordinary call we will say that we expressed our regret over the incident on the 13th.

Dr. Kissinger: That is fine. That is all right. We should not look for an opportunity to say anything. (Laughter) There is practically no chance of your being seen. (To Mr. Lord) Correct?

Mr. Lord: That's right.

Dr. Kissinger: I'm glad to see my old friend (Mr. Guo). I hope the Ambassador will come here.

Mr. Guo: I came on very short notice.

Dr. Kissinger: I know about the system—we will work it out.

Mr. Ji: Mr. Solomon and Mr. Romberg are working this out.

(There was some more light talk during which Dr. Kissinger said that US policy wouldn't change with Mr. Lord's absence although it would be less efficient. He was counting on Mr. Lord's getting bored on the outside and also on the good sense of his Chinese wife.)[21]

Dr. Kissinger: I saw that Ambassador Bruce arrived yesterday. We need to expand our office since 10,000 Americans want to work there. (Laughter)

You still don't know when your Ambassador arrives?

Ambassador Han: There is still no news. As soon as we do know, we will let you know. Mr. Solomon asked Mr. Ji whether the Ambassador might come while you are in Paris. (Dr. Kissinger indicates puzzlement.)

Ambassador Han: We have no news. He was just wondering if the Ambassador might come while you were away.

Dr. Kissinger: Whenever he does come he will be highly welcomed. Of course, the President will see him very soon after his arrival.

Ambassador Han: We are looking forward to that.

Dr. Kissinger: It is always a pleasure to see our friends. I will leave first and separately so that you can leave more discreetly.

(There were then cordial farewells. Mr. Lord checked to make sure that there were no people around to notice the Chinese departure. There was a brief discussion in which Mr. Lord told the Chinese that they should contact Mr. Lord the next day or two, and after that, Mr. Howe. Mr. Lord again indicated he was looking forward to seeing the Chinese on a personal basis. He asked Mr. Guo to give his warm regards to Ambassador Huang Hua and Mrs. Shi in New York. There were then very warm farewells as Mr. Lord escorted the Chinese to their limousine waiting at the diplomatic entrance.)

COMMENTARY

On 29 May, Ambassador Huang Zhen, chief of the PRC Liaison Office in Washington, had his first meetings at the White House with Kissinger and President Nixon.[22] Kissinger continued the discussion of Cambodia by repeating a proposal made to Huang Hua a few days earlier. Huang agreed to convey to the Foreign Ministry U.S. thinking about parallel talks between the Khmer Rouge and Lon Nol's representative on the one hand and Sihanouk and the USLO in Beijing on the other. Gratuitously, Kissinger threatens "to bring pressure"—more bombing—if the Cambodian insurgents refused to negotiate. However, a few days later, on 4 June, Huang suggested to Kissinger that once Sihanouk had returned from foreign travels, Beijing "can communicate the U.S. tentative thinking to the Cambodian side." Although hardly an unequivocal promise, it was the development that Kissinger had been hoping for.[23]

During this meeting and a short meeting with President Nixon the next day, Kissinger and the President proposed a formal understanding on U.S.-Chinese consultations—"[W]e would be prepared to consider some joint declaration that neither of us will engage in any negotiation against the other or that neither of us will join in any agreement without consultation with the other." The Chinese turned the offer down on 14 June, arguing that it rehashed what was already in the Shanghai Communiqué and that it would not stop the Soviets from trying to envelope China with its proposals for an "Asian security system." Nixon and Kissinger insisted on providing assurances that U.S.-Soviet détente would not undercut Chinese interests. Thus, in a letter to Zhou on 16 June, Nixon "pledged unilaterally . . . that we would not deal with others on matters affecting PRC interests without full consultation."[24]

A few days earlier, Hua Huang had presented a critique of the Prevention of Nuclear War Agreement, forcing Kissinger to provide Huang Zhen with still more assurances that the "hegemony of two large nuclear countries . . . is not our policy."[25] To reinforce the message, Kissinger provided him with the text of a statement that he had made to French President Pompidou a few days earlier explaining why U.S. policy could not aim at a condominium with the Soviets, and why the PRC's independent existence was essential to European and American security: "There is no sense in choosing the stronger against the weaker. If the Soviet Union managed to render China impotent, Europe would become a Finland and the United States would be completely isolated. It is therefore consistent with our own interests not to want, and to try not to permit, that the Soviet Union should destroy China."

However, the Nixon–Brezhnev summit in June 1973 further raised Beijing's hackles in spite of assurances from Nixon and Kissinger. The summit, another step in the collaborative U.S.-Soviet effort to institutionalize détente, was very successful, but Zhou Enlai revealed his skepticism a few days after Brzhnev left California.[26] Summoning Bruce to the Great Hall of the People, Zhou began with some discussion of modern science and the dangers of spreading nuclear secrets.[27] He then archly noted that "[n]o matter how friendly people are to each other around the Western White House swimming pool, it is impermissible to make an exhibition of their nuclear secrets." Not only did he doubt that the Soviets would honor the PNW agreement, but it raised the prospects of a superpower nuclear condominium: "Since only the two major powers were engaged in this agreement, there were grave doubts among other states as to whether these two powers wanted to dominate the world." Zhou also argued that if the Soviets and the Chinese ever went to war, the United States would initially provide the Soviets with military aid but would later "strike the Soviets from behind."

Bruce reported that Zhou's critique of the PNW was made "in sorrow but not in anger," but he was unaware that one of the Premier's key advisers, Assistant Minister for Foreign Affairs Zhang Wenjing, had written a report critical of U.S. policy. Some months later, Kissinger's China experts learned that Zhang had been arguing that Washington was stepping up its collusion with Moscow at the expense of the "world's revolutionary forces," including, presumably, China itself. Since Zhou had his own suspicions of U.S. policy, Zhang's arguments may have confirmed his concerns; however, Mao soon declared them "rubbish." After Mao announced his opinion, Foreign Minister Ji formally criticized Zhang's analysis, reaffirming the validity of Mao's "revolutionary line in foreign policy"; Zhang was forced to confess to error "in the application of ideology," and was named ambassador to Canada, where he would be far from the decision-making process.[28]

Kissinger knew nothing about Zhang's critique of U.S. policy, and Bruce's report of the conversation with Zhou almost certainly disturbed him. To allay the premier's doubts, he asked Bruce to tell Zhou that Washington had not given nuclear secrets to the Soviets, and that in the event of a Sino–Soviet war, the United States will "under no circumstances . . . give assistance to the USSR" and will "probably terminate all economic programs." To reduce suspicions further, Kissinger wanted Zhou to know that he would soon personally brief Ambassador Huang Zhen on the Nixon–Brezhnev talks.[29]

On 6 July, Huang met with Kissinger and then Nixon. An important focus of the talks was Cambodia; but prospects for a negotiation on Kissinger's terms were less favorable than ever. In the preceding weeks, Kissinger had worked frantically to preserve White House freedom of action and to prevent congressional limitations on the bombing of Cambodia; nevertheless, in late June, Congress took the extraordinary step of forcing a politically weakened Nixon to agree to a bombing halt by 15 August.[30]

The focal points of the conversation, though, were the Brezhnev–Nixon summit and Brezhnev's renewed efforts to bring Washington into an anti-Beijing understanding. Although he did not mention that Brezhnev had characterized Mao as a "treacherous fellow" or that Gromyko had sternly warned against U.S.–China military cooperation, Kissinger painted a grim enough picture. Yet, no matter how concerned the Soviets were about a Chinese threat, they eschewed the disastrous course of launching a unilateral preemptive attack on China's nuclear facilities (just as the Johnson administration had dismissed unilateral action in 1964). Indeed, Kissinger later admitted to Dobrynin that his assessment of the Soviet threat to China had been exaggerated.[31] Overwrought or not, Kissinger may have hoped to draw Beijing closer to the United States. In any event, he surely realized that his presentation would startle the Chinese, thus to soften the impact, he provided general and specific reassurances, ranging from contingency planning to Chinese access to Western technology. Kissinger, however, soon concluded that assurances were not enough; by November, he offered Zhou material assurance in the event of conflict with the Soviets.

THE WHITE HOUSE
TOP SECRET/SENSITIVE/EXCLUSIVELY EYES ONLY
MEMORANDUM OF CONVERSATION
PARTICIPANTS: USA Henry A. Kissinger Assistant to the President for National Security Affairs; Brent Scowcroft Deputy Assistant to the President for National Security Affairs; Lawrence S. Eagleburger, Deputy Assistant to the President for National Security Council Operations; PRC Ambassador Huang Zhen; Mr. Ji (interpreter)
DATE, TIME & PLACE: July 6, 1973–10:00 A.M.
PLACE: Dr. Kissinger's Office Western White House[B]

Ambassador Huang: I am very happy to see you here.
Dr. Kissinger: We are very happy to have you here though I must apologize for the weather.

You will meet people at the dinner tonight who no longer exist in the PRC. I have selected them for their impact on U.S. life. They have public influence and will talk for two years about their meeting with you. Danny Kaye will be there. He is a great Chinese cook. Remember if he mentions it tonight that I told you of his love for China and his great ability as a Chinese cook.[32]
Ambassador Huang: I want to thank you for the many fine arrangements that have been made for my trip. It is timely that I come now; a week from now I would not be able to make it. I have just received instructions to return to

---

[B] Source: *PPS*, box 329, China Exchange 14 June–9 July 1973.

Peking for a period of time. I will probably be there to welcome you when you arrive.

[Kissinger informs Huang that he would like to visit China beginning on 6 August and to announce the visit on the 12th or the 14th of July; the Ambassador agrees to pass the information to Beijing.]

Dr. Kissinger: Before Mr. Ji translates, let me ask a question. Is the Ambassador a General?

Ambassador Huang: Certainly.

Dr. Kissinger: That's what I thought but someone argued with me that you were not.

Ambassador Huang: I was in the same profession as General Scowcroft.

Dr. Kissinger: One thing I have noticed about the U.S. Army is that there are very many intelligent colonels and very few intelligent generals. I have been watching for Scowcroft's deterioration ever since he was promoted to General.

Ambassador Huang: From the standpoint of generals, I can say that there should be more intelligent generals. As you know, we have removed all ranks in our army.

Dr. Kissinger: The General's union. I didn't give you a chance to translate, Mr. Ji.

Ambassador Huang: While we are on the subject of speculation, let me discuss the visit of Prime Minister Zhou En-Lai to the U. S. There has been a great deal of speculation in the press, including one report on June 27 from San Clemente that the Prime Minister might consider a visit to the Western White House since it would not be so detrimental to our "principled stand."

Dr. Kissinger: You must understand that we had nothing to do with those stories.

Ambassador Huang: The U.S. side must understand that it still has relations with the Chiang group. Last year a message of congratulations was sent to Chiang from President Nixon, and the Chiang group still has an embassy in Washington. Under these conditions, how would it be possible for our Prime Minister to visit the U.S.? A visit to San Clemente would only be using the side door or the back door. I should also tell you that the Prime Minister has no plans to visit the U.N.

Dr. Kissinger: The stories did not come from us. We have always officially denied them.

Ambassador Huang: My personal recommendation is that it is beneficial when Ziegler says there are no grounds for such speculation, as he recently did.

Dr. Kissinger: That's our position. As the President has said, he is willing to visit China again. But it would be difficult for us when there is no intermediate meeting in Washington. It would have eased matters if something took place between the first Presidential visit to Beijing and the next Presidential visit, which we are prepared to do in 1974.

Ambassador Huang: This can be discussed in Beijing.

Dr. Kissinger: Yes; we will stop all speculation in the meantime. How should we proceed? We have a number of concrete problems to discuss. I want to review the Brezhnev visit and one particular matter arising from it. Further, there are Cambodia, Korea, and a number of minor things.

Ambassador Huang: I'll finish up and then listen to you. The other thing I want to discuss is Cambodia. I have a paper here to give you. (Hands over paper, text of which follows.)

"The Chinese side informed the U. S. side earlier that as Samdech Norodom Sihanouk was visiting in Africa and Europe, it was yet infeasible for the Chinese side to communicate to him U.S. tentative thinking on a settlement of the Cambodian question. Although the Chinese side had informed the U.S. side that negotiations between Samdech Sihanouk and the Phnom Penh traitorous clique would be impossible, the U.S. side nevertheless openly refused to negotiate with Samdech Sihanouk, which enraged him all the more. However, according to news reports, U.S. government officials have recently made some disclosures on this question, which have given rise to various speculations. At the same time, it is learned that the Lon Nol clique has gone to the length of spreading the rumor that the Phnom Penh authorities will enter into official negotiations with the National United Front of Cambodia very soon, with the United States and the Chinese Communists serving as go-betweens. In spreading such utterly groundless assertions, the Lon Nol clique harbours ulterior motives, widely attempting to confuse public opinion and forestall the settlement of the Cambodian question. The Chinese side is of the view that such a turn of events is extremely disadvantageous to seeking a settlement of the Cambodian question and will even cause trouble. The Chinese side cannot but bring this to the serious attention of the U.S. side."

Ambassador Huang: This message was received before Prince Sihanouk returned to Beijing.

Dr. Kissinger: (reading paper) He is certainly enraged.

Ambassador Huang: Since you always indicated in the past that you didn't want to talk to him, he is angry.

Dr. Kissinger: Yes, but you have received several communications from us. These were before his return to Beijing.

Ambassador Huang: Now that Sinahouk has returned to Beijing, we will hand over your thinking to him.

Dr. Kissinger: I gather he had not received this by the time of his arrival.

Ambassador Huang: By the looks of it, no.

Dr. Kissinger: I did not know that the Prime Minister could speak French.

Ambassador Huang: He was in France.

Dr. Kissinger: I had forgotten. He made some comments in French about us.

Let me give you our view on Cambodia. First, we cannot control what the Lon Nol people are saying. But they do not know what we have said to you; the proposals we have made to you. It is just speculation on their side.

I want to speak frankly. What we have proposed to you — a ceasefire, if necessary for only 90 days, we believe takes care of the situation. We have no interests in Cambodia other than what the Prime Minister said to Ambassador Bruce the first time he saw him.[33] This is our objective. We have no objection — in fact, we would welcome it — if the Government in Phnom Penh is on very friendly terms with Beijing and would refuse to participate in great power hegemonial activities in Southeast Asia.

As I have expressed before, it is a delicate problem for us as to how to manage the transition. If we are pushed into an undignified position, it will only strengthen the forces in this country who will oppose other things we may judge it necessary to do over the next three or four years. So we think it important that the matter in Cambodia be ended in a way not necessarily wounding for the U.S. We take great care not to embarrass you publicly. We really think it is not in our interest to create a situation which is unnecessarily difficult for either side.

Ambassador Huang: I will report this to my Government. Our attitude has already been made clear by the Prime Minister to Ambassador Bruce. As the Prime Minister said, all sides should respect Cambodia's sovereignty. We cannot negotiate about Cambodia. That must be between you, those now in power in Phnom Penh, and Sihanouk.

Dr. Kissinger: We're not asking to negotiate with you, but we have made suggestions as the basis for a solution. If the Prince proposes a cease-fire before my arrival we could stop bombing, and then reach a solution satisfactory to everyone's needs.

Ambassador Huang: It is up to the Prince. It is not for us to predict.

Dr. Kissinger: No, but our thinking could be mentioned to him.

Ambassador Huang: I can only report. It depends thereafter on my Government.

Dr. Kissinger: Of course.

Ambassador Huang: The Prince said a great deal at the airport.

Dr. Kissinger: I know. The guns have been going off all over Beijing these days. The Prime Minister, for example, made some remarks to our Congressional delegation the other day.[34]

Ambassador Huang: I have not seen this.

Dr. Kissinger: I'm not criticizing. He bracketed us, but he hasn't hit us yet.

Ambassador Huang: We haven't heard anything of this.

Dr. Kissinger: No? What he said was in the spirit of what you said before. It was new to the Congressmen, but not to us.

Let me say a few words about Brezhnev. I take it rather seriously. I want to tell it to you as it happened. I want first to discuss our conversations about China. Brezhnev sought for a week to see the President without me.

Ambassador Huang: You are a dangerous man.

Dr. Kissinger: Brezhnev is persistent but not subtle. He did see the President for about 30 minutes alone at Camp David. His comments about China were not favorable, but you may know that. But on the last day—on Saturday—Brezhnev had three hours with the President at which I was present. We talked about China at great length.[35] It was his initiative. During the first part of the meeting he violently attacked the Chinese leadership and gave us his explanation of the Lin Bao affair. I won't discuss that unless you want me to.

Ambassador Huang: It's up to you.

Dr. Kissinger: It was in that context that he told us about the nonaggression treaty about which you had already informed us. He said he would publish it at a suitable interval after his return as an example of the bellicosity of the PRC.

On Lin Bao, the only thing that may be of interest is that he said he would be prepared to let us see their investigative report. We said we were not interested.

He then discussed a number of things. He said it would be intolerable to imagine a Chinese nuclear capability in 15 years equal to what the Soviets have today. This, he said, would be intolerable and unacceptable to the USSR. He suggested we cooperate on this problem, as he had hinted at Zavidovo. Now he was making a formal and more explicit proposal.

He proposed as well that the U.S. and USSR begin exchanging information on your nuclear program. We said we would not exchange military information and were not interested. Brezhnev then asked if we are prepared to exchange other information on China. We said we could not make one country the subject of regular exchanges. They could always tell us what they had on their minds, but we would make no such undertaking. Brezhnev then said he expected our relations with you to improve, and that they could not object to this. But if military arrangements were made between the U.S. and the PRC, this would have the most serious consequences and would lead the Soviets to take drastic measures. Those were the key points.

They asked if we were planning any military arrangements. We replied three times that we have made no military arrangements, but we said nothing about the future. We do this as a question of principle. Neither of us has any plans along these lines, but we don't believe the Soviets can tell us with whom we can have arrangements.

The meeting was between Brezhnev, the President, myself, and the Soviet interpreter. We have told no one in our Government of this conversation. It must be kept totally secret. We have not told Ambassador Bruce, but I would have no objection if, when you return, you talk to Ambassador Bruce about it. But no one else should be present

Ambassador Huang: I won't say anything to Bruce. You discuss it when you are there. As for us, as the President said to me last time, the Chinese side is very careful.

Dr. Kissinger: Brezhnev told us that only those in the room would hear of this conversation. But that evening, Gromyko asked to see me and asked what I thought of the Brezhnev conversation. (laughter)

He asked if I understood Brezhnev's proposal about China. I said that I understood it to have something to do with military arrangements between us. Gromyko then said I had misunderstood. Brezhnev not only meant military arrangements, but also political arrangements directed against the USSR. I asked what was meant by political arrangements, and who determined whether they were directed against the USSR. Gromyko was very evasive. I then called his attention to the Shanghai Communique and told him that we had an understanding not to make agreements directed at other parties.

It is my impression that the Soviet Union was quite serious about some of the matters we discussed previously. They were more openly brazen and brutal than I would have thought possible.

Under these conditions we think it is very important that we understand each other and what our intentions are. Your Prime Minister mentioned to Ambassador Bruce that you think in the event of a Sino-Soviet war we would give arms and supplies to the Soviet Union. That is absurd. We have no interest in supporting the stronger against the weaker.

Ambassador Huang: The Prime Minister said that?

Dr. Kissinger: (Reading from Ambassador Bruce's cable of June 26) "In the beginning, the U.S. would maintain a position of non-involvement, but give military supplies to the USSR. Then, after waiting until China had dragged out the USSR for a period of time, the U.S. would strike the Soviets from behind." If China was attacked by the USSR, we would certainly cut off all credits to the Soviets. The second part of the Prime Minister's remarks might be true, but certainly not the first part. Under no circumstances would we give military or other supplies to the Soviets if they attacked the PRC. We would certainly cut off all economic ties, but we don't know whether that would be enough.

We must do the maximum we can to deter an attack on China. I used the [Prevention of] Nuclear [War] Agreement in a press conference to say that no attack on China would be conceivable that would not threaten peace and security. There would have been an unbelievable uproar in the Congress without the Agreement. So don't attack the Agreement too much. Give us a chance to use it in the one way we want. I think we have out-maneuvered your allies on this one.

I have set up a very secret group of four or five of the best officers I can find to see what the U.S. could do if such an event occurred. This will never be publicly known. I tell it to you in the strictest confidence. The group is only being formed this week. I talked to the Chairman of the JCS [Joint Chiefs of Staff] about it when he was here this week. I am prepared to exchange views on this subject if it can be done in secret.

Further, I have talked to the French Foreign Minister about our interest in strengthening the PRC. We will do what we can to encourage our allies to speed up requests they receive from you on items for Chinese defense.

In particular, you have asked for some Rolls Royce technology. Under existing regulations we have to oppose this, but we have worked out a procedure with the British where they will go ahead anyway.[36] We will take a formal position in opposition, but only that. Don't be confused by what we do publicly. In the future, now that we have our military establishment understanding the problem, we can handle these problems in a different way.

When I come to Beijing I think we should discuss this complex of issues rather seriously. That is, how we can do the maximum to deter an attack without providing an excuse to undertake it.

You above all should understand what our policy is. If we wanted to cooperate with the USSR, then we would not have to be so complicated. We are trying to gain time and be in a position for maximum resistance should it happen. This is our position. I most say that we considered our discussions with the Soviets quite ominous.

Ambassador Huang: I will report to my Government. As to the US–Soviet Nuclear Agreement, I have already told you our position.[37]

Dr. Kissinger: I know. It does not give us any great pain. It would be worse if you supported the Agreement. I just want you to understand our position. But don't tell our Congressmen that it is just a scrap of paper. We want to use it. You can criticize it in other ways.

Ambassador Huang: Our Prime Minister said that?

Dr. Kissinger: Our newspapers so report. As I have said, we don't object to criticism. The Soviets would think something was wrong otherwise.

Ambassador Huang: Our experience has been that it means nothing to the Soviets when they sign a paper.

Dr. Kissinger: I understand. Its purpose is in terms of our own problems; it has no impact on the Russians. But if I had said an attack on China threatened the U.S., there would have been a major uproar in the absence of the Agreement. But with the Agreement it was possible to say this relatively quietly.

I have to talk to the press now. What should I say about our meeting? That we had a review of the situation, and that we had a friendly talk? Nothing more specific? Do they know you are returning to China?

Ambassador Huang: Not yet.

Dr. Kissinger: The press will now say I have upset you so much you are returning to China.

Ambassador Huang: Others will say that I am so happy that I am returning to report.

(Break for meeting with the press and the President.)

Dr. Kissinger: I have just had a report from Ambassador Bruce about the Prime Minister's meeting with the Congressmen. He did say what I reported, but he was provoked by our side. He did not volunteer his comments, they insisted on raising it. We understand that he has no choice but to express his view when asked. Then the Senators repeated it to the newsmen.

Our Congressmen do not have a capacity for keeping confidential information, and Senator [Warren] Magnuson knows nothing about foreign policy, which makes it worse. We will have a chance to deal with it in our channels.

We have told you our views on Korea. I suppose that the Prime Minister will discuss it with me when I get there.

Ambassador Huang: Did Dr. Kissinger see what our Prime Minister said about Korea at the Mali reception? He supported Kim Il Sung's 5 points.

Dr. Kissinger: Yes, but that was a general statement. Now, however, we have to decide how we will deal with specifics — UNCURK [United Nations Commission for the Unification and Rehabilitationi of Korea] and the UNC [United Nations Command] — over the coming years.[38]

Ambassador Huang: You can discuss this in Beijing.

Dr. Kissinger: You mentioned in an earlier conversation the possibility of an exchange of chancery sites. It is complicated legally, but we would be prepared to facilitate an exchange when you are ready.

COMMENTARY

Kissinger and Huang discussed possible sites for the PRC's chancery in Washington and U.S. grain sales to China then walked to President Nixon's office, where they continued discussion on the summit and U.S.-PRC relations.[39] After Brezhnev's departure, Nixon had remained in San Clemente and resisted requests by the Senate Watergate Committee for access to his papers, which was focusing on the question "what did the President know and when did he know it?" Although Nixon had written to Committee Chairman Sam Ervin (D-N.C.) that he "must and shall resist" their efforts to induce him to testify or turn over White House documents, his worst troubles were ahead. Within a week, committee staffers learned about Nixon's tape recording system from former White House aide Alexander Butterfield.[40]

Availing himself of the chance to play the statesman, Nixon offered Huang more assurances to counteract Kissinger's bad news. After asserting his pivotal role as decisionmaker — "Dr. Kissinger never spoke for himself alone" — Nixon defended détente as a matter of basic U.S. interest but he also reassured Huang that no U.S.-Soviet agreements would be made at Beijing's expense.

On Cambodia, Nixon urged Chinese assistance in a settlement; but, given the Congress' recent action on the bombing, his words about "the possibility of the conflict spreading" must have seemed hollow. Huang's response to Nixon's appeal was perfunctory, as was his reaction to the reassurances about the Soviet danger. No doubt, he lacked instructions for responding to such extraordinary news. After all he had heard, he may have wanted to file a report with the Foreign Ministry as quickly as possible.

On 18 July, Kissinger's efforts to negotiate a settlement preserving some portion of the Lon Nol government took a dive: the Chinese informed the

"U.S. side" that its ruthless bombing of Cambodia and intensified support for the "Lon Nol clique" had "all the more enraged Samdech Sihanouk" against American policy. These circumstances made it "obviously inappropriate" for Beijing to communicate Kissinger's thinking about a settlement to Sihanouk. As long as the United States held the "key" to a settlement, it was its responsibility to make the requisite policy changes.[41] This note made Kissinger indignant. Believing that the Chinese were going back on their word—if in fact "can communicate" was a promise—he informed the USLO through the back channel that the note "was substantially more brutal" than anything he had heard from PRC officials. Furthermore, he wondered whether the Chinese note signaled some more fundamental change in the PRC's U.S. policy. The fact that Beijing had not responded to his proposal that his trip be announced on 16 July did not help. Kissinger surmised that this amounted to a de facto cancellation. In a fit of pique he grumbled to his staff, "[t]o cancel a Kissinger trip was a major international event"—only to learn a few hours later, that his trip was still on Beijing's agenda.

On 19 July, Kissinger reviewed the situation with his staff. While he assumed that the bombing halt explained the change in Beijing's stance on Cambodia, some of his advisers were not so quick to draw conclusions. In any event, Kissinger remained determined to let the Chinese know that he felt let down. A week later, Scowcroft told Hans Xu that "this was the first time in the development of our relationship that the Chinese word has not counted."[42]

THE WHITE HOUSE TOP SECRET/SENSITIVE/EXCLUSIVELY EYES ONLY
MEMORANDUM OF CONVERSATION
PARTICIPANTS: Henry A. Kissinger; General Brent Scowcroft; Lawrence Eagleburger; Winston Lord; Jonathan T. Howe; Richard Solomon; Peter W. Rodman
DATE AND TIME: Thursday, July 19, 1973 11:00–11:46 A.M.
PLACE: Dr. Kissinger's Office The White House[C]

Mr. Kissinger convened the meeting in order to discuss the note received from the PRC the previous evening (Tab A)—its implications with respect to

---

[C] Source: *PPS*, box 328, China Exchanges 10 July–31 Oct. 1973.

Cambodia, his prospective trip to Peking, and the course of Sino-U. S. relations; and how the U. S. should respond.

Mr. Kissinger began by pointing out that the note had to be read against the background of the course of the U.S.–Chinese relationship over the past several months. This note was clearly sent as a cancellation or postponement of the Kissinger trip and an opting-out by the Chinese of any involvement in negotiations for a Cambodian settlement. This was a complete reversal of the Chinese position on both counts.

On each and every previous Kissinger trip to China the Chinese had proposed that he meet with Sihanouk. Sihanouk has now said, in a speech on July 10, that we should negotiate with the Khmer Rouge and not with him, *Mr. Solomon* interjected. That is true, *Mr. Kissinger* replied. But on each previous trip, especially in February 1973, Cambodia had been discussed extensively. At the end of May we had made a proposal and the Chinese had said they would convey it to Sihanouk once he returned from his travels. Their message of June 4 went to the extraordinary length of reciting our proposal back to us to make sure they understood it correctly—something they had never done on any other subject. Therefore this note represented a reneging on a clear assurance.

What had happened in the interim? Mr. Kissinger asked. The Congressional vote to cut off the bombing had destroyed the balance in Cambodia. It was clear the Chinese couldn't deliver.

The bombing cut-off had fundamentally changed the situation in Cambodia. Formerly, Sihanouk's utility to the Khmer Rouge had been that he gave them legitimacy which they had not had. Now they didn't need legitimacy; they saw they could win. Sihanouk's utility to the Chinese had been that he gave them influence over the Khmer Rouge and could resist other outside influences. The utility of the Chinese to us was that they had some control over Sihanouk. Sihanouk's utility to us was that, once he returned to Cambodia, he might be able to keep things balanced. Ironically the Chinese needed the Lon Nol group—this was a restraint on Sihanouk and on the Khmer Rouge. The Congressmen had totally misjudged the situation. Now this was all lost. Sihanouk couldn't deliver the Khmer Rouge and the Chinese couldn't deliver Sihanouk.

With respect to the trip, the Chinese had virtually agreed in June that it would take place in early August. They had invited us to choose any date we wanted; we had then proposed August 6. They had spread the word around that it would be early August and had even leaked the date of August 6th to the press in Beijing. But then Huang Zhen was called back the beginning of this month and we received the note that they couldn't reply on a date until he got to Beijing. We had yet to receive a reply to our proposed dates for the trip and for the announcement. We had first proposed July 16 for the announcement. But July 16 had come and gone. The Chinese had to know that this delay in replying, and the turn-around on Cambodia, meant a postponement.

This was a conscious decision, Mr. Kissinger concluded. The question was whether it reflected only the Cambodian issue or something more fundamental that was happening to the relationship. [General] Brent [Scowcroft] had told Han Xu that Dr. Kissinger's authority would be undermined if he came back empty-handed on Cambodia and that he and the President were the key men who embodied American support for China for the right reasons. All this talk about 25 years of mutual estrangement was crap. What the Chinese wanted was support in a military contingency. We might not be able to pull it off, but at least he and the President understood this. Alex Eckstein and other chowder-headed liberals loved China but if you asked them about military actions in a contingency they'd have 600 heart attacks. Liberals kept talking about how isolation was so psychologically disturbing to the Chinese. It might have been psychologically disturbing to us, but it wasn't to the Chinese. For 3,000 years it didn't bother them to be isolated. They've been self-contained more than they've been in contact with the rest of the world, and they have the self-assurance to handle it quite well.

To cancel a Kissinger trip was a major international event. It had to be a major decision for them. To assess this question—this was the real reason Mr. Kissinger had called together this group.

Mr. Solomon pointed out the disastrous [Senator] Magnuson conversation with Zhou Enlai. Zhou had been visibly angered by Magnuson's attempt to engage him with the Congress against the President. Magnuson had talked for 45 minutes about Cambodia in spite of everyone else's efforts to get off the subject. While Zhou attacked the US–Soviet nuclear agreement, and uttered some harsh words about the Cambodian bombing, Magnuson stressed the role of Congress in cutting off the bombing and repeatedly urged Zhou to "Be patient. It'll be over soon." Jenkins and Holdridge, Mr. Solomon noted, thought that the tone of the note may have reflected their irritation at Magnuson's performance. *Mr. Kissinger* said he had thought that was a stupid point. There was something more fundamental underlying this. He suggested that from a coldly calculated Chinese point of view they now saw a paralyzed President unable to provide firm support in matters affecting their security. This may have made them now question the value of our relationship. *General Scowcroft* emphasized that the Chinese wanted firm action from the U.S.

Mr. Solomon turned again to the Cambodian aspect. Sihanouk had displayed his own powerlessness and admitted he could be only a figurehead in asserting that we should now talk to the Khmer Rouge. This was probably true. In addition, the Chinese might not want him to expose his weakness in negotiations with us, as they probably hoped to use him as a point of influence in Cambodia in the future. Nor would the Chinese leadership want to expose themselves to criticism from domestic or foreign sources for pressuring an evidently successful "people's war" into compromising negotiations on the eve of an apparent victory. Certainly not before a Party Congress.

Mr. Eagleburger suggested that the unfortunate juxtaposition of press leaks here about the "delicate negotiations in progress" and the Kissinger trip to Beijing may have provoked a change in the Chinese attitude. He asked if some members of the Chinese leadership might not be saying that China had, wittingly or unwittingly, been used by the Americans to obtain a 45-day extension of the bombing.

Mr. Kissinger responded that the bombing cutoff was the decisive thing, not the bombing extension. We had been bombing the bejesus out of them since May. There had in fact been no intensification of the bombing since the Congressional vote. *General Scowcroft* confirmed this. Next to us, *Mr. Kissinger* continued, the ones most hurt by the bombing cutoff were the Chinese. Before, our bombing gave them and Sihanouk something they could deliver to the Khmer Rouge, namely a bombing halt worked out with us. Now if the Chinese try to exert their influence for a settlement it comes across as a brute big-power play between us and them.

Mr. Lord commented that to him the language in the note didn't seem especially harsh. *Mr. Rodman* mentioned that the language was their standard line on Cambodia, which was not new. They had always been relatively abusive to us on Cambodia in their public statements. *Mr. Kissinger* said he was sure the Chinese didn't like the bombing. But this was nevertheless in marked contrast to all their previous exchanges with us on the subject and with the experience we had had with them on Vietnam. On Vietnam when they had harsh things to say in a message, they would always have other things to say, or would make clear in other ways that this did not hurt our relationship. This time, the failure to reiterate the invitation, and indeed the failure to reply at all to our date proposal, was a major step, and very puzzling.

Commander Howe noted that we had established a clear link between movement on Cambodia and the trip. They were on the spot and couldn't deliver. By commenting only on Cambodia they may have been trying to make a clean break and separate the two issues. They wanted to make a "principled stand. " *Mr. Lord* asked what the tone of the previous few months had been. *Mr. Kissinger* reiterated that it had been totally positive and that this note was something new. *Mr. Lord* asked how they had taken the Brezhnev visit. They had taken it all in stride. *Mr. Kissinger* replied. They didn't like the nuclear agreement but had said so in very restrained fashion. *General Scowcroft* pointed out how extensively we had consulted with them on that.

Mr. Solomon stated that there was no other evidence of a basic shift in the line toward the U.S. On the contrary, three days before, Mao himself had taken the unusual step of receiving a Chinese–American nuclear physicist, and then Zhou had had a banquet for him. This was an unmistakable signal to the Chinese people and overseas Chinese that the Sino–U. S. relationship was still on. And Madame Mao's appearance with Ambassador Bruce at the basketball game a few weeks before showed that the very people who might have been challenging the rapprochement with the U. S. were now solidly lined up with it. *Mr. Kissinger* commented that this was all people to people stuff and did not exclude a shift in the political line.

Mr. Kissinger returned to the issue of the Chinese seeing a paralyzed President. They might want to provide themselves with a little more flexibility, particularly with respect to the Russians. There was no question about the significance of turning off a Kissinger trip, particularly after the Brezhnev summit. *Mr. Rodman* pointed out that the Chinese message was a response to a question we had put, namely, what could we expect on Cambodia? They were giving us an honest answer. We had linked the trip with Cambodia. It was now being left to us how to respond. *Mr. Kissinger* reiterated that the Chinese response was unmistakably a postponement of the trip. They could have done any one of a number of things to take the edge off the Cambodian note. Responding in any way to our proposed date would have done this. They could have said, "We can't do anything for you on Cambodia but we are glad to have you on August 6 — or some other date." *Mr. Rodman* suggested that they might not want to propose August 6 knowing it was now impossible for us to come. *General Scowcroft* stated that there were a hundred other ways they could have played it.

Mr. Eagleburger concluded that we were simply not going to be able to answer Mr. Kissinger's question as to why the Chinese had behaved in this way.

The discussion then turned to how to respond. It was agreed that we should answer the Cambodian note in strong terms and also postpone the trip. *Mr. Kissinger* said that we should have Bruce deliver a tough note on Cambodia which would express regret that for the first time in our relationship the Chinese word had not counted. We should just list all the things they had said before—their assurances that they would convey our proposal to Sihanouk. There had been no change in the situation. The idea that we had to communicate with Sihanouk through Mauritania was absurd. Sihanouk was in Beijing. And the Chinese themselves had said they couldn't contact Sihanouk when he was abroad because it wasn't secure.

We should try to find out what their message means about our relationship. We should have Bruce go in and sound out [Deputy Foreign Minister] Qiao Guanhua about the status of our relations generally. We should say we are asking Bruce to have a general review of Sino–American relations. If they answer, we'll find out. Even if they give us no answers, that in itself is an answer. Either way, we learn something. We should have Bruce deliver a stern message on Cambodia and then raise the other questions orally. We should do that next week, on the 24th or 25th.

It was agreed that we had no choice but to postpone the trip with a cool note. On the 21st we should give a note to Han Xu here doing this, Mr. Kissinger said. There was some discussion about whether we should propose a date after September 1, or propose "some time in the fall" or ask them to propose a time period. The note should be "ice cold." The second question was whether we should propose the text of a joint announcement or ask them for their proposal on an announcement. This would put them on the spot. A formal announcement would have a heavy impact. But we had to have some announcement, Mr. Kissinger said, or at least some answer to give to press queries, because as August went by there would surely be a flood of press questions. We could just say that because of scheduling difficulties the two sides agreed to postpone until September.

Postscript: At 5:00 p.m. on July 19, Han Xu delivered a second Chinese (note Tab B) proposing that Mr. Kissinger come on August 16. By the end of the day it was tentatively decided to respond to the two Chinese notes in sequence, as they had done—replying to Cambodia on one day and proposing a September trip on the second day. It would be done here, on paper, with Han Xu. There was now no need for Bruce to raise "fundamental questions" with Qiao.

COMMENTARY

In the wake of the Cambodia affair and U.S. remonstrances about the PRC's word "not counting," David Bruce reported that relations with the Chinese were a bit "cooler," although the Chinese "obviously want to proceed toward further normalization." That the Chinese delayed agreement on dates for Kissinger's visit continued to annoy Kissinger—he thought it "discourteous"—until they settled on 26 October. Another snag developed, however, that made Kissinger's advisers wonder even if there were deeper problems in the relationship. On 26 September the Chinese Foreign Ministry asked Bruce to order the U.S. Marine Guard security detail to leave China because they had "made themselves conspicuous as members of the Marine Corps." The Chinese had initially approved the presence of the Marines (no other embassy in Beijing had military guards), but the soldier's presence in uniforms soon led to complaints. The Marines, in deference to Chinese sensitivities about foreign military forces, reluctantly began to wear street clothes. But they attracted Chinese attention yet again when they had set up a bar-nightclub in their quarters, the "Red Ass Saloon," which quickly became a lively social center for entertainment-starved foreigners. The Foreign Ministry renewed complaints about foreign troops.[43]

Kissinger recognized that the dispute over the Marines could turn a minor issue into a major headache, so he asked Beijing to delay the order so he could discuss it with Zhou personally. However, his anticipated late October visit ended up being delayed until November; then Secretary of State Kissinger—the Senate had confirmed him on 21 September—asked Zhou Enlai to accept yet another postponement after Egyptian and Syrian forces launched a surprise attack on Israel on 6 October.[44]

As the Middle East crisis unfolded, Kissinger regularly kept Ambassador Huang abreast of the situation and of his strategy to prevent a "victory for Soviet-supported arms," as well as his support for an airlift "to show that we can intervene more rapidly than they can." By 19 October, when Kissinger believed that Israel was "winning rather decisively," he told Huang that he was about to leave for Moscow in order to arrange a cease-fire with the Soviets. As a preparation for finalizing the agreement, Kissinger stopped in Israel, where he seems to have tacitly encouraged the Israelis to gain more ground. Thus, soon after Kissinger's return from the Middle East, the cease-fire collapsed. Israel launched a major offensive and encircled Egypt's Third Army on 23 October.[45]

The next evening, as the Israeli encirclement continued and rumors of cease-fire violations ran rampant, Brezhnev sent the White House a letter urging joint American–Soviet intervention to stop the fighting. If Washington rejected joint action, "we should be faced with the necessity urgently to consider . . . taking appropriate steps unilaterally." Although some saw menace in Brezhnev's language, he was not tryint to threaten; instead, he was appealing to Nixon to induce the Israelis to abide by the cease-fire. Having ruled out independent military action, Brezhnev's language about "appropriate steps" was purposefully vague.[53]

Kissinger has since said that Brezhnev's letter was "in effect an ultimatum," but even at the time he knew that the Soviets would not intervene unilaterally; as he told Ambassador Huang, Brezhnev's letter was a bluff. Nevertheless, he believed it necessary to react militarily to Brezhnev's letter for two reasons: first, to squelch any thinking in Moscow about an independent Soviet role in the Middle East settlement, and, second, to give cover for U.S. pressure on Israel to observe the cease-fire, thus preventing a decisive Israeli victory. An intoxicated Nixon, reeling from the "Saturday night massacre" and congressional preparations to launch impeachment proceedings, delegated authority to Kissinger to act. With his NSC colleagues, Kissinger ordered a worldwide alert of U.S. military forces, including strategic nuclear and air defense forces.[47]

The next day, Kissinger caught up with Huang and briefed him on the Brezhnev letter, the alert, and U.S. strategy for a peace settlement. Huang was plainly a pro-Arab partisan; nevertheless, Kissinger wanted the PRC to note that his policy was plainly anti-Soviet but conciliatory toward the Arabs. Thus, he emphasized the importance of American policy for simultaneously meeting Arab grievances and containing Soviet influence. As the following months would show, Kissinger's determination to squeeze the Soviets out of the Middle East peace process would increase Cold War frictions. Whether Kissinger actually believed that such a development was compatible with peace in the region remains to be determined.

U.S. Department of State
TOP SECRET/SENSITIVE/EXCLUSIVELY EYES ONLY
MEMORANDUM OF CONVERSATION
PARTICIPANTS: Dr. Henry A. Kissinger Secretary of State; Joseph J.
Sisco Assistant Secretary for Near Eastern and South Asian Affairs;
Arthur W. Hummel Acting Assistant Secretary for East Asian and
Pacific Affairs; Winston Lord Director of Planning and

Coordination; Ambassador Huang Zhen Chief of PRC Liaison Office; Han Xu PRC Liaison Office; Ji Chaozhu Interpretor, PRC Liaison Office
DATE AND TIME: Thursday, October 25, 1973 4:45 P.M.–5:25 P.M.[D]

Amb Huang: You were up all night.

Secretary: Your allies tried to throw their weight around last night. I thought I would bring you up to date on what has been happening for the benefit of the Prime Minister.

First, let me tell you about the situation last night and today, and then I'll go back to the Moscow trip. First, Mr. Ambassador, our policy has been what I told you the first night. We have one principal objective, to keep the Soviet military presence out of the Middle East and to reduce the Soviet political influence as much as possible. I know you are going to disagree with these objectives violently. (Laughter.)

Amb Huang: Not necessarily.

Secretary: But we will pursue them regardless of your recommendations.

Amb Huang: I watched your entire TV press conference today.[48]

Secretary: (To Mr. Sisco.) The Prime Minister says I am the only man who can speak a half an hour without saying anything.

I was not offended by what he said, simply that he gave away my secret.

Amb Huang: You are very much interested in these words of the Prime Minister, and Qiao Guanhua also told you how the Prime Minister explained them.

Secretary: Let's go through yesterday. We received in the morning some Soviet complaints that the ceasefire was being violated. We believed them and, therefore, we brought very great pressure on Israel to stop what they were doing. But then we found out that Israel was not doing anything.[49] We also found out that the Egyptians were not doing anything, that it was a rather quiet day. All day long the complaints were getting louder and louder in a way that we couldn't do anything about.

At four o'clock I saw Dobrynin, and he discussed with me only the question of how we get the political negotiations started. At the end, we discussed what would happen at the Security Council, and he said the only instructions to their representatives were to vote for the resolution about the ceasefire. At 7:30, Dobrynin called me and said they had changed instructions now and

---

[D] Source: *PPS*, box 328, China Exchanges 10 July–31 Oct. 1973.

would vote for the resolution introduced by somebody else that the Soviet and American forces be introduced into the Middle East. We told them we would veto such a resolution. You remember we called you and recommended that you might consider vetoing, too.

At 10:15 we received a message from the Soviet Union which was very brutal in language and which, in effect, said that we should immediately agree to send a joint force with them into the Middle East, and if we didn't agree to send a joint force with them, they would send Soviet forces alone. We were not prepared to send a joint force with the Soviet Union because of the impression of condominium, because our objectives were not the same as theirs, and because we did not want to establish the principle that Soviet combat forces could be transported over long distances into foreign countries.[50]

So I called the Soviet Ambassador and told him he would get an answer later, and I called a meeting of the National Security Council. That is when we put our military forces on the alert. We moved our fleet to the eastern part of the Mediterranean and put another aircraft carrier into the western part of the Mediterranean.[51] And only after we were sure that the Soviets would have picked up all these movements did we send them a reply, in which we said we were prepared to send individual observers, but not combat personnel, only as part of the UN observer force.

But if the Soviet Union would act unilaterally, it would have the gravest consequences and would violate the principles we signed and violate Article II of the Treaty for the Prevention of Nuclear War. I know you won't like me to invoke that treaty. So we used the treaty as I told the Prime Minister we would use it. And we also told the Soviet Ambassador that we would not receive any other communication until we had replied to this one.

So at the United Nations today you know what happened. We refused to join any resolution unless it excluded permanent members from any force. So now the Soviet Union is excluded from sending a force except as part of the United Nations. About one and one-half hours ago we received a reply from the Soviets that they were sending 70 individual observers and no military contingents.

Amb Huang: That would mean that you will also send individual observers?

Secretary: Maybe, but we haven't decided yet. Our major concern was that they had alerted 7 of their 8 airborne divisions. (To Sisco.) Was it 7 out of 8 or 6 out of 7?

Sisco: I think it was 7 out of 8 but I'm not sure.[52]

Secretary: They had assembled all their air transportation to move them. We are not concerned with individual personnel in Egypt—they have been there before—but we were determined to resist introduction of combat units.

Now about our strategy. As far as the discussions in Moscow were concerned, they dealt only with the Middle East and only with the Security Council resolution. There was no other subject. I don't think their affection for you has increased in recent months, but it was not a subject they pursued. Our major concern was that, since they were defeated, not to push matters to the point where it would produce a military confrontation.

Amb Huang: Who was defeated?

Secretary: Basically, the Egyptians were defeated and, therefore, so were the Russians. We weren't asking for a ceasefire. We will now pursue the policy I discussed with the Vice Foreign Minister of strengthening our relations with Arab countries. I am considering stopping in a few Arab countries, specifically including Cairo, on the way to Beijing. And I wanted to ask you whether it might be possible for you if we entered China the way I did on my first trip through Pakistan. I thought I would go from Cairo to Teheran to Rawalpindi to see President Bhutto and go up to Beijing from there. (There was some discussion among the Chinese.) You will have to ask your government. Or maybe we could come around that area and go to Shanghai.

Amb Huang: We will report this to our government and tell you very quickly.

Secretary: Of course. We think this is an opportune moment to visit those countries and it fits in with the general views expressed by Qiao Guanhua when I last saw him.[53] And it will be in the spirit that we discussed that I would be making those stops.

This is what I wanted to inform you of and, of course, answer any questions you might have.

Amb Huang: Thank you for the information about this. We will report this immediately to Prime Minister Zhou Enlai. I would like to ask from your point of view what you estimate the developing situation in the Middle East to be.

Secretary: My honest view is that the Soviet Union has suffered a major strategic defeat, and that's why they tried to bluff us last night. For the third time now its friends have lost most of the equipment the Soviet Union gave them. Even the Arab leaders have had to learn that they can get military equipment from the Soviet Union, but if they want to make diplomatic progress, they have to deal with us.[54] And since we are not anti-Arab we will help them now make diplomatic progress. So we now have a very good position to reduce the Soviet political influence.

This is our assessment of the outcome. They will bluff us from time to time and make some threatening noises, but their nerves are not as good as their bluffs.

Amb Huang: What are the United States and the Soviet Union planning to do in the future?

Secretary: There will be formal cooperation between the Soviet Union and us to encourage negotiations. The Soviet Union will try to create the impression that they pushed us into it. But since the Soviet Union can deliver nothing, we will have our bilateral discussions with the Arabs as well. You must distinguish appearance from reality. There may be some face-saving things, but we will determine for ourselves what will be done. You know the Western concern with face.

Amb Huang: The Orientals are very much concerned with face, with self-respect.

Very honestly speaking, I would like to say that the practice of the United States and the Soviet Union that they were doing during the Security Council meetings of the 22nd and 23rd, of putting in a resolution agreed upon by themselves, but not letting other countries consult or receive instructions from their governments, is a practice we find intolerable. And Vice Minister Qiao Guanhua made that quite clear in the Security Council. At the Security Council meeting, others didn't even want him to finish his speech.

Secretary: I hope our representative didn't bring any pressure on you.

Amb Huang: But practically both the U.S. and the Soviet Union pushed the resolution in the Security Council without giving time to the other members to consult or to ask instructions from their governments.

Secretary: I agree with you. This was an exceptional circumstance in which the Egyptian forces would have been completely wiped out if the war continued another 24 hours.

Amb Huang: I don't agree with that estimate. From the very beginning our views were different on this point. The U.S. said at the very beginning that in 72 to 96 hours the Arabs would be defeated.

Secretary: I underestimated.

Amb Huang: It went on for 16 or 17 days, and as Qiao Guanhua has made very clear, it was a big victory for the Arabs. It was not the six-day war of 1967. On this point we differ. I do not wish to go further.

Secretary: We have different public assessments, but we still have to have realistic private assessments. I underestimated the length of time, but I did not underestimate the outcome.

Amb Huang: But there is a fundamental difference of assessments here. We look at the perspective of which side is just and which side is not just. Also, we consider that, while weapons are important, people who use the weapons are even more important.

You can see that the Arab peoples have, during the past several decades, suffered humiliations, ever since the British trusteeship of Palestine in 1947. And in the creation of Israel there were two states—one in Palestine and one in Israel—with the support of the big powers on the 5th of June 1948. On the second day, Israel launched attacks on the Arab states and the Arabs in the Palestinian area, about one million, were driven out homeless. And for these several decades the Palestinians and Arabs are without their homes and have to live in refugee camps; After the war in 1967, our Arab friends felt humiliated. That was why the Arab people suffered so much in the 1967 war. The Soviet Union gave them weapons, but they did not let them use them. The purpose was to control them. Under the circumstances, of course, the Arab people could not have their concerns met. Under the provocation of Israel, the Arabs fight back, as the Vice Minister made clear in his speech at the Security Council. He pointed out that the Arabs fought very heroically, and they victoriously hoisted the Egyptian flag east of the Suez. And on the Golan Heights it was not so easy for Israel; the Syrians put up a very firm struggle. Mr. [Moshe] Dayan claimed that the Israeli forces would take Damascus, but they did not. And the Palestinian Arabs, too, put up a heroic struggle. Other Arab countries and peoples participated in the battle. And the unity and strength of the people have increased. I'm not very clear on the present situation.

There is strength in the situation of the Arab people. At this or that time, there may be military setbacks, but I do not share your assessment that they have been defeated. We are firmly convinced that the side of justice will finish with victory. So long as territories are not restored and so long as the legitimate rights of the Palestinian Arabs have not been resolved there cannot be peace. Regarding what the U.S. and the Soviet Union did, I am frankly expressing my views. In the end, the Arabs will certainly be victorious.

Secretary: We are not anti-Arab. Our principal objective is to prevent Soviet influence, as I told you on the first day. We take very seriously what the Vice Minister said in New York. You will see that we will pursue a very active policy toward the Arabs. I agree with you that they have wiped out the humiliation of the past years, and they fought very heroically.

Amb Huang: I just wanted to say these things, and then I won't go on any longer. We are old friends. We have differences of view, but we are old friends. And you do know that we do sympathize with the just cause of the Arab people.

Secretary: We are not asking you to abandon this.

Amb Huang: And as we said in the past, we are not against the Jewish people; we are opposed to Zionism and Zionist aggression. That's what the Arabs say, too.

And what is more, I myself being a soldier, I don't believe the theory that weapons decide everything. Because if the weapons were more decisive, then the Chinese revolution would never have been victorious. And George Washington would never have been victorious. And many others, too.

Secretary: And Winston Lord would be deprived of all hope of taking over the State Department.[55]

Mr. Ambassador, our present plan is to leave here on the 5th or 6th of November and then go to Cairo and then into China. If you could let us know at your convenience whether we can come in via Pakistan, it would be a sentimental journey. (Laughter)

Amb Huang: I will immediately report this.

Secretary: Of course, I will be happy to go into greater detail with the Prime Minister when I am there.

(As the Chinese were moving toward the door) You will not disagree with what we did last night, Mr. Ambassador. (Laughter) I don't want you to get too nervous.

Amb Huang: We will report this immediately. I personally think that this (travel to Arab countries) would be a good idea.

(The Secretary then went over parts of the itinerary, adding Saudi Arabia as an example of another country that he might visit.)

Notes

1. See Nelson D. Lankford, *The Last American Aristocrat: The Biography of David K. E. Bruce* (Boston: Little, Brown, 1996), and Hood to Lord, 15 March 1973, Critic 1516332, National Archives, Record Group 59, U.S. Department of State Records Policy Planning Staff (Director's Files), 1969–77 (hereafter referred to as *PPS*, with archival box number and file information), box 329, China Exchanges 1 Jan. 1973–14 April 1973.

2. See Memorandum of conversation 29 March 1973, *PPS*, box 329, China Exchanges 1 Jan. 1973–14 April 1973. On 16 April, Kissinger told Ambassador Huang Hua, that "we we would like to put one man from the intelligence agency in the Liaison Office. We will identify him so you can watch him. (slight Chinese laughter) We promise he will undertake no other activity but to be a channel of communication." CIA officer James Lilley became the official at the USLO in Beijing who handled special communications. Lilley served as the U.S. Ambassador to China.

3. For a useful overview of Kissinger's transition to his new role, see Walter Isaacson, *Kissinger: A Biography* (New York: Simon and Schuster, 1992), pp. 490–510.

4. See Kissinger to the President, "My Visit to Peking," 3 March 1973; memcon, 16 April 1973, *PPS*, box 328, China Exchanges 15 April 1973–15 May 1973; and Henry Kissinger, *Years of Upheaval* (Boston: Little, Brown, 1982), p. 277. For major developments in the negotiation of the PNW agreement, see Raymond Garthoff, *Détente and Confrontation: American–Soviet Relations from Nixon to Reagan* (Washington, D.C.: Brookings Institution, 1994), pp. 376–86.

5. See William Burr and Jeffrey Richelson, "A Chinese Puzzle," *The Bulletin of the Atomic Scientists* 53 (July–Aug. 1997), pp. 42-47; "U.S. and China to See a 'Strategic Partnership,'" *Washington Post*, 30 April 1998.

6. For "unnerving," see Eagleburger to Kissinger, 18 July 1973, *PPS*, box 328, China Exchange 10 July–Oct. 31, 1973.

7. See Memcons, 27 May and 4 June 1973, box 381, PRC–Cambodia, Secretary Kissinger; Kissinger to Ambassador Bruce, 19 June 1973, box 328, China Exchange 14 June–9 July 1973.

8. See George C. Herring, *America's Longest War: The United States and Vietnam, 1950–1975*, (New York: McGraw-Hill, 1996), p. 300. According to the U.S. Strategic Bombing Survey, the Army Air Force dropped 161,425 tons of bombs on Japan proper (a total of 583,962 tons were dropped on Japanese forces elsewhere in the Pacific and mainland Asia). See United States Strategic Bombing Survey, *The Effects of Stratagic Bombing on Japan's War Economy* (Washington, D.C., Over-all Economic Effects Division, 1946), p. 35. For a useful account of the legislative politics of the Cambodian bombing halt, see Randall Bennett Woods, *Fulbright: A Biography* (Cambridge, Eng.: Cambridge University Press, 1995), pp. 632–38. For Kissinger's very defensive justification for the bombing, see his *Years of Upheaval*, pp. 347–48.

9. See Kissinger, *Years of Upheaval*, p. 339. For a measured assessment of U.S. responsibility for the Cambodian situation, see Herring, *America's Longest War*, pp. 261–62.

10. For "total humiliation" see Milton Osborne, *Sihanouk: Prince of Darkness* (Honolulu, Hi.: University of Hawaii Press, 1994), pp. 225–26, Also see Ben Kiernan, *How Pol Pot Came to Power: A History of Communism in Kampuchea, 1930–75*, pp. 360–61, 391–92; Garthoff, *Détente and Confrontation*, p. 366. See also William Bundy, *A Tangled Web: The Making of Foreign Policy in the Nixon Presidency* (New York: Hill and Wang, 1998), 391–92.

11. Bruce to Kissinger, 19 Agust 1973, PPS, box 328, China Exchanges–10 July–31 October 1973. See memcon, 25 Oct. 1973, at p. 166 of this volume.

12. For a history of the Watergate affair, see Stanley I. Kutler, *The Wars of Watergate: The Last Crisis of Richard Nixon* (New York: Knopf, 1990). For the wiretaps, see Isaacson, *Kissinger: A Biography*, pp. 497–500.

13. Seymour Hersh's article on Kissinger's role in approving wiretaps of his NSC aides and others appeared in the *New York Times* a few days later; it may have made Lord even more interested in leaving Kissinger's staff: Isaacson, *Kissinger: A Biography*, pp. 498–500. Nevertheless, Lord chose to stayed on.

14. Jonathan Howe, Peter Rodman, and Richard Soloman all worked in Kissinger's NSC staff. Solomon, a China specialist, later prepared a significant classified study on U.S.–

China negotiations that includes significant material on the Kissinger period. See Richard H. Solomon, *Chinese Political Negotiating Behavior, 1967–1984 An Interpretative Assessment*, December 1985, RAND Corporation, copy at *NSA*.

15. For some of Brezhnev's specific accusations, including cannibalism, see *Kissinger, Years of Upheaval*, p. 233.

16. For developments in the SALT II negotiations before the June 1973 summit, see Garthoff, *Detente and Confrontation* pp. 369–70.

17. From mid-May through mid-June 1973, Kissinger met in Paris with Le Duc Tho to discuss the implementation of the Paris agreement; for Kissinger's account, see his *Years of Upheaval*, pp. 327–33.

18. Kissinger may be referring to his efforts to maneuver Secretary of State William Rogers into resigning so that he himself could take control of the State Department.

19. This is a reference to proposals to restrain Chinese sales of highly competitive textile products in U.S. markets. See Briefing paper, "Economic and Trade Relations," n.d., *PPS*, box 370, Secretary Kissinger's Visit to Peking, 10 OPct. 1973, S/PC Mr. Lord.

20. After several years of effort, columnist Marquis Childs had won Beijing's approval for a visit to China; he interviewed Zhou on 20 May. For his account, see Marquis Childs, *Witness to Power* (New York: McGraw-Hill, 1975), pp. 222–40.

21. The well-known writer Bette Bao Lord, author of *Spring Moon: A Novel of China* (Boston: G. K. Hall, 1982) and *Legacies: A Chinese Mosaic* (New York: Knopf, 1990), among other books.

22. See memcon, 29 May 1973, *PPS*, box 328, China Exchanges 16 May 1973–13 June 1973.

23. See Kissinger, *Years of Upheaval*, p. 352; memcon, 4 June 1973, *PPS* box 381, PRC–Cambodia Secretary Kissinger.

24. See Peter Rodman to Kissinger, "Consultation Clause in Peking Trip Communiqué," 9 Oct. 1973, *PPS*, box 374, China–Sensitive July 73–Feb 74.

25. Among other points made in their note, the Chinese argued that the draft PNW agreement "still aims at the establishment of U.S. nuclear hegemony over the world." Further, the agreement will spread a "false sense of security" in Europe and the United States, where it "will have a demoralizing effect on efforts to strengthen defense." See Note, 27 May 1973, *PPS*, box 328, China Exchange 16 May–13 June 1973.

26. For accounts of the summit, see Kissinger, *Years of Upheaval*, pp. 286–300; Nixon, *RN: The Memoirs of Richard Nixon* (New York: Grosset and Dunlap, 1978), pp. 877–86; and Garthoff, *Détente and Confrontation*, pp. 360–403.

27. See David Bruce to Henry Kissinger, Beijing 005, "Meeting with Zhou Enlai," 26 June 1973, *PPS*, box 328, China Exchanges 14 June–9 July 1973.

28. See Richard Solomon to Kissinger, "The Current State of U.S.–PRC Relations: Parallelism in International Affairs; Shaky Bilateral Ties," 31 Dec. 1973, *PPS*, box 330, China Exchanges 1 Nov. 1973–21 March 1974. For Zhou's suspicions, see Dick Wilson, *Chou: The Story of Zhou Enlai, 1989–1976* (New York: Viking, 1984), p. 285.

29. See Kissinger to Dick Kennedy, 28 June 1973, *PPS*, box 328, China Exchanges 14 June–9 July 1973.

30. For Kissinger's account of the bombing halt, see his *Years of Upheaval*, pp. 355–61. For the legislative politics, see Woods, *Fulbright*, pp. 632–38.

31. Anatoly Dobrynin, *In Confidence: Moscow's Ambassador to America's Six Cold War Presidents, 1962–1986* (New York: Times Books, 1995), p. 277.

32. Besides Danny Kaye, others scheduled to attend the dinner included Rosalind Russell, Bob Hope, Kirk Douglas, Gary Grant, Irving "Swifty" Lazar, Billy Wilder, *Los Angeles Times* publisher Otis Chandler, and MCA president Sidney Sheinberg. See Memcon, 4 July 1973,

33. On 18 May, Zhou told Bruce that their governments shared the goal of a "peaceful, neutral, and independent Cambodia" where the Democratic Republic of Vietnam had no bases. See Kissinger, *Years of Upheaval*, p. 351.

34. Senator Warren Magnuson (D–Or.) had recently led a congressional delegation to China. During a meeting with Zhou, Magnuson had reportedly upset the premier by focusing the discussion on Cambodia and congressional plans to halt the bombing and refusing to move on to other subjects. According to one account, "By the end of the session Chou was visibily angered at both the content of the discussion and the fact that he had been put in the position of appearing to play Congress against the White House." When asked by Magnuson when he would visit the United States, "Chou snapped back with asperity, 'Frankly, I must tell you that I cannot come because Chiang Kai-shek has a representative there." See Richard H. Solomon to Kissinger, "The U.S. Congressional Delegation's Tour of China: It Might Have Been Worse," 18 July 1973, *PPS*, box 328, 10 July–31 Oct. 1973.

35. For Kissinger's published account of Brezhnev's efforts to spark talks on China, see *Years of Upheaval*, pp. 394–95.

36. "Existing regulations" is a reference to the Paris-based Coordinating Commmittee, (COCOM), where U.S., Japan, and European allies met routinely to discuss problems involving the export of sensitive goods to the Soviet bloc and the PRC. In this instance, the Chinese wanted to purchase Rolls-Royce Spey aircraft engines. Recognizing that COCOM would not approve the transaction, the British had informed Kissinger that they were going ahead anyway and asked for his assent. The British and the Chinese completed an agreement for the sale in December 1975. Robert S. Ross, *Negotiating Cooperation: The United States and China, 1969–1989* (Stanford, Calif.: Stanford University Press, 1995). p. 89.

37. This is a reference to the Chinese note critiquing the PNW Agreement. See Note, 27 May 1973, *PPS*, box 328, China Exchange 16 May–13 June 1973.

38. Established by General Douglas MacArthur on 24 July 1950, the United Nations Command [UNC] was the means for U.S. direction of military forces that UN members committed to the Korean War. The UN established the commission for the Unification and Rehabilitation of Korea [UNCURK] on 7 October 1950 a few days after U.S. and allies forces invaded North Korea. James F. Schnabel, *United States Army in the Korean War, Policy and Direction: The First Year* (Washington, D.C., Office of the Chief of Military History United States Army, 1972), pp. 103, 194. During 1973, the North Koreans, with Chinese support, were pressing the United Nations to dissolve both the UN Command and UNCURK as well as to force the withdrawal of U.S. forces from South Korea. While the United States was flexible on UNCURK, it opposed troop withdrawals and abrupt action on the UNC because of its role in enforcing post-Korean War armistice arrangements. See Department of State Briefing Paper, "Korea," n.d., *PPS*, box 370, Secretray Kissinger's Visit to Peking October 1973.

39. See Kissinger Memorandum for the President's File, "Meeting with Ambassador Huang Zhen, Head of the PRC Liaison Office in Washington, Friday, July 6, 1973, 11:30 a.m.," *PPS*, box 329, China Exchanges 14 June–9 July 1973.

40. For the course of the Watergate investigation during the summer of 1973, see Kutler, *Wars of Watergate*, pp. 350–82. For "resist," *Public Papers of the President of the United States Richard Nixon, 1973* (Washington, D.C.: Government Printing Office, 1974), p. 637.

41. Note, 18 July 1973, *PPS*, box 328, China Exchanges 10 July–31 Oct. 31, 1973.
    See Bruce to Kissinger, 23 July 1973, Peking 023, *PPS*, box 328, China Exchanges 10 July–31 Oct. 1973. But see also Solomon to Kissinger, "Mao and Chou Under Pressure? Some Recent Pieces in the Chinese Puzzle," 24 July 1973, *PPS*, box 328, China Exchanges 10 July–31 Oct. 1973.

42. See Kissinger, *Years of Upheaval*, p. 366.

43. See Solomon to Kissinger, "PRC Order to Remove Marine Guards from USLO," and "Your Meeting with PRC Liaison Chief Huang Chen . . . ," 26 and 28 Sept. 1973 respectively, both in *PPS*, box 328, Chinese Exchanges 10 July–31 Oct. 1973. For the Marine's social role, see John H. Holdridge, *Crossing the Divide: An Insider's Account of Normalization of U.S. - China Relations* (Lanham, Md.: Rowman and Littlefield, 1997), pp. 124–26. "Red Ass" was in honor of the Navy Sea Bees ("red ass engineers") who set up the USLO offices.

44. See memcon, 29 Sept. 1973, *PPS*, box 328, China Exchanges 10 July–31 Oct. 1973. For important accounts of the October War and its diplomatic context, see Victory Israelyan, *Inside the Kremlin During the Yom Kippur War* (University Park: Pennsylvania State University Press, 1995); William B. Quandt, *Peace Process: American Diplomacy and the Arab-Israel Conflict Since 1967* (Washington.: Brookings Institution, 1993), pp. 148–82; Garthoff, *Détente and Confrontation*, pp. 404–57; and Janice Gross Stein and Richard Ned Lebow, *We All Lost the Cold War* (Princeton, N.J.: Princeton University Press, 1995).

45. See memcons, 6, 15, and 19 Oct. 1973, *PPS*, box 348, China Exchanges 1 July–31 Oct. 1973.

46. See Garthoff, *Détente and Confrontation*, pp. 423, 430–31. See also Israelyan's account in *Inside the Kremlin*, pp. 165–70, 190–95.

47. *On Saturday evening, 20 October, Nixon* had Special Prosecutor Archibald Cox, Attorney General Eliot Richardson, and Deputy Attorney General William Ruckelshaus fired. For the impact of Watergate and Nixon's drunken condition, see *Garthoff, Détente and Confrontation, pp. 425–26, note 78, and* Stein and Lebow, *We All Lost the Cold War*, pp. 247, 480–81. For Kissinger's strategy in calling an alert, see Garthoff, ibid., pp. 430–33.

48. In his press conference, Kissinger emphasized the U.S. and Soviet "special responsibility" to avoid armed confrontation and his opposition to the "unilateral introduction by any great power, especially by any nuclear power, of military forces into the Middle East." See Kissinger, *Years of Upheaval*, pp. 594–95

49. The Israelis were doing nothing, that is, other than sustaining their encirclement of Egypt's Third Army and seizing the Egyptian naval base at Suez. See Garthoff, *Détente and Confrontation*, pp. 421–22.

50. For Kissinger's account of Brezhnev's message and the subsequent U.S. alert, see his *Years of Upheaval*, pp. 583-91. For discussions of Brezhnev's message, see Garthoff, *Détente and Confrontation*, pp. 423-33; Stein and Lebow, *We All Lost the Cold War*, and Quandt, *Peace Process*, pp. 173-74. Apparently, Brezhnev put in the sentence about unilateral action only to prod Washington into accepting a joint force; he had no intention of following it up. See Garthoff, *Détente and Confrontation*, p. 428.

51. Kissinger signicantly understates the alert's scope. Besides naval actions, the National Security Council put Strategic Air Command and North American Air Defense Command nuclear forces on a higher state of alert. See Garthoff, *Détente and Confrontation*, p. 427. For more on the alert and its context, see Lebow and Stein, *We All Lost the Cold War*, pp. 246-51.

52. The Soviet army's airborne troops had seven divisions of somewhat less than 8,000 soldiers each. Their alert status had nothing to do with Brezhnev's letter; the Soviet Defense Ministry had initiated it earlier in the war, on 10 October, as a normal contingency measure. Israelyan, *Inside the Kremlin*, pp. 190-93; and Garthoff, *Détente and Confrontation*, p. 424.

53. This is a reference to Kissinger's meeting with Qiao in New York earlier in the fall; see Kissinger, *Years of Upheaval*, pp. 681-82

54. In other words, given the strength of U.S. ties with Israel, only the United States would have the political leverage needed to help the Arabs regain lost territory. See Quandt, *Peace Process*, p. 179.

55. The inspiration for this wisecrack is obscure. However, in his new capacity as Director of Planning and Coordination (eentually changed to Director, Policy Planning Staff), Lord had important responsibilities such as reviewing key telegrams to ensure that they conformed with policy. Kissinger may have jokingly equated that assignment with "taking over the State Department." Kissinger, *Years of Upheaval*, p. 441

4

In Search of Strategic Alliance:

Kissinger in Beijing, November 1973

Henry Kissinger made his first appearance in Beijing as secretary of state on 10 November 1973 when he arrived for long-delayed talks with Zhou and Mao—his sixth trip to Beijing in a little over two years. No senior Chinese official other than Ambassador Huang Zhen had met—or would meet—with Nixon or Kissinger in Washington as long as Taiwan had a diplomatic presence there. Kissinger certainly had good reason to meet with Mao and Zhou, but they must have taken great satisfaction in the fact that he had to come to them, much as in the past, foreign diplomats from "barbarian" states had to "pay obeisance and deliver tribute" to China's imperial throne.[1]

The coolness that PRC officials had shown after the June 1973 summit and the discord over Cambodia made reassurances to Mao and Zhou a major task for Kissinger during his visit. Recognizing further that the Chinese were concerned about Watergate and its implications for the continuity of U.S.–PRC relations, Kissinger labored to reassure the leadership that China remained critically important to the United States, that Washington was determined to "constrain" Moscow in the Middle East, and that normalization was on track, despite glitches concerning Taiwan. Moreover, to bolster the relationship, Kissinger held secret talks with Zhou over ways and means to provide indirect access to U.S. strategic warning systems so that Beijing could improve its defenses against the Soviet Union. After the talks ended, Kissinger believed that they had gone successfully; he reported to Nixon that the atmosphere was "cordial" and that the discussions showed a "deeping of the close identity between you and the Chinese leaders' strategic perspectives on the international situation."[2]

However, while Kissinger's power was ascending, Zhou Enlai's position was deteriorating. In 1972, doctors had discovered that he had stomach cancer; though he stayed active throughout 1973, to those in the know—which did not yet include Henry Kissinger—Zhou's future was plainly uncertain. Much remains to be learned about political developments during this period. Mao and Zhou saw eye to eye on the opening to Washington, but apparently

Zhou's opposition to the ultra-Left caused him to lose favor with Mao, who still retained his regal authority. Party radicals targeted the Premier indirectly in an anti-Confucian campaign they unleashed with Mao's blessings, which put Zhou on the defensive, forcing him to spend much time deflecting newspaper attacks. By November, Kissinger perceived the change in Zhou's status; he reported to Nixon that "his role was considerably more subordinate to Mao's."[3]

However much Zhou's status may have been diminishing, Kissinger's memoir account in *Years of Upheaval* may have gone too far in characterizing him as more or less "passive" during the talks.[4] "Passive" does not describe Zhou's request that Kissinger "exercise some influence" over the military junta that had overthrown Salvadore Allende's Socialist government in Chile on 11 September, "or his remark that "[t]hey shouldn't go in for slaughtering that way. It was terrible." Zhou was was faintly assertive on 12 November when he pointed out to a chagrined Kissinger that a U.S. Navy cruiser, the USS *Oklahoma City*, had just "intruded" by sailing through the Taiwan Straits about 25 kilometers from the mainland. Kissinger could only admit "that there is no defense against stupidity."

Apart from such contretemps, Kissinger had reason to be happy about his dialogue with Mao and Zhou. Unlike earlier in the year, criticism, suspicious comments about U.S.-Soviet relations were a minor theme in the talks.[5] Moreover, Mao and Zhou, unlike Ambassador Huang Zheng, appreciated Kissinger's strategy. As Mao explained to Kissinger, "[O]ur Ambassador . . . mentioned this support of the Arab world, but he didn't understand the importance of U.S. resistance to the Soviet Union." Zhou's view was consistent with this: not only did he give explicit support for the military alert, but he applauded Kissinger's efforts to exclude the Soviet Union from bilateral negotiations such as the cease-fire agreement. Most likely this meeting of minds was central to Kissinger's conclusion about a "deepening of the close identity" between U.S. and Chinese "strategic perspectives."[6]

Although Kissinger's memoirs gives a reasonably full account of the exchanges on foreign policy issues, nowhere does he mention his extraordinary initiative to strengthen strategic links and possibly to counter Beijing's annoyance about the U.S.-Soviet summit. Soon after he arrived, he made a proposal that, had the Soviets learned of it, would have disrupted détente, possibly in disastrous ways. In keeping with his exaggerated assessment of a Soviet military threat to China, Kissinger proposed secret U.S.-China military cooperation, "ideas on how to lessen the vulnerability of your forces and how to increase the warning time" of a Soviet attack—exactly what the Soviets had warned against months before. Zhou, who at the last Party Congress had stressed the need for preparations against surprise attack, was plainly interested in the proposal; he met with Kissinger several times to discuss a possible hotline as a means to provide strategic intelligence information. However, the Chinese did not respond to Kissinger's offer; it was not until 1998 that they would sign a hot line agreement with the United States.[7]

U.S.–Taiwan relations elicited some questions from Zhou, but not enough to cause Kissinger to worry. Zhou questioned the State Department's approval of more consulates for Taiwan—a decision that Kissinger later admitted was a "bureaucratic goof"—as well as the decisions to supply Taiwan with capability to produce its own fighter jets. Overall, though, he did not press for a rapid solution of the Taiwan problem, because China already had Nixon's pledge to normalize U.S.–PRC relations in 1976. As Mao said, the Taiwanese "were a bunch of counterrevolutionaries," and Beijing could "do without Taiwan for the time being."

For Kissinger, the communiqué issued as his visit closed gave further grounds for a relaxed approach to U.S.–Taiwan relations. Noting the importance of expanding trade and other contacts, it emphasized that the normalization of relations could be "realized only on the basis of confirming the principle of one China." Some ambiguous remarks by Zhou inspired Kissinger's hope that Beijing might allow the U.S.–PRC relationship to develop despite the fact that Washington continued to maintain a "substantial relationship" with Taiwan; the condition, he thought, was that the United States must pay lip service, through a "nominal juridical framework," to the principle of one China. The implication was that even if Washington and Beijing did not formally exchange ambassadors, the United States could continue to enjoy political and military relations with Taiwan while U.S.–China political and economic relations would deepen.[8]

If Kissinger believed that he could drink his Taiwanese and Chinese "mao tai" more or less simultaneously, he was mistaken. As he would learn over 1974 and 1975, even if the Chinese said there was no rush to normalize, they would take no steps to upgrade relations unless Washington severed political ties with Taiwan. For Beijing, true recognition of the one-China principle required more than a "nominal juridical framework."

During his visit, Kissinger had tried to resolve some bilateral issues, such as the blocked assets and claims problems, and was optimistic that they would be resolved "in about a month" (it took almost six years).[9] His greater concern, however, was the outlook for post-Zhou, post-Mao China; as less familiar figures took leadership roles, he said, "we have no assurance that the PRC will continue its present policy toward us."[10] Moreover, U.S. politics, Watergate in particular, were starting to impinge on the relationship. Kissinger reported that while Mao made light of it, the Chinese were worried about congressional attacks on Nixon; in particular, they were "wary of our domestic and Congressional mood which they see potentially leading to American disengagement from the world." However valid Beijing's concerns about prospective U.S. isolation were, Zhou's assessment of a central problem that had precipitated the U.S.'s foreign policy debate was acute. As he told Kissinger, "Your government had overstretched itself."

Kissinger arrived on 10 November, and the Chinese hosted a banquet in his honor that evening. The short meeting he held with Zhou and Marshal Ye Jianying is not even hinted at in the memoirs. The record of the discussion exemplifies the system of control Kissinger used to ensure that only officials with a "need to know" learned about the most sensitive discussions: shortly after the visit, Winston Lord prepared a collection of transcripts for limited distribution among the State Department's East Asian specialists, but he did not include a copy of it. A copy did, however, end up in Lord's files.[11]

Kissinger briefed the two Chinese leaders in very general terms, on the substance of anti-Chinese proposals the Soviets had made earlier in the year. He suggested that Washington could provide the Chinese with information that would reduce their exposure to a possible Soviet attack on their military forces. Noting that he had already commissioned special studies on this problem, he offered to share the findings.[12]

Prior to this meeting, Arms Control and Disarmament Agency Director Fred Iklé sent Kissinger a brief report on possible areas of strategic intelligence cooperation with the Chinese. Iklé asserted that U.S. intelligence on Soviet forces was better than China's, and Washington might be able to detect Soviet preparations "hours before the Chinese could." Iklé had suggested that a hotline arrangement for providing strategic warning information would be the best way to strengthen China's nuclear forces without enhancing their "capability against us." Washington, he said, could make high-resolution photos from Skylab available to the Chinese in order to "improve their current target information of the USSR," thus increasing their forces' effectiveness.[13] Kissinger may already have been thinking along similar lines, but the drift of the ACDA paper is extremely close to the proposals he actually made to Zhou.

THE WHITE HOUSE
TOP SECRET/SENSITIVE/EXCLUSIVELY EYES ONLY
MEMORANDUM OF CONVERSATION
Participants: Prime Minister Zhou Enlai; Ye Jianying, Chairman of the
    Military Affairs Committee; Vice Prime [*sic*] Minister Qiao
    Guanhua; Tang Wensheng, Interpreter Shen Zouyun, Interpreter;
    Henry A. Kissinger, Secretary of State; Winston Lord, Director of
    Planning and Coordination, State Department
DATE AND TIME: Saturday, November 10, 1973, 9:25 P.M.–10:00 P.M.
PLACE: Great Hall of the People, Beijing, Peoples Republic of China[A]

(As the group was walking toward the meeting room, Marshal Ye indicated to
the Secretary that he now had heavier burdens as Secretary of State. The
Secretary replied that it was more complicated, but the direction of policy
was the same. There had been major personnel changes.)

[Kissinger briefs Zhou along much the same lines as the reports he had given Ambas-
sador Huang Zhen regarding Brezhnev's overtures on China and Chinese nuclear
capabilities during U.S.–Soviet meetings in May and June 1973 (see chapter 2).]

Secretary Kissinger: . . . Since then, the Soviet Union has tried on three or
four occasions to exchange information on China with us by putting it in the
context of a discussion on strategic nuclear limitations. The way they do it is
to say they should be entitled to have equality with the United States, and, in
addition to this equality, enough weapons to destroy China. And those
weapons must increase each year because of the Chinese situation.

I tell you this, Mr. Prime Minister, not out of altruism, but because I believe
the destruction of China by the Soviet Union, or even a massive attack on
China by the Soviet Union, would have unforeseeable consequences for the
entire international situation. (The interpreter indicated that there was not
total understanding of this point.) I don't tell this out of abstract altruism
because I believe it is in our interest to prevent such an attack. You know as
well as I do, Mr. Prime Minister, the consequences on Japan, Europe, South
Asia, and the Middle East if such an attack even had the appearance of success.

Before these conversations, I believe the Soviets had a generalized hostil-

---

[A] Source: National Archives, Record Group 59 (hereafter referred to as *PPS* with archival box number and file
information), Department of State Records, Policy Planning Staff (Director's Files), 1969–77 box 380, Lord
China File Exclusively Eyes Only.

ity toward China, but I did not believe they had a specific plan. You may have had another idea. I do not now exclude the possibility of some specific ideas.

Now, as a result of these conversations, I ordered some studies in our government that only four or five people know about, of what we know about what such a threat could be, and what from our knowledge could be done to prevent it, and of what help we could be in ways that are not obvious, because I don't think a formal relationship is desirable for either of us. These would be of a technical nature. I don't have those papers with me here now, but I have them in my guest house. We have some ideas on how to lessen the vulnerability of your forces and how to increase the warning time, and I repeat that it has to be done in such a way that it is very secret and not obvious.

If the Prime Minister is interested, I can have Commander Howe, or in some respects I could mention the details in a small group — either to the Prime Minister or someone he designates. This is not something that involves reciprocity or any formal relationship, but advice based on our experience and some regularized intelligence information. (The interpreter questions the meaning of "regularized.") "Regularized intelligence information" means the regularized information from us to you, not the other way.

Apart from that, I thought it might be of some importance to you to know the state of mind of Brezhnev as stated to us. As far as we are concerned, we don't believe we can permit this, though it is a very difficult problem how to work out in practice.

Prime Minister Zhou: During your recent short visit, it was probably not raised again.

Secretary Kissinger: No, he raised it again. He raised the question of exchanging military information again.

Prime Minister Zhou: They have satellites that can survey China every day.

Secretary Kissinger: I know .

Prime Minister Zhou: And they still want it?

Secretary Kissinger: Our belief is their photography is not as good as ours. But I think what they want is an indication from us that they would use as a symbol of cooperation rather than using it. They want us to accept the desirability of destroying China's nuclear capability or limiting rather than the information itself. But the exchange of information is not a big problem, as that obviously we won't do, and they probably have what they need.

Prime Minister Zhou: Even though the Middle East was so tense, they still discuss such an issue?

Secretary Kissinger: When I was there it was during the ceasefire discussion.

Prime Minister Zhou: It was before our alert. You went originally for the ceasefire.

Secretary Kissinger: Yes.

Prime Minister Zhou: They invited you?

Secretary Kissinger: At that time there was no question of military pressure on us. The military pressure started four days later, and since then, they have not raised it.

Prime Minister Zhou: It was only mentioned during the visit.

Secretary Kissinger: During my visit and not since then.

Prime Minister Zhou: I believe they would suggest such matters to Japan, too.

Secretary Kissinger: It is conceivable. In any event, even if they don't, if they started on this course, it is in my judgment not clear what Japan will do. We have not heard that they have proposed anything like this to Japan.

Prime Minister Zhou: They always wanted to get Japan brought closer to them and away from us. They know they can't severe relations completely between you and Japan, but at least they want to get Japan closer to them than to you.

Secretary Kissinger: Yes

Prime Minister Zhou: We have also said to Japan that if they want to exploit Siberia, it is better to be done with you than alone. I believe Prime Minister [Kakuei] Tanaka will tell you that when he meets you.

Secretary Kissinger: That is our view, too.

Prime Minister Zhou: I told them that if they do, it is better to do it with the United States. We said we do not fear their exploiting Siberian resources. The only thing is that we are afraid that they might be taken in.

Have you found some difficulties within the Soviet leadership at present, among the three or four of them?

Secretary Kissinger: No, because we always deal with Brezhnev.

Prime Minister Zhou: Yes, he monopolizes the scene.

Secretary Kissinger: At first we always dealt with Kosygin or Podgorny and Brezhnev. Gromyko is a functionary and not a leader.

Prime Minister Zhou: Suslov doesn't take part in the negotiations.

Secretary Kissinger: Only once when the President was in Moscow. We have no special information on that. Our people think he's more ideological and less bureaucratic than the others. He's ideological and less bureaucratic than the others, but I don't know how we would know that.

Prime Minister Zhou: He knows historical theory, but he follows the other line of thinking. He explains other peoples' theories. The Soviet party history has been changed three times, and all three times under his guidance.

Secretary Kissinger: That I didn't know. I knew it had changed three times; I didn't know he did it.

Prime Minister Zhou: He is the one who finalized the draft, so he is that kind of author who follows the others.

Secretary Kissinger: There is no outstanding intellectual leader in the Soviet Union.

Prime Minister Zhou: No. [T]hey don't have any. It is impossible to have any, because they are so oppressive.

Thank you anyway for your information and for your notification. Anyway, Ambassador Huang Zhen has passed on what you have told him, and we have taken note of that. At present, though they are quite busy on day-to-day policies and other matters, they have to curse us everyday in the newspapers anyway. There are some people here in our party who read and study the materials, but we don't have the time to go through them all.

[Kissinger and Zhou then agree to begin their talks with a small group meeting of five or six participants. Kissinger reminds Zhou that if Marshal Ye wants to see the special intelligence studies, either Lord or Howe will provide them.]

COMMENTARY

The following afternoon, Kissinger and Zhou meet for a longer discussion; Kissinger provides a lengthy tour d'horizon on U.S.–China relations and U.S. foreign relations.[14] In his memoirs, Kissinger describes himself as dominating the conversation: he shares with Zhou his thinking on the Middle East, Western Europe, Southeast Asia, and other areas. What he does not mention in his memoirs, however, is his litany of assurances concerning Taiwan (mostly a restatement of secret pledges that Nixon had made in 1972), or his exposition of the U.S. plans to withdraw nuclear and other military forces, including U-2 aircraft, from the island.

His assurances on Taiwan are more or less boilerplate. Zhou, however, is interested in why Washington is allowing Taiwan to establish new consulates, and in the U.S.–Taiwan agreement to provide capabilities to produce F-5E fighter jets. Kissinger will provide more information on the jets and more assurances that Taiwan will not be able to strike the PRC with them. In explaining the Taiwanese consulates, Kissinger adroitly claims that Taipei's efforts to establish more regional offices was a "reflection of the reduction of their position in the United States, not an attempt to increase it."[15]

The following excerpts from the Kissinger-Zhou discussion during the afternoon of 11 November disclose what else he left out of his memoir account: discussion of Japan and U.S.-Soviet economic détente as well as comments that were critical of West German policy. The Soviets would have been dismayed by his observation that his economic détente strategy was more a question of "promises" than of actually making a difference for Soviet economic strength. Kissinger may have made that statement simply to allay Chinese concerns about U.S. policy, but if he was in earnest, his skeptical view of U.S.-Soviet economic relations helps explain why the Nixon and Ford administration's elaborate efforts at economic détente made so little progress.

Secretary Kissinger: My views on Japan are that what we discussed last February are [*sic*] still true—that Japan is at a crucial point and necessity will drive it to decide between a more traditional nationalism and maintaining its present orientation. And it has many temptations. It is very much affected by the Middle East oil situation.

Prime Minister Zhou: I believe about 80 percent of its oil comes from the Middle East.

Ambassador Ingersoll: Eighty-five percent I would say; that is only about 40 percent from the Arab countries and 45 percent from Iran.

Prime Minister Zhou: Yes.

Secretary Kissinger: It has temptations from the Soviet Union. It has temptations by its own economic strengths. And it is concerned that it will be left alone in any arrangement that we make with the Europeans. This is one reason why we may try to find a formula to associate Japan with our efforts in Europe. The intention is not to link it militarily with Europe but primarily psychologically, to prevent a total sense of isolation.

Prime Minister Zhou: And have you expressed support or are you waiting to see the outcome of events with regard to your joint exploration of Siberia?[16]

Secretary Kissinger: One problem is that no one knows exactly how much natural gas there is. There is some dispute between what the Soviets have told us and what some experts have said.

We have just authorized a loan which will be a joint American/Japanese exploration in Siberia to get a precise determination of what is involved. We have agreed in principle to make it a joint project with the Japanese. And we believe, for political reasons, it would be undesirable to have the Japanese so completely dependent on Soviet political decisions. And the Soviet Union will probably be more reluctant to tackle both the United States and Japan simultaneously than Japan alone. We have a problem in our Congress whether we can get any support for these long-term investments in the Soviet Union And that will not be decided until the early part of next year.

Prime Minister Zhou: Their salesmen don't seem to be very effective.

Secretary Kissinger: Soviet salesmen?

Prime Minister Zhou: That is the impression we received both from West Germany, Japan and from you. Is the data and the material of the salesmen credible?

Secretary Kissinger: There are some questions in our mind about the reliability of these figures. The second question we have is to what degree we want to commit massive American investments in the Soviet Union. Our strategy up to now, quite candidly, has been to do enough to give the promise of future investments but not so much as to make a strategic difference in their situation.

Prime Minister Zhou: That is a very complicated strategy.

Secretary Kissinger: That is true.

Prime Minister Zhou: Ambassador Ingersoll will be, of course, very familiar with the lesson that General Secretary Brezhnev taught Prime Minister Tanaka. He brought out his map and began his lectures.

Secretary Kissinger: He has only one lecture. And I have heard it ten times.

Prime Minister Zhou: He came at the same time when Brezhnev went to visit Bonn.

Secretary Kissinger: It is dangerous to underestimate German shortsightedness. My apologies to the Vice Minister.[17]

Prime Minister Zhou: Perhaps you say that out of your unhappiness with the present Brandt Government.

Secretary Kissinger: That too, but it is a historical phenomenon. The Germans have had only one leader of stature — that was Adenauer[18] . . .

Prime Minister Zhou: Yes, because he had been active.

Secretary Kissinger: Who, Adenauer?

Prime Minister Zhou: Adenauer.

Secretary Kissinger: He knew the importance of it, but he never let himself be deflected. While Brandt, if he persists in his present policy, will have given the Soviet Union veto over German policy.

Prime Minister Zhou: There is such a danger. And the opposition party did not carry out the elections very well either.

Secretary Kissinger: No. They had very incompetent leadership. You met their best man but he is not very energetic, Schroeder. He is their best man.

[If Zhou met with Kissinger Sunday evening, the record of discussion is not available, they do, however, hold a lengthy talk on Monday afternoon, before Mao summoned them.[19] After Kissinger tries to mitigate Zhou's concerns about future Taiwanese jet production, they circle around the thorny problem of how to advance U.S.-China relations while Washington maintains an embassy in Taiwan. Zhou wants to see some development, but as Kissinger acknowledges, Washington is not yet ready to do what Japan had done to normalize relations, that is, break off formal diplomatic and military relations. If the United States and China were to establish diplomatic relations ahead of the 1976 schedule, something more "flexible" than the Japan formula is needed; he suggests a plan that would reaffirm the Shanghai Communiqué principle of "one China" while allowing Washington to "maintain relations" with Taiwan.

Zhou seems to be amenable to Kissinger's suggestion and that evening they seek to formulate as they pull the communiqué together. They also begin to probe the bilateral and international problems Kissinger had raised the day before, as well as the complex private claims and assets issue. In the following excerpt from the Monday afternoon discussion, Zhou's questions about the prospects for a Middle East settlement segue in out and out of a discussion of the Vietnam War. Zhou rightly emphasizes the difficulties of the Middle East situation; Kissinger is overconfident that he can reach a settlement.]

Prime Minister Zhou: . . . I hope that in this case you would not spend such a long time as four and a half years as you settled the Vietnam question.

Secretary Kissinger: No. It is a different problem. We were directly involved in Vietnam.

Prime Minister Zhou: The direct involvement, of course, is one of the reasons, but that was left over. It was left over by your predecessor. But you yourself had made some mistakes. Perhaps you would not agree to what I say. I would not say it very straightforwardly because we understand this possibility. It is inevitable that human beings will make mistakes.

Secretary Kissinger: We may have. I think if the North Vietnamese had proposed the settlement that we achieved in the end in the first year we would have accepted it at any point. Our difficulty was that the North Vietnamese always asked us to overthrow a friendly government and that we could not do.[20] That was the one thing I have always told you, Mr. Prime Minister, that it was a point of honor with us.

Prime Minister Zhou: This question again is left over historically. The responsibility should not remain entirely on your present Administration.

Secretary Kissinger: This problem is easier from one point of view and more difficult from another. It is easier because no one is asking us to destroy a friendly government. But now all parties accept the existence of Israel which is essential for us too.

Prime Minister Zhou: I think that it would not be so quick that all parties would recognize the existence of Israel.

Secretary Kissinger: All parties to which I have talked accept the existence of Israel.

Prime Minister Zhou: But the party with which you have discussions, the number is not so big. You think so. It is not so easy. While the fighting was going on, there was an ill wind of break in diplomatic relations with Israel on the part of African countries. This was part of a just voice on the part of the Africans, and you cannot say they are not correct. Because you cannot expect everyone to be like us who have combined principles with realities. We objected to the establishment of Israel to start with. Now the population of Israel has reached 2.5 million and as we know perhaps reached 3 million—can you drive them to the sea? No. So when your press people ask me about it, I answer them, "of course not." I ask them how can there be any strength in things like that in the world. That is why one is bound to find some way to settle this question. Would that be a reason to have the Palestinians driven out? This question should also be settled.

Secretary Kissinger: I agree this question should be handled.

Prime Minister Zhou: It would not be fair if this question would not be settled at the same time. Only when these two questions are settled can there be any co-existence, and a peace to be spoken of. Otherwise, there would be no co-existence. This is why that we agree to your having direct dealings with the Arab States. This is just a first step. But I think, although the first step has been taken, the journey will be even longer than the journey you traveled when you first came to China to prepare for the visit of President Nixon. Because it only took half a year for your President to come for a visit to China.

Secretary Kissinger: I think it will take more than a half a year but not half a year to show progress. We can show progress in less than half a year.[21]

Prime Minister Zhou: There might be some progress, but it is not so easy to settle the question because it is very complex.

[The exchange over the Middle East turns to the energy crisis and from there to nuclear arms control issues and then to the question of Soviet "expansionism." Rather than dwell on the implications of a nuclear Japan, Zhou and Kissinger shift to arms control problems and their mutual interest in containing Soviet foreign policy ambitions. Kissinger is confident that the West could check any military or political moves, in part because Soviet policy is "not very intelligent." However, he explains, the "West Euro-

peans are the weakest link in terms of their understanding," so he must find ways to outmaneuver both them and the Soviets. Thus, Washington has to "keep slightly to the left of the Europeans" on détente policy so European countries will not make separate deals with Moscow. Conceding Zhou's point that the "people might not comprehend" U.S. strategy, Kissinger suggests that the danger can be reduced if Washington deprived the Soviets of "symbolic successes" by bogging them down in negotiations.[22]

Before they go to see Chairman Mao, Zhou engages Kissinger in a brief exchange on the problem of imperial overstretch. While discussing "isolationist" currents in the opposition to Nixon, Zhou observes that it is not only the Democrats who want to change the U.S. international role: the Nixon administration itself has "contracted a bit, retracted a bit" in order to focus on the "main questions." Even so, the Soviets, after spending "a lot of money and a lot of energy," remain a formidable power. Acknowledging that the United States has overstretched, Kissinger provides a sketchy explanation: "It was partly inexperience and partly the weakness of every other country."

Zhou cuts the discussion short by announcing that it is time to meet with Mao and then stuns Kissinger with a delicate announcement: a few hours earlier, the U.S. Navy guided-missile cruiser, the USS Oklahoma City, *had sailed through the Taiwan Straits uncomfortably close to the mainland. Kissinger can only fume that "it should not happen at anytime this close, and it should not happen while I am in China under any circumstances."]*

COMMENTARY

After a short drive, Kissinger and Zhou arrived at Mao's residence for what turns out to be nearly a three-hour meeting, apparently the longest talk that Mao held with a foreigner for some time. Mao has largely recovered from his illness of nearly two years earlier (he is not yet seriously encumbered by the Parkinson's disease that would soon disable him). Kissinger later reported to Nixon that the Chairman "looked much healthier and thinner than last February when in turn he looked much better than during your trip." Thus, "he moved and walked unaided and used his hands continuously and expressively as he talked in his slow, low, gravelly tones."[23]

In *Years of Upheaval*, Kissinger provides a vivid description of his third encounter with Mao, noting his "mocking, slightly demonic smile," his dominance of the Chinese side, and Zhou's deference; he also remarks on Mao's exceptional conduct of the talks, which David Bruce described as "the most extraordinary and disciplined presentation he had ever heard from a statesman."[24]

Kissinger's summary brings across some of the major points covered in his talk with Mao, but he hardly does justice to the variety of issues that they addressed. His account also sidesteps a central theme in the discussion—the "realistic possibility" that the Soviets could attack China because "above all [they] want to destroy your nuclear capability." Although Mao laughs this off—he compares China's nuclear forces to a "fly of this size"—Kissinger maintains that "if this eventuality were to happen, it would have very serious consequences for everybody." Consistent with this line of thought, an important part of the discussion that follows is about how to deter such an attack.

THE WHITE HOUSE
TOP SECRET/SENSITIVE/EXCLUSIVELY EYES ONLY
MEMORANDUM OF CONVERSATION
PARTICIPANTS: Chairman Mao Zedong; Prime Minister Zhou Enlai;
  Foreign Minister Ji Pengfei; Assistant Minister of Foreign Affairs
  Wang Hairong; Tang Wensheng , Interpreter Shen Zuoyun,
  Interpreter; Henry A. Kissinger, Secretary of State; Ambassador
  David Bruce, Chief U.S. Liaison Office; Winston Lord, Director of
  Planning and Coordination, Department of State
DATE AND TIME: Monday, November 12, 1973 5:40 P.M.–8:25 P.M.
PLACE: Chairman Mao's residence, Beijing, People's Republic of
  China[B]

(There was informal conversation as Chairman Mao greeted the Secretary, Ambassador Bruce, and Mr. Lord in turn while the photographers took pictures. The Chairman said that he had not seen the Secretary in a long time and that he now had a higher position. The Secretary responded that the Chairman looked well, and the Chairman commented that he was fair. To Ambassador Bruce, the Chairman commented that he was advancing in age like him, but younger. Ambassador Bruce responded that he was not much younger. To Mr. Lord, the Chairman noted that he was very young.)
Chairman Mao: What did you discuss?
Prime Minister Zhou: Expansionism.
Secretary Kissinger: That's correct

[B] Source: *RG 59, PPS,* box 372, Mao Book Dec. 1975 Mr. Lord.

Chairman Mao: Who's doing the expanding, him (indicating the Secretary)?

Prime Minister Zhou: He started it, but others have caught up.

Secretary Kissinger: The Foreign Minister criticizes us from time to time for the sake of equilibrium, but I think he knows the real source.

Chairman Mao: But that expansionism is a pitiful one. You should not be afraid of them.

Secretary Kissinger: We are not afraid of them, Mr. Chairman. Every once in a while we have to take some strong measures as we did two weeks ago.

Chairman Mao: Those were not bad, those measures. At that time, we were not yet able to persuade Egyptian Vice President Shafei. He came here and said that they had no confidence in you. He said you were partial to Israel. I said not necessarily. I said that those of Jewish descent are not a monolithic block; for example, we cooperated with Engels and not with other Jewish capitalists.

Secretary Kissinger: The problem in the Middle East is to prevent it now from being dominated by the Soviet Union.

Chairman Mao: They can't possibly dominate the Middle East, because, although their ambition is great, their capacities are meager. Take, for instance, Cuba. You intimidated them, and they left.

Secretary Kissinger: And since then we've done that a second time, although we did not announce it.

Chairman Mao: Recently?

Secretary Kissinger: Recently. They moved several submarines, and we moved several ships, and they left.[25] I'm very suspicious that this country wants to have some relations with us. At the beginning it was done through delegations sent by Castro. At that time, the head of the Delegation was Rodriguez. He led a delegation of six Latin American compatriots to China to try to make peace with us on behalf of the Soviet Union. The second time they tried to make peace through [Nicolae] Ceausescu of Romania, and they tried to persuade us not to continue the struggle in the ideological field.

Secretary Kissinger: I remember he was here.

Chairman Mao/Prime Minister Zhou: That was long ago.

Prime Minister Zhou: The first time he came to China. (said in English)

Chairman Mao: And the second time Kosygin came himself, and that was in 1960. I declared to him that we were going to wage a struggle against him for ten thousand years. (laughter)

Interpreter: The Chairman was saying ten thousand years of struggle.

Chairman Mao: I also declared to him that neither of us two were socialists, and that we had been labeled by you (Soviet Union) as being dogmatists and that this is anti-Marxist. So I said let us also give you a title, and that is "revisionism." (laughter) And, therefore, neither of us is Marxist. And this time I made a concession to Kosygin. I said that I originally said this struggle was going to go on for ten thousand years. On the merit of his coming to see me in person, I will cut it down by one thousand years. (laughter) And you must see how generous I am. Once I make a concession, it is for one thousand years. (Zhou and Mao confer.)

And then there was another time, also Romania, and a Mr. Bordeolovski came also to speak on behalf of the Soviet Union.[26] This time again I made a concession of a thousand years. (laughter) You see, my time limit is becoming shorter and shorter.

And the fifth time the Romanian president Ceausescu came again — that was two years ago — and he again raised the issue, and I said "this time no matter what you say, I can make no more concessions." (laughter)

Secretary Kissinger: We must adopt Chinese tactics.

Chairman Mao: There is now some difference between you and us. I do not speak with such ease now because I've lost two teeth. And there is a difference between your and our activities, that is, we just hit back at everything that comes. And we seized upon the fact that the agreement reached between Prime Minister Kosygin and us has never really been implemented, that is, the September 11, 1969, agreement at the Beijing Airport.

Secretary Kissinger: I explained to the Prime Minister, going in the car or elsewhere, that our tactics are more complex and maybe less heroic, but our strategy is the same. We have no doubt who is the principal threat in the world today.

Chairman Mao: What you do is a Chinese kind of shadow boxing. (laughter) We do a kind of shadow boxing which is more energetic.

Prime Minister Zhou: And direct in its blows.

Secretary Kissinger: That is true, but where there is a real challenge, we react as you do.

Chairman Mao: I believe in that. And that is why your recent trip to the Arab world was a good one.

Secretary Kissinger: The Chairman is learning English.[27]

Chairman Mao: Why is it in your country, you are always so obsessed with that nonsensical Watergate issue? (There is much laughter on the Chinese side as the interpreter tries to explain that she couldn't really translate the Chairman's wording for "nonsensical" which really meant "to let out air." Prime Minister Zhou asks Mr. Lord if he knew the meaning of the Chinese word "pee." Mr. Lord said "no" and the Prime Minister said that he could ask his wife. The Chinese side explained that it was an adjective used to qualify the incident.)

The incident itself is very meager, yet now such chaos is being kicked up because of it. Anyway, we are not happy about it.

Secretary Kissinger: But not in the conduct of foreign policy, Mr. Chairman, which will continue on its present course, or in our capacity to take actions in crises as we've shown.

Chairman Mao: Yes. And even in the domestic aspects, I don't think there's such an overwhelming issue for you and the President.

Secretary Kissinger: No. For me there is no issue at all because I am not connected with it at all. The President, too, will master it.

Chairman Mao: What I mean by domestic aspects is your inflation, rising of prices, increase in unemployment, because it seems that the number of unemployed has been cut down by an amount and the U.S. dollar is relatively stable. So there doesn't seem to be any major issue. Why should the Watergate affair become all exploded in such a manner?

Secretary Kissinger: There are many complex factors, including the fact that there are many old style politicians who dislike the President because he pursues unorthodox policy. And too many intellectuals have become nihilistic and want to destroy everything.

Chairman Mao: For instance, James Reston and Joseph Alsop are all now triggered against President Nixon. I can't understand that.

Secretary Kissinger: I can understand James Reston because he follows others, and he is always a reflection of the fashionable view. Joseph Alsop—I think—that was a brief aberration, and he will return to his original position very soon.

Chairman Mao: Do you think they are writing articles, for instance, in trying to taste public opinion?

Secretary Kissinger: They all like to think that they are running the country. And they play President alternately every other day and take turns at it. (Laughter.) If we had paid attention to them, Mr. Chairman, I'd never have been here on my first trip. (laughter) Everything important has been done against their opposition.

Chairman Mao: Yes. People say that Americans can keep no secrets.

Secretary Kissinger: That's true.

Chairman Mao: I think Americans can very well keep secrets.

Secretary Kissinger: That's basically true, Mr. Chairman, but you may be sure that as long as we keep the information in the White House, you can be sure that nothing has ever come out of our discussions.

Chairman Mao: Take the Cuban incident, for instance. Take, for instance, your visit to China. And another situation would be your recent dealing with the Soviet Union. In all these cases, secrets were kept quite well.

Secretary Kissinger: That's true. Things we can keep in my office, we can keep quite well. But there are no secrets with the Soviet Union. We always tell you everything we are doing with the Soviet Union. There is nothing we are doing with the Soviet Union that you don't know. You can count on that for the future.

The Soviet Union likes to create the impression that they and we have a master plan to run the world, but that is to trap other countries. It's not true. We are not that foolish.

Chairman Mao: You are always saying with respect to the Soviet Union something we are ourselves always saying. And your views seem approximately the same as ours, that is, there is the possibility that the Soviet Union wants to attack China.

Secretary Kissinger: Well, Mr. Chairman, I used to think of it as a theoretical possibility. Now I think it is more a realistic possibility, and I've said it, especially to your Prime Minister and also your Ambassador. I think they above all want to destroy your nuclear capability.

Chairman Mao: But our nuclear capability is no bigger than a fly of this size. (laughter)[28]

Secretary Kissinger: But they are worried about what it will be ten years from now.

Chairman Mao: I'd say thirty years hence or fifty years hence. And it is impossible for a country to rise up in a short period.

Secretary Kissinger: Well, as I have said on many occasions, and as I said to the Chairman last time, we believe that if this eventuality were to happen, it would have very serious consequences for everybody. And we are determined to oppose it as our own decision without any arrangement with China.

Chairman Mao: Their ambitions are contradictory with their capacity.

Secretary Kissinger: That may be true.

Chairman Mao: Beginning from their Pacific Ocean, there is the United States, there is Japan, there is China, there is South Asia, and westward there is the Middle East, and there is Europe, and the Soviet forces that are deployed along the lines through Siberia way up to the Kurile Islands only account for one-fourth of their forces.

Prime Minister Zhou: East of the Urals.

Secretary Kissinger: A little closer to one-half. Two-fifths maybe.

Chairman Mao: Excluding the Middle East, that is. The Middle East would be counted on the other side.

Secretary Kissinger: I see.

Chairman Mao: But that includes Kazakstan, the Uzbek Republic, Urquiz and other small republics.[29] Also, some other minority nationality troops stationed in the East.

Secretary Kissinger: We know where every Soviet division is. And we have occasionally discussed some of this with you. But I agree with the Chairman . . .

Chairman Mao: (Before translation [of Kissinger's statement has begun]) They have to deal with so many adversaries. They have to deal with the Pacific. They have to deal with Japan. They have to deal with China. They have to deal with South Asia which also consists of quite a number of countries. And they only have a million troops here — not enough even for the defense of themselves and still less for attack forces. But they can't attack unless you let them in first, and you first give them the Middle East and Europe so they are able to deploy troops eastward. And that would take over a million troops.

Secretary Kissinger: That will not happen. I agree with the Chairman that if Europe and Japan and the U.S. hold together — and we are doing in the Middle East what the Chairman discussed with me last time — then the danger of an attack on China will be very low.

Chairman Mao: We are also holding down a portion of their troops which is favorable to you in Europe and the Middle East. For instance, they have troops stationed in Outer Mongolia, and that had not happened as late as Khrushchev's time. At that time they had still not stationed troops in Outer Mongolia, because the Zhenbao Island incident occurred after Khrushchev. It occurred in Brezhnev's time.[30]

Secretary Kissinger: It was 1969. That is why it is important that Western Europe and China and the U.S. pursue a coordinated course in this period.

Chairman Mao: Yes.

Secretary Kissinger: Because in that case, nobody will be attacked.

Chairman Mao: Japan's attitude is also good.

Secretary Kissinger: That's very important, yes.

Chairman Mao: And the attitudes of major European countries are not bad either.

Secretary Kissinger: Their attitude is better than their courage. (Prime Minister Zhou explains something in Chinese to Chairman Mao.)

Chairman Mao: The main trouble now is those small Nordic countries. (The interpreters then corrected.) No, mainly the Benelux countries.

Secretary Kissinger: The Benelux countries and the Scandinavian countries, and there's some ambiguity in the evolution of the German position.

Chairman Mao: In my opinion, Germany is still a part of the West and will not follow the Soviet Union, while Norway is quite fearful of the Soviet Union. Sweden is a bit wavering. Finland is slightly tended [*sic*] to be closer to the Soviet Union.

Secretary Kissinger: Because of its geographic position, not because of its conviction.

Chairman Mao: That's correct. And they were very courageous during that war.

Secretary Kissinger: Very.

Chairman Mao: They are the country of one thousand legs [lakes?].

Secretary Kissinger: That's true.

Chairman Mao: The Soviet Union first carved out a part of their country and then gave it back, and that country is not one to be easily offended. Because they are hemmed in too close to the Soviet/Finish border.

Prime Minister Zhou: Why were they cut off?

Secretary Kissinger: They did take part. They were in the Karelian Isthmus.

Chairman Mao: And even during the time of Hitler's occupation of Poland, Stalin still did not dare attack some of the countries that used to exist along the Baltic Sea.

Secretary Kissinger: But he took them shortly afterwards.

Chairman Mao: That was because Hitler attacked Poland, and the Soviet Union seized the opportunity to act in such a manner. They tried an agreement of cooperation. The Soviet Union was able to resist that opportunity to seize these three countries.

Perhaps these three representatives have embassies in your country.

Secretary Kissinger: And they still do, Mr. Chairman.

Chairman Mao: And the Soviet Union did not ask you first to abolish those embassies before they established diplomatic relations with you.

Secretary Kissinger: That is correct.

Chairman Mao: In 1933.

Secretary Kissinger: In 1933, those countries still existed, and we established diplomatic relations in 1933.

Prime Minister Zhou: It's not so convenient for them to go to the United Nations.

Secretary Kissinger: They are not in the United Nations.

Prime Minister Zhou: They probably have some nationals residing in your country.

Secretary Kissinger: Yes. I frankly . . . they have ambassadors and are accredited, but I don't know what they do.

Ambassador Bruce: They don't do anything. One of them appears, I think it is Estonia, once a year, and gives an annual day reception. (laughter)

Secretary Kissinger: You're quite right. It has not affected our diplomatic relations with the Soviet Union.

Chairman Mao: Let's discuss the issue of Taiwan. The question of the U.S. relations with us should be separate from that of our relations with Taiwan.

Secretary Kissinger: In principle . . .

Chairman Mao: So long as you sever the diplomatic relations with Taiwan, then it is possible for our two countries to solve the issue of diplomatic relations. That is to say like we did with Japan. As for the question of our relations with Taiwan, that is quite complex. I do not believe in a peaceful transition. (To the Foreign Minister.) Do you believe in it?

Secretary Kissinger: Do I? He asked the Foreign Minister.

Chairman Mao: I'm asking him. (the Foreign Minister.) (Prime Minister Zhou said something that was not translated.)

They are a bunch of counterrevolutionaries. How could they cooperate with us? I say that we can do without Taiwan for the time being, and let it come after one hundred years. Do not take matters on this world so rapidly. Why is there need to be in such great haste? It is only such an island with a population of a dozen or more million.

Prime Minister Zhou: They now have 16 million.

Chairman Mao: As for your relations with us, I think they need not take a hundred years.

Secretary Kissinger: I would count on that. I think they should come much faster.

Chairman Mao: But that is to be decided by you. We will not rush you. If you feel the need, we can do it. If you feel it cannot be done now, then we can postpone it to a later date.

Secretary Kissinger: From our point of view we want diplomatic relations with the Peoples Republic. Our difficulty is that we cannot immediately sever relations with Taiwan, for various reasons, all of them having to do with our domestic situation. I told the Prime Minister that we hope that by 1976, during 1976, to complete the process. So the question is whether we can find some formula that enables us to have diplomatic relations, and the utility of it would be symbolic strengthening of our ties, because, on a technical level, the Liaison Offices perform very usefully.

Chairman Mao: That can do.

Secretary Kissinger: What can do?

Chairman Mao: (Before translation) It can do to continue as now, because now you still need Taiwan.

Secretary Kissinger: It isn't a question of needing it; it is a question of practical possibilities.

Chairman Mao: That's the same. (laughter) We are in no hurry about Hong Kong either.[31] (laughter) We don't even touch Macao. If we wanted to touch Macao, it would only take a slight touch. Because that was a stronghold established by Portugal back during the Ming Dynasty. (laughter) Khrushchev has cursed us, saying why is it you don't want even Hong Kong and Macao. And I've said to Japan that we not only agree to your demand for the four northern islands, but also in history the Soviet Union has carved out one and a half million square kilometers from China.

Secretary Kissinger: As I see the problem of diplomatic relations, Mr. Chairman, it's this. On the question of Taiwan, I believe we have a very clear understanding to which we will stick. So the problem we have is . . . also, the Liaison Offices are doing useful work at this time. So the only question is whether at some point either or both of us thinks it is useful to demonstrate symbolically that our relationship is now normal in every respect. In that case, we should find a formula to make it possible, but it is not a necessity.

Chairman Mao: We have established diplomatic relations with the Soviet Union and also with India, but they are not so very good. And they are not even as good as our relations with you, which are better than our relations with them. So this issue is not an important one.

The issue of the overall international situation is an important one.

Secretary Kissinger: I agree with the Chairman completely and on that we must understand each other, and I believe we substantially understand each other.

Chairman Mao: Our Chief of our Liaison Office was talking to you about grand principles and referred to George Washington's opposing Britain.

Secretary Kissinger: Yes, he made a great speech to me a few weeks ago. I'd heard it before from the Prime Minister.

Chairman Mao: That set of language can be cut down. And we are now facing a contradiction. On the one hand, we have supported various Arab countries against Israeli Zionism. On the other hand, we have to welcome the U.S. putting the Soviet Union on the spot, and making it so that the Soviet

Union cannot control the Middle East. Our Ambassador Huang Zhen mentioned this support of the Arab world, but he didn't understand the importance of U.S. resistance to the Soviet Union.

Secretary Kissinger: Well, I took him by surprise, and he repeated the formal position from the United Nations. (laughter) And I understand that publicly you have to take certain positions, and it is not against our common position that you do so. But the reality is that we will move matters toward a settlement in the Middle East, but we also want to demonstrate that it was not done by Soviet pressures.

So, whenever the Soviets press we must resist apart from the merits of the dispute. Then when we have defeated them, we may even move in the same direction. We are not against Arab aspirations; we are against their being achieved with Soviet pressure.

Chairman Mao: Exactly

Secretary Kissinger: And that is our strategy right now.

Chairman Mao: And now there is a crucial issue, that is the question of Iraq, Baghdad. We don't know if it is possible for you to do some work in that area. As for us, the possibilities are not so very great.

Prime Minister Zhou: It is relatively difficult to do that. It is possible to have contacts with them, but it takes a period of time for them to change their orientation. It is possible they would change their orientation after they have suffered from them. They've already suffered once, that is with regard to the coup.

Secretary Kissinger: You can do good work in Iran, and Iran is active in Iraq. And we have encouraged the Shah to establish good relations with you. Our strategy with Iraq is first to try to win Syria away from it, and then to reduce its influence in sheikdoms along the Persian Gulf. And then when it sees it can achieve nothing by leaning to the Soviet Union, then we will move toward them. But first they have to learn that they gain nothing from their present course.

Chairman Mao: And this country it contains no banks or coasts of the Arab gulf, that is the Persian Gulf. Recently, your naval ships have gone in that part of the world. I said that was good.

Secretary Kissinger: They are still there, and we will keep them there a little longer.

Chairman Mao: That is one carrier.

Secretary Kissinger: A carrier and escort ships.

Chairman Mao: And the Soviet Union often passes through the Japanese straits, for example, the Tsrumi Straits eastward to the vicinity of the Midway

Islands. And they go in and out of the Japanese Islands. Sometimes they test their missiles in the Pacific Ocean, too.

Secretary Kissinger: Yes.

Chairman Mao: In my opinion, their aim is to tie down a portion of your strength in the Pacific Ocean to avoid your sending a large number of troops westwards.

Secretary Kissinger: First, we don't mind their testing missiles in the Pacific, because this makes it very easy to find out what their characteristics are. As for the fleet, our difficulty about operating in the Indian Ocean and the Arab Sea has been that we have not had a base in that area. But we have now developed an island called Diego Garcia as a base, and we have also discussed with Pakistan the possibility of building a port. And we are establishing very close relationships with the Shah of Iran. And I believe you will see we will be stationing more ships in the Indian Ocean from now on.

Chairman Mao: Why is it that Iran is favoring the Soviet Union's Asian collective security system?

Secretary Kissinger: First, of the leaders in that area that I know, the one who understands the Soviet danger best is the Shah of Iran. And he's buying very large numbers now of military equipment from us in order to defend himself against the Soviet Union and also to be able to protect Pakistan. So if he sat here, Mr. Chairman, he would agree completely with your analysis or the situation. But he has a tactical problem, and he wanted to say that he was for peace in general. I think he made a mistake, but he is not really for an Asian security system.

Prime Minister Zhou: He will be arriving in China during the first three months of next year. (The Prime Minister and the Foreign Minister discuss the date.) It's going to be postponed. It is not going to be so early.

Secretary Kissinger: He is very much interested in good relations with China, and we have recommended it very strongly. And he sees your attitude and our attitude about Pakistan and Afghanistan.

Chairman Mao: It seems to me that the comparatively weaker place in the contemporary international situation would still be Iraq.

Secretary Kissinger: Iraq right now is the most difficult place in that area.

Prime Minister Zhou: (Laughing) Quadaffi went to Iraq to stir up something there.

Chairman Mao: What have they done now?

Prime Minister Zhou: He has gone and returned. He went there to persuade them not to accept a ceasefire.

Secretary Kissinger: Quadaffi is not the most stable intellect that leads countries right now.

Chairman Mao: He is a man I do not understand. There's another, that is South Yemen. The President of South Yemen approached me.[32] He said he wanted to sever diplomatic relations with the Soviet Union. He asked me my opinion. I was not taken in by him and said he must be prudent. Now they are tying themselves very closely to the Soviet Union.

Secretary Kissinger: Very closely tied to the Soviet Union. And they are stirring things up all over the Gulf.

Chairman Mao: Do you have diplomatic relations with them?

Secretary Kissinger: We have technically diplomatic relations with them but no useful influence. But we give assistance to Muscat and Oman and North Yemen in order to contain them. (The interpreter and Prime Minister Zhou explain the location of Muscat and Oman to the Chairman.)

Chairman Mao: Let's discuss something about Japan. This time you are going to Japan to stay a few more days there.

Secretary Kissinger: The Chairman always scolds me about Japan. I'm taking the Chairman very seriously, and this time I'm staying two and a half days. And he's quite right. It is very important that Japan does not feel isolated and left alone. And we should not give them too many temptations to maneuver.

Chairman Mao: That is not to force them over to the Soviet side.

Secretary Kissinger: And not force them into too many choices for example, between us.

Chairman Mao: That would not come about.

Secretary Kissinger: Not from our side either. (not translated)

Chairman Mao: Their first priority is to have good relations with the United States. We only come second.

Secretary Kissinger: We have no objection to good relations between Japan and China. We want to prevent them from moving too close to the Soviet Union.

Prime Minister Zhou: And they should not be taken in.

Secretary Kissinger: That's why if they do something in the Soviet Union, we sometimes join them, so they are not all alone in facing the Soviet Union.

Chairman Mao: And we also encourage them to do things together with the United States to avoid their being taken in.

Prime Minister Zhou: Recently, Tanaka and others paid a visit to the United States. Was that on the West Coast or in Hawaii?

Secretary Kissinger: No, he went to Washington before they went to the

Soviet Union during the summer. Our relations now are better than they were when I was here last time. They are no longer so nervous. (laughter)

Chairman Mao: They are afraid of you and you should try to lessen their fear. [T]he Soviet Union is doing its utmost to go all out to win them over, but Japan is not so trustful of them.

Secretary Kissinger: No, they had a very bad historical experience, and that is very fortunate for all of us. And the Russian temperament doesn't harmonize very well with the Japanese.

Prime Minister Zhou: During Tanaka's visit to the Soviet Union, the Russians acted very stupidly.

Chairman Mao: They didn't have any discussions the first two days.

Chairman Mao: They only made proposals about the resources of the Soviet Union.

Prime Minister Zhou: They lectured them.

Secretary Kissinger: Yes, they did that to us, too. It creates the impression they are trying to buy us. But the proposal is that we have to invest there for ten years, and only after everything is built, then they'll start paying us back. (laughter) We have not yet agreed and there is no prospect of an early agreement to any of their big projects.

Chairman Mao: And that includes most favored nation treatment [MFN]. Now it is put on the shelf. I thought it was good upon hearing that news. I think it is best to put it on the shelf for a longer period of time.

Secretary Kissinger: But we would like to have MFN for China. (laughter)

Chairman Mao: Not necessarily. So long as the Soviet Union doesn't get it, that would be enough. (laughter)

Secretary Kissinger: The prospects of that legislation are not very promising.

Chairman Mao/Prime Minister Zhou [simultaneously]: Is that so?

Secretary Kissinger: It won't be taken up again until February. That's in the House. And then it must be taken up in the Senate. But all in all, it seems it will be finally passed if not next year, the year after. The big problem, Mr. Chairman, is not the MFN clause, because the Soviet Union doesn't have goods to sell us. The obstacles to Soviet trade is not our duties, but the low quality of Soviet products.

Chairman Mao: But they can give you energy which you need.

Secretary Kissinger: Mr. Chairman, that is not exactly accurate. Even if they were able to produce the natural gas they have claimed, and there is still some dispute about that, it would only amount to about five percent of our needs. And it would take ten years to deliver. And within that ten-year period, we will have developed domestic alternatives, including natural gas in America. That makes it much less necessary to import natural gas in quantities.

Chairman Mao: That would be good.

Secretary Kissinger: The problem is credits more than MFN. And those we have controlled very rigidly. We haven't given any credits.

Chairman Mao: I'm lacking in knowledge and cannot understand this problem. I cannot understand this. Probably what you said is correct. At present, the Soviet Union seems in need of such great amounts as $8 billion in credits.

Secretary Kissinger: Yes, and we've given them up to now $330 million. They want $8 billion dollars just for natural gas.

Chairman Mao: Your President issued the Nixon Doctrine at Guam, I believe, and we see that you are gradually realizing his policy in putting out the flames of war in Southeast Asia. In this manner, you will be able to achieve a greater initiative.

Chairman Mao: That is correct.

Chairman Mao: What you issued was a new Atlantic Charter. (There was some discussion of the translation of this word and the difference between "Charter" and "Constitution.") But they mean the same thing.

Secretary Kissinger: I would think we will realize the basic objective of that proposal within the first half of that year. Most of the Charter is already drafted in the military sphere; we've almost completed a draft, and in the political sphere, we've almost completed drafting it. The economic one requires more work.[33]

Chairman Mao: In the economic field, there are some contradictions.

Secretary Kissinger: Yes. That's true, but they have to be overcome too, because of the great need, and I think we can work them out. Our press always concentrates on disagreements. Those diplomats who are willing to talk publicly are usually least reliable, and their reports are always published. But basically, we are making good progress.

Chairman Mao: That is why I believe it will be greatly difficult for the Soviet Union to seize Europe and put it on its side. They have such ambition but great difficulty.

Secretary Kissinger: I think it is very difficult for them to seize militarily, and if they attempt it, they will certainly have to fight us. (Chairman Mao talks to Prime Minister Zhou.)

The greatest danger with the Soviet Union is where they either move land armies quickly, as in Czechoslovakia, or make a sudden air attack in areas where they think we will not do anything.

Chairman Mao: Take, for instance, the manner of their actions in Czechoslovakia, It is completely unseemly. For instance, they engaged in intriguing against Czechoslovakia; they sent civilian aircraft and used troops in the civilian aircraft.

Secretary Kissinger: To control the Prague Airport.

Chairman Mao: Later they sent troops there. Others thought they carried civilian passengers in that aircraft, but they sent troops. In that manner, they were able to control the Prague Airport. They sent troops there and reduced Czechoslovakia to inertia.

Secretary Kissinger: That's true. That's exactly how it happened.

Chairman Mao: And, therefore, in my opinion, with regard to the Soviet Union, it has a great ambition—and that is, it wishes to seize in its hands the two continents of Europe and Asia, and North Africa and elsewhere, but they will have trouble doing that.

Secretary Kissinger: As long as countries that are threatened stay united. (Chairman Mao toasts everyone with his tea.)

Chairman Mao: They made use of the opportunities when both of your feet were stuck in the quagmire of Southeast Asia. And in this, your President can't take all the blame for that. The Johnson Administration was responsible for that.

Secretary Kissinger: Where did they take advantage of their opportunity?

Chairman Mao: That is to enter Czechoslovakia.

Prime Minister Zhou: And also India.

Chairman Mao: And I don't pay so much attention to these minor things. That is, they have so-called nonaggression pacts with Egypt, Iraq and India, like the Treaty of Friendship with India. I don't believe that settles things. Therefore, we would not agree to any such treaties when they propose them to us.

Secretary Kissinger: Yes. I have noticed that.

Chairman Mao: And there are some people here who are commenting that you had lost an opportunity to take action when you did not do so when Egypt chased out Soviet military personnel. The commentary goes that at that time you should have assisted Egypt a bit. Upon hearing that I thought further. I thought that because at that time both your feet were in the whole of Southeast Asia, and you had not yet climbed out.

Secretary Kissinger: You are quite right, Mr. Chairman. There were two problems. We had our election. And, secondly, we were still in Vietnam, and we couldn't tackle both at once.

Chairman Mao: That is so. You are now freer than before.

Secretary Kissinger: Much more.

Chairman Mao: And the philosopher of your motherland, Hegel, has said—I don't know whether it is the correct English translation—"freedom means the knowledge of necessity."[34]

Secretary Kissinger: Yes.

Chairman Mao: Do you pay attention or not to one of the subjects of Hegel's philosophy, that is, the unity of opposites.

Secretary Kissinger: Very much. I was much influenced by Hegel in my philosophic thinking.

Chairman Mao: Both Hegel and Feuerbach who came a little later after him.[35] They were both great thinkers. And Marxism came partially from them. They were predecessors of Marx. If it were not for Hegel and Feuerbach there would not be Marxism.

Secretary Kissinger: Yes. Marx reversed the tendency of Hegel, but he adopted the basic theory.[36]

Chairman Mao: What kind of doctor are you? Are you a doctor of philosophy?

Secretary Kissinger: Yes. (laughter)

Chairman Mao: Yes, well, then won't you give me a lecture?

Secretary Kissinger: I think the Chairman knows much more philosophy than I. And he has written profoundly about philosophy. I used to shock my colleagues, Mr. Chairman, by assigning essays from your collected works, in my courses in the 1960s at Harvard.

Chairman Mao: I, myself, am not satisfied with myself. The main thing is that I don't understand foreign languages and, therefore, I am unable to read books of Germans or Englishmen or Americans.

Secretary Kissinger: I can't read German in its original form. I must translate into English, because it is too complicated in its original form. This is quite true. Some of the points of Hegel—quite seriously—I understand better in English than German, even though German is my mother language.

Prime Minister Zhou: Because of the intricate structure of the German grammar, it is sometimes gets misinterpreted if one doesn't understand the grammar correctly. Therefore, it's not easy to understand the German language and especially the reasoning of various works.

Chairman Mao: (To Prime Minister Zhou) Don't you know some German?

Prime Minister Zhou: I learned in my youth; now I've forgotten it.

Secretary Kissinger: German sentences are long, and the grammar is involved. Therefore, it's easier to understand English than German. One of the characteristics of the German language . . .

Prime Minister Zhou: Yesterday, a few of those who know German were joking together that German sentences are so long in length that there are quite a few pages, and one does not understand the sentences until you find the final verb, and the verb is at the very end. That, of course, is exaggerated. One sentence does not take several pages.

Chairman Mao: Did you meet Guo Morou who understands German? Now we are discussing Hegel, and I give you an opinion.

Secretary Kissinger: I don't know the gentleman that the Chairman was mentioning.

Chairman Mao: He is a man who worships Confucius, but he is now a member of our Central Committee.[37]

Let's go back to Hegel. In Hegel's history of philosophy, he mentioned Confucius who he showed great disrespect. He showed more respect for Lao-tze, but he showed the greatest respect for the philosophy of Indian Buddhism.

Secretary Kissinger: I don't quite agree with him (the Chairman) on that last point. That's a very passive philosophy.

Chairman Mao: And I also believe that that was not a correct way of saying. And this is not only true of Hegel.

Secretary Kissinger: There is a sentimental love affair between Western intellectuals and India based on a complete misreading of the Indian philosophy of life. Indian philosophy was never meant to have a practical application.

Chairman Mao: It's just a bunch of empty words.

Secretary Kissinger: For Ghandi, nonviolence wasn't a philosophic principle, but because he thought the British were too moralistic and sentimental to use violence against. They are nonsentimental people. For Ghandi it was a revolutionary tactic, not an ethical principle.[38]

Chairman Mao: And he himself would spin his own wool and drink goat's milk.

Secretary Kissinger: But it was essentially a tactical device for him.

Chairman Mao: And the influence of Ghandi's doctrine on the Indian people was to induce them into nonresistance.

Secretary Kissinger: Partly, but also given the character and diversity of the English people, it was only a way to conduct the struggle against the British. So I think Ghandi deserves credit for having won independence against the British.

Chairman Mao: India did not win independence. If it did not attach itself to Britain, it attaches itself to the Soviet Union. And more than one-half of their economy depends on you. Did you not mention during your briefings that India owes ten billion dollars in debt to the U.S., or was that all debts?

Secretary Kissinger: That was all debts together. It's not $10 billion but closer to $6 billion. I will have to check. I thought it was $10 billion to everybody, of which India owed 60 percent. But you may be right. I have to check. (To Lord: can you check, Win?)

Prime Minister Zhou: That includes the rupee debt.

Secretary Kissinger: Including the rupee debt, that is correct. Yes. And one can mention the dollar debt, too.

Chairman Mao: I recall your President told us the various debts at the World Bank were $10 billion.

Secretary Kissinger: Yes. When one includes the unilateral debts and the rupee debts and the bilateral debts, then it is $10 billion and probably a little more even.

Chairman Mao: That is also something you've imparted to me. In the past, I had not known that. And if you come to China again, besides talking politics, talk a bit of philosophy to me.

Secretary Kissinger: I would like that very much, Mr. Chairman. That was my first love, the study of philosophy.

Chairman Mao: Perhaps it is more difficult to do now as Secretary of State.

Secretary Kissinger: Yes.

Chairman Mao: And they say you are a galloping horse whose hooves never stop. (laughter)

Secretary Kissinger: He (Prime Minister Zhou) called me a "cyclone." (laughter)

Chairman Mao: There is a cyclone around the world.

Secretary Kissinger: Your Vice Foreign Minister told me your views, Mr. Chairman, about the Arab world when he talked to me in October, and I paid great attention to them.

Chairman Mao: That is the matter of my discussions with the Vice President of Egypt which was somehow gotten hold of by Lord Qiao. (laughter)[39]

Secretary Kissinger: He didn't tell me who he had talked to.

Chairman Mao: It was [Egyptian Vice President] Shafei. Did you see him?

Secretary Kissinger: I saw [Anwar] Sadat and two or three others.

Chairman Mao: At that time I was trying to persuade him to get closer to you, because I noted that after you announced your position as Secretary State and you'd only been that a few days, you met the Arab Foreign Ministers and later on invited them to lunch. Only the Foreign Ministers of Iraq Syria, Libya, and South Yemen declined. I think even Egypt accepted.

Secretary Kissinger: That is correct.

Chairman Mao: That is why I was following behind you. (laughter) I was very happy that you entertained those Arab Foreign Ministers.

Secretary Kissinger: Yes. It was my first official function.

Chairman Mao: And your predecessor, the previous Secretary, I think did not do so.

Secretary Kissinger: He was interested, but I don't think he ever had them as a group.

Chairman Mao: And these Arab countries, which spread up from the Atlantic to the Persian Gulf, account for more than a hundred million people.

Prime Minister Zhou: The population is now one hundred and fifty million.

Chairman Mao: And they are composed of 19 countries.

Secretary Kissinger: And we are making a major effort to improve our relations with them and take this very seriously.

Chairman Mao: And the difficulties are also great because these countries are both united and engaged in internal struggles. It is not so easy to deal with.

Secretary Kissinger: Libya quarrels with all its neighbors.

(Prime Minister Zhou leaves the room.)

Chairman Mao: Perhaps he's that kind of cock that loves fighting. That's the way Khrushchev cursed us. He said we were a cock that liked fighting.

Secretary Kissinger: He did not have a very successful visit here in 1959.

Chairman Mao: We fell out by 1959. We began to fall out in 1958 when they wanted to control China's seacoast and also China's naval ports. And during my discussions with them, with their Ambassador, I almost slammed the table, and I gave him hell. (laughter) And he reported that to Moscow and Krushchev came. At that time, he put forth the notion of a joint fleet, that is, for the Soviet Union and China to form a joint naval fleet. That was the suggestion he raised. And at that time, he was quite arrogant because he had seen General Eisenhower who was then President, and he attained the so-called "spirit of Camp David." And he boasted to me in Beijing that he got to know the President and the two English words concerning President Eisenhower were that he was "my friend." (To Ambassador Bruce: You knew that?)[40]

Ambassador Bruce: No, I never knew that.

Chairman Mao: And also a piece of news. Since then, he never came again. But he had been to Vladivostok, and he went there from China.

Prime Minister Zhou: There he made an anti-China speech.

Chairman Mao: None of the present leaders of the Soviet Union have been as far eastward as Vladivostok. Kosygin himself has said he is not quite clear about matters in Siberia. (The Chinese check the time.)

Prime Minister Zhou: It's been two and one-half hours.

Chairman Mao: And there's another issue I would like to discuss with you. It seems today we have talked all too long. Over two and one-half hours. We have taken up time originally set aside for other activities. (Note: He meant Ambassador Bruce's reception.) The question I would like to discuss is that I am quite suspicious that if the Democratic Party comes into office, they will adopt the policy of isolationism.

Secretary Kissinger: That is a very serious question, Mr. Chairman. I think there may be trends now among the intellectuals and some Democrats in the direction of isolationism. On the other hand, objective realities would force them to understand that there is no alternative to our present policy. Now, what damage would be done until they learned this, and whether they would continue with the same tactical complexity, this I don't know. But I think they would pursue the present course. (The last sentence is not translated.)

Chairman Mao: Then you seem to be in the same category as myself. We seem to be both more or less suspicious.

Secretary Kissinger: I'm suspicious, and I have some questions about some leaders. But I believe the overwhelming necessity of the situation will force us to return to the policy we are now pursuing.

But this, Mr. Chairman, is why I believe we should use this period, when all of us are still in office and understand the situation, to so solidify it that no alternative will be possible anymore.

Chairman Mao: And this is mainly manifested in that one point—that is the advocacy of troop withdrawals from Europe.

Secretary Kissinger: Yes.

Chairman Mao: This will be a great assistance to the Soviet Union.

Secretary Kissinger: We will not carry it out in our Administration. It occurs in two things, the troop withdrawals from Europe and maybe less of a willingness to be very brutal very quickly in case there is a challenge.

Chairman Mao: What you mean by "brutality" is probably going to war.

Secretary Kissinger: If necessary, but . . .

Chairman Mao: I am not happy you are putting up a diplomatic front to me.

Secretary Kissinger: If necessary, but our experience has been that, if they know we are going to war, they draw back. Up to now, they've always been afraid of us.

Chairman Mao: Because I also think it would be better not to go to war. I'm not in favor of that either, though I'm well known as a warmonger. (laughter)

If you and the Soviet Union fight a war, I would also think that would not be very good. If you are going to fight, it would be better to use conventional weapons, and leave nuclear weapons in the stockpile, and not touch them.

Secretary Kissinger: We will not start a war in any event.

Chairman Mao: That's good. I heard you put forward the opinion before that you want to gain time.

Secretary Kissinger: We want to gain time, but we also want to be in a position that, if the Soviet Union attacks any major areas we discussed, we can resist. And it's in those circumstances we have to be prepared.

Chairman Mao: That's entirely correct. As for the Soviet Union, they bully the weak, and are afraid of the tough. (Laughter as he points to Miss Wang and Miss Tang.) And you shouldn't try to bully either Miss Wang or Miss Tang because they are comparatively soft.

Secretary Kissinger: Mr. Chairman, in my experience they are not very soft. They also don't carry out the Chairman's advice. (laughter)

Chairman Mao: She (Miss Tang) is American, while she (Miss Wang) is a Soviet spy.[41] (laughter)

(The Chairman then got up unassisted and escorted the Americans to the outer lobby. He said goodbye to the Secretary, ambassador Bruce, and Mr. Lord in turn, and asked photographers to take pictures. As he shook hands with the Secretary, he said "and please send my personal greetings to President Richard Nixon." The Secretary said he would do that. Ambassador Bruce and Mr. Lord indicated that it was a great honor to see Chairman Mao. The Chairman mentioned to Mr. Lord that he had met him before, and Mr. Lord acknowledged this.)

[The day before Kissinger leaves for Japan, he and Zhou meet again, with a larger group of U.S. and PRC officials, to review bilateral matters and to clarify other contentious issues such as the PNW Agreement.[42] Before formal discussions begin, Kissinger apologized to Zhou for the Oklahoma City incident. He cannot, however, promise that such incidents will never occur again: "I can't think of what new stupidity people are thinking up."

When Kissinger reviews his case for the PNW Agreement, Zhou takes a softer approach than earlier in the summer. Not only does he concede that the agreement could facilitate anti-Soviet interventions in areas where Washington lacks a "formal treaty," he explains that "we had to make criticism because we think it is necessary for the Third World countries to have such an understanding." Zhou goes on to protest the Chilean junta's terrible slaughter of Allende's supporters. Kissinger does not deny that there were executions, but he claims there were not as many as Zhou has claimed; he promises to look into it.[43] *Zhou has other questions about Chile, as the following excerpt indicates.]*

Prime Minister Zhou: . . . did [the CIA] have a hand in the coup?

Secretary Kissinger: They would not have a hand in the coup, but it is true they could not control the situation.

Prime Minister Zhou: They could only control one thing. Remember when your charge d'affaires in Laos during the recent coup ran to this airport and told the official of the coup.[44]

Secretary Kissinger: That's true. In Laos, we attempted to restrain the situation. In Chile, it was the incompetence of the Allende government. We would not give assistance, would not make their task easier, but we did not have anything to do with the actual coup.

Prime Minister Zhou: But that government itself was much too complicated. Allende himself admitted that if one wanted to seize political power in the true sense of the word . . . but on the other hand their subordinates made great publicity. And those Communists in that country wanted the Soviet Union to supply them with weapons. Whereas those Che Guevarists in Cuba that took up arms found themselves divorced from the masses by doing quite similarly those activities which they carried out in their Cuban guerrilla forces. They thought that once they had weapons in hand, they could kill some people and burn down some houses.

[Kissinger's response to Zhou's query about the CIA in Chile is evasive: he knows very well that he has done all he could to push the agency to undermine Allende.[45] *Zhou does not question him further on the point; instead, they digress into a fascinating discussion of Che Guevara, the Allende government, and Latin American revolutions. Both have low opinions of Che: Kissinger sees him as "silly" because he had no "political hope" to influence the situation in Zaire or Bolivia; Zhou thinks he was "mad" for asking for Chinese help in building a huge broadcasting station to support his guerrilla activities, and paranoid for having believed that "the peasants in Boliva were all spies." As for the Allende government, Zhou believes that it made too many promises and did not prepare to deal with the economic problems created by nationalizations.]*

Prime Minister Zhou: . . . we give only limited support to Latin American countries' revolutions. We are still learning .

Secretary Kissinger: I hope you don't learn too fast.

Prime Minister Zhou: You don't have to be afraid of that. It takes time to have the people rise up.

Secretary Kissinger: I am in favor of very careful long studies by our Chinese friends.

Kissinger's and Zhou's conversation next turned to the more prosaic issue of the blocked assets and foreign claims settlement. For Kissinger's advisers, a settlement was necessary to improve the climate for large-scale corporate trade and investment operations in China as well as a condition for conferring most-favored-nation status to China. Already corporations such as M. W. Kellogg had exported entire plants, and executives from others, such as Monsanto and General Electric, were going to China for discussions. Encouraged by the possibility of big-ticket sales, David Bruce advised Kissinger that settling the blocked assets and claims issue could enable U.S. banks to finance PRC "imports of whole plants and equipment on a 'deferred payment' basis."[46]

Although Zhou was committed to China's modernization, he was not ready to settle the claims and assets issue. Not only was he worried about possible lawsuits by aggrieved holders of old railroad bonds, a risk that the Americans downplayed, but there was the problem of the $17 million in blocked assets that foreign banks had more or less illicitly returned to the PRC. The Americans wanted China to return the money in order to make the claims settlement viable, but Zhou may have worried about attacks from the radicals if he signed off on a restitution agreement. These problems, along with the lingering problem of U.S.-Taiwan relations, made it easy for the Chinese to defer a settlement until 1979, during the Carter administration.[47]

On the claims and blocked assets issue, Kissinger would leave empty handed but in his final substantive talks with Zhou, on Tuesday evening and Wednesday morning he tried to resolve other issues, such as the Marine Corp presence in Beijing, and consummated his bid for closer strategic cooperation.

The complete record of the Tuesday-night meeting is unavailable. Apparently Winston Lord made part of the transcript ("Marines, Southeast Asia,") available to State Department Far Eastern specialists, while sequestering a transcript of additional discussion in an entirely different file. Given the abrupt way that the latter document begins, it seemed that more was said than the available record shows. This is another example of Kissinger's system of information control: by having his closest advisers creating sanitized records of a meeting, Kissinger could restrict knowledge of the details of the most sensitive discussions. Of course, as Lord would later observe, this procedure meant wasting valuable time: "It was like juggling a double or triple bookkeeping system."[48]

The following excerpt from the more widely distributed record of the late Tuesday evening discussion shows that Zhou was receptive to Kissinger's request that the Prime Minister countermand the Foreign Ministry's early decision that the boisterous Marine Corps security leave Beijing. For Kissinger, sending the marines home would set a bad precedent and was inconsistent with the traditions of U.S. diplomacy. Although Bruce appreciated the Marines' contribution to the otherwise boring social life of embassy staffers, Kissinger was not amused.

Ambassador Bruce: I have got to confess that these Marines are a gay lot of people. There are six of them in one room. (Ambassador Bruce tells about their dances and the fact that their female neighbors appreciated it.) [laughter all around]

Secretary Kissinger aside to Commander Howe: Can't you square this away with Zumwalt? We are not running a rest camp. They have just got to be brought under control.

[After some joking about the possibility of Peoples' Liberation Army units providing security to the PRC's liaison office in Washington—it would serve as a "distraction" from Watergate, Kissinger says—Zhou sardonically added that perhaps some Red Guard units could be sent to Washington: "Perhaps your long haired youth would pay visits to them." Not wanting to turn a relatively minor issue into one that disrupted U.S.–China relations, Zhou agreed that the Marines should stay, while Kissinger acquiesced to Zhou's request that the guards refrain from wearing uniforms. But this did not settle matters; Zhou's shaky position meant that his control of the Foreign Ministry was less than perfect. Within a few weeks, Ambassador Bruce would report "obviously exaggerated complaints over the Marine Guard." Soon the Marines would be gone. [49]*

For Kissinger, a more urgent issue was the future of the U.S. client state in South Vietnam. U.S. forces were no longer fighting, but Kissinger wanted to prolong the "decent interval" between the American withdrawal and the eventual collapse of the Saigon regime. He asked the Premier to use his influence to prevent "a major offensive." That much Zhou promised; and the devastating attack the Americans feared did not come. Instead, National Liberation Front and North Vietnamese forces took on the Saigon army in a series of smaller engagements and regained ground they had lost in earlier battles. As Zhou noted, and Kissinger acknowledged, "small frictions" were unavoidable.* [50]*

Before a brief discussion of the recent student-led revolution in Thailand, the talk inevitably turned to the Cambodian question. Zhou wondered why the United States persisted in supporting the Lon Nol regime. For Kissinger, the administration's credibility remained paramount, although he continued to have "no objection" to the return of Prince Sihanouk.]*

Prime Minister Zhou: You have no treaty obligations to Lon Nol as you have with Thieu and the military dictatorship in Bangkok has undergone changes but they won't be of very major portions. It would be relatively better if that area could be one of peace and neutrality.

Secretary Kissinger: I will speak frankly. Our major problem with Cambodia is that the opponents of President Nixon want to use it as an example of the bankruptcy of his whole policy. So if there is a very rapid collapse, it will be reflected in our other policies. That frankly is our only concern.

Prime Minister Zhou: Why is it that Senator Mansfield is in favor of letting loose and allowing Sihanouk to return?

Secretary Kissinger: Senator Mansfield is first of all an isolationist in the classical tradition. He is a true isolationist from the Middle West. Secondly, he has a sentimental attachment to Prince Sihanouk which is not related to reality and not reciprocated in any way. Because I think the Prince is a very shrewd calculator.

[The following document was closely held by Lord; it is an excerpt from the still unavailable full transcript of the late Tuesday evening discussion shows Kissinger continuing his effort to develop a "tacit alliance" with Beijing by proposing arrangements to provide early warning of a Soviet attack. Although Zhou was plainly interested in Kissinger's proposition, he withheld comment until the next morning.]

THE WHITE HOUSE
TOP SECRET/SENSITIVE/EXCLUSIVELY EYES ONLY
MEMORANDUM OF CONVERSATION
PARTICIPANTS: Zhou Enlai, Premier of the State Council; Ye Jianying, Vice Chairman, Military Affairs Commission, CCP; Vice Minister Chai Hongging; Tang Wensheng, Staff (Interpreter); Mrs. Yang Yuyuh; Military Interpreter; Secretary of State Henry A. Kissinger; Ambassador David Bruce; Commander Jonathan T. Howe; Mrs. Wilma G. Hall, Notetaker.
Date and time: Tuesday, November 13, 1973 10:00 P.M.-12:30 A.M.
PLACE: The Great Hall of the People, Beijing.[C]

Secretary Kissinger: Now we could be of help in two ways.
—One, if the war should be prolonged in the obvious way, we could be helpful by supplying equipment and other services.

[C] Source: *PPS*, box 381, President's China Trip.

—What I want to discuss today is what we can do to shorten the period of vulnerability.

One way of shortening the period of vulnerability is to point out certain areas which any force has to keep in mind in defending itself. One problem any country has is early warning. With respect to bombers, that means an air defense that can not be saturated. And with respect to missiles, it means getting sound warning of missile launching.

Now any help we would give you in our mutual interest should be in a form that is not easily recognizable. With respect to missile launches, we have a very good system of satellites which gives us early warning. The problem is to get that information to you rapidly. We would be prepared to establish a hotline between our satellites and Beijing by which we could transmit information to you in a matter of minutes.

Prime Minister Zhou: Through the satellites?

Secretary Kissinger: Well, the information goes to Washington and then to Beijing. We could do that in one of two ways that would not attract attention.

—We could just announce the establishment of a hotline just as we have with Moscow, Japan, etc. But yours would be of a special nature but that would not be generally known. This would enable you to move your bombers and if possible you could move your missiles if you knew an attack was coming. You would then need good communications from Peking to your various bases, but we could probably help with that in some guise.

—Another way is to sign between ourselves an agreement on accidental nuclear war, the same as we have signed with the Soviet Union, and also establish a hotline.

I am simply thinking of methods of establishing a hotline to Peking that would not attract attention. We could also give you the technology for certain kinds of radars but you would have to build them yourselves.

* * *

Prime Minister Zhou: As for the specific matter you wished discussed, I will have to study it. And tomorrow morning before you leave, I will pay a visit to you and say farewell. I think there are some things that would be useful to us. Although the human factor is decisive in war, the practical also counts.

COMMENTARY

After their disucssion concluded, Kissinger and Zhou met until the early hours of the morning to work out the final details of the communique on their talks. Kissinger readily characterized it as a "positive" document: it extended opposition to "hegemony" to anywhere in the world, not just the Asia-Pacific sphere. It also called for "frequent contact at authoritative levels", thus suggesting a more positive Chinese response to Nixon's earlier invitation on consultations. Moreover, it included the statement "confirming the principle of one China" that Kissinger hoped would give Washington more flexibility in dealing with both Taiwan and Beijing.

Having hardly slept, Kissinger and Zhou nevertheless met early Wednesday morning to conclude their discussions about a few sensitive items, such as policy toward Japan, the Premier's appeal for more U.S. aid to Pakistan, and the strengths and weaknesses of Senate foreign policy leaders. Given that two unconnected transcripts of this meeting are in the files, it is likely that the full record remains to be disclosed.

As Kissinger departed for Tokyo, Zhou left him with his thoughts on the possible direction of Japanese policy. Japan, he said, had another choice besides the two Kissinger mentioned earlier in the week, "traditional nationalism" or the present alignment with the West. Both Beijing and Washington had to ensure that Tokyo did seek shelter under a "different nuclear umbrella" such as Moscow's. To prevent the Japanese from seeking shelter under a "different nuclear umbrella" such as Moscow's — Zhou urged Kissinger to make sure that Tokyo maintained its alignment with the West.

Apparently their hour of conversation was long enough to allow Zhou to discuss some scenarios for possible Soviet attacks before addressing Kissinger's hot line proposal. He agreed that such data would be "intelligence of great assistance," but suggested that it could be risky for China. Kissinger can only agree when Zhou observed that the proposal would have to be implemented in "a manner so that no one feels we are allies." Zhou also pointed out that satellite communications could be decoded; Kissinger's response is not recorded here.

Kissinger had already presented Zhou with draft texts for agreements on a hotline or accidental nuclear war as potential cover for the intelligence linkage, so he was ready to move forward. But Zhou wanted to study the issue further with Marshall Ye, China's highest ranking military official — and, no doubt, with Mao. He told Kissinger that Huang Zhen would give Washington the response and that the ambassador would be returning to Beijing for consultations.

Given bitter Sino-Soviet tensions and dissent within the Chinese bureaucracy about Mao's U.S. policy, Kissinger's proposal was potentially explosive. Zhou assured Kissinger that only a few officials would learn about it, but

Zhou was on his way out and not in a strong position to see the proposal through the decision-making process. No doubt, Huang Zhen was in fact brought into the discussions; but he did not return to Washington for some months. In any event, there is no evidence to suggest that he or any other Chinese official ever responded to Kissinger's proposal.[51]

Over the coming year, U.S.-China relations would begin to cool. In a report to President Ford a few years later, Kissinger observed that around the turn of 1973-74, "some voices in Peking may have asserted that China was 'tilting' too far toward the United States." He believed that Mao's policy was coming under great pressure; whether his proposal and Zhou's interested response encouraged some influential Chinese to conclude that the leadership was going too far is not known.[52]

TOP SECRET/SENSITIVE/EXCLUSIVELY EYES ONLY
MEMORANDUM OF CONVERSATION
PARTICIPANTS: Prime Minister Zhou Enlai; Tang Wensheng,
    Interpreter; Secretary of State, Henry A. Kissinger; Commander
    Jonathan T. Howe, NSC Staff; Mrs. Bonnie Andrews, Notetaker
DATE AND TIME: Wednesday, November 14, 1973 7:35 A.M.-8:25 a.m.
PLACE: The Guest House Peking
SUBJECT: Japan, Congress, Pakistan[D]

Prime Minister Zhou: I wish to discuss with you our assessment of Japan. You mentioned two probable alternatives. There is a third alternative because they are under your nuclear umbrella and they have a very clear conception. And when you arrive on Japanese soil you will see that without the American umbrella, you will see what state they would be in. Then they would be under a different nuclear umbrella. I think that is a tendency that both of us should try to deviate. And the more farsighted statesmen of Japan must see the danger.

Of course, we don't think it would be possible for you to tell them all of your own plans with regard to your nuclear umbrella over Japan. You have a defense treaty with them and you can't tell them all the details but we feel you can come very close to them. Because at the present they cannot leave your nuclear umbrella or your energy resources; and to them their needs are not

---

[D] Source: *RG 59, PPS*, box 372, Secretary's Conversations in Peking November 1973.

confined to energy but to all resources of their economy. Their main short-coming is that some of their statesmen tend to be shortsighted, but I believe that in the turmoil of the world persons of great stature will gradually emerge. You have also included them in the economic aspect of the new Atlantic Charter. That will reassure them. They will meet with new difficulties and they have various odd notions.

Secretary Kissinger: They specialize in that.

Prime Minister Zhou: You cannot ask too much out of consideration of their foundations. If the foundations are comparatively shallow, then you must have imagination and also when you have such hodgepodge public opinion. They are perhaps not second to us. (To you.)

Secretary Kissinger: Their public opinion is even more complex than ours and their government has even less freedom of action. In foreign affairs our government has greater possibility for action.

Prime Minister Zhou: Although Congressional action has limited your President to war only 60 days, it would be temporary.[53]

Secretary Kissinger: Yes. And in practice, it will not make much difference, because what will they do if we go into a war?

Prime Minister Zhou: But you would have to report that to them.

Secretary Kissinger: Yes, but you can't hide a war.

Prime Minister Zhou: Some of your measures do not seem too scientific.

Secretary Kissinger: Once we are in a war, they cannot stop us.

They could have always stopped us in Vietnam by withholding appropriations. But while they made unbelievable amounts of noise, they voted the appropriations each year.

Prime Minister Zhou: That is the result of your constitutional system because various members wanted to make their views known to their constituents.

Secretary Kissinger: You saw Senator [Warren] Magnuson.

Prime Minister Zhou: And this time the second visit of Senator [Mike] Mansfield has been postponed. When there is a good time you might reconsider and tell us the result. We will also determine when the appropriate time would be. We don't think it would be good to have it put off indefinitely.

Secretary Kissinger: I agree. We don't have any objections to Mansfield.

Prime Minister Zhou: And Senator [Henry "Scoop"] Jackson.

Secretary Kissinger: Jackson will be quite an experience. I meant, it would be helpful.

Prime Minister Zhou: He is a Republican?

Secretary Kissinger: No, he is a Democrat. If I may make a suggestion as a friend about Senator Jackson. He is a friend of mine. You will find that he agrees with you completely about the Soviet Union but he has enemies in America who are more pro-Soviet but who are not against you. So, he should be handled in a way that when he comes back from here he doesn't take such an extreme position that he alienates men like Senator [William] Fulbright whom we need and who is his enemy.[54]

Prime Minister Zhou: (laughs questioningly) Oh?

Secretary Kissinger: It is a complex situation, but I think he should come.

Prime Minister Zhou: Another issue would be that of South Asia which the Chairman mentioned to you the other night. And that is that we will be in great favor of your assisting Pakistan and building a naval port in Pakistan. Of course, that would take time but it would be a significant step. And as you told us, and as Prime Minister Bhutto and other Pakistani friends have mentioned, you are also considering how to assist them in military ways. We cannot help them much because our arms are light weight. We have small arms but not heavy arms. You have heavy arms. The Soviet Union is always wanting to break through that knot. In South Asia it would be through India/Pakistan. And in the Middle East—it would be Iraq. And we can see that at present their greatest ambitions are there and to link the chain.

Secretary Kissinger: We have a tough time with our Congress on Pakistan—and their attitude is ridiculous. You should talk to Senator Mansfield when he comes.

Prime Minister Zhou: They are probably favorable toward India.

Secretary Kissinger: Yes.

Prime Minister Zhou: Perhaps it is the national character of the Americans to be taken in by those who seem kind and mild.

Secretary Kissinger: Yes.

Prime Minister Zhou: But the world is not so simple.

Secretary Kissinger: On Senator Mansfield. If he comes, I might perhaps offer another thought. And we know it is difficult for him not to see Prince Sihanouk but it could help us if he does not receive too much ammunition from the Chinese side on Cambodia.

Prime Minister Zhou: We understand. Perhaps he is partial on certain smatters.

Secretary Kissinger: Right, he is singleminded.

Prime Minister Zhou: But as a man, he is quite honorable.

Secretary Kissinger: Yes, he is a fine and decent man.

Prime Minister Zhou: And when he feels that your President is correct or when you are able to convince him, he is not obstinate. Perhaps you now, as

Secretary of State, can play that role. Because you will now meet with Congress.

Secretary Kissinger: Yes and now I am doing that systematically. And as the Prime Minister may have noted, many Congressmen have made favorable comments supporting our foreign policy since I became Secretary of State. And when I return, I will meet with four Congressional Committees and with the leaders.

Prime Minister Zhou: We wish you success and also success to the President.

Secretary Kissinger: Thank you and thank you for the reception we have received as always.

Prime Minister Zhou: It is what you deserve. And once the course has been set, as in 1971, we will persevere in the course.

Secretary Kissinger: So will we.

Prime Minister Zhou: That is why we use the term farsightedness to describe your meeting with the Chairman.

Secretary Kissinger: We maneuver more than you but we will get in the same direction.

Prime Minister Zhou: That is dialectic but we understand. Perhaps you need to maneuver. We want to be more straightforward.

[Before adjourning, they agree to release the communiqué at 10:00 P.M. Japan time. Zhou asks that Kissinger give his regards to the Nixons as well as to Japanese Prime Minister Kakuei Tanaka and Foreign Minister Masayoshi Ohira.]

THE WHITE HOUSE
TOP SECRET/SENSITIVE/EXCLUSIVELY EYES ONLY
MEMORANDUM OF CONVERSATION
PARTICIPANTS: Prime Minister Zhou Enlai; Tang Wensheng, Interpreter; Secretary of State, Henry A. Kissinger; Commander Jonathan T. Howe, NSC Staff; Mrs. Bonnie Andrews, Notetaker
DATE AND TIME: Wednesday, November 14, 1973 7:35 A.M. – 8:25 A.M.
PLACE: The Guest House, Beijing[E]

Prime Minister Zhou: And only by viewing it in that manner can we remind ourselves not to slacken our vigilance. That is the same for the coastal areas,

---

[E] Source: RG 59, *PPS*, box 381, President's China Trip.

for they are bound to come by the flanks. And because they have been here before, they [are] more familiar with the coastal areas of China. And, therefore, we must envisage that there will be a period when we will have to be fighting alone and that will be the basic military concept.

Before we had spoken about four quarters attacking us at the same time.[55] We are not talking about that now.

Secretary Kissinger: You would be wasting your resources to be protecting yourselves against us.

Prime Minister Zhou: So we are not going to go into detail now but we have put forward such a proposition. And under those circumstances, if as you envisaged it would be possible for you to cooperate with warnings, that would be intelligence of great assistance. And, of course, there are also communications networks. But this must be done in a manner so that no one feels we are allies.

Secretary Kissinger: I agree.

Prime Minister Zhou: And, therefore, indeed that would require very good consultations. The word "concrete" consultations (in the communiqué) is a correct one indeed.

Secretary Kissinger: Mr. Prime Minister there is no way we can establish a hot line secretly.

Prime Minister Zhou: Yes, I understand that.

Secretary Kissinger: But once the line is established, we can give it the purpose you described yesterday and that can be kept secret.

Prime Minister Zhou: And because it is so concrete and complex an issue, we need to study it before we can consult you further. One of the levels of such consultation would be as the document yesterday said (referring to the Joint Communiqué) at "authoritative levels." That was your proposed sentence and we thought it should be used. It was also put into the language that will be published that we would engage, while not negotiating on behalf of third parties, in concrete consultations. Now that you are Secretary of State perhaps you may not find you have so much time as before. But we also appreciate the fact that you have stayed only one-half days in the other countries and you have stayed four days here. After traveling in a cyclone to the others, you stay here four days. And the result of that is that we are meeting here this morning. And, therefore, besides your coming in person, we will have contact with each other in the Liaison Office. That would be Ambassador Bruce here and Huang Zhen there. And that would be done only through him and one interpreter. And he will know because he is a military man and he understands fighting. In this sense he will not be speaking in abstract ways and dwelling on grand principles. And on our part here, myself, Marshal Ye, and the Vice Minister, Cai Hongjing, whom you met the other day, would be the only ones involved. Of course, when we go into the details of this work, then we might also want to add some others. Your side already includes the Secretary of Defense and the Chairman of the JCS and his assistant.

Secretary Kissinger: But your Ambassador should talk only with me. Because those who know do not know what I have told you. And, frankly, so that you understand, I will tell my colleagues only each step as we decide it—not more. In that way there is the least danger of a leak.

Prime Minister Zhou: Yes. Because we know that you can keep secrets, but you must be very strict when you want to do that.

Secretary Kissinger: Yes.

Prime Minister Zhou: And on our side, of course, the main persons would be myself and Marshal Ye and also our assistants. And even if the decision would be made by our side, everything will be done with this channel.

Secretary Kissinger: We are confident that you know how to defend secrets.

Prime Minister Zhou: Because these secrets are slightly different than the other subjects and must be treated accordingly. And also when there are communications through the air, they can be of various types. Because communications through the air are not confined to one type now but to various types and then people can decode the messages. And I think that is all I might say for now. And as for the next step, when we have finished considering the matter, we will ask Ambassador Huang Zhen to contact you. Perhaps he will have to come back in the interim so we can discuss it.

* * *

Prime Minister Zhou: As for the matter you mentioned yesterday, the signing of the treaty for war, that is the treaty that you signed last year on the visit to Moscow.

Secretary Kissinger: Yes, and you understand that we don't care about the treaty, we just wanted an excuse to sign a hotline agreement. And the Soviet Union could not object since they signed the same treaty with us.

Prime Minister Zhou: We will have to study such issues because taking the nature of our country if we want to adopt such a course of action that would have great impact internationally. They know we are not talking empty words.

Secretary Kissinger: Why don't I . . . we have rewritten the treaty to adapt it to Chinese conditions. If you would want me to, I could leave a copy here or I could give it to your Ambassador in Washington.

Prime Minister Zhou: If it is too inconvenient, it can wait.

Secretary Kissinger: The principal obligation of the treaty is that if either side launches, they can communicate it rapidly to the other side. And that also is our interest in suggesting it. It has the advantage of creating an obligation of informing each other of an unauthorized launch, of detecting something which is unidentified on radar. But we are also prepared to establish a hot line directly without a treaty. Our thought would be to link our end of the hotline to the satellite and then work out with you how this could go quickly and directly to you. Here are the two documents, one is linking a hotline and an accidental war agreement. The other is simply the hotline. You can have them both together or separately. (Hands over documents attached at Tab A.)[56]

[Kissinger never had another extended discussion with Zhou, and he never received a response to his hotline proposal. Nevertheless, his optimism about the results of his trip, his confidence that he could oust the Soviet Union from Middle East negotiations, and his conviction that the world configuration of power was fundamentally advantageous for the U.S. position enabled him to tell U.S. ambassadors a few days later that "it is extremely in our interest, I believe to keep the present world going as long as possible."]

Notes

1. The quotation from U. Alexis Johnson, *The Right Hand of Power* (Englewood Cliffs, N.J.: Prentice-Hall, 1984), p. 555.
2. For Kissinger's account of the talks, see his *Years of Upheaval* (Boston: Little, Brown, 1982), pp. 678–99. For the importance of reassuring the Chinese, see "Scope Analysis: Sustaining the Momentum of U.S.–PRC Normalization: Preparing Ground for Hard Choices," n.d., National Archives, Record Group 59, Department of State Records, Executive Secretariat Briefing Books, 1958–1976, box 192, Secretary Kissinger's Visit to Peking October 1973 (1 of 2)
3. For political developments, see Richard Evans, *Deng Xiaoping and the Making of Modern China* (New York: Viking, 1993), pp. 193–96. See also Steven Ross, *Negotiating Cooperation, The United States and China, 1969–1989* (Stanford, Calif.: Stanford University Press, 1995), pp. 63–65; Kissinger to the President, "My Visit to China," 19 Nov. 1973, National Archives, Record Group 59, State Department Records, Policy Planning Staff (Director's Files), 1969–77 (hereafter referred to as *PPS*, with archival box number and file information), box 374, China–Sensitive Special WL File Misc. and Reports Nov 1974.
4. See Kissinger, *Years of Upheaval*, p. 687.
5. See Kissinger to the President, "My Visit to China," 19 Nov. 1973.
6. See ibid.
7. Harry Harding, "The Domestic Politics of China's Global Posture, 1973–78," in *Chi-*

na's Quest for Independence: Party Evolution in the 1970s, ed. Thomas Finger, (Boulder, Colo.: Westview, 1980), p. 96.

8. See Kissinger to the President, "My Visit to China," 2 March 1973. See the exchange between Kissinger and Zhou in memcon, 12 Nov. 1973, 3:00 P.M.–5:30 P.M., *PPS,* box 372, Secretary's Conversation in Peking, Nov. 1973. Kissingesr, *Years of Upheaval,* p. 692, where Kissinger speculates that Mao might have hinted at the possibility of a "separate legal status" for Taiwan.

9. See Kissinger to the President, "My Visit to China," 19 Nov. 1973, *PPS,* box 374, China-Sensitive-Special WL File.

10. See ibid.

11. See "Index of EA Conversations," n.d., box 380, Exclusive Eyes Only — Lord China File. For the more widely distributed file, see *PPS* box 372, Secretary's Conversations in Peking, Nov. 1973.

12. This may be the report mentioned by Robert McFarlane in *Special Trust* (New York: Cadell and Davies, 1994), p. 150.

13. See Director, Arms Control and Disarmament Agency Fred Ikle to Secretary Kissinger, "Your Trip to Peking: Arms Control Aspects," 22 Oct. 1973, attached to Solomon to Kissinger, "Director Ikle's Memorandum . . . ," 1 Nov. 1973, *PPS,* box 370, Secretary Kissinger's Visit to Peking S/PC Mr. Lord, vol. 2 (folder 2 of 2).

14. See memcon 11 Nov. 1973, *PPS,* box 372, Secretary's Conversations in Peking, Nov. 1973.

15. The Northroup Corporation later built the F5E factory in Taiwan; see Nancy B. Tucker, *Taiwan, Hong Kong and the United States, 1945–1992* (New York: Twayne, *Uncertain Friendships,* 1994), p. 145.

16. The joint project to develop Siberian natural gas fields involved Armand Hammer's Occidental Petroleum, El Paso Natural Gas, and Tokyo Gas. However, the ceiling on U.S. Export-Import Bank credits to the Soviet Union scuttled the plan because it depended on $100 million each from the Japanese Export-Import Bank, a consortium of private banks, and the U.S. Bank. See Carl Blumay with Henry Edwards, *The Dark Side of Power: The Real Armand Hammer* (New York: Simon and Schuster, 1992), p. 250.

17. Qiao had received his Ph.D. from the University of Göttingen in Germany.

18. Zhou's depiction of Konrad Adenauer as "active" was most likely a reference to the Chancellor's strong opposition to Soviet policy toward Germany.

19. See memcon, 12 Nov. 1973, *PPS,* box 372, Secretary's Conversations in Peking, Nov. 1973.

20. It was not until October 1970, however, that Nixon began to deemphasize previous demands for North Vietnamese withdrawal from the South. See William Bundy, *A Tangled Web: The Making of Foreign Policy in the Nixon Presidency* (New York, Hill and Wang, 1998), p. 206.

21. Kissinger's biggest accomplishment within six months was the Israel–Syria disengagement agreement signed 31 May 1974. See William B. Quandt, *Peace Process: American Diplomacy and the Arab–Israel Conflict Since 1947* (Washington, D.C.:Brookings Institution, 1993), pp. 213–14.

22. Kissinger quotes his statement about "slightly to the left" in *Years of Upheaval,* p. 686, but does not disclose his strategy of negotiations with Moscow.

23. See Kissinger to the President, "My Visit to China," 19 Nov. 1973.

24. See Kissinger, *Years of Upheaval*, pp. 688–94.

25. This is a reference to one of the last incidents concerning Soviet submarine access to the Cuban naval base at Cienfuegos. The event apparently took place in May 1972, not as recently as Kissinger suggests. For the controversy, see Garthoff, *Detente and Confrontation*, pp. 87–95, 338–41.

26. Bordeolovski not further identified.

27. Apparently Mao had made his last statement in English.

28. By 1973, the Chinese had some 79 bombers and 65 intermediate- and medium- range missiles for delivering a stockpile of about 150 weapons. This was indeed a "fly" compared to the thousands of ICBMS, SLBMs, and bombers in the American and Soviet stockpiles. See Robert S. Norris et al., *Nuclear Weapons Databook*, vol 5: *British, French, and Chinese Nuclear Weapons* (Boulder, Colo.: Westview Press, 1994), p. 359.

29. Urquiz is generally known today as Kirquiz.

30. Zhenbao (Chienpao) Island, known as Damansky Island to the Russians, was one of the larger islands located on Sino–Soviet border rivers that figured in the border dispute. It was the scene of eight incidents between Soviet and Chinese forces during January and February of 1969. See Garthoff, *Détente and Confrontations*, p.230.

31. Mao could be patient because the British leasehold for Hong Kong was due to expire in 1997.

32. Salim Ali (1934–1978) was chairman of South Yemen's Presidential Council during 1969–78.

33. For Kissinger's account of the abortive aattempt to draft an "Atlantic Declaration," see his *Years of Upheaval*, pp. 700–707.

34. George Wilhelm Friedrich Hegel (1770–1831), German philosopher of idealism and dialectical thinking, taught at the University of Berlin from 1818 until his death. For useful discussions of his thought, see George Lichtheim, *Marxism: An Historical and Critical Study* (New York: Columbia University Press, 1982), pp. 3–12, and Shlomo Avineri, *The Social and Political Thought of Karl Marx* (London: Cambridge University Press, 1968), pp. 8–40.

35. A one-time student of Hegel, Ludwig Feuerbach (1804–1872) became a critic of his teacher's philosophic idealism and developed a materialist philosophy that would influence Marx. See Avineri, *Social and Political Thought of Karl Marx*, pp. 8–12.

36. Thus, Marx drew upon Hegel's dialectical method but moved from an emphasis on the play of an "absolute spirit" on human consciousness and history to an emphasis on human labor, proposing that humanity made its history, produced and reproduced itself, and created its social relations, through the nature-ordained necessity to work.

37. This is a reference to then-ongoing anti-Confucius campaign.

38. For a different view of Gandhi's commitment to non-violence as a "total moral commitment" and not just a tactical question, see Judith M. Brown, *Gandhi: Prisoner of Hope* (New Haven: Yale Uniersity Press, 1989), p. 388.

39. Apparently a disparaging reference to Deputy Foreign Minister Qiao Guanhua.

40. For Mao's tense meetings with Khrushchev during the latter's third and last visit to China, see William Taubman, "Khrushchev vs. Mao: A Preliminary Sketch of the Role of Personality in the Sino–Soviet Split," *Cold War International History Project Bulletin* 8–9 (Winter 1996–97), p. 245.

41. During a basketball game attended by Mao and officials from the U.S. Liaison Office, Mao referred to Nancy Tang and Wang Hairong as "those spies," most likely because he believed, correctly as it turned out, that they were in league with his wife, Jiang Qing. See John H. Holdridge; *Crossing the Divide: An Insider's Account of Normalization of U.S. - China Relations* (Lanham, Md.: Rowman and Littlefield, 1997), p. 151.

42. For the full record, see memcon, 13 November, 4:30 – 7:15 p.m., *PPS*, box 372, Secretary's Conversations in Peking, November 1973.

43. Assistant Secretary for Latin American Affairs Jack B. Kubisch subsequently prepared for Kissinger a briefing paper on "Chilean Executions" for use in briefing Huang Zhen. Drawing on confidential information from within the junta, it stated that there had been some 320 "summary, on-the-spot executions" carried out between 11 and 30 September 1973, with total number of dead, as of mid-November about 1,500. On 24 October, the junta said that it would no longer carry out summary executions, but Kubisch observed that "there are no indications as yet of a disposition to forego executions *after* military trial." See Lord to the Secretary, "Information for the Chinese," 20 Nov. 1973, *PPS*, box 330, China Exchanges 1 Nov. 1973 – 31 March 1974. Corrections on the "talking points" prepared for Kissinger for briefing Chinese officials shows that he decided not to mention the executions.

44. The coup attempt, apparently generated by "right-wing pressures" on Prince Souvanna occurred on 20 August 1973. See State Department Briefing Paper, "Laos," n.d., *PPS*, box 370, Kissinger Visit to Peking, Oct. 1973.

45. For a succinct account of the Nixon administration's policy toward Chile, see William Robinson, *Promoting Polyarchy: Globalization, US Intervention, and Hegemony* (Cambridge, Eng.: Cambridge University Press, 1996), pp. 159 – 63.

46. See USLO to SecState, Peking 1171, 6 Oct. 1973, *PPS*, box 370, Kissinger Visit to Peking, S/PC Mr. Lord, vol. 1 (folder 1 of 2).

47. See Ross, *Negotiating Cooperation*, pp. 74 – 75.

48. See Walter Isaacson, *Kissinger: A Biography* (New York: Simon and Schuster, 1992), p. 208. For the more widely distributed record of the Tuesday night meeting, see memcon, "Marines, Southeast Asia," 13 November 1973, *PPS*, box 372, Secretary's Conversations in Peking, November 1973. For the closely-held excerpt from the same meeting, see memcon, 13 November 1973, *PPS*, box 381, President's China Trip, reproduced below.

49. See Richard Solomon to Kissinger, "The Current State of U.S. - PRC Relations," 31 Dec. 1973, *PPS*, box 330, China Exchanges 1 Nov. 1973 – 31 March 1974.

50. See George Herring, *America's Longest War: The United States and Vietnam, 1950 – 75*, (New York: McGraw-Hill, 1996), p. 291. In the weeks before Kissinger's visit, State Department intelligence suggested that, while the Democratic Republic of Vietnam leadership had not finalized its decision, it was likely to decide in favor of large-scale military action. See, for example, Ray S. Cline to the Secretary, "Prospects for a Communist Military Offensive This Dry Season," 26 Oct. 1973, *PPS*, box 370, Kissinger Visit to Peking.

51. For the record of this discussion, see memcon 14 Nov. 1973, 1:00 A.M. – 2:20 A.M., *PPS*, box 372, Secretary's Conversations in Beijing Nov. 1973.

52. For the communiqué's text, see *U.S. Department of State Bulletin*, 69 (10 Nov. 1973) pp. 716 – 17. For Kissinger's analysis, see Kissinger to the President, "My Visit to China," 19 Nov. 1973.

53. See Department of State Briefing Paper, "Hot Line Issues and Talking Points," Oct. 1975, *PPS*, box 373, Visit of Secretary Kissinger to Peking, 19–23 Oct. 1975 Bilateral Issues Book S/P Mr. Lord.

54. See Kissinger to the President, "Your Trip to the People's Republic of China: A Scope Analysis . . . ," 20 Nov. 1975, *PPS*, box 380, China notes.

55. This is a reference to the War Powers Resolution vetoed by Nixon on 24 October; Congress overrode the veto on 7 November. See "President Nixon's Veto of War Powers Measure Overridden by Congress," *U.S. Department of State Bulletin* 69 (26 Nov. 1973), pp. 662–64.

56. For Fulbright's friendly working relationship with Kissinger, see Randall Woods, *Fulbright: A Biography* (New York: Cambridge University Press, 1995), pp. 575–76, 646–47. For Fulbright's disagreements with Henry Jackson, see ibid., pp. 642–44.

57. When Zhou first met with Kissinger, he identified four threats to China's security — India, Japan, the Soviet Union, and the United States.

58. One document was entitled "Memorandum of Understanding Between the Governments of the United States and the Peoples' Republic of China Regarding the Establishment of a Direct Communications Link"; the other was entitled "Agreement Between the United States and the People's Republic of America."

5

"What Are 3,000 MIRVs Among Friends?":

Kissinger in Moscow, March 1974

When Henry Kissinger returned to Moscow in March 1974, his discussions with Leonid Brezhnev were not so informal as they had been during his May 1973 visit. Nor did Brezhnev vent his indignation to Kissinger about the Chinese as he had at Zavidovo, although the Soviets did convey a few quiet hints of concern. Unlike Kissinger's wide-ranging conversations with the Chinese with their often surprising digressions, the Moscow talks were rather more structured and focused, largely because Kissinger was there to prepare the agenda for President Nixon's forthcoming visit, which required diligent efforts to work through complex issues, including arms control, commercial-financial relations, and the Conference on Security and Cooperation in Europe [CSCE]. Kissinger later told the British that he found the Soviets basically "obnoxious," but the transcripts reveal how Cold War antagonists could negotiate affably and share in each other's jokes.

At the time of Kissinger's visit, U.S.–Soviet relations were becoming strained, even though the Nixon administration and the Politburo remained strongly committed to developing a nonadversarial relationship. Tensions over the Middle East complicated U.S. and Soviet foreign relations, and domestic U.S. pressures threatened economic cooperation. The March 1974 talks revealed these and other difficulties, as well as a continuing deadlock in the strategic arms limitations talks. Yet, in spite of disagreements and rivalries, neither side had any practical alternative to détente, and both wanted to make sure that it remained "irreversible."

Despite this mutual determination, President Nixon was mortally wounded by his Watergate cover-up. Not only had former top aides, such as Attorney General John Mitchell and Chief of Staff H. R. Haldeman, been indicted on conspiracy charges, but the House of Representatives had authorized the Judiciary Committee to conduct an impeachment inquiry. These developments disturbed the Soviets, because they seemed to threaten the stability of U.S.–Soviet relations. Nixon had personally assured Ambassador Dobrynin—and written General Secretary Brezhnev to the same effect—that he was determined to stay in office; but this was not the whole story, the Soviets soon learned. In January, Dobryin learned from Vice President Gerald Ford that if Nixon left office, Kissinger would remain as secretary of state. No matter who was president, U.S.-Soviet relations would presumably remain on course.[1]

Brezhnev's future was also in question. Although his political position was strong—his skills at consensus building and his personal control over relations with the United States were unchallenged—State Department officials believed that he had serious health problems. A top-secret study of the succession problem faced by an aging Soviet leadership reported that Brezhnev may have collapsed after a recent trip to Cuba. With his high-blood pressure, history of heart trouble, and weight problems, as well as heavy drinking and smoking, the report said, "We should not be surprised if he died or became physically incapacitated in the next year or two." This prognosis was not unique to Brezhnev: most of his aging cohort—the "gerontocracy"—were in poor health. Yet, even if the leadership changed, the department anticipated that "whoever succeeds Brezhnev would appear to be susceptible to the same pressures which led the Soviets to pursue détente."[2]

While nuclear arms and U.S.-China relations had encouraged the Soviets to move closer to the United States, some issues made détente more difficult. The Soviets were especially disgruntled by Kissinger's Middle East shuttle diplomacy. A special Geneva Conference sponsored by Washington and Moscow had lasted only one day and Kissinger excluded the Soviets from his efforts to facilitate the pullback of Israeli forces from the Suez Canal and to negotiate Syrian disengagement. Kissinger might have worried that his quest for unilateral U.S. diplomatic advantage would prompt greater Soviet activity in the region, but as he would note to close advisers, Moscow had been far from assertive.[3]

U.S.-Soviet relations were beginning to fall afoul of a developing network of labor leaders, old social democrats and Trotskyites turned "neo-conservative," and congressional and Defense Department hard-liners who sought to limit economic cooperation and to preserve narrow strategic advantage. At the forefront of these movements was presidential hopeful Sen. Henry "Scoop" Jackson (D-Wash.) who was successfully translating his fierce criticisms of SALT and Soviet emigration policies into legislative obstacles to détente. Jackson was already making progress with an amendment to the trade bill: the Jackson-Vanik Amendment, co-sponsored with Rep. Charles Vanik (D-Ohio), would link the extension of most-favored-nation

(MFN) status for the Soviet Union to freer conditions for emigration of Soviet Jews. In December, the House of Representatives had passed the amendment, and in early 1974, Jackson was steering it through the Senate. Jackson forces were also threatening to scuttle substantial Export-Import Bank credits to the Soviets, the foundation of economic détente.[4]

Nixon and Kissinger had privately acknowledged that Jackson–Vanik had a constructive impact on Moscow's emigration policy, but Jackson began to raise his demands. They feared that the amendment's blunt linkage of trade concessions with Soviet domestic policy would wreck the administration's effort to manipulate MFN and other economic benefits they sought to use as "carrots" to foster Soviet foreign policy restraint. As Kissinger prepared for the Nixon summit, he scrambled to negotiate with Jackson and his colleagues while privately encouraging the Soviets to loosen restrictions on emigration. Before leaving for Moscow, he described Jackson's view of him as a "hostile country"; he had not yet realized that the Senator was implacably opposed to compromise.[5]

Arms control remained critical to détente, and the centerpiece of the Brezhnev–Kissinger meetings were the SALT II negotiations. U.S. and Soviet delegations had met in Geneva since late 1972 to achieve new constraints on strategic nuclear delivery systems, but the talks had deadlocked. A basic problem was the status of multiple independently targetable reentry vehicles (MIRVs), a technology in which the United States enjoyed a substantial edge. The U.S. Air Force and Navy had already deployed thousands of MIRVs on Minuteman III missiles and Poseidon submarine-launched ballistic missiles, and the Soviets were determined to catch up. They did not even begin to test until the summer of 1973–five years after the first U.S. MIRV tests.[6]

MIRVs had been a SALT issue from the beginning, and influential U.S. arms control negotiators had argued early on for an outright ban as a way to check the spiraling U.S.–Soviet arms race. Kissinger had acquiesced in Nixon's decision to reject a MIRV ban during the SALT I talks, but now that the Soviets were developing their own he would lament to the press that "I wish I had thought through the implications of a MIRVed world more thoughtfully in 1969 and 1970 than I did."[7] Now he wanted the SALT process to constrain MIRV development so that Soviet warheads would not threaten Minuteman forces and significantly erode the United States' superiority in warheads.[8] Yet, Brezhnev found the MIRV limitations that Kissinger would offer him in March 1974 unacceptable. There was no chance that the forthcoming Moscow summit would include the signing of a SALT agreement.

On a few arms control issues, negotiations could be, and were, completed in time for Nixon's visit to Moscow. One was the decision to forgo one of two permitted anti-ballistic missiles sites allowed in the 1972 Antiballistic Missile Treaty; the other was the "threshold" test ban limiting underground nuclear tests, which was extremely controversial in Washington because of strong support for testing at the Pentagon and in some quarters of Congress. Last minute negotiations, mostly on the U.S. side, led to agreement on a 150 kilo-ton threshold for nuclear tests, although the U.S. Senate would never approve the treaty.[9]

Kissinger's memoirs provide important source material on the SALT talks, but in them he omits any mention of Brezhnev's persistant efforts to remove nuclear weapons from the Mediterranean, which Kissinger side-stepped. He also passes over U.S.–Soviet discussions of two significant negotiations on European issues, the historic Conference on Security and Cooperation in Europe [CSCE] and the negotiations on Mutual and Balanced Force Reductions (MFBR). Both issues, but especially CSCE, were of great concern to Europeans on both sides of the Cold War because they related to such central issues as security of frontiers, human rights, and the formidable armies confronting each other in Central Europe.[10]

In his talks with the Chinese, Kissinger had described the CSCE as "meaningless" at best, at worst an enterprise that could give a potentially dangerous opening to the Soviets.[11] However, with Brezhnev he could not be too devious because Moscow had a tremendous investment in European dé-tente; it was determined to get an agreement that would codify the postwar status quo, including the division of Germany. Kissinger, responding to Brezhnev's suspicions that Western European delegations were taking positions that subverted the Soviet Communist Party's political monopoly, offered assurances: "The United States will use its influence not to embarrass the Soviet Union or raise provocative issues." Yet, he was more cautious in response to Brezhnev's call for an early completion of the CSCE in order to link it to Nixon's visit. Kissinger did not want the conference to end too soon; as he would tell the British, as long as the Soviets were engaged in important talks with the West, the negotiations were "something . . . to restrain them in the future."

While the CSCE plodded along, the MBFR talks, which began in October 1973, were stalemated by incompatible negotiating positions. The West was focusing on cuts in U.S. and Soviet ground forces in Central Europe; the Soviets wanted West European forces as well as air and nuclear forces brought into the negotiations. Washington was willing to consider some reductions in nuclear weapons to match cuts in Soviet tank force, but the Soviets were not ready to discuss tanks. As neither Brezhnev nor Kissinger could find a way to expedite the talks, they could only agree to let them continue.

The available U.S. records of Kissinger's March 1974 visit to Moscow show that even when the discussions were heated, they remained cordial. The one antagonistic discussion, on the morning of 26 March, was devoted to the Middle East. Brezhnev read Kissinger the riot act. Kissinger could say nothing that would lessen Breshnev's objections to the U.S. policy of excluding the Soviets from the Middle East negotiations; and he certainly would not tell him the truth. In spite of this political chasm, the Kissinger–Brezhnev meeting crystallized plans for another heads-of-state summit that kept the lines of communication open at the highest level and gave more impetus to the détente process.

Before Kissinger went to Moscow, he held a meeting with his top advisers on Soviet policy and arms control issues. Among them were State Department Counselor Helmut Sonnenfeldt and States' Intelligence and Research (INR) Director William Hyland. Sonnenfeldt—perhaps the only one in the room who dared call Kissinger "Henry"—was an old colleague from army days, a Soviet expert at State Department INR during the 1950s and 1960s, and a key player on the NSC staff before returning to State. Sonnenfeldt's expertise made him indispensable, but his relationship with Kissinger was uneasy as is evidenced by the latter's jibes in Brezhnev's presence. Sonnenfeldt had brought Hyland, a CIA Soviet expert, to the NSC Staff where he had stayed until Kissinger went to State in 1973.[12]

No one in the room had to worry about diplomatic niceties or questions from nosy journalists, so the tone of the meeting was brutally frank; Kissinger, in particular, rages about his critics and the government bureaucracy. His interaction with top advisers provides an extraordinary picture of the key dilemmas of U.S. détente policy at midpoint—the impasse in arms control, Soviet resentment of the U.S. role in the Middle East, and the linkage between Soviet emigration policy and commercial relations. The latter led Kissinger to fulminate that the "the same sons of bitches who drove us out of Vietnam . . . [are now trying] to destroy détente and assert that it is our moral obligation to change internal Soviet policies." This conviction—that a state's "legitimacy" in the international system does not depend on the way it treats its citizens—put him at odds with the human rights component of the U.S. political tradition that motivated anti-Vietnam War protest as much as it did the crusades against dictatorships of the 1970s. Thus, it was natural for left-liberals such as Sen. George McGovern (D–S.D.) to challenge Kissinger's support for the dictatorial Thieu–Ky regime and push for Jackson–Vanik type approaches: they were following a consistent human rights policy.[13]

The staff meeting opened with Kissinger making caustic statements about U.S.–European relations. Since 1973, the United States and the European Community (EC) had been holding desultory conversations, stemming from Kissinger's "Year of Europe" initiative for a joint U.S.–E.C. declaration on transatlantic policy coordination. But U.S.–European tensions, spurred by domestic political developments and policy differences during the October War, had turned the declaration into a bureaucratic exercise.[14]

SECRET/NODIS/EYES ONLY[15]
Memorandum of Conversation
DATE: March 18, 1974 TIME: 11:40 A.M. PLACE: Secretary's Office
SUBJECT: The Secretary's Visit to the Soviet Union
PARTICIPANTS: The Secretary; Helmut Sonnenfeldt, Counselor of the Department; Arthur Hartman, Assistant Secretary for European Affairs; William Hyland, Director for Intelligence and Research; Lawrence S. Eagleburger, Executive Assistant to the Secretary; Brent Scowcroft, White House; Jan Lodal, White House; Denis Clift, White House[A]

(Sonnenfeldt, Hartman, Hyland, Scowcroft enter Secretary's office.)
Secretary: Art, I want the Europeans to understand beyond any doubt that the President is not coming in April. Not in any circumstances. Even if they give us the God damned EC declaration on a golden platter. The President is not going to Europe.

[After further discussion of the EC declaration, the talk turned to the MBFR and the CSCE negotiations.]

Secretary: Hal, did you hear about this MBFR VP meeting? The God damned Defense Department is becoming as cynical about MBFR as about SALT. We cut 29,000 men with no equipment and they cut 68,000 with their equipment. Then we put a ceiling on equipment so we are not penalized and

---

[A] Excised copy released through Freedom of Information Act request to Department of State, copy at National Security Archives (hereafter referred to as *NSA*).

they are. And to top it off, since Reforger is independent of MFBR, we have the right to send 50,000 troops into Europe each year for four months, so we withdrew 29,000 and have the capability to put in that 28,000 plus 31,000 more during the non-winter months when combat is most likely.[16] Do you really think that position can be negotiated? I am willing to try it but I don't think it has much of a chance.

Hartman: The important thing is to link US–Soviet reductions in the first phase with a second phase.

Sonnenfeldt: In the first phase we get US–Soviet reductions, a commitment to the principle of general equality and ceilings on other than US and Soviet forces.

Secretary: Wait a minute. Let me get this straight. Ten to fifteen percent cut in the first phase of US-Soviet forces; a ceiling on the rest of the participants; and a commitment to a common ceiling in the second phase, but what do we do about the God damned Russian tank army?

Sonnenfeldt: That is probably a non-starter. Unless we are willing to negotiate nuclear weapons, the Russians are going to refuse to talk about pulling back a tank army. So you keep the nuclear option in abeyance until you can buy something in SALT with it. Do you agree, Bill?

Hyland: Yes.

Secretary: What will be the Allied reaction?

Hyland: They have agreed. One of our strengths in MBFR is that we have carefully developed an Allied consensus so they don't have any room to bitch.

Secretary: Not until we get an agreement with the Soviets. I want you and Hartman to go to NATO after we go to Moscow. You may want to go to London first but I definitely want you to go to NATO.

Sonnenfeldt: Who were you looking at?

Secretary: You and Hartman, I have read the CSCE memo, unless there is a new one.

Sonnenfeldt: There is a new one.

Secretary: Then I haven't read it.

Sonnenfeldt: We have to be very careful on negotiating a CSCE summit with the Russians.

Secretary: I agree.

Hartman: I discussed this with the British in London last weekend and suggested we don't tie ourselves down firmly against a CSCE summit. Our political leadership may decide that they want one at the last minute.

Sonnenfeldt: And we may be able to use it as a sweetener for SALT.

Secretary: But [German Chancellor Willy] Brandt will probably recommend it himself.

Sonnenfeldt: That depends on what happens in Basket III.[17] They are now doing minuets in Geneva on the subject of Human Contacts. All the Europeans who drove us into the conference are now saying, and they repeated it when I was at NATO, that they have to have something on Human Contacts for their parliaments so they are getting themselves in the position of demanding exactly what the Russians cannot give. But the issue on Basket III is being narrowed to some extent.

Hartman: Our proposal.

Secretary: What is our proposal?

Hartman: To make some reference in the principles to laws and regulations to avoid reference to customs and to insert a cross reference in the preamble to Basket III linking it to the principles.

Sonnenfeldt: But as Brezhnev said to Stoessel, Basket III is chickenfeed. What really matters to the Russians is the principle of inviolability of frontiers. But I think we are going to have to let the Europeans bleed themselves on that one.

Secretary: Who is siding with the Germans against the Russians on that issue?

Hartman: All the Europeans are backing the Germans.

Hyland: I think the Russians will buy some reference to peaceful change as long as it isn't juxtaposed with language on borders.

Sonnenfeldt: This is really the Germans' problem. We shouldn't get out in front of them.

Secretary: Hal, can we do a back channel to Bahr saying that in view of my trip we would like a rundown of his talks in Moscow and at the same time can we ask Von Staden officially if the German position is the same as Scheel outlined to me at dinner.

Sonnenfeldt: We have got some debriefing of the Bahr visit to Moscow but it hasn't been very specific nor helpful.

Secretary: (Looking at CSCE memo) Shouldn't we ask for a Soviet draft? Both of us should submit drafts.

Sonnenfeldt: That's right.

Secretary: But what bothers me about all of this is that the Soviets are getting nothing out of détente. We are pushing them everywhere and what can I deliver in Moscow?

Sonnenfeldt: We are in bad shape.

Secretary: Why, what do you mean?

Sonnenfeldt: There is going to be no trade bill and we will get clobbered on the Ex-Im credits issue.

Secretary: Then God damn it, we are going to have a public brawl with them. The same sons of bitches who drove us out of Vietnam and said it would be immoral for us to tamper with the North Vietnamese internal system now try to destroy détente and assert that its our moral obligation to change internal Soviet policies.

Sonnenfeldt: Will you get anything out of [Senator] Jackson and Ribicoff this week?

Secretary: Nothing. Could someone get me the Jackson paper.[18] Every time I ask for it, it is at the White House.

Sonnenfeldt: Which Jackson paper at the White House? Unless there is a different one, you returned it to me. (Showing the Secretary his memo) Is this what you mean?

Secretary: Campbell thinks he has a moral obligation to keep my papers at the White House.[19] Every time I ask for one, it is over there.

Sonnenfeldt: There is nothing we can do with Jackson now as far as I can see.

Secretary: You are absolutely right. Jackson has obviously been convinced that I am a hostile country. He won't go below 100,000 on the immigration issue before I go to Moscow because he obviously thinks he wouldn't get it. If I can't deliver the 100,000, then he may accept a smaller number.

Sonnenfeldt: You are going to have to talk to Dobrynin and get a piece of paper which contains a commitment on credits.

Secretary: Haven't you heard Jackson's latest—he says if we deliver everything he wants on immigration, then he will deliver MFN and do his best on credits—but he is not so sure on that issue. On the Ex-Im thing, what are they trying to do? What is their purpose?

Sonnenfeldt: They say that we are giving away billions of dollars of credits to the Soviet Union which ultimately is underwriting their defense budget and thus weakening our security.

Hyland: It is the same old cold war argument against trading with the communists.

Secretary: That point of view simply supports the Soviet view that there is really no way of effectively dealing with the United States. Given their system, they have tried to be fairly reasonable all across the board. You can look at no place where they have really tried to make serious trouble for us. Even in the Middle East where our political strategy put them in an awful bind, they haven't really tried to screw us. Their tactics haven't been exactly brilliant but they haven't been particularly destructive either.

Sonnenfeldt: I assume Dobrynin wants to ride back to Washington on the airplane. It will be a nice full aircraft.

Secretary: I might take my two kids along too.

Sonnenfeldt: Good. That should put you in a good mood.

(Clift and Lodal enter.)

Secretary: Let's talk about SALT. Jan, I read your paper and I like it.

Sonnenfeldt: There is a slightly revised version of what you would give Dobrynin at Tab A.[20]

Secretary: (Looking at memo) I don't find it at Tab A.

Sonnenfeldt: That is the wrong paper. That's Art's CSCE memo.

The theory is to try to force some reaction out of the Russians on the MIRV question.

[Large portions of the discussion of SALT, about 105 lines, have been excised from this document.]

Secretary: . . . but these bastards on the hill ignore the fact that 400 Jews were leaving the Soviet Union in 1969 and now say that 30,000 a year is inconsequential.

Sonnenfeldt: Of course, they say it is their pressure which forced the number to 40,000 and that, if we keep after the Russians it will go up even higher.

Secretary: Whose bright idea was it that I negotiate this with Richard Pearl [*sic*]?[21] Whose memo was that?

Sonnenfeldt: What memo?

Secretary: I don't negotiate with staff members.

Sonnenfeldt: Whose memo was that?

Scowcroft: Peter Rodman's.

Sonnenfeldt: There are too many memos floating around.

Secretary: I think this SALT memo is OK. We can't go to the Russians with one specific cynical proposal after another. We have to give them something realistic but I think the paper at Tab A goes too much into numbers.

Sonnenfeldt: It is really the NSDM [National Security Decision Memorandum], Henry.[22]

Secretary: I understand that, but I don't give a God damn about the NSDM.

Sonnenfeldt: I think we have to make one more stab with the Russians on the issue of equal MIRV throw weight.

Secretary: I agree, but I want one sentence which sums up our position at Geneva. I don't want all this detail.

Sonnenfeldt: That is another way to do it.

Secretary: I think that is the best way. I like the alternative to the bracketed portion, the one that includes the procedures.

Lodal: Oops. I was supposed to give you pages that took that part out.

Secretary: I like the procedures part.

Lodal: We can put it in either way.

Sonnenfeldt: You are talking about the tics at Tab A?

Secretary: Yes. What I want to give the Russians is something to start the SALT process working smoothly. I do not want to give them a final position and tell them to take it or leave it. Trade is no good, SALT can't go down the drain. I want to say these are our ideas and we are eager to get yours. Anyway, no matter what we do, the [Joint] Chiefs [of Staff] and Jackson will shoot the hell out of us so we might as well do what is right. Bill, would you do a memo on the Soviet situation.

Sonnenfeldt: Do you want to give a piece of paper to Dobrynin on SALT before we leave?

Secretary: I think so. Almost certainly. Before Wednesday. Now Denis, what are the problems with bilateral agreements?

[The discussion turns to specific agreements that can be signed at the summit, including the threshold test ban, a long-term economic agreement, space cooperation, and an umbrella agreement on energy. When Kissinger learns of delays in an energy agreement, he roars that "I don't want any waffling by the God damned bureaucracy. I want specific proposals to give to the Russians but no God damned waffling."]

Clift: Another area of cooperation is space. Doctor [James] Fletcher of NASA is very much in favor of a second US–Soviet space launch. That would be a real benefit to the United States since it would keep NASA alive during this period.

Secretary: I could give that to Brezhnev. With his mentality he would like it. Do they still want the President to travel in Russia again?

Sonnenfeldt: [Nikolai] Patolichev mentioned something to that effect when he was here.

Secretary: If the President is impeached, will the Russians want to go on with it?

Hyland: I think they will if the President decides he wants to.

Secretary: How, what about this HUD [Department of Housing and Urban Development] proposal.

Clift: Lynn has some reservations about general cooperation.

Secretary: Every stinking, God damned bureaucrat in this town has reservations about cooperation with the Russians. I am not asking about their reservations. I am not asking about their reservations. I am asking what they can do.

[More discussion on the umbrella agreement on energy in which Assistant Secretary of Treasury Charles Cooper plays a lead role.]

Secretary: Brezhnev needs to have something to report to the Politburo. I have to give him a little analysis about what is possible in this field, but he is totally incompetent to discuss detail. If I tell him that Simon should talk to Isokov (*sic*) or whatever his name is, he will go jumping around the room mumbling and we won't come away with a thing.[23] That is totally the wrong way to deal with him. Brezhnev's contribution will be to deliver the Politburo. Mine has to be to explain to him why it is in our and the Soviets best interests to reach an agreement.
Sonnenfeldt: That is what Cooper is supposed to be doing for you.
Clift: It is not really hard to recast my memo.
Secretary: It is not useful if it is not written for conversations with Brezhnev. I need a ten minute exposition of what we think we can accomplish.
Sonnenfeldt: And you know what he will say.
Secretary: The big projects. This is all the more reason to give him an analysis which convinces him there is something to be gained from the small ones. I now have to swear in the first bearded assistant secretary of the State Department.[24]
Sonnenfeldt: Perhaps not the first, Charles Evans Hughes was Secretary of State in 1900 and he had a tremendous beard.[25]

COMMENTARY

Kissinger's memoirs provide a reasonably full account of his talks with Brezhnev in March 1974, but, the transcripts show points that he elided, such as Brezhnev's strong aversion to U.S. nuclear "forward based systems" [FBS] deployed in NATO Europe and adjoining waters.[27] "Who are these aimed at?" Brezhnev asked. With SLBMs in the Mediterranean, he complained, Washington could strike targets in much of European Russia and beyond, as far as Baku and Tashkent. While Kissinger tried to soothe Brezhnev by talling him that the U.S.'s "entire policy . . . is based on the proposition that neither side [can] attempt to achieve military superiority over the other," in other settings he would suggest that the United States enjoyed relative strategic superiority. Taking numbers of warheads and missile accuracy into account, Kissinger later told a NATO audience, "the results of analyses [of] a first strike show that if you have to choose military establishments, you would not necessarily choose the Soviet side."[28]

Kissinger was preoccupied with Middle East negotiations and lacked time for any careful study of arms control options, so he settled for a a SALT negotiating position that would deflect attacks from critics. Rejecting Soviet proposals for cuts in FBS, he focused on MIRVs. Partly in order to placate Senator Jackson—a sharp critic of SALT I's unequal features—Kissinger sought an agreement that permitted "a high degree of equivalence" in central strategic nuclear delivery systems (ICBMs, SLBMs, and long-range bombers). The problem was that these proposals were nonstarters: they codified the United States' strategic advantage in MIRVs. So, rather than submitting another "cynical proposal," Kissinger had one developed that he hoped would get negotiations "working smoothly." The new proposal was based on each sides' advantages—"offsetting asymmetries"—thus preserving the Soviet lead in ICBMs while protecting the U.S. advantage in MIRVs. Further, to check Soviet MIRV development, Kissinger insisted on a specific ceiling on heavy ICBMs with MIRVs.[29]

Kissinger had told the press that there was a possibility of a "breakthrough" that would move the talks forward, but nothing of the sort happens, at least not in the sense of a workable compromise. Despite Kissinger's claims about Brezhnev's competence, the transcripts show the General Secretary completely engaged in the minutiae of SALT. Nevertheless, amid the verbal sparring, some differences were narrowed; notably, Brezhnev did come round to consider an agreement that would permit a slight U.S. advantage in MIRVed ICBMs of 1,100 to 1,000. The transcripts suggest that Kissinger was interested in the proposal until a "slight insurrection" in his staff led to reconsideration. Kissinger did not mention this in his memoirs, nor did he take credit for suggesting the 1,100 figure to Brezhnev in the first place.

THE WHITE HOUSE
SECRET/NODIS
MEMORANDUM OF CONVERSATION
PARTICIPANTS: Leonid I. Brezhnev, General Secretary of the Central Committee, CPSU; Andrei A. Gromyko, Member of the Politburo of the Central Committee, CPSU, and Minister of Foreign Affairs of the USSR; Anatoly F. Dobrynin, Ambassador to USA;

Andrei M. Aleksandrov, Assistant to the General Secretary; Georgi M. Korniyenko, Member of the Collegium of the MFA; Chief of USA Department; Victor M. Sukhodrev, USA Department, MFA (Interpreter); Andrei Vavilov, USA Department; Oleg Sokolov, USA Department; Henry A. Kissinger, Secretary of State and Assistant to the President for National Security Affairs; Walter J. Stoessel, Jr., Ambassador to the USSR; Helmut Sonnenfeldt, Counselor of the Department of State; Arthur A. Hartman, Assistant Secretary of State for European Affairs; William G. Hyland, Director - INR; Jan M. Lodal, NSC Senior Staff; Peter W. Rodman, NSC Staff
DATE AND TIME: Monday, March 25, 1974 11:05 A.M. - 1:57 P.M.
PLACE: Brezhnev's Office, Council of Ministers Building The Kremlin
SUBJECTS: US–Soviet Relations; SALT; Other Arms Control[B]

(The Secretary's party arrived at 11:00 A.M. and was greeted by the General Secretary in his office. Press and photographers were present. There was a brief period of picture taking and pleasantries.)

US–Soviet Relations

Brezhnev: Dr. Kissinger, I expect we should devote as little time as possible to protocol matters and get down to concrete things right away. But I can't deprive myself of the pleasure of expressing my profound satisfaction at this new visit of yours to the Soviet Union, and I know it will be useful. Your previous ones have, and this will I'm sure be of good service to our peoples and states.

But I guess our situation is made easier by the fact that this is not our first meeting. We have accumulated some experience in negotiating, and it is not the first stage—it is the development of negotiations that have been taking place since 1972 and 1973.

But previously I talked to a Dr. Kissinger who had one title; now he has two titles, while I am stuck with my one. Isn't that true?
Gromyko: Just one! (Laughter)
Kissinger: We will make special allowance for that.
Brezhnev: Let me say a couple of words about the development of our relations in the recent past.

[B] U.S. Department of State Freedom of Information Act release, copy at *NSA.*

Kissinger: Certainly I would like to express appreciation for myself and my colleagues for your courtesy—especially that you let me bring my children. We feel that having worked together these many years we have a good foundation for the future.

Brezhnev: That is certainly true. We have laid a good foundation. And I will not now speak about those who want to shake or destroy that foundation. And I believe when those people become more mature they will apologize to their own people for the harm they are trying to do.

We have always been and always are according hospitality to our guests, but I would like to call attention to another aspect of our meetings: I hope this round will be useful in preparing for the forthcoming visit by President Nixon to Moscow. We are preparing not in a purely formal way, but we will sign agreements that will break new ground.

We should speak less on minor points and more on the really important policy issues.

Kissinger: I agree.

Brezhnev: And if from that point of view we consider the state of our relationships in the past several years, if we look at them in a big way, casting aside the minor points—and I know there are important internal problems—in general, we can say they are developing in a positive way. (Kissinger nods yes.) It wouldn't be in our best interests not to admit we have had to go through quite a few difficulties and complexities in the past, but what we have achieved in our relationships has withstood the test of time, and in a complex situation.

And therefore I wish to reemphasize that at this point we still have more grounds than before to stress the exclusive importance of our meetings with President Nixon and the importance of the agreements and understandings they produced. I should like to heavily emphasize, and I repeat emphasize, that the entire Soviet leadership stands today as hitherto on the principles expounded to President Nixon in the documents and in our previous meetings. Without going into the various details of what is taking place in the United States—and we hear and read a lot about it—we see that President Nixon is displaying firmness and resolve to move ahead on the course we have charted, to move ahead toward further deepening of relationships between the Soviet Union and the United States. But having said that, I cannot fail to say that in order to move further ahead we have to overcome a few difficulties and obstacles which are integrally linked to improving relations with us and improving the atmosphere in the world. And that fact may well come to be one of the difficulties we face. But I feel sure the experience of the past will help us find correct solutions without violating the principles we have agreed upon.

(Brezhnev plays with a dome-shaped brass object on his desk. He lifts off the top. It reveals six brass cartridge-like objects pointed upward. He removes the cover from one of those and it reveals six cigarettes.)

Kissinger: Is that a MIRV? (laughter)

Brezhnev: No, it's for cigarettes. It's more peaceful than it looks.

Kissinger: One of our intelligence experts will now say we know there are six MIRVs on the Soviet missiles.

Gromyko: That's what we do from friendship.

Kissinger: It's better than much of our intelligence.

Brezhnev: We have no secrets from each other.

Let me say I am very grateful to President Nixon for his recent message (President's letter of March 21, Tab A). It was one I read with great interest, and I replied right away (Tab B).[30] I am glad Ambassador Dobrynin was able to discuss it.

Kissinger: The President was very glad to receive it, and sends his warm personal regards.

Brezhnev: Thank you. Since I knew you would be empowered to conduct these negotiations with me (Kissinger smiles to Sonnenfeldt) I didn't go into any of the details of the subjects. I frequently recall the conversation we had, especially at San Clemente, when the President emphasized the very good and very friendly relations that had been coming into being between us. That we very much retain, and in my reply I wanted to tell him we maintain that spirit.

I would like to say a few words on the substance of the matter at hand.

Kissinger: Please.

Brezhnev: The basic substance is that, in order not to spoil the past, and in order to secure further advance in the future, we must ensure that the forthcoming visit of President Nixon to this country be of no lesser significance in its content than our two previous meetings. On the contrary, we must show our two peoples that all we have done in the past has built a secure foundation. If we slipped back, that would be a bad sign for our two peoples. And these words I link with the grand strategy of our state and our party. We have always said, particularly after the 23rd and 24th Party Congresses, that our policy is not built on momentary considerations. And this relates not merely to the question of, say, economic ties, but first and foremost to the basic policies of peace and the necessity to save mankind from the scourge of thermonuclear war, and that must be the focal point of all our discussions.

I believe that in the course of our discussions there will be quite a few questions we will want to raise. (Kissinger nods yes.) I would like to ask you, Dr. Kissinger, what you would prefer to start out with.

Kissinger: Mr. General Secretary, we agree with everything you have said. When we first met, almost two years ago, to prepare for the summit between you and President Nixon, we were at the very beginning of a totally new relationship. You and President Nixon recognized that whatever differences exist, our two countries have a very special responsibility to bring about peace between ourselves and peace in the world. This conviction has been strengthened by the events of the past two years and it is the fundamental guiding principle of our relations, which we are determined to follow in all our dealings with the Soviet Union.

Brezhnev: I am very pleased to hear that.

Kissinger: In addition, there has grown up a degree of personal confidence between President Nixon and the General Secretary which is unusual among leaders of great powers and which we are sure will be a further guarantee of our relations. So the most important thing is to reaffirm that the President and the Administration are determined to pursue the course even when occasionally there are disappointments, and against all opposition in the United States. Our basic objective is to make the pattern of our relations they have developed in the past two years irreversible, no matter what happens.

Brezhnev: (Interrupts Sukhodrev's translation.) We should cross out the word "disappointments." "Complications" is better.

Kissinger: It is a better word.

Brezhnev: Because I have never seen President Nixon disappointed with what we have done. Only [Senator] Jackson.

Kissinger: Right.

Brezhnev: And he is not America.

Kissinger: And that will be proved in the next two years.

(Sukhodrev finishes his translation of the Secretary's remarks above.)

Brezhnev: That is a word I certainly like—"irreversible." And I say so not only on my behalf but for my entire Party and people. I could fit you out with an artificial mustache and beard and you could go in any part of the country, and anybody you ask would come up with those words. And I say that to truly emphasize that this policy of détente, of improving relationships with the United States, is one approved by the Soviet people. You know why this is so. It requires no complex explanation.

Kissinger: So it is in the United States. There are groups and individuals in the United States who have always opposed these policies. And there are other groups who have taken our successes for granted, so they think they can have both peace and an anti-Soviet policy. But we will not be deflected from the course that you and the President agreed to at the two summit meetings. We will reinforce it at the next summit meeting. And we agree with the General Secretary that the next summit meeting must be worthy of its predecessors, with their agreements on strategic arms limitation, the agreement on prevention of nuclear war, and other agreements.

I want specifically to emphasize that we will observe and carry out to the best of our ability every understanding we have made, whether on trade or on specific geographic areas.

The General Secretary asked me what we should discuss here. We believe . . .

Brezhnev: That is, what we should start out with.

Kissinger: Well, the Foreign Minister mentioned this morning, and I agreed, that we might discuss this morning strategic arms, and this afternoon the Middle East. If that is still your wish, we agree with your proposal. On other topics, we are prepared to discuss anything in our relations, but we think the problem of force reductions in Central Europe is ripe for progress, and on the European Security Conference we are prepared to discuss how it can be brought to a rapid conclusion at the appropriate level. We are prepared to discuss a long-term trade agreement, as well as other issues in our bilateral relations that are appropriate to cover.

Brezhnev: I certainly believe that during so pleasant a meeting as this, neither side should restrict the range of questions to discuss, and both should feel free to raise any matter that seems useful to discuss. Both sides should proceed this way.

Kissinger: I agree.

Brezhnev: We are indeed prepared to begin by discussing any question, and it is my view that the question of strategic arms is the most complex and most appropriate. It would be better still if Dr. Kissinger could arrange to work out and even sign a whole series of important agreements and bring them back to President Nixon. (Gromyko make[s] a comment to Brezhnev.) But the Foreign Minister says not sign it, only initial. He wants to initial them himself.

Gromyko: No, I want to leave something for the summit.

Kissinger: If we make progress here, whatever we agree to here we will certainly maintain.

Brezhnev: I certainly agree. If we reach agreement on certain issues, we should maintain them. Otherwise we are not honest partners.

Kissinger: If we are to discuss strategic arms, I have one associate waiting outside who is a technical expert, and I would like to bring him in.

Brezhnev: Certainly.

(Hyland goes out to fetch Lodal. Hyland returns alone; Lodal can't be found. Hyland goes out again. Hartman goes out to retrieve Hyland. Hyland returns, goes out again.)

Kissinger: We have no simple problems.

Gromyko: We can assure you we have not gone in for a kidnapping exercise.

Kissinger: One Foreign Service officer was just kidnapped in Mexico, and they're demanding $500,000.[31] But I don't know one that's worth $500,000, so we're refusing to pay. We're prepared to proceed without him.

(Lodal arrives. The Soviets had kept him in a waiting room at the other end of the corridor. Dr. Kissinger introduces him.)

Brezhnev: (to Lodal) Dr. Kissinger didn't want you to be present, but I insisted on your being present.

Lodal: Thank you.

Kissinger: Provocateur! I have trouble enough with discipline on my staff.

Brezhnev: I told you I had difficulties—I used to talk with you when you were only Assistant to the President for National Security Affairs. Now you are Secretary of State, too. And you have other titles too.

Kissinger: What other titles? I don't mean what they call me in the newspapers.

Brezhnev: Let's have some of those snacks first. (Snacks are served.)

Kissinger: I had lost 2 kilos before I came.

Brezhnev: You look well, honestly.

We can start our discussions.

Kissinger: Please.

Strategic Arms Limitation Talks

Brezhnev: We start with strategic arms.

Kissinger: Please.

I gave to your Ambassador, Mr. General Secretary, some ideas which we developed to advance the discussion (Tab C, US note of March 21). I don't know if we should use those as a starting point.[32]

Brezhnev: I think we should basically proceed from the fact that our delegations discussing the matter find themselves deadlocked. They have engaged in discussions but have not moved very far.

Past experience has shown that this is the time for decisions to be taken at a higher level.

Kissinger: That is our view.

Brezhnev: I would just like to make an observation here: If we let our purely military men into this sphere we'll end up with an unprecedented arms race; I say that in a full sense of responsibility. Your military men and ours are the same. You can't really blame them. What they say is, we don't care about all these policies, and there is the Secretary of Defense saying the United States has to be militarily stronger. And there are others in the United States echoing these views and saying "We have to talk to the Soviet Union from a position of military strength."[33]

Surely, Dr. Kissinger, if we let ourselves be carried away by that kind of talk, all our discussions will come to nothing. What we have based ourselves on in the past, and the greatness of what we have achieved, is that we first of all achieved a freeze of existing arms and agreed on reductions, but without changing the balance. Only on that basis can we maintain coexistence.

So let us endeavor to decide something at this level without giving new instructions at Geneva. If we achieve something, our delegates will talk a different language.

Kissinger: I agree, this is the best way to proceed.

Brezhnev: But I really would like you to pay attention to this fact, all those statements about the United States needing to be strong.

Aleksandrov: (Correcting Sukhodrev's translation) Stronger.

Brezhnev: Unless we put a stop to this kind of talk in the United States, people will become accustomed to this need, that is, the need to talk to the Soviet Union from a position of strength. And not for the record, perhaps, but let me say that living generations of Americans have never experienced war on their own territory and never experienced a fascist advance as far as Stalingrad—so they are prone to this kind of talk. Americans have not had 20 million deaths from war.

Gromyko: Think of how many widows and orphans there are.

Brezhnev: In Belorussia, every fourth person died in the war. That is why we in this country—I can't speak for the United States—are very sensitive to these issues. I have emphasized this to everyone—to Chancellor [Willy] Brandt, for instance. Even if the Senate didn't appropriate additional sums of money to the Pentagon, and if the Pentagon didn't always shout about it, it would still be a very sensitive subject for us. But the sensitivity is heightened by these statements. We can't help it.

I would like to emphasize, Dr. Kissinger, you and I don't have an easy task before us, but we are duty bound—I repeat, duty bound—to find an acceptable solution, a solution which will give no advantage to either side. That is the principle we agreed on with President Nixon, and I would like to see it observed.

Kissinger: Mr. General Secretary, the entire policy of the Administration is based on the presupposition that neither side can achieve military superiority over the other and should not attempt to achieve military superiority over the other. If either tries to talk to the other from a position of strength, it will be a disaster for our two peoples and for all mankind. I have made this point in every public statement, and so has the President. Since we speak here as friends, I can tell you certain circles in the United States have taken advantage of certain domestic developments to say things that would be difficult to permit otherwise. But the basic direction of our foreign policy is fixed. And of course our people are also watching Soviet developments, and as the Soviet Union develops new weapons, they are used as a justification for our new weapons.

Brezhnev: I don't quite agree on that, and here is why:

By the time the SALT agreement was signed, the United States already had its multiple reentry vehicles and we were behind the United States in that field. But nonetheless we did agree to sign the agreement on that score, proceeding from the most humane goal, which is embodied in the preamble of that (agreement). And we undertook not to introduce any new missile systems and we accepted certain conditions for those, and those are being scrupulously observed.

Kissinger: We don't question that.

Brezhnev: By the beginning of next year, perhaps I or perhaps someone else will be entrusted with making the relevant report, but we will accurately report what is taken out of commission and made into submarines. But we are not making any new weapons.[34] It was agreed we both could engage in certain improvements but without any increase in diameter or any new systems. We have developed a MIRV but that is all that is taking place. So it is wrong to say we are devising something new. Even if something is being invented, we are not deploying anything in contravention of the agreement.

President Nixon said there are new submarines being developed in the United States, but while there are 42 . . .

Kissinger: 62.

Brezhnev: Yes, 62, we won't develop any new ones.

Kissinger: If you want to make it 42, we won't object.

Brezhnev: We scrupulously observe that. We know you are making MIRVs on the submarines and replacing Poseidons with Minutemen.[35]

Kissinger: No.

Brezhnev: You're installing new missiles in place of older models.

Kissinger: That is true.

Brezhnev: Within the limits of the improvements allowed by the agreement. So it is wrong to conclude that we're doing anything in contravention of the agreement. So as of this time, it is certainly a fact you are ahead of us in multiple warheads. As this is one aspect that can't lend itself to control by national means of detection.[36] Since you were ahead, we assume you have more. If we have to apologize for something we're not doing . . . The numbers you have are in excess of what we have. I'm not complaining about that. We should both scrupulously observe the agreement. You are refusing to take into account forward-based systems. Who are these aimed at? Not against France, because France can't declare war on the United States.

Kissinger: But this may change if things keep up!

Brezhnev: Or Holland or Belgium, or the GDR or the FRG. I can show you a map. You said the agreement should relate to American missiles that could reach the Soviet Union and Soviet missiles that could reach the United States. That is the significance of those forward-based missiles. (He shows a small map.) They can reach Tashkent, or Baku.

Kissinger: The submarines?[37]

Brezhnev: Yes. And air bases. More than one-half of the European part of the Soviet Union is within range of those.

Kissinger: We have to separate the problems. First of all, if M. Jobert makes more of his speeches, we'll need some of those missiles against France.[38]

Brezhnev: You can't blame me for that! No speech ever caused destruction; only weapons have.

Kissinger: This shows submarines?

Brezhnev: It shows all kinds of bases and ships.

Kissinger: So this line is the range of the submarines, and they're being counted. They are part of the agreement. They are not forward-based systems. They are counted in the Interim Agreement.

Gromyko: But they are pointed at us—whether submarines or carrier-based aircraft. The first agreement left aside strategic aviation.

Kissinger: I agree with that. That's a separate problem.

These are our fighter aircraft?

Brezhnev: It's not a good picture, is it? Those are European-based aircraft carrying nuclear weapons. Then nothing else remains for us but to have our aircraft carrying nuclear weapons or missiles.[39]

Kissinger: I have two separate problems, Mr. General Secretary. According to our estimate, you're developing four new missiles.[40] That's not in violation of the agreement. In fact, one of them impresses our people very much, and if that's only an improvement, I'd hate to see what a new system looked like. In fact, if I see Mr. Smirnov, I'll congratulate him on this new system.

Brezhnev: I can reply in place of Mr. Smirnov, and I can say we're not making a single new missile. We are improving our missiles.

Kissinger: It's just a question of definition. It's such a great improvement that to our people it looks like a new one. But I won't debate it. But we're not saying it's in violation of the agreement.

Brezhnev: Let us not proceed from what people think but from official statements of governments, and from what lends itself to control.

Kissinger: I agree.

Brezhnev: If we really get down to business, we should proceed from the assumption that in the time left before President Nixon's visit, our delegations will hardly be able to proceed without us.

We will hardly be able to work out a solution that can be a permanent agreement.

Kissinger: I agree.

Brezhnev: Let me suggest, perhaps then we could undertake to enter into a new arrangement where the first operative paragraph—after the preamble—says that the two sides have agreed to prolong the provisional agreement in its full measure, let's say, until the year 1980. That's the first point. That is, both remain with the existing levels. But just that alone would not exactly satisfy certain circles in US.[41]

Kissinger: Not in its exact details.

Quite candidly, this would be quite impossible in present conditions in the United States. It would strengthen Senator Jackson, quite frankly.

Brezhnev: So then, after this, we could have a second paragraph couched in the most categorical terms, which would say roughly that the two sides undertake that their delegations will continue their work to convert the provisional agreement into a permanent one. But even that would not be enough, I gather. Since these multi-warheads are constantly in the news, let's decide on a certain number of warheads on certain number of missiles.

Korniyenko: The number of missiles to be equipped with multiple warheads.

Gromyko: That will be MIRVed.

Brezhnev: They could be listed in quantities or in percentages. For example, the United States will be entitled to MIRV 1,000 missiles and we will be entitled to MIRV 1,000 ICBMs.

[Discussing in more detail his proposal—which would extend the Interim Agreement until 1980—Brezhnev says that each side would have freedom to mix, that is, to determine which proportion of ICBMs or SLBMs would carry MIRVs. He goes on to discuss the difference between deploying new missiles and modernizing old ones.]

Brezhnev: (Draws a silo diagram on a piece of paper) Say we had a silo launcher and our designer invents a narrower one; it's not a new missile. So we're free either to reconstruct this or install it on a submarine.

Kissinger: Now I understand the difference between a new missile and an improvement. I have to compliment your designers; they've used the existing space with great skill.

Brezhnev: I can just say you have some very wonderful designers too. They've put Minuteman III in the same hole, though it is a new rocket.

Kissinger: (laughs) All I can say is, I hope you never come up with a new missile.

Brezhnev: Yours too.

Kissinger: But basically we both have the same problem. Could I take a two-minute break?

Brezhnev: Certainly.

(There is a break in the meeting from 12:58–1:02 P.M. At a table near the wall, they look at a blow-up of a picture taken of Major General Brezhnev in Red Square at the Victory parade on June 24, 1945. The meeting then resumes.)

[Brezhnev suggests that if the United States approves his proposal for 1,000 MIRVed missiles, negotiations could continue over a permanent agreement to sign when he returns to Washington in 1975.]

Brezhnev: . . . Also, and concurrently, we could also reach a new understanding on ABM systems. Under our agreement, you remember we both agreed the United States was building one ABM area and the Soviet Union was building one, and both were entitled to build another. So we could refrain from building the additional ABM area and agree we both stay with the one we have. Further, you've been working on the B-1 bomber, and we are building our plane, the 160.[42] We could agree to cease work on the 160 on our side if you agree to cease on the B-1.[43]

   If we want to proceed towards détente, all those would be elements of détente.

That could of course be part of a separate understanding, but I am just mentioning them in one package.

Let us reach an agreement to end underground nuclear testing. Let us agree, say as of an agreed date, say 1975, 1976, or 1977, we shall both cease underground nuclear tests and call upon all others to do so. Say by January 1, 1976. And we would add a paragraph that if other nations do not discontinue testing, then each of us will be free to act at our own discretion.

Also, we could enter into an agreement that United States and Soviet Union could agree to withdraw all nuclear systems from the Mediterranean.

Kissinger: Ban them?

Brezhnev: Withdraw them. We'd withdraw all nuclear weapons carriers, and you too. Both surface vessels and submarines.

Kissinger: Missiles, or anything?

Gromyko: Carriers of any type of nuclear weapons.

Brezhnev: Of course, conventional naval vessels would be permitted to remain in the Mediterranean.

There, Dr. Kissinger, you have before you a program for strengthening security, and equal security for both sides.

(Kissinger and Sonnenfeldt confer.)

[After Brezhnev suggests an agreement not to commission new missile-launching submarines such as the U.S's Trident, Kissinger states that the U.S. side might accept the Soviet proposal to eliminate one ABM site. They also discuss in more detail the possibility of restrictions on heavy bombers such as the B-1.]

Brezhnev: Dr. Kissinger, all that from a purely human standpoint is aimed at lessening the temptation to increase nuclear weapons on both sides.

(Gromyko gives Brezhnev a paper.)

It turns out, on the one hand, that we write and sign very good papers and proclaim very good objectives, and on the other hand we listen to our staffs and we build the Trident and B-1 long-range bombers, and we on our side build the (Tu-)160 bomber with long-range nuclear missiles. When the people get to the bottom of what is happening, they will start criticizing us.

Kissinger: Let me turn to the 1,000 missiles that the General Secretary mentioned. There are a number of problems in connection with this.

One, the fact that you have more warheads on each of your missiles than we do. Or will have. And each of the warheads is of greater weight.[44]

Secondly, you do not yet have multiple warheads for submarines. So if you put all your permitted warheads on land-based missiles, then by the end of this period, you will be free to put multiple warheads on all your submarines. And since there is only a certain amount you can do anyway, this only means that we are only endorsing your existing program. The end result would be that on land-based missiles you would have many more warheads than we do.

Brezhnev: Dr. Kissinger, I listen to you and I hear the exact words of our general staff when they report to me. But vice versa. Our people say the Americans have more than we do.

Kissinger: True.

Brezhnev: And you have 12 on a rocket.

Kissinger: What 12?[45]

Brezhnev: They say the Americans are putting multiple warheads on their older missiles. So in your place I keep seeing our chief of the general staff reporting on developments in the United States. What is a warhead? One block with a capacity of a million tons. When you divide it into six warheads, the capacity will no longer be a million tons. The whole thing becomes weaker by half.

Then there are those in the military who believe it is better to have one warhead but a bigger one, and there is another school of thought who think the more the better. But what is the difference between one kiloton and 50 kilotons? Both mean death and destruction. In World War II, you dropped two and wiped out populations.

I read the American press quite attentively and I don't think anybody in the United States is so critical of the agreement. What they are proposing has nothing to do with the agreement.

Kissinger: No, there is increasing criticism—but we should not debate it. Most of it is by dishonest people, I must say.

Brezhnev: Undoubtedly.

Kissinger: But that is an American domestic complexity.

Brezhnev: What do you suggest in place of it?

Kissinger: We gave you our ideas in the note to your Ambassador on Thursday. (The note is at Tab C.)

We don't exclude a limit on the number of missiles that can be MIRVed, and we would have to make some calculations to see whether 1000 or 900—that clearly is not unacceptable. And you would certainly listen to a counter proposal on this.

Brezhnev: I am waiting for it.

Kissinger: I have just heard your idea for the first time. Let me think about the number for a while. Our basic problem is that it would have to be based on an agreement on how many would have to be land-based.

Brezhnev: This is not something—MIRVing—that can be done in just one year, so it is hard to predetermine at once the number of landbased missiles.
Kissinger: Since we may have completed 80% of our MIRVing, while you haven't even started, the practical result is that we would have to stop for five years while you were given time to catch up. That is how it would be seen in America.
Gromyko: But you will have advantages in that situation. You have got it in your pocket already.
Kissinger: Yes, but then why is it in our interest to tie ourselves to figures we have already?
Gromyko: Otherwise, the whole question of limitations will simply soar. It will be an unlimited race.
Kissinger: If the Soviet side could accept some of the principles in the paper we gave to the Ambassador, then we could consider an upper ceiling. Then we could consider numbers.
Brezhnev: Although within the limits of the agreement you have already in fact violated the balance of forces.
Kissinger: How?
Gromyko: Of this proposed agreement. Now we have agreed not to build any new missiles until 1977. But improvement is permitted, and you want to deprive us of any chance to improve it.
Kissinger: I think, Mr. General Secretary, we are arguing semantically about new missiles and improvements. My briefers tell me about your new systems. We do not have any change of that same magnitude. We are not saying it is a violation of the agreement, Mr. Brezhnev. I can only answer in the same vein.
Brezhnev: You have built an entirely new type of missile. Instead of one warhead, now each carries five.
Kissinger: Mr. General Secretary, your information is wrong. We don't have a missile with five or with 12.[46] That is not the basic point. Mr. Gromyko thinks it is three. That is because he takes trips. Whenever I think he is at Las Vegas he is at missile bases.
Gromyko: I haven't yet been allowed into a single missile base.
Kissinger: I'll take you there once.

Our Ambassador asked for so many appointments, I am surprised he hasn't asked to see a missile base.

So that—since your Foreign Minister is as usual correct—we have three on our land-based and you have six on yours, we think the equivalence ought to be established on the basis of warheads. On submarines, we have more warheads.

Another way of doing it is to set an upper limit on MIRVed missiles, with a sublimit for ICBMs for each side, and the sublimit could generally be established on a differential basis.

Gromyko: You mean a sublimit for submarine-based missiles and another sublimit for land-based missiles?

Kissinger: Yes. Automatically.

(Both sides confer)

Dobrynin: We will have to consider 1,000.

Kissinger: We have to consider 1,000, 1,100, 900. 1,100 would be easier for us. We could accept 1,100 now.

My various colleagues are having heart attacks along the table because I am accepting things so quickly. (Both sides confer.)

Dobrynin: Do we want to take a lunch break?

Kissinger: We could certainly — without going back to Washington — we could accept 1,100 if there was a subceiling below that.

Dobrynin: What is the number?

Kissinger: That we would have to discuss. I agree to an interval, because I have a slight insurrection on my staff.

Gromyko: We will issue a communique to the press about our meetings at the end of the day.

Kissinger: Good. We won't report back to Washington yet.

Gromyko: I have a list of subjects.

Kissinger: When we come back, what will we talk about? Because I have to know whom to bring.

Brezhnev: We should continue with this, then we have to talk about the Middle East.

Kissinger: I will bring these people, then the Middle East people will be told to stand by.

(The meeting then ended.)

COMMENTARY

After breaking for lunch, Brezhnev and Gromyko met Kissinger and his party that afternoon, and they continued their discussion of nuclear arms control issues.[47] On antiballistic missiles — one ABM site only for each — and on the threshold ban of underground nuclear tests, they made some progress. But on SALT II, the debate continued. Kissinger frankly observed in his assessment of Brezhnev's proposal for high limits on MIRVed ICBMs that a ceiling on land-based MIRVed missiles was essential for mollifying Pentagon concerns about Soviet capability to destroy U.S. Minuteman forces. But Brezhnev objected to Kissinger's thinking about a sub-ceiling because it "puts us in such a position of unequality [sic]."

Brezhnev also sought assurances that Washington would not deploy the new B-1 bomber and the new Trident SLBM if the Interim Agreement was extended. Kissinger was responsive, but Brezhnev's proposals for the withdrawal of nuclear weapons-carrying submarines and aircraft carriers from the Mediterranean met without success. Brezhnev appeared to be dismayed about the risk posed by nuclear forward-based systems—"Don't think that's something out-of-a pack of cards—it's nuclear weapons"—but Kissinger agreed only to "study" the proposal. For him, naval deployments, nuclear or otherwise, were integral to U.S. global strategy. He did not explain, as he would to NATO officials, that because nuclear-armed naval forces, along with aircraft, could be alerted easily and were much more visible than "missiles stuck in the ground", they were a more "politically useful" way to employ Washington's "relative" strategic superiority.

The discussion then turned to an extended review of the negotiations at the Conference on Security and Cooperation in Europe. Though Kissinger had little regard for the CSCE, he was quite careful: Brezhnev saw the conference as confirming the post–World War II political and territorial status quo (including Germany), but Washington's European allies wanted to use the CSCE process—especially the discussions on human contacts ("Basket III")—to advance human rights principles and chip away at Soviet bloc internal controls.[48] Soviet negotiators at Geneva had hinted that concessions on Basket III would be forthcoming, but Brezhnev made it clear that he would negotiate an outcome that safeguarded internal political controls. He revealed his suspicions when he warned, "if anyone is counting on being able to interfere in our internal affairs through the Conference, those hopes are to no avail."[49]

Brezhnev, tired of the conference, wanted an early agreement. He suggested that if the CSCE were to complete its work by the time of the June summit, the President would have a useful "political asset." Kissinger played his cards very carefully; overt cooperation with the Soviets would anger European allies, but open support for Allied positions would alienate Brezhnev and weaken détente. Given's Kissinger's disinterest in a human rights agenda, it was easy for him to favor a low U.S. profile in the negotiations at Geneva.[50]

The next day, when they moved on to other subjects, Kissinger experienced Brezhnev's rage over Washington's Middle East policy. No transcript of this meeting is available, but Kissinger later reported that Brezhnev had accused him of ignoring the spirit and the letter of the Geneva Conference by totally excluding Moscow from the negotiations. Brezhnev further insisted that the United States move the pending Syrian–Israeli negotiations to Geneva so the Soviets could participate. A telegram Kissinger sent to Israeli Ambassador Dinitz the same day gives a hint of the meeting's tone: "My three and one-half hour meeting . . . with Brezhnev and Gromyko . . . is [sic] the toughest and most unpleasant I have ever had with the Soviets. They are clearly in a state of high agitation about our role in the disengagement negotiations and the success of our diplomacy."[51] Nevertheless, Kissinger rejected Brezhnev's arguments and declared that the Syrian–Israeli talks would fail if they were folded into the Geneva Conference. He did not share his basic assumptions with Brezhnev, that he would personally control the negotiations and that Moscow's role would be peripheral, at best.[52]

When they regrouped in the afternoon, discussion returned to arms control, CSCE, and the MBFR agenda.[53] Kissinger and Brezhnev quickly reached understandings on the threshold test ban and on ABM cuts, but not on Brezhnev's proposal for a withdrawal of nuclear-armed ships and submarines from the Mediterranean. Kissinger was similarly unresponsive to Brezhnev's suggestions for the inclusion of weapons systems in proposed initial force reductions; Washington was not ready to introduce the nuclear issue in the MBFR talks.

The following excerpt shows that when the discussion turned to the CSCE, Brezhnev poked fun at the language and methods of diplomacy:

Brezhnev: Dr. Kissinger, I have derived great pleasure hearing the two Foreign Ministers talk at length with each other, and I keep thinking "How are they able to do this?" My conclusion is that I can never be a Foreign Minister. I would have to set aside a couple of years to study the most complicated words from every encyclopedia in the world and insert them one after the other in each phrase. I will set aside a couple of years and maybe then I will be up to it.

My second conclusion is that Foreign Ministers speak in such an interesting way but resolve nothing.

Kissinger: That gives them job security.

Brezhnev: I am really thinking of volunteering for one of these commissions in Vienna. It will be a school of practical study.

Gromyko: But not on Basket III.

Brezhnev: The other day I phoned Comrade Gromyko and I said "My deeply respected Andrey Andreyevich . . ."

Kissinger: The President never says that to me—but then I am not in office as long as he.

Brezhnev: And I said, "I was quite convinced that as soon as I telephoned, you would raise your phone and reciprocate. And I was so impressed I ventured never to forget that. I was impressed by your gesture for me, and you can be assured of my feelings for you for many years. And availing myself of this opportunity, I would like to know how you feel and at the same time inquire about the health of Lydia Dmitrievna, your spouse, and please pass on to her my best wishes, and please let me express my hope that the forthcoming telephone conversation will give you the greatest pleasure and bring forth no problems. Because my many years of experience give me every confidence you are directing every effort toward these goals that I and my colleagues are seeking, and I am sure our conversation will be a success. Now I will say a few words—but I forget one thing." But he then broke into conversation saying, "I entirely reciprocate your feelings." And I said, "Andrey Andreyevich, if I were not assured of your feelings I would not have called."

Kissinger: He would say to me, "I essentially reciprocate your feelings."

Brezhnev: My call was to find out when your plane was coming. (laughter) He said, "It is coming one hour late." We talked twenty-two minutes. But I wanted to hear the two Foreign Ministers talk to each other.

Kissinger: But I am a new Foreign Minister . . .

Brezhnev: I have one shortcoming: I like a precise discussion. But we talked for twenty minutes about our mutual respect and admiration, and we concentrate on the last word. So I listened to you most attentively. You agreed to inform each other. I will inform President Nixon, Korniyenko, Sonnenfeldt.

Kissinger: I knew Sonnenfeldt was communicating with somebody, because he is not communicating with me.

Brezhnev: I haven't ever been able to suspect Sonnenfeldt of ever engaging in clandestine activity. The only thing I can guess is that he writes you notes and tells you "Don't agree to anything they say." .

Kissinger: What really happens is, I move my lips and he speaks.

When I speak to your Foreign Minister, he never says, "I entirely agree." The most I get is, "I essentially agree with you."

Brezhnev: As I see it, that is again a case of his reciprocating your words.

"Thank you, Mr. Kissinger, for thanking me for my gratitude. I am deeply indebted to you. Thank you for my hearing of these words so pleasant to my soul."

That is what is called a respite or disengagement.

Kissinger: I don't think I would achieve this felicity of phrase.

Brezhnev: (Referring to Rodman) What is he writing this for?

Kissinger: We need this for our diplomatic language training.

Gromyko: I don't know what he is writing.

Kissinger: We will initial it. We will introduce it into our Foreign Service charm course.[54]

[As the discussion on CSCE continues, Brezhnev shows his impatience with the slow progress of the talks and concern that Basket III might impinge on the Soviet Union's internal political controls. Revealing more than a trace of big power chauvinism but also a fear of losing control to outside influence, Brezhnev went on an unusual tirade about the Netherlands's proposals for freer contacts between East and West: "What kind of proposal is it if they want to arrogate to themselves the right to open theaters in the Soviet Union without any control by the Soviet administration? . . . It's just wrong to have ideas like that."

Kissinger makes private assurances that the United States will find the final conference document "acceptable," he does not promise to work for an early denouement of the negotiations, let alone prior to Nixon's visit. As for Soviet concerns about internal controls, he suggests that Brezhnev is worrying too much: "I don't think the Soviet system will be changed by the opening of a Dutch cabaret in Moscow."

Discussion of MFBR issues very quickly reveals that both sides are uncomfortable with the prospect of a powerful Germany in a more unified West European community. Brezhnev, recounting a conversation with Pompidou, says that a "Europe without boundaries" will be one where "every one . . . would have to learn German," to which Kissinger responds, "[t]hat might be one result of the current tendencies." Likewise, both men wonder why the French support a tighter European community when it "will lead to the domination of Scheel," in other words, West Germany. These exchanges show that, in spite of the Cold War, trace elements remained of the World War II grand alliance: both Moscow and Washington want to avoid an "overstrong" Germany that can threaten European stability.[55]

After discussion on economic cooperation, during which Kissinger assured Brezhnev that he would circumvent Senator Jackson, the two have a final lengthy meeting on SALT on 27 March.[56] The mood remained amicable, but they could not reach a settlement on the focus of their discussion, SALT.

For Kissinger, Brezhnev's proposal for about 1,000 MIRVed missiles on each side is far too high because it would give Moscow too great an advantage in deploying MIRVs: "Our concern is to get some figures that are a realistic limit and are not simply the maximum program of both sides." However, Brezhnev is worried about the U.S. advantage in warheads; he is not ready to accept what Kissinger see as an essential feature of an agreement with "realistic limits," namely, ceilings on MIRVs for heavy missiles and submarines. At the most, Brezhnev is willing to let Washington know when the MIRVing of Soviet submarines begins. It will take another round of negotiations later in the year before the two sides agree on ceilings for MIRVed missiles.]

SECRET/NODIS
THE WHITE HOUSE
MEMORANDUM OF CONVERSATION
PARTICIPANTS: Leonid I. Brezhnev, General Secretary of the CPSU
 Central Committee; Andrei A. Gromyko, Member of the Politburo
 of the CPSU Central Committee, Minister of Foreign Affairs of the
 USSR; Anatoliy F. Dobrynin, Soviet Ambassador to the U.S.; Andrei
 M. Aleksandrov, Assistant to the General Secretary; Georgi M.
 Korniyenko, Member of the Collegium of Ministry of Foreign Affairs
 Chief, USA Department; Mikhail D. Sytenko, Member of the
 Collegium of Ministry of Foreign Affairs Chief, Near East
 Department; Oleg Sokolov, USA Department; Viktor Sukhodrev,
 USA Department (Interpreter); Dr. Henry A. Kissinger, Secretary of
 State, Assistant to the President for National Security Affairs; Walter
 J. Stoessel, Jr., U. S. Ambassador to the USSR; Helmut Sonnenfeldt,
 Counselor of the Department; Arthur A. Hartman, Assistant
 Secretary for European Affairs; William G. Hyland, Director,
 Bureau of Intelligence and Research, State Department; Jan M.
 Lodal, Senior Staff Member, NSC; Peter W. Rodman, NSC Staff
DATE AND TIME: Wednesday, March 27, 1974 5:50–9:10 P. M.
PLACE: General Secretary Brezhnev's Office Council of Ministers
 Building The Kremlin
SUBJECTS: President's Visit; SALT; Middle East; Other Arms
 Control; Vietnam; Economic Relations and Energy; Scientific and
 Technical Cooperation[C]

Brezhnev: I keep trying to learn this diplomatic language: I am having a hard time. I am an engineer by profession. It is an arduous but honorable one. In another ten meetings, I will be able to speak diplomatic language even in English.

How are your children?
Kissinger: Marvelous. My daughter loved the gift you sent her.

[C] Source: U.S. Department of State Freedom of Information Act release, copy at *NSA*.

Brezhnev: What did they like best?

Kissinger: My daughter liked the Kremlin best; my son liked the Pioneer Club best.

[Brezhnev notes that the fog would have made it unpleasant to visit his country dacha at Zavidovo, despite preparations made for Kissinger's visit there.]

Kissinger: I appreciate the thought.

I am sure the boar are grateful.

Brezhnev: I wasn't able in this brief period to get a full report on all you talked about today. So perhaps in this conversation we could revert to some of the most important questions we have discussed. Not all, but the more important ones.

Kissinger: I agree.

Brezhnev: And Dr. Kissinger and your friends, I do this from President Nixon's message, where he lays particular emphasis on the questions he feels to be the most important.

There are certain other matters—like the artificial heart—but those are scientific matters, and the scientists will understand each other better than we can. I did inquire from our people about progress in cancer control, and I was told there is broad cooperation already.

Kissinger: Yes.

Brezhnev: I know ceilings are a subject Dr. Kissinger specializes in.

Kissinger: I specialize really in subceilings.

Brezhnev: Now I know. Can they be low ceilings, like 2.20 meters?

Kissinger: Architecturally, I like high ceilings; for MIRVs I like low ceilings.

Brezhnev: My view is exactly the opposite. (laughter)

The Secretary of the Party Committee in my town, his name was Svirsky. We were doing our best to strengthen the Party organization in the country-side, so we sent urban party men out to the villages. They would think up any excuse not to go. Some said their wife was sick, some said they had piles, etc. Svirsky said: "That is fine. Now we have exchanged views on this subject. You have given me the benefit of yours. So it is all arranged. You go." (laughter)

That is a good principle.

Now if we turn to what we feel are the most important questions, I think we agree the first is limitation of strategic arms. Then the Middle East. Then economic cooperation. And then the European Conference. So perhaps we should talk about some of those.

[Brezhnev and Kissinger discuss the dates for Nixon's visit in late June. To avoid a conflict with Supreme Soviet elections in mid-June, they agree that Nixon should arrive on 24 June.]

Brezhnev: That date seems to be acceptable. As to length, I would like to leave that to the President's hands.

Gromyko: As long as he can stay.

Brezhnev: About six weeks, I would say.

Kissinger: That has many possibilities!

Brezhnev: Congress can take a rest then.

Kissinger: I was going to say that.

Brezhnev: They are all tired anyway.

[Brezhnev says he would like Nixon to stay for seven or eight days: the weather is good at that time of the year, so he can take him to the Crimea, including a visit to the Yalta Palace. "He can really breathe there."]

Brezhnev: . . . Now for the most complicated question of all—it is time for tea and cookies.

(A waiter comes in. The Soviets ask for a "MIRVed" plate of snacks.)

There was a time everyone was scared about flying saucers.

Kissinger: One family in the United States thought one landed in their backyard.

Brezhnev: It was probably something the neighbors threw over. I threw a saucer once in the air and tried to get it to fly. It broke and my wife complained. (laughter)

SALT

As I recall, on the subject of MIRVs, yesterday you suggested we should have 1,000 and we 600. I felt that was quite unjust. So I made a counterproposal that you should have 1,000 and we have 1,000 too.

Kissinger: That is characteristic of our negotiations—that we don't accept proposals unfavorable to the other side.

Brezhnev: Of course we only put forward constructive proposals.

We agreed we would think it over overnight. I hope you had pleasant dreams.

On this I rely on the reports in your press, which say our talks have been friendly and in a constructive spirit.

Kissinger: And businesslike.

Brezhnev: Why spoil this very friendly atmosphere? It is not in the interests of either side.

(Tea is brought in. Brezhnev counts the slices of lemon.)

How many warheads here? One-two-three . . . six! You tested one like this.

[They cross swords again over the numbers of warheads on MIRVed missiles. Brezhnev and Kissinger continue to wrangle over how to extend the 1971 Interim Agreement and how "to preserve the balance so neither side acquires any advantage." When Brezhnev points out that Kisssinger's proposal preserves the U.S. lead in numbers of MIRVs, Kissinger concurs. Brezhnev then complains that, before fitting out the 62 submarines authorized by the Interim Agreement, Moscow had to destroy 210 land-based missiles—an overall loss of more warheads.]

Kissinger: Yes, Mr. General Secretary, but the missiles you have to destroy are a type on which you cannot put multiple warheads.

Gromyko: But we would be entitled to replace them with a more modern type.

As I said yesterday, your military may have their doctrine and ours have their own. But neither has anything to do with political negotiations.

Kissinger: The problem, Mr. General Secretary, is that even the missiles you are permitted are about 1,400, or maybe a little more. Of the characteristics most suitable for MIRVs, on those you can put either five or six warheads now and God knows how many later.

Brezhnev: The same God doesn't know how many you can install. You have missiles carrying ten already. We don't have any yet. So even today, each one of yours equals two of ours. That is the honest method of approaching this.

Kissinger: First, unless we are only making debating points, the missiles that are comparable are the land-based. You can install warheads on more of yours and each of your warheads is more powerful than ours.

[Brezhnev argues that it would take years before the Soviets catch up with the number of MIRVs the United States has, and he proposes to extend the provisional agreement until 1980. The United States can have 1,100 MIRVed launchers, the Soviets 1,000. Brezhnev further asserts that the proposal has political advantages: it will hold the "line on limiting strategic arms," is consistent with the principle of preventing nuclear war, and will allow Washington to complete its MIRV deployment. "What else can you ask for the Soviet Union to do? How can you ask for more when you already have a clear superiority?"]

Brezhnev: . . . I would request that you transmit the substance of my remarks to President Nixon. I think he will think it over and appreciate the significance of our position.

Kissinger: Let me sum up, so I understand.

Brezhnev: Certainly.

Kissinger: In this total figure, it is not specified in each category how many in that category can be MIRVed—how many ICBMs of what type or how many submarines of what type.

Brezhnev: That would depend on the desires of each side.

Kissinger: But they don't even notify each other about their intentions.

Brezhnev: I don't know. We should think that over. We will, of course, report to you when we scrap some land-based missiles.

Kissinger: That is a different matter.

Brezhnev: But it is very important.

[Kissinger points out the complexity of differentiating between MIRVed or non-MIRVed SLBMS, and argues that "we would have to consider every boat [i.e., submarine] you have capable of accepting that missile as carrying MIRV." Therefore, supposing that Soviet submarines can carry 400 missiles, they "would have to be deducted from the 1,000." Brezhnev suggests a special clause on the exchange of information to help resolve this problem.]

Brezhnev: . . . [M]eanwhile we know you have a vast superiority over us in MIRVs. But we proceed from the fact that we have an agreement on Prevention of Nuclear War, and we know we won't have a nuclear war between us. It is only guided by such a lofty spirit of confidence between us that we can make such a proposal.

Let us have a ten-minute break.

Kissinger: Good.

(There was a break from 7:07 to 7:26)

Kissinger: I was explaining our military proposals to my colleagues who have never heard it. You know what I think, Mr. General Secretary? Quite honestly, both our military people have painted a picture of the situation that is rather one-sided. Your people emphasize the number of warheads; our people emphasize the weight of your warheads.

Brezhnev: I don't know how well you are familiar with the concept of the weight of warheads and with what percentage of the weight is lost when you MIRV that warhead. But I do.

Kissinger: I know.

Brezhnev: I have made a little calculation. Our proposal actually means if we agree you are allowed the total number of missiles you have, plus an additional 100 you get, plus the figure we have to scrap for our submarines, it means the United States will have—and this is an exact figure–the United

States will be entitled to MIRV 64 percent of all the missiles it is allowed to have, whereas the Soviet Union will be entitled to MIRV only 42 percent of the missiles we are allowed. If you ask your military experts, they will give the same figures.

Kissinger: Yes, but if I ask my military men, they will probably say it proves that in our last agreement you took advantage of us because it allowed you a greater number of missiles that you are allowed to MIRV.

Brezhnev: Yes, well, people can invent anything to say but you can say you have discussed this with the Russians and this is the agreement you have come to.

Kissinger: If [sic] this form I don't believe we can make progress with these figures. We don't want to get an advantage in ICBM warheads. Because, for example, if we had an equal number of MIRVed ICBMs, you would have roughly twice the number of warheads. But this could then be compensated for by submarine missiles. So our concern isn't that. Our concern is to get some figures that are a realistic limit and are not simply the maximum program of both sides. Because the General Secretary himself said he wasn't sure he could MIRV as many.

I am just being analytical, Mr. General Secretary.

But without an agreement, we could MIRV 500 more Minutemen easily, and after 1977 we could deploy Trident missiles on land. So we would accept a limit on our number of both; by extending the Interim Agreement we would accept a limit on numbers and a disadvantage in numbers which gives you the possibility of more over a period of time.

Brezhnev: That is a logic I don't understand, because it doesn't meet the figures. I would ask you to report back to the President.

Kissinger: I will report this to the President. Maybe we can develop some counterproposal, and then we will see where we are.

Brezhnev: One other matter. You asked about information about our intentions as to how many submarines we intend to fit out with these missiles. I am not denying the validity of that suggestion. Let me think it over. It may turn out to be acceptable.

Kissinger: Let me say Mr. General Secretary, if that is acceptable, then I think we will be approaching an agreement. At least, this thing will look different.

Brezhnev: I can say we would not be concerned about whatever figure you mentioned—whether 2,000, 3,000 missiles—because we proceed from our agreement in good faith not to use nuclear weapons. So I would never have raised it. But then I hear first one speech by an official in the United States that "we must be stronger," then another speech, and then Congress is increasing military appropriations. That I feel is in violation of our understandings.

Kissinger: I understand this, Mr. General Secretary, but we are attempting to prevent a runaway arms race in the United States.

Brezhnev: You say so, but on the other hand your military appropriations are growing, and you are mobilizing public opinion behind the idea the United States must be stronger. Which leads Americans to believe the United States is militarily weak and the United States stands on feet of clay.

Kissinger: (laughs) There is certainly merit in what the General Secretary is saying. I am not arguing every point the General Secretary makes.

Brezhnev: I recently spoke in Alma-Ata, and I will be making my election speech. What if I get up and make a speech: (He gets up and gesticulates): "Comrades, we must make every effort; we must be stronger than America." Then the military men will say, "Give us the money."

Kissinger: (laughs) If you said that, Senator Jackson would give you wide publicity in America.

Brezhnev: Senator Jackson again!

Kissinger: Of our military budget, of course, the greater part of the increase is due to inflation and most of it goes to personnel. The President never said more than that we will never be number two, never that we must be stronger than the Soviet Union.

Brezhnev: Perhaps we could end the discussion of that subject on that. We feel that could provide a good basis for our meeting.

Kissinger: If you could think over the submarine issue, and we will think over the numbers issue. (They query.) Assuming we accepted your figure for MIRV, and if you could then consider giving us information of how many will be on submarines, then we could think the matter over very seriously.

Brezhnev: I told you I couldn't rule out the possibility of our informing you whenever we install the first MIRV on submarines. Maybe there is something reasonable in this.

So I take it, if we quite honestly inform you on the subject, this wouldn't mean imposing any limits on us.

Gromyko: Within the limits.

Brezhnev: Let's say, within the 62 submarines allowed, we will tell you whether one or five are being MIRVed.

Dobrynin: Just inform you. No limits.

Kissinger: No, you will have the right to determine the limits in each category.

Gromyko: You are trying to introduce the notion of a ceiling through the back door.

Kissinger: (laughs) I have tried to explain to you the problem of a ceiling introduces itself the minute you have started testing a submarine missile.

[Kissinger goes on to argue that even though the Soviets cannot MIRV their current ICBM arsenal, they are developing "new" or "improved" ICBMs that can take MIRVs.]

Brezhnev: It is the same type of rocket. But fitted with MIRV-type warheads, in the same silo. For a new type missile, you need a new silo, that is natural. And you know that.

Kissinger: You think they go in the same silo?

Brezhnev: Only in existing silos, otherwise it would be a violation.

Kissinger: We thought you would make them deeper, which is not a violation.

Brezhnev: If we had widened the silos, you would have complained.

Kissinger: So, should I continue with our reasoning?

Brezhnev: I think the main thing is, you should inform President Nixon that that is our proposal. That is as far as we can go. And we proceed from the assumption that neither of us will attack each other [*sic*]. If you need them, it is because maybe you think China will attack you. For us, the greatest guarantee is our intention of never attacking you.

In fact, Dr. Kissinger, I can tell you our military men have certain fears about a violation of the agreement, as far as widening of silos is concerned, to house new-type rockets. You know what those fears are based on? The fact that in the United States about 500 land-based launchers have been covered up. And we made two representations about that.

Kissinger: But we have stopped that.

Brezhnev: That is still going on.

Kissinger: That is impossible.[57]

Brezhnev: That introduces certain questions. It is not something I really wanted to mention but it is a fact. Let us act in good faith.

Kissinger: Mr. General Secretary, I have to check this, but we ordered it stopped, and if it is not stopped, it violates orders. But I wasn't accusing you of violating the agreement. That wasn't our point. The only point I was going to make was that for the purposes of the agreement, for the purposes of verification, once you test a missile with MIRV, we have to assume it is MIRV'd because we have no way of verifying whether it is or is not.

Brezhnev: I have replied that it is a matter of military doctrine. We ourselves may decide to MIRV only half of them. We will be proceeding not from anything to do with the United States but from something to do with our other potential opponent. So what we are talking about is what each side is entitled to.

Kissinger: Okay, so how do we know you have deployed only half of your MIRVs?

Brezhnev: Dr. Kissinger, I am not rejecting your proposal about mutual information. It may turn out to be acceptable. I am not rejecting it. Let's think it over.

Kissinger: All right. We will both think it over.

Brezhnev: After all, we have undertaken to inform you we are scrapping a certain number of land-based missiles to build submarines. Maybe we can go on to a broader agreement on exchange of information. But I am not in the position now to give you the exact answer.

Kissinger: No, I understand. Let's leave it at that point

Middle East

Brezhnev: Now, Dr. Kissinger could we finish the discussion on the question of the Middle East, by agreeing that we will cooperate with one another completely as was initially agreed upon by our two sides? And I stress the word "cooperate," and by that I mean not simply inform each other. That should characterize our relationship in the Middle East.

Kissinger: I had a brief talk with your Foreign Minister today, and we agreed we would have a full exchange on the occasion of his visit to Washington. On the Middle East. And we are prepared to cooperate, to answer your question, and not to seek to achieve a unilateral advantage.

Brezhnev: We certainly have no aim to achieve any unilateral advantage. Unless you consider the assurance of the security of Israel and all Arab states a unilateral advantage.

Kissinger: I consider our objectives in this area compatible.

Brezhnev: That is what I think. But we should act accordingly.

Kissinger: I agree we should coordinate our moves.

[A brief discussion of the threshold test ban leads to an agreement that the experts should develop specific proposals on the anticipated threshold level of tests. Brezhnev wants to discuss proposed limitations on military weather-modification efforts, but Kissinger demurs because his side is not prepared. Both sides agree to prevent North

and South Vietnam from breaking the Paris agreement, and the discussion turns to economic and energy cooperation agreements. Brezhnev suggests possibilities such as a U.S.-financed pulp mill or tin-smelting operations: the Soviets would repay credit by exporting the end-product to the United States. (Another example he offers is an ammonia production operation supported by Armand Hammer.) Kissinger's assessment is "positive," but he observes that such ventures depend on credits—and some would like to cut them back. After briefly discussing scientific cooperation, perhaps involving energy or a joint space mission, they review the communiqué on their meetings.]

Kissinger: Does Korniyenko draft for both sides now? Did you know he is joining my staff for a year? On the basis of equal torture for both sides. We will trade Sonnenfeldt for Korniyenko if you will get an additional man who can read upside down.

(Brezhnev goes out for a few minutes, returns.)

Kissinger: (To Gromyko) I will talk to the British about that European Security Conference. I will send a message to you on Friday.

Gromyko: Good.

Kissinger: I think it is still bureaucracy. I will talk to [British Foreign Minister James] Callaghan tomorrow. They probably haven't had time to study it.

Brezhnev: Really, Dr. Kissinger, I find the thought rather dull that you are leaving tomorrow.

Kissinger: I always enjoy our meetings.

One possibility that occurred to me, Mr. General Secretary. If we make some progress on SALT, I would be prepared to return for a couple of days in May.

Brezhnev: You know, I was thinking about that. But I decided not to mention it. But I really thought we might need one more meeting, to finalize or almost finalize some of the documents. I didn't think it would be on SALT, because I thought we had already settled that.

Kissinger: What are 3,000 MIRVs among friends? (laughter)

But still we have to write down the small print.

Brezhnev: I don't think I will live to see the day when we have 300 MIRVs in our favor.

Gromyko: To make things fair, we should be given 1,100 and you 1,000.

Kissinger: You will end up with more warheads. We will write down our considerations, because I really think I haven't had a chance to give them to you. Our analysis of the problem.

Gromyko: Whenever you give us something in writing it looks very negative. Conditioned reflexes.

Brezhnev: What we gave you was really our final position. It means we are really giving you the maximum. I really should be fired from the Council of National Defense and all my other posts. You just think it over, how far I have gone. I for one—you absolutely never expected me to say what I have done. We have completed our discussions in a friendly way; I am sure you didn't expect me to go so far. (laughter) When you tell President Nixon, I am sure he will give you a third post, in addition to the two you have.

[After each side confers and studies the draft communiqué, they agree it should be released at 7:00 P.M. Moscow time.]

Brezhnev: This might disappoint you, but I have no intention of considering any new proposals on SALT.
Kissinger: We have to now.
Brezhnev: Maybe something will come out of the information problem.
Kissinger: Exactly. If we can do something with the information problem. This is the direction my mind is now working.
Brezhnev: I believe you. And I hope so.
(After an exchange of pleasantries, they close the discussion.)

COMMENTARY

On his way back from Moscow, Kissinger's first stop was London where he gave the newly elected Labor government's foreign minister, Callaghan, a briefing on the Moscow talks.[58] The meeting signaled some repair of an uneasy Anglo–American relationship under the Conservatives, whose independent policy during the October War Kissinger had found "most obnoxious." As a sign that the famously special relationship was to improve, Kissinger disclosed in his own memoirs what the State Department saw fit to censor in the text that follows, that in Kissinger's presence, Callaghan told his Foreign Office subordinates, he wanted no more "mutual needling."[59]

Kissinger's presentation of the Moscow talks was fair enough, albeit with a decidedly upbeat spin: "Détente as a policy is very much on course." That statement was in stark contrast to his comments before the trip—"what bothers me . . . is that the Soviets are getting nothing out of détente." Perhaps both statements were too strong: détente was having its troubles and its economic underpinnings were in danger, but key negotiations on SALT and CSCE were moving forward with promising gains for both sides.

In talking to the British Kissinger's assessment of the Soviets was hardly glowing:

> As everybody knows, the Soviet leaders belong to the most unpleasant group one can deal with. Their capacity to lie on matters of common knowledge is stupendous. I have already pointed out (at lunch) their comments about our domestic situation.
>
> Leaving aside the atmospherics, and except for their inherent obnoxiousness, their attitude was really very good. A great effort was made to have the atmosphere extremely cordial.

These indiscreet comments may well have captured Kissinger's true feelings about the Soviets. Central to Kissinger's and Nixon's thinking about détente was the need to accept contradictory ideas about the Soviets, as rivals as well as partners. In a world where "the most reliable tie we have to the Soviet Union is the mutual reluctance to engage in nuclear war," both men found it imperative for the superpowers to find ways to minimize antagonisms and to establish modalities of political and economic cooperation.[60]

Notes

1. For Watergate-related developments during late 1973 and early 1974, see Stanley Kutler, *The Wars of Watergate: The Last Crisis of Richard Nixon* (New York: Knopf, 1990), pp. 415–70; Anatoly Dobrynin, *In Confidence: Moscow's Ambassador to America's Six Cold War Presidents, 1962–1986* (New York: Time Books, 1995), pp. 303–6.

2. See U.S. State Department, "The Soviet Succession Problem, Background Paper," March 1974, FOIA release, copy National Security Archives (hereafter referred to as *NSA*). For Brezhnev's direct control over foreign policy, see U.S. Central Intelligence Agency, Research Study, "The Soviet Foreign Policy Apparatus," June 1976, copy at *NSA*.

3. For background on Kissinger's "shuttle diplomacy," see Walter Isaacson, *Kissinger: A Biography* (New York: Simon and Schuster, 1992), pp. 546–51; William B. Quandt, *Peace Process: American Diplomacy and the Arab-Israel Conflict Since 1947* (Washington, D.C.:Brookings Institution, 1993), pp. 183–222. For "disgruntled," U.S. State Department, "Briefing Paper, Middle East," March 1974 (copy at *NSA*).

4. See Raymond L. Garthoff, *Détente and Confrontation: American-Soviet Relations from Nixon to Reagan* (Washington, D.C.: Brookings Institutions, 1995), pp. 461, 471; Henry Kissinger, *Years of Upheaval* (Boston: Little, Brown, 1982), pp. 985–96; and Isaacson, pp. 611–21. For an incisive portrait of Jackson and the anti-détente network, see Mike Bowker and Phil Williams, *Superpower Detente: A Reappraisal* (London: Royal Institute of International Affairs, 1988), pp. 156–19. For the major study of Jackson-Vanik, see Paula Stern's *Water's Edge: Domestic Politics and the Making of American Foreign Policy* (Westport, Conn.: Greenwood, 1979).

5. See Isaacson, *Kissinger: A Biography*, pp. 613–14; *Détente and Confrontation*, pp. 368-

69; and Richard Nixon, *RN: The Memoirs of Richard Nixon* (New York: Grosset and Dunlap, 1978), pp. 875–76.

6. For Soviet MIRV testing, see Lawrence Freedman, *U.S. Intelligence and the Soviet Strategic Threat* (Boulder, Co.: Westview, 1977), p. 170. For background on MIRVs, see Daniel Ruchonnet, "MIRV: A Brief History," U.S. Department of Energy, Feb. 1976, copy at *NSA*.

7. See Garthoff, *Detente and Confrontation*, pp. 155–61; and Freedman, *U.S. Intelligence*, pp. 170–72. For one important proposal on a MIRV ban, see Ronald Spiers, "Preferred ABM/MIRV Limitations in SALT," 13 March 1970; copy at *NSA*.

8. For superiority, see State 148542 to U.S. Embassy Belgrade, "Secretary Kissinger's July 4 Report to North Atlantic Council on 1974 Summit Meeting," 10 July 1974 (hereafter *State to Belgrade*; copy at *NSA*).

9. See Garthoff, *Détente and Confrontation*, pp. 471, 476–77.

10. For background on the CSCE and MBFR, see ibid., pp. 527–42; and Bowker and Williams, *Superpower Detente*, pp. 90–93.

11. For "meaningless," see memcon, 16 April 1973, Policy Planning Staff (Director's Files), 1969–1977 (hereafter referred to as *PPS*, box 328, China Exchanges 15 April 1973–15 May 1973. In November, Kissinger had told Zhou that the Soviets were trying to "undermine [the Europeans] by such measures" as the CSCE. See memcon, 12 November 1973, 3:00–5:30 P.M., *PPS* box 372, Secretary's Conversations in Peking, November 1973.

12. For the Kissinger–Sonnenfeldt relationship, see Isaacson, *Kissinger: A Biography*, pp. 40, 55, 185–86.

13. For McGovern's support of the Jackson–Vanik approach, see Bowker and Williams, *Superpower Detente*, pp. 153–54.

14. For Kissinger's account, see his *Years of Upheaval*, pp. 700–34.

15. "NODIS" means "no distribution" without the approval of authorized officials at the National Security Council or the State Department.

16. What rankled Kissinger was that not only were the Pentagon MBFR proposals blatantly unequal, as long as the U.S. Army continued its annual REFORGER strategic mobility exercises, any cuts would be fictitious. REFORGER's purpose was to demonstrate a capability to "rapidly reinforce Central Europe" by airlifting and sealifting thousands of U.S. troops across the Atlantic. See U.S. Army Command, *REFORGER 88: Leader's Reference Guide* (Ft. Riley, Kansas, Headquarters, 1st Infantry Division, 1988).

17. The CSCE talks focussed on three sets of problems, known as "Baskets." Basket I concerned security and border issues, Basket II concerned East-West economic relations, and Basket III referred to East-West human contacts. For a comprehensive account by a participant in the CSCE negotiations, see John Maresca, *To Helsinki: The Conference on Security and Cooperation in Europe* (Durham, N.C.: Duke University Press, 1987).

18. The reference is obscure but possibly concerns a position paper on Jackson–Vanik.

19. Richard Campbell was Kissinger's personal assistant on the NSC staff.

20. Tab A refers to one of the items, a position paper on the SALT II talks, in the briefing book prepared for Kissinger's use in this meeting; it may well be the same document mentioned in endnote 41.

21. A reference to Richard Perle (b. 1941), one of Sen. Henry Jackson's principal aides on the

Senate Armed Services Committee staff during 1973-80. Under the Reagan administration, he served as assistant secretary of defense for international security affairs.

22. This is a reference to National Security Decision Memorandum 245, signed by Kissinger on 19 Feb. 1974 (hereafter *NSDM 245*), which sets forth the U.S. SALT position, emphasizing equal overall aggregates (21,350 ICBMs, SLBMs, and heavy bombers), equal ICBM/MIRV throw weight. Kissinger emphasized the importance "of controlling MIRV's on ICBM's promptly . . . to preserve the survivability of deterrent forces and reduce the risk of nuclear war." See Garthoff, *Détente and Confrontation*, p. 468, and National Security Decision Memorandum 245, Kissinger to the Secretary of Defense et al., "Instructions for the SALT Talks, Geneva," 19 Feb. 1974 (copy at *NSA*). James C. Fletcher (1919-1991) was administrator for NASA during 1971-77. Nikolai Pattolichev (b. 1908) had served as Soviet minister for foreign trade since 1958. James Lynn (b. 1927) served as secretary for housing and urban development during 1974-75.

23. Clift had just mentioned a Soviet official named Osipov, and Kissinger had confused the name. Clift's reference may have been to Georgii I. Osipov (1906-1980), a member of the Communist Party Central Committee during 1968-80.

24. On 18 March, Kissinger swore in Foreign Service Officer Donald B. Easum (b. 1923) as assistant secretary of state for African affairs. Easum served as assistant secretary until December, when Kissinger fired him because of policy disagreements over southern Africa. Easum went on to serve as ambassador to Nigeria during 1975-79. For Kissinger and Easum, see Garthoff, *Détente and Confrontation*, p. 564, n. 26.

25. Sonnenfeldt here confuses Hughes, who wore a beard, but was secretary of state during the 1920s, with the also hirsute John Hay, who was secretary during 1898-1905.

26. For Kissinger's character sketch of Brezhnev, see Henry Kissinger, *White House Years* (Boston: Little, Brown, 1979), pp. 1138-41.

27. For Kissinger's account of his March 1974 trip to Moscow, see his *Years of Upheaval*, pp. 1020-25.

28. See *State to Belgrade, copy at NSA*.

29. See Garthoff, *Détente and Confrontation*, pp. 468-69, and *NSDM 245*. Using the present Minuteman III deployment as a baseline, under the two-to-one ratio the United States would have 550 silos while the Soviets would have 270. Also part of the proposal was a subceiling on the number of Soviet heavy ICBM launchers with MIRVs; the United States suggested 15 percent. Among other features, the two sides would agree to measures "to assure that modifications in ICBN launchers . . . will be appropriately constrained at all ICBM complexes, so as to increase confidence that MIRV missile limitation are being observed." See U.S. Note, 21 March 1974, State Department FOIA release; copy at *NSA*.

30. Neither letter was included with the original FOIA releases.

31. John Patterson, the U.S. vice counsel at Hermosillo, had been kidnapped on 22 March, not by left-wing guerrillas as had been thought but by an American ex-convict. Patterson's body was found in the Sonora desert on 8 July. See *Facts on File, 1974* (New York: Facts on File Inc, 1974).

32. U.S. Note, 21 March 1974, State Department FOIA release; copy at *NSA*.

33. This is a reference to hawkish positions taken by James Schlesinger (b. 1929), who served as secretary of defense during 1973-75.

34. A reference to terms in the SALT I agreement that gave the Soviets the right to increase the size of their SLBM force in exchange for taking older ICBMs, such as SS-7s, out of commission.

35. Brezhnev is referring to Poseidon submarine-launched ballistic missiles (SLBM), the generation of SLBMs that replaced Polaris missiles and whose deployment began in 1971. Armed with 16 missiles, each carrying about 10 MIRVs, Poseidon submarines could strike targets between 2500 and 3200 nautical miles away. See Graham Spinardi, *From Polaris to Trident: The Development of Fleet Ballistic Missile Technology* (New York: Cambridge University Press, 1994), pp. 40, 106. By the 1970s, the U.S. Minuteman force had stable numbers at 1000, although the force composition changed as the Air Force replaced older missiles with the MIRVed Minuteman III: see Robert S. Norris and Thomas B. Cochran, *Nuclear Weapons Databook: US-USSR/Russian Strategic Offensive Nuclear Forces, 1945-1996* (Washington, D.C.: Natural Resources Defense Council, 1997).

36. A reference to the various technical intelligence programs, such as overhead satellite photography, RADINT (radar intelligence), and ELINT (electronic intelligence), used to verify arms control agreements.

37. This is a reference to Poseidon submarines patrolling the Mediterranean and North Sea.

38. A career civil servant, Michael Jobert (b. 1921) was France's foreign minister during 1973-74. For Kissinger's difficult relations with him, see his *Years of Upheaval*, pp. 162-66.

39. In 1974, U.S. forces in NATO Europe and allies there had about 165 light bombers and some 1,250 fighter/ground-attack aircraft, as well as some 350 intercepters and 275 reconnaissance aircraft. In the same categories, the Warsaw Pact had 250, 1,500, 2,100, and 500. See *The Military Balance 1974-1975* (London: International Institute for Strategic Studies, 1974).

40. This is a reference to four experimental LCBMs planned for inclusion in the Soviet arsenal, including the SS-x17, SS-x18, and the SS-x19. See Central Intelligence Agency, History Staff, *Intentions and Capabilities: Estimates on Soviet Strategic Forces, 1950-1983*, ed. Donald P. Steury (Washington, D.C.: Central Intelligence Agency, 1996), p. 334.

41. It would not satisfy them, presumably, because it would codify the disparity favoring the Soviets in numbers of missiles.

42. The TU-160, later known as the Blackjack A bomber, was the Soviet equivalent of the U.S. B-1 heavy jet bomber. The Soviets completed testing the Blackjack A in the early 1980s and deployed it later in the decade.

43. Research and development work on the B-1 bomber was well underway. The first test flight took place on October 26, 1974, but President Carter canceled the B-1 in 1977 before large-scale production and deployment occurred; President Reagan later reinstated the B-1.

44. For example, the SS-18 ICBM model 2 carried up to eight reentry vehicles with warhead yields (generally proportionate to weight) ranging from 0.6 to 1.8 megatons. See U.S. Air Force, *A History of the Strategic Arms Competition, Vol. 3: A Handbook of Selected Soviet Weapon and Space Systems*, June 1976; copy at *NSA*. By comparison, yields for the MIRVed warheads on Minuteman III were about 170 kilotons each.

45. Brezhnev is referring to Poseidon SLBMs, which had 10 MIRVs, but were capable of carrrying 12.
46. Soviet intelligence was slightly off: Minuteman III could carry 3 MIRVs, not 5.
47. See memcon "SALT, Other Arms Control; CSCE," 25 March 1974; copy at *NSA*.
48. For background on the CSCE, see Garthoff, *Détente and Confrontation*, pp. 527–32; Bowker and Williams, *Superpower Detente*, pp. 90–93; U.S. State Department Briefing Paper, "CSCE," March 1974; copy at *NSA*.
49. John J. Maresca, *To Helsinki: The Conference on Security and Cooperation in Europe, 1973–1975* (N.C.: Duke University Press, 1987), p. 93.
50. For U.S. strategy, see U.S. State Department Briefing Paper, "CSCE," March 1974; copy at *NSA*.
51. See U.S. Embassy Moscow telegram Secto 17, 26 March 1974; copy at *NSA*.
52. See Moscow 4346 and 4360 to SecState, "U.S.–Soviet Middle East Talks," both dated 26 March 1974; copies of both at *NSA*.
53. See memcon, "Other Arms Control; CSCE; MBFR; Economic Relations," 26 March 1974, U.S. Department of State Freedom of Information Release; copy at *NSA*.
54. This is a reference to the two-week course at the Foreign Service Institute taken by newly appointed ambassadors.
55. For "overstrong" Germany and the nature of the de facto post–World War II settlement that rested on Germany's partition, see Anton W. DePorte, *Europe Between the Superpowers: The Enduring Balance* (New Haven: Yale University Press, 1979), p. 142–65.
56. Before heading to that meeting, he and Gromyko held a brief discussion on West German breaches of the 1971 Quadrapartite Agreement on Berlin. See U.S. Department of State, memcon, "Federal Environmental Office in Berlin," 27 March 1974; U.S. Department of State Briefing Paper, "Berlin," March 1974 (copy at *NSA*); and Garthoff, *Détente and Confrontation*, p. 138.
57. This exchange dances round each side's tacit awareness of the other's capabilities to verify arms control agreements with overhead satellite photography—perhaps the most effective of the "national technical means" of verification. Brezhnev was correct: the U.S. Air Force had been covering up the missile silos. See Garthoff, *Détente and Confrontation*, pp. 503–4. For the role of U.S. KH-9 satellites in arms control verification, see Jeffrey T. Richelson, *A Century of Spies: Intelligence in the Twentieth Century* (New York: Oxford University Press, 1995), pp. 330–31.
58. Memcon, "Results of Moscow Visit, Including SALT, CSCE, MBFR, and the Middle East"," 28 March, 1974; copy at *NSA*
59. Kissinger, *Years of Upheaval*, p. 933.
60. "East Asia Chiefs of Mission Conference November 14–16, 1973, Tokyo Japan," 117, copy in U.S.–Japan Collection at *NSA*.

6

Firing Cannons:

Beijing – Washington, 1974

The period between Henry Kissinger's November 1973 and November 1974 visits to Beijing was an awkward and uncertain one for Sino–American relations. While the United States was going through the turmoil of the Watergate crisis, Chinese political elites were engaged in intense conflict over the direction of economic and social development. The PRC leadership was concerned that Watergate could throw their relationship with Washington off course, and it also wondered whether U.S. détente policy might impair Beijing's vital interests. While Kissinger still perceived a "tacit alliance," meeting transcripts show that his rapport with Zhou's de facto successor, Deng Xiaoping, was not the best, and that he knew that internal Chinese political conflicts, or the wrong moves by Washington, could weaken ties with Beijing. Even though Deng Xiaoping would affirm that relations were "good," his firing of rhetorical "cannons" in the direction of the United States was only a symptom of what senior U.S. officials perceived as a "cooling off" in relations, notwithstanding progress in strategic intelligence cooperation. Moreover, on the crucial issue of normalization of relations, by the year's end a stalemate had developed, raising the possibility that Sino–American relations could stagnate until one side or the other made concessions over Taiwan.[1]

During the first months of 1974, the ongoing Watergate crisis raised concern in Beijing just as it had in Moscow. As Deng explained to Kissinger in April 1974, the Chinese leadership was "not happy" about Watergate, to the point of finding it "incomprehensible." Although Deng was discreet enough to say that Watergate would not affect U.S.–PRC relations, the NSC staff had learned from their contacts with Chinese diplomats that Beijing might be wondering if Nixon would be able to make "further major initiatives" on China. Kissinger's advisers speculated whether the Chinese might even reconsider their relationship with Washington because of doubts about Nixon's capability to "act in a strong manner in foreign policy."[2]

The resolution of the Watergate crisis—Nixon's resignation on 8 August

1974 — brought to power Gerald Ford, a somewhat more conservative Republican who had honed his political skills and learned political caution through years in the House of Representatives. If the Chinese worried about a new president changing policy, however, both Ford and Kissinger would personally assure Mao and Zhou that they intended to sustain the special relationship Nixon had forged. Yet Ford had his own future to consider, and with all his problems — an emerging deep recession and uproar over his pardon of Nixon — he had to think seriously about the domestic political effects of any foreign policy moves, especially after he chose to seek election in 1976. The implications of his political plans for U.S.-PRC relations were not immediately evident, and they collided with Nixon's pledge for full diplomatic normalization with China in 1976, which meant that Washington would have to break off relations with Taiwan, an "old friend" with substantial political influence in the United States.[3]

However tumultuous U.S. politics were in 1974, Chinese observers of U.S. policy had the advantage of a reasonably transparent government and press. Richard Solomon, Kissinger's chief China specialist, was not so fortunate when it came to Chinese internal developments; he had to rely on educated guesswork. Solomon did not know of Zhou's fatal illness or of Mao's developing estrangement from the premier; nevertheless his analysis of the struggle between Zhou and a coalition of party radicals and military leaders over the course of Chinese development was astute. Solomon thought that Zhou sought to tackle China's economic backwardness and military vulnerability while preserving Communist Party supremacy and fighting to restore the power, chipped away during the Cultural Revolution, of state organizations. Moreover, Mao had rehabilitated the pragmatic Deng Xiaoping, a victim of the Cultural Revolution who had enraged radicals with his aphorism that it "is not the cat's color but his skill at catching mice that counts." In Deng, Mao gave Zhou a deputy with great organizational expertise and an interest in learning techniques of economic development from the West. It was precisely those techniques that party radicals were trying to thwart.[4]

Solomon perceived that while Zhou and his allies were trying to consolidate their position, they wanted to avoid giving their opponents, some of whom were questioning the direction of relations with Washington, the "added ammunition that would come with a more visible relationship" with the United States. Thus, by the spring of 1974, Solomon saw "greater aloofness and lack of cooperation" by the Chinese at the operational level even though senior officials were saying that relations were fine. Besides the Foreign Ministry's aloof posture on the claims and assets negotiations and on expediting semiofficial exchanges (visits by governors and congressional delegations), in April the Chinese reneged on the agreement over the Marine Guards. After a petty incident, the Foreign Ministry insisted that the Marines go; they did, and the Liaison Office replaced them with civilian State Department security officers.[5]

As Kissinger's advisers saw it, the policy and philosophical differences that both sides had "submerged" during the first phase of contacts had "surfaced publicly with some sharpness" at a time when Beijing's doubts about U.S. power and policy were growing. Whatever the Chinese leadership may have thought about Kissinger's warnings during 1972-73 of the Soviet threat to China, now they were downplaying the Soviet threat to themselves. Deng showed little concern about superpower collusion against China; his rhetoric focused on U.S.-Soviet rivalries and Moscow's danger to the West. Assistant Secretary of State for Far Eastern Affairs Arthur Hummel, Winston Lord, and Richard Solomon saw in this an "element of gamesmanship, an attempt to downgrade our central lever." They speculated that the Chinese were trying to give themselves more freedom of action and reduce "pressure to make political compromises."[6]

Deng's equanimity about "great disorder under heaven" in a speech he made at the United Nations raised hackles in Washington as did the growing rhetorical attacks on superpower hegemony and imperialism. The "Chinese emphasis on justice and struggle" was opposed to "our emphasis on peace and stability." Also troubling the China hands was the PRC's endorsement of economic development strategies based on national independence and "self-reliance." For Kissinger and his advisers, "unrestrained economic nationalism" was a threat to the "interdependence" that characterized the modern world economy.[7]

Not surprisingly, the Taiwan problem remained a difficult one in U.S.-PRC relations. Zhou had already incurred Mao's wrath in 1973 by suggesting the possibility of a "peaceful" liberation of Taiwan; for that and other reasons, Mao had charged Zhou with taking a "capitulationist" stance toward Washington. In February, Washington raised suspicions when Kissinger approved the appointment of a senior Foreign Service officer, Leonard Unger, as the new U.S. ambassador to Taiwan. The Chinese saw this as a move to keep Washington-Taipei relations at a high level, and soon Beijing initiated a pressure campaign on Washington for a resolution of the Taiwan problem. That the campaign started from the top was evident in the tough language the chastened Zhou used in conversation with Zambian president Kenneth Kaunda: progress in the relationship would be slow "as long as the U.S. is giving blood transfusions to Taiwan." Throughout the year, Chinese officials told Washington, directly or indirectly, that breakthroughs in such areas as trade and exchange depended on U.S. action to withdraw recognition of Taiwan and to consolidate diplomatic relations with the PRC.[8]

Although Washington was moving forward in substantially reducing the U.S. military presence in Taiwan, Kissinger's advisers—Solomon Lord, and Hummel—were looking closely at the next step, the details of breaking diplomatic relations with the Republic of Taiwan and establishing them with mainland China. While the advisers were willing to take such steps, they believed that those steps would have a heavy political cost—notably the opposition of the U.S. Taiwan lobby. Hoping that the PRC would show some flexibility, they believed that the least damaging option overall was to establish a consulate or a liaison office; but they also knew that Beijing would consider any relationship with government-to-government connotations as violating the "one China principle."[9]

Even more important—the "cutting edge" of normalization—was the problem of how to preserve the security of Taiwan, an "old friend." Since his first meetings with Zhou in 1971, Kissinger had emphasized the importance of a resolution of the Taiwan problem through "peaceful negotiations" and had encouraged Beijing to consider making statements to that effect.[10] While expecting U.S. arms sales to Taiwan to continue, Kissinger's advisers also believed that a politically workable arrangement—one that buttressed U.S. credibility and avoided problems with the Taiwan lobby—would require PRC guarantees for a "peaceful resolution" of the Taiwan situation. It took months before Kissinger's China hands could get their distracted boss to approve substantive studies on normalization, but by August 1974 he accepted that PRC guarantees had to be part of a U.S. normalization package.[11] Accordingly, he advised Ford that the Chinese would have to be told that "we are not committed to delivering Taiwan to Beijing rule and that U.S. public opinion will not allow us to make unilateral decisions about the future of 15 million people."[12]

In the end, the optimum Taiwan settlement that Kissinger's China specialists suggested would require some willingness, an unlikely possibility, by PRC leaders to "publicly [tie] their hands" on Taiwan. Indeed Kissinger found Chinese authorities stiffening their terms for a deal and asserting more strongly than ever that Washington must follow the Japan model of breaking all political and military ties with Taiwan. As for guarantees on peaceful change, later in the year Deng insisted that Taiwan was "an internal matter . . . in which no one has the right to interfere." Guarantees were out of the question; the Chinese would, however, let the Americans determine their own schedule for normalization.

Deng's position came as no surprise to the Americans, who anticipated a possible deadlock on the specifics of a normalization deal. But Kissinger was acutely aware that, two years earlier, U.S. authorities had pledged that 1976 would mark the year when Washington would recognize China. With Nixon gone and a new, politically cautious president looking toward a 1976 election campaign, a move toward diplomatic recognition on the schedule that Nixon had indicated could be politically risky.

Even if prospects for diplomatic relations were shaky, the strategic relationship that Kissinger had anticipated during his 1973 visit became more tangible. The details remain murky, but it seems that intelligence cooperation with China against the Soviet Union expanded: Beijing secretly provided Washington with access to important sites for gathering intelligence on the Soviet Union as a *quid pro quo* for secret data provided by Kissinger's staff.[13]

An important development in the U.S.-PRC relationship during 1974 was Vice Premier Deng Xiaoping's visit to New York in April, his first appearance in the United States. A year earlier, Deng had been living in internal exile, one of the millions purged during the Cultural Revolution, but Mao had ordered his rehabilitation. It was a virtual state secret, although well known to Chinese Communists, that Mao had personally apologized to Deng for what had happened during the 1960s. Although Deng had traveled abroad in his youth, this visit marked his first exposure to the United States. It was also Henry Kissinger's first encounter, under informal circumstances, with a man who was to become, by fits and starts, the key decision-maker in China for the next two decades.[14]

As deputy to Zhou, Deng now had acting responsibility for foreign affairs and his visit gave him an opportunity to appraise the state of Sino-American relations. Publicly, however, he was in New York to participate in U.S. discussions on international development. In a fiery speech on 10 April, Deng articulated Mao's theory of "three worlds": the superpowers, the other industrial nations, and the developing countries, including China which had no superpower pretensions. He denounced the imperialist superpowers, of which the Soviets were the "especially vicious" example, and called for "revolution" and "liberation" from their hegemony.

Deng's tough rhetoric, even with its implication that the United States was the less vicious superpower, caused concern; but when he met privately with Kissinger he volunteered that Sino–American relations were "good"[16] and even encouraged U.S. Middle East diplomacy. That Beijing still leaned toward Washington undoubtedly gratified Kissinger, but he nevertheless began to form an unfavorable opinion of Deng. Kissinger later compared Deng unfavorably with Zhou Enlai: Deng, he said lacked Zhou's "grasp of history" and his deft handling of diplomatic discourse; and his personal style was "rather frontal and somewhat acerbic." Kissinger also saw a "lack of self-assurance" on Deng's part: a man who had known political exile was unlikely to "range very widely from his brief" much less take innovative positions. Certainly, the conversation on 14 April had its share of awkward pauses, though, as one American later noted, Deng warmed up as the evening progressed.[17]

In spite of this meeting's significance, Kissinger did not see fit to mention it in his memoirs. With Deng in power at the time *Years of Upheaval* went to press, Kissinger presumably erred on the side of caution when it came to describing a political leader from whom he might need favors someday.

DEPARTMENT OF STATE
TOP SECRET/SENSITIVE/EXCLUSIVELY EYES ONLY
MEMORANDUM OF CONVERSATION
PARTICIPANTS: Deng Xiaoping, Vice Premier of the PRC; Qiao Guanhua, Vice Foreign Minister of the PRC; Ambassador Huang Hua, PRC Permanent Representative to the UNGA; Z hang Hanzhi (F) (Acted as Interpreter); Luo Xu (F) (Acted as Notetaker) Guo Jiading (Acted as Notetaker); Henry A. Kissinger, Secretary of State; Joseph P. Sisco, Under Secretary of State; Brent Scowcroft, Major General, National Security Council; Winston Lord, Director, Policy Planning Staff, Department of State; Arthur W. Hummel, Jr., Deputy Assistant Secretary (EA) Department of State; Charles W. Freeman, Jr. (EA/PRCM), Department of State (Acted as Notetaker)
SUBJECT: Secretary's Dinner for the Vice Premier of the People's Republic of China
DATE AND TIME: Sunday, April 14, 1974, 8:05 P.M. – 11:00 P.M.
PLACE: Secretary's Suite, Waldorf Astoria Hotel, New York City[A]

[A] Source: National Archives, Record Group 59; Department of State Records, Policy Planning Staff (Director's Files), 1969-77 (hereafter referred to as *PPS*, with archival box number and file information, box 374, China — Sensitive Special WL File, Misc Reports, Nov. 1974.

(The Chinese party arrived at 8:05 and were escorted to suite 35A by Mr. Freeman. When the party was seated, the conversation began.)

Secretary Kissinger: It is a very great pleasure to meet you, Mr. Vice Premier. I understand that the Vice Foreign Minister has taken up the same step recently as I . . .

(At this point the press was admitted to take photographs and the conversation was broken off briefly.)

Vice Premier Deng: This is a very large group of press we have here.

Secretary Kissinger: They are asking me to shake hands. (Shakes hands with the Vice Premier and the Vice Foreign Minister.) They want us all three to shake hands at once. Your photographers are much better disciplined than ours, I'm afraid.

Vice Premier Deng: We shouldn't listen to their orders.

Secretary Kissinger: But we have to listen to their orders. Otherwise they will print the worst picture that they take.

(The press was escorted out of the room.)

[After a brief discussion of his travel plans, Deng asks if he may smoke. After Kissinger assents, noting that he did not smoke, Deng says that "you've missed something."]

Secretary Kissinger: I concentrate on other vices. How is your back coming along, Ambassador Huang?

Ambassador Huang: So-so.

Secretary Kissinger: Have you used the doctor that I arranged for you?

Ambassador Huang: I am keeping him on standby.

Secretary Kissinger: He's afraid if he uses our doctor he will install a microphone in his back.

Vice Premier Deng: I believe of all who are present here tonight your earliest acquaintance was Ambassador Huang.

Secretary Kissinger: Yes. He met me at the Beijing Airport in 1971. He may have forgotten this, but he gave me some very valuable lessons in how to negotiate. When we meet with the Russians to discuss a communique, they suggest that each side put forward its maximum position and that we then try to discuss a way of bridging the difference. But Ambassador Huang suggested that we write our real positions down at the outset, and that in this way we could more easily reach agreement. And it was as he said it would be.

Vice Premier Deng: You've had quite a few years of experience in dealing with the Soviet Union.

Secretary Kissinger: Yes. Quite a few years. It is always very fatiguing and always the same. On the first day the atmosphere is very pleasant. On the second day there is an explosion. On the last day, two hours before the departure, when they see that we will not abandon our position, they become accommodating and pleasant. It is always the same.

Vice Foreign Minister Qiao: (In English) Dialectics!

Secretary Kissinger: Well, I don't want to get into that with the Vice Foreign Minister. You still owe me a poem.

Vice Foreign Minister Qiao: That's right.

Vice Premier Deng: I also have quite a bit of experience with the Soviet Union.

Secretary Kissinger: Oh, in what years?

Vice Premier Deng: Well, I have been to the Soviet Union seven times.[18]

Secretary Kissinger: Then you have been there once more than I have. Tell me, are they always so very difficult? Do they yell at their allies as well as at others?

Vice Premier Deng: In my experience we could never reach agreement.

Secretary Kissinger: We can reach agreement but only very slowly. Their idea of arms control is that we should start from the base which we have now, but they should have five years in which to do what they want.

(At this point Mrs. Kissinger entered the room and was introduced to the guests.)[19]

We've just been talking about negotiations with the Soviet Union. The Vice Premier has been to the Soviet Union on seven occasions. His experience has been that the Soviets never agree to anything. We have reached some agreements with them.

Vice Premier Deng: You are more advanced than I am.

Secretary Kissinger: But I know that, now that I have explained all this, the next time I am in Beijing the Vice Foreign Minister will yell at me just to see what the result is.

Vice Premier Deng: You must have had quite a few quarrels with him by now.

Secretary Kissinger: Negotiations with him are always hard but reasonable. And we can reach agreement. For example, on the Shanghai Communique, we spent many, many nights going over the details of the language together.

Vice Premier Deng: Each side should speak its mind. That is what is most important.

Secretary Kissinger: But in those negotiations I had had so much mao tai that I was negotiating in Chinese.

Vice Premier Deng: Then you have that in common with the Vice Foreign Minister. He also likes to drink mao tai.

Vice Foreign Minister Qiao: If you had drunk a lot, it was not my fault.

Secretary Kissinger: But you were not defeated in those negotiations. (Pause)

You know, I have had same complaints from Mr. Gromyko about your speech the other day.

Vice Premier Deng: Was he very dissatisfied?

Secretary Kissinger: He felt he was being attacked and he wanted me to answer on both our behalfs.

Vice Foreign Minister Qiao: (In English.) Very clever tactics! Secretary Kissinger: But even if you listen very carefully to what I am going to say tomorrow, you will not hear much criticism.

Vice Premier Deng: I got acquainted with Mr. Gromyko in 1957 for the first time.

Secretary Kissinger: Has he changed much since then? What is your opinion?

Vice Premier Deng: He is not one of the people who decide policy in the Soviet Union.

Secretary Kissinger: That's right. In my experience he has been used as a straight man for Brezhnev. He never expressed an opinion himself on the negotiations except on technical matters.[20] Lately he has become somewhat more assertive because he is now on the Politburo. . . .

Vice Premier Deng: Brezhnev was also not one who decided policy before 1964.

Secretary Kissinger: Correct. And he was not supposed to understand foreign policy at that time. After what he did to Khrushchev he has been very, very careful about going away on vacation.[21]

[Kissinger escorts his guests into the dining room where he introduces Joseph Sisco and Brent Scowcroft. "Mr. Sisco is my alibi on the Middle East."]

Vice Foreign Minister Qiao: You mean if you achieve success, it belongs to you but if you fail, the failure is Sisco's.

Secretary Kissinger: But the one who is really responsible for what has happened in the Middle East is the Vice Foreign Minister. Last year we talked about the Middle East question, and I have followed the outlines of that conversation since in what we have done.[22]

Vice Foreign Minister Qiao: Last time I met you, we talked according to what Chairman Mao had said to the Egyptian Vice President. You have two hands. You should use both. Give one to Israel and one to the other side.

Secretary Kissinger: We have been following the policy we discussed then.

Vice Premier Deng: That is true. Both hands should be used.

Secretary Kissinger: Exactly!

Vice Premier Deng: In your view is there any hope for disengagement now between Syria and Israel?

Secretary Kissinger: I hope that in the next three weeks we will make considerable progress on this. As you know, I talked yesterday with the Chief of the Syrian Military Intelligence and today I talked to the Israeli Ambassador. In about two weeks, I will go to the Middle East and try to do for the Syrians and the Israelis what I did with Israel and Egypt. And for your information, the Syrian has told me that after disengagement has been achieved, they will turn towards Iraq and work to reduce the Soviet Union's presence in Iraq. You remember that I discussed this with Chairman Mao and Premier Zhou as a long-term strategy.

Vice Premier Deng: Exactly so! President Asad of Syria has visited Moscow lately. What influence do you think that will produce on the situation?

Secretary Kissinger: The Soviet Union has been very eager to play a major role in the negotiations, and they have been conducting themselves with the delicacy for which they are well known. For example, when I was in Moscow, Brezhnev yelled at me for three hours, saying that they must take part in the negotiations. The difficulty is that the Arabs and Israelis do not want the Soviets in the negotiations. While I was in Moscow I sent Asad a telegram asking what he wanted. He replied he wanted the same handling as we had given in the case of the Egyptians. I believe he went to Moscow to balance off the visit of his representative to Washington. But we have no impression of any change in the Syrian position. In fact, Gromyko suggested that I should meet him in Damascus, but when I asked the Syrian in Washington what he thought about this, he said he was not in favor of it. Everything now depends on whether we can succeed in getting the Israelis to agree to withdraw from part of the Golan Heights. (Note: The Chinese interpreter omitted the words "part of" in the Chinese).[23]

Secretary Kissinger: This is mao tai. Mr. Vice Premier, we welcome you to New York. It is a very great pleasure to see you here.

Mr. Sisco: This is the first time I've had it.

Secretary Kissinger: If you were like the Vice Foreign Minister you would drink it bottoms-up every time.

Mr. Lord: I believe that with mao tai we could solve the energy crisis!

Vice Premier Deng: But could we also solve the raw materials crisis?

Secretary Kissinger: I think if we drink enough mao tai we can solve anything.

Vice Premier Deng: Then, when I go back to China, we must take steps to increase our production of it.

Secretary Kissinger: You know, when the President came back from China he wanted to show his daughter how potent mao tai was. So he took out a bottle and poured it into a saucer and lit it, but the glass bowl broke and the mao tai ran over the table and the table began to burn! So you nearly burned down the White House!

Actually, in about two weeks I'll be in the Middle East again.

[Kissinger provides Deng with more details of the Middle East peace talks, noting that Washington would try to induce the Israelis, "who are very difficult to deal with," to withdraw from the Golan Heights in stages. Withdrawal from all of Golan cannot be asked for yet because it would "lead to a stalemate, and the Soviets would come back in." However, he says, "[i]f we are successful in these disengagement talks, we can hope to reduce Soviet influence in Syria, as we did in Egypt."]

Vice Premier Deng: If the Soviet Union succeeds in Syria, then the Soviets will have three places in the Middle East on which they can rely: Syria, Iraq and Southern Yemen.

Secretary Kissinger: We are trying to prevent this from happening in Syria. And, we are already working on Southern Yemen. We think the Egyptians will help us in this.

Vice Premier Deng: Chairman Mao touched on this point in his discussions with you. Our attitude is that, on the one hand, we support the Arabs, but, on the other hand, we work with you to fix the bear in the north together with you.

Secretary Kissinger: That is exactly our position. If we can get into a position in which we can disagree on the Middle East, that would show there had been progress. Afterwards, that is after there has been a settlement, of course, we can expect to have some disagreements.

(The Chinese interpreter had some difficulty with this sentence and there was a brief discussion in Chinese over how to interpret it.)

Secretary Kissinger: I have not seen Ambassador Huang Zhen since he returned, but I plan to see him next week.

Vice Premier Deng: There has been no change in the relationship we have so far. (Note: The Vice Premier's original statement did not contain the words "so far." These two words were added by the Chinese interpreter.)

Secretary Kissinger: We continue to attach the utmost importance to good and friendly relations between the United States and the Peoples Republic of China. We intend to pursue the course of normalization of our relations, as I have said in my talks with Chairman Mao and Premier Zhou.

Vice Premier Deng: This policy, and the principles on which it is based, are personally supported by Chairman Mao. I believe that from your two long talks with Chairman Mao you ought to have this understanding. The last time you met him you talked for three hours, I believe.

Secretary Kissinger: We went into great detail in those discussions, so I never pay any attention to the newspaper accounts of our relationship. In our experience, the Chinese word always counts.

(The Secretary toasted the Vice Foreign Minister.)

Vice Premier Deng: Now that you have drunk all this mao tai, your speech tomorrow is bound to be excellent.

Secretary Kissinger: It will be moving! I shall probably attack the superpowers! I am glad that the Vice Premier has confirmed what the Vice Foreign Minister has already said to Ambassador Bruce in Beijing. Our relationship has not changed.

Vice Premier Deng: I have read the record of your talk with Chairman Mao Zedong. It was very explicit. You had a discussion of the relationships between the United States and China from a strategic point of view. The only difficulty is on where the Soviet strategic focus is. On this point, we have some differences, but these differences do not matter, for practice will show where the true focal point is.

Secretary Kissinger: Exactly. Wherever the first focal point is, the next focal point is obvious. If the focal point is in Europe, then the next is on China. If the focal point is China, then the next one is Europe. If the focal point is on the Middle East, then the next is also obvious.

Vice Premier Deng: In the East we have talked to the Japanese— our Japanese friends—about this. They do not seem to realize this point. They seem to think that the Soviet intentions in the East do not include them. For example, in our discussion of the Tyumen project—the exploitation of oil fields in Siberia—the Japanese said they would have to reconsider their position so as not to offend the Chinese. But they did not really think that their interests would be affected by this development.

Secretary Kissinger: The Japanese do not yet think in strategic terms. They think in commercial terms.

Well, I am particularly glad tonight to see my old friends from China. Speaking from our side, we can confirm every detail of our discussions with

Chairman Mao and with Premier Zhou, and we can confirm the direction on which our policy is set. We have had some debate with our European allies to make them realize the facts and to be realistic. But this does not influence our long-term strategy. It does not influence our desire to construct a strong Europe. But you, as old friends, understand this. The French have been taking a rather short-term viewpoint. You have talked to them recently, I believe. But this cannot influence the realities of the United States and the Soviet position vis-a-vis Europe. This is nothing but a quarrel within the family.

Vice Premier Deng: Just so. There are minor quarrels, but the unity remains.

Secretary Kissinger: Well said.

Vice Premier Deng: But if you were to show more consideration for the Europeans, would there not be a better result?

Secretary Kissinger: Depends to whom. They are very much divided.

Vice Foreign Minister Qiao: What we mean—we are not much qualified to speak on the European question—what I mean is, mostly consideration for France. Speaking frankly, we know that you have some opinions against the French. But must it be so open? That's the first point. The second is that we wonder whether you could show more consideration to the French. They have a very strong sense of self-respect and national pride.

Secretary Kissinger: The problem is that we started out working with France because we have believed the French were in many ways most supportive of Europe and they were the best on this point.[24] So with regard to every move we made in the Middle East we went to the French and got their approval. Then we discovered they were opposing us on every point—every detail—behind our backs. In our last conversation the Vice Foreign Minister said that we have a coordinated strategy. But the French have no strategy, only tactics. So in the Middle East they have been working to undermine us. This is of no advantage to anyone, not even to the French. So we decided that it would be useful to make it public—to bring it out in the open where the issues could be clarified.

Vice Premier Deng: That is good—if it does not continue in the open.

Vice Foreign Minister Qiao: I tell you quite frankly that when I read your talk to the wives of the Congressmen I was very alarmed.

Secretary Kissinger: You know, I have never persuaded anyone of what really happened on that occasion. It is the perfect example of what happens in an unplanned economy. I arrived at my office and found that I was scheduled to talk to the Congressional wives, so I screamed at my colleagues and objected. But it was on the schedule, so I went to see them. I thought that no three of them could ever agree on what I said and that I would be safe. About two thirds through the talk I joked that I was glad to see no press there.[25] It was then that I found that there were press there. Everyone thinks this was very carefully planned. But you are right. I do not intend to repeat that particular speech.

[Kissinger rises to toast the health of Mao, Zhou, and guests, and he observes that the "most important mission I have engaged in was my first trip to Beijing" because U.S. - PRC "normalization . . . is a major factor in the protection of world peace."]

Secretary Kissinger: . . . I am always at a disadvantage with the Vice Foreign Minister. The Vice Foreign Minister has studied philosophy. And he has studied Hegel, but I have only studied as far as Kant. I am sure that it's all right with the Vice Foreign Minister if I criticize France, but not Germany. He would not let me get away with that.

Vice Premier Deng: Why is there still such a big noise being made about Watergate?

Secretary Kissinger: That is a series of almost incomprehensible events, and the clamor about it is composed of many people who for various reasons oppose the President.

Vice Premier Deng: Chairman Mao told you that we are not happy about this. Such an event in no way affects any part of our relations.

Secretary Kissinger: I assure you we have carried out our foreign policy without regard to the Watergate incident, and we will continue to carry it out regardless of Watergate.

Vice Premier Deng: We do not care much about such an issue.

Secretary Kissinger: In our foreign policy we continue to have very wide support from the American public. When I first met the Prime Minister I spoke of China as the land of mystery. Now the U.S. must seem a very mysterious country.

Vice Premier Deng: Such an issue is really incomprehensible to us.

Secretary Kissinger: It has its roots in the fact that some mistakes were made, but also, when you change many policies, you make many, many enemies.

[Deng rises to return the toast to Dr. Kissinger and U.S. - Chinese friendship, and he notes that since the 1971–1972 visits, "relations between our two countries can be said to be fine." After some comments by Kissinger about coverage of Chinese politics by Hong Kong newspapers, Deng explains the anti-Confucian campaign as a means to "emancipate the people's ideology from old thinking."]

Secretary Kissinger: Our newspapers have said that this is directed against individuals, living individuals, and not against ancient individuals.

Vice Premier Deng: There is some ground in what they say. When you criticize a conservative ideology, then, naturally, it will affect some working staffs — some people who represent the conservative ideology being attacked.[26]

Secretary Kissinger: I have been observing your foreign policy for a long time, and I conclude that it has always been consistent. We, of course, do not comment on your internal policies and your internal situation.

Vice Premier Deng: Those comments in the newspapers are not reliable.

Secretary Kissinger: Of that, I am sure.

(Pause.)

Mr. Gromyko asked me about the situation in China, and I told him we see no change in your foreign policy.

(Pause)

You know, one reason I never take Sisco to China is that I never fail in China, so I don't need him. But I did take one of his associates, Mr. Atherton, last time.

(Pause)

[There is a brief discussion of the 24 Dynasties histories — a compilation of the various official histories originally prepared by dynastic historians — that the PRC has presented to the State Department]

(The party adjourned to the sitting room.)

Secretary Kissinger: The last time I was in this room was when the Arab–Israeli war started. Sisco woke me up at 6:00 a.m. He said, if you can get on the telephone you can perhaps stop it. I thought anyone with this kind of judgment deserved to be promoted.

Vice Foreign Minister Qiao: The last time we met here also, didn't we?

Secretary Kissinger: I have this for when I come up to the U.N. Mr. Lord is still working on my speech for tomorrow, but I tell you if I say anything significant at all that will be a mistake.

Vice Foreign Minister Qiao: Not because of the mao tai!

Secretary Kissinger: I thought with your permission, Mr. Vice Premier, we might review a few problems. We have already talked about the Middle East, and now I would summarize our discussion as follows: We agree with your assessment that the three Soviet strong points in the Middle East are Syria, Iraq and South Yemen. We are bringing about substantial changes in Egyptian foreign policy. For your information we have reason to believe that the Egyptians will abrogate their treaty with the Soviet Union this year. This is, of course, very confidential. But I have never read a leak in a Chinese newspaper!

[Kissinger discusses U.S. plans for economic aid to Egypt, noting that he will try to encourage Western European support as well through West Germany, the Netherlands, and Britain. Support could also come from Kuwait and Saudi Arabia and even China: "It is up to you." The Egyptians "are working with us on the South Yemen problem. Syria will work on the Iraq problem, and so will Iran, which is also active in Oman. We think we can reduce Soviet influence in the area systematically."]

Secretary Kissinger: . . . The Soviets are extremely anxious about our efforts. I may agree with them to some face-saving thing, which would not, however, affect the substance. For example, I may agree to meet Gromyko in Geneva before I go to the Middle East. I will not tell him anything and, in fact, I will not be able to tell him anything because I will not yet have gone to the Middle East. I will do this to prevent them from agitating their supporters in Syria.

[Kissinger discusses his plans to visit the Middle East in about two weeks; besides Israel, he will visit Iran, Kuwait, and some of the Gulf emirates. After a discussion of possible Iranian supply of tanks to Pakistan, the discussion turns to Iraq.]

Secretary Kissinger: We are leaving them to sit there. We are keeping them occupied so they can't intervene in Syria. We told President [Houari] Boumedienne that at the right moment we were prepared to make a move toward Iraq but it is a little premature at the moment. After Syria is a little closer to us we can approach Iraq.

Vice Minister Deng: When the Vice President of Egypt visited China, we touched on this question of giving some assistance but we never got into details. They did not raise it directly with us.

Secretary Kissinger: Because they are not ready yet.

Vice Foreign Minister Qiao: But, they raised the question of light weapons.

Vice Premier Deng: In this respect, our power is very limited.

Secretary Kissinger: We recognize that. Should the Egyptians talk to you? Or do you want to stay out of it?

Vice Premier Deng: We adopted a positive attitude when we talked to them.

Secretary Kissinger: Wouldn't it be better to talk directly with the Egyptians than through us?

Vice Premier Deng: We've kept very good relations with the Egyptians, so that would be easy.

Secretary Kissinger: That is very useful! Very good!

[There is more discussion of military aid to Pakistan; Congressional opposition has led Kissinger to encourage the Shah to help Karachi. After Deng asks why the Shah has given more aid to India than to Pakistan, Kissinger replies it was "inconceivable" but he will investigate.]

Secretary Kissinger: In all my discussions with the Shah he has always considered India a major threat to his security.
Vice Premier Deng: The reality probably is so.
Secretary Kissinger: Yes. But now there is so much money in the Moslem countries we will see what we can do to get Pakistan military aid.

[Deng wants the United States to do more to help Pakistan; Kissinger understands Pakistani anxieties but notes the "many legal restrictions." There follows some discussion of Indian–Pakistani–Bangladeshi talks and the resolution of the problem of Pakistani prisoners. On Soviet–Indian relations, Kissinger observes that the Indians are "trying to loosen" their Soviet connection and "trying hard to get closer to us."]

Vice Premier Deng: How was your trip to Moscow?
Secretary Kissinger: That was the next question I wanted to discuss. You know that the President will be going to Moscow in June. We discussed arrangements for the visit and the agreements we might reach during it. The trip followed the pattern I have described to you. That is, there was a very good first day and the last half day was very good. But, the day and a half in the middle was not so good at all. It is very curious. I have been to the Soviet Union six times. I have always had the experience of being yelled at, but I have never made any concessions after having been yelled at; so I conclude that Mr. Brezhnev does it for the Politburo and not for any concrete purpose.

[Kissinger reviews the plans for the Nixon–Brezhnev summit, noting that there will be no major agreements but minor ones on heart disease, space flight, and exchange of long-term economic information. On the threshold test ban, the proposed 100 kiloton limit will have no impact on the U.S. nuclear program because "we hadn't planned to test anything above that limit." He also points out that the United States has rejected Soviet proposals for an appeal to other testing countries.]

Secretary Kissinger: Whatever we do with them will be bilateral, and there will be no appeal to the Peoples Republic of China.
Vice Foreign Minister Qiao: (In English) You have done it right.

[On the SALT talks, Kissinger anticipates no agreement because of the wide differences in the U.S. and Soviet positions. While he does not specifically mention the dispute over MIRV limits, Kissinger noted that "in effect, what the Soviet Union has proposed to us

is that they give us a limit but not have one immediately for themselves. The limit they have picked for us is what we already have in our arsenal." He also characterizes as "nonsense" press reports about Soviet strategic superiority. Not only does Washington have a lead of almost six to one in nuclear warheads, but its missiles are more accurate.]

Secretary Kissinger: . . . But you read so much nonsense in the American press. Even I sometimes get scared when I read these reports! So far the Soviet Union does not have any multiple warheads on its missiles. They are testing them, but they do not have them. I will give you some figures sometime on this in a smaller group. I can't have Hummel find it out.

Vice Premier Deng: I also feel in this respect it is hardly possible that you could reach agreement.

Secretary Kissinger: I may be wrong, but I see no sign that an agreement will be concluded. We may be able to achieve an optical agreement.[27] The issue of inspection is very hard. We have made an interim agreement. Frankly, the number of launchers is not so very important. Each launcher has many weapons on it. For example, each missile on our submarines has 10 warheads that can be independently targeted with very great accuracy. So you can't make judgments on the basis of the numbers alone any more. Therefore, an agreement is quite difficult. The Soviets have still not started to test multiple warheads on their submarine-launched missiles. On land, they are testing three types. We think that by year-end they may complete the testing of one of these. But, then they must produce it. They have not done so yet.

Vice Premier Deng: As far as we are concerned in our relations with the Soviet Union, that is, on the eastern part of our border, there has been no change. It is still the same. There seems to be no change in deployments.

Secretary Kissinger: I think there has been a slight change, but I am not sure. I thought they had added three divisions recently, but I will check.

Maj. Gen. Scowcroft: Yes. That's right.

Secretary Kissinger: Three divisions are not significant.

Vice Premier Deng: Basically, they have not changed.

Secretary Kissinger: That is our impression as well.

Vice Premier Deng: There are one million Soviet troops deployed on our very, very long border, and they are scattered all over the place. They use this simply to scare people with weak nerves! I believe that, when you discussed this with Chairman Mao, he said even one million was not enough for defensive purposes and for an offensive purpose they must increase them by another million.

Secretary Kissinger: It depends on what they want. If they want to take all of China, that is right. It depends on what their objective is.

Vice Premier Deng: If they occupy some places on the border, what is the significance of that? They would simply get bogged down.

Secretary Kissinger: I have no estimate that they have any such intent, but it could be that, at some point, they would try to destroy your nuclear capacity. I'm not saying that they definitely plan it, but I say that that would be conceivable.

Vice Premier Deng: Chairman Mao has said that our nuclear power is only that much (holding up narrow gap between thumb and forefinger). But, we thank you very much for telling us all this.

[During a brief discussion of bilateral relations, Deng says there are no "significant" issues; both he and Kissinger agree that the temporary return of David Bruce to Washington and Huang Zhen to Beijing will be "normal." Kissinger says he has wanted Bruce's advice on European issues.]

Vice Foreign Minister Qiao: I said to Ambassador Bruce once, wondering about his involvement with Europe—he said—I liked his answer—that just because he knew the grandfathers of the European leaders, this was no reason to put him in charge of European affairs. But I am sure this was not a criticism of you.

Secretary Kissinger: Ambassador Bruce is a good friend of mine.

Vice Foreign Minister Qiao: I asked Ambassador Bruce if this was true and he said yes.

Vice Premier Deng: Anyway, we are going along the track of the Shanghai communiqué.

Secretary Kissinger: So are we.

Vice Premier Deng: Do you think of any issue on bilateral affairs which we should discuss?

Secretary Kissinger: (To Hummel) Is there anything else? (To Deng) On Korea, we are now talking with the South Koreans about the removal of the UN Command. We think you and we should stay related to the armistice in order to influence our friends in this situation.[28] (Note: The Chinese interpreter rendered the sentence simply as "we should influence our friends in this situation." She did not mention the armistice agreement in this context.) We are also prepared in principle to make a statement on the withdrawal of our forces along the lines of the Shanghai communiqué statement. But, we cannot withdraw immediately. After we have worked out the details with South Korea, we will let you know informally. We appreciate your acts with respect to the U.N. Command last year very, very much, and particularly appreciate the meticulous way in which you carried out our understanding.[29] Our Ambassador to the UN is a little excitable—Scali—but Ambassador Huang will understand. He had several heart attacks along the way. He has very great respect for Ambassador Huang.

I want you to know I have been thinking about the phrase in the last communiqué which we issued in Beijing. We can discuss the meaning of this through Ambassador Huang Zhen, or later in the year, if I take my annual trip to Beijing.

Vice Premier Deng: (The Vice Premier indicated inconclusively that this topic could be discussed with Ambassador Huang Zhen.) What is to be done on the Taiwan question?

Secretary Kissinger: We are continuing to reduce our presence there as I told you. We are thinking of methods of how we can give effect to the principle of one China as expressed in the last communiqué. We have not worked out all our thinking yet, but we are willing to listen to any ideas you have. You drafted the phrase.

Vice Foreign Minister Qiao: I think on this question, I understand the essence of the question. I participated in the drafting of the communiqué and in the drafting of this language. The essential meaning is as Chairman Mao told you. The normalization of our relations can only be on the basis of the Japanese pattern. No other pattern is possible. So, I might also mention that, with regard to the present relations between our two countries, my view is that our relationship should go forward. It should not go backward. I talked frankly on this with Ambassador Bruce. We had a friendly talk on this.

Secretary Kissinger: I am aware of what you said to him. We keep this very much in mind.

Vice Premier Deng: With regard to this question, there are two points. The first point is that we hope we can solve this question relatively quickly. (Note: Chinese interpreter rendered this in English as "as quickly as possible.") But, the second point is that we are not in a hurry on this question. These points have also been mentioned to you by Chairman Mao.

I suppose we have discussed everything that we have to discuss tonight. We have taken up a great deal of your time. You must be tired. Tomorrow, you must speak at the UN.

Secretary Kissinger: I must make sure to say nothing at all. I think I am on the verge of achieving success in this with the dedicated assistance of my associates. Please give my regards and those of the President to our friends in China and especially give my respects to Chairman Mao and the Prime Minister. (The dinner ended at approximately 11:00 P.M. The Secretary escorted his Chinese guests to the elevator.)

COMMENTARY

Almost immediately after Nixon's resignation, if not earlier, Kissinger began making plans for a trip to China in the fall of 1974. To reassure the Chinese about the continuity of U.S. policy, and also to counterbalance high-level meetings with the Soviets that were already on the agenda, Kissinger hoped to schedule at least two trips—one in September and the other later in the year. More than merely symbolizing the value of the U.S.-PRC relationship, Kissinger hoped that a trip in December or early January would allow for a focus on the normalization issue.[30] As it turned out, he only went once, in late November. But to "try to get some elbow room on Taiwan formulations," he scheduled a special meeting in October with an old friend, Vice Foreign Minister Qiao Guanhua, who was in New York for the U.N. General Assembly.[31]

By this time, there had been important personnel changes in U.S.-PRC relations, aside from Nixon's resignation and Ford's ascendancy. It was no longer a secret that Zhou was ill; he had been hospitalized since June, when Mao had finally given permission for him to receive surgery.[32] On the U.S. side, Ford had nominated George Bush to replace David Bruce as the next chief of the Liaison Office in Beijing. This was to the surprise and disappointment of Bruce, who was growing weary of his assignment but had wanted to set his own date for leaving. It was, however, a consolation prize to Bush for being chosen as vice president. Thus, the meeting with Qiao gave Kissinger an opportunity to reintroduce Bush, in a sometimes condescending fashion, to U.S.-China relations: "You are learning more about international politics this evening than you ever did at the U.N."[33]

Kissinger found during the talk with Qiao that the Chinese might not give him much "elbow room" on the Taiwan problem. He argued strongly that the Japan model for normalization did not necessarily apply to the United States because of its historic connections with Taiwan and U.S. concerns for the credibility of alliance commitments: "It is important that we not be seen as throwing our friends away." Qiao nevertheless cited Mao and insisted that a sharp break in diplomatic relations with Taiwan was the necessary starting point for normalization. Since U.S.-Chinese contacts were "already warm," even without diplomatic ties, "we can either solve this problem, or leave it as it is." Kissinger observed that it might be necessary to postpone normalization because a controversy could only benefit the Soviet Union. It was this exchange that led Kissinger's advisers to predict that when Kissinger visited Beijing in late November a "deadlock" on normalization could ensue. The outlook was not promising.[34]

Although Kissinger was no doubt reassured by Qiao's acknowledgment that Moscow remained China's number-one enemy, some of the discussion—and not only the exchange on normalization—made the advisers feel "slight uneasiness." They recognized that the U.S.-China relationship had a profoundly "unsentimental" basis, but the Chinese were nevertheless acting in ways that could thwart important U.S. interests. Qiao expected U.S. help in counterbalancing Moscow, but he had showed "unhelpfulness" on Cambodia. Moreover, his U.N. speech assailing détente and superpower hegemony, endorsing Third World revolutions, and favoring the oil-producing nations generated concern that Beijing was trying to "organize a third force against us for the longer haul."[35]

Kissinger arrived with his usual phalanx of Secret Service agents at Beijing airport on his way back from the Vladivostok summit, where Brezhnev and Ford met for the first time and reached agreement on the outline of a SALT II agreement.[36] He was in a confident mood because he believed that the strengthened U.S.-Soviet relationship from the success at Vladivostok would "help . . . us enormously" in—that is, give him leverage with—Beijing. When he arrived, however, he found he had very little leverage: He did not get to see Mao, and Deng gave no ground on normalization. On the contrary, Deng's sharp questioning of détente and U.S. policy generally suggested a certain strain in the relationship.[37]

One area where Kissinger found the Chinese particularly cooperative, though, was intelligence sharing. As was customary during these visits, U.S. officials provided intelligence briefings to the Chinese. Thus, Kissinger's military aid Robert McFarlane spent three days with a senior Chinese military officer reviewing hundreds of pages of U.S. intelligence information. Apparently, either during this visit or somewhat later in 1975, the Chinese began to provide something in return: They apparently secretly provided Washington with access to sites in China so that U.S. intelligence agencies could directly monitor the Soviet Union.[38]

Though Kissinger's China experts had advised him that the PRC leadership was "under substantial pressure to consolidate their relationship" with the United States, Deng had no interest in diplomatic give-and-take on normalization; he simply sustained the hard-line. Kissinger was prepared to negotiate on various formulations for guarantees, to no avail; whether Deng wanted to negotiate is not known. The China experts later concluded that he was stalling, perhaps to avoid a debate over a controversial issue before the meeting of the National People's Congress early in 1975.[39]

Deng was in fact in no position to engage in serious negotiations over Taiwan. Mao had just nominated him to be first vice premier, making him in effect Zhou's successor. This move infuriated Mao's wife, Jiang Qing, and the Party radicals; with dangerous enemies watching Deng's every step, U.S. observers could tell that he was uneasy. Whenever Deng spoke, he glanced back at his Chinese associates, as if checking that he was saying the right thing. Even if Deng's private thinking on Taiwan was more flexible, avoiding "capitulationism" was high on his agenda.[40]

Kissinger and Deng began their discussions in the mid-morning of 26 November.[41] After some small talk and some speculation on the successor to Japanese Prime Minister Kakuei Tanaka, who had just resigned, Kissinger indicated that he would like to discuss "the whole question of normalization."[42] Regarding specific bilateral issues such as the blocked assets/foreign claims settlement, Kissinger observed that he was "indifferent" about the details and that they were important only for symbolizing "our overall relationship." In any event, Washington was not going to push for a settlement: "When you want to settle them . . . , you let us know and we will find a way." Although Deng and Kissinger agreed to discuss sensitive issues such as normalization in a smaller group setting, as the following excerpt shows, Deng did not hold back and started to "fire cannon" because of mistakes on the U.S. side concerning Taiwan:

Vice Premier Deng: . . . Outside there are many opinions in the world and a lot of talk saying that our relations have chilled and our speed has slowed down. But in the essence I believe that both sides hold that the progress of our relations has been normal.

But we should also say it is not correct to say that there is no ground whatsoever for such talk. For instance, the Doctor mentioned yesterday and also in October in his discussions with the Foreign Minister that our cannon are sounding more frequent.

Secretary Kissinger: Yes, and also becoming more accurate.

Vice Premier Deng: And it is only natural that there should be some speculation and talk when you send an Ambassador to Taiwan, and when they increase the number of their consulates in the United States.[43]

Secretary Kissinger: Especially since you will never believe that some of our actions are the result of stupidity and not planning. I never knew about the consulates until it had been done.

Vice Premier Deng: As for our views on the question of normalization, I believe the Doctor and other American friends are familiar with these: that is, the Japan way. And in this aspect, you have expressed the desire that we on our side should put forward specific mode of how we should do it. But actually we have given our opinion long ago: that is, the Japan way. On our side we would also hope that you on your side can move forward a few steps.

Secretary Kissinger: Mr. [Vice] Prime Minister, the point in reflecting about what you said—you have given us a general idea, which is the Japan way. But it is always said the Japanese imitate us. Now you are forcing us to imitate the Japanese. This is a new style. But we can accept that basic principle. But we have a number of special circumstances which the Japanese do not have. And at various stages of our relationship we have found means, which were consistent with your principles, which also took into account our necessities. It is perhaps not proper to ask you to make a specific proposal on an issue that is of such profound principle to you.

I remember when we drafted our first communique, on my very first visit, when I did not have the pleasure of knowing the Foreign Minister, I was still being treated gently by the Chinese. But Ambassador Huang Hua, with whom I was drafting the communique, before we started working on the text said let us have a frank talk about what we must have, each of us, and when we do we can find the words. And it worked out that way.

And I think that within the framework of the Japanese model we should have a frank talk of some of our necessities consistent with your principles, and then see whether we can find some way to reach our goal. After this then we can put forward a specific proposal.

Vice Premier Deng: We perhaps can go into more detail in the smaller groups.

Secretary Kissinger: I agree.

Vice Premier Deng: But I must first fire a cannon.

Secretary Kissinger: At me?

Vice Premier Deng: Well, empty or full, as you like. That is, on this issue, as we see it, you owe us a debt. We don't have to discuss it now.

Deng did not explain what the debt was, but the implication was that Washington owed Beijing for its patience on the Taiwan issue and the pace of normalization. Whatever Deng's precise meaning, he went on to reiterate what he, Mao, and Zhou had said in the past: they would welcome an early settlement of the Taiwan issue, but "they are not so much in a hurry." In almost the same breath, Deng also quoted Mao as having said that "we pay special attention to international issues," suggesting that broader world context — for example, the challenge of Soviet policy — made it necessary for the Chinese to wait for full normalization.

Deng and Kissinger then settled arrangements for some of their advisers to meet separately for talks on technical bilateral issues and agreed to begin discussions on international issues in a smaller group.

THE WHITE HOUSE
SECRET/NODIS/XGDIS
MEMORANDUM OF CONVERSATION
PARTICIPANTS: Deng Xiaoping, Vice Premier of the State Council of
the People's Republic of China; Qiao Guanhua, Minister of Foreign
Affairs; Amb. Huang Zhen, Chief of PRC Liaison Office,
Washington; Wang Hairong, Vice Minister of Foreign Affairs; Lin
Ping, Director, Department of American and Oceanic Affairs; Tang
Wensheng, Deputy Director, Department of American and Oceanic
Affairs; Zhang Hanzhi, Deputy Director, Department of American
and Oceanic Affairs; Qian Dayong, Counselor, PRCLO,
Washington; Zhu; Dr. Henry A. Kissinger, Secretary of State and
Assistant to the President for National Security Affairs; Amb.
George Bush, Chief, U. S. Liaison Office; Donald Rumsfeld,
Assistant to the President; Winston Lord, Director, Policy Planning
Staff; Philip Habib, Assistant Secretary of State for East Asian and
Pacific Affairs; Richard Solomon, National Security Council Senior
Staff; Peter W. Rodman, National Security Council Staff; Karlene
Knieps, Department of State (notetaker)
DATE AND TIME: 11:15 a.m.–12:20 p.m. Tuesday, November 26, 1974
PLACE: Great Hall of the People, Beijing[B]

Deng: So how should we commence? I suggest we listen to the Doctor first, because you have traveled to so many lands.
Kissinger: Perhaps we should have a general review of events since we last met. I'm deciding whether to read the black (briefing) book, which has 400 pages, or the green book, which has 200. (laughter)

[B] Source: *PPS*, box 370, Secretary Kissinger's Talks in China, 25–29 Nov. 1974.

Deng: It is up to you.

Kissinger: Let me review the international situation as we see it, as it has developed during the year.

I agree with the analysis of Chairman Mao that we should make progress in normalization, but also that there is an international environment which brought us together in the first place and which determines in many respects our relationship.

In this respect, the factor in which we both have an interest, and which has produced some common fronts, is your ally and northern neighbor.[44] In this respect, our assessment has not changed since last year. We believe Soviet purposes are still essentially hegemonial. We don't think it is particularly fruitful to debate in which direction the primary thrust is going, because in which ever direction it goes, the ultimate consequence will be the same. And therefore, we believe the principal necessity is to keep in mind the overall objectives and the means to prevent them from being realized,

In this respect, we have to keep in mind—and I'm being very frank with you—a very complicated domestic situation. For the United States to take strong actions in crises, it is necessary to do so from a position of having demonstrated to our people that we have exhausted every avenue for peace. I think Chairman Mao, last year, said the United States plays complicated games, and China too plays complicated games, but more energetically. (laughter)

Deng: I think he had discussed actually the difference between shadowboxing and boxing in the Shao lin style, which is more energetic.

Kissinger: Yes, shadow-boxing. But it was a profound observation. We have to do a lot of shadow-boxing to get into a position to take action when we are in a crisis. I say this only so you will distinguish between appearances and reality. We will not permit a strategic gain for Soviet power. We will attempt to reduce Soviet power where we can. We do not, however . . . At the same time we go through many stages which create either diplomatic obstacles to the extension of Soviet power or which [sic] psychological and political obstacles against Soviet military action. We do not intend to create a condominium with the Soviet Union, because such a policy—by removing all obstacles to Soviet expansion—would eventually, with certainty, turn against us.

So events of this past year fitted this pattern. We have made a number of agreements with the Soviet Union on limiting arms competition to some extent, and certain technical cooperation on specific subjects. But this has enabled us, at the same time, to prevent any further extension of Soviet power.

If we were in a position of open confrontation with the Soviet Union it would create the domestic situation I have described. And in addition, in each European country, the European left would be able to polarize the political spectrum by labeling us as the source of world tensions. Our present policy forces the Communist parties of Italy and France to support NATO, and (this is) despite their domestic battle on purely domestic issues.

[Noting that the Vladivostok SALT agreement shows that Moscow "is not as strong as it sometimes pretends," and the U.S.-European relations continued to improve, Kissinger turns to the Middle East situation. He describes how he has tailored his step-by-step approach so as not to create a strong domestic reaction, and explains that "[o]ur policy is to produce progress that returns Arab territory to Arab control, but gradually at a pace that doesn't produce paralysis of our foreign policy because of the domestic reaction. And we will not do it under Soviet pressure at all."]

Deng: Have you decided with the Soviet Union when the Geneva Conference will be convened?

Kissinger: No.

Deng: I think the Soviet Union thinks it should be quicker and they will be attending.

Kissinger: Yes, we spent 4 months preparing for it, and then it met one day, after which we closed it. (laughter) The Soviet Union always urges us to hold it. Eventually, it will have to take place. I don't think it can possibly be before March.

As long as the Arabs think they are making progress outside the Conference, they will be in no hurry to get there. No one wants it except the Soviet Union. They have an Ambassador in Geneva, Vinogradov, who spends all his time waiting for a conference that doesn't take place. We occasionally send Ambassador Bunker once every two months to keep him company there doing nothing. But we have not agreed on a resumption date. The earliest I could foresee would be March—unless there is a total breakdown in the secret discussions now going on between Egypt and Israel and the other Arab countries and Israel through us. And I don't foresee such a breakdown.

On Iran, as I have said, things have developed in the direction of my discussions with Chairman Mao and the Prime Minister last year. (Refreshments are brought in.)

I was getting worried. No food was coming in for 20 minutes. (laughter) I didn't see how I was going to live through it. (laughter) (to Rumsfeld) See, I have gained 5 pounds here on every visit.

We can discuss that in great detail too. I mean about Iran, not about food. (laughter)

[Kissinger discusses his recent visit to India, where he emphasized the importance of restraint, then notes plans to resume cash arms sales to Pakistan. "I will probably have to shoot half of Mr. Lord's staff before we can execute this."]

Kissinger: . . . We are prepared in principle to discuss these issues with you, and to explain our views to you. They are areas in which we know you are sensitive to some statements that have been made by us. We are not indifferent to cannons that are fired at us with respect to these issues. And I think we should attempt to avoid unnecessary confrontations, because we have to solve the energy problem, not for ourselves, but because if it continues in its present form it will lead to the political disintegration of Western Europe. We can solve it for ourselves easily—relatively easily. And this cannot be a matter of indifference to the People's Republic. It has for us nothing to do with the Third World against the industrialized world, and we don't think it should be approached from a strictly theoretical point of view. But while I am here I am prepared to discuss it in greater detail.

So this is the general situation. I have spoken for 50 minutes, which is what doctors do. I would propose, as we continue our discussions—in addition to normalization, we could pick an area for discussion in greater detail—the Soviet Union, the Middle East.

There is another issue which I leave it up to the Chinese side whether it wishes to discuss, and that is the problem of Cambodia. We don't insist on discussing it. I have the impression that whenever it is raised it creates a degree of irritation on the Chinese side, which is uncharacteristic—and in addition to being uncharacteristic is out of proportion to the intrinsic importance of the subject being raised. From this I conclude the Chinese side considers us more than usually stupid on the issue of Cambodia. (Laughter) and that you must have the impression we are missing some point that should be perfectly obvious. So I thought, if you want to, we could give you our analysis.

Because in one respect we are really not in disagreement. We are not opposed to Sihanouk. We have no interest in Sihanouk returning to Cambodia as a figurehead for Hanoi. But we would have no objection to him if he could head a truly independent government. And if you want to, we could have an exchange of views on this subject—if you promise me not to get irritated.

Qiao: I don't think we have ever become irritated.

Kissinger: No, not personally. No, we understand your interest in Sihanouk and we are prepared to discuss it.

So this is the international scene as we see it, quickly. And then in our subsequent discussions we will go into more detail on each area.
(They confer.)

Deng: On this issue you would know we support Samdech Norodom Sihanouk and the resistance forces within the country and we support their position. And to put it frankly, we think if the United States is to place its hopes on Lon Nol or on any force you think would replace Lon Nol, that is not reliable.

Kissinger: We think it is possible to produce a negotiation, at the end of which Sihanouk could quite possibly emerge as the controlling factor. We think it is [not] in his own interest to be totally dependent on one force. He should have many forces, factors to play with.

Deng: That is your idea.

Kissinger: It is our idea that it is possible to achieve a solution in Cambodia in which Sihanouk could emerge as the dominant force, yes.

Deng: As you wanted to discuss this specifically, we can.

Kissinger: All right.

Deng: But I think that is all for this morning.

Kissinger: That is probably right.

Deng: How should we proceed this afternoon?

Kissinger: It is up to you. We have not discussed normalization and we are prepared.

[They agree to meet at 3:30 PM at the Guest House to discuss bilateral relations and normalizaion. Kissinger says he will add Gleysteen and drop someone else in order to keep the number of participants the same.]

Deng: An agreement on quantity and not quality! (laughter)

THE WHITE HOUSE
WASHINGTON
TOP SECRET/SENSITIVE
MEMORANDUM OF CONVERSATION
PARTICIPANTS: Deng Xiaoping, Vice Premier of the State Council, People's Republic of China — Henry A. Kissinger, Secretary of State and Assistant to the President for National Security Affairs . . . [45]

DATE AND TIME: Tuesday, November 26, 1974 3:45-5:00 P.M.
PLACE: Great Hall of the People, Beijing, People's Republic of China
   Peking, People's Republic of China
SUBJECT: Normalization[C]

Secretary Kissinger: They outnumber us today.
Vice Premier Deng: Some more on our side are coming. I don't think you will ever outnumber us because we have 800 million.

[Kissinger thanks Deng for the tours of the Forbidden City given to his family. When Kissinger notes that Nancy Kissinger, his wife, is going to receive an acupuncture demonstration, Deng discusses the history of the technique.]

Secretary Kissinger: Who would have thought if you stick a needle into somebody it would help him? No other civilization thought about that.
Vice Premier Deng: Shall we come back to our subject? We will listen to the Doctor. All right?
Secretary Kissinger: Let me discuss the subject of normalization. I understand that Mr. [Philip] Habib has already had a talk on the bilateral relations.

I am confident that our side can keep multiplying the complexities as long as your side can. It is something we are very good at.

[Kissinger reviews the 1971-72 commitments to the PRC and notes that Washington has been observing them, for example, by undertaking substantial force reductions in Taiwan.]

Now the problem is how we can complete the process. I would like to divide it into a number of parts:—There is the problem of the diplomatic status of Taiwan, and of course of the diplomatic relations between us. —There is the problem of our military forces on Taiwan.
—And there is the problem of our defense commitment to Taiwan.

Our problem is different from the situation of Japan, or for that matter from the situation of any other country with which you have normalized relations, in two respects:

First, there is a formal defense relationship. Secondly, there is a rather substantial group in the United States that historically has been pro-Taiwan.

Together with your cooperation we have been able to neutralize the pro-Taiwan element in the United States by moving step-by-step in a very careful

---
[C] Source: *PPS*, box 370, Secretary Kissinger's Talks in China, 25-29 Nov. 1974.

manner. But what we have to keep in mind for our common interest is to prevent Sino-American relations from becoming an extremely contentious issue in the United States.

It is not in your interest, or in that of the United States, to have emerge a Senator or Senatorial group which does to Sino-American relations what Senator Jackson has attempted to do to United States-Soviet relations.

I am speaking very frankly to you so that we understand each other exactly. After I have put my considerations before you, you will of course give me yours. Then we will see if we can solve the problem. I am here to remove obstacles, not to hide behind them.

We believe, as I have said, that while cannons have been fired—mostly in one direction—we have also had common fronts.

As the Premier said yesterday, they were mostly produced by the "polar bear."

We do not want to jeopardize that possibility (of developing common fronts with the PRC) given the dangers that may be ahead, and keeping in mind what Chairman Mao said to me last year of the two strands—normalization, and the international environment.

Now having said this, let me go back to the specific issues between us.

First, on the issue of the diplomatic status: We are prepared to solve this on substantially the Japan model; and with the one variation that it would be easiest for us if we could maintain a liaison office in Taiwan and an embassy in Peking. Except for that we would follow the Japan model.

With respect to the presence of (U.S.) troops on Taiwan, we are prepared to remove all our troops from Taiwan. We would like to agree with you on a schedule, a time-frame within which this will be accomplished—by which we would reduce the forces by half by the summer of 1976, and the remainder to be removed by the end of 1977.

Incidentally, what I am discussing is not something to which we want to agree—we can agree to it hear, but it should not be announced until the end of 1975, the agreement we make. But we want to come to an understanding about it now, that this is what would happen.

Now that leaves the last problem, which is our defense relationship to Taiwan. And this is a problem to which, in all frankness, we have not come up with a good answer.

Our problem is this: on the face of it, it is of course absurd to say one has a defense arrangement with a part of a country one recognizes, that is, which belongs to that country.

Secondly, we obviously have no interest in maintaining a strategic base on

Taiwan after we have established diplomatic relations with Beijing and recognized Beijing as the legal government of all China.

But as I told the Foreign Minister in New York, we need a formula that enables us to say that at least for some period of time there are assurances of peaceful reintegration with (*sic*) can be reviewed after some interval in order to avoid the difficulties which I have described.

If we can, this would mean that we would have accepted Beijing as the (legal) government (of China). We would have withdrawn our recognition from Taiwan, we would have broken diplomatic relations with Taiwan. We would have withdrawn our troops from Taiwan. All that would remain is that we would have some relation to peaceful reintegration.

Speaking here frankly and realistically, the political and psychological effect of breaking relations is that our defense relationship will be eroded by the act of recognition. But we need a transition period for our public opinion in which this process can be accomplished without an excessive domestic strain.

These are our basic considerations. If we agree on the principles, we can then see what formula can then be worked out.

Vice Premier Deng: Is that all?

Secretary Kissinger: This is the essence, yes.

Let me emphasize one point. To us the question of the defense commitment is primarily a question of the way it can be presented politically. It is not a question of maintaining it for an indefinite period of time.

Vice Premier Deng: Well, actually this law was formulated by yourselves. Is that so?

Secretary Kissinger: Which law?

Vice Premier Deng: You are the ones who make the law. That is, the law of that defense commitment you have with Taiwan. That was fixed by yourselves.

Secretary Kissinger: Of course. That is absolutely true.

Vice Premier Deng: Well, since you can formulate a law, naturally you can also do away with it.

Secretary Kissinger: That is also true. Our point is not that it could not be done. Our point is that for reasons I have explained to you, it is not expedient to do—well, the act of recognition in itself will change the nature of that arrangement because you cannot have a defense treaty with part of a country.

Vice Premier Deng: I have noticed the consideration which the Doctor has just mentioned. And I understand that all of these imaginations the Doctor has discussed with the Foreign Minister while he was in New York in October.

Secretary Kissinger: That is correct.

Vice Premier Deng: And I believe in principle the Foreign Minister gave you the answers on our side concerning the principal matters. In essence your imaginations—your considerations—cannot be considered as being in accord with the Japan model.

And we feel that in essence it is still a variation of one China and one Taiwan.

Secretary Kissinger: Why is that?

Vice Premier Deng: Well, this is primarily that you just reverse the position, change the position of the liaison office. The present situation is that we have established a liaison office in Beijing—we have established our liaison office in Washington and you have established one in Beijing. And you keep an embassy in Taiwan. This in itself indicates there has not been the necessary conditions for the normalization of relations.

In other words, if you change this order, that is, to have an embassy in Beijing and a liaison office in Taiwan, it is not the way to correct the problem.

People will come to the conclusion that it is actually a variation of one China and one Taiwan. Therefore, we find it difficult to accept this formula.

And just now you touched upon the question of the defense treaty. That is, the defense treaty which you have with Chiang Kai-shek on Taiwan. Of course, if we are to achieve the normalization of relations between our two countries and abide by the course set in the Shanghai Communique, then the treaty you have with Taiwan must be done away with.

The reasons actually have been given by the Doctor yourself just now.

Secretary Kissinger: The defense treaty can have no international status after the normalization of relations.

Vice Premier Deng: But still it has a substantial meaning.

So it appears that time is not ripe yet to solve this question, because according to your formula, it would not be possible for us to accept this method of normalization. It still looks as if you need Taiwan.

Secretary Kissinger: No, we do not need Taiwan. That is not the issue. I think that it is important to understand. That would be a mistake in understanding the problem.

What we would like to achieve is the disassociation from Taiwan in steps, this process would be rapidly accelerated by the ideas which we have advanced.

Vice Premier Deng: And the other question is the way (method) to solve the Taiwan problem. As for solving the Taiwan question, suppose you have broken diplomatic relations with Taiwan. Then the Taiwan question should be left with us Chinese to solve among ourselves.

As to what means we will (use to) solve the Taiwan question, I believe Chairman Zedong made it very clear in his talk.

Secretary Kissinger: Chairman Mao, if I understood him correctly, made two statements: One was that he believed that the question would ultimately have to be solved by force. But he also stated that China could wait for one hundred years to bring this about, if I understood him correctly.

Vice Premier Deng: That was true. He did say that.

Of course, the number of "one hundred years" is a symbolic one.

Secretary Kissinger: Of course, I understood this. I was going to say that in one hundred years I will not be Secretary of State.

I have to say this occasionally to give some hope to my associates. I understood it was symbolic. I understand also that after normalization that any attributes of sovereignty in the relationship between Taiwan and the U.S. have to be eliminated.

Vice Premier Deng: Chairman Mao Zedong made it very clear that the solving of the Taiwan problem is an internal affair of China, and should be left to the Chinese to solve.

[Discussion along these lines continues inconclusively; Kissinger suggests that the Chinese also owe the Americans a debt for "starting the process" in 1971 that led to China's admission into the United Nations. Deng reminds Kissinger of Mao's statements that "we do not believe in peaceful transition." Then the Chairman said we can do without Taiwan—we can wait for one hundred years to solve the problem. And the Chairman also said, 'As for the relation between you and us, I do not think that will take one hundred years to solve.' I think from this conversation the meaning is clear."]

Secretary Kissinger: I agree. This is exactly my recollection of the conversation. From this I also made certain deductions, produced by my brain which is somewhat slower than that of the Chinese. I have never had a Chinese contradict me on my statement. (laughter)

I remember once Prime Minister Zhou Enlai made the comment that I was intelligent, and I said by Chinese standards you mean I am of medium intelligence. He did not contradict me either. (laughter)[46]

COMMENTARY

Despite disagreements over the normalization process, the next day started on an upbeat note, with Deng and Kissinger agreeing that President Ford would travel to China sometime in 1975: a terse communiqué issued at the end of Kissinger's stay would announce Ford's visit.[47]

During a short, insubstantive meeting with Zhou at the hospital, however, Kissinger learned that a meeting with Mao would not be "convenient."[48] Mao was not in Beijing—he was going blind and, as his doctors learned, suffering from the effects of Lou Gehrig's disease (amyotrophic lateral sclerosis). No one dared tell him that his illness was fatal. He had been away from Beijing for months trying to treat his ailments, though he refused professional medical care, even for his cataracts. Nevertheless, he had in fact received some foreign visitors, including Imelda Marcos and Denmark's Prime Minister Paul Hartling.[49] Kissinger's "nonvisit" with Mao was very likely intended as a slap in the face and was reported as such in the international press.[50]

The transcripts of Deng's and Kissinger's second round of meetings show the usual wide-ranging discussion, from nuclear weapons, detente, and the Middle East, to Sino–Soviet relations, Eurocommunism, Cambodia, and the energy crisis. The talks remained difficult, however; Deng's digs at U.S. negotiations with the Polar Bear suggested that he retained the terrier instincts for which Mao valued him as a combatant against Soviet "revisionism."[51] Kissinger held his own, though. To show confidence in U.S. power, he expounded on U.S. strategic superiority; and he dodged a major debate over whom the Soviets threatened the most, China or the West, no doubt to avoid revealing any concern about a possible loss of leverage. Perhaps to keep the Chinese on edge, he briefed Deng on Brezhnev's latest anti-Chinese overtures. Deng took the bait; his preoccupation with the Soviets very likely reassured Kissinger that his triangular diplomacy retained its basic validity.

TOP SECRET/NODIS/XGDS
MEMORANDUM OF CONVERSATION
PARTICIPANTS: Deng Xiaoping, Vice Premier of the State Council, People's Republic of China; Qiao Guanhua, Minister of Foreign Affairs; Amb. Huang Zhen, Chief of the PRC Liaison Office, Washington, D.C.; Wang Hairong, Vice Minister of Foreign Affairs Tang Wensheng, Deputy Director, Department of American and

Oceanic Affairs; Lian Zheng bao, (Notetaker); Dr. Henry A.
Kissinger, Secretary of State and Assistant to the President for
National Security Affairs; Amb. George Bush, Chief of the U. S.
Liaison Office, Peking; Winston Lord, Director, Policy Planning
Staff; Bonnie Andrews, Secretary's Office (Notetaker)
DATE AND TIME: Wednesday, November 27, 1974 9:45-11:32 A.M.
PLACE: Guest House #18 Beijing
SUBJECT: President's Visit; Nuclear War; SALT; Yugoslavia[D]

*[After Kissinger observes that "most Americans" did not understand Qiao's U.N. at-
tacks on the superpowers, he raises questions about a possible Schlesinger visit to
China. The Soviets had repeatedly invited U.S. Secretaries of Defense for visits, but
Washington had always turned them down. "So if we begin using our Secretary of
Defense for diplomatic travels, he will begin going to places that I don't believe are
desirable."[52] While not ruling out Schlesinger's visit, Kissinger suggests instead either
a visit by other cabinet members or a presidential visit. Deng welcomes the possibility
of a Ford visit, and they agree it should take place during 1975. An announcement of
Ford's visit will be included in the communiqué.]*

Kissinger: . . . Now, I wanted to tell you one other thing that I have already mentioned to your Ambassador for your information. When I was in
Moscow in October, Brezhnev made a proposal for a new treaty to us and
repeated it in more detail to President Ford in Vladivostok. And it is a rather
novel and ingenious proposition. The proposal is as follows: the U.S. and
Soviet Union should make a treaty with each other in which they will defend
each other against any attack by any other country or they will defend each
other's allies against nuclear attack from any other country.[53]
(Meeting temporarily interrupted by Chinese girl opening outer door.)
Kissinger: I have people in the other room but they will join us for the later
discussion
Translator: They must be able to hear me because of my loud voice.
Kissinger: We asked for a practical explanation of how this would operate.
 The practical explanation is that in any use of nuclear weapons, regardless
of who initiates it, in a war between the Soviet Union and another country or
between the U.S. and another country, or between an ally of each, then the
U.S. and Soviet Union would have to help each other, and if physical help is
not possible, then they would have to observe benevolent neutrality. We
think it has two, well three, general purposes. The first is to undermine

[D] Source: *PPS*, box 370, Secretary Kissinger's Talks in China, 25-29 Nov. 1974.

NATO, because it would specifically oblige us to cooperate with the Soviet Union against our allies if nuclear weapons were involved.

Secondly, it would force those Arabs who are afraid of nuclear weapons being used by Israel into an alliance relationship with the Soviet Union.

And third, I think, China. Those seemed to us the three purposes, together with the general impression of condominium.

We did not accept a serious discussion of this proposal. Nor will we.

Qiao: Actually your treaty on preventing nuclear war could be interpreted in this way also.

Kissinger: No, absolutely not.

[Kissinger goes on to explain the difference between the latest Soviet proposal, "aimed at a kind of nuclear condominium" and the 1973 Prevention of Nuclear War Agreement.]

Deng: Their goals and purposes have been constant all along.

Kissinger: And their diplomacy clumsy and obvious.

Deng: But their purpose is also very clear. And their goals are clear. And we think their purposes can only be these: First of all, to utilize the signing of such an agreement with you to develop their own nuclear weapons to standards either equivalent to yours or surpassing yours. And the reason they are expressing such interest in signing such an agreement naturally shows that they have tasted a sweet taste out of such agreements. If I recall things correctly, you signed your first treaty pertaining to nuclear matters in July 1963. At that time I was in Moscow carrying on negotiations between our two parties, and on the very day I was leaving you signed that treaty.

Kissinger: We were not informed about all your movements at the time. (laughter)

Deng: And it must be said that at that time the level of Soviet weapons were lagging a considerable distance behind yours. But in the eleven years since, I must say they have been able to reach a level about the same as yours.

Kissinger: That is not exactly correct, and I will explain that to you.

It is inevitable that a large industrial power increase the numbers of its nuclear weapons. And it is the characteristic of nuclear weapons because of their destructiveness that beyond a certain point superiority is not as effective as in conventional weapons.

But in numbers, diversity, accuracy and flexibility, our nuclear weapons will be considerably superior to the Soviet Union for the whole period of the arrangement which we signed in Vladivostok. And I will explain that to you if you want, or some other time while I am here. That is true both in numbers and characteristics.

Qiao: I would like to add a few words if possible. We thank the Doctor for telling us of Soviet intentions, but as we have said many times, we do not attach such great importance to such treaties. We still have a treaty with the Soviet Union that has not been outdated yet and now they have now [*sic*] proposed to us a new treaty for mutual non-aggression. Of course, how we will deal with this new treaty will have to be seen. But on the whole, we do not attach such great importance to such matters. And the decisive fact is not any treaty but a policy, the principles and the lines.

Deng: But I haven't finished now. I have only mentioned the first goal of the Soviet Union. The second is, as Dr. Kissinger mentioned, to try to divide the U.S. from its allies, which you have discovered or perceived. But it seems that although you have revealed this point, they will never give up this goal, whether in the past, present or future. And the third purpose will be to maintain the monopolistic status of your two countries in the field of nuclear weapons.

And they will try to use this point not only to compare with your country but also intimidate countries with only a few nuclear weapons and thus reach their aim of hegemony.

So our overall view of such treaties is that we attach importance to their political significance, and as always our attitude toward such matters is that we believe they are not of much consequence, and we are not bound by any such treaty or agreement. And as the Doctor has repeated many times, your aim is not to bind others either.

Kissinger: In every meeting with the Soviet Union in discussing proposals directed against China such as nuclear testing and nuclear proliferation, we have always avoided formulations whose purpose is directed against third countries.

Deng: But even if they were so, even if they succeeded, what role would those treaties play? They would not be able to play much of a role. And if they signed such agreements, they would still be waving their baton, and if they don't sign they would still have nuclear weapons. As for our nuclear weapons, as Chairman Mao says, they are only so much "gesturing with fingers."[54]

Kissinger: We have never discussed nuclear weapons with you from our side.

Deng: That is right.

Kissinger: We inform you of Soviet overtures not because you should pay attention but because if they should ever tell you, you will know what is happening. And also we have an understanding with you not to do anything with the Soviet Union without informing you. And so we inform you of things with them whether you attach significance to them or not. And we are not asking you to do anything about it.

There is one other matter that came up in Vladivostok that I wanted to mention to you. The Soviet proposed to us to have consultations on Japanese–Chinese relations and to prevent them from becoming too close. We have refused this, and we have told the Japanese in a general way about this, and have told the Japanese about our refusal.

Deng: So from this too we can see the aims of the Soviet Union. You know, their Foreign Minister, Mr. Gromyko, has a characteristic of which we were told by Khrushchev in 1957 when Chairman Mao went to Moscow.

Khrushchev introduced Gromyko to us, and he told us that Gromyko had a lot of things in his pocket. And Khrushchev told us that this fellow Gromyko could produce this formula today, and tomorrow, and he has so many things he can produce that that is his major trait — that was Khrushchev's introduction of Gromyko. And it seems that Brezhnev has learned that trait from Gromyko and has a lot of things in his pocket too.

As for our dealings with the Soviet Union, we do not rely on our nuclear weapons. And we don't have very much skill other than digging tunnels and having rifles.

Kissinger: That is entirely up to you; the agreements we sign have nothing to do with China except the one on preventing nuclear war which to us gives us legal possibilities. But the agreement, or the tentative one in Vladivostok, we consider very favorable in the overall strategic balance. It is up to you if you comment or not. It has nothing to do with the People's Republic of China.

Deng: I would like to raise a question. We have heard the Doctor say that the recent meeting and the recent signing of such an agreement was a great breakthrough. Was it really so? To be more specific — how reliable can it be — how reliable are the prospects for ten years of detente and a cease of competition in the military field?

Kissinger: First of all, you have to understand that we have to fight on many fronts. And our domestic strategy is to isolate our left, if that is a proper thing to say in the People's Republic.

Deng: We like those on the right!

Kissinger: The ones on the right have no choice but to be with us anyway. The ones on the right are no problem with us.

Deng: Isn't Mr. Heath of Great Britain a well-known man on the right?

Kissinger: Oh, yes.

Deng: And wasn't Mr. Adenauer of your former father-land a well-known man of the right? And in France, De Gaulle, Pompidou and Giscard, Tanaka, and Ohira are famous men on the right. We like this kind, comparatively speaking.

Kissinger: We send our leftists to Beijing.

Bush: I don't think I understand that.

Kissinger: The Ambassador is a left-wing Republican. No, he is here because he has our total confidence.

But it is important in the U.S. to isolate and paralyze those who would undermine our defense program and who generally conduct what I consider a stupid policy. And we can do this by pursuing policies which adopt their rhetoric.

And to answer your question: I do not believe that this guarantees ten years of detente—not for one minute. But I do believe that if detente breaks down, or when it does, we will be better able to mobilize our public opinion having made every effort to preserve peace rather than being accused of having provoked them.

Deng: On our side we don't believe it is possible to reach detente—still less maintain ten years of detente. And we don't think there is any agreement that can bind the hands of Russia.

Kissinger: No, but there is no way they can violate this agreement without our knowing it. I don't think it was a very intelligent agreement for them. They have two choices: they can either respect the agreement, in which case we preserve a certain strategic advantage, or they can violate the agreement, in which case we have the psychological and political possibility of massive breakout ourselves, which we would not have otherwise for domestic reasons.

Deng: As we see it, it is still necessary to have vigilance.

Kissinger: There is no doubt about that for us.

Deng: That would be good.

Kissinger: I once studied the foreign policy of Metternich, and he said the trick to dealing with Napoleon was to seem to be a fool without being one. There is no question—in terms of our domestic situation, it is, strangely enough easier to get Congress to give funds for limits in agreements than to get funds for the same amounts without an agreement. (To Bush.) Do you think so, George?

Bush: Yes, I do.

Deng: There is something else I would like to ask about your SALT agreement. Does it mean strategic arms? Does it apply only to nuclear arms?

Kissinger: Yes, and only those with an intercontinental range.

Deng: That means that only those strategic weapons are included, not others.

Kissinger: According to the definition of the agreement.

Deng: But outside that agreement, what is meant by strategic weapons? For example, conventional weapons have been considered strategic?

Kissinger: No.

Deng: Then we differ a bit here. Because here is the question of whether a future war would be a nuclear war.

Kissinger: What do you think?

Deng: We don't think so necessarily.

Kissinger: I agree. But I would like to say, as I said to the Chairman and Prime Minister, we would consider any sign of expansion of the Soviet sphere—either to the West or East, whether countries were covered by treaty or not, as a threat to our long-term security. It has nothing to do with our affection for the countries covered—but strategic reality. Secondly, we don't care if that expansion comes with conventional or nuclear weapons.

Deng: You know there is a story, after Khrushchev came to Beijing. He came to Beijing in 1954, and he gave us this reasoning: During that visit, aside from boasting of his corn planting, he also boasted about the uselessness of naval vessels. He said that in the missile era naval vessels were nothing other than moving targets and they would be finished off at once.[55] And the Soviet Union actually ceased to build their Navy for two or three years. But they very quickly rectified that. And since then, while energetically developing their nuclear weapons, they are at the same time continuing to build their conventional weapons and their Navy also.

[The Chinese emphasize the Soviet Union's growing naval presence in the Indian Ocean and elsewhere, but Kissinger dismisses the Soviet navy, noting that during recent Middle East crises, it "maneuvered with great clumsiness" and that Moscow's "panicky behavior" during the crisis confirmed its naval vulnerability.]

Kissinger: Be that as it may, but in conventional land strength, we do not underestimate the Soviet Union. They are very strong in conventional land strength. In naval strength they are absolutely no match for us. We have hysterical admirals who, when they want money, say that no matter what country we are in war against, including Switzerland, that we are going to lose. But in reality, the only way the Soviet Union could hurt our fleet in the Mediterranean is with their land-based aircraft. And if they did that, that would be a general nuclear war. But if it is a naval battle, our carriers can strike theirs with so much greater distance and force, that there is absolutely no possibility for them to survive.

Deng: But from our discussions with some Europeans, they seem much more worried than you—not just on naval forces but on the whole question of conventional forces.

Kissinger: On the question of conventional forces, everyone has reason to worry. On the question of naval forces, I believe we are far superior.

Deng: But the Soviet Union develops itself with greater speed. If the Soviet Union launches a war, it might not be a nuclear war; it might quite possibly be a conventional war. Under this condition, conventional weapons should not be neglected.

Kissinger: I completely agree. That is a problem the western countries do have, not in naval forces but ground conventional forces. But you will notice that we have increased the number of our divisions recently.

But it is a problem. There is no question.

Deng: But your increase is proportionately much smaller than the Soviet Union.

Kissinger: That is true. But I think it would be extremely dangerous for the Soviet Union. First of all, in Europe, the Soviet Union could not achieve a decisive victory without a very large battle and in those circumstances we would use nuclear weapons.

Deng: But under those conditions, where the Soviet Union has the same destructive strength as you, would it be easy for you to make up your minds?

Kissinger: The Soviet Union does not have the same destructive force as we.

Deng: Not even enough strength for a first strike?

Kissinger: No. Let me explain the composition of the forces to you because there is so much nonsense written in the U.S. by people with specific purposes in mind that there is a very misleading impression created.

We have 1,054 land-based missiles, 656 sea-based on submarines, 435 B-52 bombers. 300 F-111 bombers which are never counted for some reason. This is just in the strategic forces. In addition, we have over 500 airplanes in Europe and over 700 airplanes on aircraft carriers.

Starting in 1979 we are going to get at least 240 new missiles on submarines—the so-called Trident submarine.

Deng: Aren't you violating the treaty?

Kissinger: No. I will explain the treaty in a minute. And at least 250 new bombers, the B-1. But the number 240 and 250 are only planning numbers. Once we begin producing, we can produce as many as we want.

Now of those missiles, the only ones that will eventually become vulnerable to attack are the 1,000 land-based ones. This cannot happen before 1982. I'll explain to you why in a minute. And before that can happen we will be producing the Trident missile which will be in serial production by 1979. And we don't have to put it on a submarine; we can put it on land if we want to.

So the Soviet Union would have to be insane to attack 1,000 missiles when we would have 1,500 and more left over even if they destroy all the land-based missiles—which they also couldn't do.

Deng: So for either side to use nuclear weapons against the other, it is a matter for great care by both sides.

Kissinger: That is without question. I was answering the question about the Soviet Union being able to make a first strike. My argument is that that is impossible.

Let's look at the reverse. The U.S. has about 30% in land-based missiles, the rest either at sea or on airplanes. I would also like to tell you, we are planning to put long-range missiles into our airplanes—something the Soviet Union cannot do because they don't have airplanes large enough to do that. The Soviet Union has 85% of its force in land-based missiles. And its sea-based missiles, up to now, are very poor. And it has only 120 airplanes that can reach the U.S., and we don't think they are very well trained. In fact, under the agreement they have to reduce their numbers. They can compose their forces any way they want—but the level we have agreed on is 2,400 for both sides. It is below their level and above ours—if you don't count overseas weapons. So they will have to reduce their forces. We think they will get rid of their airplanes, but we don't know.

Deng: But they will not violate the agreement when they improve qualitatively.

Kissinger: Yes, but neither will we.

Deng: So you still have your race then.

Kissinger: But we have planned our forces for the 1980's and they have planned their forces for the 70's. By the early 1980's, both land-based forces will be vulnerable. And 85% of theirs are land-based while only 35% of ours are land-based. Secondly, they are making all their improvements in the most vulnerable forces, namely in the land-based forces. We are making ours in the sea-based and air-based forces—which are not vulnerable, or much less vulnerable. For example, on their submarines, they have not begun to test a multiple warhead—which means they could not possibly get it before 1980 into production. Which means, in turn, we will be, in accuracy and technical procedures, 10 to 15 years ahead of them.

Deng: We are in favor of your maintaining a superiority against the Soviet Union in such aspects.

Kissinger: And I repeat that if we launched a first strike against them we could use overseas forces which are added to the strategic forces that I gave you.

Deng: I thought what we were exploring today was the position of nuclear and conventional weapons.

Kissinger: I just wanted to answer the Foreign Minister's statement that they could first attack us. But it is true that it is more difficult to use nuclear weapons today than 15 years ago. This is without question true.[56]

Qiao: What I was saying was this: At present if the Soviet Union should launch an attack with conventional weapons on not necessarily a large scale, on a medium scale, for you to use nuclear weapons under those circumstances would be a difficult thing to make up your minds about.

Kissinger: It is more difficult now than 10 to 15 years ago. It depends on where the attack takes place.

Chiao: As we discussed in New York, if there are changes in Yugoslavia—they need not make a direct attack, but if they incite pro-Soviet elements to bring in the Soviet armed forces—what would you do?

Kissinger: Yugoslavia? I went to Yugoslavia after our talk and talked to Marshall Tito and his colleagues about exactly this problem. For one thing, we will begin selling military equipment to Yugoslavia next year. We are now studying what to do in such a case. We will not let it happen unchallenged. It will not be like Czechoslovakia or Hungary. We have not yet decided on the precise measures. But we believe that if the Soviet army is permitted to move outside its sphere, it will create appetites that might not stop. This is why we reacted so violently when they mobilized their airborne divisions during the Middle East crisis.[57] Because it was our judgment that once permitted to operate far from their territory in foreign wars, not in internal quarrels, there would be no end to their appetites.

Deng: In our opinion, not only the Middle East is explosive but also the Balkan Peninsula. And this is an old strategy of the Czar.

[Kissinger then observes that if there is a CSCE conference in 1975, Ford plans to stop in Romania and Yugoslavia to "make clear the American interest in the independence of these two countries. But we have unannounced this, obviously." Deng and Kissinger agree to continue discussions in a larger group setting.

During the next hour, Deng expounds on Sino-Soviet relations, noting that Moscow "continues to use military threat and subversion" against China.[58] When he asks about the CSCE, Kissinger dismisses it: "It cannot be a success. . . . There will be no substantive agreement of any kind." Returning to the dispute with Moscow, Deng tries to persuade Kissinger that "we don't pay much attention" to the Soviet threat.]

Vice Premier Deng: . . . The Soviet military strength in the East is not just directed against China. It is also directed against Japan and your Seventh Fleet, your air and naval forces. And if they are going to attack China, as the Chairman has discussed (with you), it will be impossible to take over China with just one million troops. They will have to increase their troops by one million, and even that would not be sufficient because if they are going to make up their minds to fight with China, they will have to make up their minds to fight for 20 years. The Chinese have no great virtue, but they do have (the virtue of) patience.

Secretary Kissinger: They have a few other virtues.

Vice Premier Deng: They also have "millet plus rifles"—and tunnels.

Secretary Kissinger: I have never seen the tunnels.

Vice Premier Deng: Hasn't Ambassador Bush done this for you? He is shirking his responsibilities.

Ambassador Bush: Not yet. I am delighted to know that I can see them.

Vice Premier Deng: The next time you can write a report to the Doctor about the tunnels.

Secretary Kissinger: Don't encourage him. Between him and the Ambassador in India [Patrick Moynihan] I have nothing to do but read cables—although the Ambassador in India publishes his in the newspapers.

Vice Premier Deng: So that is the order of relations between the Soviet Union and China. As for the strategic emphasis of the Soviet Union, we see it as "a feint toward the East to attack in the West"—to attack in Europe. It doesn't matter if we have different views, we can see what happens.

Secretary Kissinger: I think the strategic situation is the same. If they attack in the East it will be a threat to the West, and if they attack in the West it will be a threat to the East. The danger is the same either way. We don't need to decide this abstractly.

Vice Premier Deng: But this strategic assessment has its practical side, especially with the Western European countries. We have exchanged views on this many times.

Secretary Kissinger: I don't believe Europe could be indifferent to an attack in the East. I don't believe you could be indifferent to an attack in the West.

Vice Premier Deng: We agree to this view. An attack in any quarter is of significance to other areas too. But to establish a strategic point of view and preparations will be of significant importance, especially to your allies in Europe. Because without (these preparations), they will suffer. When we say the emphasis is in the West, it does not mean we will ignore our own defenses.

Secretary Kissinger: We agree, and we will add to our preparations too. Unfortunately, as you know, some of the leaders in Europe are not the most heroic right now. You have met them and can form your own opinions. But we will do our best. I might add something about the oil problem: The U.S. has two options. Economically, we can deal with the problem on our own better than in cooperation with others. But the reason I have made several specific suggestions and proposals is because I believe if Europe continues to suffer a balance of payments drain, they will lose so much confidence that they will not be able to resist Soviet pressures. And if they take money from countries like Libya and Algeria, this will continue the process of their political demoralization. So you should understand that the proposals I have made, and our policies, have nothing to do with economic considerations, because economically we would be better off making bilateral agreements with the Saudis, and we could leave Europe alone. We do this because we feel the defense of the West will be weakened if these countries are demoralized by their economic condition.

Vice Premier Deng: So, I think we spent quite a lot of time this morning. We must have something to eat, otherwise our stomachs will make revolution.

[Deng and Kissinger break for lunch then meet later in the afternoon for wide-ranging discussions on Europe, the Middle East, South and Southeast Asia, and international oil politics. The following excerpt captures the dialogue after Deng emphasizes the importance of strong European allies to deter the "Polar Bear" and of U.S.— European partnership based on "equality."]

Secretary Kissinger: I agree with you. I always say that the People's Republic is our best partner in NATO. (laughter) If you want to arrange seminars here for visiting European Ministers, I can mention a few who would benefit by it. (laughter) You had a very good effect on the Danish Prime Minister, although his nerves may not be up to your considerations.

Vice Premier Deng: We had very good talks.

Secretary Kissinger: Very good, very good.

Vice Premier Deng: Actually, the Prime Minister of Denmark really fears war very much.

Secretary Kissinger: Anyone who plans to attack Denmark doesn't have to prepare for a 20-year war or build so many underground tunnels. (Laughter)

But seriously, we know your talks with the European Ministers are very helpful and we appreciate them.

[They then turn their conversation to Eurocommunism, which worries Kissinger because Italian and French Communist Parties are following a strategy of appearing "moderate and very responsible."]

Secretary Kissinger: . . . When you analyze our foreign policy you have to understand we have to do certain things and say certain things designed to paralyze not only our Left but the European Left as well. But we are opposed to, and we shall resist, the inclusion of the Left in European governments. We shall do so in Portugal because we don't want that to be the model for other countries. And we shall do so in Italy. And of course in France.

[While Deng was more phlegmatic about Eurocommunism — they would be "teachers by negative example" — Kissinger emphasizes the administration's determination to "resist" because Communist electoral victories in France or Italy would have a "serious" impact on NATO and on German politics. Showing his deep-seated suspicions of the German Social Democrats, he claimed that Italian or French Communist successes "will strengthen the Left wing of the Social Democratic Party, which is very much influenced by East Germany."

A long discussion of the Middle East situation and U.S. negotiating efforts ensues, in which Deng urges a more even-handed approach. Kissinger agrees that he needs to do more to take Arab goals into account, but he nevertheless cautions that "there will be ups and downs, especially when 15 Arabs get together in one room — because they can't always make a distinction between epic poetry and foreign policy." Deng suggests that Kissinger should not underestimate the Arabs.]

Vice Premier Deng: Actually the position of the United States in the Middle East, the weakest point of the U.S. is that you support Israel against the Arab world, which has a population of 120 million, and on this point the Soviet Union is in a better position than you.

Secretary Kissinger: I accept that impotence never gives you a good position. Israel is both our weakest point and our strongest point. Because when all is said and done, no one else can make them move. Because the Arabs can't force them, and the Soviets can't do it. And anyone who wants progress will have to come to us. And this even includes the Palestinians.

[On South Asia, Kissinger and Deng agree on the need for U.S. engagement with India to give New Delhi an alternative to Moscow and to make it easier for Washington to provide Pakistan with military aid. On other Third World issues, the talks show little affinity. Deng rejects Kissinger's proposal for a new Cambodian coalition involving

*Sihanouk and some of Lon Nol's supporters.[59] On energy issues, Kissinger warns
Deng that Chinese support for the oil producers could hurt Europe and Japan and
impair China's security, but Deng does not let go of the issue.*

*Finally Deng reiterates his three principles of normalization: it can occur only on
the basis of the Japan model, once Washington ends its defense treaty with the Nationalist regime, Taiwan will be an "internal matter" for the Chinese to solve; and "any
kind of reviewing or guarantee or any kind of involvement in the process we will not
accept." However, he says, if Washington still needs time because it "needed Taiwan"
and had "domestic difficulties," Beijing could wait.]*

Vice Premier Deng: I don't think we can finish our talks on this issue this
time.

Secretary Kissinger: I don't think so either.

Vice Premier Deng: So, shall we stop here? And you'll have a little rest, and
I'll invite you to taste the well-known Peking mutton [at a restaurant for din-
ner].

Secretary Kissinger: I'm looking forward to it. I've never had it.

*[After working out final procedures for preparing the communiqué, they agree to meet
in a small group the next day.]*

Kissinger toured the Forbidden City the next morning and met Deng later in
the afternoon.[60] They discussed the Middle East negotiations in some detail,
which led to a review of bilateral relations, including the claims and assets
issue. Deng objected to the way in which U.S. negotiators were invoking
U.S. law and argued that "U.S. law doesn't govern China." Kissinger puck-
ishly observed, "There are some Congressmen who think that China is a
suburb of Chicago." Kissinger wanted to avoid an "acrimonious negotiation" and said that he sympathized with Deng's concerns.

On normalization, Kissinger found no change in Deng's position; the Vice
Premier restated the PRC's three basic principles and added that "it is for the
one who has tied the knot to unfasten it." Beijing, he said, will wait until
Washington is ready to settle on the basis of the three principles. For Kissinger, the problem was not accepting those principles, which he did, but
"how to implement them." Deng had stated that China would not "undertake any commitments or make any promises in internal affairs," and Kissinger suggested the possibility of a "general statement of your unilateral
intentions" on Taiwan. Deng asked, "[W]hat are we to say in it?" He did not
want to pursue the discussion any further.

In an intense discussion of the international situation, Deng revisited his themes of a Soviet threat to the West: "The Polar Bear is after you." World war is a danger but "would it necessarily be a bad thing?" he asked; "bad things can turn into good things." They had a sharp exchange, excerpted below, on the U.S. role in world politics. Deng took issue with Washington's "forefront" position, while Kissinger advised the Vice Premier not to hit himself with his own cannon fire.

Deng: . . . Another matter is that which the Doctor has repeatedly mentioned the question of firing cannons. It seems the Doctor is very concerned about cannon fire.

Kissinger: I dig tunnels very deeply.

Deng: I am in favor of that. Cannons must be fired. And the Doctor has mentioned that the frequency and accuracy of the cannon fire has been raised and since the accuracy has been raised, it is quite unclear that cannon fire can not afford to cease. We think there might be a necessity to study the matter of whether or not the cannon fire is reasonable. And, therefore, I think it might be of some use to raise this point to your attention. That is, that in many issues now, the United States is in the forefront. Doctor has mentioned many time[s] here the energy question and the food issue. The United States is always in the forefront. You mention the fact that it is Western Europe and Japan and other countries that are most affected by the crises, but they are not in the forefront.

Kissinger: They are also not in the forefront of military defense.

Deng: Of course, it isn't in all issues that the United States is in the forefront, but in the recent period of time, you have been in the forefront on many important issues. On the contrary, the Soviet Union has been hiding behind. For instance in Cyprus and the Middle East, you have also been in the forefront. And no matter how you look at the issue in the Middle East, for the U.S. to foster Israeli expansionism, which is what it is, in essence against 120 million Arab people — from the political point of view, you are bound to be in a weaker position. Of course, the Doctor has repeatedly explained that this is because of domestic issues. No matter out of what reason, so long as the Arab countries are not able to regain their lost territory, the principle issue remains unsolved. Tactics will not be able to settle the problem, the Communique will not be able to solve the issue. There is already some similarity between this and the Indochina issue and the Korean issue too. I don't think that the Doctor will take these views to be ill-intentioned.

Kissinger: No. Mr. Vice Premier, I have summed up our views on many of these issues. The Vice Premier was finished, I understood?

Deng: Yes.

Kissinger: I have summed up the US view on many of these issues. I could perhaps say one or two words. First of all, I agree with the Chairman, who, I believe, is a very great man. In any event, that it is important to be prepared for war and it is our policy to prepare for all eventualities and not to rely on the words of others or their assurances for peace. And in this analysis and in the manner of the quotation you just mentioned to me, we agree with his analysis of the overall situation.

Whether the attack comes in the East or the West is a subsidiary issue in this respect because wherever it comes it is ultimately intended for us and in this analyses [sic] I agree. If it comes first in the West, it still will affect the East and if it comes first in the East, it will still affect the West. And in either case it will affect us, but this is not a difference between us. The practical consequences for us—we have to do the same things in either case. With respect to the United States being in the forefront. That is imposed on us by the particular necessity of the various analyses you have made. The Vice Premier has correctly pointed out that neither Europe or Japan is in the forefront of the energy problem, even though they are the primary victims. They are also not in the forefront of the defense problem, even though they are the primary victims according to your own analysis. For a variety of reasons, it would be interesting to discuss sometime, neither [sic] of these societies are in a position to take a leading role for their own survival without strong American support. This is a historical reality. And if they were to separate from the United States, they would very soon become impotent and what one could call *syntensizid* [?] or *finlandized* [sic]. And therefore, they are not capable of being a second world under the present circumstances by themselves. It would be much more convenient for us if they could be. And in any event, we believe in what the Vice Premier said earlier—on equal partnership. And therefore the energy problem—I wanted to report our view that neither Europe or Japan can play a strategic role in which you and I agree—if at the same time they are demoralized by economic pressures which are beyond their capacity to solve. This is why we are in the forefront.

On the Middle East, I have explained to you our tactics, which are complicated. I agree with you that unless there is a fundamental solution, a tactical solution is not going to be permanent. So, on this we are agreed, and I have explained to you what our strategy will be and their strategy will lead inexorably to a radical solution. The Vice Premier knows himself, from his own experience in political and military warfare that if one accumulates enough minor changes, sooner or later a fundamental change becomes _____ .[61]

As for Cyprus and the Middle East and the Soviet role, the Soviet Union will not be able to create anything. It can only make noise. We would prefer not to be in the forefront on these issues, and in Cyprus we tried to push Britain into the forefront and that produced its own complications. As to firing cannons, we recognize the necessity and we have our own tunnels and you will consider that you should not hit your own fortifications.
Deng: They haven't.
Kissinger: I am not saying they have, so we rely on you for this.
Deng: You can study our cannons.
Kissinger: We generally do not do any counterbatting fire. But more fundamentally, I think we have had a very useful, very beneficial exchange and in what I consider a friendly spirit of many subjects of common interest. . . .

That evening Kissinger hosted a banquet for the Chinese. Kissinger's private observations about Qiao's and his own toasts pithily expressed the state of Chinese-U.S. relations near the close of 1974. He described Qiao's toast as "somewhere between friendly and correct." Of his own toast he said, "I tailored my remarks accordingly, giving them a modest upbeat quality." With all the cannons fired that year, though, only the sense of a common adversary could sustain a strictly unsentimental relationship.[62]

Notes

1. For "tacit alliance," see "People's Republic of China," 14 Aug. 1974, National Archives, Record Group 59; Department of State Records Policy Planning Staff (Director's Files), 1969–1977 (hereafter referred to as *PPS*, with archival box number and file information), box 376, China—Sensitive 1 Jul–16 Aug 1974. For stagnation in Sino-American relations beginning in 1974, see Stephen Sestanovich, "U.S. Policy Toward the Soviet Union, 1970–1990: The Impact of China," in *China, the United States, and the Soviet Union: Tripolarity and Policymaking in the Cold War*, ed. Robert S. Ross (Armonk, N.Y.: M. E. Sharpe, 1993), pp. 12–144.
2. See Solomon to Kissinger, "Peking Sends the U.S. Some Warning Signals," 16 Feb. 1974, *PPS*, box 330, China Exchanges 1 Nov 1973–31 March 1974; Lord and Hummel to the Secretary, "Your Meeting with Deng Hsiao-ping and Ch'iao Kuan-hua," 12 April 1974, *PPS*, box 376, China–Sensitive—Feb–April 1974. See also USLO 870 to SecState, 24 May 1974, *PPS*, box 376, China—Sensitive 1 May–30 June 1974.
3. For an insightful discussion of Ford as president and as a politician, see Anatoly Dobry-

nin, *In Confidence: Moscow's Ambassador to America's Six Cold War Presidents, 1962-1986* (New York: Times Books, 1995), pp. 320, 338-341.

4. See Solomon to Kissinger, "The PRC's Domestic Political Situation and Foreign Policy as a Context for Your Meeting with Deng Hsiao-p'ing and Ch'iao Kuan-hua," 12 April 1976, *PPS*, Box 376, China—Sensitive—Feb.-April 1974; U.S. State Department Bureau of Intelligence and Research, Research Study, "The Chinese Leadership After the National People's Congress," 13 Feb. 1975, *PPS*, box 375, China—Sensitive Chron Jan.-Feb. 1975. For the political scene around the time of Deng's rehabilitation, see Li Zhisui, *The Private Life of Chairman Mao: The Memoirs of Mao's Personal Physician* (New York: Random House, 1994), pp. 575-79, and Richard Evans, *Deng Xiaoping and the Making of Modern China* (New York: Viking, 1993), pp. 189-93.

5. See Robert S. Ross, *Negotiating Cooperation: The United States and China, 1969-1989* (Stanford, Calif.: Stanford University Press, 1995), p. 65; Solomon to Kissinger, "Confucius and the State Governors' China Trip: Is Peking Debating Foreign Policy?" 25 Jan. 1974, *PPS*, box 330, China Exchanges 1 Nov. 1973-31 March 1974; John Holdridge, *Crossing the Divide: An Insider's Account of Normalization of U.S.-China Relations* (Lanham, Md.: Rowman and Littlefield, 1997), p. 126.

6. See "Background and General Approaches for Your Talks with the Chinese," n.d., *PPS*, box 371, Secretary's Visit to Peking, Bilateral Issues S/P Mr. Lord, Nov. 1974; Department of State, "Issues/Talking Points, Soviet Union," *PPS*, box 371, Secretary's Visit to Peking, Third Country Issues Nov. 1974; and Hummel, Lord, and Solomon to the Secretary, "Imperatives for Planning and Action on the China Issue," 24 May 1974, *PPS*, box 376, China—Sensitive 1 May-30 June 1974.

7. See "Background and General Approaches for Your Talks with the Chinese," n.d., *PPS*, box 371, Secretary's Visit to Peking, Bilateral Issues S/P Mr. Lord, Nov. 1974; "Speech by Deng Hsiao-Ping, Chairman of the Delegation of the People's Republic of China. . . , 10 April 1974, *PPS*, box 371, Bilateral PRC Officials, 22 April 1974; Secretary Kissinger, "An Age of Interdependence: Common Disaster or Community," *Department of State Bulletin* 71 (14 Oct. 1974), p. 502.

8. See Lord and Hummel to the Secretary, "Your Meeting with Deng Hxiao-ping and Chiao Kuan-hua," 12 April 1974, *PPS*, box 376, China—Sensitive—Feb-Apr. 1974; unsigned memorandum to Kissinger, "Indicators of PRC Internal Debate and Desire for Movement on the Taiwan Issue," 23 May 1974, *PPS*, box 376, China—Sensitive 1 May-30 June 1974; Hummel, Lord, and Solomon to Secretary, "Your Meeting with Ch'iao Kuan-hua—Dinner, October 2, 1974," 27 Sept., *PPS*, box 376, China—Sensitive Chron 17 Aug-Oct. 1974; Robert Ross, *Negotiating Cooperation:* p. 77; Nancy B. Tucker, *Taiwan, Hong Kong, and the United States, 1945-1992: Uncertain Friendships* (New York: Twayne, 1994), pp. 126-27.

9. See Solomon to Secretary Kissinger, "'Confirming the Principle of One China': Next Step in the Evolution of U.S.-PRC-ROC Relations," 19 Jan. 1974, *PPS*, box 371, China—Secretary Kissinger.

10. "Private Statements Made by PRC Leaders to Secretary Kissinger or President Nixon Regarding the Peaceful Liberation of Taiwan," n.d., *PPS*, box 372, PRC Nov. 1974.

11. See Richard H. Solomon to Secretary Kissinger, "'Confirming the Principle of One China': Next Step in the Evolution of U.S.-PRC-ROC Relations," 19 Jan. 1974, box

371, China—Secretary Kissinger; Hummel, Lord, and Solomon to the Secretary, "Imperatives for Planning and Action on the China Issue," 24 May 1974, *PPS*, box 376, China—Sensitive 1 May–30 June 1974; and "Normalization of U.S.–PRC Relations and the Future of Taiwan," n.d., *PPS*, box 372, PRC Nov. 1974.

12. See Briefing paper for President Ford, "People's Republic of China," 14 Aug. 1974, *PPS*, box 376, China—Sensitive 1 Jul–16 Aug 1974.

13. See Robert McFarlane, *Special Trust* (New York: Cadell and Davies, 1994), p. 151.

14. See Solomon to Kissinger, "Political Background Analysis of Deng Hsaio-p'ing," 12 April, *PPS*, box 371, Bilateral PRC Officials, 22 April 1974. Although Solomon reported that Zhou played a major role in bringing Deng back to power, more recent accounts suggest that Mao was the prime mover and that Zhou's illness (of which no U.S. official was aware) was a motivating factor. Li, *The Private Life of Chairman Mao*, pp. 575-76; and Evans, *Deng Xiaoping*, p. 188.

15. See Evans, *Deng Xiaoping*, pp. 198-99; "Top Chinese Who Made a Comeback," *New York Times*, 11 April 1974; "Speech by Deng Hsiao-Ping . . ." April 10, 1974, *PPS*, box 371, Bilateral PRC Officials 22 April 1974. For "taking the temperature," see Solomon to Kissinger, "Political Background Analysis of Deng Hsaio-p'ing," 12 April, *PPS*, box 371, Bilateral PRC Officials, 22 April 1974.

16. For concern about China's toughening stance, see Lord and Hummel to the Secretary, "Your Meeting with Deng Hsiao-ping and Ch'iao Kuan-hua," 12 April 1974, *PPS*, box 376, China—Sensitive—Feb–April 1974.

17. The fact that Deng's party arrived for dinner ten minutes late on purpose may not have helped his mood. See Hummel to Winston Lord, "Random Notes on HAK–PRC Dinner, April 14," 15 April 1976, *PPS*, box 380, Exclusively Eyes Only—Lord Chron File. For comments on Deng, see Kissinger to the President, "Your Trip to the People's Republic of China: A Scope Analysis for Your Discussions with Chinese Leaders," 20 Nov, 1975, *PPS*, box 380, China Notes. According to a biographical sketch, Deng "has shown a lack of confidence in his conversations with visitors, seeking reassurance from accompanying PRC advisers." See "Deng Hsaio-p'ing," 4 April 1974, *PPS*, box 376, China—Sensitive Feb.–April 1974.

18. For discussion of Deng's critical role in Sino–Soviet relations and the ideological warfare of the early 1960s, see Vladislav Zubok, "'Look What Beautiful Chaos in the Socialist Camp': Deng Xiaoping and the Sino–Soviet Split, 1956–1963," *Cold War International History Project Bulletin* 10 (March 1998), pp. 152-61.

19. Henry Kissinger and Nancy Maginnes had just gotten married only a few weeks earlier, on 30 March. See Walter Isaacson, *Kissinger: A Biography* (New York: Simon and Schuster, 1992), p. 587.

20. Kissinger's predecessors had characterized Gromyko in similar if more expressive ways as far back as the 1950s. In March 1959, Secretary of State John Foster Dulles said that negotiating with Gromyko over Berlin would be "bleak and barren" because the real decision-maker was Nikita Khrushchev. See Memorandum of conversation, 20 March 1959, U.S. State Department, *Foreign Relations of the United States, 1958-1960*, vol. 8 (Washington, D.C.: U.S. Government Printing Office, 1993), p. 513.

21. A reference to Brezhnev's role in the overthrow of Soviet Premier Nikita Khrushchev in October 1964, which occurred after Khrushchev returned from a holiday.

22. For Kissinger's account of that conversation, see his *Years of Upheaval* (Boston: Little, Brown, 1982), pp. 681-82.

23. Notetaker Charles Freeman had good Chinese language skills; Kissinger was finally allowing Foreign Service professionals with interpretive abilities to attend meetings with high-level Chinese figures.

24. For Kissinger's account of U.S.-French relations during 1973-74, see ibid., pp. 163-81, 707-735.

25. Among other things, Kissinger said that Washington's major foreign policy problem was not "how to regulate competition with its enemies" but how to eliminate "endless competition" with allies, for example, U.S.-French disagreements over oil policy. His most controversial remark was that "there have been, very rarely, fully legitimate governments in any European country since World War I." Later, chagrined, he said, "I have the impression that during this week I have done more for European unification than any man since Jean Monnet." With respect to his comments on political legitimacy, he said that he had been trying to say that "no government that entered World War I recovered its legitimacy as a result of [the] devastation." "U.S. Seeks to Soften Kissinger's Remarks" and "Kissinger Acts to Undo His Gaffe on Europe," See *Washington Post*, 13 and 15 March 1974 respectively.

26. "Working staffs" refers to the Chinese officials who were targets of the latest ideological campaign. For the anti-Confucian campaign as perceived by U.S. officials, see Holdridge, *Crossing the Divide*, p. 146, and Kissinger, *Years of Upheaval*, pp. 680, 696.

27. "Optical agreement" refers to one that lacks substance and is for the sake of appearance.

28. The Chinese had been pressing for removal of the U.N. Command on behalf of the North Koreans, but the UNC's role in administering the armistice agreement made Kissinger reluctant to dissolve it without any agreement on alternative arrangements. See U.S. Department of State Briefing Papers, "Korea," Nov. 1974, and "Issues/Talking Points UNC Alternatives," Nov. 1974, *PPS*, box 371, Secretary Kissinger's Visit to Peking Third Country Issues, Nov. 1974.

29. In 1973, the PRC worked with Washington to develop a compromise proposal on Korea that met the North's goal of abolishing the United Nations Commission on the Unification and Rehabilitation of Korea (UNCURK). See Briefing Paper, "Korea," Nov. 1974, *PPS*, box 371, Secretary Kissinger's visit to Peking, Third Country Issues, Nov. 1974.

30. See memcon, "The Secretary's Travel Plans," 15 Aug. 1974; memcon, 16 Aug. 1974; both in *PPS*, box 331, China Exchanges 9 Aug.-31 Dec. 1974.

31. See Kissinger to Bush, WASH80, 4 Nov. 1974, in *PPS*, box 331, China Exchanges 9 Aug.-31 Dec. 1974.

32. See Li, *The Private Life of Chairman Mao*, pp. 582-83.

33. For the transcript of this talk, see memcon, 2 Oct. 1974, *PPS*, box 376, China—Sensitive—Chron 17 Aug.-Oct. 1974. For Bruce's departure, see Holdridge, *Crossing the Divide*, p. 144, and Nelson D. Lankford, *The Last American Aristocrat: The Biography of David K. E. Bruce, 1899-1977* (Boston: Little, Brown, and Co., 1996), pp. 384-86. See also George Bush, *Looking Forward* (Garden City, N.Y.: Doubleday), pp. 129-30.

34. "Your Dinner Conversation with the Chinese," 3 Oct. 1974, *PPS*, box 376, China—Sensitive— Chron: 17 Aug.-15 Oct. 1974.

35. See ibid. For Quiao's speech, see *New York Times*, 3 Oct. 1974, and "Speech by Ch'iao Kuan-Hua, Chairman of the Delegation of the People's Republic of China . . . ," 2 Oct. 1974, *PPS*, box 376, China—Sensitive—Chron 17 Aug.-15 Oct. 1974.

36. Bush, *Looking Forward*, p. 134. Given Beijing's tight control, Bush found Kissinger's security team "excessive" in numbers. For more details on the Vladivostok summit, see chapter 7 of this volume.

37. William Hyland, *Mortal Rivals: Superpower Relations from Nixon to Reagan* (New York: Random House, 1987), p. 78. For "helping us enormously," see Scowcroft to the President, "HAK Talks with the Chinese," 27 Nov. 1974, *PPS*, box 372, Secretary Kissinger's Talks in China, 25-29 Nov. 1974; for Chinese ambivalence, see Ross, *Negotiating Cooperation*. p. 77.

38. See Peking 91 to White House, George Bush to the Secretary, "China's Internal Scene on the Eve of Your Visit," 18 Nov. 1974, *PPS*, box 331, China Exchanges 9 Aug.-31 Dec. 1974.

39. See "Normalization of U.S.-PRC Relations and the Future of Taiwan," n.d., *PPS*, box 372, PRC Nov. 1974; and Philip Habib et al., "U.S.-PRC Relations and Approaches . . . ," 3 July 1975, *PPS*, box 379, China—Sensitive July-Sept. 1975. For the formulations of possible joint U.S.-PRC or unilateral U.S. or PRC guarantees prepared for Kissinger's use in negotiations, see "Conceptual Approaches to Formulating U.S. and PRC Statements on the Security of Taiwan," n.d., *PPS*, box 371, Secretary's Visit to Peking Bilateral Issues, S/P Mr. Lord, Nov. 1974.

40. See Evans, *Deng Xiaoping*, p. 203; Ross, *Negotiating Cooperation*, p. 78; and Holdridge, *Crossing the Divide*, p. 152.

41. For the full text, see memcon, "Introductory Tour d'Horizon Japan; Bilateral Relations and Normalization," 26 Nov. 1974, 10:20-11:02 A.M., *PPS*, box 370, Secretary Kissinger's Talks in China, 25-29 Nov. 1974.

42. Tanaka had resigned because of allegations about improper land transactions and newspaper stories about a mistress. Deng and Kissinger agreed that they would prefer Mayasoshi Ohira (1910-1980), because "he would support the policy we are familiar with." Deng observed that Takeo Fukuda (1905-1995) "would be voted for by the Soviet Union. . . .Their relationship is growing closer day-by-day."

43. This is a reference to the appointment of senior Foreign Service Officer Leonard Unger (b. 1917) as ambassador to the Republic of China. Unger had previously served as Ambassador to Laos and then to Thailand.

44. "Your ally and northern neighbor" is a facetious reference to the Soviet Union.

45. The same Chinese and American officials as in the 11:15 A.M. meeting attended this one as well.

46. Kissinger made this flattering but humorously self-deprecating comment in a number of conversations with the Chinese.

47. See "Text of Joint Communiqué," n.d., *Department of State Bulletin* 71 (23 Dec. 1974), p. 907.

48. See Ross, *Negotiating Cooperation*, pp. 78-79, and Holdridge, *Crossing the Divide*, p. 157. According to Bush, when the Chinese said that a meeting was "not convenient," it meant that "you could see the official when hell freezes over." Bush, *Looking Forward*, p. 136.

49. See Ross, *Negotiating Cooperation*, pp. 78–79; Holdridge, *Crossing the Divide*, p. 157; and Li, *The Private Life of Chairman Mao*, pp. 580-88. "Dane Finds Mao Clear-Minded and In Good Humor," *New York Times*, 22 Oct. 1974.

50. Noting the absence of a Kissinger–Mao meeting, the *New York Times* reported that "there was no hint" that Mao "was indisposed or otherwise preoccupied," and "it seemed that the Chinese, in a typically indirect manner, were indicating their displeasure over the lack of momentum in the relationship." See "President Plans a Visit to China in Second Half of '75," *New York Times*, 30 November 1974.

51. For Deng as an "ideological terrier," see Zubok, "'Look What Beautiful Chaos in the Socialist Camp,'" p. 152.

52. Kissinger of course does not mention his intense rivalry with Schlesinger, which no doubt informed his thinking on finding an alternative to a Schlesinger visit. It is likely that the Chinese were aware of this rivalry and may have been trying to manipulate Kissinger by suggesting it.

53. During the Moscow summit in June, Brezhnev had tried out with Nixon his proposal for a nonaggression pact. This time Nixon was interested, but Kissinger ignored his instructions to follow up through the back-channel. See Raymond Garthoff, *Detente and Confrontation: American–Soviet Relations from Nixon to Reagan* (Washington, D.C.: Brookings Institution, 1994), p. 478.

54. A wry description of China's limited nuclear weapons capabilities.

55. It is possible that Deng confused Khrushchev's 1954 visit to Beijing with the one in 1958, during which strategic nuclear issues were the subject of debate between Khrushchev and Mao. See Vladislav Zubok and Constantine Pleshakov, *Inside the Kremlin's Cold War: From Stalin to Khrushchev* (Cambridge, Mass.: Harvard University Press, 1996), pp. 219–20.

56. This is a tacit reference to the "taboos" that made many U.S. government officials and military officers view nuclear weapons to be all but unusable. For thoughtful discussions, see Peter Gizewski, "From Winning Weapon to Destroyer of Worlds: The Nuclear Taboo in International Politics," *International Journal* 51 (Summer 1996), pp. 397–418; and Richard Price and Nina Tannenwald, "Norms and Deterrence: The Nuclear and Chemical Weapons Taboos," in *The Culture of National Security: Norms and Identity in World Politics*, ed. Peter J. Katzenstein (New York: Columbia University Press, 1996), pp. 116–52.

57. This is somewhat misleading as stated because the Soviets had put airborne divisions on alert nearly two weeks before the U.S. alert on the morning of 24 October 1973. Garthoff, *Detente and Confrontation*, p. 424.

58. For full text, see memcon, "Sino–Soviet Relations; Europe," 27 Nov. 1974, 11:40 A.M.–12:20 P.M.; PPS, box 370, Secretary Kissinger's Talks in China.

59. While Kissinger still made claims about a Khmer Rouge alignment with Hanoi, a telegram sent out under his name in April suggested conflict between "xenophobic" Khmer communists and the Vietnamese. See Ben Kiernan, *The Pol Pot Regime: Race, Power, and Genocide in Cambodia Under the Khmer Rouge, 1975–1979* (New Haven: Yale University Press, 1996), pp. 24-25.

60. See memcon, 28 Nov. 1974, 4:00–6:15 P.M., PPS, box 372, Secretary Kissinger's Talks in China, 25–29 Nov. 1974.

61. The stenographer missed some words, possibly, Kissinger said a "qualitative one." If so, he was referring to the Marxist–Leninist precept that enough quantitative changes can produce a qualitative one.

62. See Scowcroft to the President, 29 Nov. 1974, *PPS*, box 372, Secretary Kissinger's Talks in China, 25–29 Nov. 1974,

7

Trials of Détente:

Washington–Moscow, 1974–75

As relations with China cooled, the U.S.–Soviet détente came under more and more pressure—precisely what Gerald R. Ford, who became president when Richard Nixon resigned on 8 August 1974, did not need. Ford was a more conservative Republican who had learned political caution through years in the House of Representatives. Like Nixon, Ford was committed to making détente irreversible, and he retained Henry Kissinger in his policy-making roles. Yet continuing pressures from Sen. Henry Jackson and the Pentagon as well as the exigencies of reelection politics made the new president averse to taking any foreign policy risks that could expose him to right-wing criticism. Even the signing of the Helsinki Treaty, the outcome of the Conference on Security and Cooperation in Europe [CSCE] and a key moment in the history of détente, did not offset the forces that complicated détente during 1974 and 1975—bureaucratic and political pressures on the domestic front and U.S.–Soviet rivalries in the Middle East and elsewhere on foreign fronts. Kissinger's shortcomings in negotiating with Congress, his ambivalence to economic détente, and his determination to exclude the Soviets from the Middle East peace process did not make the situation any easier, and he admitted that the United States shared in the blame. In October 1974, after Brezhnev read off a litany of grievances about U.S. policy, Kissinger responded, "What burns me up is that a lot of what the General Secretary has said is true."

Only weeks before his resignation, Nixon had traveled to Moscow for his last summit meeting with Brezhnev. Their talks yielded no extraordinary accomplishments, but a number of lesser agreements on the ABM treaty and nuclear testing, among other issues, helped to provide a "little momentum" to détente.[1] SALT II, however, remained stalled. As much as Nixon believed it was essential to constrain Soviet nuclear forces, neither he nor Brezhnev could agree on the numbers of MIRVed missile launchers that an agreement would sanction. Nevertheless, they agreed that Brezhnev should come to Washington in 1975, and that in the interim they would hold a "mini-summit" in a third country to reach a SALT agreement.[2]

However, as soon as Ford decided to seek election in 1976, the growing domestic opposition to détente made him extremely careful when it came to U.S.-Soviet relations. Some of his own tendencies—a visceral commitment to a strong military posture, some concern about Soviet intentions, and long congressional experience that disposed him to look at foreign policy issues first "through the prism of domestic policy"—reinforced this caution.[3] Indeed, Ford's political caution ultimately precluded the realization of Nixon's and Brezhnev's goal of making quick progress on a SALT II agreement. In any event, in spite of the fact that Kissinger had to adjust to the new president's policymaking style, the two worked comfortably together.

To demonstrate the new president's commitment to détente, and also to reason with its critics, on 19 September 1974, Kissinger made a major statement to the Senate Foreign Relations Committee.[4] Kissinger's testimony included arguments in favor of economic incentives to encourage Soviet restraint, but he could not outmaneuver Senator Henry Jackson. On October 18, only days before Kissinger was to leave for meetings with Brezhnev, Jackson sabotaged an elaborate deal that Kissinger and Dobrynin had worked out in advance, which the White House hoped would enable Jackson to support MFN for Moscow. Jackson disclosed a supposedly confidential exchange of letters with Kissinger that the latter hoped would reduce the pressure by providing some assurances, however ambiguous, on forthcoming changes in Soviet policy. When Jackson released the letters, he crowed that he had achieved a "historic understanding [on] human rights," and that the Soviets had agreed to allow as many as 60,000 Jews to emigrate annually.[5]

The Soviets, who had made no explicit concessions on numbers, were startled by Jackson's maneuver and by the White House's inability to check him. When Congress passed the Trade Bill, with the Jackson-Vanik intact, and an Export-Import Bank bill that substantially curtailed credits to Moscow, the Soviets were further "shocked" that Ford and Kissinger had acquiesced. As Anatoly Dobrynin wrote years later, Brezhnev and his colleagues "could not imagine an American president who was not exactly a supreme ruler." The Soviets would have been even more disturbed had they realized that Kissinger had not even fought against legislative measures to restrict credits: he had completely lost track of the issue. If Kissinger had formerly seen domestic political pressures for a credit ceiling as a possible bargaining chip, he had now lost the freedom to offer the economic benefits that, he believed, would give Moscow an interest in restraint.[6]

The trade credits fiasco said much about the relatively low priority that Kissinger had given to economic détente as well as about the administrative hazards of making one person both Secretary of State and National Security Adviser; it did incalculable damage to détente by casting doubt on Washington's reliability as a partner.[7] For Kissinger, Jackson–Vanik was the worst form of linkage because it denied him the power to use economic benefits, "carrots," to foster cooperation in Moscow and to place subtle restraints on Soviet foreign policy. U.S. and Soviet policymakers were determined to find ways to make détente work, but, with economic diplomacy effectively undercut, avenues of bilateral cooperation had become much narrower. Moreover, Kissinger's inability to restrain Jackson and his allies would do much to bring about one of his major anxieties—closer connections between Western Europe and the Soviet bloc. This development had considerable influence on the way the Cold War unfolded during the early 1980s.

In a key area, the Middle East, significant cooperation had become all but impossible because Kissinger was determined to negotiate limited agreements between the principal adversaries while excluding the Soviets from the peace process.[8] Although Brezhnev acted more calmly than he had in March, the transcripts of the October meetings show him warning of instability in the region—a "powderkeg"—and insisting that the Geneva conference be reconvened to allow Moscow a role in the peace process. It is doubtful that Kissinger's blandishments to the General Secretary—"neither of use can gain a permanent advantage [in the region] at the expense of the other"—provided any consolation. Brezhnev almost certainly fully understood that Kissinger had no intention of abandoning the short-term diplomatic advantages he had cultivated so assiduously since the October War.

With potential for accord in economics and the Middle East so limited, strategic arms control remained the area where significant progress was conceivable. When Kissinger arrived in Moscow in 24 October 1974, both sides wanted to find ways to break the stalemated SALT process. Indeed, a deal that Kissinger, Brezhnev, and Gromyko struck in October set the stage for the general agreement that Ford and Brezhnev reached at Vladivostok in November. Not only did the two sides agree on an overall ceiling of 2,400 strategic missiles and bombers for each, but they reached an accord on something that had stymied Brezhnev and Kissinger in March—a sublimit for MIRVed missiles. Moreover, in light of Brezhnev's earlier complaints about nuclear weapons in the Mediterranean, Ford threw him a bone: Washington would close its submarine base at Rota on the Spanish coast, which had served as the staging area for Poseidon submarines sailing east through Gibraltar.[9]

For both Ford and Brezhnev, reaching and finalizing the Vladivostok agreement involved political conflict; neither of them could rest on his laurels and start planning a Washington summit to sign a SALT II treaty. Soviet Defense Minister Marshal Grechko and his military colleagues were well aware of the Soviet inferiority in MIRVs, and they strongly opposed any constraints on ICBM construction; Brezhnev was able to compel their acquiescence because they did not want an open fight. The Vladivostok accord soon came into question in Washington, too, and the growing domestic political hostility to détente made finalizing it all the more difficult. Indeed, Jackson started attacking the agreement on the grounds that 2,400 delivery vehicles was too high, as did liberal arms controllers. Wanting to see lower levels of Soviet strategic forces, Jackson argued for deep cuts to bring the numbers down to 1,700. Ultimately, the agreement had enough support in the U.S. executive branch to make the numbers stick.[10]

Pentagon officials endorsed Kissinger's numbers, but, wary of his negotiating style, they watched him very closely. One issue where military officials were especially vigilant was Kissinger's handling of the Soviet Backfire bomber, aptly described by Raymond Garthoff as the "albatross of SALT II." The Soviets designed Backfire for regional missions in Europe and Asia; if refueled in flight, though, it could have reached continental U.S. targets. The Soviets lacked the tanker force that could support their 50 Backfires for such long-range missions, but the Pentagon nevertheless insisted that it was designed for both medium- and long-range attacks.[11]

Kissinger recognized Backfire's limited capabilities, and when he met with the Soviets in October, he excluded it from the categories of weapon systems counted under SALT II ceilings. Though he told U.S. journalists in a background press briefing in December 1974 that "the Backfires would be in a completely different category," his commitment to this position was shaky; he later used his control of the record to deny that he had made any such assurances.[12] Pentagon demands that Backfire be counted in the aggregates ultimately forced him to put it back on the negotiating table, to Moscow's great displeasure.[13]

These disagreements over Backfire prolonged the SALT negotiations, as did a major disagreement over the standing of cruise missiles—especially the bomber-launched air to surface version. Since late 1973, if not earlier, Kissinger had shown an interest in the air-launched cruise missiles (ALCMs), both as a bargaining chip in the SALT talks and also as a means for U.S. bombers to suppress the air defenses that protected important Soviet targets.[14] Serious disagreements over cruise missiles surfaced only when U.S. and Soviet officials began to draft an aide mémoire to describe the understanding that Brezhnev and Ford had reached at Vladivostok. The Americans argued that the SALT II totals should include only air-launched "ballistic" missiles that could strike targets deep in the Soviet homeland; the Soviets saw cruise missiles as a "new channel" in the nuclear arms race and wanted to limit them by including in the 2,400 aggregate all ALCMs whose ranged exceeded 600 miles. Although both sides agreed on language that enabled them to finalize the memorandum, Kissinger and the Pentagon rejected significant limits on ALCM deployments.[15]

Although the SALT II talks were extremely frustrating for the negotiators, Moscow and Washington sustained the dialogue, and there was no danger of a breakdown. Another area where East–West cooperation promised significant agreement, even if Kissinger had little use for it—"They can write it in Swahili for all I care"—was the Conference on Security and Cooperation in Europe. Brezhnev, on the other hand, remained anxious to wrap up the conference and attend the high-level signing ceremony. For the Soviets, the agreed-upon language about the inviolability of European boundaries thus validated the post-World War II territorial outcome—in their eyes, the CSCE's basic purpose.[15a]

As the possibility of a final agreement approached, Gromyko persuaded the Soviet politburo that on all counts the CSCE would benefit Moscow because it ratified postwar boundaries and offered the possibility of greater economic cooperation. As long as the CSCE guaranteed each country's right to its own laws, Gromyko argued to Brezhnev and his colleagues, its human rights provisions would not weaken the Soviet political system. "We are masters in our own house," he told the Politburo.[16]

Neither Gromyko nor, for that matter, Henry Kissinger anticipated the degree to which the CSCE Final Act, signed in Helsinki in July 1975, would encourage dissidents throughout the Soviet bloc. Although Helsinki was a historic moment in Cold War history—one that Ford declared to be a "triumph" for the West—its immediate positive implications for bilateral U.S.-Soviet relations were slight. Indeed, Ford received not credit for Helsinki but renewed harsh attacks from Senator Jackson and the reinvigorated Republican right for signing another "Yalta" agreement "sanctifying and consolidating the Soviet sphere of influence." With the 1976 elections beckoning, Ford's competitors could not resist using the politics of anticommunism to chip away at political support for détente.[17]

The Soviet leadership, with its worries about U.S.-China relations, long-term need for Western capital and technology, and desire to avoid confrontation with Washington, had no practical alternative to détente. Yet the Politburo did not understand its political vulnerability in the United States and was hardly prepared for any reverses in relations with Washington. Complicating the situation were Brezhnev's grave health problems, just as State Department intelligence had estimated. Only Kremlin insiders knew, however, that at the time of the Vladivostok summit, Brezhnev had had two grand mal *seizures, signifying a developing atherosceloris of the brain.*[18] *He had enough stamina to stay in power into the next decade, but not enough acuity to address tensions in U.S.–Soviet relations creatively.*

What made the summit possible in the first place were the Brezhnev-Kissinger talks in Moscow during October 24-26, 1974. Before he had left, Kissinger and the Soviets had reached general agreement on the parameters, if not all the details, of a SALT agreement that would be the summit's highlight.[19] Despite this favorable development, after Kissinger arrived in Moscow, it did not take long for Brezhnev to start listing his grievances over U.S. decisions and developments and to pound the able. Kissinger soon joined him in doing so; both appeared frustrated and angry with Senator Jackson's machinations (even if Kissinger was less than candid in discussing them).

TOP SECRET/NODIS
MEMORANDUM OF CONVERSATION[A]
PARTICIPANTS: Leonid Il'ich Brezhnev, General Secretary and Member of the Politburo, CPSU Central Committee; Andrey A. Gromyko, Minister of Foreign Affairs; Member CPSU Politburo; Anatoly Dobrynin, USSR Ambassador to the United States; Andrey M. Aleksandrov-Agentov, Aide to General Secretary Brezhnev; Georgiy M. Korniyenko, Chief, USA Department, Ministry of Foreign Affairs; Oleg Sokolov, USA Department, Ministry of Foreign Affairs; Viktor M. Sukhodrev, Second European Department, Ministry of Foreign Affairs (Interpreter); Henry A. Kissinger, Secretary of State and Assistant to the President for National Security Affairs; Walter J. Stoessel, Jr., U.S. Ambassador to USSR Counselor of the Department, Department of State; Arthur A. Hartman, Assistant Secretary for European Affairs, Department of State; Winston Lord, Director, Policy Planning Staff, Department of State; William G. Hyland, Director, Bureau of Intelligence and

---

[A] Source: State Department Freedom of Information release; copy at National Security Archive (hereinafter referred to as NSA).

Research, Department of State; A. Denis Clift, Senior Staff Member, National Security Council

TIME AND DATE: Thursday, October 24, 1974 11:00 A.M.-2:00 P.M."

PLACE: Old Politburo Room, Council of Ministers Building The Kremlin, Moscow, USSR

SUBJECT: Secretary Kissinger's Visit to USSR, October 1974

Introductory Remarks

Kissinger: (Shaking Brezhnev's hand) You're looking well.

Brezhnev: I keep getting younger. You know, when you get as old as I am, it becomes natural. I see that you have placed Ambassador Walter Stoessel to your left (seated at table).

Kissinger: That's true.

Brezhnev: You know, we would never criticize your Ambassador. He is highly respected.

Kissinger: We're seated this way because I am to the left of Sonnenfeldt.

Brezhnev: Ah, everyone in a position of advantage.

Kissinger: I've told the Ambassador that he is the first one whom we tell everything.[20]

Brezhnev: How does he know? We tell him everything.

Gromyko: We tell him everything until there is no more to tell him.

Kissinger: That I'm sure of.

Brezhnev: How is Mrs. Kissinger?

Kissinger: She is fine, and she very much appreciates your hospitality.

Brezhnev: The first thing that came to my mind when I got up and looked out the window this morning was that the weather is so bad. I thought: This will spoil Mrs. Kissinger's sightseeing. The second thought was a pleasant one: This time, too, Dr. Kissinger won't get to Leningrad (laughter).

Kissinger: At least I will know now that Leningrad exists. But this will make me even unhappier.

Brezhnev: Maybe on your next visit I'll take your wife around Moscow, and you'll go to Leningrad.

Kissinger: You will negotiate with my wife?

Brezhnev: I am sure she would be easier to negotiate with than you are.

Kissinger: I saw what you told Secretary [of the Treasury William] Simon about me.

Brezhnev: That was a good discussion; I liked him.

Kissinger: Yes, he's a nice man, but you told him I don't make concessions.

Brezhnev: Dr. Kissinger, you are starting out our conversation by saying what isn't true! I did say what I thought of you to Secretary Simon and Mr. Kendall . . .

Kissinger: I know, it was very friendly.

Brezhnev: To both I said very positive things.

Kissinger: I appreciated it.

Brezhnev: It's no secret. I said what I did in the hope that it would be brought to the attention of your President. I am sure Secretary Simon and Mr. Kendall will bring it to his attention.

Kissinger: Your views were reported to the President, and I appreciated it very much.

Brezhnev: That makes me very pleased.

Kissinger: I was touched personally.

Brezhnev: You know, it wasn't said as a deliberate or pointed remark. The subject came up naturally.

Kissinger: I appreciated it very much, and they did report your remarks to the President.

General Review of Bilateral and International Issues

Brezhnev: We are today beginning our eighth meeting. May I first voice my satisfaction at this fact. Let me again say from the outset that, as in our other meetings, we have a very responsible mission—that is, to agree on various matters relating to further improvement in the relations between our countries in all fields.

I am deeply conscious of the great trust invested in me by our Central Committee and our Government in that I have been authorized to conduct these complex, difficult discussions with you. Our discussions have steadfastly served to advance relations between our countries. I trust you will appreciate that it is my intention to make every effort in that direction.

Of course, negotiations are negotiations. Each side is equally free, as in the past, to set out our points of view. The important thing is the results in negotiations. In the course of our talks there can be arguments and disputes. On the whole, our talks since 1972 have played a positive role—and continue to have such a role—in improving our relations. I would say in brief that, on the whole, relations between our two countries have developed in the spirit of the accords negotiated in the past few years.

Since our last meeting, there have been quite a few important events both in the United States and, indeed, in the world. I would like to start out by saying a few words on this. Then we can move on to easy subjects such as warheads and missiles and other bilateral matters.

Kissinger: The General Secretary taught me much about warheads during our meetings in March.

Brezhnev: You know, I'll think I'll tell you something about them, that you don't know this time, again. In fact, some of these things I have learned from your experts.

Kissinger: I'm glad they're telling someone.

Brezhnev: I have nothing but words of gratitude for them. Well, what I would like to say first is that from our very first meeting and until today, I believe that the U.S. side has no grounds to reproach us for any lacking in good faith to fulfill our obligations. And this is something I relate not only to our agreements but also to our general line of policy and the official statements made both by myself and my colleagues. We have never made any statements in any way interfering in internal U S. affairs. Even when there have been some complicated events, we have never exploited them.

Kissinger: I wish I could say that the same was true on our side.

Brezhnev: For the time being, I have no reproaches to make, but if you are patient we will come to all of that in good time.

I wish to stress that in all of our official statements, our public statements, I have had several opportunities to emphasize to our Party and to our Government to follow the line of seeking improvements with the United States in all fields.

Naturally, this cannot involve such things as matters of ideology, but, in that line, we have even made references to and cited Lenin in discussing US–USSR relations. I emphasized this principle in my speeches to the German Democratic Republic, Alma Ata and Kishinev, and in other statements I have made in the past period.[21] I also emphasized this point in my remarks to the US–USSR Trade and Economic Council. Our aim is the achieving of a steadfast improvement in relations. This is something you can see in our public statements and in our press, although the press does criticize certain aspects of your policy. Of course there have been on our part certain critical remarks, not on domestic matters but on questions of international policy.

Everytime I have met with you I have understood our meetings to mean that I am meeting with the official representative of the United States Government—whether you were in the position you held or in the position you now hold. I saw our meetings as discussions between two States.

Most Favored Nation Treatment

Brezhnev: And now, Dr. Kissinger, I would like to turn to certain matters, features to which our attention cannot fail to be attracted.

Now I do not know wherein lie the reasons for the United States' failing to live up to its obligations and agreed positions. I don't know how you will explain this, but I would like to say we have been concerned and we have been put on our guard by several factors. While we have followed the course of improved relations, the United States has taken actions not following that line.

I would like to start by mentioning the first fact, a fact on which we had agreement between the two sides. Proceeding from a reciprocal desire to improve relations between our two countries in all spheres and from the principle of equality between the two sides, we reached agreement sometime ago that the Soviet Union was to be accorded Most Favored Nation treatment. And, in return, we agreed to repay the Lend-Lease debts.[22] Everything was agreed and crystal clear two and one-half years ago. Yet we do not see any part of that agreement fulfilled. Several days ago, I read that the United States had decided to accord MFN to several countries including China. But, regarding the Soviet Union, MFN would be accorded only as a special favor and only for 18 months. Let me say frankly that we cannot accept that "gift" (hits table with hand). We see it as a discriminatory practice that we cannot agree to. I wish to emphasize that!

Middle East

Brezhnev: That is the first question. Now, there is another fundamental issue that I also wish to mention. You will recall . . .

Kissinger: (As [Viktor] Sukhodrev begins translation). I've already got the interpretation, and I don't want to hear it.

Brezhnev: Sonnenfeldt, don't divert his attention. You will recall Dr. Kissinger the conversation we had at San Clemente on the Middle East — not the details, just the gist. At that time, maybe I was tactless in being as insistent as I was — as the guest — but I felt I had to stress the dangers of the situation. I said that there could be no peace in the Middle East without a genuine settlement of the problem.[23] Now, as a politician I suppose I should have been happy to receive subsequent confirmation from your side that I was right. But, that didn't make a settlement any easier.

We felt that through the United Nations framework that had been developed, we had achieved an understanding on an approach that could settle the Middle East problem with due respect for the legitimate rights of all states in the region, including the rights of Israel.

The situation took a different turn. You began your travels. You played upon countries to disunite them. I believe you have now convinced yourself that nothing will come from such attempts. Your side violated an understanding on an agreement in that region.

Grain Sales

Brezhnev: Now, turning to a third fact—one that is virtually unprecedented—that of our purchases of grain in the United States.[24] We had signed contracts when your President announced that he was nullifying the contracts. This is difficult to conceive of, but even more so when both sides want improved relations. Even then we gave a positive reply. We displayed patience; we pretended it was unimportant. We proceeded from the desire not to complicate the situation for the President but to help him.

Facilitation of Business

Brezhnev: Finally, we are doing our best to assist U.S. businessmen in the Soviet Union. We are allowing them to make the visits they want, to meet the people they want, and we are facilitating the signing of contracts. Much has been done. We have a trade turnover of some $1 billion dollars. But, we have noticed of late that our business representatives, who used to be accorded cordial treatment in the United States, have not been allowed to visit open engineering plants—plants that have nothing to do with war production. All of this cannot help but influence our thinking about the direction that U.S. policy is taking toward the Soviet Union.

Soviet Emigration/Soviet Jewry

Brezhnev: And now, a few other matters. I am not alone in observing the progress that has occurred in US–USSR relations. Our Party and our people follow these events. (Brezhnev puts on glasses and reads document.) Here we have an exchange of letters between Senator Jackson and you. These letters are written in clever diplomatic terms, but the undertones are that the Soviet Union has given an undertaking concerning the departure from the USSR of Soviet citizens of Jewish origin—a figure of 60,000! You know that the Soviet

Union has not given an obligation in terms of numbers. We have said we would not erect barriers; we are not. (Brezhnev reads document, then holds it up to Secretary Kissinger across table.) I have official proof on this from our Minister of Internal Affairs. This is as of this October. Even if I were to allow all who want to leave, I see that only 14,000 want to go. This document also says that there are 1,815 applications pending. Even if I were to add those figures, I still get 15,000 whereas Jackson cites 60,000. Where am I to get those applicants? I will have a copy of this given to you—the latest official figures regarding emigration. The import of this is that Jackson has won a great victory over the White House and that he has managed to extract certain concessions from the Soviet Union.

Now, I want to return for a moment to the MFN question.

Kissinger: (As Sukhodrev begins translation.) What burns me up is that a lot of what the General Secretary has said is true.

Brezhnev: Dr. Kissinger, you must know me well now after eight meetings. I never take things out of thin air; what I have said has substantial grounds. And also, what I have said makes me think that the United States is not doing all it can to improve relations. We do see difficulties of a domestic character on the U.S. side. That is why we disregard minor issues. However, there are some issues which by their nature affect relations between states. This is an occasion when one state talks to another state.

Returning to MFN, there are some groups and individuals in the United States who pretend that we are begging for MFN as some kind of special concession that we can't get by without. Of course, we can both note the increase in trade that has been of benefit for both sides—an increase of $1 billion with contracts for several billion dollars signed. It is very doubtful that a U.S. business man would sign a contract that is not to his advantage. I would go on to say that we have broad, long-term economic relations with the Europeans and with Japan. With them we have dozens more contracts than with the United States. This is a factor to be taken into account. I would emphasize that interests of the United States and of U.S. businessmen in business relations with the USSR.

Returning to the Middle East, the method you have chosen can only in the final analysis confuse matters, cause them to be more complicated than they were before the October war. At one stage what you were doing seemed not too bad. But now when you analyze Arab interests, you have to conclude that there can be a new flare-up, worse than October. We believe that only through the understanding we reached earlier can we bring our influence to bear and work to bring peace. In the past, this proved true in Vietnam. The situation there is still complicated, but there is no war. I could show you official documents from the Vietnamese saying that they won't violate the Paris Accords. If we did it in Vietnam, we can do it in the Middle East.

CSCE

Brezhnev: One last matter affecting us is that of the All European Conference. If you have any reproaches regarding our position I'm sure you will make them. There are no hidden dangers in the USSR position, no one-sided advantages. The Conference must serve the interests of all the participants. But, how is the United States acting?

I don't want to criticize your President, but, in practice, we don't feel that at Geneva the United States is acting vigorously with the Soviet Union to bring the Conference to a successful conclusion. I am sure that if the United States and the President wanted to act, agreement would be achieved rapidly. The United States and Soviet Union would not be showing hegemony, but would be safeguarding peace in Europe. If the United States took a stand, your friends would act. Now we have new delays, another interval. Then they will say it is too cold, then too hot. It is being dragged out. We feel the United States is far too passive. In words, the United States says it wants to act. At the conference, the United States sits in silence. France takes one position. The FRG [Federal Republic of Germany] has its position. We think the United States should take a resolute position. The Netherlands, Turkey and others are dragging it out. But, when questions regarding our territory to the Urals are raised, then European Security is really not the subject.[25]

Please excuse me for discussing these questions and leaving easy matters such as nuclear issues, but all that I have raised here has an important bearing on confidence between the two countries. It has not all been negative. Some of your statements we have valued. Your statement to the Congress and your statements to newsmen, those we have valued highly indeed.

Dr. Kissinger, I must ask your forgiveness for starting out with all these questions. I got carried away. I forgot to ask you to give our very best regards and respects to the President and to express my appreciation for the fact that in the first day of his Administration he sent me a message expressing his desire to continue the improvement in our relations. I sent him a reply at the time of Foreign Minister Gromyko's visit to the United States. Please put these remarks at the first place in our conversation.

Kissinger: I thought the General Secretary was going to say that after these introductory remarks he would move into substance.

Brezhnev: We can do that after lunch.

Kissinger: Mr. General Secretary, first of all . . .

Brezhnev: Really, Dr. Kissinger, there have been some major events. Every month there have been new events that we cannot disregard. And, I do not regard as ordinary, run-of-the-mill events what has happened inside the United States. Whether we want it to or not, all of this affects our relations. These problems depend on the position each side takes.

I have no need to describe the events in this country. Things are very normal. We regularly publish figures regarding our economic affairs. We are now developing final figures for the fifth Five Year Plan for 1975. We have discussed this plan and had a meeting of the Council of Ministers which I attended and addressed. In some fields there are, perhaps, certain hitches. Everyone wants to be allocated as much money as possible. Some have over-fulfilled the plan, and, of course, we don't punish them for that. At the close of the Five Year Plan, we will have a Party Congress, at the end of 1975 or in 1976—we haven't decided. During our Congresses we review not only foreign policy but also domestic affairs.

In short, if I were graphically to portray the basic trends—and Ambassador Stoessel can bear me out—the line would be an upward one. We would prefer an even steeper upward line, but the trend of the line will without question be upward. And, as we develop economically, we are broadening and expanding our economic and commercial relations with a number of nations.

On October 15, it was ten years since I was vested with the great trust of our Party and became the head of the Central Committee of the Party. I received thousands of congratulatory letters and messages, but that is not what I wish to emphasize. And, in this 10 years—a little more than 10 years—we have had no rise in retail prices in such staples as bread, butter, sugar, rice and other staples. Not by one Kopek has there been any rise in rent, and this is something we take pride in. I say this not in any way to contrast the situation in this country with other facts . . .

Kissinger: There has not been one cent of increase in my salary during the same period.

Brezhnev: That is bad! How severely they are exploiting you. Dr. Kissinger, I have to complain that in these 10 years my salary hasn't increased one Kopek. They are all exploiters.

Kissinger: Dobrynin or Gromyko?

Brezhnev: Dobrynin is a nice man.

Kissinger: Gromyko is always at his country house.

Brezhnev: We should lower Kissinger's and Gromyko's salaries.

Gromyko: Dr. Kissinger's point was misunderstood.

Secretary Kissinger's Response to Points Raised.

Kissinger: Mr. General Secretary, I appreciate the frankness of your presentation. When I arrived at the airport yesterday I said I was coming here to meet friends. In the 7 or 8 times I have been here there has developed a relationship of confidence that enables us to speak frankly.

Secondly, I had intended to congratulate the General Secretary on the October 15 anniversary.

Brezhnev: Thank you.

Kissinger: I believe the General Secretary will go down in history as someone who has done much for his people and for the peace of the world. I want to say that while we have spirited debates, we know his commitment to peace and to improved US–USSR relations.

Brezhnev: Let me interrupt to say that you need have no doubts in that regard. I still have some more life — at least 20 years — and throughout I will be steadfast.

Kissinger: I was going to say that when we meet on his 20th Anniversary he will have even greater accomplishments.

Brezhnev: I agree. Then we will not drink tea but cognac.

Kissinger: I have been asked by President Ford to convey his warm regards . . .

Brezhnev: Thank you.

Kissinger: He is firmly committed to the continuation of the policies already established. He is looking forward to meeting you in Vladivostok.

Brezhnev: I am looking forward to it also.

Kissinger: I think your Ambassador will already have given you his own judgment. But in terms of personalities, I believe a constructive personal relationship can be developed.

I am sure that by the time you visit the United States next summer, Mr. General Secretary, many of the problems you have mentioned will have been substantially overcome. At any rate, a cardinal principle of the foreign policy of the Ford Administration is that we want to make relations between the United States and Soviet Union irreversible. And, when we have difficulties and occasional disagreements, we should keep in mind that since 1972 we also have made enormous achievements.

Now, before returning to the specifics of your points, I want to thank you for receiving me when you have another visitor from abroad. I know that this adds to the difficulties of your calendar. It is a courtesy we appreciate very much.

With regard to your remarks, Mr. General Secretary, let me group my answers in two categories—those issues that more or less result from the American domestic situation and those issues which more or less reflect the international situation.

In the first category, I place MFN, grain, visits to factories and Senator Jackson. If you can make Senator Jackson a foreign problem for me I would be delighted. (laughter) We would be glad to arrange for his emigration without reciprocity, as a unilateral concession to any country. If he comes here you can keep him on national security grounds without problem.

I do not doubt, Mr. General Secretary, that your Ambassador has given you a good description of the U.S. domestic situation. And, of course, it is also clear that the U.S. domestic situation is not what the foreign policy of the Soviet Union can be based on. It is also true that the Soviet Unions has shown extraordinary restraint in commenting on the U.S. domestic situation. I should like to say a few words so that the General Secretary can understand the context of the actions taken.

First, I was, as you know, a close collaborator of President Nixon. I believe, as I have said publicly, history will treat President Nixon more kindly than have his contemporaries. It is true, for whatever reason, that the last phase of his Presidency created so many tensions that in the U.S. Congress much of this is only becoming evident today. The Congress is traditionally controlled by the personal popularity of the President. This balance wheel was removed during the last year. Therefore, it was difficult. Many things have been done by the Congress in the last months that would never have been possible in a normal Presidency.

Brezhnev: That we have noticed.

Kissinger: I say this not to change the facts but to help in understanding. When the new President came in, he was immediately caught up in an election campaign for the new Congress. But, I want to tell the General Secretary the following. I think, as you will see for yourself, my personal relationship with the new President is at least as close as that with his predecessor. You will judge that yourself. We are both determined as soon as the election is over to have a showdown with the Congress on who controls foreign policy.

Brezhnev: That will be this fall?

Kissinger: It will really begin after the meeting in Vladivostok, really in January 1975. There is no sense in fighting with the old Congress. The old Congress comes back November 18 for two to three weeks. We will get the Trade Bill from the old Congress. But, the fundamental issues will be fought in January.

In your assessment of the situation, bear in mind that the President until the election had to be a transition President. But he has already started on a much tougher set of speeches yesterday. It is important to understand that starting in January we will be going back to 1972 conditions instead of the conditions you saw in 1973–74.

That is why your meeting in Vladivostok is of importance.

Now, let me speak of the domestic issues you raised—in increasing order of importance. For example, visits to factories by Soviet personnel. I consider a universal law unaffected by ideology the stupidity of bureaucracy. While you were talking, I was raising hell with my associates, left and right, and neither I nor they had ever heard of it. It certainly does not reflect a new national policy. I would suggest Mr. General Secretary that rather than spending time here we have the following understanding. Any visit to which either the General Secretary or the Soviet Government attaches importance, if the Ambassador calls me, and unless there are reasons such as looking at the warheads of our missiles, we will, of course, approve.

Brezhnev: There can certainly be no question of us wanting to look at warheads. Any such authorization would have to come from the Politburo and the Politburo would not approve, and, as the Foreign Minister says, it is not without danger to look at warheads.

Kissinger: That's true, At any rate, if there is any visit to which the Ambassador attaches importance you can be certain it will be arranged. And, if it is refused at a lower level, that refusal will not be final: I should add that our Agricultural Delegation complained that it could not see certain things during its recent visit—it's not one-sided.

Brezhnev: I don't know about it.

Kissinger: Let's leave it that if either side attaches importance, we will notify each other through our Ambassadors.

Brezhnev: I agree.

Kissinger: I assure you there has been no change in policy.

On the subject of grain purchases, I suppose Secretary Simon has explained what happened. We were confronted with a situation where, in the judgment of our people, if the contracts had been agreed to there would have been a sharp increase in prices. This would have led the Congress to impose export controls which would have meant no grain for the Soviet Union.

Brezhnev: I don't think we should spend time on this issue here. The fact is that from the press reports we know that the United States sold China 10 million tons and you sold to others. Why was it that there was no problem with regard to those countries but only with the Soviet Union? Perhaps it wasn't 10 million tons, five million, it doesn't matter. The crux of the matter is in the unprecedented nature of the action. To some countries you sell grain, with the Soviet Union you discriminate.

We have contracts, up to $2 billion in contracts with your companies. The question in our mind is: If the President vetoes the grain deal, then, perhaps, he will veto others of these contracts. That is what is important, not the precise tonnage of wheat or corn. We ship grain to Poland, the GDR, Bulgaria, one million tons here, 600 thousand there. The point is that this is unilateral discrimination.

Kissinger: In the field of grain I don't want a debate. One of the useful roles I can perform is to help us understand motivations.

Brezhnev: Dr. Kissinger, you will recall we took a calm attitude; we gave a calm and quiet reply.

Kissinger: We appreciate this, and the General Secretary will know from the Ambassador that I made a public statement saying that the fault lay with the United States and not with the Soviet Union.

[Kissinger proposes joint consultations on Soviet grain requirements so that "sudden" orders do not disturb price levels. Brezhnev explained the Soviets' inability to provide figures because they have not yet determined the agricultural budget under the Five Year Plan; moreover, compilation of figures for the current year grain harvest is not yet complete. Kissinger suggests further discussion at Vladivostok on a more definitive solution.]

Brezhnev: Not to continue this discussion, but I just remember that the United States sold several million tons to Iran.

Kissinger: Let me tell you that an order was placed for 400,000 tons at the time of your order. We stopped that order together with yours.

Brezhnev: I was talking about general background sales to Iran and China while the Soviet order was vetoed.

Kissinger: No, no. We vetoed all foreign orders. We reduced Iran's order to 200,000 tons. You're getting 2.2 million tons.

Dobrynin: It is a small country.

Kissinger: But an ally.

Most Favored Nation Treatment

Kissinger: Our attitude on détente was stated in my statement to the Congress. Secondly, it is true that as part of the general Congressional difficulties, the opponents of US–USSR relations have organized very active opposition.

On MFN, it was in this room, or a similar room, that we agreed on MFN and Lend-Lease together in 1972. I had never heard of the Jackson Amendment: at the time. Nor had I ever mentioned Jewish emigration. I have stated publicly on numerous occasions that we have a moral obligation on these issues quite independent of any other consideration. And, almost anything Senator Jackson does to the Soviet Union he has done to me. He doesn't only claim he has defeated the Soviet Union; he claims he has defeated me.

What happened last Friday was a trick of Jackson's. We didn't know what he would do when he stepped on the White House press podium.[26] That doesn't make us look good, but I can assure you we won't get tricked twice.

On the substance of the matter, Soviet officials never said anything to us other than what you have said today. You have said, Mr. General Secretary, and your Foreign Minister has repeated numerous times, that no obstacles would be placed in the way of those seeking either applications or visas.

Gromyko: Except on grounds of national security.

Kissinger: Exactly correct. You have consistently refused to give a specific figure. In the letter I wrote Senator Jackson, no figure was used. My letter said what is true, that visas would be issued in relation to applications received. Jackson then said that this meant 60,000. The White House issued a statement on Monday, which I do not know whether you have seen, in which we stated specifically that the Soviet Union had never given us figures, that all the Soviet Union had done was to give us the principle for applications and visas. We said that we are not bound by the Jackson figure, that we would only take it under consideration. The Administration, under extremely difficult circumstances, attempted to fulfill a promise to the Soviet Union, and I regret the behavior of Senator Jackson. I want to assure you on behalf of the Administration that the figure of 60,000 is not our figure, nor do we consider it your figure. All you have told us is that no obstacles would be placed in the way of applications or visas, except national security.

Brezhnev: And that we are fulfilling scrupulously.

Gromyko: But, generally, the formula used by the White House in saying it takes into consideration the Jackson figure gives grounds for a one-sided interpretation of the Jackson figure.

Kissinger: No, no. Jackson said that the Congress would apply certain standards. We said that we would take that into consideration

Gromyko: All you have said is in the statement, but it does give grounds for interpretation. I have just read it.

Kissinger: I want to make clear that as far as the Administration is concerned our understanding is that no obstacles will be placed in the way of either applications or visas, except for security, and I repeat that as far as the Administration is concerned, the only thing that governs visas is the number of applications. That has been our understanding. The Administration has no other position. If there are no other interferences, the Administration has no right to any objections.

Brezhnev: There is also reference in the letter to harassment involving the applicant and his job.

Kissinger: I was told this by your Foreign Minister.

Gromyko: There is no harassment.

Kissinger: I didn't say there is harassment.

Gromyko: I deny having said it.

Dobrynin: But there is still the implication in the letter.

Kissinger: The intention of the Administration was to state those things we had been told in order to make MFN possible. There is a mistake that I made, in retrospect. I have believed and have said publicly that it was a mistake for the United States to involve itself in an internal Soviet issue.

I never briefed the press on our discussions. If I had it would have been apparent that he yielded to your point of view, not vice versa. We told him that if necessary he could refer to the letter in the Senate, but not release it at the White House. His manner is as humiliating for me as it is for you (hits table with hand). The press is saying that Kissinger has been defeated by Jackson. I'm as angry as you are. (Secretary Kissinger leaves the room for three minutes.)

Gromyko: Should we continue after lunch, at 5:30 P.M.?

Kissinger: You're saying that you're ending this discussion in the middle of my most eloquent speech?

Brezhnev: I have just been handed a most sensational document. At last I can expose Dr. Kissinger.

(Sukhodrev read the text of a communiqué on "businesslike and constructive" U.S. – Soviet talks).

Kissinger: Front pages of newspapers all over the world will have to be redone.

Brezhnev: Yes.

[They discuss the details of the communiqué and plans for the announcement of the Vladivostok summit.]

Kissinger: Mr. General Secretary, on a personal basis, I believe this meeting between you and President Ford will be very important. You will have a longer meeting next summer, but it can affect events in the interim. Perhaps we can have a few words on how to do it so that it is most successful. You can count on me to do everything toward this end.

The President is going with good will. His methods are different than his predecessors, as your Ambassador will have told you.

Brezhnev: I am as before.

Kissinger: You two will get along well. Don't you agree Anatol?

[Discussing summit arrangements, Brezhnev proposes that Soviet helicopters carry the U.S. and Soviet delegations from the airport to the meeting site outside of Vladivostok: "We guarantee absolute safety."]

Kissinger: I'm not worried, but our security people will raise hell and will insist on our helicopters.[27]

Brezhnev: You'll be welcome. I know your helicopters in the United States. If you could have seen the helicopter I used with Brandt. His face turned as white as this napkin. The only kind of helicopter they had was the kind that their police use. The whole thing was vibrating.

We will work it out.

Kissinger: As long as it doesn't land on Chinese territory.

Brezhnev: But I don't think your Secret Service could believe I want to lose my life in a helicopter crash!

Kissinger: We will work it out.

Brezhnev: You have a lunch to go to; you're late. Mr. Gromyko is a punctual man.

Gromyko: I have to be there first to receive the guests.

(Meeting ended at 2:00 P.M.)

[That evening, Kissinger and his party returned to the Kremlin for discussions on economic issues, the CSCE, and the Middle East while saving an "easy" topic, arms control, for the next day.[28] As they spoke about Jackson-Vanik and the latest threat to economic détente, a Senate proposal to limit sharply Export-Import Bank credits to the Soviet Union, Kissinger tried to assure Brezhnev that the administration would prevail in the domestic debate over U.S.–Soviet relations. Optimistically, Kissinger informed Brezhnev that after the election, he would "provoke a confrontation" with forces critical of détente; they could "be defeated."

As he had in March, Brezhnev told Kissinger that he was "sick and tired" of the slow

CSCE talks, and he appealed for the United States to take a more active role in the negotiations.

Kissinger, however, was unwilling to support a more vigorous U.S. role in Geneva, but he did agree with Brezhnev that it was time to sound out the Germans and other U.S. allies to see if it would be possible to finish the CSCE by March. By early December, though, he was content to let the conference drag on for as long as Washington could avoid blame. "I wouldn't mind extending it beyond the next extension," he said, because a delay will restrain Soviet conduct: "They may not want to blow up the Middle East before the European Security Conference." The conference continued into the summer; discussions took months to conclude.[29]

Kissinger's and Brezhnev's discussion of the Middle East situation that evening would generate some fascinating exchanges, for example, the following excerpt on how much foreknowledge the Soviets had of the Egyptian attack on Israel in October 1973.]

Kissinger: I agree. I agree the situation is dangerous. And I've told the General Secretary that his analysis in San Clemente (in 1973) was more correct than ours.

Brezhnev: On my honor, I did not at that time know there was going to be a new war on that date. I had no discussion with the Arabs, either at that time or any other time, up to the beginning of the October War. I simply saw the situation developing.

Kissinger: I personally believe it, though there are many in America who do not.

Brezhnev: You certainly have my word.

Kissinger: No, I believe it. And I've had our intelligence people do an analysis of all the information we can piece together, and I believe it.

Brezhnev: Nothing. Nothing.

Kissinger: We think you knew about three days before.

Brezhnev: Even less than that. We were simply notified, at such a time and in such a form that we were absolutely deprived of any possibility of doing anything about it. . . .[30]

Kissinger: My honest belief is that until San Clemente you attempted to restrain the Arabs. After San Clemente you made no further effort to restrain them, but you did not particularly know they were going to attack. You even mildly encouraged them, but without specific knowledge they were going to attack.

Brezhnev: I deny even a mild form of encouragement. You know the events that occurred. Sadat by his own volition asked us to withdraw our military advisers.[31] And we did it without a word. And that was a political action.

Kissinger: That we didn't know about. . . .

[Their talk on the Middle East crisis does not prompt any concessions from Kissinger on reopening the Geneva talks, despite Brezhnev's warning that the region was a "powderkeg." Kissinger is far from candid when he told the Soviets that "whatever we have done has not had any intention of hurting the Soviet Union." He cannot reveal to Brezhnev his basic axiom of Middle East diplomacy, what he had told Deng Xiaoping the preceding April: "If we are successful in these disengagement talks, we can hope to reduce Soviet influence in Syria, as we did in Egypt."

The talks on 24 October close with Brezhnev voicing his distress over recent U.S. statements about a need for the strongest possible defense posture. In this excerpt, Brezhnev poses some troubling questions.]

Brezhnev: . . . do you believe or admit of the possibility of atomic war between our two nations? Or the possibility of atomic war anywhere in the world, for instance in Europe or elsewhere? Hearing my question, you would be entitled to ask me my view. On that thought, I wish you pleasant dreams.
Kissinger: Without hearing my answer?
Brezhnev: No, not today.
Kissinger: But now suspense will make you very sleepless.
Brezhnev: No, I'll sleep.
Kissinger: I'll answer tomorrow. I'll ask Sonnenfeldt.
Sonnenfeldt: Now I can't sleep!

COMMENTARY

The transcripts from the next day of discussions—about the possibility of nuclear war, as well as SALT II negotiations—remain classified.[32] Nonetheless, certain developments could only heighten Brezhnev's concern about U.S. nuclear policy. Publicly announced changes in U.S. nuclear targeting policy ("Schlesinger Doctrine"), for example, were intended to grant the President more nuclear attack options in event of war. Moreover, in June 1974, the Senate had supported the administration's request for funding to support improvements in ICBM accuracy for better capability to strike Soviet ICBM silos and command posts. It is possible that the Soviets learned of Kissinger's musings at NATO meetings over the advantage of "relative" nuclear superiority.[33]

The transcript of Kissinger's and Brezhnev's final round on SALT, however, has been declassified. It shows Brezhnev and the Soviets reaching agreement on Kissinger's latest proposal for equal aggregates of 2,200 strategic delivery vehicles and limitations on the number of MIRVed missiles, a bow to Senator Jackson's emphasis on equality. While it would enable the United States to preserve temporarily its lead in MIRVs, the high threshold for equal aggregates would appeal to Brezhnev because it did not require large cuts in Soviet forces.[34]

Before Brezhnev discussed SALT with Kissinger during the evening of 26 October, he had secured the Politburo's approval of equal aggregates. He had also met privately with Kissinger and Sonnenfeldt to rehash Soviet proposals for a nuclear nonaggression pact; during the talk Brezhnev played with a model cannon which finally went off with a "loud bang." They then discussed SALT with a larger group and Brezhnev suggested a deiling of 2,400 launchers by 1985, a number that was close enough to Kissinger's 2,200 to be acceptable.[35]

THE WHITE HOUSE
TOP SECRET/SENSITIVE/EXCLUSIVELY EYES ONLY
MEMORANDUM OF CONVERSATION
PARTICIPANTS: Leonid L Brezhnev, General Secretary and Member of the Politburo, CPSU Central Committee; Andrey A. Gromyko, Minister of Foreign Affairs; Member CPSU Politburo; Anatoly Dobrynin, USSR Ambassador to United States; Andrey M. Aleksandrov-Agentav, Aide to General Secretary Brezhnev; Georgiy M. Koriyenko, Chief, USA Department, Ministry of Foreign Affairs; Viktor M. Sukhodrev, Second European Department, Ministry of Foreign Affairs (Interpreter); Oleg Sokolov, USA Department, Ministry of Foreign Affairs; Henry A. Kissinger, Secretary of State and Assistant to the President for National Security Affairs; Walter J. Stoessel, Jr., U.S. Ambassador to USSR; Helmut Sonnenfeldt Counselor of the Department, Department of State; Arthur A. Hartman, Assistant Secretary for European Affairs, Department of State; William G. Hyland, Director, Bureau of Intelligence and Research, Department of State; Jan M. Lodal, Senior Staff Member, National Security Council; A. Denis Clift, Senior Staff Member, National Security Council
TIME AND DATE: October 26, 1974 7:10 P.M.–10:20 P.M.
PLACE: Old Politburo Room The Kremlin, Moscow[B]

[B] Source: Gerald Ford Library, Trip Briefing Books and Cables — Ford, Nov. 1974, Japan, Korea, and General.

(The meeting began at 7:10 P.M. following a 4:30–7:00 P.M. meeting in General Secretary Brezhnev's office involving Brezhnev, Gromyko and Sukhodrev on the Soviet side and Kissinger and Sonnenfeldt on the U.S. side.)

Brezhnev: Our colleagues don't know what we decided on. I want to review it. Tomorrow morning, we're leaving for Zavidovo for a hunting trip. It was Sonnenfeldt's idea. Dr. Kissinger agreed; I was very pleased. I certainly wouldn't mind if all the others present joined us.

Well, unfortunately because of other matters, we weren't able to meet this morning, but we didn't lose too much time. Since the basic objective of this meeting is to debate the principles which could form an agreement, we should talk about the principles. The details can be elaborated later, but not the major issues. So, if you agree, we can spend some time discussing those principles.

Kissinger: I agree.

Brezhnev: Do you have anything new to tell me for the U.S. side?

Kissinger: I have given you the substance of our position yesterday, Mr. General Secretary.

Brezhnev: No, I meant maybe something more interesting that may have happened in the United States. I haven't been able to follow events there.

Maybe Jackson's invented something new. Maybe you have something new by way of instructions.

Kissinger: Any instructions that Jackson sent me would have to be sent to our Secret Service first. They might explode.

Brezhnev: So, in short, there has been nothing new in the United States since our last meeting—anything new in Ethiopia, perhaps?

Kissinger: The Emperor is still alive and well.[36]

Brezhnev: You're a very humorous man.

Kissinger: The Emperor of Ethiopia makes the longest toasts of any man.

Brezhnev: I've met him, but I've never had the occasion to hear his toasts.

Kissinger: His private conversation is like his toasts. His speech is like King Faisal's.

Brezhnev: I haven't had the pleasure of listening to it.

Kissinger: Faisal or the Emperor?

Brezhnev: The Emperor.

Kissinger: I can tell you that King Faisal thinks that Moscow is run from Jerusalem.

Brezhnev: I liked the photo of you two.

Kissinger: He made an exception for me.

Brezhnev: See the privileges you enjoy!

Well, let's get down to the specifics we wanted to discuss. First, by way of summing up, from the political point of view we can state that both sides reaffirmed their determination to make every effort to improve relations between their countries in accordance with preview agreements, and to endeavor to make that progress irreversible. And, I feel that this is in line with the President's wishes.

And, secondly, as I see it, to those ends, both sides will do all they can not only to develop their bilateral relations but also in international matters to closely coordinate and maintain a parallel line with respect to the European Security Conference and the Middle East.

And, thirdly, we agree that the agreements signed in 1972 and 1973 retain full validity. The two sides underline their determination strictly to observe them, especially so far as the question of strategic arms is concerned, without allowing any violation of those agreements through the very end of their duration.

And fourthly, the two sides have agreed for the purpose of preventing the danger of thermonuclear war and in the interests of peace not only between the two countries but also the peace of the world, to prepare for signing next year a new agreement on strategic arms to run until 1985. The following basic principles should underline that new agreement. Each side should by the termination of the duration of the new agreement—i. e., by the end of 1985— have an equal quantity of strategic arms vehicles, that number to be 2,200 (corrects himself) that number to be 2,400 strategic arms vehicles.

The Soviet Union, considering the geographic and other factors, will be entitled to carry out its program of vehicles to a limit of 2,400 strategic vehicles, choosing at our discretion where those vehicles are to be placed—that is, land-based, sea-based or placed on bombers.

Within the same period, the United States will fulfill its program or plans de facto of 2,200 strategic arms vehicles with the same right of choice as to how they are to be distributed, but with the understanding that by the end of 1985 the total quantity of strategic arena vehicles on each aide should be equal.

The United States and the Soviet Union agree that the total quantity of MIRVs should be equal by the end of 1985 and amount to 1,320 on each side.

Each side undertakes in this period to act in accordance with previously concluded agreements and not to violate previous agreements on either side including new strategic arms vehicles. But both sides shall be entitled in accordance with previous agreements to carry out modernization and improvement of existing land-based ICBMs as provided for in the agreement of 1972.

Brezhnev: Do you understand this, Sonnenfeldt?

Kissinger: We understand. We are awed by your ability to do it without paper in front of you.

Brezhnev: Well, everything is so clear, one doesn't need any paper.

Kissinger: I'm impressed.

Brezhnev: After the end of the duration of the previous accord—that is, after 1977—the United States will be entitled up to the end of 1985 to build other, more modern submarines of the Trident class to the amount of 10 such submarines. The Soviet Union in the same period of time will also be entitled to build 10 modernized submarines of the Typhoon class.[37] The number of missiles on these submarines on each side should be part of the total quantity of strategic arms vehicles provided for in the agreement.

The United States will build its B-1 bombers carrying missiles with a range of not more than 3,000 kilometers. The total number of missiles of these bombers will be determined by the United States, but also will be part of the total number to be included by the end of 1985. The Soviet Union will be entitled to take a decision at its own discretion as to whether to build a strategic bomber capable of carrying nuclear weapons vehicles, or instead to deploy such vehicles on land or in submarines. The proportion of these numbers may be subject to additional understandings which, for example, in substance means that if one aircraft can carry 20 missiles this does not mean that if they are not used on planes they must be replaced by the same number of land-based launchers—for example, there may be 15 or less.

The two sides have agreed that the total number of missile-armed vehicles should be equal on both sides but with due account taken of the third country vehicles of such countries as are allied with the United States by the end of 1985.

The aforesaid has been initialed by Kissinger and Gromyko to be subsequently signed by President Ford and General Secretary Brezhnev.

(At the conclusion of Brezhnev's presentation in Russian, the following dialogue took place—prior to Sukhodrev's translation.)

Brezhnev: After you have heard this, we can ask for some cognac to be brought in and some hot frankfurters and have a drink. It's worth drinking; I have forwarded such a mutually worthy agreement.

Kissinger: Mr. General Secretary, without having heard the translation, my colleagues and I are extremely impressed over the way you have all the elements of such a position in your head. We would have to draw diagrams.

Brezhnev: This is easy. There are more complicated things.

Kissinger: Before I have heard the translation . . .

Brezhnev: I don't think we should argue about one rocket here, 17 there, where the cement dries quicker—yours doesn't seem to dry at all. However, I am sure your concrete is quite dry by now. I'm sure it won't rain while you install new missiles.

Kissinger: Dobrynin, who reads our Defense Budget, knows we are not putting new missiles in silos.

Brezhnev: Pity poor Comrade Dobrynin having to write reports about Comrade Kissinger having a net over his house. What's the matter; is your roof leaking?[38]

Kissinger: Will you translate, or should I sign it in Russian?

Brezhnev: Let's do that! (He offers Secretary Kissinger a pen.)

(Sukhodrev then translates Brezhnev's SALT proposal, as set forth in the paragraphs above.)

Brezhnev: We can say the aides have agreed to be guided by the aforesaid principles in their further working negotiations on this issue.

Kissinger: Let me first ask a few questions.

Brezhnev: Please.

Kissinger: First, this is a serious proposal which gives us a base for discussion, and obviously serious work has been done which also tries to understand our point of view. There are aspects which give us difficulties. But, it gives us a framework in which to talk.

[Kissinger's asks about the aggregates, and Brezhnev confirms that the forces of neither side would exceed them during the 1977–85 period. Kissinger repeats his question whether the United States would ever have more than 2,200 launchers under the agreement.]

Brezhnev: Well, do you want to ask me all your questions first, making it easier? Otherwise, you'll start undressing me article by article.

(Brezhnev gestures as if stripping off his clothes.)

Kissinger: No, no. I'm not debating.

[Kissinger repeats his question about exceeding the aggregates and asks if it would be possible for the United States to modernize SLBMs other than those deployed on the 10 Trident submarines. Although Brezhnev has said that Moscow will also deploy a new SLBM—the Typhoon—both sides would scrap their old submarines. He tells a puzzled Kissinger that they could not be replaced with new ones because they were "morally obsolete."]

Kissinger: As I understand it, each aide is free to compose a force up to 2,400.

Brezhnev: Yes.

Kissinger: But, if you can't build new silos and if you can't replace old submarines, you have not got a choice. I am not arguing; I am trying to understand.

Brezhnev: Dr. Kissinger . . .

Kissinger: I'm not debating; I am trying to understand.

Brezhnev: To be absolutely frank, let me explain why we want our total number at 2,400 and yours at 2,200. You will realize that unless we set those levels we will have to scrap a certain number of our land-based missiles.

Kissinger: I understand that.

Brezhnev: That's all there is to it.

Kissinger: I understand . . .

Brezhnev: So there will be factual equality even if it will appear on paper that we have more than you do. That's the mechanism. There it is laid bare before you.

Kissinger: One other question: I don't understand this business of missiles on bombers. Would you count any missile? Supposing there is a missile with a range of 100 kilometers, does that count too?

Brezhnev: Well . . . (Brezhnev confers with Gromyko and Korniyenko.) Well, Dr. Kissinger, in our previous agreement there was no mention of bombers. So when I mention bombers today I did not mean old types of bombers; I was referring to nuclear missile–carrying bombers.

Kissinger: In other words the B-1?

Dobrynin: The B-1 type. Now you don't have a B-1 type with nuclear missiles.

Kissinger: You won't count B-52s in this program?

Brezhnev: Generally speaking that is one point we should give additional thought to. (He again confers with Gromyko, Korniyenko and Dobrynin.) So, since it is a new matter not covered in the previous agreement, we need not elaborate right now.

Who knows, maybe as we go into the program further you might want to scrap your program and we might not go ahead with our program.

Kissinger: I understand. Let me . . .

Brezhnev: Because, I guess that one of the reasons why under the previous agreement we were given a certain advantage in the number of missiles was because you had an advantage in bombers.[39]

Kissinger: That's correct. I understand. May I have an answer to my first question?
Brezhnev: You have no further questions?
Kissinger: I have questions for technicians, but no other questions worthy of your attention.
Brezhnev: There are no questions in your mind about MIRVs?
Kissinger: We have noticed that you have said nothing about heavy missiles.
Brezhnev: They shouldn't be mentioned.
Kissinger: That is something we can negotiate.
Brezhnev: I don't think we should end our discussions as to the number of 1,300. On your bombers, you may want to have MIRVed missiles. You may want one heavy instead of smaller ones. Let's consider it settled.
Kissinger: Don't assume that the things about which I ask no questions are agreed. I have to discuss them with my associates. It just means that I understand it. As I told you, there are many positive elements in your proposal.
Brezhnev: Well then, how do we end our work?
Kissinger: First, can we put your proposal in writing?
Brezhnev: Your associates have it in your notebooks.
Kissinger: That's an unreliable way of proceeding, but we can take it from our notebooks.
Gromyko: Well, you didn't give us any formal documents.
Kissinger: No, but we gave a written document to Dobrynin.
Gromyko: At some stage it can be done.
Kissinger: It just makes it harder for us to study, but we can put it together from our notes.
Brezhnev: Well, Dobrynin will have this as a working paper.
Kissinger: Good enough, a working document.
Brezhnev: He hasn't the right to alter a single word but he will have the . . . One question: How many missiles do you plan to put on the B-1s. I ask this out of curiosity, not subject to controls.
Kissinger: Yes, but you count them.
Brezhnev: Of course. What they are are airborne launchers. Come here. (Brezhnev gestures to Secretary Kissinger; they both rise and Brezhnev leads the way to a large wall map of the world. He points to the USA and the USSR.) They can enter either from your own territory or the territory of your allies.

You fly to a certain point and launch your missiles. They cover a certain part of the territory and thus they are airborne launchers.
Kissinger: But that is not the purpose of the B-1, because if so it wouldn't be

built as a supersonic bomber. If we wanted to shoot a missile with a range of 5,000 kilometers we would stay out here. (He points into an area in the vicinity of the United States.)

Brezhnev: That's exactly what I say, they are nothing but an airborne launcher. Another thing you can fly over the Pole like we can; that's a reply to your question.

Kissinger: I have to get to the hot dogs before Sonnenfeldt does.

Brezhnev: I have a question: Why fly at all?

Kissinger: You mean, why should we fly when we can launch a missile from the United States?

Brezhnev: Why build the B-1?

Kissinger: I have been asking our Generals that one for years.[40]

Brezhnev: That's why I say if you want it go ahead. That's why I said we will be entitled to build an equal number.

The other point to further confuse matters, what about installing rockets in the Arctic and covering them with snow?

Kissinger: We have a bomber which plays the national anthem of the country it is flying over.

(They both return to the table.)

Brezhnev: Dr. Kissinger, your question is really warranted. Yours question about us giving you a piece of paper with our position set out. I told you Comrade Dobrynin would have a piece of paper. I agree that at some point you will have such a paper.

Kissinger: It doesn't have to be signed. It would enable us to study your proposal.

Brezhnev: So, so, please don't understand me as having said there will be nothing in writing.

Kissinger: Would you answer the first question: At no time after 1977 will you have more than 2,400?

Brezhnev: Dr. Kissinger, by the end of 1985 the total number on each side will be the same. We will be equal. Throughout that period we will not have a number in excess of 2,400, but account will be taken of the missiles at the disposal of your allies.

Kissinger: How?

Brezhnev: In the total quantity of missiles.

Kissinger: On whose side?

Brezhnev: Both. Our allies have neither missiles or submarines capable of carrying nuclear arms.

Kissinger: The Chinese do.

Brezhnev: That changes things. If we have reached that point then let's have a drink, a toast. Sonnenfeldt! (Sonnenfeldt downs his drink.) That's an honest man; all the others have nets over their glasses. (To Hyland) Are you the guy who puts the nets over the missiles?[41]

Kissinger: What is the compensation for the missiles of the allies you're thinking about?

Brezhnev: There's no compensation; we will count them in the total number.

Kissinger: (laughs) On your side or on ours?

Brezhnev: Your side. Now, if and when Mr. Wilson comes to the Soviet Union and tells me Great Britain is going to join the Warsaw Treaty, then we will add his missiles.

Kissinger: Does that mean we are to deduct France and Great Britain from the 2,200 or is that deducted before?

Brezhnev: No, they are already incorporated in the 2,200.

Kissinger: I understand. My question is: Under those 2,200, can we have 2,200 U.S. systems or 2,200 minus the French and British?

Dobrynin: The 2,200 can all be American.

Brezhnev: We regard that as the total number of rockets aimed against us.

Kissinger: 2,200 minus the 64 British?

Brezhnev: Dr. Kissinger, we unfortunately don't have any ally we can either add or subtract.

Kissinger: I wonder by what theory you explain an advantage of 200, and then subtract the British force.

(A 25-minute recess.)

Brezhnev: This recess has deprived us of all of our pleasure. Let me make a correction as to numbers and in doing so reply to your questions as to what 2,200 means — that is, purely U.S. or not. By way of equalization, the 2,200 will be purely American missiles after the numbers have become equal.

Kissinger: I understand: 2,400 minus the U.K. force. Mr. General Secretary, may I make a suggestion. I believe we should proceed as follows. I will speak frankly, and I believe Dobrynin will confirm the correctness of what I say. If we put this proposal in its present form to our bureaucracy, it will lead into a process in a way most unfavorable to the Soviet Union — and not useful to the talks at Vladivostok. I propose that Ambassador Dobrynin is given a rough piece of paper when he comes to Washington and that we keep the discussion for the time being entirely in this channel. Because then we can refine many considerations. I think there are positive elements in your proposal that we can take seriously. There are some considerations that we have that you may take seriously. I would prefer to handle this in the channel until after the meeting in Vladivostok. I proposed that Dobrynin and I have a number of meetings in Washington about this—not to negotiate, but to clarify points. Then you and the President can talk in Vladivostok. And, I do this in order to prevent those people who are looking for difficulties to cause trouble because I believe there are many aspects here we can take very seriously. And, I will work on it only with my closest collaborators—all who are in this room. But, we will say you haven't given us a formal proposal; this is a sign that we are taking you seriously. Otherwise, we will have Senator Jackson. You know what will happen—he will hold hearings.

Brezhnev: I agree with you on one condition: that whatever amendments you make will not be in the nature of fundamental new proposals or new in principle. Because I don't want this forthcoming—this first—meeting with the President to begin with a dispute.

Kissinger: If it looks difficult, we will eliminate it from the agenda and have further discussions. There would be no surprises at Vladivostok. I can give Dobrynin our considerations and then, if it looks difficult, we will just defer it. But, we are not intending to come up with anything radically new. I think we have come closer together in this visit than ever before. And, our intention will be to narrow the distance further, not to widen it. But, if on analyzing your proposal we find difficulties, we will defer discussion. But my expectation is that we will come closer together. Our considerations will be in the area in which I have asked questions; so they will be quite predictable.

Brezhnev: You did understand what I said about the B-1s?

Kissinger: Yes, but we will have to study it because I don't have a precise answer. I want to study the range of missiles and other matters. For example, I know we have some missiles that are only air defense, short distance. This is why I would like to analyze it before giving my reply. But I understand the principle.

Brezhnev: When I refer to the B-1s, I was referring only to bombers carrying strategic missiles.

Kissinger: I understand, but this is what I would like to study.

Brezhnev: Of course. Then I will have one question to ask Dr. Kissinger face to face. Here, I would like to express appreciation and satisfaction that we have worked constructively and usefully.

Kissinger: I believe we have worked seriously and that we have made good progress. We will try to work by all available means to come to an agreement by the time you visit the United States in 1975, and we will do our utmost to make the meeting in Vladivostok a success—and the beginning of close co-operation between you and President Ford.

Brezhnev: Thank you. That is what I want!

Please do not forget not only the substance of this discussion on missiles but also what we discussed on the first day. I know you have not forgotten, and I won't discuss it any more. I endeavored to set out our position as clearly as possible, and I trust you will not disagree.

Kissinger: I take it seriously. I talked with your Foreign Minister at luncheon telling him, for example, there is a chance I will visit Ankara next week, and I promised to be in touch afterward.

Brezhnev Good. Those very small minor amendments to the overall com-muniqué we've made in the belief that it might be useful in terms of Vladi-vostok.

Kissinger: I agree. You understand our problem on MBFR.

Brezhnev: We can accept it.

Kissinger: And we accept. If you make many more concessions like this you'll have Alaska by next year.

(Sukhodrev translates; Gromyko translates again and Brezhnev and Soviet side laugh.)

[While discussing the phrasing of the communiqué and the timing of its release, Kiss-inger and the Soviets spar a bit over a sentence on the Geneva Conference. They agree that it should read "the early convening . . . should play a useful role in finding" a Middle East settlement.]

Brezhnev: (The General Secretary gets up and walks around to the Ameri-can side of the table.) It remains to shake hands. (He shakes the hands of the U.S. participants.).

Kissinger: And to say that we will meet in one month's time.

Brezhnev: I attach great importance to that meeting, and I appreciate that the President wants to have a working meeting. It is a big step forward toward my visit to Washington, and I believe that the meeting will be instrumental in terms of the political situation in the United States.

Kissinger: That's no longer so important.

Brezhnev: The important thing is that Ford and Kissinger shouldn't be un-der fire—only Sonnenfeldt!

(After the meeting concluded at 10:20 P.M., Kissinger and Brezhnev had a private discussion.)

COMMENTARY

Kissinger immediately wired Ford telling him that the proposal was a "major step forward toward a SALT agreement" because it could enable Moscow and Washington to reach mutually agreeable principles on totals, MIRVs, and "possibly a few other issues." Nevertheless, he worried that the Pentagon could "shred" the proposal in its present form, so he advised Ford to keep the details confidential: tell Secretary Schlesinger only that the Soviets had responded in a "conciliatory fashion." Kissinger further told Ford that Brezhnev wanted a friendly meeting at Vladivostok in order to "sustain forward movement" in U.S.-Soviet relations. Yet he also cautioned the President that it "remains to be seen whether sufficient flexibility can be mustered on both sides to bring SALT positions into real negotiating range."[42]

In the following weeks, Kissinger and Dobrynin gave more precise shape to the proposal that Ford and Brezhnev signed off on at Vladivostok. That understanding was essentially an accord for the framework of a SALT agreement, limiting levels of strategic delivery vehicles to 2,400 each and the right to deploy MIRVs on only 1,320 of them. Although the statesmen reached a tolerably acceptable settlement, Kissinger's fears came true: officials on both sides imperiled the deal by taking hard-line positions on Backfire bombers and cruise missiles.

Before negotiating positions on SALT started to harden, economic détente unraveled. In mid-December, as the Senate began to finalize the Trade Bill incorporating Jackson-Vanik, the Soviets denounced "any attempts . . . to interfere in internal affairs that are entirely the concern of the Soviet state." While Kissinger had hoped that a deal was still possible, Dobrynin told him that if Congress passed Jackson-Vanik, Moscow would not comply with the 1972 Trade Agreement.[43] Congress drove more nails into the coffin of economic cooperation by limiting Export-Import Bank and other U.S. government credits to #300 million. Weeks later, during meetings with his staff, Kissinger admitted that he "frankly wasn't watching the Ex-Im bill" because of his preoccupation with Jackson-Vanik. But he knew that the Senate's action was unacceptable to Moscow: $300 million was "in effect no credit."[44]

Once Congress passed the trade bill, Ford signed it into law in early January, although he made clear his objections to its discriminatory features. The confrontation with Congress that Kissinger had promised Brezhnev never occurred. With credits limited and MFN available only under onerous conditions, on 10 January the Soviets told Washington that they considered the 1972 Trade Agreement void. Washington's failure to carry out the 1972 Trade

Agreement would hurt U.S.-Soviet détente, but Brezhnev could make the decision to repudiate the agreement without too much anguish. U.S.-Soviet trade was not as important for Moscow as it had been a few years earlier; it was finding more dependable trade partners and billions in credits from the U.S.'s commercial rivals in Western Europe, especially West Germany.[45] Thus, as superpower détente stagnated, economic cooperation between Moscow and Western Europe advanced—an outcome that Kissinger found troubling.

Various developments in the following months—the fall of South Vietnam and consequent hypersensitivity about U.S. credibility, growing U.S.-Soviet rivalries in the Third World, and the deadlock over SALT II—made the climate for détente more difficult, although both superpowers continued to affirm its fundamentals. It was in this context that Kissinger went to Geneva in early July 1975 to participate in foreign ministers-level decisions on a meeting of heads of states to sign the CSCE's Final Act, what became known as the Helsinki Treaty. The ministers scheduled a meeting in Helsinki for late July and approved the Final Act's text. Basket I included language on basic principles—human rights, non-intervention, and borders (inviolability and peaceful change)—as well as provisions for military confidence building measures. Basket II covered East-West economic cooperation, while Basket III provided for humanitarian cooperation, including family reunification and free dissemination of information.[46]

The ensuing Helsinki Conference was one the great moments of East-West détente, but the Gromyko-Kissinger talks in Geneva showed that old Cold War anxieties and suspicions endured. In an aside to Ambassador Dobrynin, Kissinger disclosed his concern about U.S.-Soviet rivalries: "We shouldn't compete for the Third World. All they do is kick us around. We're not competing with you." Dobrynin did not respond, and Kissinger did not elucidate his remark. In light of the unfolding Angolan drama, Kissinger's claim about not competing was far from true. During the months after Portugal's April 1974 revolution, its Angolan colony headed for independence: rival nationalist groups, all basically left of center, struggled for position and violated the letter and spirit of a January 1975 agreement to form a transitional government. Holden Roberto, the leader of the Front for the Total Liberation of Angola (FNLA), had received modest CIA funding since the 1960s; covert assistance expanded considerably when Kissinger approved $300,000 in January 1975. Indeed, up until July 1975, the FNLA seemed likely to prevail over its chief opponent, the Popular Movement for the Liberation of Angola (MPLA), which had received modest Soviet and Cuban support over the years. By the spring of 1975, though, the Soviets began to increase aid, and Cuba began to send military advisers to allow it to compete with the FNLA.[47]

For the first half of 1975, Soviet support for the MPLA caused very little concern: Kissinger saw modest competition as business as usual under détente, and the U.S. client was winning. However, when Kissinger met Gromyko in Geneva, the FNLA was beginning to lose battles, and Kissinger found the competition more annoying. Looking at Angola through a Cold War lense, he decided that U.S. credibility was at stake. He overruled the State Department's skeptical African experts and asked the CIA to provide a covert action plan for Angola in two days. On 18 July, President Ford approved the plan; within two weeks, the FNLA was receiving U.S.-financed weapons from Zaire enabling its units to restore, if only temporarily, their edge over the MPLA.

After the CSCE's work was completed, Gromyko and Kissinger met through the early afternoon of 11 July to review other issues, starting with the Middle East. Although Kissinger was making headway in his step-by-step Middle East diplomacy, e.g., by negotiating Israeli forces out of the Sinai, the Soviets remained dissatisfied with the U.S. monopoly over Mideast diplomacy. To bring Moscow back into the peace process and to prevent the regional "tinderbox" from exploding again, Gromyko argued for reconvening the Geneva Conference. While Kissinger made vague assurances, he was not interested in reconvening Geneva because "there will be a tremendous pressure to do something rapidly that we may not be able to do." To Gromyko's emphasis on the Palestinian problem, Kissinger noted condescendingly that if Syrians, Palestinians, and other Arab delegations meet in the same room, "all together they intoxicate each other."[48]

Kissinger and Gromyko then had a private meeting, where the latter handed over a letter from Brezhnev to Ford raising concerns over Secretary of Defense James Schlesinger's public statements on first use of nuclear weapons. Declaring that the United States would use nuclear weapons first in event of a massive Soviet attack on Western Europe, Schlesinger saw an avowed first-use policy as essential to deter war: "If one accepts no first-use doctrine, one is accepting a self-denying ordinance that weakens deterrence."[49] These statements were standard U.S. nuclear doctrines, but to Brezhnev they seemed inconsistent with détente. Ford's response to Brezhnev remains unavailable; no doubt, he did his best to mollify him, but the sensitivity of this issue must have made it difficult.

Kissinger and Gromyko also spoke more or less frankly about China and Japan. The two countries had been talking about a peace and friendship treaty, and both superpowers were monitoring the situation closely. In the past, Kissinger had rebuffed a Soviet proposal for consultations on Sino-Japanese relations, but the stagnation in U.S.-PRC relations may have encouraged him to tell Gromyko that overly close relations between Beijing and Tokyo was in neither superpower's interest.[50] He did not, however, disclose another tenet of U.S.-Japan relations—the inadmissibility of a Soviet-Japanese alignment—which he had spelled out to both Mao and Zhou. While neither a Tokyo-Moscow nor a Tokyo-Beijing alignment was a near-term prospect, Kissinger opposed a more independent or nationalistic Japanese policy that could weaken the strong U.S.-Japanese ties that he and his associates regarded as a condition for stability and economic development in East Asia.[51]

On China, Kissinger was taciturn: he was not going to discuss the details of Washington-Beijing relations with the Foreign Minister of the PRC's chief enemy. He was more candid in expressing his thought that, as China became more powerful, it could become "more difficult." He had said as much to U.S. ambassadors a few years earlier: once the PRC had developed a formidable nuclear capability "they will have more options"and less need to lean on Washington—and "our problem will become more complex."[52]

THE WHITE HOUSE
SECRET/NODIS/XGDS
MEMORANDUM OF CONVERSATION
PARTICIPANTS: Andrei A. Gromyko, Member of the Politburo of the
    Central Committee of the CPSU and Minister of Foreign Affairs of
    the USSR; Viktor M. Sukhodrev, Ministry of Foreign Affairs
    (Interpreter); Dr. Henry A. Kissinger, Secretary of State and
    Assistant to the President for National Security Affairs; Peter W.
    Rodman, NSC Staff
DATE AND TIME: Friday, July 11, 1975 1:10-2:02 P.M.
PLACE: Secretary Kissinger's Bedroom Intercontinental Hotel
SUBJECTS: Brezhnev Oral Message; SALT; UNGA; China and Japan;
    FRG-Brazil Nuclear Deal; Bilateral Relations[C]

[C] Source: State Department Freedom of Information release; copy at NSA.

Gromyko: (To Sukhodrev in Russian.) Give me the letter.

Mr. Secretary, I wish to hand to you an oral message from General Secretary Brezhnev to President Ford in connection with the repeated utterances made by your Defense Secretary Schlesinger. We have called your attention to it. Frankly, we are surprised at this, and all the Soviet leadership, including General Secretary Brezhnev, are concerned at this.

Let me repeat: This is an oral message. Let me give you an official Russian text and a working translation (Tab A).

[The "working translation" read as follows.[53]

Esteemed Mr. President:

I have to address you once again on a question which has already been the subject of an exchange of views between us in Vladivostok and in subsequent correspondence.

I am referring to statements made by high United States officials, particularly by your Secretary of Defense, which are not only whipping up the arms race but also envisaging a possible use of nuclear weapons by the United States against the Soviet Union and other states-members of the Warsaw Treaty.

Despite the assurances to the opposite received by us, statements of that kind, far from ceasing, are becoming ever more frequent and ever more challenging. The US Secretary of Defense is tinkling almost incessantly like a bell. Hardly a day passes without him saying something on that score. Now he talks about using tactical nuclear weapons in Europe, now about making 'selective strikes' against the Soviet Union. Finally, a few days ago he bluntly announced the possibility of the United States being the first to use nuclear weapons against the Soviet Union.

You will agree, Mr. President, that the picture thus [*sic*] emerges looks more than strange. Is it not high time to put an end to that?

On the one hand, we are settling ourselves against the common goal of preventing a nuclear-missile war and have concluded a fundamental agreement on this matter. In Vladivostok we agreed to regard precisely this direction of mutual efforts by our countries as the central one in Soviet–American relations for the future as well.

On the other hand, statements are being made in the United States by leading officials who are openly impressing upon the public the idea of a possibility, and almost the inevitability of such a war. After all, your Defense Minister is speaking day after day precisely about laying down rules for the conduct of a nuclear war, not about preventing such a war.

Do not such statements testify to a desire to proceed in a direction which runs counter to the one our countries have decided to follow[?]

We have been given various kinds of explanations in connection with these statements. But the fact remains that such statements—and surely there is a definite policy behind them—are still being made.

The question is how are we to react to these statements. It does not seem hard to understand what it would mean for both our mutual relations and for the state of affairs in the world at large if statements like those by the United States Defense Secretary began to be made in the Soviet Union, too.

This question, is, I repeat, very serious, it deals with matters of principle, with the intentions of our countries toward each other. That is why complete clarity here is very much in order.

Both my colleagues and I hope, Mr. President, that you will treat the considerations we have set forth with all the attention this entire matter deserves.]

Kissinger: (reads it) It will be brought to the immediate attention of the President. Speaking frankly, it is not unhelpful that you sent this because they don't reflect the views of the President. Frankly, they reflect an attempt by a Cabinet member to play politics in an election year. But it is not unhelpful.

Gromyko: I would like just to express my hope—and I know this is what the General Secretary would want me to say—that it will be treated with utmost seriousness.

Kissinger: It would not be inappropriate for the General Secretary to raise it with the President at Helsinki, and it will be treated with utmost seriousness.

[Gromyko notes that SALT II talks continue at Geneva but the delegations have had little to discuss; he asks Kissinger to give instructions to U.S. envoys so the two sides will have something to talk about.]

Gromyko: Then there is this question: Just before this year's Regular Session of the United Nations General Assembly there will be a Special Session devoted to international economic problems, continuing the discussions in the UN framework on these topics. What in your view should be discussed there? And would it be a good idea to have consultations on what should be discussed? This is not by way of a positive statement.

Kissinger: No, I understand. I'll give a speech next week warning against confrontation tactics in the UN, and specifically not regarding the Soviet Union but the new countries. We will be making proposals on raw materials, and so on, which we are prepared to discuss with you. We believe we should not let the new countries dictate on these questions. But we will put forward our proposals—and we will not move from these positions, I can tell you.

[The two discuss their plans to attend U.N. sessions in the fall, and Gromyko accepts Kissinger's invitation to Washington for a meeting with President Ford.]

Gromyko: . . . Earlier you remember we spoke about the possibility of Vietnam joining the UN. You remember?

Kissinger: Yes.

Gromyko: What is your view: What do you think about both joining the UN—the Democratic Republic of Vietnam and South Vietnam?

Kissinger: If both Koreas join, we would be in favor of it.

Gromyko: This is still your position?

Kissinger: Yes.

Gromyko: If it is done, what about just the DRV?

Kissinger: [Thinks] I don't totally exclude this. Let me think about it.

Gromyko: In the Asiatic area, what is happening? With your friends the Chinese and Japanese?

Kissinger: The Chinese are very anxious to have the President go there. We are thinking now of November or December, maybe late November, and before then I will go there before the President. Six weeks before.

Gromyko: Will there be negotiations with Mao?

Kissinger: We don't expect any spectacular results.

Gromyko: Will it be a short or long visit?

Kissinger: We haven't discussed it. They would like a week. We may cut it, less than a week.

Gromyko: Do you have any information about the possibility of an agreement or no agreement between the Chinese and Japanese on friendship? Earlier we discussed what is the intention of the Japanese on this question of. . . .

Kissinger: Hegemony.[54]

Gromyko: Hegemony, and what the Chinese have in mind on this question.

Kissinger: My prediction is—and this is not based on information—is that they will probably make this.

Gromyko: Make this?

Kissinger: Make this agreement.

Gromyko: So the Chinese will succeed.

Kissinger: This is not based on information but on the Japanese character.

Gromyko: The Japanese Prime Minister is not strong?[55]

Kissinger: He is not strong. He will visit Washington in August. We are not encouraging any excessively close ties between China and Japan.

Gromyko: It strikes the eye that [Japanese Prime Minister] Miki [Takeo] rather underrates the sharp edge that China wants to direct against the Soviet Union—you know best the situation as regards the United States.[56]

Kissinger: We have no interest in this.

Gromyko: This surprises us. We have no idea why Miki underrates this. We would have no objection—although we don't request it—if you could mention our view to the Japanese Prime Minister when you see him. Japan has relations with its other neighbors including the Soviet Union, and it would seem that that would be a factor the Japanese would take into due account. But it seems he is not.

It isn't that we are so alarmed by this. We have been frightened and frightened again and we can stand up for ourselves! But we would like to have normal friendly relations with Japan, and we think it would be the best interest for Japan.[57]

Kissinger: I've told you it is important for our two countries to keep a long term perspective in mind. I am convinced that by the 1980's the identity of interest will become self-evident. Now it is self-evident with respect to nuclear weapons; by the 1980's it will be true of many political issues. We shouldn't lose sight of this fact.

Second, we consider it dangerous to have too close relations between China and Japan. Not normal relations, but an axis between the two would be dangerous.

Third, the hegemony clause could be used some day against us. It doesn't name the country. I don't exclude that our relations with the Chinese will be more difficult in five years, certainly in ten. It is a historical accident that our relations with the Chinese are somewhat better now than yours.

Gromyko: Somewhat!

Kissinger: But as China grows stronger, it can become more difficult for us too.

Gromyko: I listened to that with great interest. And I do believe here that we are faced with serious problems, serious both for our leadership and for the United States, and these are questions which should interest the United States too, if you really want to look into the future of your relations with nations of Asia. And I'm sure in your position you do.

Our attention has been drawn to one fact, and trying to assess the significance of that fact we cannot come to any optimistic conclusion—and that is the agreement between West Germany and Brazil to provide nuclear reactors and either equipment.[58] Our assessment is like that of others—that Brazil is on the path to the production of nuclear weapons and wants to use the help provided by West Germany. Am I right that this isn't a theoretical problem but a problem of practical policy? it concerns our two states as parties to the Non-Proliferation Treaty [NPT]. Incidentally, Germany is party to the NPT, but Brazil is not.

You are located closer to Brazil geographically and politically. And we believe you are more aware of how West Germany is breathing in this matter.[59]

Kissinger: We don't believe Brazil has decided to build nuclear weapons but this deal creates the possibility and we are concerned for the future. When a complete fuel cycle is provided, it provides the possibility to obtain fuel. But we are concerned and have expressed our concern publicly.

We had hoped this suppliers' conference would agree on safeguards.[60] But if it doesn't, we would be prepared to exchange views bilaterally, because it is a dangerous development.

Gromyko: We would be prepared for an exchange of views.

Kissinger: All right. Shall we have lunch?

Gromyko: As regards our bilateral relations, I remember very well what you said to me in Vienna, and I expressed my views and don't want to repeat myself. We are continuing the line that developed particularly at the two summit meetings. True that there are occasional statements made in the U.S. that are not quite in accord with that line, but the President and you on behalf of the President have reemphasized that that line is the same. This cannot but evoke a positive response on our part. We believe if we continue on the course, our two nations can look confidently into the future and advance confidently on the path we have taken in recent years. It would be in the interests not only of the peoples of the United States and the Soviet Union, but of all nations. In fact, not even [Maltese Prime Minister] Mintoff could distract us from that.[61] I wanted to repeat this view.

Kissinger: We appreciate this. We, too, believe this is in the interests of peace, and the necessity for it will grow, as I said, in the coming years. The position of our President is growing stronger, almost by the week, so by the time President Ford leaves office, in 1981, it will be a permanent feature of the world scene.

Gromyko: You are optimistic.

Kissinger: All the polls show that if elections were held now, he would win overwhelmingly. Unless there is a collapse of the domestic situation. All our people say it is improving.

Gromyko: What is the situation in the Democratic Party?

Kissinger: Humphrey is mentioned. Jackson is still a possibility; Kennedy is mentioned as a possible compromise.

Gromyko: But he has not announced himself. Is it possible?

Kissinger: I don't think it's possible, but I don't exclude it. I think he is waiting for 1980. They will hurt themselves by fighting among themselves while the President is conducting his office.

(Everyone gets up.)

Gromyko: For the conference to be finished would make possible many things.

Kissinger: I've instructed our Ambassador to tell the other delegations that after two years of effort, to permit one clause to hold it up makes no sense.

Gromyko: What does it mean—"contacts?" Everybody has contacts all the time. Nobody can take decisions.[62]

Kissinger: I agree.

Gromyko: This was a good meeting.

(At 2:02 P.M. the conversation ended and the party joined the rest for luncheon.)

COMMENTARY

Kissinger's prediction that détente would be a "permanent fixture of the world scene" in 1981 was wildly mistaken but one that he tried to validate with his persistent efforts to negotiate a SALT II agreement under decidedly unfavorable conditions. At Geneva, Kissinger and Gromyko had discussed SALT II, and when Gerald Ford attended the Helsinki Conference in late July, he met twice with Leonid Brezhnev to consider SALT and other bilateral issues. By then, the Backfire and cruise missile problems had complicated the negotiations in ways that none of the principals could have anticipated a year earlier. Brezhnev and Ford got along very well at Helsinki, but neither their talks nor a subsequent round of negotiations in Washington and New York in September significantly bridged the gap in negotiating positions.

While Kissinger sought to avoid the substantial limitations on cruise missiles sought by Moscow, the Soviets insisted that Backfire be kept out of the negotiations. Kissinger was willing to treat Backfire as a "hybrid" weapons system (rather than a strictly strategic bomber) that could, along with U.S. ship-launched cruise missiles, be the subject of special limitations. Bromyko, however, was unenthusiastic: "we wouldn't cry if our non-heavy bomber spends its life in a state of loneliness, without American companionship." He also lamented that Kissinger was "clinging to those cruise missiles" but the U.S. side was unwilling to accept Gromyko's proposals to treat longer-range ALCMs as strategic systems subject to the SALT aggregate. Although Kissinger made proposals designed to "come closer" to Soviet positions on cruise missiles, the talks were deadlocked.

After Gromyko returned to Moscow, Ford kept the discussions going by restating Kissinger's latest proposal in a letter to Brezhnev, but it made no difference. In late October, Brezhnev turned down the offer in a strongly worded response. By the time that Kissinger was back in Moscow with new proposals, his power had been diminished, and the Angolan situation was casting a pall over détente.[63]

Notes

1. Raymond L. Garthoff, *Détente and Confrontation: American–Soviet Relations from Nixon to Reagan* (Washington, D.C.: Brookings Institution, 1994), pp. 475–80.
2. For Nixon's account of the summit, see his *RN: The Memoirs of Richard Nixon* (New York: Grosset and Dunlap, 1978), pp. 1023–39.
3. The quotation is from Dobrynin; for an insightful discussion of Ford as president, see Anatoly Dobrynin, *In Confidence: Moscow's Ambassador to America's Six Cold War Presidents, 1962–1986* (New York: Times Books, 1995), pp. 320, 338-341. For Ford and defense spending, see Nixon, *RN*, p. 1025.
4. See Henry Kissinger, *American Foreign Policy* (3d ed., New York: Norton, 1977), pp. 143–76.
5. See Paula Stern, *Water's Edge: Domestic Politics and the Making of American Foreign Policy* (Westport, Conn.: Greenwood, 1979), pp. 154–65, and Walter Isaacson, *Kissinger: A Biography* (New York: Simon and Schuster, 1992), pp. 616–18; and Garthoff, *Détente and Confrontations*, pp. 506–8.
6. See Dobrynin, *In Confidence*, p. 337. Kissinger observed at the time that when Nixon and Treasury Secretary John Connally negotiated the trade agreement in 1972, the Soviets "were never even told there was a possibility of congressional difficulty." See Transcript of Secretary's Staff Meeting, 3 January 1975, National Archives, Record Group 59, Department of State Records, Transcripts of Secretary of State Henry A. Kissinger's Staff Meetings, 1973–77 (hereafter referred to as *Staff Meetings* with archival box number), box 5.
7. See Mike Bowker and Phil Williams, *Superpower Detente: A Reappraisal* (London: Royal Institute of International Affairs, 1988), p. 164, and Garthoff, *Détente and Confrontation*, pp. 518–19.
8. For developments between March and October 1974, see William B. Quandt, *Peace Process: American Diplomacy and the Arab–Israel Conflict Since 1947* (Washington, D.C.: Brookings Institution, 1993), pp. 203–29.
9. For Vladivostok and the SALT process during Ford's first year, based on the available memoirs and interviews with participants, see Garthoff, *Détente and Confrontation*, pp. 494–505. For Ford's account of Vladivostok, see Gerald R. Ford, *A Time to Heal: The Autobiography of Gerald R. Ford* (New York: Harper and Row, 1979), pp. 213–18. Trident SLBMs were due to be deployed in the late 1970s, and their increased range reduced Washington's reliance on overseas submarine bases near the Soviet Union.

10. See Center for Foreign Policy Development, Thomas J. Watson Jr. Institute for International Studies, "SALT II and the Growth of Mistrust, Conference No. 2, The Carter-Brezhnev Project," Conference at St. Simons Island, 6–9 May 1994, pp. 17, 179–80, and William G. Hyland, *Mortal Rivals: Superpower Relations from Nixon to Reagan* (New York: Random House, 1987), pp. 99–100.

11. See Garthoff, *Détente and Confrontation*, pp. 498–500.

12. See ibid.; Isaacson, *Kissinger: A Biography*, p. 628; and Jack Mendelsohn to Ambassador Johnson, 17 Dec. 1974, State Department FOIA release, copy at National Security Archive (hereafter referred to as *NSA*).

13. Garthoff, *Détente and Confrontation,* pp. 498–500, and Jack Mendelsohn to Ambassador Johnson, 17 Dec. 1974. For the CIA's analysis of the Backfire, see NIE 11-3/8-74, *Soviet Forces for Intercontinental Conflict Through 1985,* vol. 1: *Key Judgments and Summary,* 14 Nov. 1974 (copy at *NSA*).

14. For an essential compendium of information on cruise missiles, see Richard K. Betts, ed., *Cruise Missiles: Technology, Strategy, Politics* (Washington, D.C.: Brookings Institution, 1981). For Kissinger's interest and *rammed down,* see Robert J. Art and Stephen E. Ockenden, *The Domestic Politics of Cruise Missile Development, 1970–1980,* pp. 360, 395, and Ford *Time to Heal,* p. 300.

15. See Garthoff, *Détente and Confrontation*, pp. 497–98; Charles Zemach to Mr. Lord, "Our 3:00 P.M. Meeting on SALT," 3 December 1974, Policy Planning Staff Records, 1969–77 (Director's Files) (hereafter referred to as *PPS,* with archival box number and file information), box 347, Dec. 1974.

15a. See Secretary's Staff Meeting, 9 Dec. 1974, *Staff Meetings,* box 7. For a knowledgeable account of the Geneva talks, see John J. Maresca, *To Helsinki: The Conference on Security and Cooperation in Europe, 1973–1975* (Durham, N.C.: Duke University Press, 1987).

16. For Gromyko's statement, see Dobrynin, *In Confidence,* p. 346.

17. See Dobrynin, *In Confidence,* p. 347, and Leo P. Ribuffo, "Is Poland a Soviet Satellite? Gerald Ford, the Sonnenfeldt Doctrine, and the Election of 1976," *Diplomatic History* 14 (Summer 1990), pp. 390-91.

18. See U.S. Department of State Briefing Paper, "Soviet Views of Detente," June 1974 (copy at NSA), and Dobrynin, *In Confidence,* p. 329. For signs of Brezhnev's failing health at the Helsinki summit, see Genscher, *Rebuilding a House Divided,* pp. 100–101.

19. See Dobrynin, *In Confidence,* pp. 322-23, 327.

20. Kissinger had ill-treated Stoessel's predecessor Jacob Beam by cutting him out of back-channel arrangements, e.g., by visiting Moscow in April 1972 without notifying the embassy. *Isaacson, Kissinger: A Biography,* p. 411.

21. Alma Ata is the capital of Khazakstan, the former Soviet Kazakh Republic, while Kishinev is the capital of Moldova, the former Soviet Republic of Moldovia. For the texts of Brezhnev's speeches, see "Brezhnev Speaks Out on Farm Policy," *Current Digest of the Soviet Press,* 26 (10 April 1974), pp. 1–5; "Brezhnev's Visit to the G.D.R.," ibid., 26 (30 October 1974), pp. 1–5, and "Brezhnev's Speech in Kishinev," ibid., 26 (6 November 1974), pp. 1–5.

22. At the 1972 summit, the Soviets agreed to pay $722 million in World War II lend-lease debts over a thirty-year period. See Garthoff, *Détente and Confrontation,* p. 345.

23. For an account of Brezhnev's statements at San Clemente on the Middle East problem, see Henry Kissinger, *Years of Upheaval* (Boston: Little, Brown, 1982), pp. 296-99.

24. Earlier in the month, Ford had canceled $500 million in contracts that the Soviets had signed with U.S. grain merchants to prevent large wheat purchases from destabilizing commodity prices à la the "great grain robbery" of 1972, when Moscow's purchase of most of the U.S.'s surplus grain reserve drove up U.S. domestic prices.

25. This is a reference to the CSCE debates over the territorial scope of confidence-building measures such as notification of military exercises; for further discussion, see Maresca, *To Helsinki*, pp. 168–74.

26. Kissinger's explanation was disingenuous: he had known in advance what Jackson would do after meeting with Ford. Indeed, his right-hand man, Helmut Sonnenfeldt, knew precisely what Jackson would say, and Ford had approved Jackson's release of the letters. See Garthoff, *Détente and Confrontation*, p. 501, and Isaacson, *Kissinger: A Biography*, p. 618.

27. In the end, Ford, Brezhnev, and their entourages took the train instead of helicopters from the airport to the Okeanskaya Sanatorium outside of Vladivostok, where they held their meetings. See Hyland, *Mortal Rivals*, pp. 76–77.

28. See memcon, "Jackson Amendment; CSCE; Middle East; Nuclear War," 24 Oct. 1974, 6:00–9:30 P.M.; copy at *NSA*.

29. A recent poll showed Kissinger with an 80 percent approval rating, which Dobrynin said was "Number one in history." See memcon cited in note 33, above.

30. The Soviets had two days' warning before the war started on 6 October. See Garthoff, *Détente and Confrontation*, p. 411.

31. The Egyptians expelled Soviet military advisers in July 1972. See ibid., p. 356.

32. As of this writing, records of the SALT discussions on 25 October await declassification review at the Ford Library.

33. See Garthoff, *Détente and Confrontation*, pp. 466–68; State Department telegram 148542 to Belgrade, 10 July 1974 (copy of *NSA*). For background on the new targeting strategy, in which Kissinger had more of a hand than Schlesinger, see Terry Terriff, *The Nixon Administration and the Making of U.S. Nuclear Policy* (Ithaca, N.Y.: Cornell University Press, 1995).

34. For background on the negotiating process, see Zbigniew Brzezinski to Secretary of State and Secretary of Defense, "SALT Negotiating History," 2 Feb. 1977 (copy at *NSA*), and *Détente and Confrontation*, pp. 494–96.

35. See Kissinger to Scowcroft, telegram HAKTO 33, 26 Oct. 1974, copy at Gerald R. Ford Library, Trip Briefing Books and Cables 20 October–9 November 1974 Europe, South Asia and Middle East HAKTO (2).

36. Emperor Haile Selassie had been deposed by a military coup led by Mengistu Haile Mariam in September. He would not live for long: Mengistu had him executed the following year. See Garthoff, *Détente and Confrontation*, p. 695, and "Ex-Rulers of Ethiopia Charged with Strangling Haile Selassie," *New York Times*, 15 Dec. 1994.

37. The Soviets first launched the Typhoon-class submarine, the largest submarine ever constructed, in 1980. It carried 20 SS-N-20 SLBMs, each with 6–9 MIRVs; the missile's range was about 8,300 kilometers. See Thomas B. Cochran et al., *Nuclear Weapons Databook: Soviet Nuclear Weapons* (Cambridge, Mass.: Ballinger, 1984), pp. 112–15, 141–42.

38. This is a joking reference to the light weight covers—either canvas or aluminum—that

the U.S. Air Force had put over ICBM silos, preventing the Soviets from spying on them with reconnaissance satellites.

39. For example, in 1970, the United States had 390 strategic bombers, while the Soviets had 157. See Robert S. Norris and Thomas B. Cochran, *Nuclear Weapons Databook: US–USSR/Russian Strategic Offensive Nuclear Forces, 1945–1996* (Washington, D.C.: Natural Resources Defense Council, 1997), pp. 11–12.

40. While Kissinger apparently had his doubts about the B-1, he was not about to acknowledge that he had been a proponent of air-launched cruise missiles, which the B-1 could carry, as a "bargaining chip" for SALT. See note 14, above.

41. Brezhnev may be singling out Hyland because of his CIA background.

42. See Kissinger to Scowcroft, telegraph HAKTO 33, 26 Oct. 1974, copy at Gerald R. Ford Library, Trip Briefing Books and Cables 20 October–9 November 1974 Europe, South Asia and Middle East HAKTO (2).

43. See Garthoff, *Détente and Confrontation*, pp. 510–13; Hyland, *Mortal Rivals*, p. 107; Stern, *Water's Edge*, pp. 165–93.

44. See Transcript of Secretary Kissinger Staff Meetings, 2 and 29 Jan. 1975, *Staff Meetings*, box 6, and Stern, *Water's Edge*, p. 186.

45. See William Bundy, *A Tangled Web, The Making of Foreign Policy in the Nixon Presidency* (New York: Hill and Wang, 1998), pp. 478–80.

46. See Garthoff, *Détente and Confrontation*, pp. 527–28.

47. See ibid., 556–75.

48. See memcon, "CSCE, Middle East," 11 July 1975, copy at NSA.

49. "Transcript of the President's News Conference" and "Schlesinger Says U.S. Is Willing to Use Nuclear Weapons First," *New York Times*, 26 June and 2 July 1976 respectively. President Ford had touched off the discussion during the news conference, when he refused to provide an answer to a reporter's question about first use of nuclear weapons: "I don't think it is appropriate for me to discuss . . . what our utilization will be of our tactical or strategic weapons." See *New York Times* 26 June 1975.

50. See memcon, "President's Visit; Nuclear War; SALT; Yugoslavia," 27 Nov. 1974, in chapter 6 of this volume (p. 325ff.).

51. See "East Asian Chiefs of Mission Conference November 14–16, 1973, Afternoon Session," pp. 51, 58; U.S.–Japan Collection, *NSA*.

52. Ibid., p. 61.

53. A copy of this document is available at the *NSA*.

54. This is a reference to Tokyo's and Beijing's negotiation of a Peace and Friendship Treaty. The Chinese wanted to include an "antihegemony" clause tacitly aimed at the Soviet Union; but this created an impasse in the negotiations for some months because Prime Minister Miki did not want to appear to yield to Beijing. See Briefing Paper, "Japan," November 1975, *PPS*, box 373, President Ford's China Visit, International Issues (folder 2 of 2). The Japanese did not sign the treaty until 1978, however, and unsuccessfully tried to neutralize anti-Soviet implications by insisting on conditions—for example, a clause stating that any antihegemony statement is not directed against any third country. See Yoshihide Soeya, "U.S.–Japan Relations and the Opening to China: The 1970s," National Security Archive, The U.S.–Japan Project Working Paper Series, No. 5. 1996, pp. 35–37.

55. Japanese Prime Minister Miki Takeo was the leader of the Liberal Democratic Party faction that was more interested in relations with China than with the United States. See Walter LaFeber, *The Clash: A History of U.S.-Japan Relations* (New York: Norton, 1997), pp. 330, 337.

56. "It strikes the eye" is a Russian expression meaning "it is plain to see."

57. State Department analysts believed that one reason the Miki government took more steps to improve relations with Beijing than with Moscow was to encourage the Soviets to be more flexible over bilateral problems such as the Northern Territories. See Briefing Paper, "Japan," November 1975, *PPS*, box 373, President Ford's China Visit, International Issues (folder 2 of 2).

58. For background on West German sale of reactors to Brazil, see Leonard S. Spector, *Nuclear Proliferation Today* (New York: Vintage, 1984), pp. 239–43, and his *Going Nuclear* (Cambridge, Mass.: Ballinger, 1987), pp. 199, 207–8. As it turned out, Brazil made very slow progress in carrying out its ambitious nuclear power program, and the Germans secretly implemented safeguards to prevent weapons development.

59. "How West Germany is breathing," a Russianism conveying the idea of "which way the West Germans were leaning."

60. After the Indian nuclear test in 1974, the United States took the lead in encouraging nuclear technology producers to accept a uniform code for conducting international nuclear sales to limit the danger of further proliferation. See Spector, *Going Nuclear*, pp. 7, 349–51.

61. This is a reference to Malta's prime minister Dominic Mintoff (b. 1916), who had delayed final agreement on the text of the CSCE's Final Act. See Maresca, *To Helsinki*, pp. 184–87.

62. This may be a reference to a dispute over language concerning the role of nonparticipating Mediterranean states, which held up the conference at the last moment. See ibid., pp. 185–92.

63. Backfire and cruise missiles were not the only problems complicating negotiations, but they were the most significant. Memcons on the substantive SALT talks in Geneva are not available, but see Zbigniew Brzezinski to Secretary of State and Secretary of Defense, "SALT Negotiating History," 2 Feb. 1977; copy at *NSA*. For the Helsinki talks and the Kissinger-Gromyko talks in September, see Hyland, *Mortal Enemies*, p. 124, and memcons "SALT," 19 and 21 Sept. 1975 (copies at *NSA*).

8

"We Have Some Problems with the Chinese":

Beijing–Washington, 1975–76

COMMENTARY

The collapse of U.S. client states in Vietnam and Cambodia, sharpening political conflict in Beijing, U.S. presidential campaign politics, and the faltering in U.S.-Soviet détente, all presented serious problems for the relationship with China that Henry Kissinger had cultivated so assiduously. Moreover, Kissinger learned that President Ford's political goals, more than merely complicating relations with Beijing by checking progress on normalization, would even undermine Kissinger's own standing in government. After a difficult visit to China in October 1975, Kissinger reported to Ford that relations were indeed cooling and wrote of the Chinese leadership's "insolent behavior and self-righteous lack of responsiveness."[1] The atmosphere improved somewhat after President Ford's visit, but Kissinger and his advisers could not be very optimistic about the prospects for triangular diplomacy. Despite China's displeasure with U.S. policy and the attentuation of the close consultations typical of the 1971–73 period, antipathy toward the Soviets remained central to Chinese policy; the opening to Washington met no fundamental challenge within the Chinese government.[2]

In the months after Kissinger's November 1974 visit to Beijing, relations with Beijing wobbled but then seemed to get back on track. In late 1974, complaints about the lagging normalization began to appear in the press, but Kissinger authorized a stern démarche which may have checked the sniping. Though the Chinese turned on the smiles, harsh statements about both superpowers continued to emanate from Beijing. Liaison Office chief George Bush, reporting through the back channel, worried a bit about the repercussions of the antihegemony rhetoric—for example, Foreign Minister Qiao's toast at a diplomatic dinner about the superpowers having "honey on their lips and murder in their hearts." Yet, Bush concluded, basic relations were "not worsening"; as far as Beijing was concerned, he believed, the Washington connection was "the most important game in town." However, there were no "visible signs of progress," and trade and exchange programs were only "rocking along."[3]

The political shock caused by the collapse of the Saigon regime in April 1975 had significant implications for U.S.-PRC relations. Kissinger belatedly acknowledged, during a "Today" show appearance in early May, the basic irrelevance of "credibility" and domino theories to understanding the Vietnam situation. Nevertheless, he had found it hard to give up those concepts; during the weeks before Saigon's collapse, Kissinger emphasized the importance of preserving U.S. worldwide credibility to justify his frenzied efforts to secure emergency aid for the Thieu regime. This renewed emphasis on credibility and concomitant efforts to reestablish it on the cheap, for example, the efforts to rescue the crew of a U.S. cargo boat, the *Mayaguez*, from its Cambodian captors, made Kissinger and his advisers keenly aware that allies, adversaries, and critics (mostly on the Right and especially partisans of Taiwan) would be scrutinizing the administration's diplomacy for any sign of uncertainty on international commitments. As Kissinger wrote to Ford later in 1975, the fall of Saigon had "created a context where any major change in our relationship with Taiwan which implied abandonment of yet another ally would be unacceptable" for foreign policy and domestic political reasons.[4]

Soon after the Thieu regime's collapse, it became apparent how it "cross-pressured" the Ford–Kissinger China policy. In a press conference on 6 May, Ford stated, without even mentioning U.S. relations with the PRC, that he intended to "reaffirm our commitments to Taiwan" as well as to other countries in the region (South Korea, Indonesia, Philippines).[5] This assertion ran counter to the administration's efforts to keep Taiwan out of the limelight, much less Ford's recent statement on accelerating U.S.-PRC relations; but it also suggested how well he understood the connections between Vietnam, Taiwan, and his standing with "conservative Republican activists" and overseas allies. Kissinger fully understood Ford's political imperatives; as he told his advisers, "If there's any one thing that will trigger a conservative reaction to Ford," it would be a deal with Beijing over Taiwan. The limits on normalization became even tighter in August, when Ronald Reagan—who had already attacked the administration's China policy—declared his presidential candidacy.[6]

Ford's statement on 6 May can only have irritated the Chinese: it was a clear signal that Washington still "needed" Taiwan. Although Mao and Deng had repeatedly said that China would be patient, Kissinger and his advisers recognized that Beijing was apprehensive that Washington was "stringing them along" on Taiwan. In trying to explain to President Ford in October 1975 why relations with China had cooled, Kissinger had to acknowledge that the politically determined resistance to full normalization could only make Beijing question U.S. reliability. Yet, as his advisers pointed out, when the time came for serious talks on Taiwan, Washington's negotiating position would be relatively weak; by being patient, the Chinese were putting the United States in the "psychological posture of being beholden to them for their 'generosity.'"[7]

Ford's statement did not, however, deter Deng from making it known that Beijing wanted to maintain high-level contacts with Washington. On 2 June 1975, he told visiting U.S. newspaper editors that President Ford was welcome to China whether or not he had important business to conduct.

Nevertheless, in the months before Ford's December visit, the Beijing leadership worked to lower domestic expectations about the summit and began to make increasingly sharp criticisms of U.S. policy. Only a few weeks after Saigon fell, Beijing's propaganda apparatus cast doubt on Washington's value in providing security against Moscow. In a fierce editorial, *People's Daily* condemned the Soviets as "Social-Fascists," run by a "dictatorship of the Hitler type"; the United States, it said, is "increasingly vulnerable and strategically passive." Not surprisingly, Kissinger told the Chinese that he disagreed with these digs at the administration's resolve. He found Deng Xiaoping's rhetoric in October even more disturbing. Deng charged Washington with taking a path of "appeasement" by failing to confront the Soviets. Indeed, Deng explicitly compared U.S. policy to the pre-World War II stance of Neville Chamberlain. With their contempt for détente as well as their refusal of the U.S. intelligence briefings that had been standard during Kissinger's visits, the Chinese showed that they wanted to keep some distance from Washington and preserve freedom of action in world politics.[8]

Deng's criticisms and similar remarks from Mao dismayed Kissinger and contributed to what he called the "most disdainful performance so far" in U.S.–PRC relations. Kissinger had come to Beijing, in October 1975, to negotiate a communiqué for President Ford's visit, which was to reflect the relationship's progress and show agreement on partial steps toward normalization. However, it was not until the evening before his departure that the Chinese presented him with their counterdraft; it set forth terms on normalization that precluded any partial steps, the dangers of world war, as well as approving language about revolutionary trends — "greater disorder under heaven and the situation is excellent." For Qiao, Kissinger's draft was unacceptable because it legitimated further delay in U.S. diplomatic recognition;

and Kissinger saw Qiao's counterdraft as objectionable because it was "overloaded with contentious language and disagreements," that would invite speculation about difficulties between Beijing and Washington.[9]

Thus, Kissinger never got his communiqué, and as Ford's December 1975 visit approached, he and his advisers tried to explain to the President the "cooling" of U.S.-PRC relations and the quarrel over détente. He saw a "growing doubt . . . that the United States is capable of playing the kind of major world role which will provide an effective counterweight" to Soviet efforts to encircle Beijing. Domestic political troubles, ranging from Congress's more assertive role in foreign policy to the United States' press "nihilistic mood," led him to fear that the Chinese were taking the United States "less seriously as a world power."[10]

However astute Kissinger's analysis was, normalization—or the lack thereof—was certainly a significant factor in the cooling process. He made no mention of reports that some elements in the Chinese leadership, feeling that Beijing had been "manipulated by us with the Soviet threat," may have sought more flexibility in dealings with Washington. Perhaps Mao and Deng hoped to do the same with the Americans—to manipulate them with assertions about the Soviet threat—in order to make Washington more pliable on normalization.[11]

Even with the troubles over the communiqué and Deng's and Qiao's "insolent" behavior—as if they were subordinates acting presumptuously—Kissinger saw no major crisis that could reverse the opening to China. Instead, he suspected that Deng was trying to put Washington on the defensive, and perhaps, even to provoke a postponement of President Ford's trip. Nevertheless, Kissinger assumed that the Chinese saw their association with Washington as important for providing a counterweight to Soviet power. But given Beijing's doubts, he foresaw little improvement in the near term: the Chinese would keep their relationship with the United States at the "present level—alive enough to suit their geopolitical purposes" but no more than that.[12]

In the meantime, domestic U.S. political pressures had also impaired Kissinger's position in government. Other presidential advisers recognized that press coverage of Kissinger's squabbles with Secretary of Defense Schlesinger were hurting Ford's standing and that Republican conservatives were antagonistic to Kissinger; so they proposed a cabinet shakeup. Ford fired Schlesinger (whom he disliked anyway) and replaced him with his Chief of Staff Donald Rumsfeld. Ford fired CIA director William Colby and replaced him with George Bush. Moreover, to reduce Kissinger's visibility,

Ford told him that Brent Scowcroft would replace him at the White House; Kissinger would remain secretary of state but would no longer be the central policy coordinator. A depressed Kissinger gave serious thought to resignation until Ford braced him up; but, as Kissinger would soon learn during the January 1976 SALT talks, his influence would never be the same again.[13]

The Chinese incorrectly believed that Schlesinger was wholly averse to détente, and so they interpreted his firing as a sign of appeasement. However, once the details of Ford's visit and contentions over the communiqué were settled, the atmosphere greatly improved. In Kissinger's eyes, Ford's visit had become all the more necessary in order to renew high-level dialogue and to symbolize the importance of the China connection for U.S. diplomacy.[14]

Ford's visit had the desired symbolic effect. During his four-day stay, he received a friendly reception; his talks with Mao and Deng were cordial and covered the gamut of international issues, including Angola, NATO, and the prospects for normalizing relations. Deng, more than Mao, continued to play up the differences over the Soviets, presumably to keep the Americans on the defensive. Ford and Kissinger held their own in debate and made no concessions on the schedule for diplomatic recognition: but their desire to bolster uneasy relations with Beijing made them conciliatory in their approach to normalization and receptive to Chinese requests in 1976 for high-speed computers.[15]

In the months that followed, U.S.–PRC relations remained in a holding pattern. Huang Zhen stayed away from Washington until Ford had replaced Bush at the Beijing USLO, and when Huang did return to Washington, his meetings with Kissinger were infrequent. To signal Beijing's continued interest, the Chinese invited Richard Nixon to Beijing in February 1976 but quickly discovered that this was not the best public relations move.[16]

Although Beijing's criticism of U.S. Angola policy as appeasement annoyed Washington, Kissinger and the administration continued to hold out a hand to China. In keeping with the Shanghai Communiqué, Washington continued to withdraw military personnel from Taiwan, although the White House delayed action on a National Security Decision Memorandum on overall forces withdrawal policy until after the Republican National Convention. By the end of 1976, the United States had reduced its military personnel in Taiwan from over 9,000 at the close of 1972 to a mere 1,140. And as a further sign of favoritism, the administration authorized the Control Data Corporation to sell high-speed computers to China—ostensibly for oil exploration purposes, though the computers had potential military applications, and Ford and Kissinger had approved weak controls over their use.[17]

Ultimately, Ford's and Kissinger's meetings with Deng and Mao were inconsequential compared with the extraordinary political developments going on in China.[18] Although not a hint of Deng's precarious situation came across in the meetings, his fortunes were falling again: his efforts to rehabilitate more victims of the Cultural Revolution had provoked the wrath of Mao's wife Jiang Qing and her fellow radicals. After Zhou died in January 1976, Mao nominated a nonentity, Minister of Security Hua Guofeng, instead of Deng, to be acting premier. Hua was a centrist, and the move raised prospects for more political conflict with Party radicals.[19]

In early April, demonstrations at Tiananmen Square to honor Zhou and to denounce Jiang turned into riots, which the police forcefully suppressed. Mao agreed with the Politburo that Deng was behind the "counter-revolutionary riot," and he made Hua premier and stripped Deng of all his posts. This time, Deng had made contingency plans in case of trouble: he dodge Jiang and others in the Gang of Four and immediately went into hiding with the secret protection of a friendly Politburo member.[20]

Mao's credibility plummeted after the Tiananmen Square incident. The political situation became even more volatile as the Gang renewed attacks on Hua and blocked his initiatives. Hua temporized, but Mao's death on 8 September 1976 forced a resolution of the political crisis when the Gang demanded that the Politburo make Jiang Qing premier. Hua, fearing that radical leaders would try to seize political power, had them arrested on 6 October. Without Mao, the Gang of Four had no protection, and Hua began to consolidate his position. Within a few days, Deng contacted Hua, expressed his loyalty, and provided policy and political advice. Deng's rehabilitation took some effort, but within months he was was restored to his posts and promoting the mix of political authoritarianism and "capitalist road" economics that would predominate late twentieth-century Chinese development.

For years Kissinger had worried about the impact of the passing of Mao and Zhou on U.S.–PRC relations. Months before these events began to unfold, however, a more immediate concern was the extent to which Washington could normalize relations with Beijing without antagonizing Taiwan and its U.S. supporters. In early July 1975, with a meeting with PRC Liaison Office Chief Huang Zhen scheduled, Kissinger met with his China specialists for a brief policy review. Phillip Habib, Winston Lord, and Richard Solomon had recently presented him with a secret study recommending a "serious effort" to determine whether President Ford could use his forthcoming visit for normalizing diplomatic relations with China. While the advisers opposed normalization "at any price," they did believe that an acceptable deal would help "stabilize a non-confrontation relationship," sustain Mao's anti-Soviet policy, and solidify the U.S. posture in Asia.[21]

Yet the package deal recommended by the advisers contained some innately controversial issues: keeping U.S. relations with Taiwan as close to an official level as possible, continued U.S. arms sales to Taiwan at levels to be discussed, and "a unilateral statement by Peking expressing the idea that the PRC does not contemplate the use of force in resolving the Taiwan question. Kissinger was not slow to react this study:

SECRET SENSITIVE
MEMORANDUM OF CONVERSATION
PARTICIPANTS: The Secretary, Henry A. Kissinger; Assistant Secretary [Philip] Habib; Mr. Winston Lord; Deputy Assistant Secretary Gleysteen [William Henry], Jr.; Mr. Richard Solomon, NSC; Jerry Bremer, Notetaker
SUBJECT: China
DATE: July 6, 1975[A]

The Secretary: I don't really have that much to say. I have read your paper and I just won't do it that way. It's exactly the same paper you presented me last year.
Lord: No, it isn't. The question is: On your advance trip do you make some serious effort to find their security requirements?
The Secretary: For political reasons it's just impossible for the US to go for normalization before '76. If there's any one thing that will trigger a conservative reaction to Ford, that's it.
Lord: We recognize that and felt that if the terms were decent enough perhaps it's less of a political problem.
The Secretary: I've got a problem with Panama and China.[22] I don't even agree with your intellectual thesis—that this is the right time to force it.
Lord: The last time they didn't want to discuss it.
The Secretary: Even if they did, what they said to the Professor was for domestic consumption. You can't hold a government to what they say for domestic consumption.[23]

A Source: National Archives, Record Group 59, Department of State Records Policy Planning Staff (Director's Files), 1969–77 (hereafter referred to as *PPS*, with archival box number and file information), box 332, unlabeled file.

Lord: Presumably we would make our own statement.

The Secretary: What is our legal basis for defending part of one country?

Gleysteen: There is none.

The Secretary: If that's the case, we can't afford to have it in a campaign.

Solomon: They have clearly indicated in seven or eight places recently their desire to be flexible. They're afraid Ford will cancel his trip.

The Secretary: The trip is clear. They are anxious for it but I see no flexibility on Taiwan.

Lord: We recognize there is not much room for maneuverability. The only issue is whether you try to see the terms.

Habib: It's difficult to avoid discussing during your trip.

The Secretary: But suppose they give us generous terms? What do I do then? Pocket it and say, "We'll have no deal for two years." Anyway can they go beyond what they've told this guy?

Gleysteen: No, the question is what kind of relationship would they permit.

The Secretary: We can consider that when we have to sell this to Congress. What do we say then, by the way? Are we going to continue to send arms?

Gleysteen: You have to be able to say yes.

The Secretary: But do we have a legal basis?

Gleysteen: There is no legal barrier if the host government tolerates it. That's the most crucial aspect.

Habib: They would have on a sales basis. No credit.

The Secretary: But then it is essentially within their power to stop it at any point.

Lord: We have always had this dilemma from the time we started this relationship. You have to make it clear in your unilateral statement.

The Secretary: I'm wondering where we'll be if we go down this road. I'll try to raise it with the President but I know the answer. Those guys over there won't even take on Panama right now.

Lord: The paper argues the importance of doing this from our international position, and also argues that there is a need for some serious discussion when you go there in August.[24]

The Secretary: Who said I was going in August? I am certainly not going in August.

Lord: If they give you a bad deal in return, your position would be strengthened. But if it generates an offer then I agree we have a bind.

The Secretary: What if they go to the limit?

Gleysteen: I think the chances are not very high they'd go that far. I think the terms in the pre-visit will be very tough.

The Secretary: I think we're better off saying we don't think we're quite ready. We've told them what we need.

Lord: I think we can be more concrete and say that we cannot do it without satisfaction on security.

Habib: I don't think they'll give you their last position when you are there. Won't they hold that out for the President?

Lord: No.

The Secretary: It is not their way of negotiating.

Solomon: They might make the Presidential trip conditional on something.

The Secretary: No. How would they react if he visited other countries in Asia do you think—like the Philippines and Indonesia?

Habib: If he did it on the way back, it would be no problem at all. I think that's a good idea.

The Secretary: Then it's not a special trip to China. What about Malaysia?

Habib: I think the essential ones are the Philippines and Indonesia.

The Secretary: How about Australia?

Habib: It depends on what's happening there.

The Secretary: Can they do Australia and not New Zealand?

Habib: It's difficult. The New Zealanders wouldn't understand.

The Secretary: They are the worst bores in the world.

Habib: That's because we never have any problems with them. All they ever talk about is cheese and butter.

The Secretary: And mutton. What do I want from them this evening?[25]

Lord: Do you want to discuss your trip?

The Secretary: They have to make a proposal to us.

Lord: Since the last time you've seen them, they are more nervous.

The Secretary: I noticed that whatever you said to them about Schlesinger didn't get through. They told a group of Iranians that they thought [Donald] Rumsfeld's and [Robert] Hartmann's influence was rising over mine. That's just stupid. Rumsfeld I can see, but Hartmann I don't understand at all.

Solomon: They're fed by third countries.

The Secretary: Hartmann is slipping in the White House and certainly has no relation to me.

Lord: It should be up to them to suggest something on your trip.

(Secretary is interrupted for a phone call.)

Habib: On the visit, you did put some suggested times for the President's trip and they answered that any time was all right. I suppose you could mention a specific time now.

The Secretary: Why can't they raise the visit?

Habib: I think they probably think that they've already replied to you.

Solomon: If you really want to raise their anxieties, don't mention it at all. Otherwise, you could just mention your trip which will make them only slightly less nervous.

Lord: Or ask if they've had any further word from Beijing.

Habib: His answer will be—"It's up to you."

The Secretary: I won't go next time unless they understand that I am to see Mao. I will not go through that BS again with our press.

Lord: I agree that we should not explore normalization unless we're prepared to go through with it.

The Secretary: My experience with the Chinese is to tell them exactly what our position is. Be frank with them.

Lord: Our concern is that the relationship is apt to unravel if nothing happens in the next two years.

The Secretary: I don't know. In my view, the relationship is based on their fear of the Russians.

Gleysteen: It is, but our people interpret it differently.

Habib: Another problem is your relationship to the process itself and to the understandings they've developed with you. You're the only one left. And that has meaning to them.

Gleysteen: One point that is not made in the paper is that the period of six months to a year now is a good one in Taiwan where the people are braced for a change.

The Secretary: If we could find a step toward normalization, I'd be receptive to it. But what kind of steps are there?

Lord: Things like lowering Taiwan to a Chargé level and lowering our arms supplies.

Gleysteen: You could get into some domestic problems with that.

The Secretary: Perhaps you could strengthen the unity point and find some formula to do that.

Solomon: That is always the strongest card with them. That's the core of normalization. I think they could be playing Deng as the front man.

The Secretary: If that's what they want, then we can do something along those lines.

Habib: I think you want to start this afternoon anyway with a review of what you're going to say to Gromyko and then go on the trip.

Solomon: There's only one argument for doing something and that is that if their situation dissipates so badly there, that they were to turn to the Soviets.

Doing something might enable Zhou and Mao to hold their domestic constituency for our relationship.

The Secretary: Well, I'm willing to find some step short of normalization.

[When Huang met with Kissinger the next day to review current developments, he repeated Deng's statements about the unconditional nature of Ford's visit to Beijing: "if there is a meeting of minds . . . that is fine; but if there is no meeting of minds, that is also fine." Kissinger hinted at the possibility of "intermediate steps between a full meeting of minds and no progress" in bilateral relations, but Huang did not acknowledge the hint.[26] Kissinger's advisers studied "partial steps," such as a U.S. statement on one China, a claims settlement, a hotline, and more research and educational exchanges, but the Chinese showed no interest in halfway measures, as Foreign Minister Qiao made clear when he met with Kissinger again in late September.[27] After a lengthy discussion of international issues, the conversation turned to President Ford's visit. The following excerpt shows Kissinger probing Qiao's statement about "some step forward on the basis of the Shanghai communique" and the Foreign Minister avoiding an answer.][28]

Foreign Minister Qiao: There is no question about it. We have our common ground, as is stated in the Shanghai Communique.

Secretary Kissinger: But when you said we should have some advance in our relationship, what did you have in mind?

Foreign Minister Qiao: (laughs nervously) I was just speaking abstractly. As Vice Premier Deng Xiaoping told many U.S. friends, it is useful for the two sides to have discussions. We can see if there is a step forward on the basis of the Shanghai communique. But it doesn't matter if there is none.

* * *

Secretary Kissinger: But you understand that we cannot complete the process regarding Taiwan, but we can have some progress (in other areas).

Foreign Minister Qiao: (Obviously seeking to reorient the discussion.) As friends, as this is not the first time that we have met, how do you view the world situation? Can we have peaceful coexistence; or will war break out?[29]

[Qiao's failure to respond hardly discouraged Kissinger from trying to persuade the Chinese to support partial steps toward normalization. On October 19, he arrived in Beijing for several days of talks but mainly to negotiate the communiqué for President Ford's visit. Expecting some give and take in the communiqué negotiating process, Kissinger wanted the final document to symbolize "considerable progress" in U.S.– PRC relations. His visit started off badly, however, when Qiao criticized détente in his banquet toast: "the stark reality is not that détente has started to[sic] a new stage but that the danger of a new world war is mounting." He went on to say, "[t]o base

oneself on illusions, to mistake hopes or wishes for reality . . . will only abet the ambitions of expansionism."[30]

The next morning, Kissinger met with Deng and Qiao to work out the details of Ford's visit. Qiao's toast was undoubtedly on Kissinger's mind when he reminded them that it would "serve the interests of neither side if it would appear that we were quarreling. I think we should reserve that for the UN and not for a Presidential visit." The main focus of the meeting was Kissinger's usual briefing on the world situation, including the Middle East, U.S.–European relations, and East Asia, all framed by the customary language on the need to prevent Soviet hegemony. He noted that the Chinese would prefer that the United States take an "intransigent" approach everywhere toward the Soviets, and observed that the U.S. domestic political situation prevented just that, although the administration was resisting expansionism in Angola, Portugal, and elsewhere. In this excerpt he also discussed his critics:][31]

Kissinger: . . . The very people who are attacking us, now and then, for détente—I am speaking of Americans, I will speak of foreigners later—are also telling us what is wrong in the Middle East is that we are not settling it cooperatively with the Soviet Union—which has been our whole policy to avoid. You have seen enough of our people here so that you can form your own judgment. But if we had, for example, done what Mr. Vance and his crew recommended, namely, to renounce the first use of nuclear weapons, then the effect on our relative power rationale would lead to the Finlandization of Western Europe. But it cannot be, and we do not believe it can be in the interests of any country to allow the Soviet Union to believe we would accept a major strategic change—whether it is in the East or the West—concerning the use of nuclear weapons. It is in our interest to make the Soviet Union believe that we will not acquiesce in an overturning of the equilibrium no matter what weapons are involved.

[In the course of the discussion, Deng questions U.S. grain sales to the Soviets, Western credits, and sales of technology to Moscow, and the results of the Helsinki Conference.]

Kissinger: While we have talked more than we have done in economic credits, the Europeans have done more than they have said. They have given altogether—between the Federal Republic and France—about $7.5 billion in credit. We have given them about 500 million over years.
Deng: $7 billion?
Kissinger: Yes. We have used the prospect of technology to moderate their foreign policy conduct and we are trying to employ a strategy of keeping the Soviets dependent by not selling plants but parts to them. It is the folly of the European countries that they are selling plants. Unfortunately the small

amount of U.S. credits has had the effect of throwing the business into the hands of the Europeans who have no strategy at all. For us it is not a business proposition. We are doing it for a strategic proposition . . .

Deng: . . . we have noticed that those who have been most enthusiastic in proclaiming the so-called victories of the European Security Conference are first of all the Soviet Union and secondly the United States.

Kissinger: No. First of all the Soviet Union and secondly our domestic opponents in the United States. The United States Government has not claimed any great achievements for the European Security Conference. The Soviet Union has . . . must claim success since it pursued this policy for fifteen years.

Our indications are that the Soviet Union may feel—whatever they say publicly—that they have miscalculated with respect to the European Security Conference. All they got from the West were general statements about matters that had already been settled in the past while we have obtained means of very specific pressures on matters of practical issues.

There were no unsettled frontiers in Europe. The Balkan frontiers were settled in 1946-47 in the peace conferences in Paris. The Eastern frontier of Poland was settled at Yalta. The Western frontier of Poland was recognized by both German states. There are no frontiers in Europe that are not recognized. Not all of our politicians know this but this is legally a fact.

[During a review of U.S.–PRC relations, Kissinger tries to justify his draft communiqué's emphasis on partial steps toward normalization.]

Kissinger: . . . Let me say a word about our bilateral relations. On normalization, we have made clear our continuing commitment to the principles of the Shanghai Communique, and we will suggest to you some formulations in the communique which suggest some progress in that direction. We think it is important to show some vitality and forward movement in our bilateral relationship. We do not do this because we particularly care about the level of trade between the United States and China, and we believe also that China, having survived 2,000 years of its history without extensive contact with the United States, may manage to stagger on for many more years without extensive exchange between our various cultural troupes. We can even survive your favorite songs without revolution. But to us that is not the issue. To us the issue is how to be in the best position to resist hegemonial aspirations in the West as well as in the East. And if that is the case, it is important that we show some movement in our relationship. It is difficult to gain public support for what may have to be done if China is not an important element in American consciousness, and it cannot be unless there is some improvement in our bilateral relationship. This is entirely up to you.

[Although the peppery Deng raises questions about U.S. policy in the morning, he refrains from firing cannons until the afternoon when he delivers a sharp critique that Kissinger believed Mao had directed in outline. After unfavorably comparing the current administration's policies to Nixon's, Deng takes up the theme he had emphasized a year earlier, namely, that the Polar Bear's major focus was the West, not the East: "It is out to fix the United States." The excerpts that come next show Deng going further, using language that Ronald Reagan would have relished, by attacking the Helsinki Conference and other manifestations of détente as examples of "appeasement" policy.][32]

Vice Premier Deng: . . . We have always believed that we should rely on our independent strength to deal with the Soviet Union, and we have never cherished any illusions about this. We have told this to the Doctor as well as to visiting American friends. We do not depend on nuclear weapons; even less on nuclear protection (by other countries). We depend on two things: First is the perseverance of the 800 million Chinese people. If the Soviet Union wants to attack China it must be prepared to fight for at least two decades. We mainly depend on millet plus rifles. Of course, this millet plus rifles is different from what we had during Yenan times. We pursue a policy of self-reliance in our economic construction and also in our strategic problems.

. . . By recalling history, I mean the period prior to the Second World War—the period 1936 to 1939, which is particularly worthwhile to recall. The Doctor studies history and I think is more knowledgeable than I . . . (Chamberlain and Daladier) pursued a policy of appeasement towards Hitler, and shortly after that the Munich agreement was concluded.

In pursuing such policies the purpose of Chamberlain and Daladier was obvious. They wanted to direct the peril Eastward, and their first aim was to appease Hitler so that he would not take rash actions. Their second aim was to direct the peril toward the East. The stark historical realities have brought out the failure of the policies carried out by Chamberlain and Daladier. Their policies have gone to the opposite of their wishes.

. . . So in fact this appeasement policy led to an earlier break out of the Second World War. In our contacts with quite a number of Europeans they often raise the lessons of Munich. According to our observations, we may say that the danger of such historical tragedy is increasing.

. . . In terms of strategy, Soviet weapons have far exceeded those of the

West. Also you have reached the equilibrium of weapons. In terms of total military strength, the Soviet Union has a greater military strength than the United States and the European countries put together. But the Soviet Union has two big weaknesses: One, they lack food grains; the second is that their industrial equipment and technology is backward. In the long run although the Soviet Union has a greater military strength, these two weaknesses have put the Soviet Union in a weak position. It is limited in its strength so that when a war breaks out the Soviet Union cannot hold out long.

Therefore, we do not understand why the United States and the West have used their strong points to make up for the Soviet weakness. If the United States and Europe have taken advantage of the weaknesses of the Soviet Union you might have been in a stronger negotiating position.

As for our views on the Helsinki Conference, I think you know our views, which differ from yours. We call it the European *Insecurity* Conference and you call it the European *Security* Conference. The Munich agreement pulled the wool over the eyes of Chamberlain, Daladier, and some European people. And in the case when you supply them, makeup for the weak points of the Soviet Union, you help the Soviet Union to overcome its weaknesses. You can say you pulled the wool over the eyes of the West and demoralized the Western people and let them slacken their pace. We have a Chinese saying: A donkey is made to push the mill stone because when you make the donkey to push around the mill stone you have to blindfold it.

. . . We always feel that to rely on the European Security Conference, or anything else in an attempt to appease the Russians, will fail.

. . . The most effective way to deal with the possible attack from the Russians is not what you call agreements or treaties, (not) what is written on paper, but actual preparations.

As for China, we have told you on many occasions, and I will [again] tell you frankly that China fears nothing under heaven or on earth. China will not ask favors from anyone. We depend on the digging of tunnels. We rely on millet plus rifles to deal with all problems internationally and locally, including the problems in the East.

[Kissinger is rather aggrieved by this. He notes that the administration's policy is what "President Nixon would pursue if it had not been for Watergate," and continues with a detailed justification of his stance toward the Soviets.]

Secretary Kissinger: . . . I must say I listened to the Vice Premier's presentation with some sadness. I had thought, obviously incorrectly, that some of the public statements which I had heard were said for public effect.

. . . The Vice Premier was kind enough to point out the lessons of history between 1936 and 1939. He pointed out that those in the West who tried to push the aggressor towards the East became the first victims of the attack; and that is true. But it is also true that those in the East who sought to escape their dilemma by pushing their aggressor toward the West eventually became the objects of the aggressor anyway.

. . . And when we say that the West and the East have essentially the same strategic problem, we don't say this because we have an interest in participating in the defense of the East. Anyone who knows the American domestic situation must know that this cannot be our overwhelming ambition. We say it because strategically wherever the attack occurs it will affect the other. And you act on these assumptions too.

. . . And we are saying this not to do you any favors, because you are not all that helpful to us in other parts of the world. We are doing this out of our own national interest.

. . . since I have been in Washington we have gone to a confrontation with the Soviet Union three times: Once over a nuclear submarine base in Cuba; once over the Syrian invasion of Jordan; once over the question of the alert in the Middle East in 1973 and — no, four times — once on the question of access routes to Berlin. We did all of these things on our own, without knowing what any other country, much less China, would do.

. . . The Vice Premier referred to the spirit of Munich. I have studied that period and I lived through it, as a victim, so I know it rather well. The Munich policy was conducted by governments who denied that there was a danger, and who attempted to avoid their problems by denying that they existed. The current United States policy, as we have attempted to tell you, has no illusions about the danger, but it attempts to find the most effective means of resistance given the realities we face. A country that spends $110 billion a year for defense cannot be said to be pursuing the spirit of Munich.

But the reality we face is a certain attitude that has developed in the United States and an attitude that exists also in Europe even much more.

I know some of the Europeans who you talk about. Some are personally good friends of mine. But there is no European of any standing that has any question about what the United States will do. In any threat, we will be there. Our concern is whether the Europeans will be there. It is the United States that organizes the defense of the North Atlantic and that brings about the only cohesion that exists. It was not the United States that advocated the European Security Conference. It was, rather, to ease some of the pressures on the European governments that we reluctantly agreed to it in 1971.

. . . If you follow the present investigations that are going on in America, you will see that it was the present Administration, including myself, that has used methods to prevent the Soviet Union from stretching out its hands— even if these are not your preferred methods.[33]

. . . We do not rely on the European Security Conference. And we do not rely on detente. Nor is everyone in the United States who talks against detente is a reliable opponent of the Soviet Union, because without a strategic grasp of the situation much of it (anti-detente talk) is simply politics. To talk tough is easy—to act with strength and maintain support for a strong policy over a period of time in a democracy is a difficult problem.

If the Soviet Union should stretch out its hands, we will be brutal in our response, no matter where it occurs—and we won't ask people whether they share our assessment when we resist. But to be able to do this we have to prepare our public by our own methods, and by methods that will enable us to sustain this policy over many years, and not go like [Secretary of State John Foster] Dulles from a period of intransigence to a period of excessive conciliation.

. . . Now I would like to correct a few other misapprehensions which the Vice Premier voiced, and then I will make one other observation.

One thing has to do with relative military strength. It is perfectly true that the Soviet Union has gained in relative strength in the last decade. This is not the result of the agreements that have been signed. This is the result of changes in technology, and the erroneous decision of the Administration that was in office in the 60's when the Soviet Union was building up its strategic forces. If you analyze the results of the (SALT) agreement of 1972, since 1972 the strategic strength of the United States has increased considerably relative to that of the Soviet Union. It is also true that after some point in the field of strategic weapons, it is difficult to translate military superiority into a political advantage.

With respect to the second agreement, the Vladivostok agreement, you must have translated what I said incorrectly from the German. There has been no change in the Soviet strength since Vladivostok. Since the Soviet Union does not dismantle their obsolete units, they have 2,700 units and they have had those for five years. After Vladivostok they would have to get rid of 200. Since we do get rid of our obsolete units we have somewhat less than 2400. But numbers are not so important anyway, as each (U.S.) unit can carry more warheads. Moreover, since the Soviets like big things which take room, they have about 85 to 90 percent of their forces on land, where they are vulnerable because the accuracy of our forces is improved. Less than 20 percent of our forces are on land, and they are less vulnerable. So it is not true that in the strategic balance we are behind, even though there are many newspaper articles in America written for political purposes that assert this.

In 1960 President Kennedy was elected by speaking of the missile gap, even though the Soviet Union had only 30 missiles, each of which took ten hours to get ready to fire and we had 1,200 airplanes.[34] Ever since then it has been the secret dream of every American presidential candidate to run on a missile gap campaign, so we are in danger of this issue erupting every four years.

. . . We do not object to your public posture. We think it is essentially correct, and indeed it is even helpful. We do object when you direct it against us, when you accuse us of betraying our allies and endangering the security of the world by deliberately promoting war and standing on the sidelines, when in fact we are doing actual things to prevent a war and preserve the world equilibrium.

. . . It is important that you have a correct perception of our objectives. If you think we are engaged in petty tactical maneuvers then that would be a pity for both of us. You do not ask for favors, and we do not ask for favors. The basis of a correct policy is an accurate perception of the national interest and respect by each side for the perception of the national interest of the other.

This is why we think a visit by the President here would be useful, and that is the purpose of our policy. We don't need theater, and we don't need you to divert Soviet energies — that would be a total misconception and it might lead to the same catastrophe as in the 1930s. After all we resisted Soviet expansion when we were allies, and we will resist it for our own reasons as you resist it for your own reasons.

I repeat, we attach great significance to our relations. We are prepared to coordinate. We think you are serious, and we are equally serious. On that basis I think we can have a useful relationship.

COMMENTARY

The next day, a late-afternoon discussion on the southern flank of Europe gave Kissinger an opportunity to show how stalwart the administration had been in supporting Portuguese anti-Communists, in providing military aid to Yugoslavia, and in opposing the "historic compromise" between Italian Christian Democrats and Communists. The discussion ended when Deng announced that Chairman Mao was ready to meet with Kissinger's party.[35]

The meeting's circumstances were extraordinary. Mao, the self-professed warlord and bureaucrat was plainly very ill; Kissinger later observed that the "the willpower to have a two-hour meeting was unbelievable." While Kissinger must have been gratified that Mao would see him—they had last met in November 1973—he found the meeting so "disturbing" that he nearly forgot to make the usual flattering statements. Mao could barely speak and was often far from intelligible, a symptom of Lou Gehrig's disease; Winston Lord wondered if some of his comments were the aimless wanderings of a "somewhat senile man." Nevertheless, in a somber report, Lord observed that the meeting was not only less cordial than previous talks with Mao but it clarified all that was going wrong between Beijing and Washington: the "cooling of our relationship linked to the Chinese perception of the US as a fading power in the face of Soviet advance." Certainly, the thrust of Mao's statements paralleled themes that Deng had already stressed. Mao criticized the priority that Washington had given to relations with Moscow, and he opined that the United States would take a "Dunkirk" approach rather than sacrifice itself for the defense of Europe.[36]

DEPARTMENT OF STATE
SECRET/SENSITIVE
MEMORANDUM OF CONVERSATION
PARTICIPANTS: Chairman Mao Zedong; Deng Xiaoping, Vice
  Premier of the State Council of the People's Republic of China; Qiao
  Guanhua, Minister of Foreign Affairs; Amb. Huang Zhen, Chief of
  PRC Liaison Office, Washington; Wang Hairong, Vice Minister of
  Foreign Affairs; Tang Wensheng, Deputy Director, Department of
  American and Oceanic Affairs and interpreter; Zhang Hanzhi,
  Deputy Director, Department of American and Oceanic Affairs; Dr.
  Henry A. Kissinger, Secretary of State and Assistant to the President
  for National Security Affairs; Ambassador George Bush, Chief of
  U.S. Liaison Office, Peking; Winston Lord, Director, Policy
  Planning Staff, Department of State
DATE AND TIME: Tuesday, October 21, 1975 6:25 – 8:05 P.M.
PLACE: Chairman Mao's Residence, Beijing[B]

At 5:45 p.m. during a meeting with Vice Premier Deng Xiaoping, Secretary Kissinger was informed that Chairman Mao would like to see him at 6:30. He

---

[B] Source: *PPS*, box 379, China—Sensitive—Chron Oct.-Dec. 1975.

was asked to name those members of his party, including his wife, whom he would like to have greeted by the Chairman, as well as those two officials who would accompany him to the talks themselves. The meeting with Deng lasted another 15 minutes. Then Dr. Kissinger and his party rested until 6:15, when they went from the Great Hall of the People to the Chairman's residence.

Each of the following were introduced to the Chairman in turn and exchanged brief greetings while photographs and movies were taken: Secretary Kissinger, Mrs. Kissinger, Amb. Bush, Counselor Sonnenfeldt, Assistant Secretary Habib, Director Winston Lord, Mr. William Gleysteen, Mr. Peter Rodman (NSC), and Ms. Anne Boddicker (NSC). The Chairman stood and talked with considerable difficulty. When he saw Mrs. Kissinger, he sat down and asked for a note pad and wrote out the comment that she towered over Secretary Kissinger. He then got up again and greeted the rest of the party. Then the guests were escorted out of the room except for Secretary Kissinger, Ambassador Bush and Mr. Lord.

The participants sat in arm chairs in a semi-circle. Throughout the conversation the Chairman would either speak with great difficulty, with Miss Tang and Miss Wang repeating what he said for confirmation and then translating, or he would write out his remarks on a note pad held by his nurse.[37] Throughout the conversation the Chairman gestured vigorously with his hands and fingers in order to underline his point.

Chairman Mao: You know I have various ailments all over me. I am going to heaven soon.

Secretary Kissinger: Not soon.

Chairman Mao: Soon. I've already received an invitation from God.

Secretary Kissinger: I hope you won't accept it for a long while.

Chairman Mao: I accept the orders of the Doctor.

Secretary Kissinger: Thank you. The President is looking forward very much to a visit to China and the opportunity to meet the Chairman.

Chairman Mao: He will be very welcome.

Secretary Kissinger: We attach very great significance to our relationship with the People's Republic.

Chairman Mao: There is some significance, not so very great. (Gesturing with his fingers.) You are this (wide space between two fingers.) and we are this (small space). Because you have the atom bombs, and we don't.

Secretary Kissinger: Yes, but the Chairman has often said that military power is not the only decisive factor.

Chairman Mao: As Vice Premier Deng Xiapoing has said, millet plus rifles.

Secretary Kissinger: And we have some common opponents.

Chairman Mao: Yes.

Secretary Kissinger: You said that in English and wrote it. Can I have it?

Chairman Mao: Yes. (He hands over the note he had written out.)

Secretary Kissinger: I see the Chairman is progressing in learning English. And we have some common opponents.

Chairman Mao: No (holding two fingers close together). So you have quarreled with him (pointing toward Vice Premier Deng).

Secretary Kissinger: Only about the means for a common objective.

Chairman Mao: Yesterday, during your quarrel with the Vice Premier, you said the US asked nothing of China and China asked nothing of the US. As I see it, this is partially right and partially wrong. The small issue is Taiwan, the big issue is the world. (He begins coughing and the nurse comes in to help him.) If neither side had anything to ask from the other, why would you be coming to Beijing? If neither side had anything to ask, then why did you want to come to Beijing, and why would we want to receive you and the President?

Secretary Kissinger: We come to Beijing because we have a common opponent and because we think your perception of the world situation is the clearest of any country we deal with and with which we agree on some . . . many points.

Chairman Mao: That's not reliable. Those words are not reliable. Those words are not reliable because according to your priorities the first is the Soviet Union, the second is Europe and the third is Japan.

Secretary Kissinger: That is not correct.

Chairman Mao: It is in my view. (Counting with his fingers) America, the Soviet Union, Europe, Japan, China. You see, five (holding up his five fingers).

Secretary Kissinger: That's not correct.

Chairman Mao: So then we quarrel.

Secretary Kissinger: We quarrel. The Soviet Union is a great danger for us, but not a high priority.

Chairman Mao: That's not correct. It is a superpower. There are only two superpowers in the world (counting on his fingers). We are backward (counting on his fingers). America, the Soviet Union, Europe, Japan, China. We come last. America, Soviet Union, Europe, Japan, China — look.

Secretary Kissinger: I know I almost never disagree with the Chairman, but he is not correct on this point — only because it is a matter of our priority.

Chairman Mao: (Tapping both his shoulders) We see that what you are doing is leaping to Moscow by way of our shoulders, and these shoulders are now useless. You see, we are the fifth. We are the small finger.

Secretary Kissinger: We have nothing to gain in Moscow.

Chairman Mao: But you can gain Taiwan in China.

Secretary Kissinger: We can gain Taiwan in China?

Chairman Mao: But you now have the Taiwan of China.

Secretary Kissinger: But we will settle that between us.

Chairman Mao: In a hundred years.

Secretary Kissinger: That's what the Chairman said the last time I was here.

Chairman Mao: Exactly.

Secretary Kissinger: Much less. It won't take a hundred years.

Chairman Mao: It's better for it to be in your hands. And if you were to send it back to me now, I would not want it, because it's not wantable. There are a huge bunch of counter-revolutionaries there. A hundred years hence we will want it (gesturing with his hand), and we are going to fight for it.

Secretary Kissinger: Not a hundred years.

Chairman Mao: (Gesturing with his hand, counting) It is hard to say. Five years, ten, twenty, a hundred years. It's hard to say. (Points toward the ceiling) And when I go to heaven to see God, I'll tell him it's better to have Taiwan under the care of the United States now.

Secretary Kissinger: He'll be very astonished to hear that from the Chairman.

Chairman Mao: No, because God blesses you, not us. God does not like us (waves his hands) because I am a militant warlord, also a communist. That's why he doesn't like me. (Pointing to the three Americans.) He likes you and you and you.

Secretary Kissinger: I've never had the pleasure of meeting him, so I'm not sure.

Chairman Mao: I'm sure. I'm 82 years old now. (Points toward Secretary Kissinger) And how old are you? 50 maybe.

Secretary Kissinger: 51.

Chairman Mao: (Pointing toward Vice Premier Deng.) He's 71. (Waving his hands) And after we're all dead, myself, him (Deng), Zhou Enlai, and Ye Jianying, you will still be alive. See? We old ones will not do. We are not going to make it out.

Secretary Kissinger: If I may say one thing about what the Chairman said earlier about our relative priorities.

Chairman Mao: All right.

Secretary Kissinger: Because the Soviet Union is a superpower it is inevitable that it has much priority, and we have to deal with it very frequently. But in terms of strategy we are trying to contain Soviet expansionism, and this is why in strategy China has priority for us. But we don't want to use China to jump to Moscow because that would be suicidal.

Chairman Mao: You've already jumped there, but you no longer need our shoulders.

Secretary Kissinger: We haven't jumped there. It's a tactical phase which the President will also affirm to you.

Chairman Mao: And please convey my regards to your President.

Secretary Kissinger: I will do this.

Chairman Mao: We welcome his visit. Do you have any way to assist me in curing my present inability to speak clearly?

Secretary Kissinger: You make yourself very well understood even so.

Chairman Mao: This part (pointing to his brain) is working well, and I can eat and sleep. (Patting his knees) These parts are not good. They do not ache, but they are not firm when I walk. I also have some trouble with my lungs. And in one word, I am not well, and majorally (*sic*) unwell.

Secretary Kissinger: It's always a great joy to see the Chairman.

Chairman Mao: You know I'm a showcase exhibit for visitors.

Secretary Kissinger: I've read over our conversation two years ago, Mr. Chairman. I think it was one of the most profound expositions of international affairs, and we take it very seriously.

Chairman Mao: But there's still some things which we must wait to observe. Some of the assessments I made still have to be moved by the objective situation.

Secretary Kissinger: But I think the basic assessment the Chairman made at that time insofar as the situation has developed has proven correct, and we basically agree with it. We've had a difficult period because of the resignation of President Nixon, and we've had to do more maneuvering than we would have liked.

Chairman Mao: I think that can be done. Maneuvering is allowable.

Secretary Kissinger: It was essential, but we are putting that situation behind us.

Chairman Mao: Europe is too soft now.

Secretary Kissinger: We agree with the Chairman—Europe is too soft.

Chairman Mao: They are afraid of the Soviet Union.

Secretary Kissinger: They are afraid of the Soviet Union and their domestic situation.

Chairman Mao: Japan is seeking hegemony.

Secretary Kissinger: Japan is not yet ready to seek hegemony. That will require one more change in leadership. But potentially Japan has the potential for seeking hegemony.

Chairman Mao: Yes.

Secretary Kissinger: I think the next generation of leaders, my student Nakasone, he was a student of mine when I was a professor . . . That generation will be more ready to use the power of Japan.

Chairman Mao: Europe is too scattered, too loose.

Secretary Kissinger: Yes. We prefer Europe to be unified and stronger.

Chairman Mao: That is also our preference. But it is too loose and spread out, and it is difficult for it to achieve unity.

Secretary Kissinger: Also it does not have too many strong leaders.

Chairman Mao: Oh, yes.

Secretary Kissinger: But Schmidt, who comes here next week, is the strongest of the leaders in Europe today.

Chairman Mao: France is afraid of Germany. (counting on his fingers) They are afraid of the reunification of West Germany and East Germany, which would result in a fist.

Secretary Kissinger: Yes, France prefers to keep Germany divided.

Chairman Mao: (Nodding yes) That's not good.

Secretary Kissinger: But they may unite on a nationalistic basis, East and West Germany.

Chairman Mao: Yes, we are in favor of reunification.

Secretary Kissinger: It depends under whom.

Chairman Mao: West Germany has a population of 50 million while East Germany has a population of 18 million.

Secretary Kissinger: West Germany is the strongest side materially.

Chairman Mao: But the reunification of Germany now would not be dangerous.

Secretary Kissinger: We favor the reunification of Germany, but right now it would be prevented militarily by the Soviet Union. But the US supports the reunification of Germany.

Chairman Mao: We agree on that, you and we.

Secretary Kissinger: And we are not afraid of a unified Germany, but Soviet power in Europe must be weakened before it can happen.

Chairman Mao: Without a fight the Soviet Union cannot be weakened.

Secretary Kissinger: Yes, but it is important for us to pick the right moment for this, and during the period of Watergate we were in no position to do it. And that is why we had to maneuver.

Chairman Mao: And it seems it was not necessary to conduct the Watergate affair in that manner.

Secretary Kissinger: It was inexcusable. Inexcusable. (Miss Tang indicates puzzlement.) It was inexcusable to conduct it in that manner. It was a minor event that was played into a national and international tragedy by a group of very shortsighted people. President Nixon was a good President (Chairman Mao nods affirmatively) and I'm still in very frequent contact with him.

Chairman Mao: Please convey my regards to Mr. Nixon.

Secretary Kissinger: I'll call him when I return.

Chairman Mao: So please first of all send my regards to President Ford and secondly my regards to Mr. Nixon.

Secretary Kissinger: I'll do both of these with great pleasure.

Chairman Mao: You're too busy.

Secretary Kissinger: You think I travel too much?

Chairman Mao: I was saying that you are too busy, and it seems that it won't do if you're not so busy. You cannot keep from being so busy. When the wind and rain are coming, the swallows are busy.

Secretary Kissinger: That will take me several days to understand the full significance of that.

Chairman Mao: This world is not tranquil, and a storm—the wind and rain—are coming. And at the approach of the rain and wind the swallows are busy.

Miss Tang: He (the Chairman) asks me how one says "swallow" in English and what is "sparrow." Then I said it is a different kind of bird.

Secretary Kissinger: Yes, but I hope we have a little more effect on the storm than the swallows do on the wind and rain.

Chairman Mao: It is possible to postpone the arrival of the wind and rain, but it's difficult to obstruct the coming.

Secretary Kissinger: But it's important to be in the best position to deal with it when it does come, and that is not a trivial matter. We agree with you that the wind and rain are coming or may come, and we try to put ourselves in the best possible position, not to avoid it but to overcome it.

Chairman Mao: Dunkirk.

Secretary Kissinger: Not for us.

Chairman Mao: That is not reliable. You can see that that is not the case for you now.

Secretary Kissinger: That will not be the case for us in the future.

Chairman Mao: That is not reliable. A military correspondent for the *New York Times* put out a book in August.[38]

Secretary Kissinger: Who is he?

Miss Tang: (After consultations among the Chinese) We'll look it up and tell you.

Chairman Mao: Do you think that the 300,000 troops the US has in Europe at the present time are able to resist a Soviet attack?

Secretary Kissinger: The weakness in Europe is not our troops but European troops. I think with nuclear weapons we can resist the attack.

Chairman Mao: That correspondent did not believe the US would use nuclear weapons.

Secretary Kissinger: The *New York Times* has had a vested interest in American defeats the last ten years. If there's a substantial attack in Western Europe, we'll certainly use nuclear weapons. We have 7,000 weapons in Europe, and they are not there to be captured. That is in Europe. In the US we have many more.

Chairman Mao: But there is a considerable portion of Americans who do not believe you'll use them. They do not believe Americans will be willing to die for Europe.

Secretary Kissinger: Mr. Chairman, we've come through a very difficult domestic period, partly caused by Indochina, partly caused by Watergate, in which many defeatist elements have been public. But if you watch what we've done the last five years, we always confront the Soviet Union and the Soviet Union always backs down. And I can assure you, as the President will reassure you, if the Soviet Union attacks Europe, we'll certainly use nuclear weapons. And the Soviet Union must never believe otherwise—it's too dangerous.

Chairman Mao: You have confidence, you believe in, nuclear weapons. You do not have confidence in your own army.

Secretary Kissinger: We have to face the reality that we will not have so large an army as the Soviet Union. That is a fact. And the most important fact is that no European country will build a large army. If they did, then there would not be a problem. And, therefore, we must build a strategy which is suited to that reality.

Chairman Mao: The Dunkirk strategy is not undesirable either.

Secretary Kissinger: Mr. Chairman, finally we have to have a minimum confidence in each other's statements.

There will be no Dunkirk strategy, either in the West or in the East. And if there is an attack, once we have stopped the attack, after we have mobilized, we are certain to win a war against the Soviet Union.

Chairman Mao: (Gesturing with his fingers) We adopt the Dunkirk strategy, that is we will allow them to occupy Beijing, Tianjin, Wuhan, and Shanghai, and in that way through such tactics we will become victorious and the enemy will be defeated. Both world wars, the first and the second, were conducted in that way and victory was obtained only later.

Secretary Kissinger: It is my belief that if there is a massive Soviet attack anywhere in the world, the US will become involved very quickly. And it is also my conviction that the US will never withdraw from Europe without a nuclear war.

Chairman Mao: There are two possibilities. One is your possibility, the other is that of the *New York Times*. That is also reflected in Senator Goldwater's speech of June 3 in the Senate.[39]

Secretary Kissinger: What did he say?

Miss Tang: We will send you a copy. It was during the foreign policy debate in the Senate on June 3.

Secretary Kissinger: But what was the main point?

Chairman Mao: His disbelief in Europe.

Secretary Kissinger: You have to understand, Mr. Chairman, that it is the year before the election and much of what is said is said for domestic effect. The *New York Times* has had a certain position for 20 years and it has an unparalleled record for being wrong.

Chairman Mao: It is said that the *New York Times* is controlled by a Jewish family.[40]

Secretary Kissinger: That is true.

Chairman Mao: And also the *Washington Post.*

Secretary Kissinger: The *Washington Post*—it is no longer true. (He then conferred with Ambassador Bush who pointed out that Mrs. Graham was Jewish, the daughter of Mr. Meyer.) You are right.

Chairman Mao: The proprietress is Jewish.

This Ambassador (looking toward Bush) is in a dire plight in Beijing. Why don't you come and look me up?

Ambassador Bush: I am very honored to be here tonight. I think you are busy and don't have the time to see a plain Chief of the Liaison Office.[41]

Chairman Mao: I am not busy, because I do not have to look over all the routine affairs. I only read the international news.

Secretary Kissinger: But the Chairman knows more about what is being written in America than I do. I didn't know about the book by the *New York Times* man or Senator Goldwater's speech.

Chairman Mao: You don't have the time. You are too busy.

(To Lord.) Mr. Lord, you have now been promoted.

Mr. Lord: Yes, Mr. Chairman.

Chairman Mao: (To Bush and Lord) You have both been promoted.

Secretary Kissinger: He (Bush) not yet. He will be in 1980.

Chairman Mao: He can be President.

Secretary Kissinger: In 1980.

Chairman Mao: You don't know my temperament. I like people to curse me (raising his voice and hitting his chair with his hand). You must say that Chairman Mao is an old bureaucrat and in that case I will speed up and meet you. In such a case I will make haste to see you. If you don't curse me, I won't see you, and I will just sleep peacefully.

Secretary Kissinger: That is difficult for us to do, particularly to call you a bureaucrat.

Chairman Mao: I ratify that (slamming his chair with his hand). I will only be happy when all foreigners slam on tables and curse me.

Secretary Kissinger: We will think about it, but it will not come naturally to us. If we call the Chairman a bureaucrat, it will be a tactical maneuver separate from strategy.

Chairman Mao: But I am a bureaucrat. Moreover I am also a warlord. That was the title I was given by the Soviet Union and the title "bureaucrat" was given me by the Soviet Union.

Secretary Kissinger: But I haven't seen any Soviet visitors here lately.

Chairman Mao: They are cursing us every day. Every day.

Secretary Kissinger: But we don't share the Soviet assessment of China.

Chairman Mao: (Before Secretary Kissinger's sentence is translated) Therefore, I have accepted these two titles, "warlord" and "bureaucrat." No honor could be greater. And you have said that I am a warmonger and an aggressor.

Secretary Kissinger: I?

Chairman Mao: The United States in the UN. The UN passed a resolution which was sponsored by the US in which it was declared that China committed aggression against Korea.

Secretary Kissinger: That was 25 years ago.

Chairman Mao: Yes. So it is not directly linked to you. That was during Truman's time.

Secretary Kissinger: Yes. That was a long time ago, and our perception has changed.

Chairman Mao: (Touching the top of his head) But the resolution has not yet been canceled. I am still wearing this hat "aggressor." I equally consider that the greatest honor which no other honor could excel. It is good, very good.

Secretary Kissinger: But then we shouldn't change the UN resolution?

Chairman Mao: No, don't do that. We have never put forward that request. We prefer to wear this cap of honor. Chiang Kai-shek is saying that we have committed aggression against China. We have no way to deny that. We have indeed committed aggression against China, and also in Korea. Will you please assist me on making that statement public, perhaps in one of your briefings? That is, the Soviet Union has conferred upon me the title of "warlord and bureaucrat," and the United States has conferred upon me "warmonger and aggressor."

Secretary Kissinger: I think I will let you make that public. I might not get the historically correct statement.

Chairman Mao: I have already made it public before you. I have also said this to many visiting foreigners, including Europeans. Don't you have freedom of speech?

Secretary Kissinger: Absolutely.

Chairman Mao: I also have freedom of speech, and the cannons I have fired exceed the cannons they have fired.

Secretary Kissinger: That I have noticed.

Miss Tang: You have noticed . . .

Secretary Kissinger: The Chairman's cannons.

Chairman Mao: Please send my regards to your Secretary of Defense.

Secretary Kissinger: I will do that.

Chairman Mao: I am dissatisfied that he went to Japan without coming to Beijing. We want to invite him here for the Soviets to see, but you are too miserly. The US is so rich but on this you are too miserly.

Secretary Kissinger: We can discuss it when the President is here.

Chairman Mao: Bring him along. You can bring a civilian and a military member, with your President, both a civilian and a military man.

Secretary Kissinger: Me as the civilian and Schlesinger as the military?

Chairman Mao: Yes. But I won't interfere in your internal affairs. It is up to your side to decide whom you will send.

Secretary Kissinger: Well, he will not come with the President. Maybe later.

Chairman Mao: We would like to invite him to pay a visit to the northeast of our country, Mongolia and Sinkiang. He perhaps will not go, nor would you have the courage.

Secretary Kissinger: I would go.

Chairman Mao: (Looking toward Bush) He has been.

Secretary Kissinger: I would certainly go.

Chairman Mao: Good.

Secretary Kissinger: And we have tried to suggest to you that we are prepared to advise or help in some of these problems.

Chairman Mao: As for military aspects we should not discuss that now. Such matters should wait until the war breaks out before we consider them.

Secretary Kissinger: Yes, but you should know that we would be prepared then to consider them.

Chairman Mao: So, shall we call that the end?

Secretary Kissinger: Yes.

Secretary Kissinger, Ambassador Bush, and Mr. Lord then said goodbye to Chairman Mao. Secretary Kissinger confirmed with Vice Premier Deng that the Chinese would put out a public statement on the meeting and would send the text to the US side immediately. (The Chinese statement is at Tab A.) The Americans then said goodbye to the other Chinese officials and drove away in their cars.

COMMENTARY

The next afternoon Kissinger learned that the Chinese were going to play hardball on the communiqué when Deng said that, with normalization not accomplished, "it is not the normal practice to sign certain agreements between states, for example, commercial and navigation agreements." As far as he was concerned, it "would be all right" if, for example, the claims and assets issue was "not settled in one hundred years."[42] But the Chinese held back on their formal response until midnight, when they presented Kissinger with a counterdraft communiqué. In the course of a sometimes testy exchange that lasted until 2:30 a.m., Kissinger took exception to the tough formulations on Taiwan ("entirely China's internal affair") and normalization (withdrawal all of U.S. forces from the Taiwan Straits area) as well as to the revolutionary rhetoric. Qiao pointed out that the U.S. draft was likewise unacceptable because it concealed Beijing's and Washington's different viewpoints on world affairs and overlooked the United States' "debt" on Taiwan. Only after he made a veiled threat that Ford's visit might be put off did the two sides agree to postpone announcing the visit until they had worked out an acceptable communiqué.[43]

Kissinger felt that the latest controversy was the "most annoying" and the Chinese were "insolent," but he remained confident that Beijing had "no real strategic options . . . to continuing our relationship." Qiao and Deng played tough; they even went so far as to request further delay of the announcement of Ford's visit. Ford, in turn, decided to shorten his stay and to make stops elsewhere in the region. Deng's and Qiao's last-minute agreement to an announcement suggest that they were not willing to endanger a presidential visit. Nevertheless, these sharp criticisms of U.S. policy were probably intended to push Kissinger and Ford into a more accommodating stance on diplomatic recognition. As State Department officials later observed, the Chinese "want to put us under psychological pressure by maneuvering us into a position where we want the relationship with them more than they with us.[44] Once the two sides had agreed to announce the Presidential visit, the "atmosphere returned to normal"; a White House advance party reported an "eerie feeling of unreality" because the Chinese were so cooperative and agreeable.[45]

While Kissinger had lost the battle for a communiqué, a presidential visit was far more important than the document; as he wrote, "appearances were everything." Given that, U.S.-PRC relations were not only difficult but still relatively tenuous—there were no formal diplomatic ties and levels of trade and people-to-people contacts remained low—Kissinger advised Ford to consider his visit to China as a "sustaining" one. By simply visiting China and trying to "maintain common perceptions" with the leadership, Ford could bolster the relationship and "sustain its symbolic weight."[46]

Much of the dialogue between Ford, Kissinger, Deng, and Mao was fairly pedestrian—for example, the boilerplate statements on the Soviet threat— some of it is fascinating.[47] Ford heeded Bush's advice to appear as a "straight-talking man" who can be "tough as nails with the Soviets, the Chinese, or others," so he tried to impress the Chinese with his resolve as a Cold Warrior, in combating Eurocommunism and even in his willingness to use nuclear weapons to "resist expansionism." Denying that U.S. policy had anything to do with Munich, he justified détente as essential to prevent nuclear war. Angola was then the Cold War flashpoint, and the transcripts reveal the Ford–Kissinger view of the situation as well as Mao's perspective. These exchanges also suggest that Beijing did in fact manage to pressure the U.S. into greater flexibility on normalization as well as its policy towards exports to China of high-tech items with potential military use.[48]

On his first day, Ford met with Chairman Mao. He had assumed that Mao's health would limit the meeting to a brief courtesy call, but Kissinger coached him for what would be the "centerpiece of your trip and will publicly symbolize the ongoing development" of Sino–American relations. In fact,

Ford stayed for almost two hours. After small talk, discussion turned into a detailed review of the international scene, ranging from prospects for post-Franco Spain and the Middle East to the problem of Japan and the Angolan situation.[49]

Mao asserted that "we don't have any conflicts," and he made unfavorable comparison of China's talks with the Soviets with those with Americans. This suggested that there had been no basic shift in Beijing's foreign policy, but he was rather dismissive of Ford's suggestions for joint cooperation against Moscow—"this is just talk." Moreover, he confirmed the picture of general stagnation in U.S.–PRC relations until a normalization agreement had been reached; in the next year or two, "there will not be anything great happening between our two countries."[50]

Later that day, Kissinger made a final, futile effort to get a communiqué, or at least a joint statement. Bush had advised him earlier to stop "beating the dead horse of a communiqué," but Kissinger argued that it was necessary in order to preclude "nihilistic" journalists from further speculation about a "cooling" of U.S.–PRC relations. However, Qiao was unyielding: after proffering cookies and observing that Kissinger had "put on a lot of weight," he only conceded to putting "what we think in our toasts." Kissinger wanted to tell the press that relations "are basically good and gradually improving," but he accepted Qiao's formulation: "relations are basically good and they will be gradually improving." For Qiao, until normalization had occurred, other improvement in relations—in trade and exchanges—would have to wait.[51]

Ford and Deng met the next day for further review of the international scene; their discussions moved from Europe and the Middle East to Cambodia and the *Mayaguez* affair and back to Angola. Deng said that he did not object to U.S. involvement in Angola, even if China could not participate, and he emphasized the Soviets' "tit-for-tat" approach to Angola and the need for Washington to pay attention to Soviet policy there. As the following excerpt shows, when Deng claimed that the Chinese were more experienced in dealing with the Soviets, Ford politely put him on the spot by asking what Beijing was actually doing to contain Moscow.[52]

Vice Premier Deng: . . . To speak frankly—and I hope that it will not offend you—in the dealings with the Soviet Union, perhaps we are a little more experienced than you.
The President: Let me say, Mr. Vice Premier, we have had some experience in dealing with them and we met and challenged them in a number of cases as

I indicated yesterday, and we will continue to do so. But I think it would be helpful in this frank talk with you if you could indicate the various places and ways—whether in Southeast Asia, the Middle East, or Africa—what your country is doing to meet this challenge so we can better understand how we can act in parallel.

Vice Premier Deng: (with some visible tension in his face): We have done only two things: One is to make preparations for ourselves—to make solid down-to-earth preparations. Second, we fire some empty cannons. The empty cannons include encouragement to Japan to strengthen its relations with the United States, and our encouragement of European unity and for the European countries to strengthen their relations with the United States.

And I believe you also understand that we told the Europeans that at present the total military strength of the Soviet Union is stronger than that of the United States and Western Europe put together . . .

[After wide-ranging talks on world events, including Angola—where Deng is leery of a Chinese role, though he recommends further U.S. embroilment—the discussions returned to the dilemma of U.S.–China normalization.[53]

Ford expresses his gratitude for Chinese patience on Taiwan and assures Deng that his administration will follow the Japanese model. However, he is too cautious to declare that normalization was a high priority; instead, he assures Deng that, though it will "take some time," he will be in a better position to establish diplomatic relations after the elections.[54]

Not surprisingly, Deng offered no concessions; he repeated Mao's formulations about the impossibility of a peaceful transition and declared that the whole question of Taiwan was China's own business. After providing the results of Chinese investigations into Americans missing in action in China, Deng then complains about the Dalai Lama and makes a request for high-speed computers.[55] Despite the computers' potential military applications, Kissinger is interested in breaking down restraints on sales of military-related technology to Beijing; the administration has already given the go-ahead for a pending sale of British Rolls-Royce aircraft engines to Beijing.[56] Ford's and Kissinger's eager rejoinder suggest great interest in doing more to help and perhaps to counteract some of the recent tensions.]

Deng: . . . under the present situation, some things we are interested in perhaps you find it impossible to supply. Like for instance computers of a speed of 10 million times. We do not think such issues are of great consequence.

Secretary Kissinger: Our problem is we have refused certain computers to the Soviet Union. (Deng spits into his spittoon.) I think we could approve computers to the People's Republic of China that would be of considerable quality. As long as we can at the same time maintain our policy with the Soviet Union.

Deng: I think that such issues can be discussed through trade channels. And we do not think it matters if perhaps you at the present will find it difficult to proceed; it would not be of very great consequence.

The President: Mr. Vice Premier, in principle we would be very anxious to be helpful in the computer area, and I think we can be. And certainly those matters can be discussed by the trade people, but I think with the overall attitude that we have, progress can be made in that regard.

Deng: Fine.

Secretary Kissinger: Could I make a suggestion, Mr. Vice Premier?

Deng: Okay.

Secretary Kissinger: I know your normal procedure is to do it through trade channels. But this has the consequence that you may ask for a particular model that then comes to us for decision and we refuse it for a reason that may have to do with our Soviet relationship and not the Chinese relationship. If your Ambassador could tell us informally ahead of time what you have in mind, we may be able to find a model of good quality which meets your needs which you can be sure will be approved, and we could work with the companies. Because there are many varieties which could be effective to you. If we can just find a model with technical differences to preserve the principle with the Soviet Union, then we can give it to you, and we can certainly work that out. . . . It will be with the intention of approving it, not refusing it.

The President: The Secretary has suggested the better procedure for the handling of the matter, and I would like you to know, Mr. Vice Premier, that we are very anxious to be helpful in this area. If we follow the right procedure it makes it very possible that we can cooperate.

Deng: Fine. So we think that, first of all we can study the issue and then further consider it. And we think that the solving of specific issues like this, or their all remaining unsolved, will not be of great effect to our general relations. (The Chinese all laugh.)

[Having exhausted their formal agenda, Ford and Deng turn to other issues, including Korea, Japan, more on Tibet, and Chinese agriculture and overpopulation; Deng admits, "Our country is still very backward." The discussion of Northeast Asia includes standard U.S. warnings against North Korean threats to the South as well as a brief exchange on the potential danger of Japanese militarism and the need to prevent Tokyo from playing a political or military role in South Korea. In the course of the

discussion, both Kissinger and Ford make sarcastic references about former Deputy Secretary of Defense Cyrus Vance, the leading Democrat foreign policy adviser, suggesting that they both are overconfident about 1976.]

Deng: When Mr. Cyrus Vance led a delegation of world affairs organization people to China, we discussed (Korea) with him.

Kissinger: That is like the Dalai Lama. (laughter) A government in exile. (laughter)

*　　*　　*

President: You mentioned earlier Mr. Cyrus Vance. He was a classmate of mine in Law School. I don't expect he will be back in government for some time. If ever.

COMMENTARY

Ford's visit temporarily smoothed over some tensions, but the Chinese continued to criticize détente and the "Munich-like" mentality in Washington. Ironically, in the weeks after Ford's talks with Deng and Mao, U.S.–Soviet détente deteriorated even more. The Angola situation was a significant factor, and domestic attacks on détente undermined the SALT process: Kissinger, in his weakened position, could do little to strengthen it. As détente slipped, Kissinger's advisers began to conclude that the Soviets understood very well that Beijing and Washington had not grown close together and they feared that, with Moscow's old "paranoia" about U.S. policy diminishing, Kissenger's China card lost more and more leverage in talks with the Soviets.[65]

Kissinger paid close attention to the political struggles that unfolded in the wake of Zhou's death in January 1976—most prominently, the Tiananmen Square incident and Deng's overthrow—because of the questions they raised about U.S.–PRC relations. Even before events started to get out of hand, the Chinese invited Richard Nixon to Beijing in late January, apparently to reassure Ford and Kissinger that Zhou's death and the selection of Hua Guofeng, as acting premier, foretold no important foreign policy changes.[58] However, George Bush was now running the CIA, and Ambassador Huang Zhen was staying in China until Ford sent a new liaison Chief, so high-level contacts had lapsed. There was no senior U.S. figure in Beijing to initiate talks with or even size up the new figures at the top. Finding the right person took longer than expected: it was not until March 1976 that the

White House settled on a candidate who had the prestige needed to impress Beijing—Thomas S. Gates, a Philadelphia banker who had served as secretary of the Navy and secretary of defense.

On 19 March, Ford, Kissinger, and Scowcroft met with Gates and told him that his first priority was to initiate contacts with Hua Guofeng. Gates heard some rough language from Kissinger, who seemed to resent—and perhaps even to admire—the PRC for putting the administration in a corner on normalization.

THE WHITE HOUSE
SECRET/NODIS/XGDS
PARTICIPANTS: President Ford; Thomas S. Gates, Chief-Designate of U. S. Liaison Office in Peking; Dr. Henry A. Kissinger, Secretary of State; Brent Scowcroft, Assistant to the President for National Security Affairs
DATE AND TIME: Friday, March 19, 1976 10:10-10:25 A.M. [C]

(A press session takes place first for the public announcement. Then the press leaves.)

The President: The Ambassador issue is complicated. I can only grant it for six months.[59]

Gates: That would be fine. I gather it was in part because you plan some movement and want to signal the Chinese.

Kissinger: They will interpret it that way.

Scowcroft: It will be a sign of the importance we ascribe to them.

The President: We do have to begin some movement, perhaps in 1977. But we do have to bite the bullet sometime after the election.

Kissinger: They are cold, pragmatic bastards. The President is right—we will have to move after the election. I would like to give Tom a letter either to Mao or Hua. Then we could have a verbatim report of what they say, to see if there are nuances of change. Nixon didn't record enough detail to be helpful.[60]

Gates: Hua may not have the confidence to make a policy statement.

Kissinger: Even if he reads it, it would be good. And I will give a lunch for you and invite the Chinese and put myself squarely behind you. I could also have Bush and Bruce there.

[C] Source: *PPS*, box 332, China Exchanges May–July 1976.

Gates' conversations with the premier a few months later would show that Hua was determined to follow Mao's line on U.S. policy, but events in the summer and fall of 1976 made Kissinger and his advisers wonder where U.S.-PRC relations were heading. With the 1976 campaign under way, pressures on Republicans and Democrats alike to pledge fealty to Taiwan intensified. President Ford endorsed Taiwan's participation in the Canadian Olympics, Republican politicians called for guarantees of Taiwan's security, and the Republican Party platform embraced a virtual two Chinas policy (Kissinger saw this as an "outrage" by the "yahoos"). Nor was Democratic candidate Jimmy Carter immune to the pressure: he suggested that normalization might not be possible without PRC assurances that Taiwan would be "free of military persuasion or domination."[62]

Beijing's position on normalization had been hardening since 1974, and it became even tougher during mid-1976. Thus, during a mid-July meeting with Sen. Hugh Scott (R-Pa.), an outspoken proponent of security guarantees for Taiwan, Vice Premier Zhang Chunqiao, (one of the Gang of Four) discussed military preparations for liberating Taiwan and the impossibility of "peaceful liberation."[63] In a conversation with Huang Zhen in mid-August, excerpted below, Kissinger learned just how concerned the Chinese were that the administration's position on Taiwan had slipped, even though his own position was much more moderate than Zhang's. As the following excerpt discloses, Kissinger all but repudiated the Republic platform on China, but he made it clear that he also wanted the Chinese to avoid "unhelpful discussion."[64]

Huang: I would like to say something about this (Taiwan). Recently people in the United States have made many official and non-official comments about Sino-U.S. relations.
Kissinger: Which have been official? I don't consider the Republican Party platform official.
Huang: (interrupting) I wish to say something. I have something to say. The United States invaded Taiwan (the interpreter incorrectly translated this as "committed aggression against Taiwan") thus owing China a debt. The U.S. must fulfill the three conditions of breaking diplomatic relations with Taiwan, withdrawing its military forces from Taiwan, and abrogating its defense treaty with Taiwan. There can be no exception about any of these conditions, and there is no room for maneuver in carrying them out. The delay in

normalizing relations is entirely the responsibility of the United States. The method and the time for liberating Taiwan is an internal affair of China and is not discussible. The Chinese position was clear to you even before you sought to re-open relations with us. Now Americans are saying that China's liberation of Taiwan will cripple the development of Sino–U.S. relations. They (Americans) are saying that Sino–U.S. relations will prosper only if the Chinese side takes into account U.S. concerns. This is a premeditated pretext. It is a flagrant threat against China, and we cannot accept it.

Kissinger: What is a threat?

Huang: Vice Premier Zhang Chunqiao and Foreign Minister Qiao told Senator Scott very clearly (what is a threat).[65] I think I should stop here.

Kissinger: I should point out that the statement about taking U.S. views into account doesn't apply principally to the Taiwan issue but rather to our broader cooperation. Certainly I thought reciprocity was a basic Chinese policy.

Huang: I hope we can proceed on the basis of the Shanghai Communiqué as Vice Premier Zhang pointed out to Senator Scott.

Kissinger: It is our firm purpose to do so. We will act on this basis, and not on the basis of what is written in this or that platform. (This was translated in a way suggesting the Chinese did not make the connection to the party platforms.)

Huang: You remember Chairman Mao told you in 1973 that we would have to liberate Taiwan and that we do not believe in peaceful liberation. Vice Chairman Zhang explained to Scott that the Shanghai Communiqué did not specify that the solution to the Taiwan problem would be peaceful or otherwise. May I remind you that I did not come (to see you) for this discussion but I had to say something (about the Taiwan issue).

Kissinger: I appreciate your comments. Basically Vice Premier Zhang did not say anything new. Chairman Mao and others have made the same points to us before. We appreciate that this is your basic view. Quite frankly we would not have recommended that Senator Scott open this issue with you as he did. As we told you last year, these election months in the United States are not the time for working out an agreement on normalization of our relations. We must instead move not long after our elections. I assure you we will maintain our support for the Shanghai Communiqué and will work to complete normalization. Nobody is authorized to speak for us. When we do it, we will do it at this level. I recognize there is not unlimited time. On our side we are doing our utmost to curb unhelpful discussion. We feel private discussion is better than public discussion.

COMMENTARY

This friction over Taiwan fell by the wayside when Mao Zedong finally died on 8 September. There was no other leader with comparable prestige who could play Mao's "integrative" role in Chinese politics, and he had left no means to choose a successor. The intelligence establishment tried its best to estimate the possible outcome, some anticipated competition between Hua Guofeng and Zhang Chunqiao, but others saw a collective leadership or coalition government rooted in the major political factions and institutions. The State Department's Bureau of Intelligence and Research argued that Hua was trying to "establish himself as a national figure . . . somewhat above factional squabbles [but] he has a long way to go." This report anticipated no major foreign policy changes—unless a left-leaning coalition emerged. In that event, China would take a "chauvinistic foreign policy stance which would place China more equidistant from both superpowers," supporting nationalistic economic policies and putting even more pressure on the Taiwan problem.[66]

Admidst all this uncertainty, Kissinger experienced what he saw as a personal insult when his old rival, former Secretary of Defense James Schlesinger, visited Beijing in September at the Chinese government's invitation. Schlesinger had become one of China's favorite U.S. hawks because of his vocal criticism of détente and Soviet policy. Kissinger acknowledged the PRC's anti-Soviet motives, but he nevertheless saw it as a "calculated and blatant affront" to the administration.[76] However, Kissinger's brooding over the affront was soon broken by the drama that unfolded in early October when Hua and his co-conspirators moved against the Gang of Four. Initially it was a closely held secret in Beijing, but State Department intelligence learned key elements of the story before it went public. With the radicals purged from positions of authority and the Chinese leadership stabilized around a coalition led by Hua, Assistant Secretary Arthur Hummel advised Kissinger that "the net result will be favorable from the standpoint of US interests."[68]

As the State Department was piecing together the coup story, on 12 October President Ford signed off on Kissinger's and Rumsfeld's recommendation for the sale of two Control Data Corporation computers to Beijing. The computers, though ostensibly sold for processing seismic data to advance oil and gas development, were equally well suited for missile testing or nuclear weapons design. The Soviets had accepted fairly strict safeguards for the same CDC computers, but Kissinger knew that the Chinese would not and, noting Ford's promise to "keep a friendly eye on computers," he let Beijing have its way. The approval touched off some inter-agency controversy over the risks of diversion; however, Kissinger and his advisers saw the sale as essential to demonstrate the United States' "continued interest in improving relations"; it also gave a nod to the Pentagon's interest in military cooperation with Beijing and to high-tech exporters interested in the Chinese market.[69]

A few weeks after Hua Guofeng's coup against the Gang of Four, Kissinger met with his top China experts (except for Richard Solomon) to review its implications for China's near-term development as well as for U.S.-China relations. The group consensus was that the overthrow of the radicals was likely to improve relations with Beijing. Nevertheless, perhaps reflecting his mood in light of the harsh attacks on his record during the presidential campaign, Kissinger's outlook on normalization was pessimistic.

DEPARTMENT OF STATE
Memorandum of Conversation
SECRET NODIS
Date: October 29, 1976
PARTICIPANTS: The Secretary; Philip C. Habib, Under Secretary for Political Affairs; Arthur J. Hummel, Jr., Assistant Secretary, EA; Winston Lord, Director, S/P; William H. Gleysteen, Jr., National Security Council Staff; Oscar V. Armstrong, Deputy Assistant Secretary, FA; Harry E. T. Thayer, Director, EA/PRCM (notetaker); Herbert Horowitz, Director, INR/DDR/REA
SUBJECT: Developments in China[D]

The Secretary: What is your assessment of the China situation?
Mr. Hummel: We'd like to have yours and your instructions.
The Secretary: My purpose in calling this meeting was to get an assessment of your great brains as to what is going on. I'll tell you my assessment later.
Mr. Gleysteen: Generally, we can't dispute the public press interpretations. But we have some uncertainty about the present balance.
The Secretary: How did it happen? Was there a coup?
Mr. Gleysteen: There could have been a coup, or the moderates could have

---

[D] Source: *PPS*, box 332, China Exchanges Aug. 1976–Jan. 1977/

seized on an alleged coup as a pretext, assessing that their action against the radicals could have popular support.

The Secretary: I can't see that there was a coup attempt.

Mr. Armstrong: I don't think there was actually a coup attempt, but the group of four vigorously opposed the new arrangements.

The Secretary: What new arrangements?

Mr. Armstrong: Hua and his moderate coalition.

Mr. Gleysteen: We have seen a pattern, which started just after Zhou's death. Zhang Chunqiao and the others challenged Deng; on the other side, there was opposition to Zhang.

Mr. Hummel: The Chinese are saying it was an anti-Zhou effort. This aspect created opposition to the group of four among other Chinese. But we should go back a bit. We are talking about a Maoist "struggle between two lines." There are two halves to that, the idealist versus the pragmatic. Mao has encouraged each at various times, and he has shifted from one to the other.

Mr. Gleysteen: Mao was the balancer and the giver of strength. The radicals, supported by Mao, weighed Zhou and then Deng down.

Mr. Lord: We shouldn't forget also Mao's remark that women are a pain in the neck.

The Secretary: Yes. Mao repeated it several times.

Mr. Habib: Going back to the coup, did the group of four try to rally any given military unit. I have always said the military is key in such situations. It is very important to assess where the army is going to be.

Mr. Gleysteen: There was some speculation that the radicals might be supported by one division in Manchuria and another in Shanghai. But there is no evidence that they responded.

Mr. Habib: How about the Beijing Garrison Command?

Mr. Hummel: There was a political kind of coup that they did attempt. But there was no purely military effort. Charges of a coup in a political sense are probably correct, but there was not actually a military coup attempt.

The Secretary: Hua was acceptable to the radicals at an earlier stage. Why not at a later stage also?

Mr Gleysteen: Hua was "tolerable" to the radicals but not "acceptable."

Mr. Armstrong: There is a credible report that Mao put Hua up for the job when Deng fell.

Mr. Horowitz: There was a subsequent development in that there were reports that Hua would likely become Chairman and Zhang the Premier.

Mr. Lord: Would this have been acceptable to the radicals?

Mr. Horowitz: Possibly.

Mr. Gleysteen: The radicals and Zhang Chunqiao were pushing hard beyond their real power. They didn't succeed and they gored the establishment cow in the process. The process continued, although in check; but it reopened after Mao's death. The radicals ware then trying to get to key positions and this is what the moderates probably reacted against.

Mr. Habib: Romulo said that in New York he had asked Qiao Guanhua if the military supported Hua. Qiao told Romulo yes.[70]

Mr. Lord: The military uniforms at the rally confirmed this.

Mr. Gleysteen: There were references to the Party, the people and the military. The military were the brokers.

Mr. Horowitz: After Zhou died and Deng was purged, the radicals at this point were potentiallly strong.

The Secretary: What was the significance of Deng's shift of commanders?[71]

Mr. Gleysteen: Mao, the Party and Deng wanted it done. Others admired Deng for being able to bring it about.

Mr. Hummel: After the Cultural Revolution, the military had too much power. The central military powers approved of what Deng did.

Mr. Habib: Ye reportedly was still backing Deng and was angry when Deng was ousted.[72]

Voice: Yes, and Ye went out of Beijing as a result.

Mr. Gleysteen/Mr. Hummel: Ye was respected widely. He was the only real peer of Mao.

Mr. Hummel: So now we see clearly that the military lines up with the moderates.

Mr. Gleysteen: But the military is not a simple homogenous group.

The Secretary: Who are the military?

Mr. Gleysteen: Ye and the chiefs of staff. Then there are the terribly powerful regional leaders: Chen Xilian, now in Beijing; Li Desheng in Manchuria; Xu Shiyou and Wei Guoqing in Guangzhou.[73]

The Secretary: What happens to Jiang Qing's followers in the provinces?

Mr. Hummel: There have apparently been some arrests, but the word is that most of them will fall in line behind the new leadership.

The Secretary: Will the four be killed?

Mr. Gleysteen: I doubt it. I think they will be handled like Liu Shaoqi.

The Secretary: Where are the four?

Mr. Gleysteen: In Beijing.

Mr. Armstrong: In effect, they have been excommunicated and isolated.

Mr. Hummel: They are isolated.

Mr. Gleysteen: The key thing is isolation.

Mr. Hummel: Their followers—the red guards who have been sent down to the countryside, the students—as the momentum grows, these people will be brought into line.

The Secretary: Will they get rid of the opera, so at least we won't have to undergo that again in Beijing?

Mr. Lord: There is strong evidence of increasing cultural openness.

The Secretary: Is there a psychological problem? Three leaders chosen by Mao have fallen in a row, the Politburo decimated; since 1971, the defense minister and chief of staff. Zhou Enlai was under serious attack when he was ill. Could he have been poisoned?

Mr. Gleysteen: It is very clear that Zhou was under attack since 1973.

The Secretary: Since Cambodia in 1973, everything changed. The Water Margin campaign, attack on Confucius.[74]

They have ignored Zhou since 1973; nobody mentioned Zhou again.

Mr. Hummel: Yes. Shifts of personnel must undermine the people's confidence in the government. In addition, the frequent shifts in ideological line must also be confusing to everybody.

Mr. Gleysteen: It is not hard to see the effects. Qiao Guanhua in New York was extraordinarily careful. Others also have been walking a very tight line.

The Secretary: Did Qiao know about the purge when we met in New York?

Mr. Hummel: Qiao was very subdued and defensive.[75]

The Secretary: Is Hua now in control?

Mr. Gleysteen: Hua is chairman of the board; but he has no independent source of power. He will take care. He has about a fifty-fifty chance of survival.

Mr. Hummel: If Hua fails, then there really would be a serious effect on Chinese popular attitudes.

Mr. Gleysteen: The issue of Deng's return is important, an important division point.

Mr. Hummel: One question is: will there be de-Maoization, like that following Stalin's death?

The Secretary: Is Mao's body on exhibit yet?[76]

Mr. Gleysteen: No. But I think it will be. The announcement about it came after the October 6/7 decisions.

The Secretary: Will it make a difference? Zhou was really a more popular man. Would Zhou have succeeded Mao if Zhou had lived?

Mr. Gleysteen: Yes.

Mr. Armstrong: If they were to go after Mao, it would undermine confidence too greatly; he was China's Lenin as well as Stalin.

Mr. Hummel: It would be too dangerous for them to do so.

Mr. Gleysteen: There might be, on the question of building China, no de-Maoization. But on the more controversial matters, there might be limited de-Maoization.

Mr. Hummel: After Lin Biao's fall, Lin was blamed for leading Mao astray.

The Secretary: What is the thinking about Lin Biao? I don't believe that he was on the plane.

Mr. Armstrong: We're sure he's dead, died trying to flee.

Mr. Gleysteen: Maybe his plane ran out of gas, and there were reports of a gun fight on the plane. But the more intriguing question is what was Lin Biao trying to do? Perhaps he was more pro-Soviet than Mao. But we don't know.

Mr. Hummel: It is depressing that we are constantly being surprised. However, Lin Biao himself was surprised; Deng was surprised; and Jiang Qing was surprised.

The Secretary: There are many things I blame the Department for, but not for this.

Mr. Gleysteen: It is difficult to analyze.

The Secretary: What is PRCLO [the PRC Liaison Office, in Washington] doing these days?

Mr. Habib: They are still entertaining as usual.

Mr. Hummel: But Xie Qimei recently stopped peddling the hard line.

Mr. Gleysteen: But he didn't stop until after Mao's death. PRCLO is now being jovial and cautious.

Mr. Armstrong: Other Chinese embassies, according to reports, all seem to be approving what has happened.

Mr. Hummel: We have a report from Tokyo about the Chinese deputy there. What he said about the changes being anti-Soviet are probably not true, but we probably can read it as a direct signal about relations with us.

The Secretary: What do the changes mean for foreign policy?

Mr. Gleysteen: We already have signals of a warmer attitude toward the U.S. We have a return to the "patience" line, and other signs.

Mr. Habib: Maybe that is a reaction to our opposition to the hard line.

The Secretary: I don't think that in itself would do it. But what about foreign policy?

Mr. Hummel: We can expect them to be a little softer toward the Soviets.

Mr. Gleysteen: Yes, but also softer toward us. It will be a more sophisticated policy.

Mr. Habib: Why will they be more soft on the Soviets?

The Secretary: It will be tactically wiser, enabling them to build their strength.

Mr. Gleysteen: Past policy toward the Soviets was self-damaging. There will be adjustments, but their fear of the Soviets remains.

Mr. Hummel: The USSR is still the main opponent. Relations with us are secondary. There will be adjustments of policy toward the Soviets to meet tactical needs.

Mr. Gleysteen: All this presumes that the present group can hold together.

Mr. Hummel: Changes will be glacial. When you went to China, the decision to receive you could be made by two people. Now decision-making will be bureaucratized.

The Secretary: It was those two (Mao and Zhou) plus Ye Jianying. And we were not impressed by Ye.

Mr. Gleysteen: If Lin Biao was attacking that policy, then Ye's association with you was to show military support for a pro-US policy.

The Secretary: We brought a present for Lin Biao, didn't we?

Mr. Lord: Yes.

The Secretary: . . . and we didn't know exactly who Ye was. It must have been a tremendous event in China.

Mr. Hummel: But now such decisions will be made by committees.

The Secretary: It was tense in 1971. But Zhou was in control.

Mr. Gleysteen: What they are trying to do now is to form Central Committees and National People Congress meetings, to ratify the decisions.

The Secretary: Will there be a warming of relations with the US?

Mr. Gleystsen: Yes.

The Secretary: Will the pinpricks stop?

Mr. Gleysteen: We must bring it to their attention when they give us pinpricks.

The Secretary: We already have done so. Their behavior with Schlesinger really was outrageous; they even told him of what the President said in his Beijing talks about Angola.

Mr. Gleysteen: There won't be any basic change in Chinese policy, but their behavior should be better.

The Secretary: How about Japan?

Mr. Habib: Japan will have to bite the hegemony bullet and get the treaty. They must have the election, then get the treaty.[77]

Mr. Gleysteen: This is by no means sure. The Chinese don't like [Japanese Prime Minister] Miki [Takeo].

Mr. Habib: They don't like Fukuda either.

The Secretary: Why don't they like Miki?

Mr. Gleysteen: Because he has been too nice to the Soviets.

Mr. Armstrong: And he hasn't accepted the hegemony language.

Mr. Gleysteen: I asked PRCLO about Miki and they answered that he is too good to the Soviets. Then Li Xiannian talked to [Sen. Mike] Mansfield, Mansfield said that he wanted Japan to do more, and Li said "but not too much." China fears Japan as a major power, especially a military power.

The Secretary: What about our claims offer? Will they pick it up?

Mr. Armstrong: Maybe, if other things related to normalization fall in place.

The Secretary: It is not possible to normalize. What price makes normalization worthwhile?

Mr. Gleysteen: We can't say it will be successful, but we can try.

The Secretary: What about the proposal (about Taiwan) discussed in 1974? Even if that had been accepted, it would be a fraud. And what are we going to do about it? Go to war?

Mr. Lord: Our only leverage with them is what we can do about US–China relations.

Mr. Gleysteen: The only real answer is that an attack on Taiwan is too much risk with the Soviets and with reaction in Japan and the United States.

The Secretary: We are going to have to answer the question before Congress.

Mr. Lord: The best would be unilateral statements.

(Secretary leaves the room and returns.)

The Secretary: You might be lucky after election and get a bleeding heart in here. I never believed that normalization is possible.[78]

Mr. Hummel: The PRC can put pressure on the issue, can't they?

The Secretary: They shouldn't.

Mr. Hummel: CIA is telling Gates that an invasion is not possible. But this is not the point. This is the higher range. At the lower range is the offshores, and other pressures short of invasion of Taiwan.

The Secretary: If Taiwan is recognized by us as part of China, then it may become irresistible for them. Our saying we want a peaceful solution has no force. It is Chinese territory. What are we going to do about it?

Mr. Gleysteen: The legal position is not tight. We would have recognized Taiwan as "part of China," not as a "Province of the PRC."

The Secretary: For us to go to war with a recognized country where we have an ambassador over a part of what we would recognize as their country would be preposterous.

Mr. Hummel: Down the road, perhaps the only solution would be an independent Taiwan.

The Secretary: The ideal solution would be if Taiwan decided to rejoin Beijing. If they worked out something between themselves; from our point of view this would be absolutely the ideal solution.

Mr. Armstrong: The likelihood is small.

Mr. Gleysteen: Yes. Unlikely.

Mr. Lord: China would be able to bring economic pressures on Taiwan.

Mr. Hummel: They would do that. Taiwan talking of independence would be a very serious threat.

The Secretary: Are they talking that way?

Mr. Hummel: No.

Mr. Gleysteen: If they would do so, they would be completely isolated.

Mr. Habib: What purpose would it serve?

The Secretary to Hummel: What's this about a letter from Goldwater?[79]

Mr. Hummel: You made a decision that Taiwan should not have an independent aircraft production facility.

The Secretary: This would not be in our interest?

Mr. Hummel: No.

Mr. Gleysteen: The PRC would raise hell. It would contradict everything that we have said to the Chinese.

Mr. Hummel: I have it in a memo to you. Our grounds are good.

The Secretary: What would we disapprove?

Mr. Hummel: We would disapprove their designing and building an aircraft trainer, something we would not have any control over.

The Secretary: What is the impact of the PRC changes on their domestic policies?

Mr. Hummel: There will be more for the military; a move toward economic incentives, to raise the economic growth level.

Mr. Gleysteen: But they can't increase wages too much.

The Secretary: Because there will be no goods to buy?

Mr. Hummel: They will have to cross the ideological bridge of more pay for more work in order to increase productivity.

Mr. Armstrong: They still have some of the same issues: the balance between ideological fervor and getting the job done, allocation of resources, etc.

The Secretary: Maybe Mao was right. If China modernizes, it becomes a bureaucratic state. Ideology is important. But 35 million bureaucrats. How can you run such a bureaucracy? The ideologues keep China weak, and the moderates keep China stultified. And without the left China will become not so untypical a Chinese bureaucratic state. Could they revert to having a semi-warlord state? Look at Czechoslovakia and Poland. They have more industry than they can use. If you let the other line continue, what do you have? I do not think any communist country can run an economy . . . Mao was a "monstrous" personality. Look at the October 1975 meeting; the willpower to have a two-hour meeting was unbelievable. I believe if they try to maintain the two lines that keeping the balance will not be easy.

Mr. Gleysteen: It was not balanced under Mao in recent years. Stultification may come in the long term.

The Secretary: Foreign policy has not been subtle since Zhou.

Mr. Horowitz: Domestic policy also has been without direction in the past year.

The Secretary: Is India doing better now than China?

Mr. Gleysteen: No. The Chinese are doing better than India.

The Secretary: But militarily the Chinese are falling behind . . .

Mr. Hummel: Despite the Communist bureaucracy, China could be run better than it is now.

(Hummel then asked to take up a special matter with the Secretary, and Armstrong, Thayer and Horowitz left.)

Notes

1. For quotations, see Scowcroft to the President, 21 Oct. 1975, National Archives, Record Group 59, Department of State Records (hereafter referred to as *RG 59*), Policy Planning Staff (Director's Files), 1969–77 (hereafter cited as *PPS*, with archival box number and file information), box 374, Secretary Kissinger's Trip to China, Oct. 1975; Kissinger to the President, "Your Trip to the People's Republic of China: A Scope Analysis . . . ," 20 Nov. 1975, *PPS*, box 380, China Notes.

2. For important studies of U.S.–China relations during this period, see Robert Ross, *Negotiating Cooperation: The United States and China, 1969–1985* (Stanford, Calif.: Stanford University Press, 1995), pp. 60–90, and Robert G. Sutter, *The China Quandary: Domestic Determinants of U.S. China Policy, 1972–1985* (Boulder, Colo.: Westview, 1983), pp. 22–46.

3. Bush to the Secretary, 15 Jan. 1975, *PPS*, box 375, China — Sensitive — Chron Jan. - Feb. 1975; Solomon to Kissinger, "Is the Period of Immobilism in Peking Over? Some Comments on the Current State of U.S.-PRC Relations," 27 Feb. 1975, *PPS*, box 375, China–Sensitive Chron Jan.–Feb. 1975.

4. For "nightmare," along with suggestions for private polls on Taiwan, see Bush to President Ford, 23 May 1975, *PPS*, box 331, China Exchanges 1 Jan–31 May 1975; Kissinger to President, "Your Trip to the People's Republic of China: A Scope Analysis . . . ," 20 Nov. 1975, *PPS*, box 380, China Notes. For the *Mayaquez* incident and Kissinger's statement about credibility during the spring of 1975, see Walter Isaacson, *Kissinger: A Biog-*

raphy (New York: Simon and Schuster, 1992) pp. 640–52, and Robert D. Schulzinger, *Henry Kissinger Doctor of Diplomacy* (New York: Columbia University Press, 1989), pp. 193–94.

5. See *Public Papers of the Presidents of the United States, Gerald R. Ford, 1975, Book I* (Washington, D.C.: Government Printing Office, 1977), pp. 647. Kissinger's advisers believed that Ford's statement had been "inadvertent." See Habib et al. to Kissinger, "U.S.-PRC Relations and Approaches to the President's Peking Trip . . .", 3 July 1975, *PPS*, box 379, China–Sensitive July–Sept 1975.

6. See briefing paper, "Bilateral Relations," attached to Habib et al., "Your Tour D'horizon with Huang Chen . . . ," 8 May 1975, *PPS*, box 375, China–Sensitive Chron–March–June 1975; Schulzinger, *Henry Kissinger*, p. 215; and Ross, *Negotiating Cooperation*, p. 80.

7. See Kissinger to President, "Your Trip to the People's Republic of China: A Scope Analysis . . . ," 20 Nov. 1975, *PPS*, box 380, China Notes; Habib et al. to Secretary, "A Strategy Analysis of Your Fall Meetings with the Chinese," 18 Sept. 1975, *PPS*, box 379, China–Sensitive July–Sept. 1975.

8. For the quotation from *People's Daily*, see Solomon to Kissinger, "Last-Minute Items for Your Meeting with Huang Chen," 9 May 1975, *PPS*, box 375, China—Sensitive—Chron March–June 1975; Kissinger to the President, "Possible Approaches to Your China Trip," 24 Oct. 1975, *PPS*, box 379, China—Sensitive—Chron Oct.–Dec. 1975. McFarlane's recollections of briefings during a 1975 visit suggest that intelligence exchanges may have resumed during President Ford's trip to China in December. See Robert C. McFarlane, *Special Trust* (New York: Cadell and Davies, 1994), p. 151.

9. Kissinger to the President, "Possible Approaches to Your China Trip," 24 Oct. 1975, *PPS*, box 379, China—Sensitive—Chron Oct.–Dec. 1975; Scowcroft to President, "Secretary's Talks with Chinese Officials," 23 Oct. 1975, and "China Trip," 24 October 1975, both in *PPS*, box 374, Secretary Kissinger's Trip to China Oct. 1975.

10. See Kissinger to President, "Your Trip to the People's Republic of China: A Scope Analysis . . . ," 20 Nov. 1975, *PPS*, box 380, China Notes; "Discussion of Substantive Policy Issues During Mr. Nixon's Visit to China February 1976," n.d., *PPS*, box 378, China—Sensitive— Chron 1 Jan–31 March 1976. See also Kissinger to the President, "Possible Approaches to Your China Trip," 24 Oct. 1975, *PPS*, box 379, "China—Sensitive—Chron Oct.–Dec 1975.

11. See Habib et al. to Kissinger, "U.S.-PRC Relations and Approaches to the President's Peking Trip: Tasks for the Rest of 1975," 3 July 1975, *PPS*, box 379, China—Sensitive—Chron July–Sept. 1975.

12. See Kissinger to the President, "Possible Approaches to Your China Trip," 24 Oct. 1975, *PPS*, box 379, China – Sensitive—Chron Oct. - Dec. 1975"; Kissinger to President, "Your Trip to the People's Republic of China: A Scope Analysis . . . ," 20 Nov. 1975, *PPS*, box 380, China Notes. For Beijing's annoyance, see also Nancy Tucker, *Taiwan, Hong Kong, and the United States, 1945–1992: Uneasy Friendships* (New York: Twayne, 1994), p. 127.

13. See Schulzinger, *Henry Kissinger*, 217–18; Isaacson, *Kissinger: A Biography*, pp. 668-72; Robert L. Hartmann, *Palace Politics: An Inside Account of the Ford Years* (New York: McGraw-Hill, 1980), pp. 360–64; and Ross, *Negotiating Cooperation*, p. 69.

14. For the visit as a "sustaining" one, see Kissinger to President, "Your Trip to the People's Republic of China: A Scope Analysis . . .", 20 Nov. 1975, *PPS*, box 380, China Notes.

15. For Ford's rather meager account of his talks with the Chinese, see his *A Time to Heal: The Autobiography of Gerald R. Ford* (New York: Harper and Row, 1979), pp. 335–37. For more substance, see Ross, *Negotiating Cooperation*, pp. 85–86.

16. See Lord to the Secretary, "Prospects for 1976," 4 Feb. 1976, *PPS*, box 358, 1–15 Feb. 1976; Solomon to Scowcroft, "Copies of My China Analysis for the President and Secretary Kissinger," 8 March 1976, with attachment, "Peking's Current Political Instability and Its Import for U.S.–PRC Relations," *PPS*, box 332, China Exchanges Jan.–March 1976. Scowcroft noticed that Beijing's treatment of Nixon at his departure was "somewhat more aloof" than when he arrived, and he suggested that the "Chinese now realize they have generated a good deal of ill will in the U.S." by hosting Nixon. See Scowcroft to the President, "Information Items," 28 Feb. 1976, *PPS*, box 332, China Exchanges Jan.–March 1976.

17. See memcon, "China Policy . . . ," 12 July 1976, *PPS*, box 332, China Exchanges May–July 1976; and Ross, *Negotiating Cooperation*, pp. 89–90. The substance of this National Security Decision Memorandum on Taiwan remains classified.

18. The following discussion draws on Richard Evans, *Deng Xiaoping and the Making of Modern China* (New York: Viking, 1993), pp. 212–19, and Richard Baum, *Burying Mao: Chinese Politics in the Age of Deng Xiaoping* (Princeton, N.J.: Princeton University Press, 1994), pp. 27–42.

19. See Solomon to Scowcroft, "Copies of My China Analysis for the President and Secretary Kissinger," 8 March 1976, with attachment, "Peking's Current Political Instability and Its Import for U.S.–PRC Relations," Saunders and Habib to the Secretary, "China," 22 Oct. 1976, *PPS*, box 377, WL China—Sensitive—Chron 1 Oct.–31 Dec. 1976.

20. Besides Jiang, the Gang of Foou included Deputy Premier Zhang Chunqiao, Party Vice Chair Wang Hongwen, and Politburo member Yao Wengyuan, all three of whom had risen to prominence in Shanghai, (Zang, for example, had served as mayor.)

21. See Habib et al. to Kissinger, "U.S.–PRC Relations and Approaches to the President's Peking Trip: Tasks for the Rest of 1975," 3 July 1975, *PPS*, box 379, China—Sensitive—Chron July–Sept. 1975.

22. Ongoing negotiations with Panama over the duration or extent of the U.S. presence in, or control over, the Canal Zone were stalemated; the House of Representatives had just passed an amendment forbidding the use of State Department funds for "negotiating the surrender or relinquishment of any U.S. rights" in the Zone. See Walter LaFeber, *The Panama Canal: The Crisis in Historical Perspective* (New York: Oxford University Press, 1978), pp. 185–87.

23. This may be a reference to conversations between Zhou and Chinese–American doctor C. P. Li, who suggested to Bush that Beijing might be receptive to making a statement on the peaceful liberation of Taiwan. See "Peking's Current Posture Toward Normalization," n.d., *PPS*, box 379, China—Sensitive—chron July–Sept. 1975.

24. The study cited in endnote 25 recommended that Kissinger make an advance trip in August.

25. Kissinger was scheduled to meet with Huang Zhen, but the meeting did not take place

until the next day. See Scowcroft to Bush, WASH 107, 13 July 1975, *PPS*, box 379, China—Sensitive—Chron July–Sept. 1975.

26. See Scowcroft telegram to Bush, WASH 107, 13 July 1975, *PPS*, box 379, China—Sensitive—Chron July–Sept. 1975.

27. See Habib et al. to the Secretary, "Partial Steps Toward Normalization of US/PRC Relations in Conjunction with the President's Trip to Peking," 4 Aug. 1975, *PPS*, box 379, China—Sensitive—Chron July–Sept. 1975.

28. See memcon, "The Soviet Union; CSCE; Europe; Japan; Angola; Indochina; the President's China Trip; the Global Strategic Situation; Korea," 28 Sept. 1975, *PPS*, box 379, China—Sensitive—Chron July–Sept. 1975.

29. In response to Qiao's question, Kissinger stated that war was a "possibility" and that, speaking as a historian, the prospects were "more likely than not." But, as "Secretary of State, I have to act as if war will not break out, or do my best to prevent it." See ibid.

30. See Scowcroft to the President, "Secretary's Talks with Chinese Officials," 23 Oct. 1975, *PPS*, box 374, Secretary Kissinger's Trip to China Oct. 1975; and "Banquet Given by Foreign Minister Ch'iao at Peking on Oct. 19," *Department of State Bulletin* 175 (17 Nov. 1975), p. 681.

31. For the full text, see memcon, "20 October 1975, 10:00 A.M.–11:40 A.M., *PPS*, box 374, Secretary Kissinger's Trip to China Oct. 1975.

32. For the full record, see memcon, "Global Strategy for Dealing with the Soviet Union; the Historical Lessons of the 1930s," 20 Oct. 1975, *PPS*, box 374, Secretary Kissinger's Trip to China Oct. 1975. For Kissinger's comments, see Scowcroft to President, "Secretary's talks with Chinese officials," 21 Oct. 1975, *PPS*, box 374, Secretary Kissinger's Trip to China Oct. 1975.

33. This is no doubt a reference to the Senate investigations of CIA efforts to prevent the election of Salvadore Allende in Chile.

34. In fact, the Soviets did not have 30 ICBMs in 1960; by the fall of 1961 they had only 4.

35. For the full transcript, see memcon, 21 Oct. 1975, "The Southern Flank," *PPS*, box 374, Secretary Kissinger's Trip to China Oct. 1975.

36. For "disturbing," see Scowcroft to President, 21 Oct. 1975, *PPS*, box 374, Secretary Kissinger's Trip to China Oct. 1975; and "Analysis/Highlights of Secretary Kissinger's Meeting with Chairman Mao, Oct. 21, 1975," n.d., *PPS*, box 379, China—Sensitive—Chron Oct–Dec 1975. In November 1973, the Chinese had reported the talks as "friendly," "wide-ranging," and "far-sighted." For the most recent talks, they did not use the third adjective.

37. Lord suggested that the words "were probably smoothed over and elaborated at times." See "Analysis/Highlights of Secretary Kissinger's Meeting with Chairman Mao, Oct. 21, 1975," n.d., *PPS*, box 379, China—Sensitive—Chron Oct.–Dec. 1975.

38. The *Times'* military correspondent, Drew Middleton, had recently published a book *Can America Win the Next War?* (New York: Scribner, 1975).

39. In this speech, Sen. Barry Goldwater argued that Western European weakness meant that "more and more we are assuming the role of the alliance's nuclear mercenaries." If the situation did not change, the "United States would be as well served in changing its automatic guarantees to NATO." Goldwater further observed that the "Chinese are also as disturbed as I am of the . . . distinct possibility that NATO might be held hostage

against the United States or that the United States might withdraw." U.S. Congress, *Congressional Record*, vol. 121 (Washington, D.C.: U.S. Government Printing Office, 1975), pp. 16671–74.

40. The businessman who made the *Times* an influential paper was Arthur Ochs, the son of a German-Jewish émigré from Bavaria whose family held a substantial share of *New York Times* stock for many years. For the Ochs family and the *Times*, see Harrison E. Salisbury, *Without Fear or Favor: The New York Times in Its Times* (New York: Times Books, 1980).

41. To his later regret, Bush did not take him up the offer. See Bush, *Looking Forward* (Garden City, N.Y.: Doubleday, 1987), p. 149.

42. See memcon, "The President's Visit and Communique; Bilateral Relations; Indochina MIA; Korea, South Asia," 22 Oct. 1975, *PPS*, box 374, Secretary Kissinger's Trip to China, Oct. 1975.

43. See memcon, "Discussion of the Draft communique for the President's Visit," 23 Oct. 1975, and Scowcroft to the President, "Secretary's Talks with Chinese Officials," 23 Oct. 1975, *PPS*, box 374, Secretary Kissinger's Trip to China, Oct. 1975.

44. See State Department Briefing Paper, "Normalization," Nov. 1975, *PPS*, box 372, President Ford's Visit to Peking, 1–5 Dec. 1974, Bilateral Issues. See also Ross, *Negotiating Cooperation*, pp. 82–83, which emphasizes bargaining power over normalization.

45. See Kissinger to President Ford, "Your Trip to the People's Republic of China: A Scope Analysis . . . ," 20 Nov. 1975, *PPS*, box 380, China Notes; Lord and Gleysteen to the Secretary, "Your Briefing of the Congressional Leadership . . . ," 9 Dec. 1975, *PPS*, box 379, China—Sensitive—Chron Oct.-Dec. 1975; Bush to Scowcroft, 8 Nov. 1975, Peking 136, and Red Cavaney and Dick Solomon to Scowcroft, 21 Nov. 1975, Peking 145, both in *PPS*, box 331, China Exchanges Oct. 1975-Dec. 1975. For Kissinger's efforts to negotiate a communiqué, see messages to Bush, 25 and 31 Oct. 1975, *PPS*, box 331, China Exchanges Oct.-Dec. 1975.

46. See Ross, *Negotiating Cooperation*, p. 85; and Kissinger to President, "Your Trip to the People's Republic of China: A Scope Analysis," 20 Nov. 1975, *PPS*, box 380, China Notes.

47. Ross, *Negotiating Cooperation*, p. 85, cites a participant who described it as "one of the dullest meetings he had ever attended."

48. For Bush's advice, see Bush to Kissinger, Peking 133, 6 Nov. 1975, *PPS*, box 331, China Exchanges Oct.-Dec. 1975. For the memcons of Ford's talks with the Chinese, see *PPS*, box 373, President Ford's Trip to China, 1–5 Dec. 1975.

49. For the full text, see memcon, 2 Dec. 1975, 4:10 P.M.–6:00 P.M. *PPS*, box 373, President Ford's Trip to China, Dec. 1–5 Dec. 1975. One account claims that during this meeting Mao and Ford ran out of topics before the meeting's scheduled end, but it was the Ford–Deng meeting on 4 December when that happened. See Ross, *Negotiating Cooperation*, p. 85.

50. See Ford, *A Time to Heal*, p. 336; and Kissinger to the President, "Your Meeting with Chairman Mao," 28 Nov. 1975, *PPS*, box 372, Mao Book, Dec. 1975 Mr. Lord.

51. See Bush to Kissinger, Peking 135, 7 Nov. 1975, *PPS*, box 331, China Exchanges Oct.-Dec. 1975; and memcon, "Discussion of Possible Communique: American Press and

Public Support for U.S.-PRC Relations," 2 Dec. 1975, *PPS*, box 373, President Ford's Trip to China, 1-5 Dec. 1975.

52. For the full transcript, see memcon, "The Soviet Union; Europe; the Middle East; South Asia; Angola," 3 Dec. 1975, *PPS*, box 373, President Ford's Trip to China, 1-5 Dec. 1975.

53. For the full transcript, see memcon, "Taiwan; bilateral relations; MIA; trade (oil and computers); Dalai Lama; Korea; Chinese minorities; agriculture; Amb. Bush," 4 Dec. 1975; *PPS*, box 373, President Ford's Trip to China, 1-5 Dec. 1975.

54. See Ross, *Negotiating Cooperation*, p. 86

55. Deng complained that representatives of the Dalai Lama had set up the Office of Tibet in New York. The Foreign Ministry had already protested that the office, which was registered with the Justice Department as a foreign aid, was an "undisguised interference in China's internal affairs." See Briefing Paper, "Tibet Issues and Talking Points," *PPS*, box 373, Visit of Secretary Kissinger to Peking 19-21 Oct. 1975, Bilateral Issues Book, S/P Mr. Lord.

56. See Ross, *Negotiating Cooperation*, p. 89.

57. See Hartman to Secretary, "Your Moscow Trip, January 20-23, 1976," n.d., and "Briefing Paper, China Issues and Talking Points," Jan. 1976; both are FOIA releases, copies at *NSA*.

58. See Solomon to Scowcroft, "Copies of My China Area Analysis for the President and Secretary Kissinger," 8 March 1976, *PPS*, box 372, China Exchanges Jan.-March 1976.

59. That is anything beyond six months depended on what happened in the elections.

60. That is, Nixon's accounts of his recent talks with the Chinese leadership were not specific enough.

61. See C. Arthur Borg to Philip Habib and Winston Lord, "Ambassador Gates' Discussions in Peking," 26 April 1976; USLO to SecState, Peking 936, 24 May 1976 and Peking 1048 and 1049, both 10 June 1976, all in *PPS*, box 378, China—Sensitive—Chron 1 April-30 June 1976; and USLO to SecState, Peking 1126, 23 June 1976, *PPS*, box 332, China Exchanges Mar-July 76.

62. See Hummel and Lord to the Secretary, "Your Meeting with PRC Foreign Minister Chiao," 4 Oct. 1976, *PPS*, box 372, unlabeled file; "Ford Asks Reversal on Taiwan; Olympic Body Meets Today," *New York Times*, 13 July 1976; Donald Bruce Johnson, ed., *National Party Platforms*, vol. 2 (Urbana, Ill.: University of Illinois Press, 1978), p. 989; *The Presidential Campaign 1976, Jimmy Carter*, vol. 1 (Washington, D.C.: U.S. Government Printing Office, 1978), p. 447. For "yahoos" and "outrage," see memorandum for the record, "Ambassador Gates' Meeting with the Secretary, Aug. 25, 1976," 1 Sept. 1976, *PPS*, box 332, China Exchanges (Aug.1976-Jan. 1977.

63. See USLO to SecState, Peking 1282, 13 July 1976, and memcon, "China: Comments on Taiwan by Chang Chun-chiao and Ch'iao Kuan-hua," 14 July 1976; both in *PPS*, box 332, China Exchanges, May-July 1976; SecState to USDel, State 182065, 23 July, *PPS*, box 377, China—Sensitive—Chron 1 July-31 Sept. 1976; Harold Saunders to the Secretary, "Peking's Hard Line on Taiwan," 4 Oct. 1976, *PPS*, box 377, WL China—Sensitive—Chron 1 Oct.-31 Dec. 1976.

64. See memcon, 18 August 1976, *PPS*, box 332, China Exchanges (Aug. 1976-Jan. 1977).

65. Huang may have been referring to a Senator Scott's statement that "[o]ur policy is not to

interfere in your internal affair—but we stand ready to back up our commitments to Taiwan." If there was a "resort to arms" against Taiwan, "such action would arouse 215 million Americans." See Scowcroft to the President, "Secretary Kissinger's Discussion with Ambassador Huang Cheng on U.S.-PRC Relations and the Taiwan Question," 25 Aug. 1975 (memo not forwarded), *PPS*, box 332, unlabeled file.

66. See Crowcroft to the President, "Information Items," 10 Sept. 1976, *PPS*, box 332, China Exchanges (Aug. 1976–Jan. 1977); and Bureau of Intelligence and Research, "China After Mao—Short Term Prospects," Report No. 586, 13 Sept. 1976, *PPS*, box 332, unlabeled file.

67. See USLO to SecState, Peking 1843, 15 Sept. 1976, and SecState to USDel, State 234412, 22 Sept. 1976, both in *PPS*, box 332, unlabeled file; USDel to SecState, SECTO 27325, 23 Sept. 1976, *PPS*, box 377, China—Sensitive—Chron 1 July - 30 Sept. 1975. Kissinger had told close advisers that the "Chinese were 'bloody minded' and that it was an outrage to invite him [Schlesinger], particularly to invite a man they know to have been fired by the President." When it was pointed out that the Chinese had a "habit of inviting people who were out of office," Kissinger "jokingly said that they might be inviting him next." See memorandum for the record, "Ambassador Gates' Meeting with the Secretary, Aug. 25, 1976," 1 Sept. 1976, *PPS*, box 332, China Exchanges (Aug. 1976–Jan. 1977).

68. See Hummel to the Secretary, "Developments in China—Policy Implications," 13 Oct. 1976, and Saunders and Hummel to the Secretary, "China," 22 Oct. 1976, *PPS*, box 377, WL China—Sensitive—Chron 1 Oct.–31 Dec. 1976.

69. See memcon, "CDC Computer for the PRC," 12 July 1976, *PPS*, box 332, China Exchanges May–July 1976; Robinson to the Secretary, "PRC Computer Case," 17 Aug. 1976; Hummel and Lord to the Secretary, "CDC Computer Sales to the PRC," 10 September 1976, both in *PPS*, box 377, China—Sensitive—Chron 1 July–30 Sept. 1976; Art Morrrisey to Jan Kalicki, "PRC Computers," 12 Oct. 1976; and Hummel to the Secretary, "Developments in China—Policy Implications," 13 Oct. 1976, *PPS*, box 377, WL China—Sensitive-Chron 1 Oct.–31 Dec. 1976. See also Raymond Garthoff, *Détente and Confrontation: American-Soviet Relations from Nixon to Reagan* (Washington, D.C.,: Brookings Institution, 1994), p. 764.

70. Carlos P. Romulo (1899–1985) was secretary of foreign affairs during 1968–78 and Minister of Foreign Affairs during 1978–84.

71. This is a reference to the reshuffling of the commanders of China's eleven military regions to break their hold over local affairs. See Evans, *Deng Xiaoping*, p. 198.

72. Ye Jianying, minister of defense and senior official at the military commission, was a key figure in the conspiracy against the Gang of Four. See ibid., pp. 214–16.

73. Chen had displaced Ye on the military commission. Xu, the commander of the Canton military region, and Wei, the provincial governor, had protected Deng in Canton and, as politburo members, they had kept him informed about debates in Beijing. See ibid., pp. 212, 215, 218

74. The "Water Margin," a classic Chinese story, inclues a character, Song Jiang—China's equivalent of Robin Hood—who eventually chooses to serve the emperor. In late 1975, the radicals began to attack the story because Song had "capitulated" to feudal authority. Many assumed that radicals were attacking Deng Ziaoping because he had allegedly ac-

ceded to capitalism. See David S. G. Goodman, *Deng Xioaping and the Chinese Revolution* (London: Routledge, 1994), p. 83.

75. In a few months, Qiao himself would be dropped from the Foreign Ministry because he and his wife had tried to curry favor with Qiang and had been "too vigorous in his denunciations" of Deng. See Lord to the Secretary, "Your Meeting with Ambassador Huang Cheng . . . ," 20 Dec. 1976, *PPS*, box 332 China Exchanges Aug. 1976–Jan. 1977.

76. In September 1977, a Memorial Hall opened housing Mao's embalmed body in a crystalline display case. See Geremie Barmé, *Shades of Mao: The Posthumous Cult of the Great Leader* (Armonk, N.Y.: M.E. Sharpe, 1996), pp. 25–26.

77. A reference to the "anti-hegemony"—i.e., anti-Soviet—clause demanded by the Chinese in the Japan–China friendship treaty negotiations.

78. Most likely a reference to a "bleeding heart liberal" who would approve the abrogation of diplomatic relations with Taiwan.

79. As a supporter of Taiwan, Goldwater undoubtedly questioned Kissinger's impending decision to deny the Republic of China an independent aircraft production facility.

9

"But 8,000 Cubans Running Around...":

Kissinger in Moscow, January 1976

COMMENTARY

While Kissinger was trying to reinvigorate U.S.-PRC relations, he would find that presidential politics were also having a stark impact on the course of superpower détente. The 1976 presidential campaign was under way, and Kissinger was becoming a lightening rod for criticism by Ford's opponents, whether Reagan Republicans or Henry Jackson Democrats, who questioned détente's validity. Moreover, the approaching victory of left-wing nationalist forces in Angola with Soviet aid made Kissinger furious because he saw it as inconsistent with détente and a threat to U.S. credibility. Therefore, when he traveled to Moscow in January 1976 to discuss SALT II with Brezhnev, it was at one of the most difficult moments in his negotiating relationship with the Soviets. During the talks, he failed to convince Brezhnev to curb support for Cuban forces in Angola. He had more success in narrowing differences over SALT; but arms control, the "testing ground for détente," had become more politicized than ever, making it extremely difficult for Kissinger to capitalize on a possible breakthrough in Moscow. Thus, the SALT process stagnated while the administration tried to penalize the Soviets for their conduct in Angola. Kissinger's public rhetoric began to toughen, and the essence of U.S. détente policy—a tactic to limit Soviet power—became clear.[1]

Presidential politics was an important factor limiting U.S.-Soviet relations in 1976. Only a few weeks before Kissinger's Moscow trip, public opinion polls showed that President Ford could not take his election prospects for granted: his disapproval rating was 46 percent with only 39 percent of those polled approving his conduct as president. Moveover, another poll taken in December showed how far Ronald Reagan had eroded his position specifically on the right: 40 percent of all Republicans and 27 percent of all independents planned to vote for Reagan. Running as an "outsider," Reagan supplemented his attacks on government with criticisms of Ford's China policy and Kissinger's conduct of the SALT II talks in order to strengthen his appeal to "convention going" Republican conservatives. Even with the advantage of incumbency, Ford could not be complacent about winning their votes at the convention.[2]

An astute State Department analyst suggested that U.S. – Soviet cooperation had become a political football partly because détente had been oversold earlier in the decade with "enormous public relations efforts": "we are now reaping the costs of our prior extravagance."[3] In early January, Kissinger professed willingness to bear some of the "costs" by presenting Ford with a draft letter of resignation. Kissinger correctly anticipated that Ford would reject the letter: though many Republicans had strong reservations about détente and disliked Kissinger's penchant for secrecy and ambiguity, Ford refused to give up his secretary of state or the policies that he personified. Instead, he justified détente as a compelling national interest; right-wing opposition notwithstanding, Ford told NBC news on 3 January that it would "be very unwise for a President . . . to abandon détente. I think détente is in the best interests of this country. It is in the best interest of world stability, world peace."[4]

Brezhnev had few worries about internal challenges to détente or other basic policies; as he explained to foreign journalists, Soviet "people are used to being told what is happening." Although doubts about his health had lessened since his severe problems in 1974, Assistant Secretary for European Affairs Arthur Hartman saw "major uncertainty" and assumed that Brezhnev would retire at age 70 (Brezhnev had turned 69 in December). Hartman further speculated, correctly as it turned out, that Brezhnev's recent ebullience in meeting with foreign visitors could have been the effect of drugs. He went on to observe that, "[b]ased on past observation, his mood can shift suddenly into dark depression."[5]

Since Kissinger's last visit to Moscow in October 1974, Congress had passed the Jackson – Vanik Amendment, and U.S. – Soviet plans for trade expansion had collapsed. Though Brezhnev must have been embittered by such developments, he remained committed to U.S. – Soviet cooperation, even if his ideological and political priorities would complicate his ability to make it work. The Communist Party's Twenty-fifth Congress was scheduled for late February, and Brezhnev wanted his keynote address to show progress in stabilizing U.S. – Soviet relations; a SALT II agreement and a Washington summit for signing it would be the icing on the cake. However, Brezhnev had a low tolerance for further concessions; he had already gone to the mat to convince defense officials to accept the Vladivostok agreement. Washington's interest in cruise missiles — the "new channel in the arms race"—raised serious problems for the Soviets, given that catching up with U.S. in MIRVs was already a strain.[6]

Brezhnev's dedication to superpower cooperation, was not uniform, though, and his decisions on Angola were taking their toll on détente. Traditional friendliness toward national liberation movements, rivalry with Beijing for political influence in Africa, and anxieties about formal U.S.-PRC collaboration in sustaining the FNLA contributed to Moscow's decisions in late 1974 to increase military aid to the MPLA. Moreover, Brezhnev approved even greater levels of aid in the fall of 1975; but by then he was more concerned about South Africa's intervention and growing U.S. covert support than with Beijing, which had ditched the FNLA. In December, when the Cubans began to have difficulty airlifting men and materiel across the Atlantic, the Soviets initiated a "major, new development" in their competition with Washington by supplying the long-range aircraft that enabled Havana to help the newly declared People's Republic of Angola (PRA) to defeat its opponents.[7] Although these actions were seen in Washington as extremely provocative, the Soviet leadership believed that its role in Angola was altogether compatible with détente.[8]

The rift over Angola was hardly the crisis in the Eurasian balance of power that Kissinger had forecast for the mid-1970s, but he nevertheless saw U.S. operations in southern Africa as an opportunity to bloody a putative Soviet client and thereby to revalidate U.S. credibility. During most of 1975, therefore, he showed little interest in discussing Angola with the Soviets, much less in finding ways to limit superpower competition in the region. Only rather late in the game, when the South Africans were intervening, the Cuban role was expanding, and the U.S.-supported FNLA losing, did he begin explicitly to link Angola to détente and demand that the Soviets exercise restraint and allow the Angolans to "resolve their differences without outside intervention." On 8 December 1975, Kissinger met with Dobrynin to ask for a halt to arms shipments; the next day, Ford told Dobrynin that Angola was making the administration more vulnerable to political attacks: the public, he said, saw Southern African developments as a test for détente. But Ford also believed that the stakes in Angola were too small to distort U.S.-Soviet relations, so he urged joint cooperation in encouraging an end to the fighting and mutual forbearance in arms shipments.[9]

A few days later, the Soviets did indeed halt their arms shipments. On 19 December, the U.S. Senate—which was suspicious of the CIA and its secret wars, skeptical of Kissinger's explanation for involvement in Angola, concerned over South Africa's role, and generally concerned about escalating involvement in the Third World conflict—rejected the administration's request for $28 million for Angola and, instead, banned further covert aid. The House soon passed the same legislation, which Ford reluctantly signed into law in early 1976. By late December, though, the Soviets had already resumed their shipments, and the MPLA stayed on the offensive. Soon South African forces began to suspend operations and eventually withdrew from Angola. The FNLA began to wither away, although Savimbi's UNITA managed to hold on for years. With the presence of Cuban forces backed by Soviet arms, the MPLA's position soon stabilized; by February, the Organization of African Unity had recognized it as the legal government of Angola.[10]

Kissinger, of course, was outraged that the Soviets and the Cubans had played the competitive game more effectively than Washington; he was also angry at Ford for not trying to circumvent Congress Nixon-style. He was determined to read Brezhnev the riot act when they met, but the administration had lost virtually all of its leverage to induce cooperation over Angola. The U.S. economy was still struggling with deep recession, so Ford rejected new export restrictions as a means to punish the Soviets: provoking export-dependent U.S. farmers was not on the White House agenda in an election year. Ford had already assured the American Farm Bureau Federation in early January that the Angolan situation would not prompt grain embargoes.[11]

The SALT process provided no leverage either. Kissinger made strong statements in Moscow about the damage Angola was doing to superpower cooperation, including SALT, but he was well aware that Angola and SALT had to be "compartmentalized as hermetically as possible." As he later explained in public remarks, arms control was not a "favor which we grant to the Soviet Union to be turned on and off according to the ebb and flow of our relations."[13]

Brezhnev had already invited Kissinger to come to Moscow in December to discuss SALT II. To his annoyance, however, Kissinger had to postpone the trip because the agencies could not agree on a set of SALT options to present to Ford. The new Secretary of Defense, Donald Rumsfeld, who was suspicious both of détente and Kissinger, was not going to approve a controversial SALT proposal. To preserve his freedom of action and to ensure that a SALT II agreement was politically and bureaucratically acceptable, Rumsfeld initiated a successful "stall and harass" strategy.[13] Further, critics had been charging Ford and Kissinger with condoning Soviet violations of the SALT I agreement, so the White House had to tread very carefully in developing a new proposal.[14]

By mid-January 1976, Ford had a set of options to consider. They all gave the United States a very free hand in deploying cruise missiles, so the key issue, the White House knew, would be how to treat the Backfire bomber.[15] At a National Security Council meeting, Ford approved a SALT negotiating position that took a restrictive approach to Backfire: all but the first 120 bombers produced after October 1970 would be included in the 2,400 aggregate of strategic delivery vehicles. For cruise missiles, air-launched (ALCMs), sea-launched (SLCMs), and land-launched (LLCMs) would be limited to a 2,500 kilometer range, while submarine-launched cruise missiles would be limited to 600 kilometers. As a concession to the Soviets, however, only heavy bombers would be allowed to carry ALCMs with ranges of up to 2,500. With each bomber counted in the 2,400 aggregate of strategic systems as well as in the 1,320 ceiling on MIRVed delivery vehicles.[16]

By asking Moscow to accept considerable U.S. freedom in deploying varieties of cruise missiles, Ford and the NSC were following Kissinger's original plan to use them as bargaining chips. Kissinger nevertheless had some room to haggle: by getting the Soviets to accept ALCMs and sea-launched cruise missiles, if the U.S. gave up submarine- and land-launched missiles.[17] However, Ford recognized that the Soviets would reject any plan that included the Backfire in the Vladivostok aggregate, so he authorized Kissinger to take a fallback position—creating separate limits for Backfire and tying it with constraints on SLCMs—to keep the discussion going. The transcripts that follow show serious efforts by Kissinger, Brezhnev, and Gromyko to find common ground on cruise missiles and the Backfire. It was far from easy, but when the talks concluded the possibility for compromise led close observers to believe that the two sides had achieved a "breakthrough."[18]

Ford agreed with Kissinger that agreement "was very near," but rather than push for an NSC consensus to conclude the negotiations he drew back. He was not convinced by the arguments of Kissinger's opponents at Defense, ACDA, and the Joint Chiefs, but he could not afford to ignore his secretary of defense, Donald Rumsfeld, who was turning "hard right" against SALT. Even if Kissinger could negotiate a treaty based on the fallback, the prospect of senior Pentagon officials opposing it was something that Ford refused to countenance in an election year.[19] In the following weeks, the NSC staff crafted another proposal more acceptable to the Pentagon that Ford hoped could keep the negotiations alive. But when presented with it in February, Brezhnev saw it as a step backward from Kissinger's stance in Moscow and quickly rejected it. Ford later wrote in his memoirs, "Reluctantly, I concluded we would not be able to achieve SALT agreement in 1976."[20]

Kissinger's efforts to move Brezhnev and Gromyko on the Angolan question were a much starker failure. Ambassador Dobrynin was worried that Moscow's policy was playing into the hands of détente's U.S. opponents, but Brezhnev refused to engage in substantive discussions on the subject; Gromyko saw no reason why justifiable Cuban activities should impair U.S.-Soviet relations. Kissinger, however, failed to recognize that the Cubans had broad freedom of action in the Angolan drama and acted as if the Soviets had total control of the situation. Dobrynin later called it a "dialogue of the deaf."[21]

In the wake of the Moscow talks, Kissinger was distressed by his inability to fund a covert war against Cuban forces, worried that a setback in Angola would undermine global stability by weakening confidence in U.S. power, and was determined to prevent "more Angolas," so his rhetoric and policy approach only hardened. No longer treating détente as an effort to build a "constructive relationship" with the Soviet Union, his public statements began to evoke the sterner containment rhetoric of the earlier Cold War: "The policies pursued by this administration have been designed to prevent Soviet expansion." The United States, he said, did not seek "unnecessary confrontation" with Soviet power, but "we can prevent its use of unilateral advantage and political expansion."[22]

However, Kissinger's toughened approach to Moscow only intensified Reagan's onslaught on the administration's foreign policy after his New Hampshire primary defeat. He charged that the United States "had become Number Two in military power in a world where it is dangerous—if not fatal—to be second best," and that "the Soviet Union will not stop taking advantage of détente" until there is a new president and secretary of state. Within days, Ford capitulated; on 5 March 1976, in response to a question after a speech in Peoria, Ill., he absurdly stated, "We are going to forget the use of the word détente." Ford continued to justify the substance of détente—negotiations rather than confrontation—but he also began to emphasize the importance of military power as the means to ensure that the U.S.-Soviet relationship was a "two-way street."[23] Kissinger soon began to emulate his boss: the word *détente* disappeared from his speeches.[24]

Reagan's attacks may have been the immediate cause for the administration's hardened rhetoric, but there were more substantial reasons too. Events over time had disclosed basic contradictions in the original Nixon–Kissinger conception of détente. As Kissinger had revealed to the Chinese time and time again, both he and Nixon had seen détente essentially as a tactic to regulate the Soviet Union, and, tacitly, to preserve a U.S. central role in world politics. Yet, as Kissinger sought a modus vivendi with Moscow, and even to find ways to integrate the Soviets into the international system, he was reluctant to validate their interests and objectives, which he saw as hostile to the "whole Western structure." Moreover, his deep-seated commitment to asserting U.S. credibility precluded taking Soviet interests into account; thus, when tensions arose, as in Angola, and Brezhnev did not acquiesce to Kissinger's view of restraint and global stability, détente's harder edge became clearer.[25]

Yet Kissinger and Ford found it difficult to translate tough words into tough deeds, however strong their opposition to Soviet policy in Angola. They did not want to estrange the Soviets seriously and saw economic sanctions as self-defeating; so the administration took a series of smaller steps to register its opposition over Angola. It did not ask Congress to suspend Jackson–Vanik, and Kissinger canceled several high-level meetings on economic and energy issues. Ccooperative efforts did not completely end and earlier accomplishments—SALT I limitations, the Helsinki process, and greater stability over Berlin—were not put at risk, but the combined effect of Angola and the 1976 campaign was to put détente on hold. The Soviets could only wait to see if it would be possible to arrive at a viable relationship with the next administration, whether led by Ford or one of his rivals.[26]

The transcripts that follow show serious U.S.–Soviet efforts to reach a modus vivendi on SALT II but also disclose the dhasm [over Angola. Although Kissinger had speculated at an NSC meeting that Brezhnev "could not afford a failure" of the SALT talks, if he hoped that the Soviets would make the concessions needed to finalize an agreement, he was mistaken.[27] The first round of talks in Moscow began inauspiciously when Brezhnev announced to the press that he had no interest in discussing Angola.

THE WHITE HOUSE
SECRET/NODIS/XGDS
MEMORANDUM OF CONVERSATION
PARTICIPANTS: USSR Leonid I. Brezhnev, General Secretary of the
   Central Committee of the CPSU; Andrei A. Gromyko, Member of
   the Politburo of the Central Committee of the CPSU; Minister of
   Foreign Affairs; Georgiy M. Korniyenko, Deputy Minister of
   Foreign Affairs; Anatoliy F. Dobrynin, Ambassador to the U.S.;
   Andrei M. Aleksandrov-Agentov, Assistant to the General Secretary;
   Vasiliy G. Makarov, Chef de Cabinet to the Foreign Minister; V.G.

Komplektov, Acting Chief of USA Dept, MFA; Viktor M. Sukhodrev, Counselor, Second European Dept., MFA (Interpreter); Maj. General Mikhail Kozlov, Deputy Chief of General Staff; Nikolai N. Detinov, CPSU Secretariat; U.S. Dr. Henry A. Kissinger, Secretary of State; Amb. Walter J. Stoessel, Jr., Ambassador to the USSR; Helmut Sonnenfeldt, Counselor of the Department; Winston Lord, Director, Policy Planning Staff; William G. Hyland, Deputy Assistant to the President for National Security Affairs; Arthur A. Hartman, Assistant Secretary for European Affairs; James P. Wade, Deputy Assistant Secretary of Defense for Policy Plans and NSC Affairs (and) Director of DOD SALT Task Force;[28] Peter W. Rodman, NSC Staff

TIME: Wednesday, January 21, 1976; 11:00 A.M.–1:50 P.M.
PLACE: Brezhnev's Office, The Kremlin Moscow
SUBJECT: SALT; Angola[A]

(Brezhnev entered first, wearing a blue suit, blue shirt, red patterned tie, and four medals: Hero of Soviet Union; Hero of Socialist Labor; the Lenin Peace Prize; and the Joliot–Curie Prize. The speakers stood on one side of the long table on which stood, among other drinks, bottled Pepsi. Black and white portraits of Marx and Lenin were on the wall.)

Brezhnev: (To the press.) This is a link-up of Soviet and American journalists, like Soyuz and Apollo.

(To Secretary Kissinger, as he entered.) You look much younger.

Kissinger: You look very well.

Brezhnev: Thanks for the compliment.

Kissinger: I'm fat.

Gromyko: No. You lost weight.

(The members of the Secretary's party were introduced. The press took photos.)

Brezhnev: (To Sonnenfeldt.) Here's an old acquaintance, a traveling companion.

Nicholas Daniloff (UPI): (In Russian.) When will your visit to us take place?

Brezhnev: That all depends on what Secretary Kissinger says.

Daniloff: Can you evaluate the current status of US/Soviet relations?

[A] State Department Freedom of Information release; copy at National Security Archive (hereafter referred to as *NSA*.

Brezhnev: It's hard for me to evaluate. It's up to what nice things Kissinger has to say.

Kissinger: I hope he (Daniloff) is friendlier in Russian than he is in English.

Daniloff: What are the chief subjects of your talks?

Brezhnev: The primary subject is the achievement of a new SALT Agreement. There are also questions of the reduction of forces in Europe and a general review of the international situation. The world is big, and the subjects are inexhaustible.

Reporter: Will Angola be among the subjects?

Brezhnev: I have no questions about Angola. Angola is not my country.

Kissinger: It will certainly be discussed.

Gromyko: The agenda is always adopted by mutual agreement.

Kissinger: Then I will discuss it.

Brezhnev: You'll discuss it with Sonnenfeldt. That will insure complete agreement. I've never seen him have a disagreement with Sonnenfeldt.

Murray Marder (Washington Post): The two countries each have a large event coming up on February 24, the New Hampshire primary and the Party Congress. Do you expect—(interrupted)

Brezhnev: The Congress is a great event for me, for our Party, and for the entire country. It is a great event for me as the one who gives the major report. It's a momentous occasion.

Marder: Will you report about a SALT agreement?

Brezhnev: If such an agreement is reached, I will talk about it. If an agreement is not reached by then, and there is something to report about it, I will do so. Our people are used to being told what is happening.

Reporter: Do you hope to visit Washington for a Summit in the near future?

Brezhnev: I expect to. I can't say when. If I can return to the first part of the question, let me say the basic importance of that visit is that agreement must be reached. And then Comrade Brezhnev can go to Washington and sign the agreement.

Reporter: Do you expect these talks to produce an agreement?

Brezhnev: I can't give a definite reply before the talks, but I certainly appreciate your curiosity. Your question contains your answer.

Gromyko: This is a diplomatic answer.

Brezhnev: I appreciate your interest. Thank you for your respect, and you have to realize that I can't give precise answers to questions before this conference.

(The press were ushered out and the parties sat at the table and the talks began.)

Brezhnev: I'm happy once again to welcome you here in Moscow, Mr. Secretary. A little over a year now has passed since we last met, but in the world many events have taken place of a different sort.

But the major fact is, in our view, that in spite of all the complexities that exist, our two countries have succeeded in consolidating the line of detente and the line of improvement of US–Soviet relations. That line is, I may say, now passing through a test of its durability. And it is proving, in our view, its durability and its wisdom. We appreciate that both President Ford and you as Secretary of State of the United States are upholding that line in the face of unceasing assault on it by various ill-wishers.

I wish here to place emphasis on one very important point of principle. Since today and tomorrow we are due to engage in very serious discussions, I should like to emphasize that we, for our part, remain dedicated to those fundamental agreements and understandings that have been agreed between our two countries and we are ready to continue efforts to bring about their consistent implementation. At the same time, I must say outright, that in recent months not everything is shaping up in US–Soviet relations as we would like. And I would like to stress, through no fault of the Soviet Union, there has appeared a certain hitch in the development of our relations, and that includes the preparations for a new agreement on strategic arms limitation. We regard it as not only wrong but also harmful to allow of any pause or, all the more, of any stagnation in the implementation of the joint line we have both undertaken.

I, Dr. Kissinger, would not be mistaken to say that you know full well that the Soviet Union—the Soviet Government and the entire Party, and I myself—are in favor of truly businesslike relations with the United States on a broad range of questions. And I don't know what the reasons are why objections are raised and proposals are put forth that are overly complicated. We must make an effort to improve relations on a broad front, and we have untapped resources in this respect, and we must move forward along that line. I must speak frankly. I trust you'll agree with me; that our countries have no right to slacken our efforts at ending the threat of war and ending the arms race. And there are other problems, too, requiring our joint efforts.

Dr. Kissinger, this is by no means our first meeting. We have had others. There is a good tradition that has been established in the past, and it is one of a frank exchange of views on whatever questions arise. And I'd like to suggest we discuss today whatever questions we have in the same spirit.

The newsmen a little while ago asked us what questions we would be discussing and I said one of the most important was the negotiation of a new

SALT agreement. And I trust you'll agree. So I would like Dr. Kissinger to start out on the question of SALT and set out.

I want to say I have the full text here of President Ford's State of the Union speech, but I have not yet had a chance to make a detailed study.

The floor is yours, Dr. Kissinger. Have a cookie. Just one. I really don't see they are any danger to you.

(Laughter.)

Gromyko: You see all these plates here are fully MIRV'd. (laughter)

Kissinger: The General Secretary is personally responsible for at least 15 pounds of my overweight.

Brezhnev: My God! Add that to all my other responsibilities? If that were all, it would be a lot easier.

Another thing I can tell you: I have given up smoking. It took one day to do that.

Kissinger: Where is that cigarette case that had the clock on it?

Brezhnev: I had two. I gave one away. I don't know where it is. My doctor suggested: Why don't you give up smoking? I am surprised how easy it was.

Kissinger: When the General Secretary comes to the United States, I hope he can teach my wife how to do it.

Brezhnev: I don't know whether I can do it. The urge to smoke is just vanishing. I used to do it before going to bed, but now I have the urge a little bit but still don't.

Kissinger: My wife is in the hospital and has to give it up. So she's a little irritable.

A year ago, the doctor sent her to a hypnotist as a way to get her to stop. He sent a nurse along with her. Afterwards, she came back to my office and told me about it. She lit up a cigarette while telling me about it. (laughter) But the nurse has given up smoking. (laughter)

Brezhnev: That's like a story by Zoshchenko. I remember it almost literally. He wrote short humorous stories. One dealt with the harm of smoking. A man said: I'll just give it up. It's hard, though, so someone suggested I go to a hypnotist. So I went to a hypnotist. The room was in almost total darkness. I seated myself in a chair and the hypnotist says: Take everything out of your pocket and put it on the table. I took out a pack of homegrown tobacco. He made passes with his hands and he said, don't think about anything. And I said to myself I shouldn't forget about one thing—to be sure to leave the tobacco when I left. (laughter)

That is in a collection of stories published here, by Zoshchenko.

I feel when people can joke with each other, they are in a good mood and can do business with each other. A man who can't joke isn't a good man.

Kissinger: Mr. General Secretary, I'd like first to bring you the greetings and warm regards of President Ford, who hopes my mission will succeed and looks forward to your visit to the United States soon, hopefully in the Spring.

Brezhnev: Thank you for the greetings and good wishes. And I say this in great sincerity and great respect for the President.

Kissinger: Mr. General Secretary, I first came to Moscow in April of 1972 at a very critical period in our relations. At that time, there was a sharp increase in tensions in the world. The talks on strategic arms were stalemated. Conflicts in other parts of the world, especially Southeast Asia, threatened our relationship. Nevertheless both our countries, conscious of our responsibility, worked with dedication to overcome all obstacles. What we were able to achieve in that atmosphere was a testimony to the special responsibilities we share to bring the nuclear arms race under control and to bring peace to the world at last.

In some respects this present meeting occurs in similar circumstances. For what we accomplish in the next few days, or fail to accomplish, will have a very important impact on the future course of Soviet–American relations and therefore the peace of the world.

Our countries are the strongest nuclear powers in the world. Others can talk about petty problems, but we bear a special responsibility to lessen the dangers of nuclear war, to lessen tensions that could lead to confrontation and to work together to achieve a world of greater peace.

I have had the privilege of many conversations with the General Secretary and I know he is dedicated to bringing about an improvement in our relationship and he is as conscious as we are of the special responsibility of our two countries. On our side, the President is firmly committed to improving our relations. And despite our election campaign and despite attacks by some of the leading contenders for the Presidency in both parties, he will persevere on this course.

And my presence here in the face of much criticism is testimony to the sincerity of our purpose. Nevertheless it is clear that what we accomplish here is going to be subjected to the most minute scrutiny in America.

I am also aware, Mr. General Secretary, that you will be reporting to the Party next month. Thus we both have reason to regard the outcome of this meeting as a very crucial element in both our countries' foreign policies.

We both have spoken many times of our responsibilities and of the need to make an improvement of our relations irreversible. This remains our objective. But events in the past 12 months have demonstrated this has not been achieved. The majority of Americans still believe that it is essential for world peace that the two strongest powers continue to improve relations and that they take a further step to limit strategic arms.

(Brezhnev speaks loudly to Gromyko while Dr. Kissinger continues.)

We will continue on this course. But we cannot ignore the fact that this possibility will be greatly influenced by events. Thus the first task of our meeting is to make progress on strategic arms limitation and then to make progress on other matters that divide us.

It has been over a year since the meeting at Vladivostok. New issues have arisen on both sides that were not foreseen at that time. We must not permit these issues to become obstacles to the truly historic gains achieved at Vladivostok. I've given your Ambassador a new proposal (Tab A) which deals with the issues of cruise missiles and the Backfire bomber. We believe these proposals represent a serious effort, and believe it is time that both of us approached these issues in a spirit of compromise, if we are to have any chance of concluding a new agreement.

The day of my departure from Washington, President Ford met with his National Security Council for the third time on this subject. At the end of the meeting, he emphasized to his advisers, and to me, the importance he attaches to bringing the negotiations to a successful conclusion, even though it is fair to say not all the advice he received was unanimous. It is an indication of the seriousness in which he approaches my mission and his determination to make every effort that he has approved this proposal and sent me here with instructions to exert every effort to work out a possible agreement that both sides can sign.

I hope to hear your reaction to this new approach.

Angola

But before I conclude, I would like to raise one new issue that has arisen between us.

It is intolerable to us that a country in the Western Hemisphere should launch virtual invasion of Africa. Moreover, the support of the Soviet Union to this Cuban force creates a precedent that the United States must resist. We have made it a cardinal principle of our relations that one great power must exercise restraint and not strive for unilateral advantage. If that principle is now abandoned, the prospect is for a chain of action and reaction with the potential for disastrous results.

In addition to Angola, we are also prepared to discuss the Middle East.

Brezhnev: You say that in the sense of a threat of some kind of war breaking out.

Kissinger: It is not a threat of war, Mr. General Secretary. But if every country behaves this way, it could grow into a very dangerous situation.

Brezhnev: But I think we should conduct discussions first and foremost on the SALT issue. If we raise all sorts of extraneous matters, we will accomplish nothing.

I am just sleeping in my bed and all of a sudden I hear about events in Portugal, about which I know nothing. Then I hear Costa Gomes wants to visit the Soviet Union. So I receive him. You can read the communique. We promised him trade. So what? We trade with many countries. As for the leader of the Communist Party—Alvaro Cunhal—I've never set eyes on him in my life.

Then the Angola situation comes up. Portugal grants it independence. [Agostinho] Neto approached Cuba after aggression was committed and Cuba agreed to support them. There is no Soviet military presence in Angola.[29]

It is true that before independence we agreed to sell them some tanks, but that is no secret. If you talk of catastrophic consequences for the Soviet Union, that is the wrong way to talk. I could talk of disastrous consequences for the United States in the Middle East, but that's the wrong way.

There is no way to underestimate the importance we attach to reaching agreement on strategic arms limitation. We reached an important agreement at Vladivostok. Now someone says that was nothing but a piece of paper. We should deal with it in a businesslike way.

I don't know what Andrei Andreyevich (Gromyko) thinks on this. He's the diplomat. But if President Ford were sitting here, I'd say the same thing.

I don't want to discuss the President's State of the Union Address because I have not read it. But we had a chance to discuss it yesterday. He talks about the 1976 military budget being greater than 1975, the need to have superior military power, the need to discuss questions including SALT with the Soviet Union from a position of strength.[30] I could never have admitted the thought that such a lackadaisical attitude could be given to such important agreements.

Kissinger: I agree, Mr. General Secretary, first priority should be to a new agreement on strategic arms.

Brezhnev: I agree.

Kissinger: But it is also a fact that our two countries, because of our power and because of our strategic interests around the world, have a special responsibility to show restraint. Because success by one country in one area can always be compensated by success for the other in other areas. I have never forgotten the conversation I had with the General Secretary, when he told me his father said the monument to peacemakers should be placed on the highest mountain. We should remember that the issues that seem important now may look like nothing a few years from now. Tens of millions were killed in Europe over Alsace-Lorraine, and what difference does in make today? The casualties in a future war would end civilized life as we know it.

I must tell you frankly, the introduction into Angola of a Cuban expeditionary force backed by Soviet arms is a matter that we must take extremely seriously. I agree also that we should be prepared to work on strategic arms. We have worked almost five years on this. If we do not complete it, our successors will have to. We will work with all seriousness to conclude the agreement we achieved at Vladivostok, which we do not consider a scrap of paper.

Brezhnev: That I like. If you have instructions to take a serious attitude on that. It is one thing to joke; it is another thing to take it in a serious way.

We will see how matters stand in actual fact.

You mentioned your first visit in 1972 and the situation and atmosphere at that time. You are quite right, it was complicated then. And we showed at that time that the Soviet Union wants good relations with the United States, that we don't want war, but we want peace with all nations. There could be no better proof of our dedication to peace at that time. The bombs were falling on Vietnam; Communist parties all over the world were berating the United States. We had to face the dilemma of whether to receive Dr. Kissinger and President Nixon in Moscow or not. We gave proof to that. We knew the war in Vietnam would ultimately end and it would not produce a world war. And the decision we made then is proof of our dedication. In this spirit I will be addressing the 25th Party Congress—not from positions of strength but from positions of seeking peace.

Are we here to discuss SALT? Or Angola? What do we need a success in Angola [*sic*]? We need nothing in Angola. But the whole world can read in the press that the West, and America, are sending arms and mercenaries in Angola. And you turn everything on its head. I've never been to Portugal; we are not responsible for anything there.

In Spain, there are lots of strikes going on and you can hold the Soviet Union responsible. If you have proof to the contrary, lay it out on the table.

Aleksandrov: Tell him about what you read.

Brezhnev: Recently, I read Kissinger will be going to Spain. An American delegation was there and made preparations for a new agreement on military bases. Here am I making every effort for peace, and Kissinger is going around making agreements on military bases.[31] I won't say this publicly, but this was in my head. If I were discussing strategic arms, I wouldn't go around organizing military bases, but I would go home and report to President Ford and work on a new agreement on strategic arms. So you can visit Moscow only in passing and your primary aim is to visit Madrid, you can do that if you want, but it certainly won't earn you respect in the world.

Strategic Arms Limitation Talks

Let me now, Dr. Kissinger, say a few words on substance of SALT, our principal goal. We have recently, Dr. Kissinger, already set out to the President our assessment of the state of affairs regarding the new agreement. We did this in all frankness and without beating around the bush.

Kissinger: What is the General Secretary referring to?

Dobrynin: The last letter (Tab B).[32]

Brezhnev: After all, work on preparing a new agreement has not yet been completed and therefore the Vladivostok understanding so far remains unrealized. I believe all this should be of equal concern to both sides since we do not believe the United States is interested in an agreement to any less extent than is the Soviet Union. During the negotiations already after Vladivostok, we for our part have made significant important steps to meet the United States in questions that are of particular importance to the American side, to display a readiness to seek constructive solutions to highly important problems. The United States to date has made no equal responsive steps or even steps comparable with ours.

The American side, as is evident from its latest proposals of January 14, attempts on the one hand to introduce limitations on Soviet arms that are not strategic arms at all, and on the other hand to legalize for yourself new systems that are genuinely strategic. Needless to say, such an approach complicates the process of reaching agreement.

Could we have a little five minute break?

Kissinger: I was going to propose the same.

Brezhnev: So we have achieved our first agreement!

(There was a break from 12:25 to 12:41 p.m., and the meeting resumed.)

Brezhnev: Dr. Kissinger, let me just in passing express my gratification that you have, as you say, instructions—as I have, too—to work out a mutually acceptable agreement on strategic arms. And I would like both of us to carry out our instructions in good faith, without worrying about second-rate matters. We can have different views about bombers, about 100 questions, and you could put questions to me and I to you. But let us secure an agreement and the kind of peace we want, and we can crown our efforts.

Kissinger: I agree. And that is the spirit we should conduct our discussions.

Brezhnev: Good.

(Brezhnev and Gromyko confer about the schedule.)

We are threatened with complete starvation. They have taken all our teacups and everything.

Kissinger: I'm sure you have lost many state guests to starvation in the Kremlin!

I met yesterday the Queen of Denmark who was very impressed with her visit to the Soviet Union.

Brezhnev: I didn't meet her.

Kissinger: If you start undermining royalty . . . She saw some family jewels in the Kremlin.

(laughter)

Gromyko: She was very impressive as a personality.

Brezhnev: There are some very impressive people there.

Kissinger: But when you start impressing European royalty, the sense of insecurity is great. (laughter)

Brezhnev: Women start out by looking at jewels. That is why there are so few women in politics.

Kissinger: The ones that are bloodthirsty.

Brezhnev: So, who dictates the terms of the new agreement? We've got to get down to writing a draft.

Kissinger: We made a proposal to you, to which we have not yet received a reply, in which we really attempted to meet several of your points. So we would appreciate your reflections or any counterproposal you may have. Of course, we could also sign this proposal, and then I could go to Leningrad tomorrow. If it exists.

Gromyko: Maybe Leningrad is just a legend—spread since the time of Peter the Great.

Kissinger: Since my wife saw it, I'm a little bit more convinced.

Gromyko: Couldn't that have been hypnosis? (Laughter)

Brezhnev: Like the man sitting and thinking about one thing in the world—not to forget his tobacco. (Laughter)

First of all, I would deem it necessary to remind you that the readiness to count in the number of MIRV'd missiles, in the 1,320, all missiles of such types as had been tested with MIRV's was and is contingent on mutually acceptable solutions on the other as yet outstanding questions.

Kissinger: I understand that.

Brezhnev: So I trust there is no misunderstanding on that.

Kissinger: The Foreign Minister has made it clear. I do not exclude there are one or two others in our government who believe you have conceded that. But the Foreign Minister has made it clear in every meeting we have had.

Brezhnev: Now as regards air-to-ground cruise missiles. We feel as hitherto that air-to-ground cruise missiles with a range of over 600 kilometers carried by heavy bombers must be on an equal footing with ballistic missiles of that class and must be counted in the total of 2,400 strategic armed vehicles, each one counted as one vehicle.

Kissinger: But this was always your position.

Brezhnev: That solution most effectively meets the goals of limiting strategic arms and accords with the substance of the Vladivostok understanding. Comrade Kissinger—I mean Dr. Kissinger. (laughter)

Kissinger: Maybe at the Party Congress they will do it. (laughter) I believe if the General Secretary called me Comrade Kissinger, it would not be without influence on subsequent primaries. Jackson and Reagan would be very grateful.

Brezhnev: I'm not all that familiar with all the ramifications of your election campaign. So I'd better be objective.

[Brezhnev spells out the rest of the Soviet position on cruise missiles, with several points, e.g., on ALCMs, showing some accommodation to Washington, although he also calls for banning LLCMs and SLCMs with ranges over 600 kilometers. On Backfire, Brezhnev insists that it is non-strategic but makes an important move by making assurances on its combat radius: about 2400 kilometers or 1491 miles. Kissinger jokingly observes that "If an airplane flies over the United States and drops bombs, we know it's not a Backfire."]

Brezhnev: Dr. Kissinger, not you yourself, but let's as an experiment, put Sonnenfeldt on that plane, and fill it with gas and fly it to New York. Or both, and call it MIRV'd.

That is a very substantive answer. Because my honest word is behind it.

Because if this isn't true, I would stand exposed before the whole world. Because if I say this officially and agree to have it reflected in the document, if it were not true, it would be a serious thing.

Kissinger: Let me take five minutes to discuss this.

Brezhnev: All right. I think, Dr. Kissinger, you and I have a good basis for understanding. We should not try to pull things out of each other.

Kissinger: I tell you. Our generals double the range of your Backfire; your generals cut it in half.

Brezhnev: Your generals should not control your government, any more than ours do ours. If generals were allowed to govern, there would be a world war and they wouldn't be among the living and would have no one to govern. (The meeting broke from 1:30 to 1:40 and then resumed.)

Brezhnev: Dr. Kissinger, please. Could I just say something? I want to make one suggestion. This is a very important question we are discussing. This is really the very core of our future relationship. So I would like to make this suggestion. This is a matter that I am sure requires a certain thinking and consideration and therefore a certain period of time. So perhaps we should declare a recess. All the more so since Comrade Gromyko has a luncheon party for you which will require some time. After all, it takes time to talk.

And we could perhaps resume our discussions at five o'clock this afternoon.

Kissinger: That's a better idea.

Brezhnev: I'm seeking no advantages for myself.

Kissinger: I was going to make the same proposal.

Brezhnev: (Pointing to the album which the Secretary has taken out in front of him.) What are those and I hope reasonable proposals [sic]?

Kissinger: (Handing over the album of photographs.) Those are photos we took of the General Secretary at Vladivostok and Helsinki. There are some very good pictures in it.

Brezhnev: (Looks through the album) I weighed less when I was in Helsinki than now. Now I'm 85–88 kilos.

Kissinger: The General Secretary looks very well.

Brezhnev: I try. All young people try and look that way, so I try.

Kissinger: I understand the General Secretary's speech (to the Party Congress) has to be two to three hours. That takes great stamina.

Brezhnev: Even more.

Aleksandrov: Castro once talked 10 hours!

Brezhnev: But ours will get big attention—the international part. There will be an economic section, and a part on the Party itself. As at the 24th Congress, we are setting out the program for the coming five years. And we have a very big step forward in these last five years—in the economy, in various social fields, in the spiritual field. Our own political unity of the people and the Party has gained in strength. It is a big Party, so there are quite a few things to say. About 15–15½ million members, quite a big organized force.

Kissinger: We will meet again this afternoon.

Brezhnev: Good.

Kissinger: Can I meet with the General Secretary one minute alone?

(He confers privately with the General Secretary at the end of the table.)

I'd like to say a word about that electronic problem.[33] We have not briefed our people on it. Your measurements were taken at ground level. But on the higher floors, which we will let you measure, it becomes very high. If it becomes public.

Brezhnev: The President answered me on that.

Kissinger: I'm not saying it for negotiating purposes. We appreciated your reply. If you could pay some attention to it.

And in general terms we wanted to tell the General Secretary we genuinely want an agreement. We have a difficult situation.

Brezhnev: We hope we can achieve an agreement and it will help Ford's situation.

Kissinger: Not so much Ford's situation but we have a concrete subject to defeat the opponents (of detente). I agree you have nothing to gain in Angola. We have nothing to gain in Angola. But 8,000 Cubans running around . . . You wouldn't want Hungarians running around conducting anti-Soviet activities. The meeting ended.)

[Later in the afternoon, after lunch, Brezhnev and Kissinger returned to the SALT problem, but not before a few words on China.]

THE WHITE HOUSE
SECRET/NODIS/XGDS
MEMORANDUM OF CONVERSATION
PARTICIPANTS: USSR: Leonid I. Brezhnev, General Secretary of the Central Committee of the CPSU; Andrei A. Gromyko, Member of the Politburo of the Central Committee of the CPSU; Minister of Foreign Affairs . . . US: Dr. Henry A. Kissinger, Secretary of State . . .[34]

DATE AND TIME: Wednesday, January 21, 1976, 5:02–6:30 P.M.
PLACE: Brezhnev's Office, The Kremlin Moscow
SUBJECT: SALT[B]

Brezhnev: I took a rest. I was reading some summaries, including about China, your friend.

Kissinger: They just gave you a helicopter.[35]

Gromyko: Our own!

Brezhnev: They formed a committee for the funeral of Zhou En-lai. It had 107 members, including Mao. But he didn't attend anything or speak any word on behalf of Zhou. He's probably considering his next poem.

Kissinger: The most dangerous position in the world is to be number two in China.

Brezhnev: I didn't want to discuss China.

Kissinger: If you want a smaller discussion while I'm here, we can do it.

Brezhnev: We would just get into a state of confusion. We had better stay away from it.

[To help resolve the Backfire issue, Kissinger treats respectfully Brezhnev's offer to include information on its capabilities as part of an agreement, but before he makes any further suggestions, he tries to gain some ground on the cruise missile problem. Kissinger and the Soviets agrees that submarine-launched cruise missiles with a range over 600 kilometers should be banned; moreover, they will treat bombers with ALCMs as MIRVed vehicles and count them in the 2400 aggregate. Further, ALCMs with ranges over 2,500 kilometers would be banned. To allay Soviet concerns about ALCMs on the supersonic B-1 bomber, Kissinger declares that they will deploy the same number of cruise missiles as are carried by B-52 bombers. The Soviets object.]

Dobrynin: The speed is different.

Kissinger: The speed has nothing to do with the cruise missile. The cruise missile is subsonic; the B-1 is supersonic. You don't want a bomber to outrun its cruise missile.

Gromyko: It makes no difference. The bomber delivers its missile in this length of time.

Kissinger: If you study it, I think you'll find the B-1 flies supersonically only part of the time. So you'll find that the time it takes to approach the release point is of marginal difference.

[B] State Department Freedom of Information Release; copy at *NSA.*

Brezhnev: Terrible things we're talking about—"approaching release points."

Kissinger: It should be our highest goal to prevent such an event from ever arising.

[Disagreements over LLCMs and SLCMs are still blocking an agreement, so Kissinger introduces a proposal that Ford has privately approved as a fallback. With agreement reached on the weapons systems of greatest interest to Washington (air-launched and submarine-launched cruise missiles) Kissinger tries to solve the problem of disputed systems — Backfire and ship-launched cruise missiles — by tying them together in a separate agreement. Even if Backfire cannot be treated as a strategic system, Kissinger believes that some constraints are politically necessary.

Kissinger also suggests cuts in the aggregate in 1980, from 2,400 to a level of 2,300, perhaps to meet the criticism that it left strategic delivery systems at too high a level, Brezhnev is at first resistant to changing the numbers ("it does amount to a revision of the classical Vladivostok agreement") and he dislikes "all these combinations," much less including Backfire in an agreement; but he does not want to be totally negative.]

Brezhnev: Maybe we wouldn't like to get into an impasse on this. Maybe we're a little tired after a full day's work.

Kissinger: Our theory is we would put the weapons in a gray area of similar range into a separate category.

Gromyko: You mean Backfire and surface-ship cruise missiles?

Kissinger: Yes.

Gromyko: In short, you want, in return for Backfire, to include another strategic weapon, while in principle we do not consider the Backfire a strategic weapon?

Kissinger: But we don't consider a sea-launched cruise missile of 600 kilometer range a strategic weapon.

Gromyko: It will operate just as any other rocket of that category. And you realize full well what distance into Soviet territory those weapons could reach.

Brezhnev: So I think we should give some thought to that proposal. I don't want to reject that out of hand.

Kissinger: Maybe that's a good idea. Or make a counterproposal.

Sukhodrev: On 2300.

Stoessel: On the whole complex.

(They confer. Korniyenko hands Brezhnev a paper, probably the communique on the second meeting. Both sides confer. The Soviets discuss the next day's schedule.)

Brezhnev: Shall we perhaps take a recess, and take a rest? Do you have any objection to that?

Kissinger: No. I could get to see the ballet, which I also don't know if it exists.

Gromyko: What will you do there? Compare ballerinas with Backfire?

Kissinger: I'm going to determine the range of the ballerina.

Brezhnev: But that is a methodology we don't use. And we don't even have it. (He draws a diagram.) It's a triangle. If you sit in the box, it's one distance. If you sit in the orchestra, it's another. That is land-based. (Laughter)

Kissinger: I'll make myself a forward-based system, and I want to be counted.

Brezhnev: I think we should meet tomorrow at 12:00.

Kissinger: Good. (The meeting ended. The Secretary and his party, accompanied by Ambassador Dobrynin, went directly to the Bolshoi Theatre for a performance of "Giselle" in honor of the Secretary.)

[Sometime that day, perhaps after the meeting with Brezhnev, Kissinger learned to his dismay that, at the Pentagon's request, President Ford had convened a special NSC meeting. There, Acting Secretary of Defense William Clements, the Chief of Naval Operations William Holloway, and ACDA Director Fred Ikle conveyed their uneasiness about the negotiations in Moscow. Making matters worse, Holloway said that the Navy wanted cruise missiles on submarines, not surface ships—the reverse of what Kissinger was negotiating![36] Kissinger was incensed that the NSC had met while he was negotiating, but, according to William Hyland, he then "became strangely resigned" because he "realized that . . . his role would never be the same again." Whatever Ford's intent had been in removing Kissinger as national security adviser, this bureaucratic powerplay showed to what extent Kissinger's position had indeed been "damaged."[37]

The next evening, Kissinger met with the Soviets again for one more talk on SALT. The discussion began with a little banter.

THE WHITE HOUSE
SECRET/NODIS /XGDS
MEMORANDUM OF CONVERSATOIN
PARTICIPANTS: USSR: Leonid I. Brezhnev, General Secretary of the Central Committee of the CPSU; Andrei A. Gromyko, Member of

the Politburo of the Central Committee of the CPSU; Minister of
Foreign Affairs . . . US: Dr. Henry A. Kissinger, Secretary of
State . . .[38]
DATE AND TIME: Thursday, January 22, 1976; 6:04–9:42 P.M.
PLACE: Brezhnev's Office, The Kremlin Moscow
SUBJECTS: SALT; Angola; MBFR[C]

Brezhnev: I don't think we need to ask each other questions. There is
enough to think about.

Did you convey my greetings to President Ford?

Kissinger: I did last night. I also told him we had a very serious meeting. And
he asked me to convey his greetings to you.

Brezhnev: Thank you. Maybe we could proceed a little faster today.

Kissinger: All right.

Brezhnev: Here is a match. (He lights a match and makes a motion to ignite
all his talking papers.)

Kissinger: I thought you were going to bring out your cannon.

Brezhnev: There is a cannon in my office?

Kissinger: You threatened me with it last time.

Brezhnev: As long as America threatens us, we have to threaten America.

We now have MIRVed warheads on that cannon. And one is aimed at your
house.

Kissinger: I'd better get my dog out of there. (laughter)

Brezhnev: (Looks through his papers) You have an enormous number of
forces. Horrors! I can't imagine where you get them all. And so many in Europe.

Kissinger: If your generals count like our generals count, Mr. General Secretary, there will be an amazing computation.

Brezhnev: Apart from his greetings, did the President convey anything interesting? I think I know what he said. He said, "Dr. Kissinger, go ahead and
decide all questions yourself."

Kissinger: (laughs) I fear not!

Brezhnev: The President has changed!

We discussed quite a few issues yesterday but did not discuss all of them.
Perhaps we should go through some of the other matters we didn't discuss,
and later get to the decisive ones. But considering your own desires, maybe
we could go through them.

[C] State Department Freedom of Information Release; copy at *NSA*.

Earlier Dr. Kissinger said he was afraid of me. I want to say I'm afraid of him. So I guess I'd better give him more of these cookies, to make him kinder. (He passes over a plate of snacks.) And there is one other request: Could we have Sonnenfeldt seated further in the back?

(laughter)

Kissinger: Under the table!

Brezhnev: That would be too polite. He'd be at the same level.

Kissinger: I've been trying to do that for seven years.

Brezhnev: During the war, soldiers had the habit of taking out their wrist watches and holding them out and saying: "Let's trade without looking."

Kissinger: Do you want to trade Korniyenko for Sonnenfeldt?

Brezhnev: No, it would be unfair to Korniyenko.

Sonnenfeldt: I went to one of your dentists this morning. You missed your chance.

Kissinger: They put a transmitter in. If you had to listen to everything Sonnenfeldt had to say, you'd need a whole staff.

Brezhnev: A whole Pentagon! Why did they call it that?

Kissinger: It has five sides, the building.

Brezhnev: Could I see your watch?

(Secretary Kissinger gives it to him.)

Gromyko: Very cheap, very cheap.

Stoessel: Mine is a Soviet one.

Kissinger: When we made the ceasefire in the Middle East (in October 1973), you gave me a Soviet watch.

Brezhnev: I've had this electronic watch several months now.

Kissinger: A Soviet one?

Brezhnev: Soviet made. (He hands it to the Secretary.)Very nice. (He hands it back.)

[*Brezhnev reacts to Kissinger's latest offer by disagreeing on a secondary issue— whether a B-1 with cruise missiles should be treated as the equivalent of three B-52 bombers in the count of MIRVed systems.[39] He regards Backfire and SLCMs as the key obstacles but believes that Backfire is an artificial issue. Brezhnev declares that the proposal to tie the bomber to SLCMs is "completely unacceptable." He is willing, however, to make assurances that the Soviets will not turn Backfire into a strategic weapon and will retain its radius limited; but he fundamentally objects to any numerical limits on Backfire or linking it to sea-launched cruise missiles, whose 2,500-kilometer range, he insists, places them in the category of strategic weapons. He also wants a 600-kilometer limit placed on SLCMs as well as LLCMs.*]

As for Kissinger's proposal for a reduction in total strategic systems in 1980, Brezhnev questions its meaning without constraints on cruise missile development.]

Brezhnev: . . . Now, we have given some thought to this too, and we believe that to speak about reducing the number by 100 in conditions where the right would be preserved to build thousands upon thousands of new strategic missiles, that is, cruise missiles, would simply be a self-delusion, and a delusion of public opinion.

[The political significance of actually cutting strategic forces ultimately leads Brezhnev to come round to supporting cuts even larger than the 100 Kissinger suggests. He insists that such an agreement depends on a satisfactory outcome of the cruise missile problem. With LLCMs/SLCMs and Backfire as the only significant areas under dispute, though, Brezhnev believes that they have found "room for agreement." Kissinger agrees "that we are moving toward each other on many issues": "I believe we have made significant progress on a number of important issues." He agrees to respond with counterproposals "within a few weeks."]⁴⁰

Brezhnev: But one earnest request! Don't think up any more problems. Or else you leave and suddenly I get a telegram from Washington with some entirely new problems invented. Let's be decent children of our epoch.

Kissinger: We will discuss it in the framework of our discussions here. We will review our position in light of your position.

Brezhnev: Even if you look at those through a magnifying glass, you'll see they are very good proposals. If you see it through Jackson's or Reagan's magnifying glass, it will be a very bad mirror.

Kissinger: Jackson and I meet very infrequently. I think Jackson will make peace with you before he makes peace with me.

Brezhnev: He just keeps talking as much as he can. He raises all the money he can so he speaks on radio and television. He's trying to fight Ford and trying to fight you.

Kissinger: He was on television yesterday saying I made too many concessions.

Brezhnev: We can't adapt ourselves to his views because we deal with America and the American Government—with those in whom the American people invested their trust. We want to deal with the American people, and devil take the rest. Tomorrow there will be another 10 fellows saying things.

Kissinger: There are already 12 candidates. We count them in the 1,320 total. And we promise you not to give them intercontinental characteristics.

Brezhnev: I think some of them should be put into one of these missiles.

Kissinger: So I believe, as I have said, we have made some progress. We will study it. We will look at our proposals in light of what you have said. We will study it very seriously.

Brezhnev: I appreciate that and I know that, whatever the situation is, I feel sure, and I know I'm right, the President does value your abilities in the international field very highly and I'm sure he will be influenced by what you are able to do. And you know, as many times as I've met you, I've never allowed myself to interfere in American domestic matters.

Kissinger: Except on our side.

Brezhnev: If I only could.

Kissinger: Mr. General Secretary, we've had many meetings and we've settled many important questions between us.

Brezhnev: I said at the outset, we have gone a long way. And whatever ramifications there have been, it's to the credit of the leaders of both countries that we have managed to preserve our relationship, despite the adversities of fate.

[Brezhnev is optimistic enough about SALT that he takes a step ahead and speaks about a visit to the United States once an agreement had been reached, sometime after the Party Congress. He expressed a preference for Camp David, although Kissinger observes that Williamsburg is "quieter."]

Kissinger: I see the General Secretary is very sure he'll be reelected at the Party Congress.

Brezhnev: That is hard to say.

Kissinger: You'll have to teach us.

Brezhnev: Let me say in the presence of my colleagues that I feel confident of the support of the local party people.

Gromyko: And we don't have 12 candidates!

Brezhnev: But when it comes to voting, you can reach into a hat and they're not there.

Kissinger: You need some technical assistance.

[Kissinger has been careful to keep arms control and the Angolan situation separate, during this lengthy meeting, but with the apparent progress on SALT he repeats his objections to the Cuban role in Angola and makes a few efforts to get Brezhnev to discuss the issue. Brezhnev refuses to cooperate, though, and Gromyko makes more denials than admissions.[41]]

Angola

Brezhnev: Dr. Kissinger, you know what's here? A map of our attack on the United States. (He shows the map on the wall behind the curtain.)

Kissinger: Of course. From Angola! (Laughter)

Brezhnev: Don't mention that word to me. We have nothing to do with that country. I cannot talk about that country.

(Brezhnev then moved away and Gromyko and Amb. Stoessel came up to talk with the Secretary.)

Kissinger: The Cubans were in Angola before the South Africans entered.[42] We asked you a question: if the South Africans withdrew, would the Cubans withdraw?

Gromyko: We have nothing to do with that. We have given some equipment to the legitimate government — that's all.

Kissinger: You transport the Cubans in your planes. They are chartered Soviet planes.

Gromyko: What planes are you talking about? The ones which transported equipment? We have sent no troops.

Amb. Stoessel: No, the Soviet planes used to transport Cuban troops to Angola.

Gromyko: (avoiding a direct answer) The South Africans are still there. They make no move to leave.

Kissinger: The South Africans are in the process of withdrawing.

Gromyko: If this is announced, we will react to it.

Kissinger: I wish to tell you in all seriousness that we can never accept 8,000 Cuban troops in Angola.

[As their meeting closes, Kissinger makes one last effort to put Angola on the table; he even makes threats, but Brezhnev does not take the bait.]

Strategic Arms Limitation

Brezhnev: In a friendly spirit, can I ask are you pleased with our discussions?

Kissinger: I think we made progress in our SALT discussion. You introduced interesting ideas today. It remains to be studied and to think of how to reconcile the two sides' approaches.

Brezhnev: Are we finished?

Dobrynin: Yes.

Brezhnev: I guess we can finish on that. I'd like to ask you once again to give my good wishes to the President, and my best wishes in his arduous duties.

And I trust when you report back, he will appreciate the great efforts we have made and the constructive character of our discussions.

Kissinger: You can be sure I will do this. There has been definite progress made. Your side has made a great effort. If we continue this effort on both sides, we can achieve an historic agreement.

Angola

I must say one thing. I don't want to mislead you. You said you didn't want to discuss the subject (Angola) beyond what you said at the end of the table. But we will not be able to accept the increasing number of Cuban troops and we will have to take measures in that respect.

Brezhnev: That's a diplomatic question. Discuss it with Gromyko.

We have in fact set out to the American side and to the President person-ally our approach to events in Angola. And yet the American side, as will be seen from your recent statement to our Ambassador, is continuing to depict our position in a distorted light, seeking to equalize the intervention of South African racists and assistance by the Soviet Union and other states to the legitimate government of Angola to resist aggressors and their abettors.

There are no Soviet troops. We have sold a limited number of tanks. That is the role we are playing there, and no more.

Kissinger: We asked you a question two weeks ago, to which we have not received an answer.

Gromyko: Let's meet at 9:30 tomorrow morning. You won't be asleep?

Kissinger: No. The Italian Prime Minister has never been awake in any meet-ing I've had with him. Unless we discuss women. (laughter)

Brezhnev: I trust the President will also discern interesting points that have come up in my visit.

Kissinger: I am certain. And we'll give the press a generally positive account.

Brezhnev: I guess you will be saying something to the press tomorrow.

Kissinger: Yes, along the lines I have said to you—that we have had positive discussions on SALT, that in certain important areas progress was made, that the General Secretary presented some new and interesting ideas that we will now study in Washington, and that some of the issues that we have agreed in principle here will be transferred to Geneva. In this sense.

(At this point the Secretary handed to the General Secretary a set of copies of a photograph of himself taken by David Kennerly at Helsinki, which Mr. Kennerly hoped he would autograph. Brezhnev looked them over and got up abruptly and went in the back room. Amb. Dobrynin explained that Brezhnev did not like the candid photo and went out to find a better one.)

[Sukhrodev reads a communiqué text on "useful" exchanges of views and negotiations taking place in a "business-like and constructive atmosphere," and Kissinger says that he wants Sonnenfeldt to add a few sentences.]

(Brezhnev returns with his official photo and two watches for Sonnenfeldt.)
Kissinger: (Looks at the watch given to Sonnenfeldt) This picks up whatever his tooth doesn't.
Brezhnev: This is a good photograph.
Kissinger: I'm very grateful.
Brezhnev: I think nothing should be done to cast any shadow over the work we have done together. This would be both wrong and not in the interests of either the Soviet Union or United States.
(He shows Sonnenfeldt how the watch band can be adjusted.)
    And I guarantee its accuracy.
Kissinger: I know it sends. Can it also receive? (Laughter) Between his Soviet tooth and his Soviet watches . . .
Brezhnev: It's just a watch!
    Well then, we thank you. These two days were not easy.
Kissinger: I want to thank you for taking two days from your schedule. After many changes in your schedule to set the dates of the meeting.
Brezhnev: This often happens. The most important thing is to act in good faith.
Kissinger: This you can be sure. (The meeting ended.)

COMMENTARY

The next morning Kissinger met with Gromyko to review several contentious issues in U.S.–Soviet relations—the Middle East, Angola, China, and Japan. Gromyko gave no ground on Angola, their discussion suggested that, in spite of Reagan's claims that détente had been a "one-way street," Soviet policy had been generally unsuccessful in areas widley seen as "critical" to Western interests, such as East Asia and the Middle East.[43]
    On the Arab–Israeli crisis, the most recent achievement in Kissinger's shuttle diplomacy had been the second agreement on Sinai. This involved further limited Israeli withdrawal, a U.S. role in monitoring the agreement,

hundreds of millions in economic aid to Israel, and a U.S. pledge not to recognize or negotiate with the Palestine Liberation Organization (PLO) until it recognized Israel's right to exist. The agreement quickly produced discord in the Arab world (Syrian President Assad criticized Egyptian President Anwar Sadat for yielding to Israel) and new efforts—energetically supported by the Soviets—to secure recognition for the Palestinians. Israel's hard line on the PLO prompted the U.N. General Assembly to resolve in November 1975 that Zionism was a "form of racism or racial discrimination"; the U.N. Security Council began to debate Arab–Israeli crisis policy on 12 January.[44]

In this volatile atmosphere, Kissinger held out to Gromyko the prospect of reconvening the Geneva conference, but only if the PLO recognized Israel's right to exist. Gromyko found this difficult to accept and argued that, at the least, Israel and the PLO had to make simultaneous overtures toward each other. The discussion showed Kissinger's blind spot on the Palestinian problem: rather than tackle it directly by trying to induce Israeli flexibility, he sought to dodge the issue in the hope that the PLO's appeal would fade and a more moderate alternative would emerge. In the meantime, however, he kept the Soviets out of the peace process and preserved the United States' special advantage.[45]

Kissinger probably took some comfort in Gromyko's brief report on his discussions with the Japanese leadership in Tokyo. In December, Gromyko had met Prime Minister Miki in an attempt to improve relations and to dissuade Tokyo from including an antihegemony clause in the peace and friendship treaty with China that the two countries were negotiating. The talks went nowhere, however, in part because the Soviets refused to negotiate over the status of Japan's claimed "Northern Territories"—the southern Kuriles. On 13 January, Miki took a "more pronounced pro-Beijing tilt" when he announced his support for an antihegemony clause in the treaty. As Hartman reported to Kissinger, that development would "keep Brezhnev aware of the latent vulnerability of his Asian flank."[46]

On China the picture was mixed, but Kissinger's discussion with Gromyko suggested that the situation was more favorable to Washington. Kissinger's advisers had cautioned him that while the Soviets continued to see China as a major "long-term threat," disagreements with China over détente and normalization were undermining the leverage provided by the U.S.–PRC relationship. Moreover, Zhou Enlai's death and the expected death of Mao meant that China's succession process had "greater potential for adversely affecting U.S.–PRC relations" than Moscow's already abysmal relations with Beijing. Nevertheless, the Sino–Japanese talks and Kissinger's personal approval of the U.K.'s sale of Rolls Royce engines to China—establishing the possibility of special Chinese access to advanced Western military technology—demonstrated to the Soviets that they could not be confident that Beijing would not move closer to their rivals.[47]

SECRET/NODIS/XGDS
MEMORANDUM OF CONVERSATION
PARTICIPANTS: USSR: Andrei A. Gromyko, Member of the
   Politburo of the Central Committee of the CPSU; Minister of
   Foreign Affairs of the USSR; Vasiliy V. Kuznetsov, First Deputy
   Minister of Foreign Affairs; Georgiy M. Korniyenko, Deputy
   Minister of Foreign Affairs; Anatoliy F. Dobrynin, Ambassador to
   the U.S.; Vasiliy G. Makarov, Chef de Cabinet to the Foreign
   Minister; V.G. Komplektov, Acting Chief of USA Dept., MFA;
   Valerian V. Mikhailov, Deputy Chief of USA Dept., MFA; Oleg
   Grinevskiy, Deputy Chief of Arab-Israeli crisis Dept., MFA; Oleg M.
   Sokolov, Chief of International Affairs, USA Dept., MFA; Viktor M.
   Sukhodrev, Counselor, Second European Dept., MFA (Interpreter);
   U.S: Dr. Henry A. Kissinger, Secretary of State; Amb. Walter J.
   Stoessel, Jr., Ambassador to the USSR; Helmut Sonnenfeldt,
   Counselor of the Department; William G. Hyland, Deputy Assistant
   to the President for National Security Affairs; Arthur A. Hartman,
   Assistant Secretary for European Affairs; Arthur R. Day, Deputy
   Assistant Secretary for Near Eastern and South Asian Affairs;
   Edward F. Fugit, Country Officer, Angola; Peter W. Rodman, NSC
   Staff
DATE AND TIME: Friday, January 23, 1976 9:34-11:45 A.M.
PLACE: Tolstoi House (Foreign Ministry) Moscow
SUBJECTS: Arab-Israeli crisis; Angola; Japan; China; Limitation of
   New Weapons of Mass Destruction; PNE Negotiation; [D]

Gromyko: I think we can begin, Mr. Secretary. Do you have any ideas on what we should take up? I thought the Arab-Israeli crisis.
Kissinger: Well, we must state our opinion on Angola. And then we are prepared to discuss the Arab-Israeli crisis, and any other subject you would like to discuss.

[D] State Department Freedom of Information release; copy at *NSA.*

Gromyko: Let's rather discuss the Arab–Israeli crisis, because we have had no discussions yet on that and we have discussed Angola. Unless you have nothing to discuss on the Arab–Israeli crisis.

Kissinger: I have something. But I must point out that messages on Angola at the highest level have a tendency to go unanswered, which is a new factor in our relationship.

Gromyko: What do you suggest?

Kissinger: You suggested the Arab–Israeli crisis; we suggested Angola—we can compromise on discussing peaceful nuclear explosions. (Laughter)

Gromyko: Let's do that. That means we will merely continue the discussion, not start it.

Kissinger: I'm prepared to discuss the Arab–Israeli crisis first. I just wanted to make clear we will state our view on Angola. And we still need answers to some of the questions.

Gromyko: That you have said already.

(The waiters bring in coffee and snacks.)It is very hard to discuss questions like the Arab–Israeli crisis, Angola and peaceful nuclear explosions, without coffee.

Arab–Israeli Crisis

[Kissinger states that after the U.N. Security Council debate on the Arab–Israeli crisis has concluded, the Geneva Conference should be reassembled—but not until a "common denominator" on Palestinian participation has been found. He objects to Palestinian participation at the beginning of a conference, whether preparatory or otherwise.]

Gromyko: If at the present it is impossible for you to take part in any multilateral discussions with the Palestinians, for us and others it is impossible to take part in multilateral discussions without the Palestinians.

Of course, it is conceivable that when all the parties concerned reach prior agreement, prior to the actual opening of Geneva, that it can open without the Palestinians but that as soon as it opens the Palestinians can take part in the discussion of the substance.[48] But I emphasize, prior agreement with the parties concerned would be necessary, and of course it would have to be concerted with the Palestinians themselves.

Kissinger: We do not believe conditions are right yet. We have said we can't ask Israel to negotiate with a party that doesn't accept the existence of Israel and that doesn't accept Resolutions 242 and 338.[49]

Gromyko: We know what Israel's position is in that regard and we know that the position enjoys US support. But after all, Israel never displayed a positive attitude on the question of assuring the legitimate rights of the Palestinians, and notably the legitimate demand of the Palestinians to be allowed to set up their own national state of the Arab people of Palestine. So how can Israel take the position of requiring them to recognize Israel as a state in those circumstances? If Israel wants to see the Palestinians taking that sort of position, surely Israel has to make some sort of movement in the regard I have stated.

There should be no question of the difficulty in deciding who should have to take the first move—who is to say "A." It should be easy to settle that one has to say "A" and the other has to say "B." That is what diplomacy is for. It should be a second-rate matter as long as the substance is settled. And we have sufficient ground as far as this train of thought. You remember I said this to you when I was in the United States, and in fact I said this to Israeli Foreign Minister Allon.

Kissinger: I'm not here to speak for Israel. On some points we agree with them and on some we do not. True, any progress will depend on US influence on Israel. We have proved we are prepared to do this. The United States has repeatedly declared it will not deal with the Palestinians until they recognize the State of Israel and Security Council Resolutions 242 and 338. It follows from that that if the Palestinians do this, certain policy conclusions will follow in the United States. That would not go unanswered in the United States. And that is not without significance.

Gromyko: But the Palestinians say they cannot do any such thing until Israel recognizes their legitimate rights, notably their legitimate right to set up an independent state of the Palestinian people. And this is something we know only too well. I don't know whether you know, but we certainly do. Surely the problem I mentioned—of who says "A"—is one that is going to be an impediment to progress. I therefore ask what is diplomacy for? Please tell me. What is diplomacy for, if it can't resolve the question of who says "A?"

Kissinger: That's what I am suggesting. The Palestinians should say "A."

Gromyko: This should be resolved in such a way that the prestige of no one is prejudiced. If that is the only stumbling block, surely the US and Soviet Union could organize it in such a way that "A" is said simultaneously by both sides. Surely it can't be a completely insurmountable obstacle. (Korniyenko shows Gromyko a talking paper.)

Kissinger: Is Korniyenko making trouble again?

Korniyenko: Double A instead of "A" and "B."

Kissinger: I was saying, if you understand American football, we will trade Sonnenfeldt for Korniyenko and a draft choice.

Gromyko: Double "A."

Kissinger: There are two separate problems. One is the attitude of Israel to the Palestinians; the other is the attitude of the United States to the Palestinians. The attitude of Israel to the Palestinians will lag behind the attitude of the United States inevitably, given the complexity of their domestic situation. Of course, there is no complexity in our domestic situation. If Palestinian recognition of Israel went unreciprocated for a considerable length of time, that would itself be a fact of significance. But I have said consistently that the United States would not ignore such a statement by the Palestinians.

[The discussion continues with no agreement reached except on the need for U.S. and Soviet "restraint" in the region.]

Angola

Kissinger: In that case, I'd like to state our view on Angola. We recognize that the Soviet Union has supported the MPLA for a long time. And we recognize that some of the activities in Angola have historic reason and understandable causes.

But we also believe that over a period of months, and recently, they have reached dimensions that are inconsistent with the principles we have jointly signed. We have called the attention of the Soviet Government for many months to our concerns. We have made repeated offers to stop foreign intervention. We have even said we would use our influence to bring about the initial withdrawal of South African forces, to be followed by the withdrawal of other forces.

But we are confronted by the fact that answers are evasive and many months go by.

We cannot accept that 10,000 troops be sent as an expeditionary force carried in Soviet aircraft, with Soviet equipment. We must take public notice. The tragedy is that those of us who have supported the policy of detente with the Soviet Union will increasingly be put into the position of attacking this policy.

So we believe something should be done about this before irreparable damage is caused. We have made a specific proposal over the weeks. This is our attitude, which we cannot give up.

Gromyko: First of all, I would like to say that fundamentally and in principle our attitude on the Angola question was set out on your visit to this country and personally to you by General Secretary Brezhnev.

With respect to your remarks concerning Cuba, I have no intention of discussing whatever actions Cuba is taking. We have not been authorized by the Cuban Government to speak on its behalf, but we do know that what Cuba is doing to render assistance to the legitimate Angolan Government, at the specific request of that Angolan Government—which I must say has been inflated out of all proportion in the United States—is a matter between Cuba and the legitimate government of Angola.[50]

That concerns Cuba. With respect to the Soviet Union, let me say this:

First, we have taken note—and this relates not just to the Soviet Union but to the majority of the states—that following the proclamation of Angolan independence, Angola became the victim of outside intervention, and in effect that intervention began earlier. Is it not a fact that the South African Government has introduced its military forces in Angola? If someone wants to close their eyes, nonetheless it is a fact that we see and others do. It is a fact that it is taking place. Some say they are in the process of being withdrawn. What kind of fact is that if every day we read reports that the South African forces are increasing?

So, the first fact is, there is a clear-cut case of intervention, and in fact, aggression, that is taking place against Angola by South Africa.

That is the first point. The second point is this:

The Soviet Union did assist the MPLA in its fight for the independence of Angola against the colonialists. And that is something we made absolutely no secret of. That part is a completely open book. After independence, we established relations with the new legitimate government and on that we based accordingly our policy and practical actions, regarding Angola as an independent and sovereign state. General Secretary Brezhnev told you previously that we had sold quantities—and let me say, insignificant quantities—of arms. And, incidentally, the United States—and there is ample information to that effect—has given funds and never ended giving supplies to the separatist elements in Angola that are backed by external elements which are well known. The United States has given them substantial assistance, and that fact is well known.

Thirdly, if there is any impression that the Soviet Union has virtually nothing else to do and does nothing else except talk somebody in Angola out of any contacts or to discourage any formation of any coalition government, that is a big mistake. We have spoken not a word either for or against such contacts and talks. We consider that a matter for the sovereign government of Angola themselves.

So that is the answer to your so-called proposals. Has the Soviet Union ever objected on that score? Certainly not.

And my fourth and last point:

You have hinted that the possible development of events in Angola might adversely affect Soviet–American relations. Well, if the United States wants that, then those events can adversely affect our relationship. If that's what the U.S. wants. We believe that all Soviet–American relations, and all that has been achieved, will override all momentary considerations or momentary events in Angola. So, objectively speaking, there is no reason for events in Angola to have an adverse effect on Soviet–American relations.

That is what I wanted to say to your remarks.

Kissinger: I have a few observations, Mr. Foreign Minister.

It is not true that the United States has supported what you call separatist forces. The United States gave no military assistance to those forces until after the massive Soviet support to the MPLA.[51] In fact, the United States rejected many opportunities in 1974 to give aid because we did not want to introduce the great power rivalry in Africa. Even after Soviet support started, we made proposals to you to halt it and to prevent it from getting out of hand.

We are not against the MPLA. We cannot recognize it as a legitimate government that is not recognized by half of the African states and established contrary to OAU [Organization of African Unity] resolutions.[52]

Therefore, we believe there were many opportunities, in light of our specific responsibility to insulate the problem from great power rivalry. We have offered to use our influence to get South African forces out and we asked only for assurances that other foreign forces will leave.

When there are 20 flights a week from Cuba to Angola with Soviet planes, with 200 troops a day from Cuba to Angola, it isn't something the Soviet Government can simply say doesn't concern the Soviet Union. What would the Soviet Union say if American planes brought troops to another country?

So the reality is these are facts inconsistent with the principles we signed in June 1972.

Moreover, what makes these events so tragic is that all the remarks the Foreign Minister has made overlook the situation in the United States, in which those who look for every opportunity to injure our policy will attack this—and we will not oppose it. Even those who oppose doing something in Angola propose doing things directly to the Soviet Union rather than in Angola.

It is a tragedy because the Soviet Union has nothing to gain in Angola. We have nothing to gain in Angola. Five years from now it will make no difference. I must say this is a tragedy, and I say this as one who has been the foremost defender of U.S.–Soviet rapprochement in the United States.

Gromyko: There is one point you made with which I certainly agree; the Soviet Union wants nothing whatever in Angola, and seeks no unilateral gain in Angola. We only want to see Angola as an independent and sovereign state. That's all . . .

Kissinger: It is difficult to be sovereign and independent if there are 10,000 foreign troops. 80,000 Portuguese troops faced a guerrilla war, and I wouldn't be surprised if 10,000 Cubans faced a protracted war.

Gromyko: To that I would reply that it is indeed most difficult to be an independent and sovereign state if there are in that state a mass of outside invading forces, with massive equipment, against the legitimate government. That does indeed create difficulties in the way of a sovereign and independent state.

You say we have not given a reply to your proposals. That I don't understand. What other reply do you want? You have heard our pronouncements and the reply by General Secretary Brezhnev; you've heard the pronouncements and the reply I have just given you. What other do you want?

Kissinger: The last message we received from General Secretary Brezhnev said that if the South African forces were withdrawn, the question of the Cuban forces would solve itself in a "natural way." We have asked in what you mean by a "natural way," and how would it take place. No reply has been received in over two weeks.

Gromyko: I said at the very outset that we cannot speak on behalf of the Cubans. We are not authorized to speak for them. So what you speak about is a hypothetical question—what would happen if the Cubans were withdrawn. I cannot speak about it. It is first and foremost for the legitimate government of Angola to react, and it would be seen in the response they take to the withdrawal of South African forces. But that is hypothetical, because there is no withdrawal of South African forces.

Kissinger: We received a message from the General Secretary that if the South Africans leave, the problem of the others would be settled "in a natural way." The question is: what does that mean?

Gromyko: It means exactly what it says. But you're now discussing a purely hypothetical case. There is no South African withdrawal.

Kissinger: I asked what would happen if the South Africans withdrew. Clearly, it means the South African forces must first be withdrawn.

Gromyko: The government of the People's Republic of Angola will set out its reaction after the withdrawal of South African forces. The Soviet Union is not the government of the People's Republic of Angola. But our view is as set out in the General Secretary's message, and I think the right thing to do would be to take a serious view of it.

On that note, I think I have exhausted all I have to say. Otherwise, I would just be repeating myself.

Kissinger: I want to say two things: We simply cannot accept that the government of Cuba, dependent entirely upon Soviet support in Cuba and dependent entirely on the Soviet logistical support—nor would you say if we decided to put an end to this by dealing with Cuba directly that this is a matter of no concern to the Soviet Union. Second, you cannot say it makes no difference when the intervention of the Cubans ends—they were brought in by Soviet planes and ships and you will not say when this will end.

It is a pity this has come to pass when many opportunities existed for two great powers to settle this in a farsighted way.

Gromyko: I regret the conclusions you draw. I have nothing to add to the statements on our side. It is those statements that express our opinion, and not the interpretation you give.

Kissinger: It wouldn't be the first time in history that events that no one can explain afterwards give rise to consequences out of proportion to their intrinsic significance.

Gromyko: We think no one else but ourselves can interpret our position and views. It is for us alone to set them out. Any attempt to interpret them in a wrongful manner can only be seen as regrettable.

And if on your return to the United States you start to aggravate this whole matter and make statements casting aspersions on our relations, it will not be we who will bear responsibility for the consequences. It will be the responsibility solely of the United States. I cannot believe that this meets the interests of the world situation.

Kissinger: Well, I've stated my view, and I see no need to repeat it.

Gromyko: Well, let's turn to the next question.

Kissinger: I picked the last topic; why don't you pick the next one?

Japan

Gromyko: Do we have anything at all in the Far East? Do you have any comments on that? What are your assessments? Are you expecting any surprises?

You have many friends in that area—friends who were looking out of the wrong side of their face at us.

Kissinger: You were in the Far East more recently; why don't you give your impression?

Gromyko: (laughs) That's no problem. I can say a few words. I was in Japan. While I was there I set out our position on the question of Soviet–Japanese relations. We spoke out in favor of more normal relations, in the interest of detente and peace. In short, we applied the principles that underlined U.S.–Soviet relations and that found expression in the relevant documents signed between the United States and the Soviet Union.

Of the political questions, there was one which was within our field of vision as well as of the Japanese—that was the possibility of a Sino–Japanese Treaty being signed. We gave our assessment of China's attempts to include in that treaty a clause directly aimed at the Soviet Union—and you know what I'm referring to. On the Japanese side, they gave their assessment of the situation and they, in effect, said they assessed China's claims in a somewhat different fashion. They underestimated somewhat the Chinese intentions in this respect. But the Japanese do understand our concerns. As we understand it—and they said so themselves—the negotiations have not yet been completed, and we can only guess at the further development of those negotiations, and I would refrain from any kind of forecast. We would like to believe that the common sense of the Japanese will prevail, as well as their understanding of the proper role of Soviet-Japanese relations.

We made some references to bilateral economic relations between our two countries, but no specific agreements were signed. We also took up a few purely bilateral matters and a few others—such as fishing. But not too much, because there are special commissions set up for that, and that is within their jurisdiction.

You know the Japanese frequently make reference to the so-called northern territories. References were made during this visit as well, but it was not really discussed at these meetings, because the two sides speak totally different languages and the positions were totally at variance.

As elsewhere, in Japan I made no attempt whatsoever to reach any agreement or understanding that is at variance with the interests of any other country, including the United States. You can verify that with the Japanese. I said it publicly and privately.

Are you disappointed?

Kissinger: We recognize you gained no unilateral advantage in Japan, and it was in the spirit of our relationship.

No, I appreciate your explanation, and seriously I believe it reflects the principles of restraint that should govern our relations everywhere and are the basis of our relationship.

What we have heard from Japan coincides with the Foreign Minister's statement. The Foreign Minister's conduct was consistent with our relationship. We heard nothing contradictory.

Gromyko: Can I ask one question?

Kissinger: Yes.

Gromyko: There have been references in various publications to the proposed establishment of a US–Japanese consultative body or agency dealing with armament and armed forces.[53] Can you give us some information about this? Any time we hear information that Japanese are taking steps to conserve wildlife and birds, it causes no concern. We are always prepared to cooperate with that. But when we hear something about armaments, we do display some concern, which is not unfounded.

Kissinger: All we are familiar with is that there is an agreement for the Japanese Foreign Minister and the American Secretary of State to meet twice a year. But we meet so often at international meetings that in fact there is no need to schedule special meetings. But I am familiar with no arrangement to consult on weapons. Certainly at a high level; maybe at a very low level. I'll check when I get back and let Dobrynin know.

Gromyko: The military must have bypassed the Department of State.

Kissinger: What is your source? Japan and the United States are allies. I'm not familiar with any new institution. No new institution could be set up without our approval. But I want to check and make sure there is nothing that is being misunderstood. What is your source?

Korniyenko: Something at the end of December.

Gromyko: In the press. I read something about it just before I left for Japan.

Kissinger: Anyway, no new body has been set up to deal with military questions. But I will check and let Dobrynin know.

China

Gromyko: Let us now mentally transfer ourselves to China. It's safe, of course, for you to go right into China, but for us it's more complicated. You might quite logically ask me what my views are on this question, and it's quite legitimate.

Our bilateral relations have undergone no change in recent months.

Kissinger: About China? Or are you approaching me carefully?

Gromyko: Going around! Our bilateral relations have undergone no changes in recent months.

With respect to China's foreign policy, it is very sharply leveled against us, and in fact against the line of policy jointly formulated by the Soviet Union and the United States and expressed in our joint documents. Their view is the worse it is, the better. But you know better; you were there most recently, and you patiently had to listen to a few lectures while you were there.

I was thinking when I read the reports of what you had to endure, I said to myself, I wish I could see Dr. Kissinger's face right now. I wonder how he feels.

Kissinger: Of course, you have an advantage in Beijing in that you have an Ambassador and we have only a Chief of Liaison Office. So we don't get invited to so many diplomatic functions, at least of the intensity your Ambassador does.

It is true that the Chinese expressed their attitude to our relationship and found it too good, from their point of view. Of course, they will be delighted by the events of the previous subject. But it's true: our bilateral relations (with China) are normal and developing. And during President Ford's visit, this progress was confirmed.

Gromyko: I would like to ask one question, and it is of course your right to reply or not.

Kissinger: If it were not my right, you would of course force me to answer. (laughter)

Gromyko: You are familiar with the general line of China's policy as well as its policy toward various areas of the world — the Soviet Union, Europe, Asia. You know this policy is sharply at variance and totally counter to the line we have agreed on and reflected in our agreements, and the line we have confirmed in our discussions recently.

But leading figures in the United States, at a very high level, including the President and Secretary of State, studiously avoid giving an assessment of that line, which is sharply against detente and is a line which seeks deterioration of relations between the Soviet Union and the United States. We in the Soviet leadership shrug our shoulders and wonder what reserves of patience it must take to simply endure this line and take no view. But the Soviet leadership pursues the line of peace and detente.

Kissinger: I think the Foreign Minister could not have read the toasts I gave on my visit to Beijing in October, in which on two occasions I made it clear the United States would maintain its policy in accordance with our national interests. And I made it clear even more privately. So it is clear we do not give the Chinese a veto over our policy, and as I said to the General Secretary, we remain committed to the policy we are pursuing.

We were told there is a Soviet faction in the Chinese leadership, and they will no doubt tell you we have told them we will maintain our relations with the Soviet Union.

They can see what is happening in our relationship and will be delighted. But we have made clear we are prepared to improve our relationship with the Soviet Union.

Gromyko: When is your next trip to Beijing?

Kissinger: We have not set a precise date.

Gromyko: You are about to go on an African holiday. If rumors are correct.

Kissinger: Not before the end of March.

Dobrynin: And to Latin America.

Kissinger: Latin America is first.

Gromyko: You are first going to invade Latin America and then you invade Africa.

Kissinger: No, you are forcing us into Africa in a much more active way.

[They briefly discussed the U.N. Disarmament Committee talks and ongoing U.S.-Soviet negotiations over the peaceful use of nuclear weapons—which produced the Peaceful Nuclear Explosions agreement signed in May. Talk then returns to the Vienna MBFR negotiations.[54] After an inconclusive discussion of a Soviet proposal for 2–3 percent reductions in NATO and Warsaw Pact conventional forces in Central Europe, Grompko emphasizes the importance of giving MBFR a "new lease on life." Kissinger is "not too optimistic" but agrees on the need for progress.]

Gromyko: That would be good. China will certainly have a lot to blame us for. If there is success. Mostly us.

Kissinger: China will certainly be very angry. China will certainly be very angry if there is success in SALT.

But they haven't given us any helicopters lately, so perhaps you should tell us what you are doing.[55]

Gromyko: (laughs) China gave us a helicopter because it is ours! Of course they recognized they made a mistake.

I was told Dr. Kissinger was staying for a week. Now these people tell me he's departing.

Kissinger: Always something surprising!

[Both sides review drafts of the communiqué of the visit, Kissinger suggests a minor change in wording, which the Soviets accept. After discussing what time to release the communiqué, Kissinger asks when the Soviets will be able to confirm they have done so.]

Gromyko: Another concession on our part.

Kissinger: It is amazing how you keep your country together, with all these concessions.

Gromyko: Concession after concession!

Kissinger: Everyone says you are so difficult to deal with.

Dobrynin: A total misunderstanding!

Kissinger: A total misunderstanding. I was afraid before I came that two or three days here would not be enough time for us, because of all the concessions you would be making.

(The meeting then ended.)

COMMENTARY

In spite of Kissinger's assessment of the Moscow talks for a SALT II agreement, Ford never followed through on the "breakthrough." The Pentagon was deeply suspicious of Kissinger's conduct as negotiator, and Ford inasmuch wished to insulate arms control controversies from the presidential campaign. William Hyland later described the line of action Ford took as a "clever way of killing the negotiations."[56] Thus, in a major letter to Brezhnev, Ford backtracked on understandings reached at Moscow and overlooked Soviet assurances on Backfire. Instead, he suggested agreement based on Vladivostok and temporary restraints on Backfire while deferring accord on cruise missiles, except ALCMs, until 1979. Brezhnev's response the next month was predictable: he rejected deferring any issues and treated the new proposals as a "step back" from Kissinger's last offer.[57]

Kissinger, in the interim, was careful to separate arms control from his toughening public rhetoric and from the countermeasures relating to Angola. He hoped that Ford would reconsider the February proposal and another trip to Moscow could conclude an agreement; instead, Ford decided to hold the line rather than risk controversy over SALT.[58]

If Ford believed that limiting the SALT process's political exposure, or even backing away from the word *détente*, would give him significant political advantage, he was mistaken; Reagan kept up the pressure. Flailing away at the "Ford–Kissinger" foreign policy, Reagan asserted that "it was never the word that disturbed us, it was the policy." Kissinger's toughening his approach to the Soviets was never enough for Reagan who sought an edge in the competitive campaign by targeting Kissinger himself. Reagan claimed that at Helsinki Kissinger had sold out the Eastern European "captive nations," which "should give up any claim of national sovereignty and simply become part of the Soviet Union." Citing Kissinger's historical pessimism as the cause of the administration's supposed eagerness to make agreements with the Soviets, Reagan asserted that "Dr. Kissinger . . . thinks of the United States as Athens and the Soviet Union as Sparta, and that the day of the United States is past."[59]

Kissinger was not in a position to take Reagan on and was deeply concerned about hurting Ford's prospects. He was truly "reaping the cost" of overselling détente and of his failure to establish political support for his policies. Having already started to distance himself from détente, Kissinger spent much of 1976 out of the country in an effort to reduce his visibility; by the end of August, he had traveled to nearly forty countries. His absences did not moderate Reagan's attacks or discourage Ford's campaign managers from speculating that Kissinger should not be reappointed Secretary if Ford won the election. Ford repudiated such conjecture, but when the Republican convention met in August, he acquiesced to a Reagan-sponsored rejection of Kissinger's diplomacy in the party platform rather than risk the votes he needed for nomination. Most likely angered and alienated by the Reagan Republican "yahoos" that had forced a two-Chinas position in the GOP platform (although he would one day court those same right-wing elements), Kissinger all but disengaged himself from Ford's reelection efforts. In late August he told State Department advisers that he would not "participate in any political activity" and would keep speeches to a minimum so as to maintain the "professionalism and continuity of our foreign policy" — presumably what Ford and his campaign advisers preferred.[60]

Only a few weeks before the election, Gromyko met with Kissinger to discuss SALT and encourage him to return to where they had left off in January. Kissinger was not free to stray from Ford's more recent proposal. Nevertheless, right up to the election, the Carter campaign worried that Ford would make a surprise announcement of an arms control agreement. Some years later, Ford would concede that he would have been better off if he had tried to reach a SALT agreement in 1976. Such a bold move, however, was unlikely in the overheated political atmosphere of 1976, in which right-wing attacks and concerns about U.S. credibility pushed Ford and Kissinger to draw back from détente rather than seek to reinvigorate.[71]

Notes

1. For "testing ground," see Policy Planning Staff study by P. S. Kaplan, "Beyond Detente: East–West Relations in Europe After Helsinki," 8 Dec. 1975, attached to Winston Lord to the Secretary, 10 Dec. 1975, National Archives, Record Group 59, Department of State Records Policy Planning Staff (Director's Files), 1969–1972 (hereafter referred to as *PPS*, with archival box number and file information), box 359, 1–15 Dec. 1975.

2. See Raymond L. Garthoff, *Détente and Confrontation: American–Soviet Relations from Nixon to Reagan* (Washington, D.C.: Brookings Institution, 1994), pp. 594–95. Anatoly Dobrynin's definition of Ford's strategy in 1976 as one of "appeasing the right" seems just; see Dobrynin, *In Confidence: Moscow's Ambassador to America's Six Cold War Presidents* (New York: Time Books, 1995), p. 372. For the pressure on Ford and the vulnerabilities of his presidency, see Leo D. Ribuffo, "Is Poland a Soviet Satellite? Gerald Ford, the Sonnenfeldt Doctrine, and the Election of 1976," *Diplomatic History* 14 (Summer 1990), pp. 385–403.

3. See Policy Planning Staff study, "Beyond Detente: East–West Relations . . .," 8 Dec. 1975; Mike Bowker and Phil Williams, *Superpower Detente: A Reappraisal* (London: Royal Institute of International Affairs, 1988), pp. 52–53.

4. See Gerald R. Ford, *A Time to Heal: The Autobiography of Gerald R. Ford* (New York: Harper and Row, 1979), p. 354; Garthoff, *Détente and Confrontation*, p. 605.

5. See Arthur Hartman to the Secretary, "Your Moscow Trip, January 20–23, 1976," n.d., FOIA release; copy at National Security Archive (hereafter cited as *NSA*.)

6. See ibid.; Garthoff, *Détente and Confrontation*, pp. 518, 596.

7. For scholarly debate over when the Soviets started to support the Cuban airlift, see Piero Gliesejes, "Havana's Policy in Africa, 1959–76," and Odd Arne Westad, "Moscow and the Angola Crisis: A New Pattern of Intervention," both in *Cold War International History Project Bulletin* 8–9 (Winter 1996–97), pp. 5–18, 21–32.

8. See Bowker and Williams, *Superpower Detente*, pp. 129–31; in "Moscow and the Angola Crisis," pp. 25–26, Westad notes that when the Cubans entered the fighting in the fall of 1975, the Soviets worried about the impact on détente but changed their minds after the South Africans intervened.

9. See Garthoff, *Détente and Confrontation*, pp. 577-78, 590–91; Walter Isaacson, *Kissinger: A Biography* (New York: Simon and Schuster, 1992), p. 684; Bowker and Williams, *Superpower Detente*, pp. 126–27, 130; and Dobrynin, *In Confidence*, pp. 360–61.

10. See Garthoff, *Détente and Confrontation*, pp. 570-72; and Bowker and Williams, *Superpower Detente*, pp. 127–28.

11. See Garthoff, *Détente and Confrontation*, pp. 520, 578–79; Isaacson, *Kissinger: A Biography*, p. 683; and Hartman to the Secretary, "Your Moscow Trip, January 20–23," n.d.

12. See Hartman to the Secretary, "Your Moscow Trip, 20–23 January," n.d., and Garthoff, *Détente and Confrontation*, pp. 605–6.

13. See Garthoff, *Détente and Confrontation*, p. 596; and William G. Hyland, *Mortal Rivals: Superpower Relations from Nixon to Reagan* (New York: Random House, 1987), pp.

153–55. See Margaret J. Wyzominski, "Donald Rumsfeld," in *Political Profiles: The Nixon-Ford Years*, ed. Eleanora W. Schoenebaum (New York, Facts on File, Inc., 1979), pp. 551–54.

14. For discussion of the charges, see Garthoff, *Détente and Confrontation*, pp. 503–4. Both sides had privately raised concerns about each other's practices, for example, putting covers over nuclear missile submarines and ICBM silos. Ford and Kissinger, as well as Schlesinger and Rumsfeld had concluded that there had been no intentional Soviet violations.

15. For the options, see George S. Vest to the Secretary, "SALT—National Security Council Meeting," 7 Jan. 1977, State Department FOIA release, copy at National Security Archive (hereafter referred to as *NSA*).

16. See Garthoff, *Détente and Confrontation*, p. 597; and Minutes, National Security Council Meeting, Part II of II, 13 Jan. 1976, Ford Library, National Security Council Meetings File. For further details, see Brzezinski to Secretary of Defense and Secretary of State, "SALT Negotiating History," February 1977, FOIA release, copy at *NSA*.

17. See Hyland, *Mortal Rivals*, pp. 156–57.

18. Ibid., pp. 157–60; and Garthoff, *Détente and Confrontation*, pp. 596–97.

19. See Ford, *Time to Heal*, pp. 357–58; Garthoff, *Détente and Confrontation*, pp. 598–99; Dobrynin, *In Confidence*, p. 364; and Hyland, *Mortal Rivals*, p. 162.

20. See Ford, *Time to Heal*, p. 358.

21. See Dobrynin, *In Confidence*, p. 363.

22. See Garthoff, *Détente and Confrontation*, pp. 580–81, 604–05. For representative speeches, see "The Permanent Challenge of Peace: U.S. Policy Toward the Soviet Union" in *Department of State Bulletin* 74 (23 Feb. 1976), pp. 201–12, and "America's Permanent Interests," *Department of State Bulletin* 74 (5 April 1976) pp. 425–32.

23. See Jules Witcover, *Marathon, The Pursuit of the Presidency, 1972–1976* (New York: Viking, 1977), pp. 398–402; *Public Papers of the Presidents of the United States: Gerald R. Ford, 1976–1977*, I (Washington, D.C.: U.S. Government Printing Office, 1979), p. 185; Garthoff, *Détente and Confrontation* p. 604. See also Robert Schulzinger, *Henry Kissinger, Doctor of Diplomacy* (New York: Columbia University Press, 1989), pp. 227–29.

24. A quip of Kissinger's after a speech in Phoenix shows how problematic the word *détente* had become by April 1976. When asked to interpret the word, he responded, "I just want the record to show that I am explaining the word only in response to a question." *Department of State Bulletin* 74 (10 May 1976), p. 606.

25. For a thoughtful discussion of the contradictions in détente and the failure to develop consensus, see Bowker and Williams, *Superpower Detente*, pp. 58–59, 164–67. For "whole Western structure," see Secretary's Staff Meeting, 1 July 1976, National Archives, Record Group 59, Department of State Records, Transcripts of Secretary of State Kissinger's Staff Meetings, 1973–77 (hereafter referred to as Staff Meetings, with archival box number), box 11.

26. See Garthoff, *Détente and Confrontation*, pp. 606–8.

27. Minutes, National Security Council Meeting, Part II of II, 13 Jan. 1976.

28. That Wade sat in on the talks—the first time ever that a Defense official attended such a meeting—is indicative of the decline in Kissinger's position since Ford had sacked him

in late October as national security assistant. Presumably, he had no choice but to acquiesce to an arrangement in which the Defense Department gained direct knowledge of how he was conducting the talks.

29. Brezhnev's statement was misleading because 60 Soviet military advisers had arrived in Angola on 12 November 1975. See Westad, "Moscow and the Angolan Crisis," p. 26.

30. In his address, Ford asserted that a "strong defense posture" was important to "give weight to our values and our views in international negotiations," and that "[o]nly from a position of strength can we negotiate a balanced agreement to limit the growth of nuclear arms." The proposed defense budget for fiscal year 1977 would allow for "real growth in purchasing power over this year's defense budget." "Address Before a Joint Session of the Congress Reporting on the State of the Union," 19 Jan. 1976, *Public Papers of the Presidents of the United States: Gerald R. Ford, 1976–1977*, I, p. 41.

31. The U.S.–Spain Cooperation Treaty that Kissinger submitted to the Senate reaffirmed the U.S. Air Forces' access to Spanish bases but also reduced U.S. KC-135 tankers (used to fuel Strategic Air Command bombers for long-range missions) to a maximum of five and provided for withdrawal of U.S. nuclear missile submarines from Rota. Further, the United States undertook not to store nuclear weapons or components on Spanish soil. See *Department of State Bulletin* 74 (22 March 1976), pp. 362–63.

32. This document has not been declassified yet.

33. This is a reference to microwaves that the Soviets had beamed at the U.S. embassy in Moscow; in May and June the State Department made a formal protest. See Garthoff, *Détente and Confrontation*, p. 606.

34. The same U.S. and Soviet officials who attended that morning's meeting were also in attendance.

35. In December the Chinese had returned three Soviet helicopter crewmen they had held since March 1974. See Briefing Paper, "China Issues and Talking Points," Jan. 1976; copy at *NSA*.

36. See Garthoff, *Détente and Confrontation*, p. 599; and Hyland, *Mortal Rivals*, p, 161.

37. Hyland, *Mortal Rivals*, p. 161.

38. Except for the presence of Roger Molander, on NSC's Program Analysis Staff, the same U.S. and Soviet officials who attended the previous meetings were in attendance.

39. The Soviets objected largely because a supersonic B-1 bomber would reach its launch point—where it would fire cruise missiles—faster than a B-52. To Kissinger's statement that "fifteen minutes makes no difference," Gromyko replied "No military man would agree with that . . . in a nuclear war, even minutes count."

40. The two sides did agree on relatively secondary issues—the definition of heavy ICBMs and limits on changes in the dimensions of launching silos. On the first point, conceding to the U.S. emphasis on throw weight—the total weight of an ICBM's or SLBM's reentry vehicle, including nuclear components, guidance systems, decoys, and so on—instead of launching weight, Brezhnev agreed that both throw weight and launching weight should be used to distinguish heavy missiles from light missiles. They also approved limits for one-time increases in the dimensions of missile silos: their dimensions could be increased by 10–15 percent in any direction—diameter, depth, or both—so long as the initial volume was not increased by more than 32 percent. The SALT teams in Geneva would work out these details.

41. Brezhnev and Kissinger also had a perfunctory discussion of the Vienna MBFR talks, which the Soviets believed had stalled. Brezhnev liked a recent U.S. proposal to include nuclear units in force reductions. He continued to object to earlier Western proposals, for example, withdrawal of a four division tank army. He gave Kissinger a preview of the latest Soviet offer: U.S. and Soviet forces should be reduced by a fixed percentage and other European forces on both sides should be frozen. See Garthoff, *Détente and Confrontation*, p. 536.

42. Cuban support was marginal until the South African intervention. See ibid., p. 567.

43. For other unfavorable trends, from Moscow's standpoint, for example, political differences with Eurocommunist parties, domestic pressures emanating from the Helsinki process, and waning influence in Southeast Asia, ibid., pp. 611–12. Besides Angola, the only "positive side of the ledger" for the Soviets was the acquisition of a naval facility in Somalia.

44. For background on the Middle East situation in the second half of 1975, see William B. Quandt, *Peace Process, American Diplomacy and the Arab–Israel Conflict Since 1967* (Washington, D.C.: Brookings Institution, 1993), pp. 239–45; and Briefing Paper, "Middle East Issues and Talking Points," Jan. 1976; copy at *NSA*.

45. For a thoughtful assessment of Kissinger's Middle East diplomacy, including his blind spot on the Palestinian issue, see Quandt, *Peace Process*, pp. 349–51.

46. See Garthoff, *Détente and Confrontation*, p. 617; and Hartman to the Secretary, "Your Moscow Trip, January 20–23," n.d.

47. See Hartman to the Secretary, "Your Moscow Trip, January 20–23," n.d.; and Briefing Paper, "China Issues and Talking Points," Jan. 1976.

48. Kissinger later saw this concession as a sign that the Soviets "were being hurt by the successful U.S. policy of exclusion." See Garthoff, *Détente and Confrontation*, p. 604.

49. Among other features, U.N. Security Council Resolution 242, approved 22 November 1967, called for "respect for and acknowledgment of the sovereignty, territorial integrity, and political independence of every State in the area," withdrawal of Israeli armed forces from occupied territories, and a "just settlement of the refugee problem." Resolution 338, passed 12 October 1973, on a cease-fire in the October War, called upon the parties in the conflict to implement Resolution 242. See Quandt, *Peace Process*, pp. 435–36.

50. Recent research in Cuban and Soviet sources confirms that Cuban support for the MPLA was entirely at the latter's request. See "New Evidence on the Cold War in South Africa," *Cold War International History Project Bulletin* 8–9 (Winter 1996–97), pp. 5–37.

51. The United States had begun providing military aid to the FNLA in July 1975, "before" the introduction of large numbers of Cuban troops and *before* the more substantial Soviet military assistance later in the year. Hitherto, Soviet military aid to the FNLA had been "limited." See Westad, "Moscow and the Angolan Crisis," pp. 21–32; and Garthoff, *Détente and Confrontation*, p. 564.

52. Nevertheless, within less than three weeks the OAU had recognized and admitted the MPLA-organized People's Republic of Angola. See Garthoff, *Détente and Confrontation*, pp. 571–72.

53. This is a reference to a new U.S.–Japanese consultative committee on defense policy, which Secretary of Defense Schlesinger had called for during his visit to Japan in late August. See *New York Times*, 30 Aug. 1975.

54. See Garthoff, *Détente and Confrontation*, p. 606.

55. A reference to Beijing's return of the Soviet helicopter crew. See endnote 35, above.

56. See Hyland, *Mortal Rivals*, p. 162; and Garthoff, *Détente and Confrontation*, p. 599.

57. See Brzezinski to Secretary of State and Secretary of Defense, "SALT Negotiating History," 2 Feb. 1977; copy at *NSA*.

58. See Garthoff, *Détente and Confrontation*, pp. 599–600.

59. See Elizabeth Drew, *American Journal: The Events of 1976* (New York: Random House, 1977), p. 239; Isaacson, *Kissinger: A Biography*, pp. 693–98.

60. See Isaacson, *Kissinger: A Biography*, pp. 693–99, 721–22; Secretary's Staff Meeting, 25 Aug. 1976, *Staff Meetings*, box 11. For "yahoos," see "Ambassador Gates' Meeting with the Secretary, August 25, 1976," 1 Sept. 1976, *PPS*, box 332, China Exchanges Aug.– Jan. 1977.

61. See Garthoff, *Détente and Confrontation*, pp. 599–600; Hyland, *Mortal Rivals*, p.163; and Isaacson, *Kissinger: A Biography*, p. 629.

Epilogue
"I Would Like to Be Chairman of Something"

COMMENTARY

In the weeks before he left office, Henry Kissinger began meeting with representatives of President-elect Jimmy Carter to expedite the transition from an old to a new administration. Besides traveling to Plains, Georgia, for a lengthy talk with Carter, he met with Secretary of State-designate Cyrus Vance, whom he had once privately deprecated as a "Dalai Lama," to discuss current policy issues and to introduce foreign diplomats, such as the chief of Beijing's liaison office, Huang Zhen.[1] Carter had run for office as a political outsider, but his foreign policy advisers came from the same establishment circles that had nurtured Kissinger, but with one difference: they belonged to the U. S. component of the Trilateral Commission, a new private forum for U. S., Western European, and Japanese multinational corporate executives, former government officials, and university-based savants that was beginning to influence U. S. foreign policy. A significant connection that linked Carter, Secretary of State-designate Cyrus Vance, and National Security Assistant-designate Zbigniew Brzezinski was their membership in the Trilateral Commission. Other members of the Trilateral Commission that held high-level office in the Carter administration included Treasury Secretary W. Michael Blumental and Secretary of Defense Harold Brown.

Undoubtedly, Kissinger found the transition a cheerless task. Like Ronald Reagan earlier in 1976, presidential candidate Jimmy Carter had made criticism of Kissinger's diplomacy an important theme of his campaign; in fact, an old antagonist of Kissinger, Columbia University professor Zbigniew Brzezinski, was one of Carter's foreign policy advisers who had helped to formulate the attacks about pursuing a "'Lone Ranger' foreign policy," ignoring human rights," having "been outtraded in almost every instance" by the Soviets, and having "elevated amorality to the level of principle." Carter would soon learn to see détente in a more positive light, but his advisers believed that Kissinger's fixation on an equilibrium of the major powers had skewed his thinking, making it difficult for him to look at the Third World in non-

Cold War terms or recognize the importance of human rights as a way to strengthen U.S. influence.[2]

One of Kissinger's most important patrons had been Nelson Rockefeller; however, the Trilateral commission's key sponsor was his brother, Chase Manhattan Bank chairman David Rockefeller. He had begun to organize the "trilateralists" in 1972, largely in reaction to Richard Nixon's unilateral commercial and financial policies, which Rockefeller had feared would precipitate dangerous fissures, or even economic warfare, among the industrial capitalist nations. Preaching the language of interdependence, U.S. "trilateralists" pushed for more U.S.-European-Japanese consultation and policy coordination to mitigate divisive trends. While he was in office, Kissinger was a strong proponent of unilateralist methods; after Nixon's resignation, though, and even more so once he himself was out of government, Kissinger warmed to the commission's view.[3]

Kissinger's meeting with Vance and Huang on 8 January 1977 demonstrated the importance of the Trilateral Commission, but it also provided him an opportunity to wax nostalgic about the opening to China and to banter about his employment prospects. The discussion also suggested that the new administration would have its own problems in developing relations with China. Huang was not at all diffident in telling Vance that Carter's recent statement equating Taiwan with the PRC was inconsistent with the Shanghai Communiqué. Vance corrected Carter's faux pas, but he did not tell Huang that he was in no rush to normalize relations with China. For Vance, normalization was important, but he was not willing to move closer to Beijing if it meant risking a much higher priority — reinvigorating détente with the Soviet Union.[4]

During the meeting Huang also pushed Beijing's standard warnings about the Polar Bear; he may well have known of Vance's interest in détente and perhaps was trying to test the waters. Although Vance was not responsive to Huang's rhetoric, the Chinese did eventually find that others in Carter's camp, Brzezinski in particular, had fairly strong anti-Soviet tendencies. As the new administration's halting efforts at détente faltered in 1978 and 1979, Carter, his national security assistant, and a less than enthusiastic Vance, made great strides in realizing Kissinger's vision of a de facto Beijing-Washington strategic alliance. Kissinger's triangular diplomacy had worried the Soviets, but it had not hurt U.S.-Soviet relations. In the tense atmosphere of the late 1970s, However, Carter's "China card" was a powerful factor in the decline of détente prior to the Soviet invasion of Afghanistan.[5]

SECRET/NODIS
MEMORANDUM OF CONVERSATION
TIME: Saturday, January 8, 1977; 1:15 P.M.–2:40 P.M.
PLACE: The Secretary's Dining Room; 8th Floor of the Department of State
PARTICIPANTS: Ambassador Huang Zhen, Chief of PRC Liaison Office; Mr. Qiah Dayong (Counselor at Liaison Office) (No. 3 man); Mr. Tu Shangwci (Interpreter); Dr. Henry A. Kissinger, Secretary of State; Mr. Cyrus Vance, Secretary of State-designate; Mr. Philip Habib, Under Secretary for Political Affairs; Mr. Winston Lord, Director, Policy Planning Staff[A]

[After introducing Vance to Huang and the others in his party, Kissinger makes a brief statement to the press and Vance answers a few questions.]

Secretary Kissinger: Whenever you go to Beijing, Cy, you will lose your trim figure.

Ambassador Huang: The year before, in 1975, Mr. Vance did visit China once. At that time I was in Peking, but I didn't have the opportunity to meet you.

Mr. Vance: Yes, I know. The food was superb when I was in China, and in fact I didn't gain too much weight in China.

Ambassador Huang: How long were you in China?

Mr. Vance: About three weeks. (He then gave a run-down of his itinerary, including Beijing and Shanghai. The Secretary joked about the fact that hors d'oeuvres were being served at the table.)

Secretary Kissinger: I've been explaining the processes here which are . . . sooner or later . . . Mr. Habib is the senior Foreign Service Officer. I'm sure Cy comes here with the illusion that he will run the department, but sooner or later they'll get him. (laughter)

Mr. Vance: I'm forewarned. I've known him before and worked with him before.

Secretary Kissinger: Every once in a while the Department needs a cultural revolution. (laughter)

[Kissinger reminiscences about his secret trip to China and the negotiation of the Shanghai Communiqué.]

[A] Source: National Archives, Record Group 59, Department of State Records, Policy Planning Staff Records (Director's Files), 1969–77, box 377, WL China—Sensitive—Chron Jan. 1977.

Secretary Kissinger: . . . We negotiated the Shanghai Communiqué, Cy, usually in the evenings after banquets and after a few mao tais, and I did most of the negotiating in Chinese. (laughter)

Ambassador Huang: Some of the wordings in the Shanghai Communiqué were created by you. (laughter)

Secretary Kissinger: What impressed the Chinese most about what I have even done was the formula we discussed about how to express the idea of one China. We came up with a formula that the Chinese on both sides of the Taiwan Straits maintain that there is only one China, and the US is not disposed to challenge that position.

Ambassador Huang: In the Shanghai Communiqué, as you mentioned, the US recognized that there was only one China and that Taiwan is only a part of China. So from that time the United States Government already knew the Chinese Government policy that we are firmly opposed to any plot of creating two Chinas, or one China—one Taiwan, or one China—two governments.

Secretary Kissinger: Perhaps I could sum up what I told Mr. Vance about our relationship and then the Ambassador could see if I have correctly stated it. First, I told Mr. Vance that I've always believed that our relationship with the PRC was one of the most important initiatives that was undertaken and one of the most important elements of international equilibrium. We expressed this in the Shanghai Communique and in other communiqué—our mutual concern with respect to hegemony, with respect to the dangers of hegemony in the world. And we therefore developed the practice of informing the PRC quite fully, or fully, about our planned discussions with other key countries. Chairman Mao, in several very extensive conversations with me and in two conversations with American Presidents, elaborated the Chinese point of view on the international situation which on many key points was parallel to our own.

Ambassador Huang: He met five times with you. (Chairman Mao and the Secretary).

Secretary Kissinger: We'll wait until they are finished (the waiters). These are all old friends (gesturing toward the Chinese) whom we have known now on every trip one way or another.

Mr. Vance: How many trips have you made there, Henry?

Secretary Kissinger: Nine.

Ambassador Huang: And you met the late Chairman Mao five times. Our Chairman Mao had maybe the longest talks with the Doctor, so many times, on elaborating the issues regarding the international situation, on bilateral relationship and also our views on major international issues. And we talked about our common points, with the main common point being we are against the Polar Bear. (laughter)

Mr. Vance: Yes.

(There were then brief informal mao tai toasts to old friends and new friends.)

Secretary Kissinger: With respect to the Taiwan issue, we have confirmed our commitment to the principle of one China, and we have on a number of occasions made clear that we would not support a two-China policy or a one China—Taiwan policy, or the various formulations that the Ambassador correctly mentioned. We have not found, while we were here, the exact formula (in response to the interpreter's question, he repeated the "precise formula") to complete the process but we have always understood that it's a process that needed to be completed.

Ambassador Huang: Regarding this issue, our position is very clear. We mentioned three points—sever the diplomatic relationship with Taiwan, withdraw US troops from Taiwan, and abrogate the Treaty. Since Dr. Kissinger and Mr. Vance are both old friends, and since Mr. Vance also visited China the year before, so today I would just like to frankly mention one point. Recently we noticed that in the recent issue of *Time* magazine which carried Mr. Carter's conversation with that magazine, in his conversation he openly called Taiwan "China" and even in the same breath put Taiwan on a par with the People's Republic of China. And we think this kind of remark runs counter to the principles of the Shanghai Communiqué.

Mr. Vance: As far as President Carter is concerned, let me assure you that he stands firmly behind the implementation of the Shanghai Communiqué as the guiding principle which should govern our bilateral relations. (Mr. Habib was talking to the Secretary as the Chinese waited, and the Secretary pointed out that he was, as always, getting his instructions from Mr. Habib. (laughter)

Ambassador Huang: Frankly speaking, the Shanghai Communiqué constitutes the foundation of the present Sino-US relationship and only if both sides strictly observe all the principles of the Shanghai Communiqué, then relations between our two countries can continue to be improved. Any action which goes back on the principles of the Communiqué will result in harming the Sino-US relationship.

Mr. Vance: Let me say that I fully accept the principle of one China.

Secretary Kissinger: Now we have settled this. We will go on to settle all the other issues. (laughter)

Ambassador Huang: So we have no difficulty on this.

[There is more small talk, including comments about the "weight problem" caused by too many Chinese meals.]

Ambassador Huang: Not long ago I met a very good friend, an old comrade of both of you, David Rockefeller.

Secretary Kissinger: Yes.

Mr. Vance: Yes, he's going to China.

Ambassador Huang: He introduced not only Brzezinski but Mr. Vance and Mr. Blumenthal. We were already very acquainted with Mr. Kissinger. And he told us you all belonged to the Trilateral Commission.

Mr. Vance: Right.

Secretary Kissinger: Not I.

Ambassador Huang: Mr. Vance, you are Chairman of the Board of the Rockefeller Foundation?

Mr. Vance: Yes, I was.

Secretary Kissinger: The Trilateral Commission was a government in exile. So now I'm thinking of going there, with all good wishes to Mr. Vance.

Ambassador Huang: Mr. David Rockefeller will arrive in China on January 21.

Mr. Vance/Secretary Kissinger: Yes.

Mr. Vance: I saw him the other night, and he told me he was going to China after his trip to Japan. Speaking of the Trilateral Commission, they have a meeting starting today and as they have sent all the people of the Trilateral Commission into the new Administration there is practically no one left to meet together in Tokyo.

Secretary Kissinger: Cy, I've always found that I could tell our Chinese friends the main lines of our policy — I cannot say they always agreed to every last step. It was helpful to our mutual understanding to have this kind of frank dialogue.

Mr. Vance: Well I would hope very much that we would continue this kind of frank dialogue.

Ambassador Huang: We would like to do the same.

(There was some discussion among the Chinese which was not translated.)

Mr. Vance: Could I say that President Carter has asked me to convey his good wishes to Chairman Hua and to emphasize the fact that we consider of great importance the continuing relationship between the US and the PRC.

Ambassador Huang: I will convey his kind regards to Chairman Hua, and also I would like to ask you to convey to Mr. Carter our best regards.

Mr. Vance: Thank you, I shall.

Ambassador Huang: (To the Secretary) I learned from the newspapers that you have got a lot of invitations about your future. One recent piece of news is that the Chairman of CBS will soon resign, and he will maybe ask you to succeed him. How true is that?[6]

Mr. Vance: Is that true, Henry?

Secretary Kissinger: The Chairman of CBS is a very good friend of mine, and anyone who knows him must realize that the idea of his resigning is inconceivable to him. Is it conceivable to you? (to Vance)

Mr. Vance: No.

Secretary Kissinger: He is a very good friend, and we meet often socially. I would like to be chairman of something. (laughter)

Mr. Vance: That would be fine. I would have someone to complain to.

Secretary Kissinger: It's a title that I like. (laughter)

Mr. Habib: You could be Chairman of the Central Committee.

Ambassador Huang: Chairman is like President.

Secretary Kissinger: But our constitution prevents me from becoming President.

Ambassador Huang: It reminds me that during the talks with President Nixon you told Chairman Mao about your constitution.

Secretary Kissinger: That's correct. The Chairman took a very kind interest in my political future.

[There is more small talk and some toasts; Huang discusses his recent visit to the South, and Kissinger speaks about his first trip to China.]

Ambassador Huang: Time flies so fast since the first secret trip.

The Secretary: It has been nearly six years. I remember all the communications that came to us through Pakistan.

Mr. Vance: I remember very well reading about the trip when the story broke back here. It was a very exciting moment in history.

The Secretary: I think it was the single most exciting moment for me, that trip to China.[7]

Mr. Vance: Of your career?

The Secretary: And of course it was my first acquaintance with the Chinese style of diplomacy, in which I learned, as I have said publicly, that the Chinese word counts, that one can rely on what our Chinese friends say.

Mr. Vance: Yes.

Ambassador Huang: I still remember the last time when I came to meet with you, and you mentioned this particular sentence. You told us that when you said this to the reporters you made a comparison with the other side (the Soviet Union).

The Secretary: That is correct.

Ambassador Huang: We have also said many times that very frankly our experience in dealing with the Russians is, to sum up in two sentences: first, they will bully the weak and are afraid of the strong. And that their words are usually not trustworthy. (Laughter) That is why you should never be weak. If you are weak, soft, the Polar Bear wants to get you.

The Secretary: My impression is that when you have a Secretary of State who used to be the Deputy Secretary of Defense you have someone who has an understanding of the reality of power.

Mr. Vance: That's true. I think I understand the reality of power.

The Secretary: You know I nominated Mr. Vance for this position six months before he got it. (Mr. Lord commented that he managed to get it anyway.) I was at a meeting of the Board of *Time* Magazine six months before. They asked me whom I would like to see as Secretary of State if Mr. Carter won, a contingency I was trying my best to avoid, and I said "Mr. Vance."

Mr. Vance: You see, he really is a Chairman.

[There are more toasts and small talk, during which Kissinger declares that he will give "full support" to the administration when it takes initiatives to normalize relations with China.]

Ambassador Huang: . . . our leaders talk to you continually about our view on the United States–Soviet relationship, and our view is that the United States has vested interests to protect around the world, and the Soviet Union seeks expansionism. This is an objective phenomenon which is unalterable. For instance our view on Soviet policy is that their policy is to make a feint toward the East while attacking the West.

The Secretary: I have also told the Ambassador that this may be true, but to us it makes no difference how the world equilibrium is overturned. We must be concerned with both Europe and Asia.

Mr. Vance: Yes.

Ambassador Huang: (After discussion among the Chinese) We also know your view.

The Secretary: I don't deny that it could happen that way. As you know from our campaign, the President-elect is very dedicated to strengthening the relationship between the United States and Western Europe, and building up the strength there.

Mr. Vance: (To the Secretary) I might say a word on that. Perhaps I might say a word on that. During the campaign, as Henry indicated, the President-elect said on several occasions that one of the cardinal principles of the foreign policy of the Carter government would be not only strengthening the political relationship of the United States and the countries of Western Europe but also to strengthen our NATO forces . . .

[Vance discusses plans for rationalizing NATO force level to ensure that they are properly equipped and ready for quick reaction.]

. . . You may have noticed, Mr. Ambassador, that the Navy has had the foresight to place in the White House four of the five last Presidents. (Mr. Vance and the Secretary discussed the names.)

The Secretary: Actually the last five.[8]

Mr. Vance: A monopoly.

Ambassador Huang: I think what Mr. Vance mentioned about the review and NATO forces is really very important. As we talked to Dr. Kissinger before, the Western European nations are too weak, too soft, so we should encourage them to unite and strengthen their forces. As we know, Europe is in need of the United States and vice versa. So that's why we hope you will strengthen your equal partnership. We also hope—another very important thing to take care—we hope that the Munich thinking in Western Europe should be decreased, because this kind of thinking may lull vigilance and demoralize the peoples' fighting will. If the situation is like this, the forces will have no fighting morale.

The Secretary: Well the internal situation in Europe is complicated. Well, Mr. Ambassador, you will be dealing with my friend, Mr. Vance, in the future. I'm glad you did us the honor of visiting us.

[After more small talk, Winton Lord escorts the Chinese to the diplomatic entrance.]

Notes

1. For a biography of Vance, see David S. McLellan, *Cyrus Vance* (Totowa, N.J.: Rowman and Allenheld, 1985). For Kissinger's often-solicitous relationships with establishment pillars such as Vance, see Walter Isaacson, *Kissinger: A Biography* (New York: Simon and Schuster, 1992), p. 142.
2. For the Carter campaign and Kissinger, see Isaacson, *Kissinger: A Biography*, pp. 699–703. For Vance's critique of Kissinger, see Cyrus R. Vance, *Hard Choices: Critical Years in America's Foreign Policy* (New York: Simon & Schuster, 1983), pp. 23–24. For important surveys of Carter's foreign policy, see Raymond L. Garthoff, *Détente and Confrontation: American–Soviet Relations from Nixon to Reagan* (Washington, D.C.:

Brookings Institution, 1994); John Dumbrell, *The Carter Presidency A Re-Evaluation* (Manchester, Eng.: Manchester University Press, 1993); Gaddis Smith, *Morality, Reason, and Power: American Diplomacy in the Carter Years* (New York: Hill and Wang, 1986), and Olav Njolstad, *Peacekeeper and Troublemaker: The Containment Policy of Jimmy Carter* (Oslo: Institutt for Forsvarsstudier, 1995).

3. For an important study of the Trilateral Commission, see Stephen Gill, *American Hegemony and the Trilateral Commission* (Cambridge, Eng.: Cambridge University Press, 1990). See also Dumbrell, *The Carter Presidency*, pp. 111–12.

4. For Vance's thinking about détente and U.S.–China relations at the outset of the Carter administration, see his memoir *Hard Choices*, pp. 28–29, and Robert S. Ross, *Negotiating Cooperation: The United States and China, 1969–1989* (Stanford, Calif.: Stanford University Press, 1995), pp. 100, 102–4.

5. For Carter's China policy during 1977–79, see Garthoff, *Détente and Confrontation*, pp. 758–85.

6. William Paley (1901–1990) was president of the Columbia Broadcasting System during 1928–46, chairman of the board during 1946–83, founder chairman during 1983–86, and chairman during 1987–90.

7. Kissinger would later tell others that a meeting with North Vietnamese diplomats on 8 October 1972 confirming the outlines of the Vietnam peace agreement was the most thrilling of his career. See Isaacson, *Kissinger: A Biography*, p. 448.

8. Presidents Kennedy, Johnson, Nixon, Carter, and Ford had all been naval officers, although Johnson's experience in the U.S. Navy was brief.

—Glossary of Abbreviations, Acronyms, and Terms

ABM—Anti-Ballistic Missiles

ACDA—U.S. Arms Control and Disarmament Agency

ALCM—Air-Launched Cruise Missile

B-1—U.S. strategic bomber that was in the research and development stage during the 1970s. President Carter canceled the project in 1977, although President Reagan later reinstated it.

B-52—U.S. heavy strategic bomber that has remained in the Air Force's inventory since initial deployment in 1955. Of eight models deployed, the most widely used was the B-52G, which carried 24 bombs and missiles and had a range of 10,000 miles without aerial refueling.

Backfire—NATO designation for the Soviet TU [Tupolev] 22M/26 medium range nuclear bomber, first deployed in 1974. Designed for European or Asian combat missions, Backfire's range was 5,000 miles (although with refueling, it was theoretically capable of reaching the United States, if not returning)

Cruise missile—A slow highly maneuverable missile, powered by jet engines, that takes a low altitude flight path to its target; launchable either from the ground, bombers, submarines, or surface ships.

CIA—U.S. Central Intelligence Agency

CSCE—Conference on Security and Cooperation in Europe

DOD—U.S. Department of Defense

DRV—Democratic Republic of Vietnam

EA — U.S. Department of State. Bureau of East Asian and Pacific Affairs

EA/PRCM — U.S. Department of State. Bureau of East Asian and Pacific Affairs. People's Republic of China and Mongolia Affairs

EXGDS — "Exclude from General Declassification Schedule" stipulated in President Nixon's Executive Order 11652 on classification and declassification of national security information.

FB-111 Aardvark Fighter-Bomber — Medium range (up to 4,100 miles) strategic bomber initially deployed by the U.S. Strategic Air Command in 1969. Aardvark carries either nuclear or conventional bombs as well as Short-Range Attack Missiles [SRAMs].

F-4 Phantom Jet — Twin-engine, all weather, multi-mission jet used by U.S. Air Force, Navy, and Marine Corps, capable of carrying nuclear bombs, active during 1964-91.

F-5E Tiger Jet — Air Force lightweight jet fighter, first flown in 1972 and developed to provide U.S. allies with a fighter that was not difficult to operate and could be maintained inexpensively.

FBS — Forward-Based Systems. U.S., French, or British nuclear delivery systems in Western Europe or the Mediterranean

FNLA — National Front for the Liberation of Angola. Anti-colonial movement organized by Holden Roberto in the early 1960s. It had U.S. CIA and Chinese support until it collapsed in late 1975.

FRG — Federal Republic of Germany

FUNK — National United Front of Kampuchea

GRUNK — Royal Government of National Union of Kampuchea

ICBM — Intercontinental Ballistic Missile; land-based rocket-propelled missile capable of delivering a warhead at intercontinental ranges between 3,000 and 8,000 nautical miles.

INR—U.S. Department of State. Bureau of Intelligence and Research

INR/DDR/REA—U.S. Department of State. Bureau of Intelligence and Research. Office of Research and Analysis for East Asia and Pacific

LLCM—Ground-launched cruise missiles

MBFR—Mutual Balanced Force Reduction negotiations, 1973-86.

MBFR VP—National Security Council MBFR Verification Panel. An NSC subcommittee charged with coordinating U.S. negotiating positions for the MBFR negotiations.

Memcon—Memorandum of conversation

Minuteman—U.S. solid-fueled ICBM first tested in 1961 and deployed in October 1962. Fielded in hardened concrete silos in the Great Plains states, Minuteman could carry a nuclear warhead 5,000 nautical miles. 1,000 were finally produced. Minuteman III was the third generation model, first deployed in 1970 with three MIRVS.

MIRV—Multiple Independently Targetable Reentry Vehicles. Nuclear warheads carried by the same missile that enable it to strike separate targets in succession. U.S. MIRVed missiles included the MInuteman III, Poseidon, and Trident.

MPLA—Popular Movement for the Liberation of Angola. Anti-colonial movement created during the early 1960s and supported by Cuba and Soviet Union.

National Command Authorities [NCA]—The President and the Secretary of Defense and their rightful successors.

NODIS—"No Distribution" without consent of authorized officials.

NSA—National Security Archive

NSC—National Security Council

NSDM — National Security Decision Memorandum. Nixon-Ford administration nomenclature used to describe memoranda to federal agencies reporting presidential decisions.

PPS — National Archives, Record Group 59. Department of State Records. Policy Planning Staff (Director's Files), 1969 – 77

Poseidon — MIRVed SLBM first deployed on reconverted Polaris submarines (renamed Poseidon) beginning in March 1971. Poseidon missiles carried 10 MIRVs at a range of at least 2,500 nautical miles.

PRC — People's Republic of China

Radius — Or combat radius, referring to the greatest distance an aircraft can fly with its weapons and still return to its starting point.

ROC — Republic of China

SALT — Strategic Arms Limitation Talks; U.S.-Soviet arms control negotiations during 1969 – 79. The 1969 – 1972 phase of SALT produced the ABM Treaty and the "Interim Agreement on Certain Measures with Respect to Strategic Offensive Arms," generally referred to as the SALT I Agreements. The 1972 – 1979 phase, generally referred to as SALT II, produced the SALT II treaty (never ratified in the United States).

SLBM — Submarine-Launched Ballistic Missiles

SLCM — Sea-launched Cruise Missiles

TU-160 — Soviet strategic bomber first deployed in the late 1980s; later dubbed the *Blackjack* by NATO.

Trident — Long-range SLBM developed during the 1970s, first tested in January 1977, and initially deployed on reconverted Poseidon submarines in October 1979.

Typhoon — the Soviet Union's largest missile launching nuclear submarine; first deployed in 1980, it carries 20 SLBMs that can strike U.S. targets from Russian waters.

UNC — United Nations Command

UNCURK—United Nations Commission for the Unification and Rehabilitation of Korea

UNITA—National Union for the Total Liberation of Angola. Anti-colonial grouping led by Jonas Savimbi that split off from the FNLA; its external support was mainly Chinese.

A

Abrasimov, Pyotr A. (b. 1912), Soviet ambassador to the former German Democratic Republic (GDR), 1962-71.

Adenauer, Konrad (1876-1967), Christian Democratic Party leader and chancellor of the Federal Republic of Germany, 1949-1963.

Aleksandrov-Agentov, Andrei M. (1918-95), career Foreign Ministry official; member of Brezhnev's private secretariat and his chief adviser on U.S.-Soviet relations.

Allon, Yigal (1918-80), a soldier who rose to the rank of major-general (Reserves) Israeli Defense Forces, deputy prime minister, 1967-77; and foreign minister, 1974-77.

Alsop, Jr., Joseph (1910-89), influential American writer and journalist, syndicated columnist for *New York Herald Tribune*, 1945-58 and for the *Washington Post* and *Los Angeles Times*, 1958-74.

Andronikof, Prince Constantin (b. 1916), official interpreter (Russian and English) French minister of foreign affairs, 1946-76.

Armstrong, Oscar Vance (b. 1918), director, Bureau of East Asian and Pacific Affairs, People's Republic of China and Mongolia Affairs, 1973-76.

Atherton , Alfred L. (b. 1921), a career Foreign Service officer, deputy assistant secretary of state for Near East and South Asian affairs, 1970-74; and Assistant Secretary of State for Near East and South Asian affairs, 1974-78.

B

Bahr, Egon (b. 1922), director, Press and Information Office, Berlin, 1960-66; promoted to rank of ambassador, West German Diplomatic Service, 1967; state secretary Bundeskanzleramt and Plenipotentiary of Federal Government in Berlin, 1969-72; member of Parliament (Bundestag), 1972; federal minister without portfolio attached to Chancellor Willy Brandt's office, 1972-74.

Bhutto, Zulkifar Al (1928–79), Pakistani politician, leader of the People's Party; president, 1971–73; foreign minister, 1971–77; and prime minister, 1973–77. Later executed by military dictatorship.

Blumenthal, W. Michael (b. 1926), chairman of the board and chief executive officer, Bendix Corporation, 1972–77; U.S. treasury secretary, 1977–79.

Boumédienne, Colonel Houari (1927–78), prime minister of Algeria, 1965–78; president, 1976–78.

Brandt, Willy (b. 1913), mayor of West Berlin, 1957–66; foreign minister and vice chancellor, 1966–69; chancellor of West Germany, 1969–74.

Brosio, Manlio (1897–1980), Italian politician; secretary general of NATO, 1964–71.

Brezhnev, Leonoid Ilyich (1906–82), joined Communist Party of the Soviet Union in 1931; first secretary, Communist Party, 1964–66; general secretary, Communist Party, 1966–82; chairman, Presidium of the Soviet Union, 1960–64, and 1977–82.

Bunker, Ellsworth (1894-1984), U.S. diplomat; ambassador to Vietnam, 1967–73; ambassador-at-large, 1973–78.

C

Ceauscescu, Nicolae (1918–89), first secretary, Romanian Communist Party, 1965 until his overthrow and execution in 1989; president, Romania, 1974–1989.

Chamberlain, Neville (1869–1940), British prime minister, 1937–40; Conservative Party leader; one of the architects of the Munich Pact.

Chen Chu (b.?), journalist, propagandist, and diplomatist; counselor, embassy in Moscow, 1956–59; ambassador to Ghana, 1966; director, Foreign Ministry Information Department, c. 1971–72; one of three representatives in the PRC delegation to the U.N. General Assembly, 1972–73.

Chen Xilian (b. 1913), joined the Communist movement in 1929 and rose to the rank of colonel-general in the People's Liberation Army; commanded the PLA's artillery, 1951–59; commanded the Shenyang Military Region, 1959–73; member, Politburo, 1969–80 and the Chinese Communist Party Central Committee, 1973–80.

Childs, Marquis (1903–90), journalist and syndicated columnist, *St. Louis Post-Dispatch*, 1926–44, 1954–68.

Clift, Arthur Denis (b. 1937), former naval officer; staff member for Europe, National Security Council, 1971–1973; senior staff member for Eastern and Western Europe and Soviet Union, National Security Council, 1974–76.

Cooper, Charles A. (b. 1933), a career Foreign Service officer; deputy assistant to the president for international economic affairs, 1973–74; and assistant secretary of the treasury for international affairs, 1974.

Cunal, Alvaro (b. 1913), secretary general of Portuguese Communist Party, 1961–92.

D

Daladier, Eduard (1884–1970), premier of France, 1933, 1934, and 1938–40; a signatory of the Munich Pact.

De Gaulle, Charles (1890–1970), leader of the "Free French", World War II; prime minister, 1958–59; president, 1959–69.

Deng Xiapoing (1904–94), joined Chinese Communist Party in 1929; Long March veteran; member, Revolutionary Military Council, 1950–54; held various high-level posts in Chinese government and Chinese Communist Party, including secretary, Communist Party Central Committee, 1952–67; vice premier, 1952–67; internal exile during Cultural Revolution, was brought back into leadership positions, 1973–74, including vice premier State Council, temporarily removed from office as "capitalist roader" in 1976; vice chairman, Communist Party, 1977–94.

Dobrynin, Anatoly (b. 1919), career Soviet diplomat; ambassador to the United States, 1962–86.

Dulles, John Foster (1888–1959), American secretary of state, 1953–59.

E

Eagleburger, Lawrence Sidney (b. 1930), career Foreign Service officer; after holding various posts at State, NSC, and Defense, was executive assistant to the secretary of state, 1973–77.

Eckstein, Alexander (1915–76), professor of economics, University of Michigan; member, board of the National Committee on U.S.–China relations, 1966–76 and chairman, 1970–72; policy adviser to the secretary of state, 1966–68.

F

Falin, Valentin M. (b. 1926), Soviet ambassador to the Federal Republic of Germany, 1971–78.

Fletcher, James C. (1919–91), administrator for the National Aeronautics and Space Administration, 1971–77.

Ford, Gerald R. (b. 1913), Republican member of U.S. House of Representatives, 1949–73; vice-president of the United States, 1973–74; president of the United States, 1974–77.

Freeman, Charles W. (b. 1943), career Foreign Service officer, State Department People's Republic of China and Mongolian Affairs Desk, 1971–74; deputy director for Taiwan Affairs, 1975–76.

Fukuda, Takeo (1905–95), a leader of Japan's Liberal Democratic Party; prime minister, 1976–78.

G

Gandhi, Indira (1917–84), Indian Congress Party leader; prime minister, 1966–77.

Gleysteen, Jr., William Henry (b. 1926), deputy chief of mission, Taipei, 1971–74; deputy assistant secretary of state for East Asian and Pacific Affairs, 1974–76.

Gomes, Marshall Francisco de Costa (b. 1914), chief of staff, Portugese Armed Forces, 1972–76; a member of the junta that seized power in 1974; president of Portugal, 1974–76.

Gromyko, Andrei, (1909–89), deputy foreign minister, 1949–57; foreign minister, 1957–85. During World War II, he was the Soviet Union's ambassador to the United States. He was elected to the Politburo in 1973.

Guo Morou (1892–1978), vice-chairman, National People's Congress; president, Chinese Academy of Sciences; and member of the Communist Party Central Committee.

H

Habib, Philip (1920–92), assistant secretary of state for East Asian and Pacific Affairs, 1974–76; and undersecretary of state for political affairs, 1976–78.

Haig, Jr., Alexander (b. 1924), former army officer; deputy assistant to the president, National Security Affairs, 1970–73; White House chief of staff, 1973–74.

Han Xu (1924–94), director, Foreign Ministry Protocol Department during the early 1970s; deputy head of the PRC Liaison Office, 1973–79.

Hartlig, Paul (b. 1914), prime minister of Denmark, 1973–75.

Hartman, Arthur (b. 1926), Foreign Service officer; assistant secretary of state for European affairs, 1974–77.

Hartmann, Robert L. (b. 1917), chief of staff to Vice President Ford, 1973–74; counselor to the president, 1974–77.

Holdridge, John H. (b. 1924), Foreign Service officer, deputy chief, Beijing Liaison Office, 1973–75.

Horowitz, Herbert (b. 1930), director, Department of State Office for Research on East Asia, 1975–78.

Howe, Jonathan T. (b. 1935), served as Kissinger's military assistant from 1969 to early 1974 after receiving a Ph.D. from Tufts University. Prior to his graduate work, Howe had received special training at the Navy's Nuclear Power School and had sailed on ballistic missile-launching submarines, the USS *George Washington* and the USS *Patrick Henry*.

Hua Guofeng (b. 1920), joined the Red Army in 1935; held various Communist Party positions in Hunan Province; deputy premier and minister of public security, 1975–76; premier, 1976–81; member, Communist Party Central Committee since 1981.

Huang Hua (b. 1913), studied at American Yanjing University in Beijing; translated during Edgar Snow's first meetings with Mao; career Foreign Ministry official; participant in US–PRC Warsaw Talks, 1958–60; ambassador to Ghana, 1960–65; ambassador to United Arab Republic during 1966–70; ambassador to Canada, 1971; permanent representative of the PRC to the U.N., 1971–76; minister of foreign affairs, 1976–82.

Huang Zhen (1907–89), a career ambassador in the PRC's diplomatic corps. After political liaison work with the Red Army during the civil war, he was successively ambassador to Hungary, 1950–54; ambassador to Indonesia, 1954–1961; vice minister of Foreign Affairs, 1961–64; ambassador to France, 1964–73; head of the PRC's Liaison Office in Washington, D.C., 1973–79.

Hyland, William (b. 1929), analyst with Central Intelligence Agency, 1954 to 1969; member of NSC Staff during 1969–73; director, State Department Bureau of Intelligence and Research, 1973–75; Deputy Assistant to the President for National Security Affairs, 1975–77.

J

Jackson, Henry M. (1912–83), Democratic senator from Washington from 1953 until his death. He was known to some as the "Senator from Boeing" for his assiduous work in promoting defense work in his district.

Jenkins, Alfred L. (b. 1916), career Foreign Service officer; member, National Security Council staff, 1966–69; director of Asian Communist affairs, State Department, 1970–73; deputy chief, U.S. Liaison Office in Beijing, 1973–74.

Jiang Qing (1913–91), actress who married Mao in 1938; member, Politburo, 1969–76; one of the "Gang of Four."

Ji Chaozhu (b. 1929), after spending ten years in the United States during his youth, including a year at Harvard, served as a translator for the Chinese delegation during the Korean armistice talks. Banished to the countryside during the Cultural Revolution, he was brought back for translation duties during the 1972 Nixon visit. During 1973–75, he served at the PRC Liaison Office in Washington.

Jobert, Michael (b. 1921), career civil servant, France's foreign minster, 1973–74.

K

Kendall, Donald (b. 1921), chairman of the board and chief executive officer, Pepsi-Cola, Inc., 1971–86; former chairman of the U.S.–USSR Trade and Economic Council. When Nixon joined the New York law firm of Mudge, Stern, Baldwin, and Todd in 1963, Kendall gave him his first international legal account.

Kennerly, David (b. 1947), White House photographer, 1974–77.

Kissinger, Henry A. (b. 1923), professor, Department of Government, Harvard University, 1954-69; executive director, Harvard International Seminar, 1958-69; associate director, Center for International Affairs, 1957-61; assistant to the president for national security affairs, 1969-75; and secretary of state, 1973-77.

Korniyenko, Georgi (b. 1925), was chief of the Soviet Foreign Ministry American Department, 1965-78; deputy foreign minister, 1975-77.

L

Laird, Melvin (b. 1922), member, U.S. House of Representatives, 1952-69; secretary of defense, 1969-73.

Li Deshing (b. 1916), a Long March veteran who rose to the rank of Lt. General in the People's Liberation Army; vice-chairman, Politburo, 1969-85; member, Chinese Communist Party Central Committee, 1973-85; commander, Shenyang Military Region, 1974-85.

Li Xiannan (1909-92), long-standing member of the Communist Party Central Committee; deputy prime minister, 1954-75; and became finance minister in 1957.

Lin Bao (1907-71), a veteran Chinese Communist military commander, he became the PRC's Minister of Defense in 1959; by 1969, he was designated Mao's successor. In September 1971, after allegedly plotting a coup, Lin died in a plane crash while en route to the Soviet Union.

Lodal, Jan (b. 1943), served on the NSC staff under Nixon and Ford as deputy for program analysis, the primary staff officer on arms control and defense program issues.

Lon Nol (1913-85), minister of national defense and chief of general staff, 1955-66; commander-in-chief, Khmer Royal Armed Forces, 1960; prime minister, 1963, 1966-67, and 1969-73; president and commander-in-chief, 1972-75; seized power in 1970 while Prince Sihanouk was in Europe.

Lord, Winston (b. 1937), U.S. diplomat, National Security Council staff member, 1969-73, Kissinger's special assistant, 1970-73; director, State Department Policy Planning Staff, 1973-77.

Lynn, James (b. 1927), secretary for housing and urban development, 1974-75.

M

Mao Zedong (1893–1976), helped found Chinese Communist Party in 1921; chairman of Chinese Communist Party and president, People's Republic of China, 1949–76.

Magnuson, Warren Grant (1905–89), Democratic senator from Washington, 1944–81.

Mansfield, Michael (b. 1903), Democratic senator from Montana, 1953–77.

Mintoff, Dominic, (b. 1916), prime minister of Cyprus, 1971–84.

Moynhihan, Daniel P. (b. 1927), U.S. ambassador to India, 1973–75.

Muskie, Edmund (1914–96), Democratic senator from Maine, 1959–80.

N

Nakasone, Yasuhiro (b. 1918), Japanese Liberal Democratic Party leader, who attended Kissinger's international seminar at Harvard in 1953. He later served as prime minister, 1982–87.

Neto, Agostinho (1922–79), president of the Republic of Angola, 1975–79.

Nixon, Richard M., (1913–94), Republican member, U.S. House of Representatives, 1947–51; U.S. Senator from California, 1950–53; vice president of the United States, 1953–1961; partner, Nixon, Mudge, Rose, Guthrie, and Alexander, 1964–1968; president of the United States, 1969–74.

O

Ohira, Masayoshi (1910–80), Liberal Democratic Party politician, foreign minister of Japan, 1962–64 and 1972–74.

P

Patolichev, Nikolai S. (1908–89), Soviet minister for foreign trade, 1958–85.

Penn Nouth (1906–?), a close adviser of Sihanouk; prime minister during various periods between 1948–69. He headed the Royal Government of National Union of Cambodia [GRUNK], established in Beijing in May 1970.

Pompidou, Georges (1911–74), premier of France, 1962–68; president of France, 1969–74.

Q

Qiao Guanhua (1908–83), a long-standing associate of Zhou Enlai; assistant to minister of foreign affairs, 1954–64; vice-minister of foreign affairs, 1964–74; and minister, 1974–76.

Qimei Xie (b. 1923), former counselor and minister counselor, PRC Liaison Office, 1973–81.

R

Reston, James B. (1909–95), influential columnist and reporter, associated with the *New York Times*, 1939–89.

Ribicoff, Abraham (1910–98), served as Democratic senator from Connecticut, 1963–79.

Roberto, Holden (b. 1925), Angolan nationalist leader, became leader of the National Front for the Liberation of Angola (FNLA), 1962.

Rockefeller, David (b. 1915), president, Chase Manhattan Bank, 1961–69; and chairman of the board, 1969–81.

Rodman, Peter (b. 1943), member of NSC staff, 1969–77.

Rogers, William P. (b. 1913), deputy attorney general, 1953–57; attorney general, 1957–61; partner, Royal, Koegel and Rogers, 1961–69; secretary of state, 1969–73.

Romberg, Alan D. (b. 1938), officer, State Department in Hong Kong and Washington, 1964–74; member, NSC staff, 1976–77.

Rumsfeld, Donald Henry (b. 1932), White House chief of staff for President Ford, 1974–75; secretary of defense, 1975–77.

Rush, Kenneth (1910–94), Union Carbide executive; U.S. ambassador to West Germany, 1969–72.

S

Savang Vatthana (b. 1907), king of Laos, 1959–75.

Scali, John (1918–95), print and TV journalist; diplomatic correspondent for ABC news, 1961–71; special consultant for foreign affairs to President Nixon, 1971–73; U.S. ambassador to the United Nations, 1973–75.

Scheel, Walter (b. 1919), leader of the West German Free Democratic Party; vice chancellor and minister for foreign affairs, 1972–74.

Schlesinger, James (b. 1929), chairman, U.S. AtomicEnergy Commission, 1971–73; director, Cental Intelligence Agency, 1973; secretary of defense, 1973–75.

Schroeder, Gerhard (1910–89), Christian Democratic Party politician; West German foreign minister, 1961–66; and minister of defense, 1966–69.

Scott, Hugh (1900–1994), Republican senator from Pennsylvania, 1959–77.

Scowcroft, Brent (b. 1925), deputy assistant to the president for national security affairs, 1973–75; assistant to the president for national security affairs, 1975–77.

Shafei, Col. Hussein Mahmoud El- (b. 1918), vice president, United Arab Republic, in the 1960s; Egyptian Delegate to the Organization for African Unity Summit, 1973–74.

Shahi, Agha (b. 1920), a career diplomat; Permanent Representative from Pakistan to the United Nations, 1967–72.

Simon, William (b. 1927), investment banker; deputy secretary, treasury, 1973–74; and secretary, Treasury, 1974–77.

Sihanouk, Norodom Prince (b. 1922), became king of Cambodia in 1942; head of state, 1960–70, and 1975–76.

Smirnov, Leonid V. (b. 1916), chair, State Committee for Defense Equipment, 1961–63; member, Soviet Communist Party Central Committee, and vice chairman, Council of Ministers, 1965–85.

Smith, Gerard C. (1914–94), assistant secretary of state and director, Policy Planning Staff, 1957–61; director, Arms Control and Disarmament Agency, and head, U.S. SALT delegation, 1969–72.

Snow, Edgar (1905–72), American left–liberal journalist who reported on China from the early 1930s to the early 1970s; the first correspondent to interview Mao and Zhou Enlai in 1936.

Solomon, Richard (b. 1937), a China specialist formerly affiliated with the University of Michigan; member of the NSC staff, 1971–76.

Sonnenfeldt, Helmut (b. 1926), director, Office of Research and Analysis for USSR and Eastern Europe, State Department Bureau of Intelligence and Research, 1965–69; member, NSC Staff, 1969–74, and counselor, U.S. Department of State, 1974–77.

Souvanna Phouma (1901–84), prime minister of Laos, 1962–75.

Staden, Berndt von (b. 1919), West German ambassador to the United States, 1973–79.

Stoessel, Walter (1920–86), career Foreign Service officer; ambassador to the Soviet Union, 1973–76.

Sukhodrev, Viktor (b. 1931?), Soviet Foreign Ministry interpreter from the 1950s–1980s.

T

Tanaka, Kakuei (1918–93), prime minister of Japan, 1972–79.

Takeo, Miki (1908–88), prime minister of Japan, 1974–76.

Tang Wensheng (b. 1943), also known as Nancy Tang, was born in Brooklyn, New York, where her father, the de facto head of the Chinese branch of the U.S. Communist Party, ran a Communist Chinese newspaper. She emigrated to China in 1955, served as an interpreter for Zhou Enlai during the early 1970s, and eventually became deputy head, American and Oceanic affairs at the Foreign Ministry.

Tito, Josip Broz (1892–1980), Yugoslavia's premier, 1945–53, and president, 1953–80.

U

Unger, Leonard (b. 1917), a career Foreign Service officer; ambassador to the Republic of China, 1974–78.

V

Vance, Cyrus (b. 1917), partner, law firm, Simpson, Thacher & Bartlett, 1956–61; secretary of the Army, 1963; deputy secretary of defense, 1964–67; secretary of state, 1977–80.

W

Walters, Vernon (b. 1917), Army and Defense attaché, Paris, 1967–72; deputy director, U.S. Central Intelligence Agency, 1972–76.

Wang Hairong (b. c.1940), assistant minister of foreign affairs; granddaughter of Mao's cousin, Wang Jifan.

Wei Guoqing (b. 1913?), Long March veteran who rose to the rank of major general, People's Liberation Army; member, Chinese Communist Party Central Committee, 1969–85 and the Politburo, 1973–85; first political commisar, Guangzhou Military Region, 1974–78.

X

Xu Shiyou (1906–85), joined the Communist guerilla movement in 1928 and rose to the rank of colonel–general in the People's Liberation Army; member of the Politburo and the Chinese Communist Party Central Committee, during the 1970s; commander, Guangzhou Military Region, 1974–80.

Y

Ye Jianying (1897–1986), a Politburo member and the highest ranking army general in China; vice chairman of the National Defense Council, 1954 until the mid–1960s; vice chairman, Military Council of Chinese Communist Party Central Committee; acting minister of national defense, 1971–85.

Z

Zavimbi, Jonas (b. 1934), Angolan nationalist; founded National Union for the Total Liberation of Angola (UNITA), 1966.

Zhang Chunqiao (b. 1917), Communist party activist in Shanghai; Politburo member, 1969–76; member of the "Gang of Four" purged from Communist party in 1976.

Zhang Wenjin (b. 1914), career PRC diplomat; director of West Europe, America, and Australia Department, Ministry of Foreign Affairs, 1971–72; Assistant Minister of Foreign Affairs, 1972–73; Ambassador to Canada from 1973 to 1976.

Zhou Enlai (1898–1976), joined Chinese Communist Party in 1921; premier, People's Republic of China, 1949–76; foreign minister, 1949–58.

Zoshchenko, Mikhail M. (1895–1958), a comic writer whose satires of Soviet bureaucracy enjoyed a wide audience even after he fell out of favor with authorities during the 1940s.

Zumwalt, Jr., Admiral Elmo Russell (b. 1920), Commander, U.S. Naval Forces, Vietnam, 1968–70; Chief of Naval Operations, 1970–74.

—A Note on Sources

Many secondary works and memoirs, all indicated in the endnotes, were essential for providing historical context or for filling in gaps in my knowledge on the period covered in this book. Several books, however, stand out. Until the substantially more primary source material becomes available, Walter Isaacson, *Kissinger: A Biography* (New York, 1992) will stand up as the near-definitive biography. For any student of the Nixon–Kissinger policies toward the Soviet Union and China, Raymond L. Garthoff, *Détente and Confrontation: American-Soviet Relations from Nixon to Reagan* (Washington, D.C., 1994) remains indispensable not only for its contents but as a guide to the literature. William Bundy's extraordinary study, *Tangled Web: The Making of Foreign Policy in the Nixon Presidency* (New York: Hill and Wang, 1998) appeared late in the preparation of this book but proved invaluable. Robert Ross, *Negotiating Cooperation: the United States and China, 1969–1989* (Stanford, 1995) is an invaluable guide to internal Chinese decision-making during the late 1960s and early 1970s.

Critically important for the annotations to the documents and the biographic glossary were various "who's who's." Among the most significant compilations are: *The International Who's Who*, various years (London: Europa Publications); *Who's Who in America*, 1998, 52nd ed. (New Providence, N.J.: Marquis Who's Who, 1998); *Who Was Who in America*, various years (New Providence, N.J.: Marquis Who's Who); Boris Lewytzkji and Juliusz Stroynowski, eds., *Who's Who in the Socialist Countries* (New York: K.G. Saur Publishing Inc., 1978); Jeanne Vronskaya and Vladimir Chuguev, *The Biographical Dictionary of the Former Soviet Union* (London: Bowker and Saur, 1992); Leonard Geron and Alex Pravda, *Who's Who in Russia and the New States* (London: I.B. Tauris, 1993); Wolfgang Bartke, *Who's Who in the Peoples Republic of China*, 2nd ed. (Munich: K.G. Saur, 1987); *Merriam-Webster's Biographical Dictionary* (Springfield, Mass.: Merriam-Webster, Inc., 1995); U.S. Department of State, *Biographic Register* (Washington, D.C.: Office of Operations, U.S. Department of State, various dates); and Donald W. Klein and Ann B. Clark, *Biographic Dictionary of Chinese Communism, 1921–1965* (Cambridge, MA: Harvard University Press, 1971). Thomas B. Cochran et al., *Nuclear Weapons Databook, Volume I, U.S. Nuclear Forces and Capabilities* and *Volume IV, Soviet Nuclear Weapons* (New York: Harper and Row, 1984 and 1989, respectively) is an invaluable source of data on U.S. and Soviet nuclear delivery systems.

—Acknowledgements

This book would not have been possible without the National Security Archive, which has provided the most wonderfully stimulating work environments that one could hope for. Tom Blanton, the Archive's executive director, has a full-time job keeping the organization afloat but was tremendously supportive and a source of astute advice. I accumulated numerous debts to other colleagues at the National Security Archive. Matthew Talbott, who worked as an intern during the summer of 1997, brought the Winston Lord collection and its unique contents to my attention. Donald T. Shaw scanned documents, helped with background research, and provided valuable editorial advice. Kevin Symons helped with the laborious task of scanning transcripts and also provided research assistance. Mary Burroughs cheerfully transcribed the handful of documents that resisted scanning. Malcolm Byrne, the Archive's deputy director, Vladislav Zubok, a senior fellow at the Archive, and James Woodard, a former intern provided astute comments on portions of the manuscript.

A number of friends and colleagues also commented on the manuscript or portions of it, and I am deeply obliged to them. Raymond L. Garthoff, Brookings Institution; James Hershberg, Department of History, George Washington University; David S. Painter, Department of History, Georgetown University; Carl Parrini, Department of History, Northern Illinois University; Nancy B. Tucker, Department of History, Georgetown University; and Lynn Eden, Center for International Security and Arms Control, Stanford University, generously took time from their busy schedules to provide helpful advice and to call attention to oversights. Needless to say, despite this generous assistance, I alone am responsible for all errors or shortcomings.

Any project undertaken at the National Security Archive needs to acknowledge the funders who make its work possible. I owe a special debt to the W. Alton Jones Foundation, especially George Perkovich, for its support for the Archive's work on U.S. nuclear weapons programs and nuclear proliferation in East and South Asia. Other foundations and their executives have been just as indispensable: the Arca Foundation, especially Smith Bagley, Janet Shenk, and Steve Cobble; the Compton Foundation, especially James Compton and Edith Eddy; the Ford Foundation, especially Susan Berresford; the Fund for Constitutional Government, especially Conrad Martin; the General Service Foundation, especially, Mary Estrin; the German Marshall Fund of the United States, especially Krystyna Wolniakowski; the John D. and C.T. MacArthur Foundation, especially Adele Simmons,

Victor Rabinowitz, Woodrow Wickham, Kimberly Stanton, and Mary Page; the New York Times Company Foundation, especially Arthur Gelb; the Open Society Institute, especially Aryeh Neier, Deborah Harding, Robert Kushen, and Anthony Richter; the Pubic Welfare Foundation, especially Larry Kressley; Rockefeller Associates, especially Wade Greene; the Smith Richard Foundation, especially Marin Stomecki and Samantha Ravich; the Winston Foundation for World Peace, especially John Tirman and Tara Magner. Finally, a special thanks to the Fund for Peace, its chairman, James Compton, its executive director, Pauline Baker, and its chief financial officer, Steven Dougherty, for providing the Archive with a financial haven over the years.

At the New Press, Jessica Blatt worked hard to keep me on schedule, and I am grateful for her forbearance. Thanks also to André Schiffrin for his enthusiastic interest in this project, to Grace Farrell for seeing the book through, to Ted Byfield, for phenomenally meticulous copy editing, and to Ruby Essien, for astute last-minute advice and assistance.

There are others that I must acknowledge. My debt, intellectual and personal, to Carl Parrini and Martin J. Sklar, has mounted since I first studied with them at the Northern Illinois University Department of History. I can only hope that this book goes part of the way in meeting the high standards that they have set in their own scholarship. I am also grateful to others at Northern's History Department for inspring teaching that conveyed their dedication to historical inquiry and human progress: John H. Bracey, C. H. George, Margaret George, John Higginson, J. Carroll Moody, Otto H. Olsen, Albert Resis, Marvin Rosen, and Alfred F. Young. I also must thank Lynn Eden, Keith Haynes, Jim Livingston, Larry Lynn, Steve Rosswurm, Rich Schneirov, and Paul Wolman, longtime friends from whom I keep learning. Finally, heartfelt thanks to Ming for her patience and support, and to my parents, to whom I dedicate this book.

—Index

www.ingramcontent.com/pod-product-compliance
Lightning Source LLC
Jackson TN
JSHW080852211224
75817JS00002B/2